HITLER'S HANGMAN

HITLER'S HANGMAN

THE LIFE OF HEYDRICH

ROBERT GERWARTH

YALE UNIVERSITY PRESS
NEW HAVEN AND LONDON

For information about this and other Yale University Press publications, please contact:
U.S. Office: sales.press@yale.edu   www.yalebook.com
Europe Office: sales @yaleup.co.uk   www.yalebooks.co.uk

Set in Adobe Caslon by IDSUK (DataConnection) Ltd
Printed in the United States of America.

Library of Congress Cataloging-in-Publication Data

Gerwarth, Robert.
    Hitler's hangman: the life and death of Reinhard Heydrich/Robert Gerwarth.
       p. cm.
    ISBN 978–0–300–11575–8 (hardback)
1. Heydrich, Reinhard, 1904–1942. 2. Nationalsozialistische Deutsche Arbeiter-Partei.
Schutzstaffel–Biography. 3. Nazis—Biography. 4. Germany–Politics and
government–1933–1945. 5. Czechoslovakia–Politics and government–1938–1945.
I. Title.
DD247.H42G47 2011
943.086092–dc22
[B]
                                                                                    2011013535
A catalogue record for this book is available from the British Library.

10 9 8 7 6 5 4 3

For Porscha

Contents

Illustrations and Maps

Maps

Preface

How does one write the biography of Reinhard Heydrich, one of the key players in the most murderous genocide of history, a historial figure the Nobel Laureate Thomas Mann famously referred to as Hitler's 'hangman'? This is the question I have been asking myself from the moment I first decided to embark on this book project. It was always clear to me that the writing of a Nazi biography would pose a specific set of challenges, ranging from the need to master the vast and ever-growing body of literature on Hitler's dictatorship to the peculiar problem of having to penetrate so the mind of a person whose mentality and ideological universe seem repellent and strangely distant, even though the Nazi dictatorship ended less than seventy years ago. But the major challenge lay elsewhere: namely, in the fact that any kind of life-writing requires a certain degree of empathy with the book's subject, even if that subject is Reinhard Heydrich.

Biographers often use the contrasting images of autopsy and portrait to describe their work: while the autopsy offers a detached, forensic examination of a life, the portrait relies on the biographer's empathy with his subject. I have chosen to combine both of these approaches in a third way best described as 'cold empathy': an attempt to reconstruct Heydrich's life with critical distance, but without reading history backwards or succumbing to the danger of confusing the role of the historian with that of a state prosecutor at a war criminal's trial. Since historians ought to be primarily in the business of explanation and contextualization, not condemnation, I have tried to avoid the sensationalism and judgemental tone that tend to characterize earlier accounts of Heydrich's life. Heydrich's actions, language and behaviour speak for themselves, and wherever possible I have tried to give space to his own characteristic voice and choice of expressions.

Personal records, however, are scarce in Heydrich's case. I have searched the relevant archives in Germany, Britain, the United States, Russia, Israel and the Czech Republic and that search has revealed many more sources on Heydrich's life than are often assumed to exist. Yet unlike Joseph Goebbels or the young Heinrich Himmler, Heydrich did not keep a personal diary and only fragments of his private correspondence have survived the Second World War. However there exists a remarkably large body of official documents, speeches and letters, which allow us to reconstruct his daily routines and decision-making processes in great detail.

In identifying the widely dispersed source material on which this book is based, I frequently had to rely on the helpful advice of archivists and librarians. I am very grateful for the expert assistance of the staff of several archives and libraries across the globe that have given me access to their extensive holdings and supplied me with unpublished material. These include the Institut für Zeitgeschichte in Munich, the German Federal Archives and its various branches in Berlin, Koblenz, Freiburg and Ludwigsburg, the British and Czech National Archives in Kew and Prague; the archives of Yad Vashem in Jerusalem and the Holocaust Memorial Museum in Washington DC, as well as the German Historical Institute in Moscow which greatly facilitated my access to the Reich Security Main Office files in the Osobyi Archive.

This book originated in Oxford and I remain deeply indebted to many friends and former colleagues there. Martin Conway and Nicholas Stargardt advised on this project at various stages and provided most welcome criticism on earlier drafts of the book. Roy Foster taught me a great deal about life-writing, has offered brilliant comments on the manuscript and has remained a friend and inspiration beyond my time in Oxford. Since leaving Oxford in 2007, I have become a staff member of University College Dublin, which has given me remarkable freedom to research and to write. Among my colleagues at UCD, William Mulligan, Stephan Malinowski and Harry White have been most helpful critical readers and sources of encouragement. Apart from my colleagues at UCD's Centre for War Studies, I must also thank John Horne of Trinity College Dublin for three years of happy research collaboration and for being a constant inspiration in his dedication to historical scholarship.

Outside Oxford and Dublin, Nikolaus Wachsmann, Chad Bryant, Mark Cornwall and Jochen Boehler generously agreed to read drafts of my work, as did two anonymous readers who went far beyond the call of duty in commenting on my original ideas. Their suggestions have greatly enhanced the final manuscript and I am immensely grateful to them. In Prague, I was fortunate to work with Miloš Hořejš whose ability to translate key sections of relevant Czech literature and sources has allowed me to incorporate the important work on the Nazi occupation of Bohemia and Moravia that has been published in Czech over the past two decades. In Berlin, I had the pleasure of working with Jan Bockelmann whose diligence in compiling vast quantities of German sources and literature has greatly aided the timely completion of this study. He and Wolf Beck also did an expert job in providing the two maps in this volume, while Seumas Spark helped with the index. Heather McCallum commissioned this book some six years ago and she and her colleagues at Yale University Press accompanied the production process with great enthusiasm, competence and patience. It is difficult to imagine a better publisher.

My final thanks, as always, go to my family. During my regular archival trips to Berlin, my parents, Michael and Evelyn Gerwarth, provided unfailing support, love and encouragement, for which I cannot thank them enough. Finally, my debts to my wife, Porscha, are enormous. She has read the manuscript from start to finish, and had to live with my periodic absences and constant distraction over the past five years. Dedicating this book to her is a necessarily inadequate attempt to acknowledge the depth of my love and gratitude.

Dublin, May 2011

Introduction

REINHARD HEYDRICH IS WIDELY RECOGNIZED AS ONE OF THE GREAT iconic villains of the twentieth century, an appalling figure even within the context of the Nazi elite. Countless TV documentaries, spurred on by the fascination with evil, have offered popular takes on his intriguing life, and there is no shortage of sensationalist accounts of his 1942 assassination and the unprecedented wave of retaliatory Nazi violence that culminated in the vengeful destruction of the Bohemian village of Lidice. Arguably the most spectacular secret service operation of the entire Second World War, the history of Operation Anthropoid and its violent aftermath has inspired the popular imagination ever since 1942, providing the backdrop to Heinrich Mann's *Lidice* (1942), Bertolt Brecht's *Hangmen Also Die* (1943) and Laurent Binet's recent Prix Goncourt-winning novel *HHhH* (2010).[1]

The continuing popular fascination with Heydrich is easily explained. Although merely thirty-eight years old at the time of his violent death in Prague in June 1942, he had accumulated three key positions in Hitler's rapidly expanding empire. As head of the Nazis' vast political and criminal police apparatus, which merged with the powerful SS intelligence service – the SD – into the Reich Security Main Office (RSHA) in 1939, Heydrich commanded a sizeable shadow army of Gestapo and SD officers directly responsible for Nazi terror at home and in the occupied territories. As such he was also in charge of the infamous SS mobile killing squads, the *Einsatzgruppen*, during the campaigns against Austria, Czechoslovakia, Poland and the Soviet Union. Secondly, in September 1941, Heydrich was appointed by Hitler as acting Reich Protector of Bohemia and Moravia, a position that made him the undisputed ruler of the former Czech lands. The eight months of his rule in Prague and the aftermath of his assassination are still remembered as the darkest time in modern Czech history. Thirdly, in 1941 Heydrich was instructed by the second most powerful man in Nazi Germany, Hermann Göring, to find and implement a 'total solution of the Jewish question' in Europe, a solution which, by the summer of 1942, culminated in the indiscriminate and systematic murder of the Jews of Europe. With these three positions, Reinhard Heydrich undoubtedly played a central role in the complex power system of the Third Reich.

Yet, despite his major share of responsibility for some of the worst atrocities committed in the name of Nazi Germany and the continuing interest of both historians and the general public in Hitler's dictatorship, Heydrich remains a remarkably neglected and oddly nebulous figure in the extensive literature on the Third Reich. Although some 40,000 books have been published on the history of Nazi Germany, including several important studies on other high-ranking SS officers such as Heinrich Himmler, Ernst Kaltenbrunner, Adolf Eichmann and Werner Best, there is no serious scholarly biography that spans the entire life of this key figure within the Nazi terror apparatus.[2] The only exception to this remarkable neglect is Shlomo Aronson's pioneering 1967 PhD thesis on Heydrich's role in the early history of the Gestapo and the SD, which unfortunately ends in 1936 when the SS took full control of the German police. Written in German and never translated into English, Aronson's research has left a mine of material on Heydrich's early life that no later historian in the field can ignore, but his study is not a biography and was never intended to be one.[3]

Several journalists have attempted to fill the gap left by professional historians. Although not without merit, particularly in gathering post-war testimonies of Heydrich's former SS associates and childhood friends, these earlier Heydrich biographies reflect a by now largely obsolete understanding of Nazi leaders as either depraved criminals or perversely rational desk-killers – an interpretation that built on the post-war testimonies of Nazi victims and former SS men alike.[4] The Swiss League of Nations' High Commissioner in Danzig between 1937 and 1939, Carl Jacob Burckhardt, who had met Heydrich in the summer of 1935 during an inspection tour of Nazi concentration camps, famously described him in his memoirs as the Third Reich's 'young evil god of death'.[5] Post-war recollections of former SS subordinates were similarly unflattering. His deputy of many years, Dr Werner Best, characterized Heydrich as the 'most demonic personality in the Nazi leadership', driven by an 'inhumanity which took no account of those he mowed down'.[6] Himmler's personal adjutant, Karl Wolff, described Heydrich as 'devilish', while Walter Schellenberg, the youngest of the departmental heads in the Reich Security Main Office, remembered his former boss as a ragingly ambitious man with 'an incredibly acute perception of the moral, human, professional and political weakness of others'. 'His unusual intellect', Schellenberg insisted, 'was matched by the ever-watchful instincts of a predatory animal', who 'in a pack of ferocious wolves, must always prove himself the strongest'.[7]

Such post-war testimonies of former SS officers must be approached with caution. With Heydrich, Himmler and Hitler dead, and the Third Reich in ruins, Best, Wolff, Schellenberg and other senior SS men in Allied captivity were keen to whitewash their own responsibility and to 'prove' that they had merely followed orders from superiors who were too powerful and scary to be disobeyed. Yet their characterizations of Heydrich stuck in the popular imagination, fuelled by books such as Charles Wighton's 1962 biography, *Heydrich: Hitler's Most Evil Henchman*. Wighton perpetuated a powerful myth in explaining Heydrich's murderous zeal: the myth of his alleged Jewish family background which originated in Heydrich's early youth and, despite the best efforts of his family to refute it, continued to resurface both during and after the Third Reich. After 1945, it was cultivated by former SS officers such as Wilhelm Höttl, who maintained in his autobiographical book *The Secret Front* (1950) that Heydrich ordered his agents to remove the gravestone of his 'Jewish grandmother'.[8] Others jumped on the potentially lucrative bandwagon of 'exposing' the chief organizer of the Holocaust as a Jew. Presumably to boost his book sales with sensational revelations about the SS leadership, Himmler's Finnish masseur, Felix Kersten, maintained in his highly unreliable memoirs that both Himmler and Hitler had known about Heydrich's 'dark secret' from the early 1930s onwards, but chose to use the 'highly talented, but also very dangerous man' for the dirtiest deeds of the regime.[9]

Wighton was not alone in falling for the myth of Heydrich's Jewish origins. In his preface to the Kersten memoirs, Hugh Trevor-Roper confirmed 'with all the authority that I possess' that Heydrich was a Jew – a view supported by eminent German historians such as Karl Dietrich Bracher and the Hitler biographer Joachim Fest.[10] Fest's brief character sketch of Heydrich – characteristically brilliant in style but unconvincing in content – added fuel to the popular debate about Heydrich's allegedly split personality. Fest reiterated the rumours about Heydrich's Jewish family background and attributed his actions to a self-loathing anti-Semitism. As a schizophrenic maniac driven by self-hatred, Heydrich wanted to prove his worth and became a 'man like a whiplash', running the Nazi terror apparatus with 'Luciferic coldness' in order to achieve his ultimate goal of becoming 'Hitler's successor'.[11]

Fest's characterization of Heydrich was called into question by the emergence of a second influential image of senior SS officers, which is captured in the iconic photograph of Adolf Eichmann in his glass booth in the Jerusalem District Court. Hannah Arendt's famous account of that trial and her dictum about the 'banality of evil' shaped the public perception of SS men in the decades that followed.[12] For many years, the bureaucratic 'technocrat of death' – the perversely rational culprit behind a desk – became the dominant image of Nazi perpetrators. These perpetrators focused on their duties, accepted the administrative tasks assigned to them and carried them out 'correctly' and 'conscientiously' without feeling responsible for their outcomes.[13] The mass murder of the Jews was now seen not so much as a throwback to barbarism, but as the zenith of modern bureaucracy and dehumanizing technology that found its ultimate expression in the anonymous killing factories of Auschwitz. Mass murder was represented as a sanitized process carried out by professional men – doctors and lawyers, demographers and agronomists – who acted on the basis of amoral but seemingly rational decisions derived from racial eugenics, geo-political considerations and economic planning.[14]

Such images strongly impacted on another popular Heydrich biography, first published in 1977: Günther Deschner's *The Pursuit of Total Power*. Deschner, a former writer for the conservative daily *Die Welt*, rightly dismissed the pseudo-psychological demonizations of Wighton and Fest. Instead he followed the prevalent trend of the 1970s and 1980s in describing Heydrich as the archetype of a high-level technocrat primarily interested in efficiency, performance and total power, for whom Nazi ideology was first and foremost a vehicle for careerism. Ideology, Deschner suggested, was something Heydrich was too intelligent to take seriously.[15]

If the popular perception of Heydrich as the Third Reich's cold-blooded 'administrator of death' has remained largely unchallenged over the years, the basic tenets on which this image rests have been well and truly eroded in the last two decades. First, it is now clear that ideology played a key motivational role for senior SS officers and that any attempt to dismiss them as pathologically disturbed outsiders is highly misleading. If anything, SS perpetrators tended to be *more* educated than their average German or Western European contemporaries. More often than not, they were socially mobile and ambitious young university graduates from perfectly intact family backgrounds, by no means part of a deranged minority of extremists from the criminal margins of society.[16]

Second, it is now generally accepted that the decision-making processes which led to the Holocaust developed through several stages of gradual radicalization. The idea that Heydrich consciously planned the Holocaust from the early 1930s onwards, as was still argued by his biographer Eduard Calic in the 1980s, is a position that is no longer tenable.[17] Although central to the development of persecution policies in Nazi Germany, Heydrich was only one of a large variety of actors in Berlin and

German-occupied Europe who pushed for more and more extreme measures of exclusion and, ultimately, mass murder. Nazi Germany was not a smoothly hierarchical dictatorship, but rather a 'polycratic jungle' of competing party and state agencies over which Hitler presided eratically. The 'cumulative radicalization' in certain policy areas emerged as a result of tensions and conflicts between powerful individuals and interest groups who sought to please their Führer by anticipating his orders.[18] Within this complex power structure, individuals contributed to Nazi policies of persecution and murder for a whole range of reasons, from ideological commitment and hyper-nationalism to careerism, greed, sadism, weakness or – more realistically – a combination of more than one of these elements.[19]

For a biographer of Heydrich, the revisionist arguments of the past decades pose a whole series of difficult questions. If the Holocaust was not a smoothly unfolding, centralized genocide and Heydrich and Himmler were not responsible for every aspect of the persecution and mass murder of the Jews, what exactly were they responsible for?[20] If, as some historians quite rightly suggest, the Holocaust was merely a first step towards the bloody unweaving of Europe's complex ethnic make-up, what role did Heydrich play in the evolution and implementation of these plans?[21] Even more fundamentally: how did he 'become' Heydrich?

The answers provided in this book revise some older assumptions about Heydrich's personal transition to Nazism and his contribution to some of the worst crimes committed in the name of the Third Reich. Born as he was in 1904 into a privileged Catholic family of professional musicians in the city of Halle, Heydrich's path to genocide was anything but straightforward. Not only was his life conditioned by several unforeseeable events that were often beyond his control, but his actions can be fully explained only by placing them in the wider context of the intellectual, political, cultural and socio-economic conditions that shaped German history in the first half of the twentieth century.

Heydrich was both a typical and an atypical representative of his generation. He shared in many of the deep ruptures and traumatic experiences of the so-called war youth generation: namely, the Great War and the turbulent post-war years of revolutionary turmoil, hyperinflation and social decline, which he experienced as a teenager. Yet while these experiences made him and many other Germans susceptible to radical nationalism, Heydrich refrained from political activism throughout the 1920s and was even ostracized by his fellow naval officers for not being nationalist enough. The great turning point of his early life came in spring 1931 when he was dismissed from military service as a result of a broken engagement promise and his subsequent arrogant behaviour towards the military court of honour. His dismissal at the height of the Great Depression roughly coincided with his first meeting with his future wife, Lina von Osten, who was already a committed Nazi and who convinced him to apply for a staff position in Heinrich Himmler's small but elite SS.

Until this moment, Heydrich's life might have taken a very different direction, and indeed he initially possessed few obvious qualifications for his subsequent role as head of the Gestapo and the SD. Crucial for his future development were his experiences and personal encounters *within* the SS after 1931, and in particular his close relationship with Heinrich Himmler. In other words, the most significant contributing factor to Heydrich's radicalization was his immersion in a political milieu of young and often highly educated men who thrived on violent notions of cleansing Germany from its supposed internal enemies while simultaneously rejecting bourgeois norms of morality as weak, outdated and inappropriate for securing Germany's national rebirth.

Yet his immersion in this violent world of deeply committed political extremists does not in itself explain why Heydrich emerged as arguably the most radical figure within the Nazi leadership. At least one of the reasons for his subsequent radicalism, it will be argued, lies in his lack of early Nazi credentials. Heydrich's earlier life contained some shortcomings, most notably the persistent rumours about his Jewish ancestry that led to a humiliating party investigation in 1932, and his relatively late conversion to Nazism. To make up for these imperfections and impress his superior, Heinrich Himmler, Heydrich transformed himself into a model Nazi, adopting and further radicalizing key tenets of Himmler's world-view and SS ideals of manliness, sporting prowess and military bearing. Heydrich even manipulated the story of his earlier life to shore up his Nazi credentials. He supposedly fought in right-wing militant Freikorps units after the Great War, but his involvement in post-1918 paramilitary activity was at best minimal. Nor do any records exist to prove that he was a member of the various anti-Semitic groups in Halle to which he later claimed to have belonged.

By the mid-1930s, Heydrich had successfully reinvented himself as one of the most radical proponents of Nazi ideology and its implementation through rigid and increasingly extensive policies of persecution. The realization of Hitler's utopian society, so he firmly believed, required the ruthless and violent exclusion of those elements deemed dangerous to German society, a task that could best be carried out by the SS as the executioner of Hitler's will. Only by cleansing German society of all that was alien, sick and hostile could a new national community emerge and the inevitable war against the Reich's arch-enemy, the Soviet Union, be won. The means of 'cleansing' envisaged by Heydrich were to change dramatically between 1933 and 1942, partly in response to circumstances beyond his control and partly as a result of the increasing *Machbarkeitswahn* – fantasies of omnipotence – that gripped many senior SS men, policy planners and demographic engineers after the outbreak of the Second World War: the delusional idea that a unique historical opportunity had arisen to fight, once and for all, Germany's real or imagined enemies inside and outside the Reich. While the mass extermination of Jews seemed inconceivable even to Heydrich before the outbreak of war in 1939, his views on the matter radicalized over the following two and a half years. A combination of wartime brutalization, frustration over failed expulsion schemes, pressures from local German administrators in the occupied East and an ideologically motivated determination to solve the 'Jewish problem' led to a situation in which he perceived systematic mass murder to be both feasible and desirable.

The 'solution of the Jewish question' for which Heydrich bore direct responsibility from the late 1930s was, however, only part of a much broader wartime plan to recreate the entire ethnic make-up of Europe through a massive project of expelling, resettling and murdering millions of people in Eastern Europe after the Wehrmacht's victory over the Soviet Union. As Acting Reich Protector of Bohemia and Moravia – a position he held between September 1941 and his violent death in June 1942 – Heydrich underlined his fundamental commitment to these plans by initiating a uniquely ambitious programme of racial classification and cultural imperialism in the Protectorate.

Despite his drive for the Germanization of East-Central Europe, Heydrich was fully aware that its complete realization had to wait until the Wehrmacht's victory over the Red Army. It was simply impossible from a logistical point of view to expel, resettle and murder an estimated 30 million Slavic people in the conquered East while simultaneously fighting a war against a numerically superior alliance of enemies on the battlefields. The destruction of Europe's Jews, a much smaller and more easily identifiable community, posed considerably fewer logistical problems. For Heydrich and Himmler, the swift implementation of the 'final solution' also offered a major strategic advantage vis-à-vis rival agencies in the occupied territories: by documenting their reliability in carrying out Hitler's genocidal orders, they recommended themselves to the Führer as the natural agency to implement the even bigger post-war project of Germanization.[22]

Heydrich's life therefore offers a uniquely privileged, intimate and organic perspective on some of the darkest aspects of Nazi rule, many of which are often artificially divided or treated separately in the highly specialized literature on the Third Reich: the rise of the SS and the emergence of the Nazi police state; the decision-making processes that led to the Holocaust; the interconnections between anti-Jewish and Germanization policies; and the different ways in which German occupation regimes operated across Nazi-controlled Europe. On a more personal level, it illustrates the historical circumstances under which young men from perfectly 'normal' middle-class backgrounds can become political extremists determined to use ultra-violence to implement their dystopian fantasies of radically transforming the world.

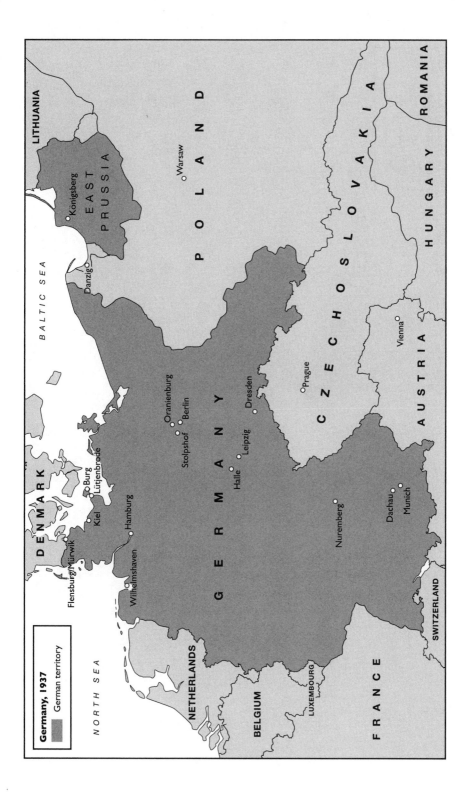

Germany, 1937

German territory

NORTH SEA

BALTIC SEA

DENMARK

LITHUANIA

EAST PRUSSIA

Königsberg

POLAND

Warsaw

Danzig

Flensburg/Mürwik

Kiel

Burg
Lütjenbrode

Hamburg

Wilhelmshaven

NETHERLANDS

BELGIUM

LUXEMBOURG

FRANCE

G E R M A N Y

Oranienburg
Berlin

Stolpshof

Halle
Leipzig

Dresden

Nuremberg

Dachau
Munich

SWITZERLAND

CZECHOSLOVAKIA

Prague

AUSTRIA

Vienna

HUNGARY

ROMANIA

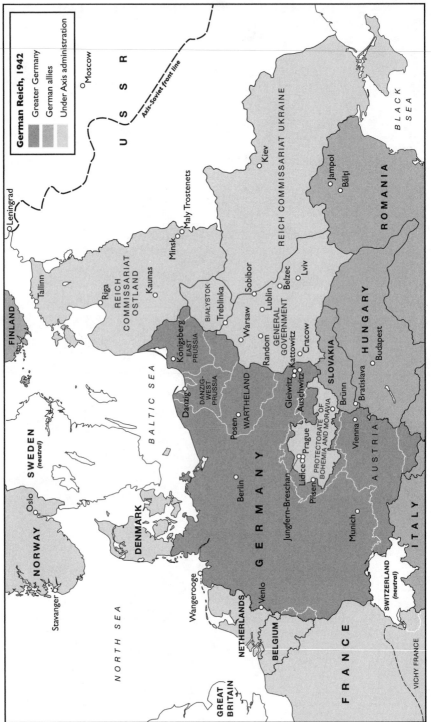

German Reich, 1942

Greater Germany
German allies
Under Axis administration

Axis-Soviet front line

U S S R

Moscow

Leningrad

FINLAND

SWEDEN
(neutral)

Tallinn

Riga

REICH
COMMISSARIAT
OSTLAND

Kaunas

Minsk

Maly Trostenets

Kiev

REICH COMMISSARIAT UKRAINE

BLACK
SEA

Jampol

Bălți

ROMANIA

NORWAY

Oslo

Stavanger

BALTIC SEA

Königsberg

EAST
PRUSSIA

Danzig

DANZIG-
WEST
PRUSSIA

WARTHELAND

Posen

BIAŁYSTOK

Treblinka

Warsaw

Sobibor

Lublin

GENERAL
GOVERNMENT

Belzec

Lviv

HUNGARY

Budapest

Random

Kattowitz

Gleiwitz

Auschwitz

Cracow

SLOVAKIA

Bratislava

Brünn

Vienna

AUSTRIA

ITALY

DENMARK

NORTH SEA

Wangerooge

Venlo

NETHERLANDS

BELGIUM

GREAT
BRITAIN

Berlin

Jungfern-Breschan

Lidice

Prague

Pilsen

PROTECTORATE
OF
BOHEMIA AND MORAVIA

Munich

SWITZERLAND
(neutral)

F R A N C E

VICHY FRANCE

CHAPTER I

◆

Death in Prague

THE 27TH OF MAY 1942 WAS A BEAUTIFUL DAY. THE MORNING DAWNED bright and auspicious over the Bohemian lands, occupied by Nazi Germany since 1939. After a long and exceptionally cold winter, spring had finally arrived. The trees were in full blossom and the cafés of Prague were buzzing with life. Some twenty kilometres north of the capital, in the leafy gardens of his vast neo-classical country estate, the undisputed ruler of the Czech lands and chief of the Nazi terror apparatus, Reinhard Heydrich, was playing with his two young sons, Klaus and Heider, while his wife, Lina, heavily pregnant with their fourth child, was watching from the terrace, holding their infant daughter, Silke.[1]

Both privately and professionally, Heydrich had every reason to be content. At the age of only thirty-eight, and as the second most powerful man in the SS behind Heinrich Himmler, he had built a reputation as one of the most uncompromising executors of Hitler's dystopian fantasies for the future of the Reich and Nazi-occupied Europe. The 'solution of the Jewish question' in Europe, with which Heydrich had been officially charged in January 1941, was making rapid progress: by the spring of 1942, the Germans and their Eastern European accomplices had murdered some 1.5 million Jews, predominantly through face-to-face shootings. Many more would die in the killing factories in former Poland where construction work for stationary gassing facilities had begun the previous winter. Despite Germany's recent declaration of war on the United States, Heydrich's future looked bright. On the Eastern and North African fronts, the German army was rapidly advancing and about to deal a number of devastating blows against the Allies. Resistance activities, to be sure, had increased throughout Europe since the German invasion of the Soviet Union in the summer of 1941, but Heydrich had good reason to be confident that these challenges to Nazi rule would strengthen, rather than weaken, the influence of the SS on

German occupation policies, where Heydrich was widely considered to be the rising star.

Contrary to his usual habit of driving to work shortly after dawn, Heydrich left his country estate at around 10 o'clock that morning. His driver, Johannes Klein, a man in his early thirties, was waiting for him in the lobby, ready to take Heydrich to his office in Prague Castle, and, from there, to the airport where Heydrich's plane was to fly him to Berlin to report to Hitler on the future governance of the Protectorate and to make more general policy suggestions on the combating of resistance activities throughout occupied Europe. As usual, they travelled the short distance to Prague in a Mercedes convertible and without a police escort. As Klein and Heydrich commenced their journey, neither of the two men could know that some fifteen minutes down the road, in the suburb of Libeň, three Czechoslovak agents from Britain were nervously waiting for them, their guns and grenades carefully concealed under civilian clothing.[2]

Secret plans to assassinate Reinhard Heydrich had emerged in London more than half a year earlier, in late September 1941. The origins of the plan have remained highly controversial to this day and have given rise to all sorts of conspiracy theories, largely because the parties involved – the British Special Operations Executive (SOE) and the Czechoslovak government-in-exile under President Edvard Beneš – officially denied all responsibility for the assassination after 1945. Neither of them wanted to be accused of condoning political assassination as a means of warfare, particularly since it had always been clear that the Germans would respond to the killing of a prominent Nazi leader with the most brutal reprisals against the civilian population.[3]

The surviving documents on the assassination reveal that the plan to kill Heydrich was primarily born out of desperation: ever since the fall of France in the summer of 1940, and the inglorious retreat of the British Expeditionary Forces from Dunkirk, the British authorities had been struggling to regain the military initiative. With no chance of being able to defeat the German army by themselves, the British hoped to incite popular unrest in the Nazi-occupied territories, thereby deflecting vital German military resources to a number of trouble spots. Hugh Dalton, the Minister of Economic Warfare, talked about creating subversive organizations behind enemy lines, while the War Office was emphatically calling for 'active efforts to combat the serious loss of confidence in the British Empire which has arisen ... following our recent disasters'.[4]

Neither Dalton nor anyone else in the British cabinet had a firm grasp of the immense difficulties and deterrents facing the underground organizations in Nazi-occupied Europe. Nor did they appreciate how complicated it was to conduct small-scale sabotage operations. The

Czechs and Poles in exile in Putney and Kensington were more realistic. They were unwilling to jeopardize their existing intelligence networks at home by organizing ambitious mass uprisings that could only fail in the face of an overwhelming German military presence. However, even when measured against the generally low levels of resistance activity in early 1941, the Czechs were seen by the British to be particularly complacent. As Beneš's chief intelligence adviser, František Moravec, admitted after the war, in terms of resistance activities in the occupied territories 'Czechoslovakia was always at the bottom of the list. President Beneš became very embarrassed by this fact. He told me that in his consultations with representatives of Allied countries the subject of meaningful resistance to the enemy cropped up with humiliating insistence. The British and the Russians, hard-pressed on their own battlefields, kept pointing out to Beneš the urgent need for maximum effort from every country, including Czechoslovakia.'[5]

The lack of Czech resistance to Nazi rule was increasingly damaging Beneš's diplomatic position and endangered his ultimate post-war objective of re-establishing Czechoslovakia along its pre-1938 borders. Beneš feared that a negotiated peace between Germany and Britain would leave the Bohemian lands permanently within the Nazi sphere of influence. After all, the British government had still not disavowed the Munich Agreement of 1938, which permitted Hitler to occupy Czechoslovakia's largely German-inhabited Sudetenland, and it consciously delayed any reconsideration of that decision to keep up the pressure on Beneš.[6]

On 5 September 1941, an increasingly impatient Beneš radioed the Central Leadership of Home Resistance (ÚVOD) in Prague: 'It is essential to move from theoretical plans and preparations to deeds . . . In London and Moscow we have been informed that the destruction or at least a considerable reduction of the weapons industry would have a profound impact on the Germans at this moment . . . Our entire position will appear in a permanently unfavourable light if we do not at least keep pace with the others.'[7] Responding to pressure from London, ÚVOD indeed maximized its sabotage activities and co-ordinated a successful boycott of the Nazi-controlled Protectorate press between 14 and 21 September. Only one week later, however, Beneš's initial enthusiasm turned into utter frustration when Hitler decided to replace his 'weak' Reich Protector in Prague, Konstantin von Neurath, with the infamous head of the Reich Security Main Office, Reinhard Heydrich. Following Heydrich's arrival in Prague in September 1941, the German authorities massively tightened their grip on Czech society: communication between the Protectorate and London temporarily ceased to exist, and the underground was paralysed by a wave of Gestapo arrests.[8]

As his ambitious plans for widespread resistance began to collapse around him, Beneš found an equally beleagured ally in the British Special Operations Executive (SOE). Launched in July 1940 and instructed by Winston Churchill himself to 'set Europe ablaze' by backing popular uprisings against Nazi rule, SOE had enjoyed very limited success in the first year of its existence. As Hugh Dalton noted in his diary in December 1941: 'Our last reports have been almost bare, long tales of what has not been done . . . I am particularly anxious for a successful operation or two.'[9] Just like Beneš, SOE was increasingly desperate to deliver some kind of success to justify its existence, particularly after its well-established rival, the Secret Intelligence Service (SIS), had demanded in August 1941 that sole responsibility for sabotage operations in enemy territory should be transferred back to SIS and its director, Sir Stewart Menzies. Perceiving the fledgling SOE as an amateurish upstart organization, Menzies and his senior staff were keen to rid themselves of the seemingly inefficient rival agency.[10]

Over the following weeks, Beneš's intelligence chief, František Moravec, and high-ranking SOE representatives met frequently to find a solution to their common problem. They co-ordinated plans to drop Czech agents trained in intelligence, communications and sabotage into the Protectorate, but a combination of bad weather conditions and lack of communication with the resistance leaders on the ground prevented concerted action. Moreover, they began to realize that even the successful deployment of trained experts in sabotage would not be spectacular enough to appease their critics. And so they came up with a much more ambitious plan: since Hitler himself was beyond their reach, they would attempt to assassinate the head of Nazi Germany's terror apparatus, Reinhard Heydrich.[11]

On 3 October 1941, two days after a secret SOE dossier described Heydrich as 'probably the second most dangerous man in German-occupied Europe' after Hitler himself, a clandestine meeting took place in London between the head of SOE, Frank Nelson, and Moravec during which details of the mission were discussed. They agreed that SOE would provide the weapons and training for two or three of Moravec's men 'to carry out a spectacular assassination. Heydrich, if possible.' The assassination of Heydrich – codenamed Operation Anthropoid – would underline both SOE's capability to deal a severe blow against the Nazi security apparatus and the determination of the Czech resistance to stand up to their German oppressors.[12]

If Beneš would have been satisfied with any spectacular act of resistance, the SOE had its mind clearly set on Heydrich as the ideal target. For their information about the target of Operation Anthropoid, British military intelligence relied heavily on the book *Inside the Gestapo*, published in 1940 by the now exiled ex-Gestapo officer Hansjürgen Köhler, who described his former boss Heydrich as:

> the all-powerful police executive of the Third Reich ... Without him, Himmler would be but a senseless dummy ... He is the man who moves everything – behind the scenes, yet with unchanging dexterity – he is the Power behind the Throne, pulling the strings and following his own dark aims. Heydrich is young and intelligent ... In short, he is the brutal, despotic and merciless master of the Nazi Police; a go-getter, whose hard certainty of aim knows no deviation ... Although he is hot-blooded and impetuous himself, he remains soberly, coldly calculating in the background and knows that the power he coveted is already his. Cruelty and sudden rage are just as severely disciplined in his make-up as his untiring activity.

Köhler's emphasis on Heydrich as the man directly responsible for 'immeasurable suffering, misery and death' was highlighted in the copy attached to Heydrich's SOE file.[13] The assassination plan devised by SOE less than a week later was already very specific: it called for a direct attack on Heydrich at a time when he would be driving from his country estate to Prague Castle, ideally at a crossroads where the car would have to slow down.[14]

Brutal German reprisals, so the somewhat cynical calculation implied, would lead to a more general uprising of the Czech population against Nazi rule. Since Beneš himself was 'apprehensive of the possible repercussions in the Protectorate', and since the British government could not be seen as officially violating international norms of warfare by sponsoring acts of terrorism, even in a war against Nazi oppression, both sides felt the 'need to produce some form of cover story'. It was quickly agreed that the assassination was to be portrayed by Allied propaganda as a spontaneous act of resistance, planned and carried out by the Czech underground at home, although the resistance in Prague itself was never informed about London's plan to murder Heydrich.[15]

As Christmas approached, three vital missions were awaiting transport into the Protectorate: Anthropoid, the team trained to kill Heydrich, as well as Silver A and Silver B, two radio transmitter groups assigned to re-establish the severed communication lines between London and the Czech home resistance. The two men selected to assassinate Heydrich were well prepared for their mission. Jan Kubiš, a twenty-seven-year-old former NCO from Moravia, had gained his first experiences in resistance activities against the Germans in the spring of 1939 when he had belonged to one of the small resistance groups that had sprung up spontaneously after the Nazi invasion. When the Gestapo tried to arrest him, he managed to escape to Poland where he met the second future Heydrich assassin, Josef Gabčík, a short but powerfully built locksmith from Slovakia who, like Kubiš, had served as an NCO in the former Czech army before fleeing the country in despair over the Nazi occupation.

Like many other penniless young refugees from Czechoslovakia, Gabčík and Kubiš enlisted in the French Foreign Legion and fought briefly on the Western Front in the early summer of 1940 before being evacuated to Britain after the fall of France. There, in accordance with an inter-Allied agreement, they were recruited into the Czech Brigade, the small military arm of Beneš's government-in-exile, numbering some 3,000 men. When SOE began its recruitment for secret operations in the Protectorate, Gabčík and Kubiš volunteered. But they were kept in the dark about the purpose of their mission. Only after months of extensive training, first near Manchester, then in the sabotage training camp in Camusdarach in Inverness-shire and at the Villa Bellasis, a requisitioned country estate in the home counties near Dorking, were they informed that they had been chosen to kill the Reich Protector himself.[16]

Although proud to be selected for such an important task, both Gabčík and Kubiš knew that they were highly unlikely to survive their mission. The journey to the Protectorate across Nazi-controlled continental Europe was extraordinarily dangerous in itself and even if they arrived safely in Prague and completed their mission, there was no escape plan. The two agents would remain underground until they were either killed or captured or until Prague was liberated from Nazi rule. Both chose to make their wills on 28 December 1941, the night their flight departed from Tangmere aerodrome, a secret RAF base in Sussex.[17]

The heavily laden Halifax, carrying nine parachutists and the crew, crossed the Channel into the dark skies over Nazi-occupied France before continuing its journey over Germany. Repeated attacks by German anti-aircraft batteries and Luftwaffe nightfighter planes interrupted the journey, but they finally arrived over the Protectorate of Bohemia and Moravia shortly after 2 a.m. Heavy snow on the ground made it impossible for the pilot to identify the designated dropping zones for the three teams. Although instructed to aim for Pilsen (Plzeň), where the parachutists were supposed to make contact with local members of the Czech resistance, the pilot accidentally dropped Gabčík and Kubiš into a snowy field near the village of Nehvizdy, some thirty kilometres east of Prague. Their contact addresses were now useless.

There were other problems, too: Gabčík seriously injured his ankle during the landing and he rightly suspected that their arrival had not gone unnoticed. Because of the lack of visibility, the Halifax had descended to an altitude of just over 150 metres before dropping off the parachutists and the bomber's heavy motors had roused half the village inhabitants from their sleep. At least two villagers saw the parachutes float down to earth. According to all the rules of probability, the Gestapo would pick up their trail sooner or later.[18] Luck, however, was on the parachutists' side that day. A local gamekeeper, sympathetic to the national cause, was the first to find them. After seeing their parachutes buried in the snow he followed their footprints to an abandoned quarry. He was soon joined by the local miller of Nehvizdy, Břetislav Baumann, who happened to be a member of a Czech resistance group and who put them in touch with comrades in Prague.[19] Baumann would pay dearly for helping the assassins. After Heydrich's death, he and his wife were arrested and sent to Mauthausen concentration camp where they were murdered.[20]

Shortly after the New Year, Gabčík and Kubiš took the train to Prague where they spent the next five months moving among various safe houses provided by ÚVOD. Their equipment, which included grenades, pistols and a sten gun, followed. In search of an ideal spot to carry out the assassination, they spent weeks walking or cycling around Prague Castle, Heydrich's country estate and the road that Heydrich used to commute between the two. By early February, they had identified a seemingly ideal spot for an attack: a sharp hairpin curve in the Prague suburb of Liběn where Heydrich passed by on his daily commute to work. The location seemed perfect as Heydrich's car would have to slow down to walking pace at the hairpin bend, allowing Gabčík and Kubiš to shoot their target from close quarters. There was also a bus stop just behind the bend where the assassins could wait for Heydrich's car without arousing suspicion.[21]

Yet the apparent ease with which the parachutists had managed to infiltrate the Protectorate made them less cautious than they should have been in the circumstances. Both Gabčík and Kubiš began sexual affairs with women they met through the families that offered them shelter, thus violating all rules of secrecy. Numerous persons and families who belonged to the wider Czech resistance circle were unnecessarily compromised by the careless use of safe houses and borrowed bicycles, articles of clothing and briefcases that would subsequently lead the Gestapo to their helpers and ultimately wipe out all organized resistance in the Protectorate. For the time being, however, Gabčík and Kubiš were lucky enough not to be discovered.

Others were less fortunate. The five parachutists of groups Silver A and Silver B, who had been airdropped only minutes after Gabčík and Kubiš on the night of 28 December, split up shortly after landing. Many of them were either arrested by the Gestapo or turned themselves in when they felt that their families were endangered. Only the group leader of Silver A,

Alfréd Bartoš, managed to re-establish contact with one of the few surviving commanders of ÚVOD, Captain Václav Morávek, and to install a radio transmitter, codenamed Libuše, which soon began beaming information on industrial production and the population's mood back to London. His reports, however, confirmed that resistance activities in the Protectorate had become 'exceptionally difficult', if not impossible, because 'for everyone politically active, there is a permanent Gestapo agent'.[22]

If another of the reasons for sending agents into the Protectorate was to facilitate the bombing of vital arms-production plants, this, too, had limited success. A plan to co-ordinate a British air raid on the Škoda works in Pilsen with the aid of the Libuše transmitter faltered. Other missions, including Silver B, failed completely. Between December 1941 and the end of May 1942, sixteen other parachutists from England were dropped over the Protectorate, but none of them completed his mission: two were arrested by police; two placed themselves voluntarily at the Gestapo's disposal in order to avoid imprisonment or torture; and some were shot or committed suicide when chased by the German police. Others simply abandoned their missions and returned home to their families. Surprised by the pervasiveness of the Nazi police state and holding poor-quality false documents, many simply panicked. In one case, a parachutist sent word to his mother that he was alive and well. The excited mother told an acquaintance, who promptly reported the news to the Gestapo. The parachutist's father and two brothers were held as hostages and threatened with execution until the parachutist turned himself in.[23]

In May Bartoš demanded that the parachute drops be halted altogether. 'You are sending us people for whom we have no use,' he told London. 'They are a burden on the organizational network which is undesirable in today's critical times. The Czech and German security authorities have so much information and knowledge about us that to repeat these operations would be a waste of people and equipment.'[24] But SOE and Beneš pressed on. Before long, to his horror, Bartoš found out about the purpose of the mission entrusted to Gabčík and Kubiš.[25] Twice in early May, ÚVOD broadcast desperate messages to Beneš entreating him to abandon the assassination, arguing that German reprisals for the killing of Heydrich were likely to wipe out whatever was left of the Czech underground:

> Judging by the preparations which Ota and Zdenek [the codenames of Gabčík and Kubiš] are making, and by the place where they are making these preparations, we assume, in spite of the silence they are maintaining, that they are planning to assassinate 'H'. This assassination would in no way benefit the Allies, and might have incalculable consequences for our nation. It would not only endanger our hostages and political prisoners,

but also cost thousands of other lives. It would expose the nation to unparalleled consequences, while at the same time sweeping away the last remnants of [underground] organization. As a result it would become impossible to do anything useful for the Allies in future. We therefore ask that you issue instructions through Silver A for the assassination to be cancelled. Delay might prove dangerous. Send instructions immediately. Should an assassination nevertheless be desirable for considerations of foreign policy, let it be directed against someone else.[26]

Two days later, Beneš's chief of intelligence, František Moravec, responded with a misleading message: 'Don't worry when it comes to terrorist actions. We believe we see the situation clearly, therefore, given the situation, any actions against officials of the German Reich do not come into consideration. Let ÚVOD know ...' The following day, on 15 May, Beneš himself sent a message to the underground without even mentioning the assassination plan:

I expect that in the forthcoming offensive the Germans will push with their forces. They are sure to have some success ... In such a case I would expect German proposals for an inconclusive peace. The crisis would be a serious one [for us] ... In such a situation, an act of violence such as disturbances, direct subversion, sabotage, or demonstrations, might be imperative or even necessary in our country. This would save the nation internationally, and even great sacrifices would be worth it.[27]

Beneš had once again succumbed to pressure from the British government. As intelligence analysts in London pointed out, 'recent telegrams from Silver A indicate that the Czech people are relying more and more on the Russians ...' – a development that posed a serious threat to British long-term interests in Central Europe. The democratic Czech underground, the report concluded, was simply not pulling its weight and was surely 'capable of making far greater efforts ...'. It now appeared 'essential, both from the military and political point of view, to take drastic action to revive confidence in the British war effort, and particularly in S.O.E., if we are to maintain the initiative in directing subsequent operations'.[28]

Gabčík and Kubiš, despite final pleas from their underground protectors to abandon the mission, decided that it was time to act. As soldiers, they felt that they were in no position to question orders that had been given to them directly by Beneš. When a Czech informer from within Prague Castle leaked to the resistance Heydrich's travel plans for a meeting with Hitler on 27 May, suggesting that the Reich Protector would then be out of the country for several weeks, Gabčík and Kubiš decided that this was the date on which to carry out the assassination.[29]

On the morning of 27 May, while Heydrich was still playing with his children in his country estate, they accordingly positioned themselves near the hairpin curve designated for the attack. Despite the warm weather, Gabčík carried a raincoat over his arm, concealing his sub-machine gun. On the opposite side of the street, Kubiš was leaning against a lamp post, two highly sensitive fused bombs in his briefcase. A third man, Josef Valčík, who had been parachuted into the Protectorate in December as a member of team Silver A, positioned himself further up the hill where he acted as lookout for the approaching car. At around 10.20 a.m., Valčík's shaving mirror flashed in the sun, signalling that Heydrich's car was approaching.[30]

As the assassins had anticipated, Heydrich's driver slowed down for the bend. When the car turned the corner, Gabčík leaped out, aiming his machine gun at Heydrich and pulling the trigger, but the gun, previously dismantled and concealed in his briefcase under a layer of grass, jammed. Heydrich, assuming that there was only one assassin, hastily ordered his driver to stop the car and drew his pistol, determined to shoot Gabčík – a fatal error of judgement that would cost him his life. As the car braked sharply, Kubiš stepped out of the shadows and tossed one of his bombs towards the open Mercedes. He misjudged the distance and the bomb exploded against the car's rear wheel, throwing shrapnel back into Kubiš's face and shattering the windows of a passing tram. As the noise of the explosion died away, Heydrich and his driver jumped from the wrecked car with drawn pistols ready to kill the assassins. While Klein ran towards Kubiš, who was half blinded by blood dripping from his forehead, Heydrich turned uphill to where Gabčík stood, still paralysed and holding his useless machine gun. As Klein stumbled towards him, disorientated by the explosion, Kubiš managed to grab his bicycle and escape downhill, convinced that the assassination attempt had failed.[31]

Gabčík found escape less easy. As Heydrich came towards him through the dust of the explosion Gabčík took cover behind a telegraph pole, fully expecting Heydrich to shoot him. Suddenly, however, Heydrich collapsed in agony, while Gabčík seized his opportunity and fled. As soon as the assassins had vanished, Czech and German passers-by came to Heydrich's aid and halted a baker's van which transported the injured man to the nearby Bulovka Hospital, where an X-ray confirmed that surgery was urgently required: his diaphragm was ruptured, and fragments of shrapnel and horsehair from the car's upholstery were lodged in his spleen. Although in severe pain, Heydrich's paranoia and suspicion of the Czechs were strong: he refused to let the local doctor operate on him, demanding instead that a specialist be flown in from Berlin to perform the urgently needed surgery. By noon, he settled for a compromise and agreed that a team of local specialists, led by Professor Josef A. Hohlbaum from the German Surgical Clinic of Prague, should carry out the operation. Shortly after midday, Heydrich was wheeled into the operating theatre while Himmler and Hitler, who had been immediately informed of the attack, dispatched their personal physicians, Professor Karl Gebhardt and Dr Theodor Morell, to Prague.[32]

While Heydrich lay in hospital, his fate uncertain, rage spread among Nazi leaders and Protectorate Germans. Police had to restrain ethnic Germans from attacking Czech stores, bars and restaurants and from lynching their Czech neighbours.[33] Officially, the Nazi-controlled press played down the significance of the attack, emphasizing that Heydrich's injuries were not life-threatening and instead reporting on the successes of the German summer offensive on the Eastern Front, most notably the recent encirclement battle south of Kharkov where more than 240,000 Red Army soldiers had been taken prisoner.[34] Privately, however, the Nazi leadership was far more agitated than it was willing to admit in public. As Goebbels noted in his diary on 28 May 1942:

> Alarming news is arriving from Prague. A bomb attack was staged against Heydrich in a Prague suburb which has severely wounded him. Even if he is not in mortal danger at the moment, his condition is nevertheless worrisome . . . It is imperative that we get hold of the assassins. Then a tribunal should be held to deal with them and their accomplices. The background of the attack is not yet clear. But it is revealing that London reported on the attack very early on. We must be clear that such an attack could set a precedent if we do not counter it with the most brutal of means.[35]

The Führer himself was entirely in agreement. Less than an hour after the assassination attempt, an outraged Hitler ordered Heydrich's deputy and Higher SS and Police Leader in the Protectorate, Karl Hermann Frank, to execute up to 10,000 Czechs in retaliation for the attack. Later that evening, a deeply shaken Himmler reiterated Hitler's order, insisting that the 'one hundred most important' Czech hostages should be shot that very night.[36]

Frank, fearing that large-scale reprisals might work against Germany's vital economic interests in the region, immediately flew to Berlin in a bid to convince Hitler that the attack was an isolated act orchestrated from London. To engage in mass killings, Frank suggested, would mean to abandon Heydrich's successful occupation policies, endangering the productivity of the Czech armaments industry and playing into the hands of enemy propaganda. Hitler, however, was furious and threatened to send SS-General Erich von dem Bach-Zelewski, head of SS anti-partisan warfare on the Eastern Front, to Prague. Bach-Zelewski, Hitler insisted, would 'happily wade through a sea of blood without the least scruple. The Czechs have to learn the lesson that if they shoot down one man, he will immediately be replaced by somebody even worse.' By the end of the meeting, however, Frank had managed to talk Hitler down. For the time being, the Führer rescinded his order for the indiscriminate killings of 10,000 hostages, but insisted that the assassins had to be captured immediately.[37]

Before his departure from Prague, Frank had imposed martial law over the Protectorate. Anyone providing help or shelter for the assassins, or even failing to report information on their whereabouts to the police, was to be killed along with their entire families. The same fate awaited those Czechs over sixteen years of age who failed to obtain new identification papers before midnight of Friday, 29 May. Anyone found without proper papers on Saturday was to be shot. Railway services and all other means of public transportation ceased. Cinemas and theatres, restaurants and coffee houses were closed. The Prague Music Festival was interrupted. A curfew was established from 9 p.m. to 6 a.m. and in accordance with Hitler's directive a reward of 10 million crowns for the capture of the assassins was announced. The Protectorate government, keen to distance itself from the assassination, pledged to double the reward.[38]

Over the course of the afternoon, the head of the German Order Police, Kurt Daluege, was ordered by telephone to assume the post of acting Reich Protector and to hunt down the assassins with all means at his disposal.[39] Fearing that the assassination attempt might be the signal for a more general uprising in the Protectorate, Daluege immediately unleashed one of the largest police operations in modern European history. Prague was completely sealed off by the German police and army. Gestapo units, reinforced by contingents from the Order Police, the SS, the Czech gendarmerie and three Wehrmacht battalions – more than 12,000 men in total – began to raid some 36,000 buildings in search of the assassins.[40] Yet although scarcely a single house was left unexamined, the police operation failed to deliver the desired results. Around 500 people were arrested for minor offences unrelated to the assassination attempt, but despite a vast number of hints (and false allegations) provided by the Czech and German population, the perpetrators were not apprehended.[41]

While the civilian population in the Protectorate was holding its breath in fear of reprisals, Beneš was ecstatic, even though the outcome of the assassination attempt remained uncertain. He immediately sent out a radio message to Bartoš, their principal contact on the ground: 'I see that you and your friends are full of determination. It is proof to me that the entire Czech nation is unshakeable in its position. I assure you that it is bringing results. The events at home have had an incredible effect [in London] and have brought great recognition of the Czech nation's resistance.'[42] Yet it was far from certain at this stage that Heydrich would succumb to his injuries. On 31 May, Himmler visited him in his hospital room in Prague. The wounded man's condition improved steadily and they were able to have a brief conversation.[43] Two days later, however, an infection in the stomach cavity set in. Had penicillin been available in Germany in 1942, Heydrich would have survived. Without it, his fever got worse and he slipped into a coma, giving rise to renewed fears in Berlin that he might die. On 2 June, Goebbels reflected on Heydrich's worsening condition in his diary and added: 'The loss of Heydrich ... would be disastrous!'[44]

A similar view prevailed in Britain: 'If Heydrich should not survive the attempt or if he is invalided for some appreciable time, the loss for the Nazi regime would be very serious indeed. It can safely be said that next to Himmler, Heydrich is the soul of the terror machinery ... The loss of the "master mind" will have serious consequences.'[45] On 3 June Heydrich's condition deteriorated further. The doctors were unable to combat his septicaemia, his temperature soared and he was in great pain. The following morning, at 9 o'clock, Heydrich succumbed to his blood infection. Hitler's 'hangman', as Thomas Mann famously called him in his BBC commentary the following day, was dead.[46]

CHAPTER II

Young Reinhard

The Heydrich Family

REINHARD TRISTAN EUGEN HEYDRICH WAS BORN ON 7 MARCH 1904 IN the Prussian city of Halle on the River Saale.[1] His names reflected the musical background and interests of his family: his father, Bruno Heydrich, was a composer and opera singer of some distinction who had earned nationwide recognition as the founding director of the Halle Conservatory, where his wife, Elisabeth, worked as a piano instructor. In naming their first-born son, they took inspiration from the world of music that surrounded them: 'Reinhard' was the name of the tragic hero of Bruno's first opera, *Amen*, which had premiered in 1895; 'Tristan' paid tribute to Richard Wagner's opera *Tristan and Isolde*; and 'Eugen' was the name of his late maternal grandfather, Professor Eugen Krantz, the director of one of Germany's most acclaimed musical academies, the Royal Dresden Conservatory.[2]

Reinhard's birth coincided with a period of rapid change and boundless optimism in Germany. Under Bismarck and Wilhelm II, Imperial. Germany had become the powerhouse of Europe: its economic and military might was pre-eminent, and its science, technology, education and municipal administration were the envy of the world. But the modernity associated with Wilhelmine Germany also had its darker sides, notably a widespread yearning to become a world power whose influence could match its economic and cultural achievements. Imperial Germany, the country of Heydrich's birth, is therefore best described as Janus-faced: politically semi-authoritarian with a leadership prepared to enhance the country's international standing through reckless foreign policy adventures, but culturally and scientifically hyper-modern.[3]

Reinhard's father, Bruno Heydrich, was a beneficiary of the almost uninterrupted economic boom that had fundamentally transformed Germany since 1871, the time at which the German nation-state had

emerged from a diverse collection of kingdoms, grand duchies, princi-
palities and free cities in Central Europe after three victorious wars
against Denmark (1864), Austria (1866) and France (1870–1). Born in
February 1863 into a Protestant working-class family in the Saxon village
of Leuben, Bruno experienced austerity and economic hardship in early
life. The path of his parents, Ernestine Wilhelmine and Carl Julius
Reinhold Heydrich, led from Leuben, where Carl worked as an impoverished apprentice cabinetmaker, to the city of Meissen, internationally
renowned for its porcelain manufactory, where the family resided from
1867 onwards. Upon his early death from tuberculosis in May 1874 at the
age of just thirty-seven, Carl Julius left behind three sons and three
daughters aged between three and thirteen.[4]

Carl Heydrich's early death left his family in an economically desolate
situation. With no inheritance to speak of, Bruno's mother was forced
to accept odd jobs to earn a living for herself and her six children.
Bruno Heydrich later recalled a 'difficult, sorrowful youth', during which
he was compelled to play the dual role of 'breadwinner and educator'
for his younger siblings, particularly after his elder brother, Reinhold
Otto, died of consumption at the age of nineteen. Finding it hard to
feed her children, Ernestine Heydrich searched for a new provider and
in May 1877 she married a Protestant locksmith, Gustav Robert Süss,
who was thirteen years her junior and just nine years older than her eldest
son Bruno. In subsequent years, it was Süss's Jewish-sounding family
name that would fuel speculation about Heydrich's non-Aryan ancestry,
even though Süss himself was neither Bruno's father nor of Jewish
descent.[5]

Given his modest family background, Bruno's decision to embark on
the career of a professional musician was unusual and required considerable talent and motivation. The professional musician, trained specifically
to perform in concert halls and operas, was a relatively recent phenom-
enon in Germany: the first full-fledged music conservatory in Germany,
Felix Mendelssohn's establishment in Leipzig, dated back only to 1843;
and the Berlin Philharmonic, soon the epitome of the serious music
ensemble, was founded in 1882. A musical education was also costly and
Bruno's mother had no money to spare. But Bruno was not easily deterred.
At the age of twelve, while still at school in Meissen, he began to play first
the violin and the tenor horn, and then the double bass and tuba. The
hobby soon turned into a much needed source of revenue as he and his
younger brother Richard supplemented the family income by singing at
local fairs. Bruno's gift as a singer did not go unnoticed and by the age of
thirteen he was already performing as a soloist in public concerts with the
Meissen Youth Orchestra.[6]

Bruno's talent and determination led to recognition from beyond the small Meissen community: in April 1879, he won a scholarship for a three-year degree in composition and singing at the prestigious Royal Dresden Conservatory, Saxony's finest establishment for musical education, which was directed by his future father-in-law, the Royal Councillor Professor Eugen Krantz.[7] In July 1882, Bruno graduated from the Dresden Conservatory with the highest honours and began to play the contrabass in the Meiningen and Dresden court orchestras. Guest performances as Lyonel in Friedrich von Flotow's comic opera *Martha* at the Court Theatre in Sondershausen (1887) and in the title roles in *Lohengrin* in Weimar (1889) and *Tannhäuser* and *Faust* in Magdeburg (1890) were followed by engagements as a heroic tenor in Stettin, Kolberg, Aachen, Cologne, Halle and Frankfurt, and then on the international stages of Antwerp, Geneva, Brussels, Vienna, Prague and Marienbad. Heydrich's success was considerable, but not sufficient to sustain a viable career as a professional tenor, particularly since he continued to support financially his mother and her four daughters, one of whom was the product of her second marriage. Even so, his early success secured him an invitation to Bayreuth, where, in the summer of 1890, he sang excerpts from *Lohengrin, Parsifal, Die Meistersinger* and *Rienzi* for Richard Wagner's widow, Cosima. In Wagner's festival theatre, built in 1871 on the green hills just outside the small Franconian town of Bayreuth, Heydrich might have had the major breakthrough of his career, but his dream of an engagement at the Bayreuth Wagner Festival was not to be. He was never asked back.[8]

Bruno Heydrich's failure to secure employment in Bayreuth has contributed to the misleading post-war assessment that he was 'a second- or third-class musician', an assessment that has been unduly influenced by his son's criminal career in the Third Reich.[9] The head conductor of the New York Philharmonic Orchestra, Bruno Walter, who met Bruno Heydrich in Cologne in the mid-1890s and who, as a German Jew, had been forced into exile by the Nazis in 1933, stated after the war that Reinhard's father had a 'charmless, no longer entirely fresh voice', and that he was regarded as a 'questionable character' among colleagues. 'The Nazi executioner Reinhard Heydrich', Walter added, 'was the appalling son of this man and, when I read about that sadist, I often think of the mediocre singer with the ugly voice . . . who was chosen by fate to sire a devil.'[10]

Walter's post-war assessment, clouded by Reinhard Heydrich's crimes in the Third Reich, stands in stark contrast to contemporary estimations of Bruno's talents, which suggest that he enjoyed high prestige among his peers. In the words of one music critic, Otto Reitzel, Bruno Heydrich's appearance as Siegfried at the Cologne City Theatre in 1896 was distinguished by 'musical infallibility', while another critic praised his performance as Fra Diavolo in Brunswick in 1901 as 'an utterly perfect impersonation'.[11] Success bred success and in 1895, the same year that he met Bruno Walter, Heydrich was offered the lead role in Hans Pfitzner's *Der arme Heinrich* in Mainz. Pfitzner had become acquainted with Heydrich in Cologne and was so impressed by his 'musically and intellectually alert' performance as Siegfried that he offered him the lead role in his new opera.[12]

Alongside his professional activities as an opera singer, Bruno increasingly devoted himself to composition, ultimately writing no fewer than five operas: *Amen* (1895), *Frieden* (*Peace*, 1907), *Zufall* (*Chance*, 1914), *Das Leiermädchen* (*The Lyre Child*, 1921) and *Das Ewige Licht* (*The Eternal Light*, 1923). Bruno's works were not among the finest compositions of the late nineteenth and early twentieth century, but the staging of several operas in the homeland of classical music, alongside the works of composers like Beethoven, Mendelssohn, Wagner and Strauss, signified considerable success in itself. In terms of style and content, his compositions were inspired by the towering example of Richard Wagner, the leading avant-garde artist of his time, whose four-part music drama *The Ring of the Nibelung* (1876) had revolutionized the international opera scene, taking musical romanticism to new and potentially insurmountable heights. The major themes of Wagner's compositions – love, power and the eternal clashes between good and evil, which he developed most powerfully in his last musical dramas, *Tristan, Die Meistersinger* and *Parsifal* – deeply impacted on Bruno Heydrich's own work, as became evident when his first opera, *Amen*, premiered in Cologne in September 1895 to great critical acclaim.[13]

Like Wagner's heroes Siegfried and Tristan, the protagonist of *Amen*, Reinhard, is an ultimately tragic figure tested by fate and by the devious deeds of the opera's villain, the peasant leader Thomas, representing the threatening rise of Social Democracy in Imperial Germany. In contrast to Thomas, the crippled villain who kills Reinhard through a callous stab in the back, Reinhard is a Germanic hero figure equipped with great moral, intellectual and physical gifts – sufficiently so for Bruno to name his eldest son after him.

The opera's success brought national recognition and a certain degree of material security, allowing Bruno to marry the daughter of his mentor, Professor Krantz, in December 1897. Reinhard Heydrich's mother, Elisabeth Anna Amalia Krantz, was twenty-six at the time of the wedding, and, in many ways, the extreme opposite of her husband. An imposingly tall and slightly overweight figure with black curly hair, Bruno was jovial and entertaining, punctuating his speech with wild theatrical gestures, whereas Elisabeth was small and of slight build, her bearing strict and well disciplined.[14] Moreover, Elisabeth was raised as a Catholic and was therefore a member of a religious minority. Catholics accounted for 36 per cent of the empire's population and inter-confessional marriages were rare. Elisabeth's mother, Maria Antonie, herself the daughter of a wealthy business family in Bautzen, had brought her children up fully cognizant of their social status as a wealthy upper-middle-class family. Her two sons were sent to London to train as merchants and acquire foreign-language skills, while Elisabeth was educated in a Catholic convent in Lugano before training as a pianist in her father's Conservatory. Such an upbringing was common for the daughters of wealthy families: in order to support the social aspirations of their husbands, especially in the educated middle classes, wives were increasingly expected to have a well-rounded education, artistic talent and musical abilities.[15] Despite the couple's different upbringings and characters, the Heydrich marriage was a love match. They shared a deep passion for music and their mutual affection was strong enough to overcome the considerable differences in social status, wealth and religious upbringing.

Encouraged by the success of *Amen*, Bruno Heydrich harboured ambitious plans for his second opera, *Frieden*, which he wanted to be staged at the Berlin Court Opera as a sign of royal endorsement. Official distinctions and royal patronage mattered a great deal in Imperial Germany, but Bruno's high-flying plans came to nothing. Instead, *Frieden* premiered in Mainz on 27 January 1907 to honour the forty-eighth birthday of Kaiser Wilhelm II. The Kaiser's lack of interest in Bruno's opera was partly due to its content: set in the sixteenth century, the three-act opera had a strongly religious subtext and revolved around Catholic notions of sin and redemption – not exactly a drawcard for the head of the German Protestant Church.[16] The mixed public reception of *Frieden* was a disappointment for Heydrich and his stage appearances became less frequent. But although a major breakthrough as a composer was to elude him, he left behind an extensive oeuvre, including five operas, several piano compositions, choral works, lyrical triplets and chamber music pieces: sixty compositions altogether by the outbreak of the Great War, securing him a more than negligible place in the history of early twentieth-century German music.[17]

Bruno's greatest success, however, was as a teacher of music. After his marriage into the Krantz family, and aided by the substantial inheritance left to Elisabeth by her father upon his early death in 1898, the Heydrichs moved to the city of Halle – the birthplace of Georg Friedrich Händel – where Bruno founded the Halle Choir School, an institution based on the famous model of Carl Friedrich Christian Fasch's internationally acclaimed Prussian Sing-Akademie. Although long established as one of Germany's finest university towns, and home to internationally renowned academics such as the economist Gustav Schmoller (1845–1917) and the Leopoldina, Germany's oldest academy for science, Halle had been a sleepy medium-sized provincial town with no more than 50,000 inhabitants for most of the nineteenth century. By the time the Heydrichs arrived, however, it had become one of Germany's booming cities whose prosperity was based on a rapidly expanding mining and chemical industry, as well as a growing number of regional banks that transformed Halle into the sixth-largest German city with a population of 156,000.[18]

Of the many beneficiaries of this radical transformation process, the middle classes prospered most. With their growing wealth, the social status attached to a distinct bourgeois culture of *Bildung* – education and cultivation through engagement with literature, music and the fine arts – increased. For all the backwardness of its political elite, Imperial Germany was a country with a hyper-modern cultural scene, a country in which these arts where widely cherished and officially promoted.[19] By the time Bruno Heydrich opened his business in Halle, music had become a middle-class commodity which formed an essential part of a bourgeois education. Its representative medium was the piano, which became an affordable asset of many middle-class living rooms in the late nineteenth century. With the shift in piano manufacture from craft shop to factory by the mid-nineteenth century, the production of pianos increased eightfold in Germany between 1870 and 1910. Their cost was accordingly cut by half and the piano became the centrepiece of middle-class cultivation. *Hausmusik* or simple compositions for amateur players was a central feature of middle-class entertainment and culture.[20]

In 1901, Bruno Heydrich's small Choir School became a fully fledged conservatory specializing in piano and singing lessons. It was the first establishment of its kind in Halle. Progress was swift in the following years. The citizens of the increasingly wealthy and fast-growing city were well able to afford to send their children to the Conservatory. Several times a year Bruno's pupils staged public concerts, which soon became an important feature of Halle's cultural life.[21] Parallel to his professional success, Bruno Heydrich managed to integrate himself fully into Halle's social circles. As in other European cities at the time, clubs and associations in Halle remained the preferred framework for middle-class social interactions. The Halle registry of 1900 listed 436 private clubs and associations, many of them learned societies that catered for the interests of the university-educated and wealthy middle classes, and arranged literature evenings, concerts, balls and similarly edifying social events. One of the most socially influential of these organizations was the Freemason lodge of the Three Sabres, whose membership included both university staff and members of the wider business community. It is unclear when Bruno Heydrich joined the lodge, but he repeatedly organized concerts on its premises in the first years of the twentieth century.[22]

Bruno was also one of the founders of the Halle branch of the Schlaraffia society, an all-male organization founded in Prague in 1859 with the purpose of advancing the arts, conviviality, and friendship across national borders. Membership of the Schlaraffia was not atypical for an artist like Bruno Heydrich. More eminent contemporaries such as the famous Hungarian composer Franz Lehár and the Austrian poet Peter Rosegger were members of the society, which operated across Central Europe. As a local celebrity, Bruno was also made an honorary member of several of the town's musical societies such as the Hallesche Liedertafel, a men's choir founded in 1834. At the Liedertafel's seventy-fifth anniversary in 1909, he composed a 'Hymn to the Men's Choir' and repeatedly staged choral performances involving both members of the Liedertafel and students from his Conservatory.[23]

Meanwhile, the Halle Conservatory continued to thrive. The number of students grew rapidly, from 20 in 1902 to 190 in 1904, requiring eleven permanent teachers, four teaching assistants and a secretary. At this point, the Heydrichs could also afford to employ two maids and a butler. Elisabeth ran the financial and administrative side of the family business, holding together what would otherwise have soon disintegrated had it been left in the hands of her artistically talented but financially inept husband, who spent money more quickly than he earned it. Bruno's musical talents and social skills, combined with his wife's fortune, secured the Heydrich family a respected place in the Halle community. They cultivated personal relationships with the Mayor of Halle and the editor of the local newspaper, the *Saale-Zeitung*. Another close family friend was Count Felix von Luckner, who would rise to fame during the Great War as one of Germany's most celebrated naval war heroes.[24]

Reinhard Heydrich was therefore born into a family of considerable financial means and social standing, a family that endeavoured to lead an orderly life characterized by regularity and hard work, as was typical for an upwardly mobile German bourgeois family at the turn of the century. While Heydrich's mother devoted herself entirely to the household and the children's wellbeing, occasionally working as a piano teacher in her husband's Conservatory, his father Bruno primarily gloried in his profession as a director. The gender-specific distribution of roles in the Heydrich household was normal for the time: the father was the unchallenged head of the family and made all important decisions concerning child-rearing and education, while the mother – together with governesses in the case of the Heydrich family – looked after the children's everyday needs. Girls, including Reinhard's elder sister Maria, were prepared for their anticipated roles as mothers and wives, whereas boys were raised as future providers and heads of their own household.[25]

Only four months after Reinhard's birth, in the summer of 1904, the Heydrichs moved into a significantly larger home. The swell of new students and the resulting space shortage had forced Bruno Heydrich to look for new premises. In July 1904, Bruno Heydrich's Conservatory for Music and Theatre moved from two separate buildings in Marienstrasse to Poststrasse, one of the more salubrious districts of Halle's city centre. This neighbourhood, with its grand-looking buildings, offered a perfect environment for the Heydrich family business, entirely focused on the educational and representational needs of the middle-class community. The new Conservatory also provided a spacious home for the owner's family and offered a larger number of classrooms and musical instruments, as well as its own rehearsal stage.[26]

Young Reinhard clearly benefited from the musical talents of his parents. As the eldest son, he would one day inherit the Conservatory, a professional destiny that required rigorous musical training from an early age. Even before starting primary school in 1910, he had learned musical notation; he could play Czerny's piano études perfectly and had begun violin lessons. His father encouraged his musical interests and in 1910, at the age of only six, Bruno and his son attended an exceptional musical highlight in the Halle City Theatre: a staging of the *Ring of the Nibelung* with the Bayreuth cast. The passion for romantic music, and for the mythical world of Wagnerian opera in particular, would remain with Reinhard for the rest of his life – a passion he shared with the future Führer of Nazi Germany, Adolf Hitler.[27]

The Heydrich family's daily life ran according to precisely determined and consistently maintained rules. Elisabeth Heydrich took both religious education and active participation in church life extremely seriously. Two conversions had turned the Heydrichs from the Protestant to the Catholic Church. On his marriage to the Catholic Maria Antonie Mautsch, Reinhard's maternal grandfather Eugen Krantz had converted from Protestantism. In the subsequent generation, the Protestant Bruno Heydrich gave in to his wife's demands and converted to Catholicism. This was not an easy decision in an overwhelmingly Protestant society. Religion, always an important force in German life, had acquired a new and heightened significance since the foundation of the German Empire in 1871. The Kulturkampf – Bismarck's unsuccessful attempt to break political Catholicism during the late 1870s and early 1880s through the persecution and arrest of hundreds of Catholic priests for using the pulpit 'for political ends' – left a bitter legacy of mutual suspicion between Protestants and Catholics.[28]

By the time of Heydrich's birth, however, the intensity of confessional antagonism was on the wane. At grassroots level, there was a tendency in popular Catholicism to move away from the insular culture of the 1870s towards an ostensibly patriotic attitude designed to counter the accusation that the main allegiance of German Catholics lay with Rome and not the Reich. Yet religion remained an important aspect of Heydrich's early life. While Protestant church attendance rates dropped significantly in the early twentieth century, the secularization process was less dramatic for the Catholic Church where observance was much more resilient.[29] The Heydrichs were part of this resilient Catholic milieu. Elisabeth, a pious Catholic, led the children in their evening prayers and on Sundays the whole family attended Mass. Reinhard served as an altar boy in the local Catholic church.[30] His consciously maintained Catholicism was one of the few oddities in his early life, particularly when measured against his radically anti-Catholic stance in the 1930s: it made him a member of a tiny minority in the overwhelmingly Protestant city of Halle. According to a census of 1905, 94 per cent of Halle's 170,000 inhabitants were Protestants. The Catholic community, by contrast, had just over 7,000 members.[31]

Another oddity of his childhood, considering his obsession with bodily fitness in subsequent years, was his physical frailty. As a child of slender and relatively small stature with a weak constitution and a susceptibility to illness, Reinhard was encouraged by his parents to take up every kind of physical exercise from an early age: swimming, running, football, sailing, horse-riding and fencing. Heydrich's life-long passion for sport began here.[32] The family's summer vacations were usually spent on the picturesque coast of the Baltic Sea, in the swanky seaside town of Swinemünde on the island of Usedom. For the Heydrich children this was surely the most exciting time of the year. They spent their holidays sightseeing, taking walks and enjoying boat excursions and days on the beach.[33]

Meanwhile the Conservatory continued to flourish: by 1907 it counted a total of 250 fee-paying pupils and the number of employees rose to nineteen. Just one year later, in 1908, the Conservatory had 300 pupils, enough to prompt the Heydrichs to consider a further enlargement of their business.[34] In April 1908 – Reinhard had just turned four – the Heydrichs moved again, this time into a much larger and grander purpose-built house in Gütchenstrasse, in which Reinhard was to spend most of his childhood and adolescence. The three-storey house in an exclusive, status-conscious location near the City Theatre testified to the increasing wealth of the family, generated by Elisabeth's income from the Dresden Conservatory and Bruno's ever-expanding Halle Conservatory, which, by 1911, reached a record high of 400 pupils and employed twenty-seven permanent teachers.[35] 'The house', a schoolfriend of Reinhard's remembered after the war, 'gave the impression of prosperity: grand wood-panelled rooms, a lot of silver dishes, the finest porcelain.' In the courtyard building, there was a large music chamber where regular soirées and concerts were given and schoolfriends celebrated Reinhard's birthday parties.[36]

A contemporary architecture critic conveyed just how large and well appointed the Heydrich family home really was:

> The Conservatory is located in leafy surroundings in the spacious three-storey wing of a splendid new building by Jentzsch & Reichardt in Gütchentrasse. The building houses a number of bright, friendly class-rooms, nearly all of them looking out on to the green gardens, a waiting room, an administration office and everything that makes up a modern school building. But the Conservatory's main attraction is the splendid hall on the ground floor, which has seating for 300 people. Spacious, bright and airy, it provides an extremely pleasant summertime abode to the many friends and sponsors, who have been coming to the Conservatory's performances for years in order to follow the progress of Heydrich's pupils. The hall, with its tasteful electrical lighting system and its ingeniously painted decorations, makes one imagine to be in one of those nice little private princely theatres that charm visitors in castles here and there ...[37]

Given Bruno's economic success and social ambitions, it had always been clear that his eldest son would attend high school. Secondary schooling at the time was reserved for a small, privileged and overwhelmingly male elite. In the early 1900s, some 90 per cent of German pupils never went beyond primary school. Of the fortunate 10 per cent attending all-boys secondary schools, some 66 per cent continued their education in the humanist *Gymnasien* which ended with the *Abitur*, the school-leaving certificate qualifying them to attend university. The remaining 34 per cent attended the *Oberrealschule*, a slightly less academic institution whose leaving certificate did not qualify its pupils for university.[38]

When the time came for Reinhard to go to secondary school, his parents decided to send him to the local *Reformgymnasium*, a relatively new institution that embodied the scientific optimism of the dynamic, future-oriented German Empire. The *Reformgymnasium* was designed to reconcile the characteristics of the classical *Gymnasium* – with its emphasis on a rounded humanist education and training in Latin and ancient Greek – with the modern educational requirements of the early twentieth century. As with the majority of the new polytechnical universities in the German Reich, the *Reformgymnasium* had its origins in the technological zeal and enthusiasm of the late nineteenth century, which in turn helped to foster Germany's leading role in the so-called second industrial revolution based on technological innovation. By the time Heydrich started secondary school, Germany had become Europe's industrial powerhouse, internationally dominant in the fields of chemistry, physics and engineering. Bruno Heydrich's decision to send his eldest son to a *Reformgymnasium* was therefore not only the result of Reinhard's good grades, but also a tribute to the technological and scientific optimism of the era. The *Reformgymnasium* was modern in yet another sense. While the vast majority of German schools at the time were denominational, the *Reformgymnasium* was not affiliated to any religious persuasion. In 1906, no fewer than 95 per cent of Protestant and 91 per cent of Catholic children were educated in schools of their own confession. Reinhard Heydrich's educational experience was therefore exceptionally modern and forward-looking in more than one sense.[39]

In addition to the main scientific subjects taught at German high schools – chemistry, physics and mathematics – great emphasis was placed on German literature and culture as well as on modern languages: French was taught from the first form onwards, Latin from the lower-fourth, and English was introduced in the lower-fifth. Unsurprisingly perhaps, given his cultured family background, Reinhard Heydrich's performance at school was above average. His results in science subjects were particularly outstanding and his career ambition as a teenager was to become a chemist. Simultaneously, he began to develop an insatiable appetite for crime fiction and spy novels, many of them serialized in newspapers. Detective novels from Britain and the United States – from Sherlock Holmes to Nick Carter and Nat Pinkerton – were a huge success in Germany and they captured the imagination of the young Heydrich. Throughout the war and the 1920s, he maintained his keen interest in the genre and put his expertise to good use when he first met Himmler in 1931. Neither of the two men had any idea of how to set up an espionage service, but Heydrich used the knowledge gained from detective and spy novels to impress Himmler to the extent that he offered him the job of creating an SS intelligence agency: the future SD.[40]

War and Post-war

In the summer of 1914 – when the Heydrichs were spending their annual holiday on the Baltic coast – the family's well-ordered world was deeply shaken by a momentous event: on 28 June the Austrian heir apparent, Franz Ferdinand, was shot in Sarajevo, aggravating an international crisis that soon culminated in the First World War. Popular enthusiasm for war in August 1914 was limited and the Heydrichs were no exception. Although confident that the war would be won, Bruno and his wife were fully aware that it also brought with it economic uncertainties for the future of the Conservatory.[41]

The full implications of the events surrounding him were difficult to comprehend for the young Reinhard Heydrich. As a ten-year-old at the outbreak of the Great War, he was part of the war youth generation – too young to be sent to the front as a soldier, but old enough to experience the war consciously as a decisive event in his personal life and in the history of his country. Even though no immediate family member had to take to the field, the war was omnipresent: newspapers and posters bombarded the home front with glorified reports on the progress of the military campaigns, photographs of prominent generals and decorated alumni of the school adorned the classrooms, and teachers announced the latest victories in school assemblies. Meanwhile, the older boys in Reinhard's school gradually disappeared to the front. By June 1915, some 80 per cent of the boys in the highest grade had volunteered for the army while those left behind in the lower grades eagerly awaited the time when they could follow their example. Like most boys of his age, Reinhard must have regarded the war as a distant adventure game from which the Germans would inevitably emerge as the victors – a belief fostered by the enormously popular penny dreadfuls that sold in millions, notably to teenage boys.[42]

While the war raged on in Eastern Europe and the distant fields of Flanders and northern France, the Conservatory's economic fortunes began to decline slowly but steadily. Due to the outbreak of the war, student enrolment stagnated and then began to shrink. By the end of 1914, Bruno Heydrich had to sack nine of his teachers, but continued to stage a number of public concerts and performances of the Patriotic Men's Singing Society of 1914, which he had founded upon the outbreak of war. His wife Elisabeth contributed to the national cause, too, by running a knitting class at the Conservatory, where Halle's middle-class wives and mothers produced clothing – mainly scarves and socks – for their soldier husbands, sons and brothers at the front.[43]

By 1915 the economic effects of war started to encroach on the Heydrichs' everyday life. Restrictions on food supplies and other essential goods became increasingly apparent. Germany had imported 25 per cent of its food supplies before 1914 and the British naval blockade effectively cut the country off from all imports. The problem was amplified by the lack of work-horses and able-bodied men on farms, and food production accordingly decreased by 30 per cent during the war. Bread rationing began in 1915 and the following year meat rationing was introduced. The pre-war average daily nutritional intake was 2,500 calories, which declined by more than half during the war.[44] For the first time in their lives, the Heydrich children experienced hunger, particularly during the Turnip Winter of 1916. At the same time, real wages fell, especially those of the middle classes, many of whom also lost their savings and were no longer able to afford a musical education for their children. The Heydrichs' holidays, too, became less exclusive. During the war, Reinhard spent his annual summer vacation in the Düben heath between the towns of Torgau and Dessau, where his parents rented a cottage from a local forester. After the Second World War, the forester's son, Erich Schultze, recalled that he and Reinhard passed their time reading history books and acquiring a rudimentary knowledge of Russian by talking to the prisoners of war working the local fields. According to Schultze, he and Reinhard also worked their way through the original French version of Charles Seignobos' *Histoire de la civilisation*, which they discussed in French, or at least attempted to do so.[45]

While the war on the Western Front stagnated and the French troops were defending Verdun with unexpected tenacity, the Heydrich family in 1916 eagerly awaited the publication of *Hugo Riemanns Musik-Lexikon*, the most complete and widely used German encyclopaedia of music and musicians at the time, which was due to appear that summer with an entry on Bruno Heydrich's life and work.[46] Anticipation turned to anger and frustration when the copy finally arrived. On opening Riemann's encyclopedia, the family discovered an entry suggesting that Bruno was a Jewish composer and that his last name was 'actually Süss'.[47] Heydrich was not a particularly political man, but the insinuation that he was a Jew – potentially damaging in a Protestant city ripe with latent anti-Semitism – prompted him to sue the encyclopaedia's editors for libel. As the lawsuit in 1916 revealed, the original entry on Heydrich (without the 'damaging' insinuation) had been altered by Martin Frey, a former pupil of Heydrich's who had been expelled from the Conservatory, in a targeted act of revenge. Frey had arranged the alteration through a relative on the dictionary's editorial team in order to harm Bruno Heydrich's reputation in the Halle community.[48] After the facts had been established, Bruno won the court case and the mention of his alleged Jewish background was removed from the next edition of the encyclopaedia. But the rumours did not disappear. Instead they gained further currency after it became publicly known that Hans Krantz, one of Reinhard's maternal uncles in Dresden, was married to a Jewish woman from Hungary called Iza Jarmy. At school, Reinhard's schoolmates began to tease him and his brother Heinz Siegfried by calling them 'Isi' or 'Isidor'.[49]

Throughout the war years, the Heydrichs placed a great deal of importance on denying these rumours, threatening those who repeated them with libel actions. Yet their own personal relations with the Jewish citizens of Halle – who numbered no more than 1,400 in 1910 – were quite normal and there is no evidence to suggest that Bruno Heydrich's attitude towards the Jews was hostile. On the contrary, Jews sent their sons and daughters to Heydrich's Conservatory; Bruno rented out the cellar of the school as a storage space to a local Jewish salesman; and his eldest son, Reinhard, became friends with the son of the cantor of the Halle Jewish community, Abraham Lichtenstein.[50]

The Heydrich scandal of 1916 is therefore indicative less of Bruno's own racist beliefs than of a general climate of mounting anti-Semitism. Although Jews were no longer subject to discriminatory legislation in Imperial Germany, unofficial discrimination against them continued when it came to access to social interaction and to eminent positions in the state bureaucracy or the upper ranks of the military. Anti-Semitism in Imperial Germany was widespread, but probably no more than in France or East-Central Europe, and it was not a clearly defined, internally consistent system of beliefs. Rather, it was a loose cluster of stereotypes drawn from a broad range of traditions that could be mixed in varying proportions. Racist anti-Semitism, the driving ideological force in Heydrich's later life, remained the affair of a small minority on the extreme fringes of German politics, and no lobby group focusing single-mindedly on the 'Jewish question' ever became an electoral success in Imperial Germany. But expressions of hostility towards Jews could be found across the political spectrum as well as in public statements from the Protestant and Catholic Churches. For the young Reinhard Heydrich, the accusation of being a half-Jew was a nuisance, but, although it may have made him hostile towards those spreading the rumours, it certainly did not turn him into a racist anti-Semite.[51]

Far more devastating than the rumours about Heydrich's Jewish ancestry was the news that the war was lost. German propaganda had suggested right up until the autumn of 1918 that victory was in sight and the peace treaty of Brest-Litovsk, which formalized Germany's victory over Russia in the spring of 1918, encouraged people to believe that the defeat of Britain and France was only a matter of time.[52] The signing of the armistice in November 1918 therefore came as a major blow and an unwanted surprise that shattered the hopes and expectations of many Germans. The suddenness of the Allied victory only months after the beginning of the initially successful German spring offensive of 1918 contributed to a situation in which many Germans refused to believe that their army had been defeated. Instead, a powerful myth gained currency across the country: the so-called stab-in-the-back legend, according to which Germany's undefeated armed forces had been betrayed by unpatriotic revolutionaries on the home front. The stab in the back had a powerful resonance in German culture, not least because the hero figure of the popular Nibelung saga, Siegfried, was slain from behind – a theme that was taken up in Wagner's *Ring* and Bruno Heydrich's opera *Amen*. Although a majority of Germans initially welcomed the end of the war and the end of the imperial system, the mood quickly changed when the revolution radicalized in late 1918 and early 1919, giving rise to shattering political upheavals and a pervasive apocalyptic mood. Two months after Germany's defeat, the extreme left-wing revolutionary Spartakists attempted to seize power in Berlin. The uprising failed and on the evening of 15 January 1919 its main leaders, Karl Liebknecht and Rosa Luxemburg, were arrested and murdered by Freikorps soldiers. Yet the revolutionary threat continued, notably in Bremen, Munich and the industrial heartlands of Western and Central Germany.[53]

By the end of February 1919, the revolutionary wave reached Heydrich's home town of Halle. Hitherto, Bruno Heydrich had not been a particularly political man – loyal to the Kaiser, national-liberal in outlook but never affiliated with any particular party. His politicization began with the German defeat and the subsequent revolution: in early 1919, he became a member of the German Nationalist People's Party (DNVP), a party with a staunchly anti-democratic, monarchist agenda. He had become political, and the momentous political changes that occurred in Halle in the spring of 1919 could not have failed to impact on his fourteen-year-old son Reinhard.

On 23 February 1919 the Central German Miners' Conference convened in Halle and proclaimed a general strike against the Provisional Reich government in Weimar. The already tense situation deteriorated further when the anti-Communist citizens of Halle responded with a counter-strike: local businessmen closed their shops, thereby cutting the city off from all food supplies. Postal services ceased to operate and policemen, doctors, teachers and other civil servants refused to work. The general strike reached its climax on 27 February, when three-quarters of the factories and mines of Central Germany were picketed. That same day, Halle experienced the largest political demonstration in its history: up to 50,000 workers demanded the resignation of the Reich government, the imposition of workers' councils and the nationalization of Germany's industrial plant. Concerned about the growing unrest in Halle – close to the city of Weimar where the deputies of the Constituent National Assembly had gathered to draft a new republican constitution – the Social Democratic Defence Minister, Gustav Noske, ordered a Freikorps unit, composed of demobilized ex-soldiers and student volunteers, to 'recapture' the city of Halle. Its commanding officer was Major General Georg Maercker, a staunchly conservative former colonial officer who had participated in the murderous colonial campaigns against the Herero and Nama in German South-West Africa before fighting on the Eastern and Western Fronts in the First World War.[54]

For Reinhard Heydrich, the experience of a feasible revolutionary threat in his home town reinforced perceptions of living through a momentous era of tangible and existential threats. Both at home and at school, the example of the Bolshevik Revolution of 1917 featured prominently in discussions about the future fate of the German Reich. Rumours about atrocities committed by Bolsheviks against the former Russian elites emanated from the East and were quickly projected on to the situation in Germany itself. The pervasiveness of such rumours can be explained only by considering the broader context of the Russian Revolution and the subsequent civil war that cost the lives of up to 3 million people. The successful consolidation of power by a determined revolutionary minority of Russian Bolsheviks during the winter of 1917–18 injected a potent new energy into the world of politics, which resulted in the emergence of equally determined counter-revolutionary forces, for whom the violent repression of revolution, and more especially of revolutionaries, constituted their overriding goal.[55]

As Maercker was gathering his Freikorps troops south of Halle, the situation escalated further when one of his officers, Lieutenant Colonel Klüber, entered the city in civilian disguise on a reconnaissance trip. When Klüber was discovered by revolutionary soldiers, he was attacked and beaten before being thrown into the River Saale and killed by a gunshot fired from the crowd that had gathered to watch the spectacle. The incident radicalized an already tense atmosphere, fuelled by atrocity stories that emanated from other parts of Germany, most notably from Berlin where conservative papers suggested that Communist insurgents had killed or wounded government troops and civilian hostages. Most of the atrocity rumours were subsequently found to be untrue or exaggerated, but they exerted a powerful influence on the public imagination, including that of young Reinhard Heydrich, who frequently cited the events of 1918–19 during his career in the Third Reich.[56]

Maercker's troops invaded the city the following morning. For several days, the troops barricaded themselves in Halle's main post office while the insurgents took over the City Theatre, just a few blocks away from the Heydrich family home. Over the following two days, Reinhard and his parents witnessed the government troops attacking the City Theatre with heavy weapons, including artillery, before finally storming the building. Maercker's troops then proceeded to crush the rebellion with utter ruthlessness, killing a total of twenty-nine people and wounding sixty-seven, many of them civilian bystanders. More than 200 people were arrested. Maercker's own troops suffered seven deaths.

On Monday, 3 March, Maercker ordered the systematic occupation of the city and declared martial law. Two days later, he set up a voluntary civil defence force from among the citizens and university students of Halle. Its primary purpose was to protect private property and maintain order in the unlikely event of further civil unrest. The formation soon counted 400 members.[57] One of the new recruits was Reinhard Heydrich, now fifteen years old and still a pupil at the *Reformgymnasium*.[58] Very little is known about his role in the volunteer force, but given his age and inexperience it is unlikely that his involvement amounted to more than a symbolic gesture – a somewhat pathetic attempt to compensate for his lack of fighting experience in the war by joining a paramilitary organization unlikely to witness real fighting. For many of the young volunteers like him, who had come of age in a bellicose atmosphere saturated with tales of heroic bloodshed but had missed out on a first-hand experience of the 'storms of steel', the militias offered a welcome opportunity to live a romanticized warrior existence without any real danger of getting killed.[59]

In the light of his subsequent career and the popular characterization of the Freikorps as a vanguard of Nazism, it is easy to overestimate the impact of Heydrich's involvement in paramilitary activities after the Great War.[60] For some of the future protagonists of the Third Reich, including Heinrich Himmler and Heydrich's future deputy, Dr Werner Best, the experience of defeat and revolution was indeed the moment of political awakening. As the eighteen-year-old Himmler noted in his diary during the revolution in his native Bavaria, the 'treason' of the home front called for a violent response and he accordingly joined the Freikorps 'Oberland', which participated in the bloody crushing of the short-lived Bavarian Council Republic in the spring of 1919.[61] Heydrich's response was less radical and indeed more representative of the war youth generation as a whole. Although unquestionably outraged by the German defeat and the outbreak of revolution, Heydrich did not become a proto-Nazi in the immediate aftermath of the Great War. Like many of his friends from school, who also joined the Halle civil defence force, he was primarily motivated by youthful adventurism and the promise of a bloodless war game against Communists who had long been defeated. His actual involvement in paramilitary activity was therefore largely confined to showing off his over-sized steel helmet and uniform to his teenage friends.[62]

Barely a year later, when Heydrich was still enlisted in the civil defence force, Halle was once more the site of bloody streetfighting. In March 1920, several Freikorps marched on Berlin to protest against their impending dissolution by the republican government and managed temporarily to install an authoritarian government under the leadership of Wolfgang Kapp, a prominent founding member of the far-right German Fatherland Party. The putsch was quickly defeated by an impressive general strike that in turn prompted the radical left in the industrial heartlands of Germany to undertake a second attempt at bringing about a Bolshevik revolution. Halle, with its sizeable industrial working class, was one of the cities affected by the uprising. For several days, the retreating Freikorps fought Communist sympathizers in prolonged street battles resulting in the deaths of dozens of men on both sides. On 23 March, government troops intervened and restored public order in Halle.[63]

Once again, there is no evidence to suggest that Heydrich actively participated in any of the fighting. There is little doubt that defeat and revolution had a politicizing effect on him, but it remains unclear just how far that politicization went. According to the post-war testimony of his childhood friend, the later SA officer Karl von Eberstein, Heydrich had already developed an 'extremely *völkisch*' attitude during the war – an attitude in which the interests of the *Volk* or German people took precedence over all other political or ethical considerations – reading radical nationalist pamphlets and history books and seeking entry into several of the now rapidly emerging racist leagues and societies in Halle.[64] Heydrich himself later claimed to have been a member of the Halle branch of the German Nationalist Protection and Defiance League (Deutschvölkischer Schutz- und Trutzbund) between 1920 and 1922. With 25,000 members in 1920, the League was the largest and most active of the countless anti-Semitic associations that sprang up in Germany after the defeat of 1918, but it was banned after the assassination of Foreign Minister Walther Rathenau in 1922.[65]

It is possible and indeed likely that Heydrich merely claimed membership in the organization after 1933 in order to prove his early commitment to right-wing politics.[66] The only existing document that supports his claim of early involvement in right-wing organizations is an undated postcard that has survived in his personal papers. The postcard's front bears an advertising text for the Teutonic Order, one of the countless tiny fringe-groups of the extreme right that blossomed in post-war Germany. On the back, an anonymous author enquires about Heydrich's commitment to the nationalist cause: 'We look forward to hearing from you again very soon. It is high time that the racially conscious and pure-blooded Germans pulled themselves together for the final deed. Are you one of us?!' The most likely explanation for this mysterious postcard is that Heydrich indeed attended a meeting of the Teutonic Order in Halle, but that he never went back, thus prompting the written enquiry. For all we know, he never responded to it.[67]

Although Heydrich hardly became a proto-Nazi or mass murderer in waiting as a result of the events of 1918–19, he most certainly subscribed to ideas that were shared by many young Germans attending school in the immediate post-war period: anti-Bolshevism, a strong rejection of the Versailles Peace accords and a refusal to accept the Reich's 'bleeding frontier' with Poland. While these ideas were something on which most Germans – from the moderate left to the radical right – could agree, Heydrich's personal experiences of the upheavals of 1918–19 also made him susceptible to an idea that would soon form an integral part of Nazi ideology: the conviction that life was a permanent and violent struggle. From 1919 onwards – first in Halle, then in the navy and finally in the SS – Heydrich was surrounded by a political milieu in which the willingness to use violence against a whole range of enemies increasingly formed a common denominator.

Reinhard shared his generation's sense of living through a crisis of epic proportions, characterized by military defeat and its political consequences, as well as by the increasing pauperization of the middle classes. Germany had lost over 2 million men in action and more than 4.1 million soldiers were wounded out of an overall population of 65 million. The country had spent the equivalent of some 40 billion dollars on the war, most of which it had borrowed from its citizens. In the Treaty of Versailles, Germany lost 13 per cent of its territory and was required to pay 33 billion dollars as a war indemnity to the victors. The post-war economic crisis went hand in hand with price inflation of a dimension unprecedented in German history. To a large extent, this inflation had domestic origins, most notably heavy borrowing during the war and an accumulation of debt that could be repaid only in the event of military victory. The financial and economic crisis that climaxed in the infamous 1923 hyperinflation when half a kilo of butter cost 13,000 Reichsmarks shook the middle classes' economic foundations and virtually wiped out the Heydrichs' cash assets. The currency reform of 1923 did little to alter this state of affairs. It became more and more difficult for Bruno Heydrich to support his family, and indeed to support his mother who continued to receive payments from her son until her death in January 1923.[68]

The inflation and the destruction of many Germans' life savings significantly reduced the ability of Halle's citizens to finance their children's musical education. The Conservatory still had 200 pupils in 1921, and the Heydrichs still managed to pay for their children's leisure actitivies, such as visits to silent films and operas or attendance at dancing lessons.[69] But by 1922 their financial crisis became apparent: in a lengthy letter to the

Halle magistrate, Bruno Heydrich begged for a state subsidy of 10,000 Reichsmarks and a reduced rate for coal, gas and electricity in order to keep the Conservatory afloat. Bruno was forced to admit that 'as a result of excessive price increases, the reduced income, and the ever-increasing attrition of our private property' his family was 'at the end of its tether'. If the war and the subsequent revolution had already undermined the economic viability of his business, the inflation deprived him of the means to subsidize the Conservatory with his family's savings. The existence of the Conservatory, the city's premier music teacher training college, was 'seriously' under threat. Bruno's letter expressed deep resentment of the rise of commercial entertainment, the advent of radio and the onslaught of 'modern times' more generally, times in which 'the general public prefers to eat *Bratwurst* than to receive a musical education'.[70]

Bruno Heydrich's request for state subsidies was turned down. At the age of sixty, he faced professional ruin and his life's work appeared doomed. Even if the stabilization of the German economy in early 1924 provided the Conservatory with a certain amount of relief, fear of radical economic and social decline would remain constant companions of the Heydrich family for the next decade.

In the Navy

After obtaining his *Abitur* leaving certificate with high marks in the late spring of 1922, Reinhard decided to pursue a career as a naval officer. Becoming a professional musician and taking over as director of the Halle Conservatory, a logical step considering his family background and his own musical talents, was no longer an attractive option in light of the business's steady economic decline. He also decided against studying chemistry, a subject that had particularly interested him at school.[71]

What exactly drove Reinhard Heydrich to join the German navy remains highly speculative. His wife suggested after the war that the young Heydrich became obsessed with the navy during his childhood holidays on the Baltic coast where he could observe the manoeuvres of the Imperial High Seas Fleet.[72] Others have emphasized the personal influence of Count Felix von Luckner, the old family friend and naval hero of the First World War whose autobiography, *Seeteufel* (Devil of the Sea), with its exciting descriptions of his adventurous voyages between 1914 and 1918, appeared one year before Heydrich finished school and was devoured by a whole generation of young German readers.[73] A third conceivable influence may have come from Heydrich's childhood friend, Erich Schultze, with whom he had spent his wartime holidays in the Düben heath. Schultze had already joined the navy as an officer cadet in 1921.[74]

Whatever the decisive childhood influence, young Reinhard had certainly been brought up in a country in which the military in general and the navy more specifically enjoyed great prestige as custodians of the empire's national security and guarantors of Germany's future destiny, a perception cultivated in school textbooks of the late Wilhelmine period.[75] The appeal of a soldierly existence remained untarnished after 1918, particularly to those young men who had no first-hand experience of trench warfare with which to compare the heroic images conjured up by the glorifying war movies and penny dreadfuls of the early Weimar years. Not only did the world of the military offer security and structure in increasingly insecure and seemingly disordered times, but the fantastical figure of the heroic front soldier, the violent 'new man' whose strict and defiant military bearing distinguished him from the despised images of an effeminate Berlin dandy or a shabby-looking Bolshevik revolutionary, exerted a powerful influence on young German men in the 1920s as a role model.[76]

Yet the German navy, once the pride and joy of German nationalists, was perhaps more tainted by the odium of treason than any other branch of the military: it was in Kiel in 1918 that the November Revolution began with a mutiny of German sailors against their officers' orders to put the Imperial Fleet to sea for a final showdown against the Royal Navy. Only after the apparently 'heroic' self-sinking of the Imperial High Seas Fleet in Scapa Flow in 1919 – a successful attempt to prevent the surrender of German warships to Britain – had the navy's reputation been restored to such an extent that it once more represented an attractive career option for the sons of patriotic middle-class families. It was the popular wartime image of the naval officer – daring, adventurous, self-controlled and attractive to women – that appealed to Heydrich, rather than the grim and underwhelming reality of a naval force reduced by the Versailles Treaty to 15,000 men and a handful of dated battleships and cruisers.[77]

The Heydrich family's attitude towards Reinhard's career choice was ambivalent. While his mother was 'very proud' that Heydrich wanted to become a naval officer, his father found it difficult to accept that his musically talented son would not take over the family business.[78] Despite his father's objections, Heydrich began his service as a naval cadet in Kiel on 1 April 1922, together with dozens of other cadets of 'Crew 22' (named after the year of the intake). The cadet training commenced with six months of harsh basic training aboard the battleship *Braunschweig*, followed by three months on the sailing vessel *Niobe*. It ended with service on the cruiser *Berlin* between July 1923 and March 1924. On 1 April 1924, Heydrich was promoted to senior midshipman and sent for officer training to the Mürwick Naval College near Flensburg.[79]

According to post-war testimonies of Heydrich's fellow cadets, unquestionably tainted by their determination not to appear to have been close to a war criminal, Heydrich remained an isolated loner throughout his time in Kiel and 'had no friends among the crew'.[80] While it is true that Heydrich found it difficult to adjust to the new environment, the reasons for his outsider status remain unclear. Some former crew members emphasized his shyness, his unusual physical appearance and his inability to cope with the physical demands of the training as explanations. 'Heydrich's appearance was of remarkable disharmony,' one of his crew colleagues remembered after the Second World War.

> His limbs somehow did not fit together. A long, narrow, and much too small head sat on a long neck, with short blond hair, a long nose, mistrustful squinting eyes, that stood very close together, and a small mouth, whose gaping lips he usually pinched together. A long upper body with almost apelike arms sat over a deep, broad pelvis, a husky build with rounded, unmuscular legs ... He appeared gangly, somewhat soft and effeminate.

Even Heydrich's learning abilities, so the same fellow officer recalled, were:

> average at best. Scholarship and thoroughness were never his thing. Perhaps he picked up on things quickly, but he was too superficial to process what he had learned and to organize it properly. However, it would be unfair merely to attribute shrewdness to him. His intelligence ... was based on logical thinking, consistent behaviour and an instinct for treating others in a way that was advantageous to himself, in recognizing opportunities for himself, in anticipating the wishes of his superiors and in his adaptability.[81]

Considering Heydrich's life-long passion for sport, it seems highly unlikely that an inability to cope with the physical demands of the training was the key reason for his outsider status.[82] Heydrich had been an active sportsman for many years before he joined the navy. He was a member of a gymnastic association in Halle, an active swimmer and a team member of his high school's rowing club. Furthermore, he had taken up fencing in his early childhood and practised daily during his time in the navy. Moreover, he was a devoted sailor, winning the Baltic Sea championships in a twelve-foot dinghy in 1927 and the North Sea championships in the same class one year later.[83]

It is more likely that Heydrich's role as an outsider among the crew members was at least partly a result of his educated middle-class background, particularly his musical proclivities and his inclination to play the violin on board whilst off-duty, a pasttime that seemed oddly out of place in the masculine world of the navy.[84] His father had given him a violin as a parting gift when he left for Kiel and Heydrich practised on it in solitude whenever he found the time. His musical inclinations repeatedly made him the target of ridicule. During his basic training in Kiel, for example, a non-commissioned training officer from West Prussia frequently woke him at night and forced him to play the Toselli Serenade on his violin. Many years later, Heydrich recalled these humiliating incidents when making condescending comments regarding the racial inferiority of the West Prussians with their 'Polish-infested' blood.[85]

Two further reasons for Heydrich's oddball status at the beginning of his officer training need to be considered. By embarking on a naval career, he had entered one of the most staunchly right-wing milieus in Weimar Germany, a milieu in which officers and NCOs compensated for the 'shameful' naval mutiny in Kiel in 1918 by taking an aggressively nationalistic stance. The naval officer corps not only played a decisive role in the Freikorps violence against Communist insurgents in 1919 and 1920, but also provided a recruiting ground for many of the right-wing terrorists that formed the infamous Organisation Consul, responsible for the assassinations of prominent Weimar politicians such as Matthias Erzberger and Walther Rathenau. Within this general climate of right-wing extremism, or so some of his naval colleagues testified after the war, Heydrich appeared oddly apolitical. If indeed he had flirted with right-wing extremism in 1918, he seems to have lost interest by 1922. When one of his fellow cadets, Ernst Werner Techow, participated in the murder of Foreign Minister Rathenau in the summer of 1922, Heydrich disappointed his roommates by displaying no interest in the case. Neither was the French occupation of the Ruhr in 1923 – hotly discussed among his fellow naval officers and the German population at large – of any concern to him. If anything, so his fellow cadet Hans Rehm testified after the war, Heydrich was considered a liberal by his colleagues and shunned for that very reason.[86] Interestingly enough, his future wife Lina gave a similar assessment of his early lack of interest in politics. After the war, Lina maintained that 'politically he was clueless ... He regarded all parties, particularly the Nazi Party, with arrogance and considered politics itself to be vulgar. In this connection he acted very much the snob and regarded his naval career as the most important thing. The rest didn't count.'[87]

Perhaps even more important for his outsider status than his apparent indifference to politics was the re-emergence of rumours about his alleged Jewish family background. 'In our class', one fellow officer cadet recalled, 'Heydrich was more or less regarded as a Jew because another crew comrade from Halle told us that his family was actually called "Süss" and that this was widely known in Halle.' Over the following years, his fellow cadets would call Heydrich the 'white Jew' or 'white Moses'. In order to counter the rumours, Heydrich maintained that he had been a member of the anti-Semetic German Nationalist Protection and Defiance League in Halle – an organization that rejected Jews as members and which had been abolished after the Rathenau assassination in 1922. Although probably untrue, the claim seems to have improved Heydrich's standing among his peers.[88]

Heydrich's position further improved after a two-month stint on the sailing vessel *Niobe* in the summer of 1923, after which he was transferred to the cruiser *Berlin*. It was here, on the *Berlin*, that Heydrich met and befriended the future head of Nazi Germany's military intelligence agency, Wilhelm Canaris, then the first officer on board. Canaris impressed the young Heydrich with his military experience: as a navigating lieutenant aboard the small cruiser *Dresden* during the Battle of the Falklands in 1914 he had managed to escape from internment in Chile in 1915 before returning home to Germany. Canaris in turn instantly warmed to the shy young man with musical inclinations and he became Heydrich's mentor over the coming years. From 1924 onwards, he frequently invited Heydrich to his house in Kiel, where Reinhard and Canaris's wife, Erika, played the violin together in a private string quartet and often entertained members of Kiel's social establishment.[89]

Heydrich also played music outside the Canaris household. According to Hertha Lehmann-Jottkowitz, a student at the Kiel Institute for Global Economics in the later 1920s, she first met Heydrich when he played the violin at the home of a mutual friend and amateur cellist. Lehmann-Jottkowitz remembered Heydrich as an extremely sensitive violinist who displayed a tenderness and sentimentality that deeply impressed his audiences. In conversation he gave the impression of being a 'superficial sailor' who had little to contribute to discussions, but he was completely transformed once he started playing the violin or discussed musical subjects.[90]

The final component of Heydrich's officer training was a six-month stint on the *Schleswig-Holstein*, the flagship of the German North Sea Fleet. In the summer of 1926, he went on a training cruise through the Atlantic and into the Western Mediterranean, visiting Spain, Portugal and the island of Madeira, where he apparently caused a minor scandal in the Officers' Mess when a British officer's wife refused to accept his invitation to dance with him.[91] Following the completion of his training aboard the *Schleswig-Holstein*, Heydrich was promoted to second naval liutenant.[92] After his promotion, he appears to have received more recognition from his colleagues and was less frequently the butt of jokes. His comrade and

roommate on the *Schleswig-Holstein*, Heinrich Beucke, recalled that
after his promotion Heydrich 'developed significantly ... His superiors
frequently gave him recognition and good evaluations. He was obliging
and showed that people could rely on him ... With every sign of recognition, his zeal increased, and so did his arrogance ... Ambition was
undoubtedly Heydrich's strongest characteristic. He wanted to accom-
plish something and others were supposed to be amazed.'[93] His childhood
friend Erich Schultze came to a similar conclusion when he met Reinhard
during a brief visit to Halle. 'We were all certain that he would go far in
the navy because of his ambition and ability. He was never content with
what he had achieved. His impulse was always for more; to do better; to
go higher. As a lieutenant he was already dreaming of becoming an
admiral.'[94]

While his relationship with the other young officers improved substantially, Heydrich began to display a noticeable arrogance towards his
subordinates – something that would increase even further during the
1930s. He approached the common sailors and non-commissioned officers
on the *Schleswig-Holstein* in an imperious and personally insulting manner,
so much so that on two occasions his behaviour nearly led to a mutiny.[95]
But, despite these setbacks, Heydrich's confidence grew and he felt that he
had 'finally settled into' his career as a navy officer.[96] During and after his
service aboard the *Schleswig-Holstein* he used his more generously allotted
leisure time for sporting activities, mainly for sailing, swimming and
fencing. According to his roommate Beucke, Heydrich exercised every
day, horse-riding and jogging through the woods at weekends:

> He wanted to become a pentathlete. He did everything with astounding
> energy while vastly overestimating his talents and skills ... He was
> already dreaming of Olympic laurels and was never ashamed to praise
> his achievements to the high heavens. When he wasn't invited to the
> Reichswehr Sport Championships, he felt completely misjudged. Based
> on the results achieved at the Championships, he 'proved' to me that he
> would have won the pentathlon ...[97]

In Heydrich's case, sporting prowess and military bearing were propelled
by a desire to gain acceptance by his peers, but he was not alone in his
enthusiasm for sport as an expression of youthful virility. By 1931 over
6.5 million Germans were members of organized sport associations. The
most popular sports for spectators were martial arts of various kinds, as
well as sports involving speed, including modern piloting, which with its
daring manoeuvres was associated with adventure, heroic bravery and
technical progress. In the popular imagination the heroic pilot, embodied

by wartime figures such as the Red Baron, stood for the mastery by man of the challenges of modern technology. Heydrich himself began to take flying lessons in the 1930s before participating as a pilot in various air raids on the Norwegian and Russian front during the Second World War.[98]

After undergoing specialist training in radio operation and wireless telegraphy, Heydrich continued to serve on the *Schleswig-Holstein* as radio officer until October 1928.[99] In 1950, his training officer at the naval communications school, Gustav Kleikamp, recalled that Heydrich's 'talents, knowledge and ability were above average'. Kleikamp also stated that Heydrich 'was always convinced of his own abilities, ambitious and able to present his achievements to his superiors in a favourable light' – a 'talent' that he would use to his best advantage in later years.[100] His ambition grew with every success. According to his roommate at the time, Heydrich tried 'to "shine" everywhere: at work, towards his superiors, towards his comrades, towards the crew, in sport, in society and at the bar. He collected a repertoire of jokes and anecdotes, and accompanied his songs on a lute. And he frequently impressed people in this way ...'[101]

On 1 July 1928 Heydrich was promoted to first lieutenant and deployed to the communications division of the Baltic Naval Station in Kiel. He now had significantly more free time, which he largely devoted to sport, music and a third area of interest: women. He had already displayed a strong interest in girls during the *Schleswig-Holstein*'s summer voyage to Spain and Portugal, and according to some of his former fellow officers he lived out his sexual fantasies in bars and brothels.[102] Back in Kiel, he repeatedly sought the company of women whom he could impress with his officer's uniform, his good manners and his musical talents. His efforts were not without success, as one of his fellow officers recalled after the war: 'He left an impression more than once, particularly on older ladies.'[103] In 1930 he made the acquaintance of a schoolgirl from Berlin whom he visited in the capital over a period of several months. This relationship was to have immense personal consequences for Heydrich.[104]

Lina von Osten

Reinhard Heydrich met his future wife, Lina von Osten, at a ball in Kiel on 6 December 1930. Born on the island of Fehmarn in Eastern Holstein, Lina had grown up in the coastal village of Lütjenbrode where her father, Jürgen von Osten, ran the local school. The Osten family was descended from Danish nobility, but had undergone a steady social decline since the German–Danish War of 1864, when Fehmarn fell to Prussia. As the second son in a family with six boys and two girls, Jürgen von Osten had

to give up all claims to the family farm and, in 1896, he moved to
the island of Fehmarn, where he met and married one of his pupils:
Lina's mother, Mathilde Hiss, whose family had lived and worked as
merchants on the island for generations. Like the Ostens, the Hisses
had seen better times. The war and the subsequent inflation extinguished
whatever was left of the family fortunes and the Ostens were forced to
live in the red-brick school building where Lina's father taught the local
children.[105]

After a childhood marked by material deprivation and uncertainty
about the future, Lina received her school-leaving certificate in Oldenburg
in 1927, before spending a year in her parents' household, during which
time her mother instructed her in cooking and other domestic duties. But
Lina was more ambitious and defied social conventions. On her own
initiative, she applied for a position at the Kiel Vocational School for Girls
with the goal of becoming a teacher – a profession which, at least in
Germany, was still largely dominated by men. In 1928 she moved to Kiel
where she lived in a girls' dormitory, the Henriettenhaus, frequently
attending social gatherings and balls like the one in December 1930
where she first met Reinhard Heydrich.[106]

Heydrich took an instant liking to the self-confident and pretty
nineteen-year-old blonde. The attraction was mutual and Heydrich spent
the rest of the evening in Lina's company before offering to escort her
back to her living quarters when the ball had ended. While they were
walking through the night, he asked for permission to see her again and
she agreed to a stroll in the local park two days later. According to her
memoirs, Lina felt instant 'sympathy' for the 'ambitious yet reserved man',
who, as she testified many years later, was 'a comrade, a friend – and really
much more'.[107]

Three days after their first date, Reinhard invited Lina to the theatre and
afterwards to a nearby wine bar. Although they hardly knew each other,
Heydrich ended the evening with a marriage proposal. Lina voiced a series
of objections – her parents had no idea of his existence and she had not
even finished school yet – but eventually she accepted. On 18 December,
Lina and Heydrich became secretly engaged, with Reinhard assuring his
fiancée that he would seek her family's approval by Christmas.[108]

That same day, a seriously love-struck Reinhard Heydrich wrote her a
letter:

> My dearest, dearest Lina! In the midst of the hustle and bustle of work
> and in a great hurry before my departure, I wanted you to know that . . .
> all my thoughts are with you. And I realize now how much I love you.
> You! I can no longer remember what it was like before. But I know only

too well what I leave behind. That is why I am looking forward all the more to the life that lies ahead of us. You! With you I could endure every sorrow! Only a few more days until Christmas Eve. The closer it comes, the more confidently I look ahead. For being straightforward and upright is the key demand I have always placed upon myself. It will thus not be difficult for me to look your father in the eye. You know, for me there is nothing worse in people whom I love than beating around the bush and insincerity. I don't hesitate to confront mean guys with the same weapons. – I can hardly wait until Saturday! Until then, much love, Your Reinhard.[109]

That weekend, Heydrich offically wrote to Lina's father, Jürgen von Osten, in order to ask for his daughter's hand in marriage. Then, over the Christmas holidays, Heydrich visited his fianceé's family in Lütjenbrode. The visit confirmed much of what Lina had already told Reinhard: the Ostens were part of northern Germany's impoverished lower aristocracy, a family that had lost all their savings in the post-war inflation. Since then, the family had compensated for lost prestige and wealth by moving, like many other German aristocratic familes that had fallen on hard times, to the extreme right of the political spectrum. Lina's brother, Hans, was an early member of the Nazi Party, having joined in April 1929 after one of Hitler's first appearances in northern Germany. At the time of Reinhard's first visit to Lütjenbrode, Hans had been a party and SA member for nearly three years.[110]

Lina, too, was already a convinced Nazi and a vehement anti-Semite when she met Reinhard Heydrich in 1930. She first attended a Nazi party rally in 1929 and was particularly impressed with the handsome young SS men in their black uniforms who guarded the stage on which Hitler was speaking that day. Reinhard may have reminded her of those imposing men on the day of their first encounter, as she described him as 'tall, manly and very self-assured in his uniform'.[111] According to her own post-war testimony, however, Heydrich lacked any interest in political parties at the time of their first encounter. Worse still from her point of view, he had never heard of Hitler's *Mein Kampf* and frequently made jokes about the leader of the Nazi Party as a 'Bohemian corporal' and the 'cripple' Goebbels.[112] Lina, by contrast, found Hitler's anti-Semitism particularly appealing. Even in the 1970s, when most people in Germany tried to disguise their former anti-Semitism, Lina openly confessed that as a teen-ager she had regarded the Polish Jews who had come into the country after 1918 as 'intruders and unwelcome guests', and had felt so 'provoked' by their mere presence that she just 'had to hate them': 'We compared living with them to a forced marriage, where the partners literally cannot bear the smell of one another.'[113]

It was through Lina and her family that Heydrich had his first proper introduction to Nazism, an ideology born in the immediate post-war atmosphere of national trauma, defeat, revolution and inflation. Most of the elements that went into its eclectic ideology – anti-Semitism, Social Darwinism and a firm belief in a strong authoritarian leadership – had already existed in Germany and many other European societies before 1914. Germany's decent into a political and economic abyss between 1914 and 1923 gave such extreme views a new urgency, and increased the willingness to use violence and murder to implement the measures which pan-Germans, anti-Semites, eugenicists and ultra-nationalists had been advocating since before the turn of the century.[114] The apparent divisiveness of Weimar politics, so Hitler's followers believed, required a firm leadership to reunite the nation in a new people's community, the *Volksgemeinschaft*. The institutions of state, society and culture would be remodelled to create a racially homogeneous nation imbued with one purpose: to make Germany great again. All those who stood in its way would be crushed. 'Community aliens' and above all Jews would be forced out of society. Weak, feeble or 'degenerate' elements would also be eliminated from the chain of heredity. Thus strengthened, the German nation would launch a war of conquest in Eastern Europe that would transform Germany into a superpower and overcome the humiliations of the previous decades.[115]

Such ideas remained those of a small number of Germans until 1929, when the onset of the Great Depression catapulted Hitler's previously tiny party of extremists into the centre of German politics, even though it never won an overall majority in general elections. By the time Reinhard met Lina, the party had achieved electoral successes of which Hitler, not even a German citizen at this point, could hardly have dreamed. In the general elections of September 1930 – barely three months before Reinhard and Lina first met – the Nazi Party had secured nearly 6.5 million votes, establishing itself as the second largest party in the German national parliament, the Reichstag.[116]

The influence of Lina and her family on Heydrich's political awakening is difficult to overestimate, but it was only in the following year, triggered by the greatest personal disaster in his life, that his complete conversion to Nazism would begin. For the time being, he was glad that he had passed the initial test of meeting Lina's parents: Jürgen von Osten could find no fault with Heydrich, not even when his future son-in-law confessed that no financial riches were to be expected from the once flourishing music conservatories in Halle and Dresden. A smart, ambitious naval officer with a seemingly secure pension and an apparently bright career ahead of him was more than the Ostens might have expected and it suited

Jürgen von Osten's image of a prospective son-in-law. An official engagement followed at Christmas, which Reinhard and Lina celebrated with her parents.[117]

Back at work after his first visit to Lütjenbrode, Reinhard wrote to his parents-in-law on 3 January 1931:

> Dear parents-in-law! Back in service and hard at work, I would like to thank you once more with all my heart for having received me so kindly and like a son in your house. I will never forget my first days in Lina's childhood home. I am so grateful to you for your consent to our engagement. I realize more and more every day that it was the right thing to do. Lina does not have to resort to secrecy in Kiel and we can be together often and get to know each other better and better without having to pay attention to the gossip of others. – Regarding our wedding date: please, please allow us to marry in September (17.!) ... There is nothing worse than uncertainty. I would be very, very grateful to you if you could agree on September – my parents, too, will be available then. Accept my sincere thanks, Your Reinhard.[118]

What Heydrich had conveniently omitted to mention to his future bride was that she was not the only woman in his life at the time – a detail that would shake the very foundations of his life.

Dismissal and Crisis

The young couple's happiness was short lived. Heydrich sent the newspaper announcement of his engagement to several friends and acquaintances. One of the recipients was a young woman from Berlin, whom Heydrich had met and befriended more than half a year earlier at a ball organized by the Colonial Women's School in Rendsburg. Since the two had enjoyed a sexual relationship over the following months and had visited each other in Berlin and Kiel, the young woman had assumed that she was herself engaged to Heydrich. Reinhard, who continued to cultivate the relationship even after he had met Lina, invited her to Kiel and, despite her request for a separate room in a hotel, encouraged her to spend the night in his living quarters. Further rapprochements probably occurred on this occasion. In any case, the young woman saw herself as compromised and reacted to the receipt of Heydrich's engagement notice with a nervous breakdown.[119]

Ever since the end of the Second World War, there has been much speculation about the identity of the young woman in question, but all that can be said with certainty is that her father must have had close connections to the navy's senior officer staff. In response to his daughter's breakdown, he lodged an official complaint against Heydrich with the Commander-in-Chief of the German navy, Admiral Erich Raeder. The complaint had serious consequences for Heydrich: in early January 1931, he was summoned before a military court of honour under the chairmanship of Admiral Gottfried Hansen, Commander of the Baltic Fleet, and invited to explain himself.[120] A broken engagement promise was a clear violation of the officer corps' code of conduct, but it was not a major offence automatically warranting the immediate dismissal of the officer in question. The embarrassing episode could have ended in little more than a reprimand for what was, after all, a 'girl's story', but Heydrich's arrogant attitude got him into trouble with the three members of the court: Admiral Hansen, his training officer Gustav Kleikamp and the senior member of Heydrich's crew, Hubertus von Wangenheim. Instead of accepting responsibility and settling for a minor punishment, Heydrich insisted that the woman had herself initiated their sexual relationship. He also denied ever having promised her marriage in return, describing their liaison in dismissive terms that annoyed the members of the court. Although no records of the court hearing have survived, having possibly been destroyed by the Gestapo in the 1930s, the proceedings were reconstructed by fellow officers after the Second World War. Heydrich's roommate in Kiel, Heinrich Beucke, recalled that 'Heydrich sought to wash his hands of the matter and to implicate [the girl in question]. His attitude before the court of honour, his lacking the guts to tell the truth, to accept the blame and to defend the woman, that was what led to his dismissal, not the actual offence itself.'[121]

One of the members of the court of honour, Gustav Kleikamp, confirmed this version and testified that Heydrich's 'proven insincerity, aimed at whitewashing himself', irritated the court more than the actual offence. The most junior member of the court, Hubertus von Wangenheim, apparently pressed for Heydrich's dismissal, arguing that his behaviour had dishonoured the German officer corps.[122]

The court concluded its deliberations by asking whether it was 'possible for an officer guilty of such unforgivable behaviour to remain in the navy', although it avoided making any recommendation itself. The matter was passed on to Admiral Raeder, who decided that Heydrich was 'unworthy' of being an officer and should be dismissed immediately. Kleikamp added emphatically: 'It was a decision which – if harsh – was recognized by all as impartial and correct and to which there was no alternative for anybody familiar with the facts.'[123]

On 30 April 1931 Heydrich's promising naval career came to an abrupt and unexpected end. 'Discharge from the navy', Lina recalled after the war, 'was the heaviest blow of his life ... It was not the lost earning capacity which weighed on him, but the fact that with every fibre of his being he had clung on to his career as an officer.'[124] At first he hoped for reinstatement, but an official appeal against the dismissal submitted to Reich President Paul von Hindenburg was turned down. Heydrich was suddenly confronted by the grim reality of being unemployed in 1931, in the midst of the Great Depression. Ejected from the navy less than a year before he would have secured his entitlement to a pension, his future looked gloomy, even though he continued to receive a severance payment of 200 Reichsmarks a month for the next two years. He locked himself in his room and cried for days in rage and self-pity.[125]

Heydrich's dismissal indeed occurred at the worst possible moment. Following the crash of the New York Stock Exchange on Wall Street on 29 October 1929, the German economic situation had deteriorated dramatically. Millions of jobless workers were plunged into terrible suffering, while German industry and trade experienced dramatic drops in turnover. The economic crisis was further exacerbated by the collapse of the last Weimar coalition government and its replacement by a minority cabinet under the authoritarian Centre Party politician Heinrich Brüning. Brüning's deflationary policies, designed to demonstrate Germany's inability to pay further reparations to the Western Allies, exacerbated the already grim situation. By the spring of 1931, there were over 4.5 million Germans unemployed, a figure that would to rise to more than 6 million by February 1932.[126]

Shortly after his discharge Heydrich and his fiancée travelled to Halle in order to inform his family of his dismissal and ask for their financial support. But bad news awaited him there as well: the Conservatory, already under serious strain since the post-war hyperinflation and the invention of modern forms of musical entertainment such as radios and gramophones, was facing bankruptcy. Bruno Heydrich, who had suffered a debilitating stroke earlier that year, was no longer able to involve himself in the running of the family business and now left most of the teaching to his wife and daughter.[127] Heydrich's parents were thus no longer in a position to support the couple. Elisabeth Heydrich, who until recently had been able to afford a maid, had to do the housework herself when not teaching the piano. Besides her husband, she now had to feed her daughter Maria and her unemployed son-in-law Wolfgang Heindorf, as well as her youngest son Heinz Siegfried, who had abandoned his studies in Dresden and his fiancée, Gertrud Werther. The failed navy career of their eldest son added to their own problems and Reinhard's parents accused him of foolishly ruining his future. In desperation Elisabeth argued endlessly with her brothers, Hans and Kurt, about selling the increasingly improfitable Dresden Conservatory, which her father, Eugen Krantz, had bequeathed to his three children. After the war, Lina vividly remembered the depressing atmosphere in the Heydrich home, where the daily worries about bills contrasted sharply with the remnants of the old furniture, expensive china and silver cutlery that testified to past affluence and social prestige.[128]

Worse was to come. In May 1931, Bruno Heydrich was informed that, after a series of complaints about falling teaching standards, his Conservatory was to be examined by a government commission. The report submitted by the commission revealed that the Conservatory no longer provided the necessary teaching level required for state certification and that his pupils had demonstrated insufficient knowledge of their craft. Physically incapacitated, financially ruined and professionally a broken man, Heydrich responded to the school authorities by admitting 'that my seminar organization and training, which I have tested for thirty years, no longer fulfils today's expectations'. He voluntarily renounced state recognition for his teaching seminar.[129]

Economic hardship also called into question Reinhard's marriage to Lina. Reinhard's mother blamed Lina for his dismissal and her own parents, too, had second thoughts about the relationship. Marrying an unemployed ex-naval officer was a far less attractive prospect than a son-in-law with high social standing and a dependable salary and pension. Although Lina refused to break the engagement, marriage was impossible until Reinhard found another job. Day after day, Lina urged her fiancé to find an appropriate career that could sustain their future life as a family.[130] Over the following four weeks, Heydrich considered and dismissed different career options and sent his surprisingly positive certificate of discharge from the navy to various potential employers:

> All superior officers state that Heydrich is a conscientious and reliable officer with a serious approach to duty ... who has undertaken zealously all duties required of him. Towards his superior officers he conducted himself openly and in a proper military manner and is well liked by fellow officers. He has treated the soldiers under his command well and justly. Heydrich is physically very fit and he is a good fencer and sailor.[131]

Heydrich did indeed receive several job offers, despite the economic crisis. A friend from Kiel, Werner Mohr, offered him an opportunity to work as a sailing instructor at the Hanseatic Yachting School in the town of Neustadt on the Baltic coast of Holstein.[132] Despite the relatively handsome monthly salary of 380 Reichsmarks, Heydrich rejected the offer from Neustadt, as well as similar offers from Kiel and Ratzeburg; he refused to become 'a sailing domestic for rich kids'.[133] It is not known why he did not jump at this opportunity, but the decisive reason appears to be that he was unable to accept the loss of his social status as an officer, as he confessed to his fiancée.[134]

In these circumstances, Reinhard's mother seized the initiative and told Heydrich's godmother, Elise Baroness von Eberstein, of her son's professional misfortunes. A formidable lady in her early sixties, the Baronness and her husband, Major von Eberstein, had met the Heydrichs at a concert in Halle shortly after their arrival in the city and they became their closest family friends, supporting the activities of the Conservatory through significant donations.[135] The Baronness immediately contacted her son, Karl, who had joined the Nazi Party in the mid-1920s and had already acquired a senior position as leader of the *Sturmabteilung* (Storm Troopers, SA) in Munich, in order to see if he knew of any suitable vacancies. Karl's response was cautiously optimistic.[136] Under the capable leadership of Ernst Röhm, and benefiting from the rising number of unemployed men in Germany, the SA had grown from just over 60,000 members in 1930 to more than 150,000 men the following year. In the civil war-like atmosphere of the early 1930s, when armed supporters of the Nazis and their opponents clashed almost on a daily basis, former officers like Heydrich, trained in military tactics, were a welcome addition to the Nazis' ranks. Yet while Heydrich's mother and his fiancée were excited by the prospect of a second career in uniform for Heydrich, he himself appears to have had initial reservations, although Lina urged him to examine this career option carefully.[137] It was not until Eberstein offered him the prospect of an 'elevated position' in the Nazi Party's headquarters in Munich that Heydrich agreed to take this path. What Eberstein had in mind was a position on the staff of Heinrich Himmler, the then still largely unknown head of the *Schutzstaffel* (Protection Squad, SS), a tiny but elitist paramilitary formation subordinate to the SA leadership of Ernst Röhm.[138]

Partly as a result of circumstances beyond his control – the military court's harsh decision to dismiss him from the navy, his family's economic misfortunes and the Great Depression more generally – and partly because of his family connections and Lina's firm commitment to the Nazi cause, the previously largely apolitical Heydrich, who had never read *Mein Kampf* or even heard of the SS before, was about to enter the most extreme paramilitary formation within Hitler's movement. He followed that path not out of deep ideological conviction, but because Nazism offered him the opportunity to return to a structured life in uniform, providing along with it a sense of purpose and a way of regaining the confidence of Lina and her family of devoted Nazis.

As a precondition for the new job, Heydrich had to join the Nazi Party, which he did on 1 June 1931. His membership number, 544,916, did not exactly make him an 'Old Fighter' of the Nazi movement, but he joined early enough to avoid the suspicion of careerism with which post-1933 members were usually confronted. Heydrich urgently requested the two letters of recommendation required for the vacancy. The first reference came from Eberstein, who assured Himmler of Heydrich's suitability: 'Very good qualifications, extended overseas commands . . . Heydrich has been dismissed from the navy due to minor personal differences. He will receive his salary for two more years, so, for the time being, he could work for the movement without pay.' Either out of ignorance or to boost Heydrich's chances of securing the job, Eberstein added that Heydrich had worked for 'three years as an intelligence expert at the Admiral's Staff Division of the North Sea and Baltic station'.[139] A second letter of recommendation was submitted by Heydrich's former commanding officer, Captain Warzecha:

> I have known the naval lieutenant Heydrich from the beginning of his service with the Reichsmarine. I was his training officer for two years during his cadet period and have had other opportunities to observe his development as an officer. I am closely acquainted with the reasons for his dismissal from the Navy. They do not prevent me from whole-heartedly recommending Lieutenant Heydrich for any position that may arise.[140]

Heydrich's application, enhanced by Eberstein's insistence that his childhood friend was an expert in espionage, arrived at a good time as Himmler was in the midst of setting up an SS intelligence service. In the summer of 1931, prompted by the Nazi Party's electoral successes and a parallel influx of new members of often questionable loyalty to the cause, Himmler felt an urgent need for the creation of such a service. He rightly feared that some of the new SA and SS members stood in the paid service of either the police or political opponents to act as spies or agents provocateurs. He realized that he needed a suitably trained officer on his Munich staff to address this problem. Having heard from Eberstein of an ex-naval 'intelligence' officer who was offering his services to the Nazi movement, he invited Heydrich for an interview.[141]

Heydrich's appointment with Himmler had already been set when Eberstein telegraphed Heydrich from Munich to tell him that the SS chief was ill. Heydrich was prepared to reschedule the appointment, but Lina urged him to travel to Munich and meet with Himmler anyway. How much this opportunity meant to Lina is clear from her memoirs, in which, thirty-five years later, she described the day of the first meeting between Heydrich and Himmler, 14 June 1931, as the 'greatest moment of my life, of our life'.[142]

CHAPTER III

Becoming Heydrich

A Second Chance

ON 14 JUNE 1931, SHORTLY BEFORE NOON, HEYDRICH ARRIVED AT Munich Central Station. His childhood friend, Karl von Eberstein, met him at the station and drove him to Himmler's poultry farm in the Munich suburb of Waldtrudering, where the Reich Leader SS was recovering from the flu.[1] The meeting was to prove a momentous one, the beginning of an eleven-year relationship of close collaboration and mutual respect. Much has been written since the Second World War about the alleged rivalry between the two men and Heydrich's apparent later attempts to sideline Himmler in pursuit of total power.[2] But the post-war testimonies of former SS officers on which this interpretation was based are generally unreliable and too narrowly focused on the apparent differences between the ideologically driven 'school master' Himmler, whose physical appearance stood in stark contrast to his own vision for the SS, and the coldly rational and supposedly only career-driven Heydrich on the other. The key witness to the myth of rivalry between the two men, Himmler's masseur Felix Kersten, alleged that next to the often indecisive and insecure Reich Leader SS, Heydrich left the impression of being made of 'sharpened steel'. According to Kersten, only the 'fact' of Heydrich's Jewish ancestry allowed Himmler to keep his first lieutenant under control.[3]

In reality, their relationship was one of deep trust, complementary talents and shared political convictions. Himmler, who was only four years older than Heydrich, also came from an educated middle-class family, his father being the director of one of Bavaria's finest secondary schools, the Wittelsbach Gymnasium. He had been called up for military service in 1917 and experienced the German collapse the following year as an officer cadet in the army barracks at Regensburg. Himmler's political awakening occurred notably earlier than Heydrich's: politicized by the war and its inglorious end, he joined Freikorps to oppose the short-lived Munich Council Republic in 1919 while simultaneously studying for his *Abitur* school-leaving certificate, which he obtained that same year. Between 1919 and 1922, he studied at Munich's Technical University, earning a diploma in agriculture. He worked for a year at a factory in Schleissheim producing fertilizer from dung but was increasingly obsessed by politics. Through old Freikorps contacts and his subsequent involvement in two radical *völkisch* and anti-Semitic societies, the Artamanen League and the Thule Society, Himmler became aware of the emerging Nazi Party, which he joined in August 1923 and in whose ranks he participated in the unsuccessful putsch in Munich that Hitler launched in November that year. In the summer of 1924, while Hitler's party was banned, Himmler became secretary to Gregor Strasser – then the second most powerful man in the Nazi Party and the leading proponent of the party's National-Bolshevik wing. While acting as Strasser's propaganda chief, he travelled by motorcycle all over Bavaria. His marriage in July 1928 to the nurse Margarete Boden, seven years older than him, enabled him to purchase a poultry smallholding in Waltrudering after Margarete had sold her share in a nursing home in Berlin.[4]

Since assuming the leadership of the (then still tiny) SS in 1929, Himmler's desire to transform it into an organization for the racial elite had been reflected in his introduction of physical selection criteria for his men. He envisaged the 'Aryan' body as the perfection of an ideal state of mankind that distinguished itself from ill and 'inferior' bodies. He desired tall, blue-eyed men who could show family trees free of 'inferior racial origin': the body was the place where one's membership of the Aryan race could be 'verified'. Unsurprisingly, Himmler was very impressed by the young applicant who presented himself on the afternoon of 14 June 1931. Blond, blue-eyed and just over six foot tall, Heydrich even surpassed the strict recruitment criteria for Hitler's SS bodyguard, the elite 'Leibstandarte Adolf Hitler'.[5]

Himmler told Heydrich about his plans to develop an intelligence service within the SS. It was only at this point that they realized that their meeting was based on a misunderstanding: Heydrich had been a radio officer in the navy, not an intelligence officer.[6] Undeterred by the realization that the applicant in front of him lacked any previous qualification for espionage work, Himmler asked Heydrich to sketch out an organizational plan for an SS intelligence agency and gave him twenty minutes to complete the task. Without any previous experience in the field of espionage, Heydrich resorted to the minimal knowledge he had gained from years of reading cheap crime fiction and spy novels, and wrapped his suggestions for a future SS intelligence service in suitably military phraseology. His minimal knowledge of espionage appears to have surpassed that of Himmler: the Reich Leader SS was impressed and hired him in preference to a second applicant, a former police captain named Horninger. Himmler's instincts served him well. Horninger turned out to be an agent of the Bavarian Political Police and was arrested after the Nazis' seizure of power in 1933, later committing suicide in prison.[7]

Heydrich's salary started at a modest 180 Reichsmarks per month – more than Eberstein had suggested to Himmler in his reference but significantly less than, for example, a skilled labourer in the chemical industry (228 RM per month), a civil service trainee (244 RM) or even an unskilled retail employee (228 RM) could expect to earn in 1931.[8] The fact that Heydrich chose this position in the SS instead of any of the better-paid jobs that were on offer was due to a number of factors: his desire to impress his wife and her family with a job in the political movement they supported, the position's quasi-military nature and the appeal of a challenging new task in a revolutionary institution that rejected the very political system which, from Heydrich's point of view, had just terminated his seemingly secure naval career.[9]

For the rest of Heydrich's life, Himmler was his central ideological and professional reference point, more so perhaps even than Hitler. Throughout his career in the SS, Heydrich remained conscious of the debt he owed to the Reich Leader SS and Himmler could rely on his unshakeable loyalty. While their relationship was hierarchical in nature, it was based not on subordination but rather on close collaboration – on a feeling of mutual understanding and the pursuit of a common goal. The nature of that goal was to change over time, as Nazi policies were gradually radicalized and escalating terror and persecution within the Reich became pan-European genocide, but throughout their shared career path the two men always knew that they could rely on each other. As Himmler himself phrased it in 1942 at Heydrich's funeral: 'I am privileged to thank you for your unswerving loyalty and for your wonderful friendship, which was a bond between us in this life and which death can never put asunder!'[10]

Although Himmler had no official deputy, Heydrich *de facto* performed this role from 1933 onwards. But Heydrich was more than Himmler's loyal paladin and vassal: he was also the man who transformed the Nazi worldview as expressed by Hitler and Himmler into concrete policies. While Himmler was anything but a weak leader and possessed a pronounced strategic talent in his dealings with other senior Nazis and his subordinates, Heydrich was his executioner – a man of deed, action and implementation. What set Himmler apart from other Nazi leaders were his deep ideological conviction and purposefulness as well as his astute manoeuvring within the political intrigues that characterized the Third

Reich. Heydrich proved himself to be Himmler's eager pupil in ideological matters, while simultaneously exhibiting an unsurpassed drive to
realize his dystopian fantasies.

Following his successful interview with Himmler, Heydrich travelled to
Hamburg, where he joined the SS on 14 July 1931. The organization was
at that time small and relatively insignificant. The SS originally served as
Hitler's personal bodyguard after his release from Landsberg Prison
where he had spent most of the year 1924 for his failed putsch attempt in
Munich the previous year. It was subordinate to the SA and remained a
subsidiary organization over the next several years, but it quickly developed a special awareness of itself as the Nazi Party guard of honour utterly
loyal to Hitler.[11]

The SS remained a miniscule organization with no more than
280 members until Himmler assumed its leadership in 1929. Driven by
political ambition and the ideological conviction that his organization
could set an example to the party by adhering strictly to the tenets of
Nazism, he designed a programme of expansion that was to develop the SS
systematically into a racial elite within the Nazi movement. He required
every prospective new SS member to supply a photograph so that he could
personally inspect the applicant's racial characteristics or 'good blood'. The
elitist character of the organization attracted a large number of young,
unemployed right-wing university graduates who had few hopes of finding
a job during the Great Depression. It also appealed to former Freikorps
officers, many of them minor aristocrats, who sought a political home after
the creation of the seemingly alien and hostile Weimar Republic. These
officers included future key players in the SS empire such as the former
Pomeranian Reichswehr officer Erich von dem Bach-Zelewski and First
Lieutenant Udo von Woyrsch, a veteran of the bitter ethnic conflicts that
ensued in Upper Silesia after 1918.[12] By December 1929, less than twelve
months after Himmler's takeover, the SS had enlisted 1,000 men. By the
end of 1930 this number had risen to 2,727; and by the time Heydrich
joined, in mid-July 1931, it counted more than 10,000 members.
Nonetheless, in comparison to the SA, which by this time was nearly
100,000 strong, the SS remained a relatively small organization.[13]

Unlike the SA, whose local leaders represented a variety of political
strands and personal ambitions within the Nazi movement, sometimes
directly challenging the authority of the party leadership in Munich, the
SS repeatedly demonstrated its unconditional loyalty to Hitler. In the
summer of 1930 and again in the spring of 1931, for example, the Berlin
SA group under the leadership of Walter Stennes staged an open revolt
against the head of the capital's Nazi Party branch, Joseph Goebbels, in
order to secure more safe seats for SA members in the forthcoming

general elections. Goebbels turned to the SS for personal protection. Although outnumbered by their SA adversaries, the SS stood by the party leadership and emerged strengthened from this internal party crisis.[14]

Heydrich thus joined the SS at an important turning point in its history, which partly helps to explain the organization's appeal for him: the SS promised a career in uniform and the opportunity for rapid advancement within a still-malleable body that promoted revolutionary views for the reordering of Germany. Even if the pay was modest, the new activity offered Heydrich, as an ardent reader of crime fiction, a job in an elite organization that boosted his shaken self-confidence. It also offered a comprehensive ideological system with a clearly defined binary world of friends and foes, and thus seemed coherently to explain an increasingly complicated world.

Over the following two weeks, between mid-July and early August, Heydrich served in the SS in Hamburg where he was thrust into a political milieu of fanatical Nazis. It was here that he first met Bruno Streckenbach, a man who was to become his close associate in future years, running the personnel department of Heydrich's terror apparatus and commanding the largest SS task force during the German attack on Poland in 1939. Born in 1902, Streckenbach had grown up in a middle-class family in Hamburg and had been deeply politicized by the war and the upheavals of its aftermath. Unlike Heydrich, he dropped out of school in 1918 to fight the revolution in Hamburg. He continued his right-wing activism throughout the 1920s while taking up temporary jobs with an importing firm and the German Automobile Club in order to earn a living. Following his membership in various small fringe groups of the far right, Streckenbach joined the Nazi Party in 1930 and became a member of the Hamburg SS in early August 1931.[15]

As a newcomer without street credibility, Heydrich had to prove himself in the meeting-hall battles with Communists and Social Democrats in the run-up to the Hamburg local elections of 27 September 1931, in which the Nazis increased the number of their city council representatives from three to forty-three.[16] On these occasions, small motorized SS units attacked party gatherings of political opponents and disappeared before the police arrived. Apparently, Heydrich quickly aquired a certain notoriety as the leader of a shock troop unit, becoming known in Hamburg's Communist circles as the 'blond beast', whose commando displayed impressive military discipline.[17] Streckenbach had greater experience in fighting Communists, Social Democrats and trade unionists on the streets of Hamburg and he undoubtedly had influence on Heydrich during his time in Hamburg. For Streckenbach, too, the encounter proved advantageous: in November 1933 he joined Heydrich's

SD, was appointed head of the political police in Hamburg and, under Heydrich's patronage, rose to become SS *Brigadeführer* (brigadier) by the beginning of the Second World War.[18]

In August, Heydrich returned to Munich to take up his new position in the Nazi Party headquarters, the Brown House. Himmler entrusted Heydrich with the development of an SS intelligence service, the future Sicherheitsdienst (Security Service or SD), which, in 1931, bore little resemblance to the sinister organization it was to become in subsequent years. Its original model was Ic – the small counter-espionage department of the German army, whose organizational structure Heydrich sought to emulate. The initial task of the SD was twofold: to gather information on political opponents, notably the Communist Party (KPD) and the Social Democrat Party (SPD), and – a more delicate issue that would repeatedly get the SD into trouble – to search for police informers and disguised Communist spies within the rapidly growing Nazi Party.[19]

The SD's beginnings were very modest: compared to the more established SA's own intelligence service, which operated separately under the direction of Count Du Moulin Eckart, the SD was a one-man organization. Heydrich was its sole staff member, setting up a basic filing system with index cards containing the names of political enemies. Due to limited funds, he was forced to share his office and his typewriter in the Brown House with Richard Hildebrandt, the chief of staff of the minuscule SS Division South, who, during the Second World War, became SS and police leader of Danzig-West Prussia.[20]

Despite this less than impressive working environment, Heydrich began to regain his confidence and relished his new responsibilities. Only one day after taking up his new position, he wrote a letter to Lina's parents, in which he sought to convince them that their doubts regarding his marriageability were now unfounded and that he had already earned the praise of his superiors through hard work. From 1 September 1931 he would receive a regular salary, enabling him to support a family and to repay money that he had borrowed from Lina's family after his dismissal from the navy:

My position and my work give me great pleasure. I can work independently and build up something new. Above all, regardless of the political situation we are currently in, this position will allow me to found a household, the goal towards which my entire work has been and continues to be aimed. From 1 September onwards, while restricting my own lifestyle appropriately, I will be in a position to redeem my debts with the highest repayments possible. I have rented a cheap, very simple room in a very good neighbourhood from an orderly old lady. My working day is extremely long ... It is likely that I will undertake extensive official journeys throughout Germany as the Reich Leader's representative in the near future and hope that I will also be able to come to Lütjenbrode. Until then, kindest regards from your Reinhard.[21]

Just ten days later, on 22 August, Heydrich announced to his mother-in-law that he would pay back the entire sum he had borrowed from her on his next visit. He himself, Heydrich emphasized with pride, had a great deal to do now that he belonged to Himmler's innermost staff and worked every day, including Sundays, until late at night:

> I am developing a large organization according to my own design, which demands all of my strength. Since I naturally spend as little as possible on myself, making only the most essential expenditures on room and board, and as I want to be able to present you with evidence of the highest possible savings in early September, you can imagine what my daily routine looks like. I probably do not need to tell you that my thoughts wander off to Lütjenbrode every free minute. Today I had joyful news: Herr Himmler, the Reich Leader SS, assured me that upon my marriage I will receive 290 Reichsmarks per month. – On quiet evenings I frequently long for the sea and the north.[22]

Although his letter was clearly written to rebuild Mathilde von Osten's confidence in his ability to sustain a family, Heydrich's description of his frenetic work schedule was probably no exaggeration since the early development and extension of the SD's responsibilities was closely linked with his vast personal ambitions. According to Himmler's future chief adjutant, Karl Wolff, the then still very 'insecure youngster' had already delivered his first lecture on enemy tactics at a leadership meeting of sixty-five senior SS officers in Munich on 26 August 1931, less than two months after entering an entirely unfamiliar working environment. In a manner that was to become characteristic, Heydrich emphasized the importance of his own task by reminding his audience that the Nazi Party was constantly threatened and spied upon both by the police and by other political parties. To counter this perceived threat, he announced his desire to build up a small group of SS men who would unmask spies within the Nazi movement. Only a few years later, after the seizure of power, Heydrich was to use similar arguments to justify an extension of SS powers: by suggesting that the national community was surrounded and penetrated by internal enemies successfully camouflaged as Nazi loyalists, he made a convincing case for an extraordinary strike force capable of uncovering and eliminating the enemies within the Nazi movement.[23]

Heydrich's suggestions were promptly implemented: an order from Himmler on 4 September 1931 called for the development of a network of agents for intelligence-gathering purposes. A passage contained in the order stating that the group would restrict its activities to non-governmental organizations was mere camouflage in case the Bavarian police caught wind of the plan.[24]

During his first months in Munich, Heydrich lived alone as a lodger in the home of an elderly widow, Viktoria Edrich, a long-standing supporter of the Nazi Party, at Türkenstrasse 23 in the bohemian district of Schwabing, where Edrich rented out rooms to unmarried SS men. In December 1931, Heydrich moved his intelligence service with three newly appointed staff members to this flat in order to protect its work from potential spies in the Brown House.[25] Over the following weeks and months, Heydrich endeavoured to install SD liaison officers in each of the individual SS regiments across Germany with orders to gather information on political enemies and report this information back to Munich. Around fifty such liaison officers were in post by the end of December 1931.[26]

Much to Heydrich's dismay, the swift progress of his work did not go unnoticed. In November 1931, the newspaper *Münchner Post* published an insightful article that blew Heydrich's efforts to keep his organization secret: the article reported on a new SS intelligence service slated to become 'a fascist Cheka' – a German equivalent to the notorious Soviet state security organization founded by Lenin in 1917 – if Hitler ever ascended to power. Even more damaging for him, the paper uncovered what it believed to be the 'real brains behind the organization: an ex-naval officer with the name of Reinhard Heydrich'. The *Post* clearly overestimated Heydrich's importance at the time, but the article convinced him that he was surrounded by spies and that he had to be more distrustful of his colleagues in the future.[27]

By the end of 1931, Heydrich had consolidated his professional future and personal finances to such an extent that he could finally marry his fiancée. On Boxing Day, the birthday of his father-in-law, Reinhard Heydrich married Lina von Osten in the Protestant church of St Catherine's in Grossenbrode on the Baltic coast. Lina's post-war description of her wedding day illustrates how strongly connected she already was in Nazi circles and how the couple made use of this formal occasion to demonstrate their political convictions:

My bridegroom was still practically unknown back then, but I was already someone in the Party. My brother was also known as one of the first hundred thousand followers of Hitler ... The SA and SS had just been banned temporarily. But the police could not easily intervene in the cemetery that surrounded the church. The SA and SS, dressed in white shirts and black trousers, formed a guard of honour all the way to the cemetery gate. The pastor was also on our side . . . [and] gave us a Luther quotation as a wedding motto: 'And though this world, with devils filled, should threaten to undo us, We will not fear, for God hath willed His truth to triumph through us.' As we marched out of the church, the organist played the Horst Wessel Song. As we left the cemetery following the wedding several guards of honour were arrested by the police.[28]

To mark the happy occasion, Himmler promoted Heydrich to SS-*Sturmbannführer* (major) – just seven days after his promotion to SS *Hauptsturmführer* (captain). In a little over fifteen months in the SS Heydrich had thus already outstripped his former military rank in the navy. Even if being a naval officer remained more prestigious than an SS career at this point, Heydrich must have felt that his life was back on track. Himmler also authorized the promised pay rise to 290 Reichsmarks, which meant that (including the severance payment which Heydrich continued to receive from the navy for a few more months) the Heydrich family had a total income of 490 Reichsmarks per month – not exactly a fortune, but a comfortable salary.[29]

Himmler's generous gesture was, at least in part, designed to encourage other SS leaders to follow Heydrich's example and to start a family with a racially suitable woman. Less than a week after Heydrich's wedding, on 31 December, Himmler issued his famous 'marriage order' in an attempt to transform the SS from an exclusively male corps into a community of carefully selected families, the SS-*Sippengemeinschaft*. Unmarried SS men – including those suspected of homosexual tendencies – were summoned to marry, but before doing so they had to apply for Himmler's approval of their chosen brides. This approval depended on a racial suitability test conducted by the SS Racial Office (the later Race and Settlement Office or RuSHA). The prospective bride and groom were both medically examined and tested for genetic disorders and fertility problems. Furthermore, they had to complete questionnaires on their family's medical history. A special form, the so-called *Rassekarte*, was used to register the racial qualities of each SS man and his future bride. Reports were then submitted to Himmler as to whether or not their mutual reproduction was 'racially desirable'.[30]

The meaning and purpose of Himmler's obsession with racial selection and breeding, which was the subject of much ridicule and criticism outside the SS, was to develop the organization as a racially superior community of husbands, wives and children. SS wives would not only ensure a stable domestic framework in which their warrior husbands could gather new energy for their militant tasks, but they would also – and more importantly – serve as the 'preservers of the species' on the battlefield of the 'birth war', thus taking a place of equal importance to their husbands within the racial community.[31] At the heart of Himmler's racial ideology stood a vulgarized Darwinian notion of 'positive' and 'negative' selection. The SS family was central to the realization of his fantasy of creating a new racial aristocracy within the 'Germanic–Nordic race', an 'aristocracy of blood and soil' that Himmler's intellectual mentor, Walther Darré, had described in a 1930 book of the same title.[32]

SS ideologues such as Darré and Himmler placed the Nordic peoples – tall, blond and blue-eyed – at the apex of the racial hierarchy in which they saw humanity ordered. Himmler had by no means invented this notion himself: the idea of a pure and superior Nordic race born to rule the world had been widespread in Germany and other European countries for decades. From the turn of the century, racial hygienists had been discussing the possibility of using racial selection to reach a higher level of human development. Basing their ideas on Darwin's theories and the subsequent publications of his cousin, Francis Galton, racial hygienists believed that they could use the selection principle to explain human history as a story of progress. For them, the key element of Darwin's evolution theory was the struggle for survival, in which only the fittest asserted themselves and survived. However, the effectiveness of the natural selection process had been so undermined by 'modern civilization' over the years that the 'unfit' were also allowed to survive, thereby passing on their flawed genetic material and potentially weakening their race as a whole. The Nazis believed that they could correct this 'degeneration' by a process of artificial selection. The reproduction of the 'unfit' should be prevented and that of the 'fit' promoted.[33]

Himmler's concept of racial selection, which in the ensuing years also formed the basis of Heydrich's convictions, was thus based, on the one hand, on traditions of positivism, and notably on the assumption that all processes in nature are scientifically explainable, and, on the other hand, on a vulgarized form of Social Darwinism that had been propagated in most Western European countries since the late nineteenth century. In terms of racial selection, the Heydrichs must have appeared as a perfect example of healthy 'Nordic qualities' – a 'beautiful couple', as Hitler remarked when he was first introduced to Lina by her husband.[34]

After the wedding, Lina accompanied Reinhard back to Munich where they rented a small house in the suburb of Lochhausen. Although the Heydrichs spent only eight months in Lochhausen, Lina immediately started to furnish the house out of her dowry and to acquaint herself with the customs of her new neighbourhood. Reinhard Heydrich joined the local football club, if only as a passive member.[35] In an ecstatic letter of 6 January 1932, he thanked his parents-in-law for hosting the wedding and described the couple's new life in Lochhausen: 'Our beautiful, spick-and-span house has now become a proper home. Out here, far from the turmoil of the big city, we find rest and relaxation after our daily work. Lina reigns supreme over her kingdom. Some visitor or another appears nearly every day.'[36] But Lina had greater difficulty in adjusting to the unfamiliar Bavarian lifestyle and her role in the SS-*Sippengemeinschaft* than Heydrich was willing to admit. She took a particular dislike to Margarete Himmler, whom she frequently met in Munich. Lina would later describe her as a 'pedestrian, humourless' woman, whose stinginess was reflected in the cheap furnishings in the Himmler home. Lina also felt lonely in the unfamiliar new environment where her daily life was largely spent without her husband. Reinhard, whose work demanded most of his time, was rarely at home.[37]

The need for reforms to Heydrich's still highly amateurish spy network in Germany became apparent in February 1932, when the SD suddenly found itself in a crisis prompted by the arrest of one of Heydrich's agents who had tried to gather secret military information from the navy command in Wilhelmshaven. Although the police investigation did not reveal Heydrich's involvement in the case, he nevertheless recognized the need to restructure his intelligence service in order to avoid further embarrassment.[38] A ban on the SA and the SS in April 1932 offered an unintended opportunity to do so. After a wave of violent SA street terror against political opponents, Reich Chancellor Heinrich Brüning officially banned the Nazis' paramilitary organizations, although the ban was subsequently lifted by his successor, Franz von Papen, just a few weeks later. During this brief period of illegality, Heydrich's department disguised itself by assuming the innocuous title of Press and Information Service (PID) while simultaneously undergoing a structural reform. Heydrich intended to make his organization less dependent on the goodwill of informers from the individual SS divisions, as well as protecting it from future interference from other party agencies. For this purpose, he undertook a number of inspection tours throughout Germany, during which he succeeded in hiring full-time staff who would now be solely responsible to (and supervised by) his office in Munich.[39]

After the ban had been lifted in June 1932, Heydrich's SD emerged strengthened. It also asserted itself against the internal competition from the SA's own intelligence service under the direction of Count Du Moulin Eckart, which ceased to exist that month.[40] At the same time, Heydrich was promoted to the rank of SS-*Standartenführer*, or colonel. The Heydrichs could now afford to move into a small city villa near the Nymphenburg Palace, which also served as the new SD headquarters with a total of eight full-time employees.[41] Lina spent little time there. During the campaign for the Reichstag elections of 31 July 1932, daily street battles raged between Communists and Nazis throughout Germany, killing over 100 people and injuring more than 4,500. Reinhard feared for the wellbeing of his wife and sent her to a small pension in the Bavarian countryside where she stayed for several weeks.[42]

Heydrich's rapid rise in the SS hierarchy and his scarcely disguised ambition earned him many enemies. At the beginning of June 1932, the old rumour of his Jewish ancestry came back to haunt him once again, this time amplified in its damaging potential by the fact that he was now working for a political organization in which anti-Semitism was a fundamental tenet of faith. It is likely that local members of the Nazi Party in Halle, jealous of Heydrich's swift ascent, had alerted the regional party leadership to the rumours. On 6 June, the Nazi Gauleiter of Halle-Magdeburg, Rudolf Jordan, wrote to the Nazi Party's organizational leader, Gregor Strasser, enquiring about 'a party member with the name of Heydrich whose father lives in Halle. There is reason to assume that his father, Bruno Heydrich, is a Jew.' As 'proof', Jordan enclosed the extract from the 1916 edition of Hugo Riemann's music encyclopaedia in which Bruno Heydrich was referred to as 'Heydrich (actually Süss)'. Jordan insisted that the party's personnel department investigate the matter.[43]

Around the same time, Heydrich's former fellow officer and member of the court of honour, Hubertus von Wangenheim, told a relative who was working in the Brown House about the rumours that had accompanied Heydrich's time in the navy. He mentioned that Heydrich had been teased by his fellow officer cadets as a 'white Jew' and 'white Moses'. Such rumours fuelled suspicions at Nazi Party headquarters.[44] Strasser immediately passed the matter on to the party's chief genealogist, Dr Achim Gercke, head of the Nazis' *Auskunft*, or Information Office. Scarcely two weeks later, on 22 June, Gercke responded with a detailed report on Heydrich's ancestry and confirmed that he was 'of German origin and free from any influence of coloured or Jewish blood'. Gercke insisted that the 'insulting rumour' of non-Aryan ancestry was entirely unfounded: 'I take full responsibility for the accuracy of this opinion and declare myself prepared to testify to it before a court should the need arise.'[45]

Despite this clarification, Heydrich was deeply shaken by the re-emergence of the damaging rumours only a year after his dismissal from the navy, rumours that threatened his carefully rebuilt professional existence. Instead of accepting the findings of Gercke with relief, he privately engaged a member of his SD service, Ernst Hoffman, to undertake further genealogical investigations. After the war, Hoffman recalled Heydrich's nervousness at each of their meetings, a nervousness which seemed 'understandable but without foundation'.[46] It was not the last time that Heydrich had to engage with the dreaded rumour: in 1940 a baker from Halle, Johannes Papst, himself a member of the Nazi Party, was sentenced to twelve months' imprisonment for spreading the libellous gossip that Heydrich was a Jew.[47]

Partly as a result of this embarrassing and potentially career-terminating episode, Heydrich devoted great energy to his work in the summer of 1932. His ambitions continued to be vast. In September, during the first meeting with the recently installed branch office directors of the SD, he declared that he intended to develop the organization into the German equivalent of the British secret service (as he understood it): 'Its task would be to gather, evaluate and verify substantive material on the objectives, methods and plans of internal enemies; and to report on potential wrongdoings within our own ranks.'[48] Compared to the reality of the situation in mid-1932, these were fantastical goals. The SD was still a tiny outfit with no more than thirty-three full-time employees and a thinly spread network of largely unpaid agents scarcely able to fulfil the tasks already assigned to them.[49]

The autumn of 1932 brought Heydrich further uncertainties. In the November Reichstag elections Hitler's party lost more than 2 million votes, triggering an over-optimistic media campaign by the republican left predicting the imminent death of Nazism. If only briefly, Heydrich must have wondered whether he had made the right decision in joining the Nazi Party. The SD's finances, always dependent on irregular payments from the party and the SA, further deteriorated in late 1932 to the extent that for a few weeks around Christmas even Heydrich's telephone was cut off due to unpaid bills. In January 1933, immediately prior to the seizure of power, the Nazi Party temporarily stopped paying the SD employees altogether. The bleak winter of 1932 clearly marked the low point of Heydrich's SS career and few people would have predicted at that time that either the SD or Heydrich had any future role to play in German politics.[50]

Seizures of Power

The events of January 1933 amounted to an extraordinary political drama, a drama that unfolded silently behind closed doors and largely out of Heydrich's sight. Backed by senior figures in the German business community and by the powerful Agrarian League of largely East Elbian estate holders, Germany's former conservative Chancellor, Franz von Papen, was looking for ways to replace his increasingly unpopular and isolated successor in office, General Kurt von Schleicher, with a right-wing coalition government that enjoyed broad popular support. The only way of establishing a viable government of the national right, as was clear to everyone involved, was to bring the strongest political party in Germany, the Nazi Party, into the cabinet. The question was whether the key players – Hitler, Papen and Reich President von Hindenburg – could agree on the price for Nazi participation in government. Although Papen initially wanted the chancellor's seat for himself, frenetic negotiations between Hitler, Papen and close associates of Hindenburg finally led to a compromise: Hitler was to lead the government as chancellor, but he was to be firmly contained by a majority of 'reliable' conservative ministers who enjoyed Hindenburg's confidence.[51]

Deprived of Hindenburg's crucial support, Chancellor von Schleicher resigned on 27 January 1933. That very same day, Heydrich was ordered by Himmler to relocate to Berlin, where he moved into a house in the salubrious Westend that served both as his private residence and as the SD headquarters in the German capital. Against the backdrop of ongoing negotiations between Hitler, Papen and Hindenburg regarding a future Nazi-led coalition government, Heydrich's task was twofold: to prepare the relocation of the SD from Munich to Berlin for the increasingly likely event of a Nazi takeover and to establish closer ties with the powerful and largely independent SS division in the capital. Just three days after Heydrich's arrival in Berlin, on 30 January, Himmler informed him that Hitler had been appointed German chancellor as head of a coalition government.[52]

Heydrich played a passive role in the largely uncoordinated events that now unfolded throughout Germany. In the lead-up to the general elections of 5 March which Hitler hoped would strengthen the electoral basis of his new government, the Nazis gradually increased the pressure on their opponents on the political left, starting with the Decree for the Protection of the German People of 4 February, which provided a means of banning opposition newspapers during the election campaign. A welcome pretext for the escalation of physical violence against Communists and Social Democrats occurred on 27 February when a lone Dutchman with a Communist past, Marinus van der Lubbe, set fire to the Reichstag building in Berlin. The Nazi leadership immediately seized upon the event as a long-awaited opportunity to wage open war on the German Communist Party.[53] Five days earlier, to deal with an alleged increase in left-radical violence, the new Prussian Minister President, Hermann Göring, had recruited some 50,000 men from the ranks of the SA and the SS as 'auxiliary policemen' with authority to carry out arrests. Now the often threatened day of reckoning had arrived. The Nazi auxiliary policemen swiftly used their newly gained powers to incarcerate thousands of real or alleged political enemies and to hold them, without judicial sanction, in abandoned factories, warehouses and basements where they were subjected to orgies of cruelty. Communists in particular were savagely repressed. Individuals were brutally beaten and tortured, sometimes even murdered, with total impunity. By April, the number of political prisoners arrested in Prussia alone exceeded 25,000.[54]

Physical coercion was directed with massive ferocity against leading Communists, Social Democrats and trade unionists, and with symbolic or exemplary force against those such as liberals, Catholics and conservatives who were less diametrically opposed to the politics of the emerging Third Reich. Jews were often maltreated, but they were not the primary target of Nazi violence. By the end of the summer of 1933, some 100,000 people, mainly opponents on the political left, had been arrested throughout Germany, with some 500–600 killed.[55]

Although the Nazi 'revolution' of 1933 claimed relatively few lives – at least in comparison with the extreme bloodshed of the following twelve years – violence and intimidation were a central component. The wave of arrests, deliberately carried out to create a climate of fear, led the victims to police prisons or, worse, to one of the many 'wild' concentration camps or informal torture cellars which sprang up across the country to deal with putative enemies. Physical violence during the first weeks of the Third Reich served a dual purpose: to eliminate the most outspoken opponents of Nazism and to intimidate those who might pose a potential threat. Nazi terror, real and threatened, had a devastating effect, but physical violence was unevenly applied in different parts of Germany where the local SA usually acted on its own initiative. In the first two months at least of the Third Reich, the terror was not co-ordinated from above.[56]

During the first few weeks of the Third Reich Heydrich remained a mere observer of political events and the terror that erupted on Germany's streets. If he and Himmler had hoped that the Nazi seizure of power would propel them into positions of influence in Berlin, their ambitions were quickly disappointed. Both were left empty-handed after the distribution of key offices in the German capital. Heydrich himself remained in Berlin until March 1933, but continued to operate on the sidelines of the major political events that took place in Germany's capital. Frustrated that the new dawn of the Third Reich had not increased his personal influence at all, he decided to launch a new initiative.

On 5 March, the day of the general elections which unsurprisingly – given the pressures on the opposition – gave the Nazis 43.9 per cent of the popular vote, Heydrich sought to make contact with Kurt Daluege, the powerful leader of SS Division East and recently appointed commissioner for special assignments in the Prussian Interior Ministry, who would later become Heydrich's counterpart as head of the Third Reich's uniformed Order Police. Daluege, so much was clear to Heydrich, was an indispensable contact who could open doors in the capital. Born in 1897 in ethnically mixed Upper Silesia, Daluege had a characteristic SS career: he had served both in the Great War and in various Freikorps formations after 1918 and joined the Nazi Party in 1922 before transferring from the SA to the SS in 1929, becoming the leader of that organization for Berlin and northern Germany. Since then, Daluege had played a key role in restraining the unruly East German SA, whose members felt that Hitler's legalistic route to power was simply too slow. Partly for that reason, Göring had selected him as the future strong man in the Prussian police apparatus and authorized him to undertake a political purge of the police force.[57]

As Heydrich understood, being directly authorized by Göring and now employed as a senior official in the Prussian Interior Ministry made Daluege relatively independent of the SS leadership in Munich. Daluege, who was busy climbing the career ladder, had little time for the unknown envoy from Munich who was also his junior in SS rank. Daluege never answered Heydrich's phone calls, and on 5 March a frustrated Heydrich wrote to complain that he had been unsuccessful in penetrating Daluege's 'protective screen' of receptionists.[58]

That same evening, Heydrich returned to Munich, where – one month after Hitler's appointment as Reich chancellor – the Nazi takeover was finally within reach. Ironically, Bavaria, the second largest German state and the original birthplace of Nazism, was the last of the *Länder* to come under Nazi control. On 9 March, one of the most prominent Nazi politicians in Bavaria, Franz Ritter von Epp, was installed in Munich as new state commissioner. The takeover was secured after Heydrich and a group of SS men threatened postal workers loyal to the hitherto ruling Bavarian People's Party with violence to ensure the delivery of the telegram announcing Hitler's appointment of Epp.[59] Epp, in turn, appointed Himmler as acting police president of Munich, and shortly thereafter, on 1 April, the Reich Leader SS assumed control over the entire Bavarian Political Police and the auxiliary police formations composed of SA and SS men. The Bavarian Political Police, which during the Weimar Republic had served to combat extremists of the radical left and right, was handed to the twenty-nine-year-old Heydrich, who quickly used his newly gained powers to transform the department into an efficient instrument of terror against real and perceived enemies of the Nazi revolution.[60]

Heydrich pursued his new task with determination, delighted that the frustrations of the previous months were finally overcome. Lina's letter to her parents of 13 March reflects some of that enthusiasm, as well as the

Heydrichs' surprise at how suddenly Reinhard had been thrust into a position of power:

> What a life! You will certainly have read about our little revolution in the newspapers. According to Reinhard's anecdotes, it must have been delightful. Let me tell you how I experienced it: on Wednesday Reinhard came home early and announced that he had to go back immediately to the Brown House, since the Bavarian government refused to submit . . . At eleven o'clock he rang me to say that I should send his pistol to the Brown House. I naturally feared the worst and got quite a shock. At 1 o'clock the government instructed the Bavarian police that they were to shoot at the SA immediately if they attempted to topple the Bavarian government on the orders of the Reich Chancellor. Then Röhm, Himmler, and Reinhard drove to Minister President [Heinrich] Held and negotiated with him for a whole hour . . . Reinhard said he felt great satisfaction that the same people who had been locking up the SA and the SS just half a year ago, who beat them down with rubber truncheons, could now no longer straighten their backs for all the bowing they did. Himmler will become the police president . . . and Reinhard – please don't laugh now – will become commissioner of the political police. I had to laugh so hard . . . In the evening SA and SS enjoyed themselves. They were entrusted with arresting all known political enemies and had to bring them to the Brown House. That was something for the lads. They could finally take revenge for all the injustice done to them, for all the blows and injuries, and avenge their fallen comrades. Over 200 are now locked up, from the KPD, SPD, the Bavarian People's Party and Jews . . . There, in the reception hall [of the Brown House], the Interior Minister stood in his socks and nightshirt, surrounded by a group of SA and SS men who couldn't stop laughing. Then they came with their big shoes and stepped on the crying Interior Minister's toes, so that he jumped from one leg to the other between them. You can imagine the scene.

Lina then described how a prominent member of Munich's Jewish community was dragged into the Brown House by a group of SS men:

> They made short work of him [*machten kurzen Prozess mit ihm*]. They beat him with dog whips, pulled off his shoes and socks, and then he had to walk home barefoot in the company of SS men . . . That will give you an idea of how they do things. Many Jesuits and Jews have fled from here. No one is dead, no one has been seriously injured, but fear, fear, I tell you.[61]

The reality was even grimmer than Lina's account suggested. Under the aegis of Himmler and Heydrich, the scale of arrests in Bavaria was proportionately higher even than in Prussia. Immediately after 9 March, a first wave of arrests rounded up real and imagined enemies of the Nazi regime, most notably Communists, Social Democrats and trade union officials – some 10,000 of them by April.[62] Jews also featured prominently among those arrested. Protests against the often arbitrary arrests were met with violence, as the lawyer Michael Siegel experienced when on 10 March, one day after Heydrich's appointment as head of the Bavarian Political Police, he lodged a complaint against the arrest of one of his Jewish clients with the Munich police. Siegel was badly beaten by SS auxiliary policemen and force-marched through the streets of the city, a placard bound around his neck: 'I will never again complain about the police.'[63]

In an attempt to transform the Bavarian Political Police into an effective instrument of repression, Heydrich quickly recruited some 152 men from various levels of the Munich Metropolitan Police. Some of them were members of the Nazi Party, but most were not. Several of the new recruits would share Heydrich's professional path until the very end, most importantly perhaps the thirty-three-year-old Heinrich Müller who would become head of Heydrich's Gestapo in 1939, a position he held until the very end of the Second World War. Müller was born in Munich in 1900, the son of a minor Catholic police official. He participated in the First World War as a volunteer from 1917 onwards and earned various decorations for bravery as a pilot. After the war, he entered the Munich Metropolitan Police in which, thanks to his great energy, he rose quickly. He was involved in the political police department, where he specialized in combating the extreme left. When Heydrich took over the Munich Metropolitan Police building on 9 March 1933, Müller was among those who offered resistance. However, rather than dismissing him from office, Heydrich decided to take advantage of his knowledge of international Communism and policing matters, despite the negative political evaluation Müller had received from the Munich Gauleitung for being loyal to the long-ruling Bavarian People's Party. The retention of non-party members such as Müller in the services of the new state police was in no way atypical. In 1933–4, the political police agencies in most German states were only sporadically restaffed with Nazi Party members.[64] Since Heydrich was not an expert in policing matters, he had little choice but to rely on the professional competence and experience of men like Müller. While he publicly described apolitical experts as ultimately expendable, in practice he could not do without them.[65]

As part of his reconstruction of the Bavarian Political Police into an ideologically reliable and efficient tool of repression, Heydrich made

extensive use of a new instrument of terror known as protective custody –
the potentially open-ended and judicially unsupervised internment of
persons in newly established concentration camps, where real or alleged
enemies of the new regime were subjected to arbitrary and unrestrained
terror.[66] Already in mid-March, an abandoned munitions factory in
Dachau, a small town sixteen kilometres north-west of Munich, had been
converted into what was going to become one of the most notorious early
concentration camps for prisoners in protective custody.[67] The day after
Heydrich was installed as head of the Bavarian Political Police, control
over Dachau (previously in the hands of the ordinary police) was transferred to the SS, which immediately unleashed an orgy of violence. Many
prisoners died as a result of maltreatment and random shootings. The
dreaded name Dachau soon became a powerful deterrent, a byword for the
horrifying though largely unspoken events known or presumed to have
taken place within the camp walls.[68]

The number of camp inmates at Dachau grew rapidly, from 170 in
March to 2,033 in May 1933, as Heydrich gleefully reported in two letters
to the Bavarian Interior Minister. By 1 August that year, some 4,152
political opponents from Bavaria were being held in protective custody,
more than 2,200 of them in Dachau. By January 1934, a total of 16,409
had been arrested, of whom 12,554 were released again, usually after severe
beatings coupled with warnings never to become politically active again.[69]
Brutal maltreatment of the prisoners in protective custody in Dachau was
the norm. Between mid-April and late May 1933 alone, thirteen camp
inmates died as a result of injuries received during their captivity.[70]

In all of this, Heydrich's actions cannot simply be understood as those
of a bloodthirsty sadist playing a preconceived role in building a totalitarian police state. Since joining the SS in 1931, he had immersed himself
in a political milieu which thrived on the notion of being locked in a life-
and-death struggle. Winning that struggle required decisive action against
enemies in respect of whom even the most unimaginable cruelty was justified. As his future deputy, Werner Best, observed, Heydrich tended to
project his own proclivity towards intrigues and violence on to his real or
alleged enemies. Finally free to move against an ideological enemy who
had supposedly enjoyed the upper hand until 1933, he considered terror a
justifiable weapon – in fact, the only adequate weapon against such evil.[71]

That Heydrich was put in charge of the imprisonment and release of
political enemies but not of the Dachau camp itself was characteristic
both of the divisions of labour within Nazi Germany in general and of
Himmler's leadership style more specifically. The Dachau camp comman-
dant was Theodor Eicke, born in 1892 and dismissed from the army after
a brief military career in 1919. Eicke, a party member since 1928, had

been sentenced to two years' imprisonment during the Weimar Republic for the illegal possession of explosives and had spent the first months of 1933 in a psychiatric asylum. As in Heydrich's case, Himmler offered Eicke a second chance and he would not disappoint his new boss.[72]

Within months, Eicke, who would become inspector of all concentration camps in 1934, created a new form of camp regime that differed profoundly from other early concentration camps of the Third Reich. The key features of the so-called Dachau system, which would subsequently provide the model for the camps of Sachsenhausen, Buchenwald and Ravensbrück, included the total isolation of the inmates from the outside world, involving above all the prevention of escapes at any cost to limit the emergence of 'enemy propaganda'; labour duties for all prisoners in order to make the system economically viable; a systemization of the previously arbitrary violence through the introduction of a penal and punishment code; and stricter supervision of the guards, who were now issued with special regulations. The desired public impression, namely that the arbitrary SA violence had now been replaced by a camp regime that was strict but based on certain rules, was also a component of this system. In reality, of course, conditions in the camp were horrifying and the violence against inmates continued to be purely arbitrary.[73]

Indeed, violent excesses occurred on such a scale that Heydrich felt the need to remind his staff in September 1934 that uncontrolled abuse of internees in protective custody would no longer be tolerated, emphasizing that 'it is unworthy' of an SS man 'to insult or to handle internees with unnecessary roughness. The arrestee is to be treated with the necessary severity, but never with chicanery or unnecessary persecution. I will prosecute severely, with the utmost rigour, offences against this order.'[74] What drove Heydrich's order was not compassion for the inmates, but a desire for stricter discipline and concern about the SS's public image. He wanted the Nazi political police to be dreaded by its enemies for its efficiency and thoroughness, but he also wanted the 'good citizen' to know that there was no need to fear his organization. The outside perception mattered far more to him than the grim reality that confronted inmates behind the closed walls of the camps.[75]

The most prominent victim of Heydrich's first wave of persecution in Bavaria was the Nobel Laureate Thomas Mann. Closely observing the dramatic political developments in Germany, Mann, who had left for a reading tour of Holland, Belgium and France shortly after Hitler's appointment as chancellor, decided to extend his stay abroad by a few months until the situation at home had stabilized. As a non-Jewish, liberal conservative, he should have had little to fear, but he had attacked the Nazis in a number of public speeches and articles in the early 1930s and wisely decided to be cautious. In late April, his house in Munich was raided by Heydrich's political police. His cars, bank accounts and private possessions were confiscated.[76]

On 12 June Heydrich went even further. In a letter to State Commissioner von Epp, he demanded that upon his return to Munich Mann should be placed in protective custody in Dachau, since the author was 'an enemy of the national movement and a follower of the Marxist idea'. As evidence, Heydrich stated that Mann had called for a general amnesty for all the revolutionaries of 1918. Moreover, he insisted that Mann's masterpiece, *The Magic Mountain* (1924), contained a 'glorifying passage' on Jewish ritual slaughter. In sum, Heydrich concluded, the writer's 'unGerman, anti-Nazi, Marxist and Jew-friendly attitude provided the reason for decreeing protective custody against Thomas Mann, which could not be carried out so far due to the absence of the accused. However, by order of the ministries all of his assets were confiscated.' When Epp enquired which ministries had authorized this step, Heydrich did not respond. By this time the SS had already developed into a largely autonomous force in Bavaria. Shortly thereafter, Heydrich employed the same arguments when he applied to have Mann stripped of his German citizenship, a procedure completed in 1936 after the SD chief's renewed request. Mann and Heydrich would never meet, but remained connected in deep enmity. It was Mann who after Heydrich's assassination in 1942 issued one of the first obituaries on the BBC, condemning him as one of Hitler's most appalling henchmen.[77]

The Thomas Mann case was an atypical example of Nazi persecution. Unlike most middle-ranked Communist or Social Democratic Party functionaries, Mann was financially independent and of sufficient international reputation to continue his career in exile without major disruptions. At the same time, however, the case was paradigmatic both of the increasing persecution of writers classified as unGerman and of the gradual expansion of terror in order to encompass more and more broadly defined enemy groups. In Bavaria, for example, the vast majority of the more than 5,000 people arrested between March and June 1933 were Communists and Social Democrats, but the target groups were soon extended. In June, Himmler and Heydrich ordered the arrest of leading functionaries of the conservative Bavarian People's Party (BVP) in order to force the party to dissolve itself. After this had been achieved and the BVP functionaries had been set free again, Bavaria still had 3,965 persons in protective custody, including 2,420 in Dachau as of August 1933. One year later, in June 1934, the number was further reduced to 2,204 people in SS custody, more than half of them in Dachau.[78]

Himmler and Heydrich had needed less than a year to create an effective system of terror in Bavaria. Towards the end of 1933, their ambition grew and they began to seek control over the political police formations in the other states outside Bavaria. Germany was a federal country with independent political police forces of varying sizes in each state, and the task of assuming control over them required patience and tactical skill. During the autumn of 1933 and the summer of 1934, the political police in most of the states were gradually brought under SS control.[79] In this process Himmler made good use of his negotiation skills and his personal contacts with local Nazi leaders to place trusted allies in key positions in the states' political police forces. The political police branches in most German states were tiny and their gradual takeover by the SS attracted little attention from the SS's political rivals. It was also helpful that the SS was widely regarded as a disciplined elite organization loyal to the Nazi Party leadership. The success of the SS in Bavaria in efficiently and quietly fighting the political opposition was now seen as a model for Germany as a whole, a model that was preferable to the uncoordinated and often spontaneous outbursts of SA violence that alienated Hitler's conservative coalition partners.

During these weeks and months, Heydrich accompanied Himmler on several trips across Germany, recruiting new staff and negotiating with political decision-makers. He made sure that the SS men appointed by Himmler as heads of the local political police forces were simultaneously recruited into the SD, enabling Heydrich to access the political information gathered by the local police commanders. Already in the spring of 1934, seven of the eleven heads of the political police forces in the individual German states were members of the SD. Heydrich recruited a large number of staff members who would share and sometimes even shape his professional path and political beliefs over the following years.[80] In September 1933, for example, he met Dr Werner Best, who would have a lasting intellectual influence on him. Born in 1903, Best had studied law and became a judge in the Weimar Republic. In 1930 he joined the Nazi Party in Hessen and directed its legal department in his spare time. When, in 1931, the authorities were supplied with the so-called Boxheim documents, which indicated that Best had made plans for a Nazi coup, he was dismissed from his judgeship. After the Nazis' rise to power, he became head of the police in Hessen where he oversaw the first arrests of political opponents, but personal differences with the new Nazi State Commissioner of Hessen, Jakob Sprenger, led to his dismissal in September 1933. It was in this situation that he met Heydrich for the first time.[81]

After the war, Best recalled his first encounter with Heydrich, a recollection that showed how far the latter had developed since 1931 when Wolff had described him as an 'insecure youth':

Heydrich was tall, of higher stature than most of his subordinates. He appeared slender, while at the same time a certain width, particularly in the hips, gave him a powerful, hefty touch. The narrow, long face beneath the blond hair was dominated by the powerful aquiline nose and the closely set blue eyes. These eyes often stared coldly, probing and distrustful, frequently disconcerting others through a flickering restlessness ... He immediately articulated his opinions and intentions with a remarkable forcefulness and thus left others no choice but either to agree and submit to his will or to undertake a counterattack for which few had the courage. In this way, Heydrich immediately forced everyone to position themselves as his friend or foe. ... The forcefulness of his demeanour and behaviour certainly left a lasting impression ... He frequently expressed his dissatisfaction towards his subordinates in exceedingly tempestuous forms and with intentionally hurtful remarks. On the other hand, when he was satisfied – particularly when a person who had originally resisted him finally submitted to his will – he could display the greatest friendliness and positively charm his counterpart. But his behaviour was always characterized by an unconcealed subjectivity and by the impetuous determination to assert himself at every moment and at any cost.[82]

Best was considerably more intellectual than Heydrich and was often surprised by his boss's lack of interest in larger philosophical questions. 'During a journey', Best recalled, 'we were talking about what we would do if for any reason we were suddenly forced to leave the public service. While I talked about studying areas of knowledge I had not previously had time for, such as philosophy or history, Heydrich declared that he would devote himself entirely to sport.'[83] Because of his intellectual superiority and Heydrich's inexperience in legal and policing matters, Best exercised a powerful influence on his superior throughout the 1930s, acquainting him with theories that appeared to support Heydrich's own value system. Through Best, Heydrich learned more about 'heroic realism', a notion propagated by Ernst Jünger and other prominent right-wing intellectuals in the 1920s and early 1930s. While it had originally emerged as a 'coping mechanism' deriving from the lost world war and from the right-wing critique of the Weimar Republic, heroic realism exerted a particular fascination on those members of the younger generation who had not been able to fight as soldiers themselves and who had thus not been permitted to prove themselves in battle.[84]

In Best's worldview, ideas emanating from hereditary biologists, demographers and racial hygienists merged with other ideological constructs of the extreme right. Heydrich's strength, so Best observed, was to translate these abstract ideas and doctrines into actual policies and to apply them rigorously. For Heydrich and Best, life was a constant struggle, a permanent state of emergency, in which the enemy was to be fought mercilessly, not out of cruelty or hatred, but out of the 'objective' biological necessity of winning the struggle of peoples for the survival of the fittest.[85]

This struggle demanded toughness, both towards oneself and towards others. It demanded the suppression of emotions and the cultivation of callousness, hardness and mercilessness towards all opponents. By being hard in the present, so they believed, they would be kind to the future. Unconditional toughness set one apart from those who had no stomach for the life-and-death struggle for Germany's survival. The keyword 'sobriety' was used to propagate an ideal of cold, pragmatic ideological soldiers whose actions would no longer be guided by irrational emotions, an attitude which also helped to conceal moments of social inadequacy or uncertainty.[86]

Over the coming years, such attitudes and beliefs would meld into a whole catalogue of 'virtues', which became aspirational for the SS as a whole and which Heydrich himself genuinely tried to live by. It was Himmler's intention that ideals such as honour, loyalty, obedience, decency and camaraderie should guide the behaviour of his SS men. Drawn from the standard vocabulary of authoritarian movements, these virtues gained special meaning in Nazi Germany, as they were increasingly deprived of their wider content. For the SS members, loyalty, for example, referred solely to their relationship with Adolf Hitler. This loyalty formed the core of a special code of honour that distinguished SS men from all others. A breach of loyalty was the gravest offence an SS man could commit and automatically resulted in a loss of honour. Camaraderie bound the organization together and made it into a unit in which conflicts and petty jealousies were unacceptable.[87]

Guided by such principles, Heydrich began to develop his characteristic leadership style, one which even his closest associates described as 'despotic'.[88] He often behaved more impulsively than the cautious Himmler and frequently bullied his way through problems. Even when among close colleagues, Best observed, Heydrich 'approached people in that enquiring, distrustful way which immediately struck everyone as his dominating characteristic', thus creating a permanently 'tense atmosphere full of mistrust and friction'. Throughout his life, he found it difficult to accept criticism, and within his immediate working environment he did not tolerate it at all. Aided by a phenomenal memory for detail, he often liked to intimidate his conversation partners by reminding them of things they had once said and long forgotten. In the most accurate post-war characterization of Heydrich's leadership style, Werner Best maintained 'that all Heydrich's subordinates feared him, yet all of them also shared a certain admiring respect for him'.[89]

Heydrich consciously cultivated this image, and the combination of fear and admiration that Best described was partly due to the fact that he appeared to live out the high demands he placed upon his men. His workdays were long: he went to his office at dawn and did not return home until late at night, usually eating dinner at work. Despite his increasingly busy schedule, he still managed to find the time and enthusiasm for daily physical exercise and he expected his men to share his enthusiasm.[90] Here, too, he tried to live up to SS ideals. The physical appearance of an SS man was seen as evidence of inner composure, masculinity and strength. The public image of an SS officer, so Heydrich believed, depended on his physical fitness, a perfectly maintained uniform, controlled behaviour and bodily posture. Public drinking in uniform was discouraged, moderation in smoking desired. Even during the war, Heydrich would insist on strict adherence to schedules for physical exercise which he himself devised for his employees. The Reich Security Main Office had its own sport facilities and all of his men were expected to attend classes twice a week, with female employees doing additional sessions on Saturdays between 8 and 10 a.m.[91]

Unlike Himmler, who alternated between fatherly reprimands and praise in his attempt to educate his men, Heydrich's leadership style was based on instilling fear and setting an example of how to live life as an SS man. He rarely gave an impression of joviality and friendly conviviality in the company of others, hardly ever drank or smoked and never indulged in expensive dinners. His self-imposed ascetism was part of the soldierly self-image that he cultivated until his death. At work, he allocated tasks to his immediate subordinates who were to carry out his orders efficiently and creatively, thus encouraging radical initiatives from below. From very early on, Heydrich promoted and lived an ideal of *Menschenführung* – the SS term for leadership – with a radical emphasis on instinct, ideological commitment and rule-despising activism that differed profoundly from the leadership ideals of the traditional administration. Personal initiative was rewarded and compromises considered acts of cowardice – an attitude that was to have fatal consequences during the unleashing of SS *Einsatzgruppen* violence in the Second World War.[92]

Although the SD was still a tiny organization with little resemblance to its later incarnation as a sinister wartime instrument of terror, by 1934 it had already begun to display characteristics of its later incarnation. Since the active persecution of the opposition remained the task of the state, and more specifically of the political police, the SD focused its surveillance and espionage activity on those supposed enemy groups that were not, as yet, the primary targets of Nazi suppression: Jews, Freemasons and the Churches. At least in part driven by the desire to justify its existence, the SD thus provided the material and ideological basis for future waves of persecution.[93] During the first few years of the Third Reich, Heydrich's SD also attracted a large number of men who differed remarkably from the typical Nazi functionary. Heydrich surrounded himself with an inner circle of men who were both significantly younger than most of the other leading personalities in the civil service and substantially better educated than the average Nazi Party member. In the mid-1930s, the typical SD leader was, like Heydrich himself, around thirty years old. Unlike Heydrich, most of them had experienced their political awakening during the early years of the Weimar Republic when they became active in far-right associations and clubs. Defying the danger of disqualifying themselves from jobs in the civil service, they tended to maintain contacts with illegal right-wing groups during their university education. The peculiar self-perception of most SD leaders was therefore based on firm ideological commitment, an emphasis on activism and efficiency, and an elitist rejection of mass organizations such as the SA or indeed the Nazi Party itself.[94]

In selecting his closest subordinates, Heydrich placed greatest importance on ideological conviction, soldierly bearing and an athletic physical appearance.[95] His personal adjutant between 1938 and 1942, Dr Hans-Achim Ploetz, was a prime example: born in 1911, Ploetz had earned his PhD in literature and fulfilled every ideological and physical precondition for the job. Tall, athletic, blond and blue-eyed, he was praised by Heydrich as an 'immaculate National Socialist'.[96] The relative youthfulness and learning of his SD recruits were an expression of Heydrich's determination to create a new efficient, professional and ideologically reliable Nazi elite, an elite by virtue of achievement, ability and discipline. This new elite was groomed to fulfil crucial tasks and roles in the Third Reich, which Heydrich was determined to consolidate and secure permanently. Much later, during the Second World War, these men would become Heydrich's preferred personnel for service in the East.[97]

Power Struggle for Prussia

By the summer of 1934, Himmler and Heydrich had brought the political police agencies in most of the German states under their control, but Prussia, the largest and most politically important German state, remained beyond their reach. Any attempt to seize control over the Prussian police would have been perceived as a direct challenge to the powerful Minister President of Prussia, Hermann Göring, who personally directed the Prussian Political Police, the Gestapo. Both Heydrich and Himmler knew all too well that they were not in a position to win that contest.[98] But neither Himmler nor Heydrich was easily deterred. In their pursuit of control over the Gestapo, they benefited from the fact that the random violence of the SA, which Göring had instated as an auxiliary police force in February 1933, increasingly threatened to damage the authority of the party and the state. This irritated not only the Nazis' conservative coalition partners but also large sections of the German population. Although reluctant to concede any of his powers to Himmler, Göring began to regard the SS as the only appropriate instrument with which to keep its much larger rival, the SA, in check. He therefore instructed the political police to use only SS men as auxiliary policemen and decided that new positions in the Gestapo should be strictly reserved for SS men.[99]

In April 1934, Göring and Himmler met to discuss the future of the Prussian Political Police. Himmler convinced Göring that he would remain in overall control of the Gestapo and that the SS would never threaten his authority. Assured of his overall control, Göring formally appointed Himmler as acting director of the Gestapo. While Himmler formally remained under Göring's supervision, control over all the political police formations in Germany now rested in the hands of the most radical party formation, the SS. Despite Göring's initial objections, Heydrich rose in Himmler's wake: on 22 April 1934, he moved back to Berlin to assume his new position as acting chief of the Gestapo office while also retaining his function as head of the SD.[100]

Immediately after taking control of the Gestapo, Heydrich transferred trusted staff from the Bavarian Political Police, including Heinrich Müller, Franz Josef Huber and Josef Meisinger, to the Gestapo headquarters in Berlin's Prinz-Albrecht-Strasse, a former Arts and Crafts school in the heart of Germany's government district that was to become synonymous with the Nazi terror state.[101] When Heydrich took over the Prussian Gestapo in April 1934, he inherited with it a sizeable bureaucratic apparatus encompassing some 700 officials and staff members in the Berlin headquarters, as well as about 1,000 further staff in the Gestapo's local branches all over Prussia.[102] Over the following three years, the number of staff would rise to roughly 7,000 employees, most of them officers in the field. Three-quarters of the employees of Nazi Germany's political police had already worked in different branches of the police during the Weimar Republic; a further 5 per cent came from other state agencies. Only 20 per cent were new recruits, mostly members or supporters of the Nazi Party.[103] In addition the political police could draw on an army of paid and unpaid informers, many of them former enemies of Nazism who bought their freedom by spying on former comrades, as well as the so-called block wardens, usually Nazi sympathizers and caretakers in apartment blocks. No fewer than 200,000 block wardens existed by 1935, each of them responsible for the political supervision of between forty and sixty households.[104] As the American journalist Howard Smith, a foreign correspondent in Nazi Germany, observed, mutual distrust quickly permeated German society as a result, creating an omnipresent accusatory climate: '"*Ich zeige Dich an, junger Mann!*" – That's the magic phrase these days: "I'll have you arrested, you imprudent young man," that and "I have a friend who's high up in the Party and *he* will tell you a thing or two!" They're like children threatening to "call my Dad, who's bigger than yours".'[105]

The conventional image of a self-supervising German society is, however, an exaggeration. Only a tiny fraction of the population of the Third Reich voluntarily provided information to the Gestapo. Denunciations of certain 'crimes' such as 'race defilement' (sexual relations with Jews) or the telling of political jokes were much more common than the denunciation of political enemies. In absolute figures, the cases of denunciation were rare; for example, not only were there only between three and fifty-one denunciations a year in the state of Lippe, where the population was 176,000, but a high proportion of the denouncers were members of the Nazi Party.[106] Even in the capital of Nazi Germany, the density of political supervision remained remarkably loose. The number of Gestapo personnel never exceeded 800 officers and operatives. In a city of 4.5 million inhabitants, this equated to no more than one agent for 5,600 Berliners.[107]

Yet although the Gestapo was never a huge organization it consciously created an atmosphere of fear and suspicion. Heydrich actively contributed to this atmosphere by portraying the Gestapo in newspaper articles and public speeches as an omnipresent organization rightly feared by the enemies of the state while simultaneously suggesting that 'honest citizens' had nothing to fear. This perception did not reflect the actual strength of the Gestapo but nonetheless successfully created a situation in which citizens refrained from committing 'crimes' out of fear of its reach.[108]

Shortly after securing control of the Gestapo, Heydrich and Himmler turned to the next obstacle that stood in the way of their growing ambitions: the SA under the leadership of Ernst Röhm. This struggle was particularly sensitive as Röhm was not only a close acquaintance of Heydrich but also the godfather of his eldest son, Klaus, who was born on 17 June 1933. Heydrich, Himmler and Röhm had been allies, even friends, in the first months after Hitler's appointment as chancellor, forming a common front against conservatives and moderate Nazis. It was the SS's gradual acquisition of the state police apparatus that drove a wedge between them. Once the SS leadership had taken control of all of the legitimate means of state repression, the SA with its illegal street violence became an inconvenient competitor in the struggle for the control of force in Nazi Germany. Heydrich viewed the SA's lack of discipline and its questionable loyalty to the Führer with growing concern: while he had some personal sympathy for the anti-establishment radicalism of Röhm and his associates, he and Himmler quickly realized that more power was to be gained by joining the growing anti-SA camp of conservatives and senior military figures who rejected the SA's ambition to become the Third Reich's revolutionary army that would ultimately replace the old Reichswehr.

The Night of the Long Knives

Heydrich was well aware that a tense mood prevailed in Germany in the summer of 1934. More than a year after Hitler's ascent to power, the severe economic crisis that had shaken Germany since the autumn of 1929 and enabled Hitler's rise was far from over. Only one-third of the 6 million people unemployed in late 1932 had found work since the Nazis had taken over the government and, gradually, the initial enthusiasm that had fired much of the population in January 1933 gave way to disillusionment. Against this backdrop, the SA, with its populist and anti-capitalist promise of a 'second revolution', represented a dangerous source of potential political unrest. Having broken the power of the left and intimidated the liberals into submission, the SA leadership also wanted to sweep aside those conservative allies – including businessmen, industrialists and bankers – who had made Hitler's ascent to power possible in the first place.[109]

Most ominously, Röhm challenged the leading role of the Reichswehr in national defence. Hitler feared a civil war and in February 1934 rejected the SA's demands, which only exacerbated the smouldering conflict. In early 1934 the SA's opponents – the party, the Gestapo and the Reichswehr – began to prepare for decisive action. From early on the SS – with a membership of around 200,000 men in the spring of 1934 – had positioned itself as Hitler's loyal executive arm for a potential strike against the rebellious and much larger SA. After taking over the Gestapo in April, Heydrich intensified his search for incriminating material against the SA leadership. In May his Gestapo and the military intelligence department in the Reichswehr ministry began exchanging material on the SA. From mid-June the SS and SD were put on high alert.[110]

At about the same time, Hitler's position was also challenged by his conservative coalition partners. On 17 June, Vice Chancellor Franz von Papen provoked a government crisis by delivering a widely circulated speech at the University of Marburg, in which he heavily criticized the

Nazis' arbitrary regime of terror, threatening the future of Hitler's government by suggesting that he would offer his resignation to President von
Hindenburg. This would have ended the coalition government appointed
by Hindenburg on 30 January 1933, leading to Hitler's dismissal as chancellor. Hitler was alarmed, knowing that in the summer of 1934 the Nazi
regime was by no means so firmly established as to survive an open
confrontation with Hindenburg and the military.[111]

Hitler solved the crisis by taking decisive action against the SA. He
calculated that by eliminating the SA leadership he could resolve the
tangle of his domestic political problems with a single blow. The threat of
a second revolution would be off the table, the majority of the population
would greet the elimination of the unruly SA with a sigh of relief and the
government alliance between National Socialists and conservatives would
emerge stronger than ever before.[112]

Heydrich's impact on Hitler's decision remains the subject of considerable controversy. According to the post-war testimony of senior SS officers,
Heydrich initiated a conscious conspiracy to destroy the SA leadership by
fabricating evidence of an imminent SA coup. Others have argued that
most of the incriminating evidence against the SA leadership was provided
by the army and that the SS played the role of executor rather than instigator. Since most of the documents relating to the Night of the Long
Knives were destroyed after 30 June 1934, the truth is difficult to ascertain.
What is clear is that Heydrich turned on the SA not only for reasons of
career advancement, as has often been alleged, but also because he and
Himmler perceived the SA as a real threat to domestic stability. They firmly
believed that factionalism made Germany vulnerable to enemy attacks.[113]

In late June 1934, the timing for decisive action against the SA could
not have been more favourable: Röhm had gone on holiday and had sent
the entire SA on summer vacation for the month of July. The SS accordingly commenced its preparations for the elimination of the SA leadership. At the beginning of the month, Dachau commander Eicke secretly
conducted rehearsals for the deployment of SS troops in the Munich area.
On 27 June the district commanders of the SS and leading SD officers
met in Berlin, where Heydrich explained to them 'that according to
confirmed intelligence reports a revolt of the SA under Röhm is being
planned'. In a fit of anger, Heydrich ranted about 'Röhm's connections to
France and the involvement of other forces hostile to the state' such as 'the
Communists, who had flowed into the SA in great numbers, and "reac-
tionary circles". The only forces that can protect the state and the Führer's
government are the SS and the Reichswehr.'[114]

Heydrich's SD provided lists with the names of the SA leaders who
were to be liquidated. While Heydrich co-ordinated the operation from

Berlin himself, he sent Best and his SD adjutant, Carl Albrecht Oberg, to Munich in order to oversee a wave of arrests in southern Germany.[115] On 30 June, the SA leadership was arrested in Röhm's Bavarian holiday retreat, Bad Wiessee. Simultaneous arrests took place in Berlin, Silesia and elsewhere. Up to 200 people were murdered, among them Röhm himself and the former Nazi Party organizational leader Gregor Strasser, who had fallen out with Hitler at the end of 1932. The SS also struck a blow against the conservative right. Those killed included Papen's secretary Herbert von Bose, the neo-conservative intellectual Edgar Julius Jung and Hitler's predecessor as German chancellor General Kurt von Schleicher, who was shot with his wife in his home near Berlin. Heydrich also used the wave of arrests to settle scores with prominent representatives of 'political Catholicism', personally ordering the murder of the leader of the Catholic Action organization, Erich Klausener. The warning to conservative and Catholic politicians not to stand in the way of the new rulers was unmistakable.[116]

The SS – and the SD in particular – emerged as the true victor of the power struggle between the Nazi Party leadership, the Reichswehr and the SA that culminated on 30 June in the Night of the Long Knives. Heydrich's SD had most likely delivered the material accusing Röhm of planning a coup in the first place and his Gestapo officers had carried out most of the murders, proving their unwavering loyalty to the Führer. In recognition of his achievements, Heydrich was appointed SS-*Gruppenführer* or lieutenant general on 30 June, at the age of thirty.[117]

Family Troubles

By mid-1934 Heydrich's professional crisis, triggered by his dismissal from the navy, was replaced by his rapid ascent in the SS. However, the financial predicament of his parents continued to cause him grief. After a brief easing of money problems in the mid-1920s, the Halle Conservatory's finances eroded rapidly. After Bruno Heydrich's debilitating stroke in 1931, his wife and daughter now ran the family business in Halle, but they did not have Bruno's reputation. In addition, the Great Depression deprived the Conservatory of both savings and pupils. After a last golden age in the 1920s, the Depression brought a crash from which institutions providing classical music education, such as Bruno Heydrich's Conservatory, never recovered. Musical education was suddenly a luxury few people could afford, particularly when the spread of gramophones offered an alternative (and much more affordable) form of home entertainment. During the Depression years, the number of professional musicians and music teachers declined dramatically, and the Heydrich Conservatory never recovered from the blow. By early 1933, the Conservatory was facing bankruptcy and the family had to move out of its mansion into a rented flat.[118]

Heydrich's brother-in-law, Wolfgang Heindorf, informed Reinhard on 6 November 1933 about his family's extreme financial difficulties and enquired whether he was prepared to give them a loan of 5,000 Reichsmarks. Heydrich must have turned down the request, as just a couple of weeks later Heydrich's mother asked him personally for at least a 'small sum of money'. Heydrich – who had asked his parents for support only two and a half years earlier – does not appear to have responded to this letter either. On 23 November his parents contacted him again, this time with a telex message sent directly to his office. Heydrich's handwritten note on the telex's margins indicate his unwillingness to deal with the matter, but eventually he sent two postal orders of 50 Reichsmarks each to his parents – far less than the required 5,000 Reichsmarks.[119]

Less than three weeks later, the money was spent and on 18 December his sister Maria contacted him again, describing their parents' financial position in the bleakest terms. Since Maria and her husband did not have the financial means to improve the situation and his parents were practically without income, Heydrich's support seemed unavoidable if he did not want his parents to starve to death.[120] Maria and her husband also asked Heydrich for money to subsidize their own existence. In June 1934, for example, Heydrich received a bill of over 216 Reichsmarks from a Halle delicatessen store, Pfeiffer & Haase, covering the expenses of the Heindorfs' wedding reception. Heydrich was furious and refused to pay.[121]

In order to gain insight into the complicated ownership structure of the Dresden Conservatory and to estimate how much money his mother as co-proprietor could expect in the event of the business's liquidation, Heydrich ordered an SD subordinate, the lawyer Dr Herbert Mehlhorn from Dresden, to advise him on possible legal strategies. Mehlhorn, a member of the SS since 1932, had entered the SD only in March 1933, but he had already become deputy head of the Gestapo in Saxony. In the summer of 1935, presumably thanks to his assistance in resolving Heydrich's family matters in Halle and Dresden, he was appointed to a senior post in the head office of the SD in Berlin.[122]

Mehlhorn's response to Heydrich's request came quickly. On 18 December 1933 he submitted his legal assessment of the situation to Heydrich's office. Mehlhorn estimated that, in theory, the share of Elisabeth Heydrich in the Dresden Conservatory amounted to 36,000 Reichsmarks. In the current economic climate, however, a sale of the Conservatory was likely to bring in far less, even if her brothers consented to sell the family business. According to Mehlhorn, her eldest brother had made a decent proposal, offering to buy her out in three instalments – 5,000

Reichsmarks immediately, 5,000 RM in five years and a further 2,000 RM in eight years. He was even prepared to pay interest on the outstanding debts at a rate of 4 per cent a year. Although the offer did not reflect the theoretical value of Elisabeth Heydrich's share in the family business, it would resolve their pressing financial problems. Much to Mehlhorn's regret, the Heydrichs had rejected the offer, insisting instead that their eldest son give them a loan until the economic situation permitted a sale of the Dresden Conservatory at a higher value.[123]

After reading Mehlhorn's report, Heydrich informed his parents that his own financial means were insufficient to meet their demands and that he had asked Himmler for a loan. He pointed out that he had already provided 700 Reichsmarks towards their living costs over the past two months – an unsustainable situation given the recent extension of his own family. In June 1933, Lina had given birth to the Heydrichs' first child, Klaus, which meant that Heydrich's modest salary now had to support a family of three.[124] Heydrich added to the letter a draft contractual agreement between his parents and himself, regulating their respective duties. According to the agreement, Heydrich offered to pay for the living costs of his parents – 65 Reichmarks for rent and 50 Reichsmarks for expenditure – until they had sold their home in Halle and the claims concerning the Dresden Conservatory had been settled. In return, he requested that his parents move to Munich and avoid accumulating any fresh debts. His parents were also to avoid 'chatter' in trading and drinking establishments that might 'endanger the livelihood of their children' – presumably a reference to the fact that both his parents and his sister's family tended to refer to Reinhard Heydrich's elevated position in the new regime whenever they bought groceries and alcohol on credit. Violations of the agreement would absolve Heydrich from his obligation to make the voluntary payments.[125]

The fact that no signed copy of the agreement exists in Heydrich's personal files and that Heydrich's parents never moved to Munich suggests that his parents rejected their son's proposal, which presumably accelerated the final collapse of the once flourishing Halle Conservatory. On 26 December 1935, Bruno Heydrich informed the Halle authorities that his Conservatory had closed down for good.[126] If anything, the constant trouble with the Conservatory and his increasingly tense relationship with his family in Halle encouraged Reinhard to distance himself further from his past life. His visits to Halle stopped altogether and he did not see his parents, now living in a tiny rented flat in one of the city's working-class districts, until the summer of 1938 when Bruno lay dying. Heydrich did not return to his hometown after his father's funeral in late August of that year, but he continued to make infrequent financial contributions to his mother's living expenses. It was only after Reinhard's death in 1942 that Elisabeth Heydrich was invited back into the family home, presumably to mind her grandchildren. For Reinhard, by contrast, the future looked very bright indeed in the summer of 1934. After nearly three years of professional uncertainty and constant relocations to short-term rental accommodation, he was now in a position to afford a generous flat in Berlin's affluent suburb of Südende. Heydrich's income was also sufficient to employ a housemaid. At the end of this highly successful year, on 28 December 1934, Heydrich's wife gave birth to their second son, Heider.[127]

CHAPTER IV

Fighting the Enemies of the Reich

In Search of New Enemies

IF THE OUTCOME OF THE RÖHM PUTSCH HAD PROVEN TO BE A THOROUGH success for Heydrich's SD and the political police apparatus, it also aroused the suspicion of influential individuals who worried that the SS was becoming too powerful – in particular, the conservatives in the military and rival Nazis like Interior Minister Wilhelm Frick, whose overall authority over the German police was gradually undermined by Himmler and Heydrich.

Although the military had emerged from the Röhm purge with some complacency, tensions soon developed between it and the SS. While Heydrich viewed the conservatives in the army as ideologically unreliable, the military resented the murder of some of its generals during the purge. By the end of 1934, Heydrich and Himmler had convinced themselves of the imminence of a military coup, and their agents assembled evidence to support this belief. They focused their suspicions on the military's own espionage department, the Abwehr, which Heydrich considered deeply unreliable, and on General Werner von Fritsch, the Commander-in-Chief of the army.[1]

Heydrich's attitude towards the Abwehr, and the murky area of foreign espionage more generally, was crucially shaped by his reading of Walter Nicolai's book, *Geheime Mächte*, first published in 1923. In his comparative study of intelligence operations during the Great War, Nicolai as head of Imperial Germany's military intelligence service essentially blamed the Reich's defeat on the lack of an intelligence agency capable of competing with similar institutions in France and Britain. Unlike its enemies, Germany had not developed co-ordinated intelligence services against its wartime enemies. The independently operating military intelligence lacked guidance from the political leadership, which did not understand its needs or support it.

What Germany needed was statesmen with the necessary determination to pursue national interests and a central, politically directed espionage service to uphold that policy. Nicolai emphasized that minorities, especially Jews, and the internationally operating Churches represented threats to national security, a view with which Heydrich enthusiastically agreed.[2]

Heydrich's critical attitude towards the Abwehr was also shaped by his ambition to control all political intelligence-gathering agencies in Germany. To date, Abwehr and police responsibilities were inextricably linked in two areas. The first was espionage and sabotage, which the Gestapo handled as crimes against the state and against property. Since no clear line separated political crimes that concerned the military from those that did not, the military Abwehr had always worked closely with the political sections of the criminal investigation police involved in those cases, the so-called Abwehr police or counter-espionage police. The two organizations shared information, but in matters primarily concerning the military the police had to accept Abwehr authority. The second problem grew from the Defence Ministry's lack of a militarized police establishment like that of other European states. Since the Abwehr had neither the authority nor the means to undertake searches and arrests in the civil sector, it had to rely on the civil police – even in cases that were clearly military-defence matters. If relations between the police and the Abwehr had been relatively smooth in the Weimar period, it was because the police had known their place. This balance of power fundamentally changed under Heydrich, whose continuous efforts to broaden his own area of responsibility at the expense of the Abwehr led to repeated clashes in late 1934.[3]

Tensions between the SS and the military reached a climax in late December 1934 when Himmler and Heydrich launched an attack on Fritsch, whom they accused of planning a military putsch against the Führer. Hitler intervened in an attempt to de-escalate the conflict and both sides subsequently made concerted efforts to ease the tensions. In a statement made in January 1935, Heydrich regretted 'the poisoning of the relationship' between the Reichswehr as 'bearer of the arms of the nation' and the SS as 'the bearer of the ideology in the state and the party'. The tensions of the past few months, so he claimed, had been the work of Germany's internal and external enemies who spread false rumours and incited hatred in order to weaken the Reich.[4]

The situation was further improved on 1 January 1935 by the appointment of a new head of the military Abwehr, Heydrich's former navy training officer and personal friend Wilhelm Canaris. Canaris, who was executed by the SS in Flossenbürg concentration camp four weeks before the end of the war because of his alleged involvement in the attempted assassination of Hitler by Claus von Stauffenberg, was still a supporter of

Nazism at the time. Like Stauffenberg and many other of the 1944 conspirators, he was an arch-conservative nationalist who had welcomed the end of the Weimar Republic in 1933 and applauded German expansionism throughout the 1930s, before the extreme criminality of the Nazi regime became apparent to him during the Second World War.[5] The Heydrich and Canaris families had become neighbours upon Canaris's arrival in Berlin and they spent much time together. Contrary to subsequent rumours, their relationship was close.[6] On 17 January, Heydrich and Canaris met for a three-hour conference to resolve the problems that had previously overshadowed relations between the political police and the Abwehr. The outcome was a ten-point agreement – the famous Ten Commandments – which specified the future division of labour between the Abwehr, the Gestapo and the SD. According to this agreement, Heydrich recognized the Abwehr's sole responsibility for military espionage and counter-espionage as well as for control and protection of military installations. In return, Canaris acknowledged the SD's competence in cases of industrial espionage and the gathering of intelligence in border areas around the Reich. He also accepted the Gestapo's sole responsibility for combating political crimes within the Reich. At least for the next few years, the working relations between the Abwehr, the SD and the Gestapo were good, and both Heydrich and Canaris sincerely sought to maintain efficient co-operation.[7]

The tensions that persisted between the SS and the Ministry of the Interior during the mid-1930s were in many ways more difficult to resolve. Despite the strategically important victory that Himmler and Heydrich had achieved during the Röhm putsch, the SS was still not in full control of the German police. Reich Interior Minister Wilhelm Frick, who remained Himmler's nominal superior, continued to argue that the newly established tools of repression under SS control – notably, the concentration camps – were merely temporary tools, created during and for the seizure of power, and that they needed to be placed back under strict government supervision as soon as the political situation calmed down. By 1935, when the Communist underground had been largely destroyed and its key personnel imprisoned, he decided that the time was ripe to dismantle the SS's extra-legal tools of repression and to return to legal means of fighting political crimes.[8]

Himmler and Heydrich, by contrast, tried to extend police power precisely at the time when the Nazi state was seemingly running out of enemies to arrest. To achieve a further expansion of SS power, they had to sell the idea of a permanent police state. In that sales campaign, the major thrust was against the contention that the extraordinary political police and concentration camp system was only a temporary response to a state of emergency.[9] The issue was not fully resolved until 17 June 1936, when Hitler formally appointed Himmler as chief of the German police. Himmler's appointment marked an important watershed in the history of the Third Reich, in terms both of centralizing the previously federal German police in his hands and of merging a paramilitary party organization, the SS, and a traditional state instrument, the police, thus creating an apparatus of political repression that was run by radical Nazi ideologues. Himmler now commanded the two most important executive organs of repression in the Third Reich, the SS and the police, which was unified under a single command for the first time. *De jure* he remained subordinate to Interior Minister Wilhelm Frick, but in the *de facto* hierarchy of the Third Reich Himmler was now answerable only to Hitler.[10]

Himmler's appointment as chief of the German police also had direct consequences for the thirty-two-year-old Heydrich: on 20 September 1936, his Gestapo headquarters in Berlin formally assumed control over the political police forces in all German states, thus creating a nationwide ministerial agency authorized to operate throughout the Reich. In addition, all criminal police and border police forces in Germany – no fewer than 9,000 men – were to be merged with the Gestapo under Heydrich's command to form a new institution: the so-called Security Police (Sicherheitspolizei or Sipo). This was not just an administrative act that more than doubled the number of men under Heydrich's command. The primary reason for the union of criminal and political police forces lay in Heydrich's and Himmler's conviction that questions of habitual criminality and political crimes could not be separated. Criminality had become a political and racial issue, as Heydrich increasingly considered deviant criminal behaviour to be an indication of 'bad blood'. Since Heydrich also remained – in the Nazi fashion of accumulating offices – chief of the SD, his joint command over that organization and Sipo gave him control over the two agencies responsible for most of the atrocities committed in Germany and occupied Europe over the following years.[11]

The victory of the SS in the power struggle with the Reich Interior Ministry was primarily the result of Hitler's decision to favour a more open-ended definition of Nazism's enemies, a definition to which Heydrich had crucially contributed and which went far beyond the persecution of the political opposition that is typical of all dictatorships. In late 1934, Himmler and Heydrich came to the conclusion that the justification of a permanent police state required a carefully elaborated scenario portraying an all-pervasive and subtly camouflaged network of enemies who made necessary an extensive and sophisticated security system to detect, expose and defeat them. In 1935, in a series of articles for the SS journal *Das Schwarze Korps* and republished in 1936 as *The Transformations of our Struggle*, Heydrich publicly defined such 'threats' and the means to combat them, indicating the need for a momentous reorientation of the Gestapo's activities. His central argument was that even after the successful elimination of the KPD and the SPD, the enemies of the German people were by no means defeated. After achieving the 'immediate goal' of Hitler's appointment as chancellor in January 1933, many Germans wrongly assumed that Nazi rule was now permanently secured. Heydrich insisted that the battle was by no means over. Instead the struggle against Germany's enemies now faced its most difficult and ultimately its decisive phase, which would require 'years of bitter struggle in order to repulse and destroy the enemy once and for all'.[12]

According to Heydrich, the 'driving forces of the enemy always remain the same: world Jewry, world Freemasonry' and 'political priests', who abused the freedom of religious expression and the spirituality of large portions of the population for political purposes. These three arch-enemies of Nazism worked towards the destruction of the Third Reich in myriad 'camouflaged ways', in which 'so-called experts' within the government bureaucracy played a key role: they informed the political enemy of legal initiatives against them and spread rumours designed to incite popular outrage against the Hitler government. At the same time, they were actively working to slow down or sabotage law-making processes and their implementation. This expanded circle of enemies, Heydrich argued, also included many university professors who allegedly indoctrinated their students with liberal ideas. Heydrich's accusations represented a massive attack against the opponents of the SS within the German civil service, who were declared almost en masse to be enemies of National Socialism.[13]

Bolshevism, which had previously been regarded as Nazism's greatest opponent, was now portrayed by Heydrich as no more than a façade behind which the real enemy lurked. The police alone, so he argued, had little chance of defeating this illusive enemy without the help of the SS – the 'ideological shock troops' of the Nazi movement.[14] Germany's life-and-death struggle against internal and external enemies would be conducted uncompromisingly and with harshness, 'even if that means that we will hurt individual opponents and even if some well-meaning people will denounce us as undisciplined ruffians'.[15] Heydrich never tired of emphasizing the need for 'utter hardness' towards oneself and against others, an attitude once again rooted in a vulgarized Darwinian under-standing of life as an 'eternal struggle between the stronger, more noble, racially valuable people and the lower beings, the subhumans'. As in every true struggle, there were only two possible outcomes: 'Either we will over-come the enemy once and for all, or we will perish.'[16]

The toughness required to achieve victory over the enemies of Nazism, so Heydrich insisted in a conversation with the Swiss Red Cross and missionary, Carl Jacob Burckhardt, placed an enormous emotional burden on him and his men, a sacrifice that was justified only by the greatness of the course: 'It is almost too difficult for an individual, but we must be hard as granite, or else our Führer's work will be in vain; much later people will be grateful for what we have taken upon us.' It was exactly the same argument, albeit under very different circumstances, that Heydrich and Himmler would use during the Second World War in justifying the mass murders by the SS task forces.[17]

Heydrich thus fundamentally reshaped and broadened the definition of the enemies of Nazism. Both Bolshevism and Freemasonry were merely 'expedient creations [Zweckschöpfungen] of Jewry'. That is why 'ultimately it is the Jew and the political cleric (which in its most distinctive form is represented by the Jesuit) who form the basis of all oppositional groups'. Such a far-reaching conception of the enemies of Nazism had consequences for the organizations designed to combat them, namely Heydrich's SD and the political police. First of all, it required a rethinking of the role of the political police in German society. Whereas in the despised Weimar Republic, the police had been restrained by misguided liberal notions of individual freedom, the police and the SS should be freed of all fetters in order to ensure the protection of the German people and their racial substance. In order to defeat an enemy lurking around every corner, the work of the police could not be restricted by law. Legal restrictions hampered the crucial success of the Gestapo's work, as did the alleged refusal of individual government authorities to co-operate. Himmler and Heydrich would ultimately succeed in their demands. Until 1945, the legal basis for police measures remained the Reichstag Fire Decree of 28 Feburary 1933, an emergency measure which had restricted significant basic rights anchored in the Weimar Constitution, such as the personal rights of prisoners, freedom of speech and the privacy of written and oral communication. Throughout the Third Reich the German police operated in a permanent state of emergency.[18]

Heydrich argued that the German police alone could not overcome the heightened threat. Instead, it needed the support and expertise of the SS, and notably that of the SD – the ideological avant-garde of the Nazi movement – in order to win the conflict. Gradually, the 'apolitical experts' in policing matters would become redundant as a new generation of ideologically committed SS men would take over their positions.[19] In contrast to traditional bureaucracy, high-ranking SS officers were not supposed simply to administer; rather they were to lead and shape Germany's future. Time and again, Heydrich insisted that the traditional bureaucrat in the civil service, focused on administrative procedures and titles, would ultimately need to be replaced by a new cast of 'political warriors', 'human material' selected exclusively on the basis of racial qualities, ideological commitment and competence.[20]

Heydrich's comments were not merely rhetorical. Throughout his career in the SS, he was to maintain a keen interest in the recruitment process for his own Security Police and SD empire, reserving his right to intervene in appointment processes in order to 'create a particularly suitable leadership corps'. He was convinced that 'the entire organization of the Security Police will be ineffective if the people serving within it do not ideologically, professionally and personally fulfil the standards which this great task demands. This will be dependent on their racial and character selection, their age, their ideological and professional training, and finally on the spirit with which these people are led to carry out all their work.'[21]

In reality, of course, it was remarkable how little expertise individual members of Heydrich's staff required to act as 'experts' in certain policy areas. His future 'Jewish expert', Adolf Eichmann, had been a salesman with little previous administrative experience before joining the SD, and the only job-specific qualification of the subsequent head of Heydrich's espionage section, Walter Schellenberg, was that he shared a passion for crime fiction with his boss. Heydrich was certainly aware of the lack of suitable personnel and actively sought to alleviate the problem. Designated training centres such as the Leadership School of the Security Police and the SD were set up in Berlin, designed to instruct the new officers in the latest investigation and modern surveillance techniques, and to create, through ideological education, what Heydrich called 'the soldierly civil servant', who would be able to fulfil 'the ideologically motivated tasks of the state and criminal police'. Their training involved them in thinking proactively about how to achieve their goals, with exam questions such as 'compile a report for the entire Reich on Jews in the livestock trade and propose your own remedies to the evil described'. Initiative and independent problem-solving were qualities that Heydrich cherished.[22] As Himmler would later remark with approval, Heydrich 'always stood by the principle that only the best of our people, the racially most carefully selected, with an excellent character and pure spirit, with a good heart and gifted with an irrepressible hard will, were suitable to perform the service of combating all that is negative ... and to bear the hardships of this responsibility'. For that reason, Himmler praised Heydrich as 'one of the best educators in Nazi Germany'.[23]

Over the following two years, Heydrich and his deputy as head of the Security Police, Werner Best, in numerous articles that appeared in the

Völkischer Beobachter and the journal *Deutsches Recht*, further developed the notion that the traditional police could no longer master the Reich's enemies. Political enemies had to be pursued preventively. In an article published in 1937, Heydrich wrote: 'The overall task of the Security Police is to protect the German people as a total being [*Gesamtwesen*], their vital force and their institutions, against any kind of destruction and corrosion. Defensively, it must resist attacks by all forces that could in any way weaken and destroy the health, vital force and ability to act of the people and of the state ... Offensively, it must probe and then combat all enemy elements in order to assure that they cannot become destructive and corrosive in the first place.' Heydrich's understanding of the tasks of the Security Police in the Third Reich was now more comprehensive than ever: it was responsible for the struggle against 'subhumans', Jews, Freemasons, Churches and other 'criminals' – indeed against 'disorder' in general.[24] The Gestapo, the SD and the general SS should further be merged into a state protection corps, a sort of 'internal Wehrmacht', in order to place the combating and pursuit of ideological enemies on a new and more solid foundation.[25] Ever since the Nazi revolution, Heydrich wrote, the German police had been given an entirely new task: the preventive protection of 'the people and the state' against all enemies in 'all areas of life'. The SD was to play a key role in this process as the think-tank of enemy persecution in the Third Reich.[26]

In the summer of 1937, Heydrich decided that it was time to disentangle the overlapping responsibilities of his two agencies, the SD and the Security Police, in an attempt to realize his aim of creating a unified state protection corps. The future division of labour between the two agencies was, at least in theory, quite simple: from 1 July 1937 onwards, the SD was to take charge of all important (and largely theoretical) questions of state security, while the Gestapo was to act as its executive arm, responsible for the persecution of political crimes.[27] The task of the SD, Heydrich insisted, was not only to analyse political crimes retrospectively, but to prevent their repetition in the future.[28] The growing importance attributed to the SD by Heydrich was reflected in its increasing size: between 1935 and 1940 alone, the number of full-time SD employees rose from 1,100 to 4,300.[29]

Heydrich's conception of the struggle against political opponents and internal enemies in the mid-1930s thus rested on four central convictions. First, the struggle against Jews, Freemasons and 'politicizing priests' had to be undertaken in a comprehensive and preventive manner in order to achieve success. Second, the work of the political police should not be made subject to any legal restrictions. Third, the Gestapo and the SD should be combined into a state protection corps. Fourth, unyielding toughness and ruthlessness were essential to secure the German state and its people from its tireless enemies. But how exactly did these ideas and concepts translate into actual policies of persecution?

The Jews

The publication of Heydrich's articles in the *Schwarze Korps* was directly connected with the 'second anti-Semitic wave', which the Nazi Party initiated in the spring of 1935 and which would ultimately lead to the promulgation of the Nuremberg Laws in September of that year. Following a temporary easing of anti-Semitic violence, a wave of apparently spontaneous local actions against Jewish property spread across the Reich.[30] While Heydrich sympathized with the overall aim of these actions, namely to terrify the Jews into emigration, he disagreed with the open brutality that was sure to antagonize a majority of the German population and trigger foreign hate propaganda against the Third Reich.

Up to this point, Heydrich had given surprisingly little thought to the Jews. To be sure, Germany's Jews had found themselves in the firing line from the very moment Hitler acceded to power on 30 January 1933. Continuing and intensifying a pattern all too familiar from the weeks before Hitler was appointed chancellor, SA and Hitler Youth members attacked Jewish individuals and shops. Within a few weeks, the regional Gauleiters had taken up the campaign, supporting organized attacks on Jewish businesses all over Germany. A national, government-sponsored boycott of Jewish businesses on 1 April 1933 was followed by a purge of the civil service.[31]

During the first two years of the Third Reich, neither the Gestapo nor the SD played a prominent role in Nazi anti-Jewish policies. The persecution of political opponents, above all Communists and Social Democrats, initially seemed more pressing to Heydrich than the Jewish problem.[32] The Nazi regime's anti-Jewish policies in the first two years of the Third Reich instead emerged as a result of a subtle interplay between Nazi Party activists and the legislative machinery, notably the Interior Ministry. The party, represented by Rudolf Hess and Martin Bormann, as well as a number of particularly anti-Semitic Gauleiters such as Joseph Goebbels in Berlin and Julius Streicher in Nuremberg, launched 'grassroots actions' against Jews, such as the 1 April 1933 boycott and the anti-Jewish riots that erupted in the spring and summer of 1935. Under the pretext of removing the reason for justified popular anger, the Interior Ministry could then react with legal measures designed to restrict the freedom of the Jewish minority even further. The Gestapo, by contrast, played no major role in the boycott of Jewish businesses on 1 April 1933 or in the subsequent anti-Semitic legislation that led to the dismissal of thousands of Jewish civil servants.[33]

This is not to suggest that Heydrich was indifferent to the Jewish question. Ever since he joined the SS, he had proved himself to be an eager ideological pupil of Himmler, and he regularly expressed his hatred toward Jews, both in public and in private. According to his wife, Reinhard became 'deeply convinced that the Jews had to be separated from the Germans. In his eyes the Jews were . . . rootless plunderers, determined to gain selfish advantage and to stick like leeches to the body of the host nation.'[34] Such views were unquestionably influenced both by his wife and by Nazi propaganda, which consistently portrayed Jews as parasites who had accumulated riches during the war and the subsequent economic crisis, while Aryan Germans had died on the front or suffered from the post-war inflation. If the Aryan German was characterized by heroism and the willingness to sacrifice himself for the greater good of the nation, the Jews were ciphers for greed and economic gain.[35]

There was therefore nothing particularly new or original about Heydrich's anti-Semitism. He subscribed to standard Nazi ideas as articulated in *Mein Kampf* and earlier works of racial anti-Semitism such as Paul de Lagarde's influential *German Writings* (1878), Houston Stewart Chamberlain's *Foundations of the Nineteenth Century* (1899) and Alfred Rosenberg's *Myth of the Twentieth Century* (1930). If race rather than religion provided the rationale for Nazi anti-Semitism, the various elements of the negative anti-Semitic stereotype that had accumulated since the second half of the Middle Ages were adopted almost in their entirety by the Nazis. The only significant addition was the accusation that Jews were responsible for the threat of the spread of Bolshevism. With little regard for logical consistency, the traditional stereotype of Jews as parasitical usurers was supplemented by a new image of Jews as subversive revolutionaries determined to destroy capitalism and overturn the social order. The Jews were thus a rootless, international force, seeking to undermine Germany from both within and without through the agencies of international Bolshevism, international finance capital and Freemasonry.[36]

Heydrich's own hatred of Jews was not shaped by an intensive study of the classic texts of European anti-Semitism, even if he did read the forged *Protocols of the Elders of Zion* and Hans Günther's *Rassenkunde des Deutschen Volkes* of 1922. He was much more conditioned by his immersion in a milieu that firmly believed in racial anti-Semitism. As Werner Best observed, his boss's strength lay in 'firmly applying the theoretical and doctrinaire assertions about enemies of the state that came from Hitler and Himmler'. In this policy area, as in all others, Heydrich proved to be a man of deed, not of ideas or theories.[37]

Heydrich's behaviour with regard to the Jewish question was characterized by a flurry of activity that intensified after 1935. Unlike Himmler,
who hardly ever mentioned the Jews in his speeches before 1938,
Heydrich became increasingly convinced that the Jews were at the centre
of a complex network of enemies that confronted the Third Reich.[38] In
search of new enemies and faced by a wave of anti-Semitic violence in
1935, Heydrich argued that while the racial legislation of 1933 had indeed
restricted the direct influence of Jewry in Germany, it was insufficient to
control permanently the 'tenacious' and 'determined' Jews: 'The introduction of the Aryan legislation has not banished the threat of Jewry against
Germany. The expedient Jewish organizations with all their connections
to their international leadership continue to work for the extermination of
our people along with all its values.' Neither the economic, the academic
nor the cultural life of Germany had been fully purged of the Jews, giving
them plenty of opportunities to expand their areas of influence.[39]

For Heydrich, this threat was closely linked to what he regarded as a
misguided notion of humanism that was widespread in Germany: the
Jew's 'work is made easier by the fact that there still are *Volksgenossen* (the
Churches even promote this attitude) who only accept the Aryan legislation under pressure and do not grasp its racial foundations. Today, only
two years after the Nazi revolution, parts of the German people are
beginning to become indifferent towards the Jew; meanwhile the Jew
relentlessly pursues his eternally unchanging goal: world domination and
the extermination of the Nordic peoples.'[40]

Until 1935, the role of Heydrich's political police apparatus was
confined to the surveillance of Jewish organizations and the execution of
new anti-Semitic legislation.[41] However, Heydrich soon displayed his
characteristic impatience and was no longer prepared to wait for new laws
and regulations. Instead he began to introduce his own police measures.
In January 1935, for example, he ordered that returning émigrés should be
interned, a directive that he clarified in March 1935: 'All persons who have
left the Reich following the National Socialist revolution for political
reasons, both Aryans and non-Aryans,' were to be regarded as émigrés and
interned in concentration camps. Women were to be deported separately
to the Moringen concentration camp.[42] From August 1935 onwards, the
regional Gestapo head offices had to keep detailed registers of Jews living
in their respective areas of responsibility.[43]

As he implemented anti-Jewish police measures, Heydrich quickly
advanced to become the central figure in SS Jewish policy. His position
was further enhanced in July 1936 when Göring appointed him to direct
the Foreign Currency Investigation Agency (*Devisenfahndungsamt*).[44]
Over the coming years, this new authority would allow Heydrich to

pursue real and alleged violations of foreign currency regulations, particularly when these 'crimes' were committed by Jews who stood under 'suspicion of emigration'. In such cases he was authorized to confiscate Jewish savings preventively. Heydrich's appointment as head of this agency was the first of a number of similar authorizations by Göring that would provide Heydrich with the tools for the persecution of Jews over the coming years. This established two competing chains of command with respect to Nazi anti-Jewish policies that would remain largely unchanged until Heydrich's death in June 1942: one from Hitler to Heydrich via Himmler and one from Hitler to Heydrich via Göring. While this second chain of command effectively undermined Himmler's authority over Heydrich, it never seems to have led to a rivalry between the two men – or at least there is no hard evidence for such a rivalry, apart from the questionable post-war memoirs of Walter Schellenberg and Felix Kersten.[45]

When it came to persecuting the Jews, both the Gestapo and the SD were primarily concerned with promoting emigration activities and preventing all 'assimilationist' activities on the part of German Jews. 'The aim of Jewish policies must be the emigration of all Jews,' an internal SD memorandum for Heydrich suggested in May 1934. In order to create the necessary pressures to induce 'voluntary' emigration, the policy document continued, the 'Jews are to have their opportunities to live in this country reduced – and not only in economic terms. Germany has to be a country without a future for Jews, in which the older generation will die off in their remaining positions, but in which young Jews are unable to live so that the attraction of emigration is constantly kept alive. The use of mob anti-Semitism [*Radau-Antisemitismus*] is to be rejected. One does not fight rats with guns but with poison and gas. The damage incurred by crude methods, especially the foreign policy implications, is disproportionate to the success rate.'[46]

The reference to poison and gas should not be misinterpreted as a road map for the Holocaust. While the document's language was redolent with metaphors of plague and parasites, its key argument was that the problem should be resolved as quietly as possible, ideally through incentivized emigration. In contrast to noisy anti-Semitic party leaders such as Joseph Goebbels or Julius Streicher, Heydrich's Jewish experts promoted a more sober (but ultimately no less radical) strategy against the Jews – a strategy that explicitly included humiliation, expropriation and expulsion in order to achieve its goal of a Jew-free Europe. Systematic mass murder was, however, still beyond the conceivable in the 1930s, even for Heydrich and his anti-Jewish think-tank within the SD.[47]

The memorandum of May 1934 suggested that Zionist organizations openly promoting emigration to Palestine should be given preferential treatment over assimilationist organizations, which argued that German Jews should weather the Nazi storm and stay in their homeland. Heydrich's own view on the assimilationists had altered since 1933. As late as March 1934, Heydrich's Bavarian Political Police had given permission to the nationalist Reich Association of Jewish Veterans to continue its work under certain conditions.[48] Ten months later, in January 1935, Heydrich changed his mind on the matter and instructed the Gestapo that the 'activities of Zionist youth organizations' were 'in line with the aims of the National Socialist state leadership' while assimilationists should be treated with 'severity'.[49]

Heydrich further expanded on the policy of differentiated treatment in the persecution of Jewish organizations in 1935. From his vantage point, the assimilationists who refused to emigrate represented the greatest obstacle to a successful Jewish policy: 'The assimilationists deny their Jewish origins either by claiming that they have lived in this country for generations and that they are Germans or by maintaining, after getting baptized, that they are Christians,' thereby trying 'to undermine Nazi principles'.[50] But how were they to be induced to leave the Reich? Heydrich at this point rejected anti-Semitic mob violence as it would both damage Germany's position abroad and provoke objections from large parts of the German population. In a report to the Reich Chancellery about anti-Semitic riots in the summer of 1935, Heydrich demanded a more orderly form of anti-Semitic policy, including notably stricter laws against the Jews: 'The reports about anti-Semitic demonstrations, which continue to arrive from all parts of the Reich, show that there is widespread and growing dissatisfaction with the hitherto inconsistent application of measures against the Jews. Those among the German people who are race-conscious believe that the measures so far taken against the Jews have been insufficient and demand altogether harsher actions.'[51]

The following month, an internal SD memorandum confirmed that a 'solution of the Jewish question through acts of terrorism' was neither attainable nor desirable:

A concerted approach to the Jewish problem is almost impossible as long as clear legislation is missing. This lack has created the conditions for repeatedly condemned independent actions. On the one hand, our people wish to see the Jews driven out of Germany in accordance with their Nazi convictions. On the other hand, no action is taken by the responsible authorities; it is an unfortunate fact that the example set by some party functionaries and their families in their personal life in relation to Jews and Jewish business does not always conform with the wishes and demands of the ordinary party member ... It should be remembered in this context that there is legal uncertainty regarding mixed marriages and race defilement. Registrars who act according to their conscience and refuse to marry such couples are often forced by the courts to do so. On the other hand those registrars who wish deliberately to go against Nazi beliefs can claim the support of official decrees. Effective laws should therefore be passed which show the people that the Jewish question is being regulated by law from above.[52]

The SD stressed above all the urgent need for legislation on citizenship, freedom of movement and the marking of non-Aryan businesses. Their criticism arose not from concern for human lives but from a wish to preserve a state monopoly of power that could not be left in the hands of party thugs. The SD and the Gestapo had an interest in radicalizing anti-Jewish policies, but made it clear at the same time that the 'solution of the Jewish question' should remain in the hands of state and party authorities, and more specifically in the capable hands of Heydrich's own apparatus.

In an attempt to co-ordinate future anti-Semitic policies, the German Economics Minister, Hjalmar Schacht, held a top-level meeting on 20 August with the Reich Justice Minister, Franz Gürtner, the Reich Minister of the Interior, Wilhelm Frick, and Heydrich and other officials in attendance. Schacht, Gürtner and Frick were all anti-Semites, but they were also concerned with legality, due process and the necessity of avoiding excesses that might invite economic and international repercussions. Schacht's demand at the meeting that 'the present lack of legislation and unlawful activities must come to an end' offered Heydrich a welcome cue. He insisted that the current situation could be remedied only by legislative measures, which would curb Jewish influence step by step. More specifically, he demanded a ban on so-called mixed marriages, the legal prosecution of sexual intercourse between a Jew and an Aryan, and special legislation restricting Jews' freedom of mobility, especially migration to large cities where it would be more difficult to police them.[53]

In a letter to the meeting's participants at the beginning of September, Heydrich formulated his demands in greater detail:

In my opinion the Jewish question cannot be solved through the use of force or the maltreatment of individuals, or through damage to personal property and other individual actions. It appears to me that it can be resolved only by gradually curtailing the influence of the Jews step by step ... Just as the influence of the Jews in the civil service, in the arts and culture has been almost entirely eliminated, their restriction must be enforced in all areas of public life. With regard to the recent violent excesses [against Jews], I consider it essential that the notion of legal

equality be abandoned, particularly in the economic sphere. I am
convinced that the individual actions across the country will die down
the very moment our *Volksgenossen* realize that the former economic
hegemony of the Jews has come to an end.[54]

Heydrich made far-ranging recommendations on how to achieve this
goal: if it proved impossible to strip the Jews of their German citizenship
altogether – a solution Heydrich favoured – then a catalogue of alternative
measures should be adopted: new laws should prohibit Jews from moving
to large cities, ban mixed marriages between Jews and Germans and
penalize extramarital sexual intercourse between Jews and Germans. State
commissions and new concessions would no longer be awarded to Jewish
businesses and Jews would be prohibited from dealing in real estate. In
addition, Heydrich proposed that Jews should no longer be issued with
new passports, since they would only use trips abroad to transfer foreign
currency illegally from Germany. Such measures would fulfil the dual
purpose of demonstrating to the German people that the government was
actively working towards the exclusion of Jews from economic life, while
also creating strong incentives for Jews to leave the Reich for good.[55]

The top-level meeting of ministers and officials on 20 August and
Heydrich's subsequent letter contradict the long-held view that the
Nuremberg Laws of September 1935 were put together hastily and
without much preparation. It instead shows only too clearly how broad a
consensus existed on future legislation long before the Seventh Nazi Party
Rally at Nuremberg in 1935 where the Nuremberg laws were passed.
The Reich Citizenship Law, the Law for the Protection of German
Blood and subsequent regulations to implement these laws largely fulfilled
most of the demands made during the 20 August meeting called by
Schacht.[56]

The Nuremberg Laws created the statutory basis for the civic exclusion
of German Jews. Yet there were certain aspects of the Nuremberg Laws
that did not satisfy Heydrich. In particular, he felt that the problem of the
Mischlinge, people of 'mixed Jewish blood', was not sufficiently addressed.
He and his racial experts advocated that even a person with one Jewish
ancestor going back to 1800 should be considered a Jew, but for the time
being such proposals seemed premature and too difficult to implement.
The Nuremberg Laws adopted a rather vague formula that encompassed
only 'full Jews' and left the question of *Mischlinge* unresolved.[57]

Nazi leaders continued to struggle with the concept and ultimate fate
of the *Mischlinge*. The Nuremberg Laws created two 'degrees' of *Mischlinge*.
The first degree consisted of Jews with only two Jewish grandparents
who were not married to full Jews and were not members of a Jewish

congregation. Second-degree Jews had only one Jewish grandparent. Initially the *Mischlinge* and Jews in so-called privileged marriages (with one Jewish and one non-Jewish partner) were spared many of the discriminatory measures aimed at full Jews. Heydrich considered this solution far too legalistic and complicated. He and his racial experts would therefore attempt to readdress the *Judenmischlingsfrage* during the war.[58]

By 1936 Heydrich had recruited a group of young, educated, self-confident and ideologically committed staff members for the small but growing Jewish desk of the SD – Dieter Wisliceny, Herbert Hagen, Theodor Dannecker and Adolf Eichmann – who began to develop an independent and comprehensive concept for a Jew-free Germany. It was their intention to harmonize the various and, to some extent, conflicting objectives of Nazi Jewish policy – from forced emigration to social and economic isolation and extortion.[59]

However, numerous difficulties persisted. The number of countries prepared to accept German Jews was not exactly large. Strict immigration quotas imposed by potential receiving countries such as Britain, France and the United States limited emigration opportunities both to well-trained artisans and to those with sufficient capital to buy a visa. Palestine – explicitly designated as a 'national home for the Jewish people' in Britain's Balfour Declaration of 1917, a formal policy statement issued by British Foreign Secretary James Balfour about the future of Palestine – remained the only territory in the world for large-scale Jewish immigration and indeed accepted more German Jewish emigrants between 1933 and 1936 than any other country.[60] Although Palestine played a key role in Heydrich's calculations, he and his staff remained concerned about the possibility of an independent Jewish state that might strengthen Jewish influence in the world to the extent that Jerusalem might become the centre of 'international Jewry' just as Moscow had become the capital of 'world Communism'. But these concerns were offset by two great advantages: first, Palestine was a place that an increasingly large number of disillusioned Jews wanted to go to anyway, so Heydrich assumed that it would be easier to convince them to resettle there than in other parts of the world. Secondly, the influence of Jewish settlers would be contained permanently by hostile Arab neighbours.[61]

That autumn, the SD put in place its own rather bizarre initiative to speed up Zionist emigration. Using Dr Franz Reichert, chief of the German News Service in Jerusalem and an SD informer, as an intermediary, Heydrich's Jewish experts made contact with a certain Feivel Polkes, a Polish Jew who in 1920 had emigrated to Palestine where he became a member of the Zionist underground organization Haganah. Between 26 February and 2 March 1937, a visit to Berlin at the SD's expense was arranged for Polkes in order to discuss the possibility of Haganah support for Jewish emigration from Nazi Germany. It was the first time that the SD was to venture into the field of international politics.[62]

The man Heydrich put in charge of the negotiations was Adolf Eichmann, who was subsequently to become notorious for his role in the wartime extermination of Europe's Jews as Heydrich's special adviser on Jewish matters. Born in Solingen in 1906 into a middle-class family, he had spent his youth in Austria after his family had moved to Linz the year before the outbreak of the First World War. After finishing school Eichmann had worked as a sales representative for a petroleum company during the troubled 1920s. Ever since his school days he was a keen supporter of pan-Germanism and came into contact with other right-wing nationalists, most notably the Kaltenbrunners, whose son, Ernst, Heydrich's future successor as head of the Reich Security Main Office in 1942, was a schoolfriend of Eichmann's. Eichmann joined the Austrian Nazi Party in 1932 and the SS shortly thereafter. Losing his job in the Depression, he moved to Germany in August 1933 and joined Heydrich's SD as a lowly official to compile information about Freemasons in Germany. His organizational talents, ruthless energy and efficiency secured his rapid promotion through the ranks. By 1936, still in his early thirties, Eichmann was working in the SD's Jewish department, where he became a self-taught 'expert' in Jewish matters, writing briefing papers on Zionism and emigration that reflected the department's ethos of 'rational' anti-Semitism which corresponded with Heydrich's own convictions.[63]

During Polkes's visit to Berlin in the early spring of 1937, Eichmann met with him on several occasions and, although Eichmann's SD membership remained secret, Polkes was certainly aware that a Nazi official was sitting opposite him. Polkes explained the position of the Zionists in Palestine and offered to provide new information on the assassination of Wilhelm Gustloff, the chief organizer of the Swiss Nazi Party, if the Nazis were prepared to make Jewish emigration from Germany to Palestine easier. Eichmann's report on Polkes's visit was presented to Heydrich, who decided that Eichmann should continue the dialogue with Polkes and travel to the Near East. Heydrich made it clear, however, that he would take no official responsibility for this journey should any information about the arrangements become publicly known.[64]

On 26 September 1937, Eichmann and Herbert Hagen started out on their journey and reached Haifa on 2 October. The trip proved disappointing. When Eichmann met Polkes on 10 and 11 October, the latter was unable to provide any information on the Gustloff assassination and merely promised to make further enquiries. As far as emigration to Palestine was concerned, he denounced newly arrived German emigrants as 'work-shy' and claimed that they were constantly planning to leave the country again. He nevertheless maintained that the Zionists 'were pleased with Germany's radical Jewish policies . . . because they ensured the growth of the Jewish population in Palestine to such an extent that it was fairly certain that in the near future Jews would outnumber Arabs in Palestine'.[65]

Hagen and Eichmann left Egypt on 19 October without having achieved their objective. Despite a lengthy report prepared for Heydrich of over fifty pages, it was clear that their trip had failed. No concrete agreements had been reached with the Zionists concerning the emigration of German Jews. Despite the failure of the trip, however, Hitler himself endorsed the SD's policy line. According to a note written by the Foreign Office and dated January 1938, the Führer restated his position to Alfred Rosenberg, the head of the Nazi Party's Foreign Policy Office, that the emigration of Jews to Palestine should be accelerated.[66] This was a considerable victory for Heydrich. In spite of Eichmann's and Hagen's failed visit to the Middle East, the SD was confident enough not only to propose its own independent solution to the Jewish emigration problem but also to attempt to put such a proposal into practice. The SD's demand to participate at ministerial level in the discussions on Jewish policies was now taken seriously.[67]

Five years after Hitler's ascent to power, the Nazis' anti-Semitic policies appeared to have been successful. Government departments had pushed ahead with the legal exclusion of Jews from public life, and special legislation for Jews had been drafted and implemented in ever finer detail. The expulsion of Jews from the economy had made considerable progress and more and more Germans of Jewish descent decided to leave the Third Reich.[68] Yet although the significant stream of emigrants continued to diminish the Jewish community in Germany, Hitler's reversal of foreign policy in early 1938, which would soon lead to the Anschluss of Austria and the occupation of the Sudetenland, would bring more Jews *into* the Reich than had left since 1933. The policy of forced emigration did not end in 1938, but it had clearly reached its limits. More radical approaches, or so it seemed to Heydrich after 1938, were required to resolve Germany's growing Jewish problem.

The Churches

Aside from the Communists and Jews, Heydrich's particular hatred in the 1930s was devoted to the Catholic Church; and he pursued the persecution of Catholic clergymen with an enthusiasm that exceeded even that of Himmler.[69] Brought up in a devout Catholic family and having served as an altar boy in his childhood, Heydrich repeatedly emphasized that he was opposed not to spirituality itself, but rather to the Church as a 'political institution', which had lent support to different 'unpatriotic' parties since the foundation of the Reich in 1871. In that sense, he was anti-clerical rather than anti-religious. Pointing to the example of the Church's resistance to the Law for the Prevention of Herditarily Diseased Offspring of July 1933, Heydrich maintained that this tradition of political agitation had continued after Hitler's seizure of power. As former Catholics, both Himmler and Heydrich knew that the creation of a 'superior' German race would necessarily involve the violation of Catholic dogma on abortion, contraception, sterilization and other aspects of the reproductive process. The Christian idea of marriage would ultimately have to be abandoned in favour of polygamy – allowing for the fertilization of more Aryan women – and a racially driven conception of human partnerships that would allow for divorce for the infertile and racially unfit. The Catholic Church's opposition to Nazi population policy led Heydrich to the view that instead of 'being a deferential intermediary between God and Man' and serving a kingdom that 'is not of this world', the Catholic Church, guided from Rome, was determined to conquer 'a worldly power position' and sow 'disharmony' among the German people.[70]

At least in this respect, there were parallels between Heydrich's perceptions of Jews and Catholics. Like the Jews, he accused the Catholics of forming more than just a confession, and both seemed to represent something alien within the German body politic. But while Catholics could be good members of the people's community if they refrained from 'Roman' politics, this option was never available to Germany's Jews. The presumption among anti-Semites like Heydrich that Jewishness retained an indissoluble core of ethnic otherness, whereas political Catholicism was an illness that could be cured, set the Jewish predicament apart.[71]

Heydrich left the Catholic Church in 1935, but had already described himself as *gottgläubig* – a believer, but not a member of a Christian denomination – as early as 1933. *Gottgläubigkeit* – Himmler's preferred expression of spirituality – came with a whole set of neo-pagan and allegedly ancient Germanic rituals: instead of the Christian baptism, newborn babies of SS parents were given a 'name dedication' ceremony representing acceptance into the wider SS family. The *Eheweihe* (marriage consecration) replaced the Christian wedding, and Easter was substituted by celebrations of the midsummer solstice, which symbolized the victory of light over darkness. Yet, even within the SS, only a minority subscribed to this new belief system: by 1938, only 21.9 per cent of SS members described themselves as *gottgläubig*, whereas 54 per cent remained Protestant and just under 24 per cent Catholic. Whether Heydrich followed the neo-pagan rituals out of conviction or merely to please Himmler is unknown, although Lina Heydrich maintained after the war that in private she and her husband often made fun of Himmler's obsession with neo-paganism.[72]

Himmler himself rarely intervened in the anti-Church measures adopted by the Gestapo and the SD, largely leaving this policy area to Heydrich. In the early years of the Third Reich, Heydrich's Gestapo and SD primarily focused their anti-clerical surveillance and persecution on the Catholic Church, which posed a greater challenge to Nazism than the largely compliant Protestant Church.[73] But Heydrich had to act carefully. In the summer of 1933, in return for the 'voluntary' self-dissolution of the Centre Party, the Third Reich and the Vatican had signed the Reichskonkordat, guaranteeing the continued existence and religious freedom of the Catholic Church in Nazi Germany. Neither the Gestapo nor the SD could be seen to act in open violation of these accords. Germany remained a deeply Christian country and public opinion mattered to Hitler.[74]

Time and again, however, Heydrich and other influential anti-Church hardliners such as Joseph Goebbels, Rudolf Hess and Martin Bormann sought to challenge the status quo and to undermine the Church's position by linking individual priests with homosexuality, Communism and paedophilia. Shortly after the seizure of power in Bavaria, for example, Heydrich moved against three priests who had expressed concern over the treatment of inmates in Dachau concentration camp. In late November, following an investigation, they admitted spreading 'atrocity stories' and were arrested. Searches of their quarters turned up the inevitable 'extensive Marxist literature' and other circumstantial evidence associating them with Communism, all of which was duly publicized. Heydrich used the case publicly to paint a picture of a Communist-infiltrated priesthood and to argue for a political police force capable of fighting such a menace.[75]

Heydrich was not the only former altar boy fighting the Catholic Church. Convinced that one had to know the enemy in order to fight him, he appointed a Catholic priest, Albert Hartl, to run the SD's Church department. Hartl, a long-time Nazi sympathizer, formally joined the SD in 1934 as a full-time officer after his position in the Catholic Church had become untenable when it became known that he had denounced a fellow priest to the Nazi authorities.[76]

In 1935 the Nazi state staged a series of trials against members of various Catholic orders, accusing them of international money laundering and immoral – that is, homosexual and paedophile – practices. Heydrich's apparatus provided the 'evidence' in most of these cases. The investigations of foreign currency offences were systematically expanded in March 1935; both the Gestapo and the SD were heavily involved in searches of monasteries and confiscated documents that could serve as evidence in the subsequent trials. By the end of 1935, some seventy clerics had been convicted in thirty trials on the basis of this material.[77]

The alleged sexual offences committed by Catholic clerics and order members were of even greater propagandistic use for the Nazi regime. Ever since 1935, Heydrich's SD had played a central role in confiscating and assembling material intended to prove the supposed homosexuality of clerics. In 1935 the Gestapo set up a special task force within its department for the handling of homosexual offences. Extensive investigations led to a wave of trials that – with a brief interruption during the 1936 Olympic Games – continued until the summer of 1937.

These trials sought to destroy the reputation of the Catholic Church and primarily targeted priests, monks, lay brothers and nuns working in primary and secondary schools. A simultaneous press campaign launched by Joseph Goebbels sought to persuade parents not to expose their children to the likely risk of sexual abuse at religious schools. One notorious and widely publicized trial in 1936 concerned the Franciscans of the Rhineland town of Waldbreitbach, who were accused of systematically abusing the children placed in their trust. Adults and schoolchildren alike were encouraged to read the lurid accounts of abuse and sexual mayhem that were allegedly at the heart of Franciscan activity. In several cities, newspaper stands were purposely lowered so that adolescents could read salacious and pornographic stories accompanied by cartoons in Nazi newspapers. All in all, 250 trials were undertaken against allegedly homosexual clergymen and order members, during the course of which over 200 Catholic order members (particularly laymen) were convicted.[78]

In the spring of 1937, the Nazis' attacks on the Catholic Church eased. The papal encyclical *Mit brennender Sorge* ('With Burning Anxiety') of March 1937, in which Pope Pius XI expressed his deep concern about violations of the 1933 Church agreement by the Nazi authorities, ended all illusions within the Nazi Party that the Catholic Church would tamely submit to the Nazi regime. Furthermore, the imminent readjustment of Nazi foreign policy towards a more aggressive strategy of expansionism in 1938 made it seem necessary to appease, rather than polarize, the home front. Hitler gradually withdrew from any direct involvement in Church politics and the fundamental reordering of relations between the Nazi state and the Church that Heydrich and other party radicals had hoped for was postponed until after the war.[79]

While Hitler abstained from making public anti-Church statements and Himmler officially instructed the SS to remain neutral in regard to Church policy, Heydrich pushed on, presumably with Himmler's blessing. On 27 May 1937 he wrote to Hitler directly, asking to be permitted to arrest dissident priests 'for the preservation of state authority' if they became politically active. One year later, in June 1938, Heydrich wrote to Hans Lammers, the head of the Reich Chancellery, stating that the Vatican was ultimately responsible for anti-German agitation from Czechoslovakia and France. But Hitler continued to insist that the solution of the 'Church problem' had to be postponed until the end of an increasingly likely international war. Only then did he want to solve the problem as the last great task of his life.[80]

No such concern applied to smaller Christian Churches. Throughout the 1930s the Gestapo devoted considerable energy and resources to the persecution of Jehovah's Witnesses, a small religious sect founded in the United States with no more than 26,000 members in Germany. The 'crimes' of the Jehovah's Witnesses consisted in refusing to participate in elections, to use the Hitler salute, to display the Nazi flag, to join Nazi organizations and to perform military service. All of these things were irreconcilable with their religious principles, which did not allow them to swear allegiance to any worldly government or to serve any country. Given their doctrinally rooted pacifism, Jehovah's Witnesses were obvious targets for Heydrich's police apparatus. They were, in fact, the only group in the Third Reich to be persecuted on the basis of their religious beliefs alone. Jews were persecuted for their race, while individual Catholics and Protestants were arrested because of their real or alleged political activism.[81]

In the course of 1936, the Gestapo increased the pressure on the group and began the systematic use of torture methods during interrogations. A first nationwide wave of arrests took place in August and September 1936. But the Jehovah's Witnesses continued to practise their religion illegally and even conducted several leaflet campaigns against the Nazi regime in December 1937. The ensuing new wave of arrests in 1938 practically destroyed all remaining organizational networks before the end of that year. Since the Jehovah's Witnesses steadfastly rejected military service after 1939, they were pursued with particular vigour during the war. It is estimated that about 6,000 of them were arrested in the course of the Third Reich and given their own concentration camp identification: a purple triangle. Hundreds of Jehovah's Witnesses died in camps and prisons due to abuse and overwork, while others were executed outright. Their suffering was immense, but ultimately their fate differed from that of the Jews: in Heydrich's view (and that of other senior Nazis) they were, after all, 'Aryans' capable of redemption.[82]

The Freemasons

In his *Transformations of our Struggle*, Heydrich included the Freemasons as arch-enemies of National Socialism alongside Jews, Bolsheviks and politicizing priests. Heydrich viewed Freemasonry, like Bolshevism, as an internationalist, anti-fascist 'expedient organization [*Zweckorganisation*]' of Jewry: 'The Masonic lodges and their related organizations, which also stand under Jewish control, have the sole purpose of organizing social life in a seemingly harmless way while actually instrumentalizing people for the purposes of Jewry.'[83]

Soon after the Nazi seizure of power, the German lodges were hit by a wave of arrests, followed by their closure. The SD began to analyse their confiscated documents and archives, including those of the Lodge of the Three Sabres in Halle, of which Heydrich's father, Bruno, had been a member.[84] By the mid-1930s, however, Heydrich had ceased to perceive Freemasonry as an acute threat. Most lodges, confronted with the Nazis' open hostility, had either dissolved themselves in 1933 or had been closed down by the Gestapo. Former members of Masonic associations, known to the police after the lodges' archives and membership lists had been seized, were at a clear disadvantage in the Third Reich, particularly if they were employed in the civil service, but they were never subjected to similarly systematic persecution as Communists or Jews. The fact that someone was a Freemason or had once belonged to a lodge did not automatically lead to protective custody.[85]

The dwindling importance Heydrich attached to the 'Freemason problem' was reflected in his organizational reform of the Gestapo and the SD in 1936: the SD's formerly independent Freemasonry desk merged with the departments for Jewry and Church affairs into a department for 'worldviews'. From the summer of 1937, Heydrich's Gestapo no longer pursued the matter of Freemasonry.[86] Instead, he perceived Freemasonry as a 'disappeared cult' worthy of preservation in a museum – not entirely dissimilar to the Central Jewish Museum that was set up by the SS in Prague in 1942 to commemorate 'a disappeared race'.[87] Heydrich ordered the establishment of a Freemasons' Museum at Gestapo headquarters in Berlin's Prinz-Albrecht-Palais, in which the Masonic lodges' confiscated cult objects, libraries, membership lists and files were on display. When, in October 1935, the Swiss emissary of the International Red Cross, Carl Jacob Burckhardt, undertook an inspection tour of German concentration camps, Heydrich explained to him that he considered the Freemasons to be primarily 'an instrument of Jewish vengeance'. Should the Freemasons get the upper hand in their struggle with National Socialism, they would unleash 'orgies of cruelty', compared to which the current measures adopted by the Nazis would 'appear rather moderate'.[88]

Two days later, Heydrich conducted his guest through his Freemasons' Museum in Berlin. In the first room, Heydrich explained to Burckhardt, were display cabinets with the names of all the world's Freemasons, ordered by country. A black-painted, windowless second room was in total darkness, Burckhardt recalled:

> Heydrich switched on a violet light and slowly there appeared all kinds of Masonic cult objects in the shadows. Pale as a corpse in the artificial light, Heydrich moved around the room talking about world conspiracies, degrees of initiation and the Jews, who, at the top of the Masonic hierarchy, were working towards the destruction of all humanity. Even darker, narrower rooms with low ceilings followed, which one could only enter bent double, to be seized by the shoulders by the bony hands of automatically operated skeletons.

By the mid-1930s, Heydrich clearly viewed the Freemason problem as an issue of the past, fit for a 'haunted house'-style museum in which he sought to impress international visitors like Burckhardt.[89]

Asocials

In an essay on the tasks of the Security Police in the Third Reich written in 1937, Heydrich argued that a close connection existed between conventional crime and the ideological threats facing the Third Reich: 'The ... subhuman doubly threatens the health and life of the body of the people [*Volkskörper*]: by violating and shaking social norms as a criminal, and by placing himself at the disposal of the enemies of our people as a tool and weapon for their plans.' Nazism's international ideological opponents, Heydrich continued, could easily recruit and instrumentalize criminal 'subhumans' because they were naturally 'inclined towards subversion and disorder'.[90]

The pursuit and arrest of 'asocial subhumans' was the responsibility of the criminal police, whose job it was to 'extirpate' 'career criminals', whose deeds Heydrich believed to indicate 'bad blood', and other social outcasts such as homosexuals and women who, having undergone abortions, were regarded as a threat to the Nazis' demographic objectives.[91] Heydrich's criminal police launched a major operation against 'habitual criminals' in 1937 and another one against more broadly defined 'asocials' (codenamed 'work-shy Reich') on 13 June 1938. In a letter of 1 June 1938, Heydrich had ordered the various branch offices of the criminal police to take '*at least* 200 able-bodied male persons (asocials)' into protective police custody. Particular attention, Heydrich insisted, was to be paid to tramps, beggars, Gypsies and pimps as well as 'persons who have had numerous previous convictions for resistance, bodily harm, brawling, disturbances of the peace and the like, thus demonstrating that they do not wish to be part of the national community'. Heydrich's order justified the mass arrests by stating that 'criminality has its roots in anti-social behaviour', but also cited a second motive: 'the strict implementation of the Four-Year Plan', the Nazi programme designed in 1936 to achieve full employment and build up military resources. The fulfilment of this plan, Heydrich insisted, did not allow 'anti-social persons to withdraw from work and thus sabotage' the economic objectives of the Hitler government. The operation fell within the context of the forced transition from a labour market to 'labour deployment', thus attempting to eliminate the alarming labour shortage that had resulted from the accelerated rearmament campaign which began in 1935.[92]

The raids against 'anti-social' fringe groups continued over the following months. By the end of 1938, a total of 12,921 asocials were being held in preventive detention and 3,231 persons were under systematic surveillance. Heydrich's rigorous campaign against asocials certainly contributed to a decline in crime rates, but more decisive was the waning of the global economic crisis, which in turn reduced the enormously inflated crime rate of the years between 1930 and 1933 to a normal level.[93]

In 'protecting' German society from asocials and political opponents, Heydrich's apparatus did not operate in isolation. Regular courts and state prisons also played a key role in repressing opposition. A whole new set of laws and decrees passed in 1933 vastly expanded the scope of existing treason laws and the applicability of the death sentence. In 1937, the courts handed down no fewer than 5,255 convictions for high treason.[94]

Those who were arrested and convicted were sent either to a concentration camp or to a normal prison depending on the nature and severity of their crime. While the concentration camps were primarily reserved for political prisoners during the first years of the Third Reich, this changed in the course of the 1930s. During 1933, some 100,000 Germans, most of them opponents of the new regime, were detained without trial in concentration camps across the Reich. By early 1935, however, the vast majority of them had been released on 'good behaviour', often after promising future political abstinence. Almost all of the early concentration camps were shut down by the end of 1933, and the number of inmates dropped to 3,000 by early 1935. It was only from 1936 onwards that the number of inmates increased again to a total of 21,000 prisoners by the outbreak of the Second World War in September 1939. The majority of camp inmates were no longer political prisoners (who tended to be confined in ordinary prisons), but 'social outcasts'.[95]

In order to accommodate the growing number of prisoners, the SS began to extend the concentration camp system. Between 1936 and 1937 the remaining early camps – Esterwegen, Sachsenburg, Columbia-Haus, Lichtenburg and Sulza – were dissolved. Dachau was the only one of the older camps to survive. Instead, the SS now began to build new and bigger camps governed by the same regulations and disciplinary code as Dachau. The 'Dachau model', designed to regiment the prisoners and dehumanize their relations with the guards, was based on a system of graded punishment for various offences, which ranged from denial of food to execution. To dehumanize relations with prisoners, the guards' behaviour was regulated to maintain distance and eliminate human contact. The first of these camps was Sachsenhausen, north of Berlin. In the summer of 1937 another camp, Buchenwald near Weimar, was built. It was followed in May 1938 by Flossenbürg in Bavaria and then, in August – after the Anschluss of Austria – by the Mauthausen concentration camp east of the city of Linz. Neuengamme near Hamburg followed in December 1938 and the women's camp at Ravensbrück, some 90 kilometres north of Berlin, opened in May 1939.[96]

Unlike Himmler, who regularly visited the concentration camps, Heydrich was rarely seen there. The only proven visit by Heydrich to Dachau, for example, occurred in the late summer of 1938, when he met another senior SS officer, the future Higher SS and Police Leader in the occupied Soviet Union, Hans-Adolf Prützmann, for dinner in the camp. The rarity of Heydrich's concentration camp visits was at least partially due to the fact that his power ended at the camp gates. While he could decide who was interned and who was released, Himmler had in 1934 entrusted the supervision of camp life throughout the Reich to Theodor Eicke, with whom Heydrich did not get on.[97] This division of labour was not only an essential part of Himmler's leadership style – his conscious decision to spread responsibility among several trusted SS officers – but also a radicalizing factor in the escalating Nazi policies of persecution. Heydrich, Eicke and other senior SS officers understandably sought to please both Himmler and Hitler, and they increasingly discovered that the best way to do so was through initiative and radicalism.

A Life of Privilege

While the Nazi police state was taking shape, Heydrich's financial situation continued to improve to the extent that the family was able to afford two houses: a family home in Berlin and a holiday house on Lina's native island of Fehmarn. The 42,000 Reichsmarks required to build the house in traditional North German style with a thatched roof and half-timbered frame were provided through a private loan from Willy Sachs, a flamboyant industrial magnate with honorary SS membership and – just like the architect, Gustav Rall – a personal friend of the Heydrich family.[98] Construction work began in the spring of 1935, and in June that year the Heydrichs celebrated the building's completion in the presence of Himmler and other SS friends and colleagues. Over the following years, the Heydrichs were to spend almost all their summer holidays there. In addition, a hunting tenancy was obtained in 1934, first at Parlow in the Schorfheide forest north-east of Berlin in immediate proximity to Hermann Göring's country estate Karinhall; then, from 1936, in Stolpshof, near Nauen in Brandenburg, where the SS maintained a small concentration camp from which Heydrich recruited slave labourers for the renovation of his hunting lodge.[99]

In February 1937, the Heydrichs left their rented Südende apartment and purchased a 700-square-metre property for a family home in Augustastrasse, not far from the picturesque shores of the Schlachtensee. The new family home, in Lina Heydrich's post-war description no more than an 'enlarged settlement house', offered nine rooms over three floors, with two of the rooms reserved for domestic servants. According to Albert Speer, Hitler's favourite architect, Heydrich's house reflected his somewhat paranoid mindset, being equipped like a fortress with police guards and alarm bells in every room. In the garden, Lina set up a playground for the children and built a henhouse for animal cultivation.[100]

The house in Schlachtensee cost a further 49,000 Reichsmarks, 10,000 of which were were provided by Himmler's 'Special Fund Reich Leader SS'. Despite the two private 'loans' from Sachs and Himmler (neither of which was ever to be repaid), the Heydrichs were obviously able to pay interest and instalments for a mortagage of 91,000 Reichsmarks and to employ two domestic servants on a permanent basis.[101]

According to Heydrich's 1936 tax declaration, he had earned 8,400 Reichsmarks the previous year, of which 1,200 RM could be offset as wages for domestic servants of a high state official. In addition, he received a 12,000 RM allowance as head of the Gestapo. The following year, his base income rose to 9,000 RM – a small fortune when compared to the average income of 2,000 Reichsmarks earned by a middle-ranked Gestapo officer. By 1937, his income totalled 15,7279.59 RM.[102] That Reinhard's salary was barely 'sufficient to live on', as Lina maintained after the war, was therefore quite a remarkable exaggeration. The financial worries of the first years of marriage, the permanent 'relocation from rental accommodation to rental accommodation' continually lamented by Lina, had clearly been overcome. And Heydrich's salary continued to rise: in 1938, he earned the considerable income of 17,371.53 RM, while simultaneously reducing the salary of his two domestic servants to a total of 550 RM per annum.[103]

The Heydrichs also benefited from Reinhard's position in other ways. During the Olympic Summer Games in 1936, for example, the family received free box seats in the Olympic Stadium. They also enjoyed privileged treatment during the Winter Games that had commenced in Garmisch-Partenkirchen on 6 February 1936. A fleet of cars and drivers was at Heydrich's disposal, as well as a plane – during the war, indeed, two planes. In addition to this, as of April 1934, Heydrich was a Prussian privy counsellor, and from March 1936 a member of the Reichstag, which brought with it an extra 6,000 RM a year.[104]

In the summer of 1937, the Heydrichs, without their children, went on a harmonious holiday in the Mediterranean together. It was a sort of delayed honeymoon and they spent it on a cruise ship, the *Milwaukee*, which brought them to Italy, Greece, Tripoli, Tunisia and Carthage. All in all, the Heydrichs were able to cultivate a lifestyle appropriate to their elevated position within the political elite of the Third Reich.[105]

Their social relations mirrored this position. The Himmlers were frequent guests at the Heydrich home, even though Lina and Margarete Himmler did not get on. Much to Himmler's and Heydrich's dismay, the two women could not stand each other. Their always tense relationship repeatedly threatened to escalate throughout the 1930s as Margarete Himmler energetically used her powers as the wife of the Reich Leader SS, repeatedly trying to advise Lina on how to be a 'proper' Nazi wife. Every Wednesday, she invited the wives of the higher SS leaders for afternoon coffee in her house in Berlin Dahlem and made it very clear that she would take offence if the invitation was declined. In response, Lina deliberately scheduled her gym classes for the wives of senior SS officers for the same day. According to Frieda Wolff, the wife of Himmler's personal adjutant, Margarete even urged her husband to pressurize Heydrich into a divorce, an idea Himmler rejected.[106]

Heydrich's ascent in the Nazi hierarchy also meant that he was frequently invited to official receptions in the Reich Chancellery, where he first came into direct contact with Hitler. However, Heydrich's relationship with Hitler was never as close and personal as that with Himmler: as a Nazi official of the second tier, Heydrich had no right to report directly to Hitler prior to his appointment as acting Reich Protector in 1941 – a right reserved for cabinet ministers and the influential Regional Party Leaders or Gauleiters. Personal encounters prior to the outbreak of the Second World War were thus confined to large official receptions in

Berlin and Munich. Later, during the war, Heydrich met with Hitler at his Bavarian mountain retreat, the Berghof, and his military headquarters in East Prussia, the Wolf's Lair. In her memoirs, Lina recalled her first encounter with Hitler during a birthday reception in Berlin. Hitler stood in the reception hall greeting his guests and, when the Heydrichs presented themselves, he stretched out both hands and said: 'What a beautiful couple. I am most impressed!'[107] It was not only Heydrich's Aryan appearance that impressed Hitler, but also his unshakeable loyalty, proven during the Röhm putsch of 1934, and his untiring activism in securing the Nazi regime from all political enemies. When Hitler famously called Heydrich 'one of the best National Socialists' and 'one of the greatest opponents of all enemies of the Reich' at his funeral in June 1942 it was no idle compliment. By the late 1930s Hitler would believe enough in Heydrich's loyalty and 'talents' to hand him responsibility for the politically sensitive issue closest to his heart: the war against the Jews. Heydrich and Hitler rarely interacted on a social level, but their 'professional' relationship was close. It was marked both by Heydrich's uncompromising loyalty towards his Führer and by Hitler's reciprocal trust in Heydrich's ability to implement the most radical initiatives of the Nazi regime's increasingly violent policies.

In 1937 Wilhelm Canaris and his family moved to Berlin-Schlachtensee and again became the direct neighbours of the Heydrichs. Reinhard and Erika Canaris revived their string quartet, and the families invited each other to evening meals, as well as taking horse rides together in the Grunewald forest. The professional disputes between Canaris and Heydrich during the negotiations over the Ten Commandments of 1935 do not seem to have damaged their otherwise friendly relationship.[108]

The seemingly harmonious family life, captured in several photographs taken in the 1930s was, however, deceptive. Heydrich confided to Karl Wolff, Himmler's personal adjutant, that Lina's constant complaints about his absences and her unfounded suspicions concerning his infidelity were annoying him.[109] Lina, too, indicated after the war that her marriage was in deep crisis in the later 1930s. As a result of her husband's constant absences, she practically lived alone with her children, repeatedly accusing her husband of having affairs with other women. According to some post-war testimonies, Heydrich indeed sought diversion from his domestic problems in extramarital affairs. Lina apparently knew about his sexual adventures, maintaining after the war that there were always 'other women in my marriage' and that her husband was keen on 'anything in a skirt'.[110]

Whether or not Heydrich accompanied the young head of the SD's department IVE (domestic espionage) chief Walter Schellenberg on frequent all-night forays through Berlin bars and brothels such as the

SS-run Salon Kitty in Berlin, as Schellenberg maintained after 1945, is impossible to establish.[111] What is certain, however, is that the Heydrich marriage after 1937 was in severe trouble, partly because of Heydrich's constant and often unexplained absences, and partly because of his suspicion that Lina's friendship with Schellenberg was more than just platonic. It was not the first or last time that such rumours emerged, and, apart from Schellenberg, Lina Heydrich is said to have had affairs with the Nazi painter Wolfgang Willrich and with Werner Best's successor in the RSHA, Wilhelm Albert.[112]

Schellenberg and Lina had become close, if not intimate, friends shortly after they first met at a state function in 1935. Lina always maintained that she merely used the handsome and recently divorced Schellenberg to arouse her husband's jealousy. But there is some reason to doubt her version of events. According to Schellenberg, a drunken evening with Gestapo chief Heinrich Müller and Heydrich took a dramatic turn when the latter told Schellenberg that his drink had been poisoned. Only after a confession concerning the nature of his relationship with Lina did Heydrich produce an antidote. In order to avoid further tensions with his boss, Schellenberg stopped seeing Lina altogether.[113]

Despite, or perhaps because of, these marital problems, Lina gave birth to their third child and first daughter, Silke, on Easter Sunday 1939. She said after the war that Reinhard 'idolized' his little daughter from the day of her birth: 'He was a proper father to his daughter. It didn't matter whether an official meeting was going on in the house or whether there was a visitor, his daughter Silke was brought to him at 6 p.m. for her goodnight kiss.' From now on, Reinhard returned more frequently to the family home in Berlin-Schlachtensee.[114]

Although not directly involved in educating his own children due to his heavy and ever-increasing workload, Heydrich had very clear ideas on how children should be educated. In a meeting with Hitler Youth girls, he stressed that education and politics were inseparable. Whereas during the Weimar Republic, 'the youths were pretty superficial, addicted to entertainment, and completely indifferent to the challenges of the future of *Volk* and Reich', education in the Third Reich was guided by clear ideological principles: 'The main tenets of our educational ideal are the uncompromising preservation of German blood, the endeavour to demonstrate an uncompromising clarity of character, to cherish truth, modesty and pride without arrogance, to inculcate a healthy ambition that demands highest achievements without being egoistic, and, last but not least, a constant endeavour to achieve the highest professional standards.' But Heydrich clearly distinguished between the education of girls and that of boys, the future political soldiers of the Third Reich. He insisted that girls 'despite all necessary self-restraint and self-control ... must never become militarized and hardened. The most attractive thing about a woman is her femininity, which in itself makes a woman beautiful. Whatever you do, always preserve your femininity.'[115]

Heydrich's stereotypical ideas about the preservation of femininity and softness reflected propagandistic Nazi gender images of women as mothers, carers and creators of homes in which their warrior husbands could find rest and regain strength. In point of fact, the reality in Nazi Germany looked very different and the number of women in permanent employment rose constantly, from 1.2 million in 1933 to 1.85 million in 1938. But female employment was not the main issue. Heydrich's ideas for educating young women, which he reiterated in his testament of 1939, were directed against a certain mentality, encapsulated by the despised image of the 'New Woman' – modern, short-haired, emancipated and smoking – propagated by left-wing intellectuals and avant-garde women's journals such as the German *Vogue* of the 1920s. The New Woman, a central feature of the perceived decadence of modernity, was to disappear once and for all.[116]

Heydrich's marital life was not the only family problem that concerned him in the later 1930s. His sister Maria insisted on several occasions that Reinhard should use his contacts to secure a job for his brother-in-law. Heydrich grudgingly complied and repeatedly found employment for Wolfgang Heindorf first in the Propaganda Ministry, and then in the Volkswagen factory and the German Labour Front. His brother-in-law was sacked from each of these jobs within six months. As a raging alcoholic who tended to submit falsified expense claims, brag about his influential brother-in-law and 'borrow' money from subordinates, Heindorf remained a constant source of embarrassment for Heydrich.[117]

By June 1939, Heydrich was at the end of his tether and ordered Heindorf to come to his office. During the meeting, he furiously attacked his brother-in-law for his inability to hold down a job, for his constant accumulation of debts and for his visible alcoholism, which he held partially responsible for the economic collapse of his family's Conservatory in Halle. Heindorf and his wife, Heydrich insisted, led an overly extravagant lifestyle. In the future they would have to make do with less.[118]

Heydrich's accusations must have infuriated Maria, for she wrote an angry letter to her brother on 30 June, complaining about the elevated moral tone that he was taking towards her and her husband:

Due to your high position, you have lost your ability to appreciate our circumstances ... to the extent that, if you are honest, you can no longer really understand and judge the abilities and shortcomings of an average citizen any more from your lofty vantage point. To be able to do that, and to think and feel like we do, you would have to live with us again for a few weeks! Excuse my radical openness, but you also tell us the truth and how you think, and I am not writing today to the SS Gruppenführer and Chief of Police Heydrich, but to my own flesh and blood, my brother ... Reinhard, tell me – what do you gain by wanting to kick me and my family down with such relish?! You don't count us among your relatives any more anyway, so if you don't help us, at least leave us in peace and do not put any further obstacles in our path ...[119]

Three weeks later, on 19 July, Maria received a brief response from Kurt Pomme, Heydrich's police adjutant since November 1934: 'The Gruppenführer refuses to have any further direct contact with you and your husband (even through letters) because he does not wish to be insulted.' Through Pomme, Heydrich further instructed Maria to leave their mother out of the dispute and ordered Gestapo surveillance of Heindorf, insisting that every incident involving his brother-in-law should be brought to his immediate attention. As the same time, he informed Heindorf's new employer that his brother-in-law required 'strong guidance' in fulfilling his tasks. Heydrich's suspicions were quickly confirmed when he received Gestapo reports that Heindorf had fallen back into 'old habits', incurring debts, arriving drunk at work and boasting about being Heydrich's relative. Heydrich gave his brother-in-law only one option: to volunteer for the Wehrmacht and to 'prove his worth in battle' – a scenario that was becoming increasingly likely as Nazi Germany prepared to go to war in the late 1930s.[120]

CHAPTER V

Rehearsals for War

The Fritsch–Blomberg Affair

IN LATE 1937, HITLER INSTIGATED A RADICAL REVERSAL IN THE FOREIGN policy of the Third Reich. On 5 November, the Führer gave a speech in the presence of the supreme commanders of the army, air force and navy, in which he emphasized the need to procure, through violent expansion if necessary, the *Lebensraum* (living space) Germany required to secure its future as a great nation. The concerns and criticisms of some of his listeners reinforced Hitler's view that he would achieve his foreign policy objectives only if he replaced with more willing helpers some of the senior conservative figures who continued to occupy key positions in the government apparatus.[1]

Just a few months later, a fortuitous opportunity arose to introduce such a comprehensive change of personnel: the scandal surrounding the Reich War Minister, Werner von Blomberg. In January 1938, in the presence of Hitler, Göring, Heydrich and other Nazi dignitaries, Blomberg had married a considerably younger woman who turned out to be a prostitute known to the police. The affair led to Blomberg's dismissal. In late January 1938, Göring, who regarded himself as Blomberg's natural successor, unexpectedly presented incriminating Gestapo material against his strongest competitor for the job: the army's commander-in-chief, Werner von Fritsch. According to Gestapo evidence, conveniently placed at Göring's disposal, Fritsch was a homosexual – a major criminal offence in Nazi Germany.[2]

Heydrich was hardly surprised by the allegations. Already in 1936, his Gestapo apparatus had gathered incriminating material on Fritsch and passed it on to Hitler. Back then, the Führer had chosen to ignore the allegations against Fritsch, and ordered the SS to destroy the police file. Heydrich had, however, ignored that order and kept a copy of the file for future reference. When Hitler and Göring tried to rid themselves of the conservative generals, he remembered the file. The allegations against Fritsch rested on thin evidence: the key witness in the case was a notorious criminal, Otto Schmidt, whose Berlin-based gang had specialized in blackmailing prominent homosexuals since 1929. Despite his youth, Schmidt had already served many years in prison for theft, forgery, corruption and blackmail, and he was currently imprisoned in a concentration camp in Emsland. According to his testimony, he had witnessed Fritsch and a Berlin rentboy, Martin Weingärtner, engage in sexual activities near Wannsee railway station. He further alleged that, when confronted, Fritsch had offered him money for his silence.[3]

Heydrich resubmitted this 'evidence' to the Führer and on 26 January Fritsch was ordered to the Reich Chancellery, where, in the presence of Hitler and Göring, he was confronted with Schmidt. Although Fritsch denied ever having met Schmidt or having engaged in homosexual practices, Hitler relieved him of his duties, along with twelve other politically undesirable conservative generals. Another forty-four generals were transferred to politically irrelevant posts. Hitler's cabinet, too, was reorganized and cleansed of potential critics: the conservative Foreign Minister, Konstantin von Neurath, was replaced by a committed Nazi, Joachim von Ribbentrop, and the Economics Minister, Hjalmar Schacht, was succeeded by the former State Secretary in Goebbels's Propaganda Ministry, Walther Funk. The Ministry of War was dissolved and replaced by the High Command of the Wehrmacht (as the Reichswehr was called after March 1935) under the obedient and ideologically reliable Wilhelm Keitel.[4]

While Hitler readjusted German policy and assumed supreme command of the Wehrmacht, Heydrich's Gestapo continued its investigations into the Fritsch case. Heydrich felt the pressure to prove Fritsch's guilt, for it was his apparatus that had raised the allegations in the first place and thus created the pretext for the restructuring of the army leadership, whose relationship with the Gestapo had now reached rock bottom. For several weeks, Gestapo agents investigated every garrison town Fritsch had ever lived in, while Heydrich's 'expert' in the fight against homosexuality, Josef Meisinger, travelled to Egypt, where Fritsch had spent his holidays in 1937, in search of incriminating evidence. None of these investigations delivered any concrete leads. Despite these setbacks, Himmler and Heydrich nonetheless assumed that Fritsch would not be rehabilitated as long as Schmidt's testimony stood.[5]

In March, Fritsch appeared before the military tribunal charged with the investigation of the case. The hearing ended with a disastrous turn of events for Heydrich and the Gestapo: under pressure from Fritsch's legal counsel, the sole prosecution witness, Otto Schmidt, admitted that he had confused General von Fritsch with a retired cavalry officer called Captain von Frisch, who confirmed that he had been blackmailed by Schmidt. Even worse for Heydrich, the court learned that the cavalry officer had admitted his 'guilt' to the Gestapo several months before, thus leaving the impression that Heydrich's apparatus had persecuted General von Fritsch despite its knowledge of the confused identity. The court concluded that Schmidt's testimony to the Gestapo was the result of 'the most extreme pressure' placed on him by investigators. Fritsch was duly acquitted and rehabilitated, but not reinstated as the army's commander-in-chief.[6]

The affair was a political disaster for the SS and particularly embarrassing for Heydrich, whose Gestapo had led the investigation. Heydrich's deputy, Werner Best, who had personally interrogated Fritsch, spoke of a severe public 'disgrace'. Others went further: Fritsch himself contemplated challenging Himmler to a duel, while the Chief of the General Staff, General Ludwig Beck, called for the immediate dismissal of Heydrich and other senior investigators. Even before the conclusion of the Fritsch trial, Heydrich began to fear and anticipate a serious response from the army leadership, possibly even a military putsch and an army raid of the Gestapo headquarters.[7] Such plans indeed existed, and a group of senior officers surrounding General Beck and Admiral Wilhelm Canaris contemplated the arrest of the entire SS leadership. Canaris's relationship with Heydrich had become more and more ambivalent over the course of the 1930s. Based on their friendship in Kiel in the mid-1920s, Canaris had wrongly assumed that, in his capacity as chief of Germany's military espionage, he could control the much younger Heydrich. When Canaris was appointed as head of the Abwehr in 1935, his predecessor, Conrad Patzig, had warned him about Heydrich and Himmler, but Canaris told him confidently: 'Don't you worry, I can handle those boys.'[8] The gradual extension of SS competences from 1935 onwards had proven Canaris wrong and increasingly undermined the Abwehr's authority. He was now prepared to see his former protégé removed from his position of power.[9] However, the putsch plans secretly advocated by Fritsch, Beck and Canaris became obsolete when Hitler pulled off a major foreign policy success: the Anschluss of Austria. For Heydrich, the military operation against Austria offered the badly needed opportunity to divert attention from the Fritsch affair and to prove that the SS was capable of collaborating with the army.[10]

Anschluss

At the beginning of 1938, Heydrich's attention turned to Austria. Eighteen months earlier, in July 1936, Hitler had concluded a formal agreement with the Austrian Chancellor, Kurt von Schuschnigg, under which the Austrians complied with Hitler's request to give the Austrian Nazi Party a number of ministerial posts in government. But while Schuschnigg regarded this as a settlement of the difficulties that had emerged in Austro-German relations following a German-sponsored coup attempt of 1934, Hitler saw it only as the beginning of a gradual process that would ultimately lead to the Anschluss with Germany. Yet for a long time Hitler did not think the moment appropriate for such a move. Throughout 1936, he ordered the Austrian Nazis to stay quiet not wanting to cause international tensions while the rest of Europe was still alarmed by the recent remilitarization of the Rhineland – the Wehrmacht's illegal entry into the previously demilitarized zone east of the German–French border.[11]

In early 1938, however, Hitler changed his mind. On 12 February, a meeting between the Führer and Schuschnigg took place in the Berghof, Hitler's mountain retreat at Berchtesgaden on the German–Austrian border. In order to intimidate Schuschnigg, Hitler had arranged for senior German police and military figures to be present, including Himmler, Heydrich, and the newly appointed chief of the Wehrmacht's High Command, Wilhelm Keitel. Hitler made it clear that military action would follow if the Austrians did not give in to his demands. The following morning Keitel was ordered to make arrangements for intimidating military manoeuvres on the Austrian border.[12] Meanwhile, Himmler and Heydrich had begun their own extensive preparations for the invasion of Austria. From January 1938 onwards, some 20,000 members of the Order and Security Police were mobilized and trained for the purpose of supporting the Wehrmacht in its task of occupying Germany's southern neighbour.[13]

Three weeks after the meeting at the Berghof, Schuschnigg inadvertently provided Hitler with a pretext for a German invasion when he suddenly announced that a referendum on Austrian independence was to be held on 13 March. To ensure a resounding yes for Austrian independence, voting was restricted to people over twenty-four years of age, thus disenfranchising a large part of the predominantly young Nazi movement. Hitler was outraged and sent an ultimatum to Schuschnigg on 11 March: the referendum's wording had to be changed to encourage people to approve union rather than oppose it. Schuschnigg was to resign as chancellor and be replaced by Arthur Seyss-Inquart, an Austrian Lawyer and Nazi activist who had been appointed as Interior Minister as a result of the Berchtesgarden agreement.[14]

Hitler did not wait for the Austrian Chancellor to make up his mind. Encouraged by Göring, he gave Keitel the invasion order. At 5.30 in the morning on 12 March, German troops crossed the Austrian border without meeting any resistance.[15] But the Nazis were not taking any chances of a repetition of the disastrous failed putsch attempt of 1934 when the Austrian Chancellor, Engelbert Dollfuss, was shot by an SS man before the coup collapsed in the face of determined opposition. Among the first to arrive in Vienna were Himmler and Heydrich, who landed at the Austrian capital's airport at 5 a.m. on 12 March, before German troops had even marched into the city.[16] Hitler had authorized Himmler the previous day to secure police control over the annexed territory. Himmler, as usual, passed on the order to Heydrich, who was instructed to supervise the first wave of arrests and to 'cleanse' the Austrian police.[17]

At a meeting at the Hotel Regina in Vienna on 13 and 14 March, the SS and police leadership – Himmler, Heydrich and the head of the Order Police, Kurt Daluege – held talks on the future of police organization in Austria. The State Secretary for Security was swiftly replaced by the leader of the Austrian SS, Heydrich's future successor as head of the Reich Security Main Office, Ernst Kaltenbrunner. Six thousand ordinary German policemen were drafted in as reinforcements, along with 1,500 Security Police agents.[18] But in general the Austrian police did not need a thorough purge. Many of them were Nazi sympathizers anyhow or at least flexible enough to adjust their political views to those of the new rulers. More than 80 per cent of the staff of the Austrian Gestapo between 1938 and 1942 came from the old Austrian police apparatus, with an additional 10 per cent from the Old Reich. A mere 5 per cent were new recruits without any previous police experience.[19]

Heydrich ordered a first wave of arrests even before the meeting at the Hotel Regina. He brought with him from Germany a team of trusted SD and Gestapo officers to eliminate the opposition and to confiscate important documents, including the police files on SS involvement in the failed Austrian putsch of 1934.[20] Heydrich's Security Police officers, armed with extensive lists of 'oppositional elements' compiled under Dollfuss and Schuschnigg, moved swiftly into action, arresting anyone thought to pose a real or potential threat to Nazi rule – 21,000 in all – on the night of 12–13 March.[21] Among those arrested were former members of the Schuschnigg government, Communists and German émigrés, but also Austrian royalists and leading ex-members of the *Heimwehren*, the conservative Home Defence Leagues. Some of the most prominent Heimwehr leaders, such as Ernst-Rüdiger Starhemberg, a descendant of the Count Starhemberg who had defended Vienna against the Turks in the sixteenth century, managed to flee the country. Others were less fortunate. Another former leader of the Home Defence Leagues, Major Emil Fey, who had played a crucial role in putting down the Nazi uprising in Vienna in 1934, killed himself with his entire family.[22]

The main immediate target was the Austrian Communists. Heydrich consciously stoked fears of a violent Communist uprising when he suggested to the newly appointed Reich commissioner for the unification of Austria and the Reich, Joseph Bürckel, that the Communist underground might stage a boycott of the impending plebiscite in order to highlight the illegitimacy of the Anschluss to the outside world.[23] By the end of 1938, the Gestapo had detained nearly the entire leadership of the Austrian Communist Party, the majority of whom were deported to concentration camps.[24] In order to cope with the new influx of political prisoners, special new facilities were made available in the recently extended Dachau concentration camp near Munich. In addition, the SS set up a camp at Mauthausen, close to Linz. It was to become the harshest of all the camps within the territory of the Greater German Reich before the invasion of the Soviet Union in 1941.[25]

Although most of those imprisoned were released over the following months, some 2,000 Austrians remained in the camps after July 1938, or so Heydrich maintained in a conversation with the Foreign Ministry's State Secretary, Ernst von Weizsäcker.[26] Alongside the first wave of arrests in Vienna, a targeted operation was launched on the night of 12–13 March designed to confiscate Jewish valuables, including jewellery, paintings and carpets. On 17 March, concerned about the safety of this new 'property of the German people', Heydrich ordered the newly established Gestapo office in Vienna to ensure the systematic registration of all captured documents and objects, threatening to 'take steps mercilessly against anyone who tries to enrich himself with the confiscated items'.[27]

The motivation for Heydrich's concern was the looting and uncontrolled terror that had been spreading alongside the 'controlled' SS police operations since the German invasion, and which ultimately reflected badly on him and his ability to control his men. Austria was not, after all, an enemy state, but an integral part of the future German Reich. Heydrich's position became even more precarious when, on 13 March, a close associate of Vice Chancellor Franz von Papen and a conservative critic of the Nazi terror in Austria, Wilhelm Emanuel von Ketteler, was drowned by the young SD official Horst Böhme, the future head of the SD in Bohemia and Moravia under Heydrich. As Goebbels noted in his diary shortly after the murder: 'Heydrich has had some very unpleasant executions carried out in Austria. That is not to be tolerated. Göring is outraged, and so is the Führer. Heydrich will not get away with this so easily.'[28]

The uncontrolled terror to which Heydrich objected for 'optical reasons' was primarily directed against Austria's Jews, the overwhelming majority of whom (170,000 out of nearly 200,000) lived in Vienna. The violence unleashed by Austria's Nazis went further than anything seen so far in the Old Reich. From the very beginning of the German invasion Jewish businesses and apartments were looted and their inhabitants maltreated. Amid the applause of bystanders, Jews were made to kneel and scrub the streets.[29] The playwright Carl Zuckmayer described the first days after the Anschluss:

> The underworld had opened up its gates and set loose its lowest, most disgusting hordes. The city transformed itself into a nightmarish painting by Hieronymus Bosch: . . . demons seemed to have crawled out of filthy eggs and risen from marshy burrows. The air was constantly filled with a desolate, hysterical shrieking . . . and people's faces were distorted: some with fear, others with lies, still others with wild, hate-filled triumph.[30]

The pogrom-like violent excesses in Austria threatened to disrupt 'orderly' Gestapo operations and to undermine Heydrich's authority. Immediately after the invasion, he ordered a special SD commando of Jewish experts, including Herbert Hagen and Adolf Eichmann, to take up their work in Vienna. The initial task of the *Sonderkommando* was to arrest Jewish officials – using a previously compiled list – and to confiscate documents from Jewish organizations and private individuals.[31] Their task was severely disrupted by the pogrom-like atmosphere in Vienna and other Austrian cities. Heydrich lost no time in threatening to arrest those Nazis who were responsible for mob violence. Annoyed that these excesses undermined his own efforts at a surgical strike against the ideological opponents of Nazism, he also undertook an exercise in damage control by publishing an article in the *Völkischer Beobachter* on 17 March. In the article, he maintained that the pogroms of the previous days had been carried out not by members of the Nazi Party but rather by disguised Communists, seeking to provide foreign hate propaganda with further material.[32]

That same day, Heydrich wrote to Gauleiter Bürckel to express his conviction that arrests should be undertaken within an 'orderly' framework and with at least the appearance of legality, arguing that it lay in the best interests of the Reich's foreign policy to depict conditions to the outside world as being as calm as possible in view of the upcoming plebiscite on 10 April.

Unfortunately, in recent days members of the Party have participated in large-scale and utterly undisciplined assaults. Today I have published a statement in the press stating that Communist supporters dressed in Nazi Party uniforms have been conducting illegal confiscations, house searches and arrests. I must point out that my comments were in fact not primarily directed against Communist supporters but rather against our own party comrades. It would be regrettable if the Gestapo was forced to arrest our own party comrades on a larger scale. I therefore urgently request that you issue appropriate instructions to all party agencies.[33]

Three weeks later, on 5 April, Heydrich felt the need to remind his SS men that 'all excesses and measures against the Jews on the part of the SS must cease'. It was not until 29 April, however, when SS leaders were threatened with dismissal if they continued to participate in these outrages, that the tide of violent incidents began to subside.[34] The experiences in Austria prompted Heydrich to issue a more general order for the entire police and SD apparatus on 14 April: although it was 'self-evident that the struggle against all vermin that infests the people and state [must be conducted] consistently and mercilessly', all measures had to be carried out in an 'orderly' way, which would reassure the general population of the 'just cause' pursued by the Gestapo.[35] This did not mean that the terror in Austria was ended – quite the contrary. The policy of 'merciless combat against all political, intellectual and criminal opponents', as Heydrich described it in the SS journal, *Das Schwarze Korps*, that April, was to be continued 'in silence'. This 'silent terror' could assume different forms, ranging from the secret night-time arrest of prominent critics of the Anschluss to restrictions on postal privacy and press freedom.[36]

When the plebiscite on the Anschluss was held on 10 April amid massive manipulation and intimidation, Heydrich's apparatus played an important role: SS men rounded up voters from their homes and marched them to polling stations where booths had been removed or were labelled with signs 'only traitors enter here', thus forcing the electorate to cast its vote in public. The SD was also in charge of collating information on 'abnormalities' and 'disturbances', which were then passed on to the Gestapo for further investigation.[37] Partly as a result of such precautions, a predictable 99.75 per cent of Austrian voters supported the Anschluss, although probably, to judge from some SD reports, only a third of Viennese voters were genuinely committed to the idea of union.[38]

Following the plebiscite, the country's new Nazi rulers rapidly introduced all of the Old Reich's anti-Semitic legislation. Jews were summarily ousted from the civil service and the professions. An elaborate bureaucracy – the Property Transfer Office, with a staff of 500 – was set up to manage the Aryanization of Jewish-owned businesses. By May 1938, 7,000 out of 33,000 Jewish-owned businesses in Vienna had been closed down; by August 1938, a further 23,000 had gone. The remaining ones were Aryanized.[39]

The Nazis also initiated the forced expulsion of Jewish populations in a manner that was far more direct than in the Old Reich. In the small eastern region of the Burgenland, bordering on Hungary, the new Nazi rulers confiscated the property of the 3,800 members of the old-established Jewish community, closed down all Jewish businesses, arrested community leaders and then used the creation of a 'security zone' on the border as an excuse to expel the entire Jewish population. Many Jews were hauled off to police stations and beaten until they signed documents surrendering all their assets. The police then took them to the border and forced them across. Since neighbouring countries often refused to accept them, many Jews were left stranded in no man's land. Fifty-one of them, for example, were dumped on a barren island on the Danube, in an incident that aroused worldwide press condemnation. The majority fled to friends and relatives in Vienna. By the end of 1938 there were no Jews left in the Burgenland.[40]

Partly in response to this mass flight, between 25 and 27 May 1938 the Gestapo in Vienna arrested nearly 2,000 Jews who were known to have criminal convictions (however trivial), sending them to Dachau, where they were segregated and particularly brutally mistreated. The police also arrested and expelled all foreign Jews and even German Jews living in Vienna. Altogether, 5,000 Jews were deported from Austria by November 1938. Thousands of others sought to leave the country by any means available.[41]

In order to speed up the process of 'orderly' Jewish emigration, Heydrich established a Central Office for Jewish Emigration on 20 August, which was based in the Rothschild Palace in Vienna and run by Adolf Eichmann, whose procedures and techniques created for this Central Office were to have a far wider application in the years that followed.[42] On Heydrich's orders, Eichmann had rushed to Vienna on 16 March as part of a special unit authorized to arrest prominent Austrian Jews. Heydrich and his Jewish experts realized that the orderly conduct of forced emigration required the collaboration of leading figures within the Jewish community itself, especially if the poorest Jews, who lacked the means to leave their homeland and start a new life elsewhere, were to be included in the plan. As Heydrich would emphasize a few months later, the 'problem was to get rid not of the richer Jews, but of the Jewish rabble'.[43]

With Heydrich's blessing and the help of forcibly enlisted members of the Viennese Jewish community, Eichmann and his team began to fast track applications for exit visas and drew on the confiscated assets of the Jewish community to subsidize the emigration of poor Jews. Frightened by the continuing terror on the streets, thousands of Austrian Jews queued to obtain exit visas. The Central Office, with its assembly-line processing of exit visas, its plundering of Jewish assets to subsidize the emigration of the poor, its application of terror and its use of Jewish collaborators became a model for Heydrich's apparatus in its subsequent dealings with the Jews.[44]

Kristallnacht

The Anschluss of Austria added some 200,000 Jews to the population of Nazi Germany. This new influx more than balanced out the roughly 128,000 Jews who had left Germany by the end of 1937.[45] It also made Heydrich's previous efforts to speed up the process of forced emigration seem pointless, particularly after the Evian conference of July 1938 at which representatives of thirty-two countries had made it clear that international enthusiasm for accepting German Jewish refugees was limited. Dissatisfaction at Nazi Party grassroots level with the 'slow progress' of Jewish emigration from Germany began to intensify. In the summer of 1938, Germany witnessed a noticeable upsurge of violence against the Jews.[46]

Among the first to feel the Nazis' newly intensified desire to rid Germany of its now increased Jewish population were the roughly 70,000 Polish Jews living in the Reich, many of whom had fled their homeland after the post-war pogroms that took place in Galicia and elsewhere. The presence of Polish Jews had been a source of increasing aggravation for the SS and police authorities since March 1938, when the Polish government nullified the citizenship of anyone who had lived abroad for more than five years – a deliberate move to prevent the return of Jews to Poland. Faced suddenly with the possibility that nearly 70,000 Polish Jews residing in Germany and Austria would be rendered stateless and trapped in German territory, the Nazi government demanded in April that Jews holding Polish passports leave the Reich. However, the authorities in Warsaw refused to allow these Jews back into Poland, and by late October Himmler and Heydrich chose to act unilaterally. During the night of 28–29 October, the Gestapo and Security Police detained and forcibly expelled 18,000 Polish Jews.[47]

Caught up in this first wave of Nazi mass deportations was a Polish master tailor named Sendel Grynszpan, his wife Rivka and their two eldest children, Esther and Mordechai, who were arrested in the city of Hanover and swiftly expelled across the German–Polish border. In Paris, Grynszpan's younger son, Herschel, heard of the fate that had befallen his family. Humiliated and outraged, he decided to act. On 7 November, in an act of revenge, Herschel shot a junior official at the German Embassy in Paris, Ernst vom Rath, injuring him severely.[48]

On 8 November, Heydrich travelled to Munich in order to attend the annual commemoration ceremony of the failed Hitler putsch of 1923 and the traditional gathering of the SS leadership corps on the previous afternoon. Himmler used the gathering to address the Jewish question, in which he had previously shown little interest. The Jews had no future in Germany, he assured his attentive audience, and would be expelled from the Reich over the next few years. Himmler did not mention the Paris incident and his insistence that the Jews would be expelled over the coming 'years' does not indicate an imminent dramatic radicalization of anti-Jewish policy.[49]

The following day, 9 November, vom Rath succumbed to his injuries. The not altogether unexpected news of his death arrived in Munich in the afternoon and was officially announced during the annual gathering of the 'Old Fighters' in Munich's City Hall that evening. The death of vom Rath provided those Nazi leaders who felt that they had lost influence over the direction of anti-Jewish policies, most notably radical Gauleiters such as Streicher and Goebbels, with a welcome cue. Hitler left the gathering without making his customary speech, but instructed Goebbels to speak instead. The Propaganda Minister used the opportunity to tell his agitated audience about the 'spontaneous actions' against Jews that had already occurred in Kurhesse and Magdeburg-Anhalt in the wake of the assassination attempt. The Führer, Goebbels proclaimed, had decided that the Nazi Party would not initiate further demonstrations, but if they happened, 'he was not going to do anything to stop them'.[50]

Heydrich was among the audience that evening in the Munich City Hall. According to the Gauleiter of Magdeburg, Rudolf Jordan, Heydrich assured the gathering after Goebbels's speech that the police would not intervene in the event of 'spontaneous' anti-Jewish riots.[51] Indeed, SS members, who had come together in many places throughout the Reich to celebrate the anniversary, participated in the riots. Whether they received instructions from Himmler or Heydrich to do so is difficult to say.[52]

The assembled regional party leaders nonetheless drew the necessary inference from Goebbels's speech and immediately called upon their party comrades in local constituencies by telex and telephone to unleash the pogrom. Heydrich returned to his hotel, the *Vier Jahreszeiten*, to confer with Himmler before calling Gestapo chief Heinrich Müller in Berlin. The exact content of their conversation is unknown, but shortly before midnight Müller set all regional State Police offices across the Reich on full alert and informed them that anti-Jewish 'actions' would begin shortly all over the Reich, 'especially against synagogues'. These incidents were not to be hindered: only looting and larger excesses were to be prevented. The State Police were to prepare for the arrest of 20,000 to 30,000 Jews, 'particularly wealthy Jews'.[53]

Less than two hours later, Heydrich followed up Müller's orders with a second telegram. He reiterated that 'demonstrations against the Jews are to be expected in all parts of the Reich in the course of this night'. The 'demonstrations' were not to be prevented. However, the police were to make sure that 'German lives or property' were not endangered and to note that 'businesses and apartments belonging to Jews may be destroyed but not looted' while 'foreign citizens even if they are Jews are not to be molested'. Furthermore, the SD was to ensure that important archival sources from synagogues were confiscated rather than destroyed. Finally, the telegram stated,

> as many Jews in all districts, especially the rich, as can be accommodated in existing prisons are to be arrested. For the time being only healthy male Jews, who are not too old, are to be detained. After the detentions have been carried out the appropriate concentration camps are to be contacted immediately for the prompt accommodation of the Jews in the camps. Special care is to be taken that the Jews arrested in accordance with these instructions are not ill-treated.[54]

Later that night, Heydrich sent out a further telegram, reiterating that looters were to be arrested immediately, but that generally participation in the pogrom would not give rise to criminal investigations against the perpetrators.[55]

The hectic sequence of orders transmitted by Müller and Heydrich indicates that the SS leadership had been surprised by the beginning and the extent of the pogrom. Throughout the Reich, Nazi activists had begun destroying synagogues and Jewish shops, demolishing the interiors of private homes, stealing their belongings and forcibly pulling Jews out of their houses, in order to humiliate, abuse and, in many cases, murder them. The official number of Jewish deaths was later estimated to be ninety-one, but the real figure is likely to be much higher. In addition, numerous desperate Jews committed suicide, and of the approximately 30,000 Jewish men who were arrested and shipped to concentration camps that night, more than a thousand died, either during their imprisonment or as a result of its long-term effects. Furthermore, an estimated 7,500 Jewish businesses, 117 private houses and 177 synagogues were destroyed, inflicting material damage of several hundred million Reichsmarks.[56] The pogrom also spread to the recently annexed Sudetenland and Austria. Forty-two synagogues were burned down in Vienna alone and nearly 2,000 Jewish families were evicted from their houses and apartments.[57]

In some ways, Kristallnacht – as the pogrom came to be known in Nazi Germany – was a frustrating event for Heydrich, partly because it undermined his attempts to organize the systematic expulsion of the Jews and partly because he was aware through SD reports that a majority of Germans did not approve of open violence against Jews. Public support for discrimination and enforced emigration did not necessarily extend to murder and mass destruction of property.[58] Furthermore, the pogroms unnecessarily aroused international protests at a time when Hitler needed calm for his expansionist foreign policy plans.[59]

Yet, while Heydrich was concerned that the pogrom had disrupted the 'orderly' conduct of emigration, he was also aware of a positive side-effect: its acceleration of the speed of emigration of frightened Jews. After inspecting Eichmann's Central Office in Vienna in November 1938, Hagen reported to Heydrich on the advantages of the policy adopted in Austria:

> The establishment of the Central Office guarantees the speedy issue of emigration visas to Jews, usually within 8 days. Furthermore, the Central Office knows the exact numbers of those who wish to emigrate, their professions, wealth etc., which will enable it to assemble the necessary emigration transportation ... According to our assessment approximately 25,000 Jews have so far been made to emigrate by the Central Office so that the overall number of Jews who have left Austria is now approximately 50,000. The establishment of the Central Office does not put an extra financial burden on the SD Oberabschnitt Donau [the SD office responsible for former Austria] because it and its employees are self-financed by the tax levied on every Jewish emigrant. In view of the success rate of the Central Office regarding Jewish emigration, it is recommended – with reference to the recent proposal of 13 January 1938 concerning the establishment of an emigration office – that the possibility of such an office is considered for the whole of the Reich as well.[60]

Hagen's report landed on Heydrich's desk at a critical time. On 10 November, one day after the Kristallnacht pogrom, Heydrich added a handwritten note to the report to the effect that the SD should draft a proposal for the establishment of a Central Office for Jewish Emigration in the Old Reich, based on Eichmann's Vienna model. While the SD's Jewish experts frantically worked on the proposal requested by their boss, Heydrich had little difficulty convincing Göring of the economic pointlessness of the mob anti-Semitism that had erupted on 9 November. He informed Göring that, according to early estimates, at least 815 Jewish businesses had been destroyed and that twenty-nine department stores had been set on fire. Of the 191 synagogues set alight, seventy-six had been completely destroyed. Göring was outraged by the damage the pogrom had done to the economy.[61]

Only two days after the pogrom, on 12 November, the future Nazi Jewish policy was discussed during a high-level conference convened by Göring in the Reich Ministry of Aviation, which he had directed as minister since 1933. Apart from Heydrich, more than one hundred representatives of various state and party agencies participated in the conference, many of them more senior than Heydrich. Following long discussions about the economic implications of the pogrom, Heydrich called for an accelerated emigration of Jews from Germany. He pointed to the previous success of his Central Office for Jewish Emigration in Vienna and recommended the creation of a similar office for the entire Reich. Heydrich maintained that by the end of October about 50,000 Jews had been expelled from Austria, a figure that was, in fact, lower than that subsequently established by historians: more recent research shows that about half of the approximately 190,000 Austrian Jews had left their country by May 1939.[62] If implemented, Heydrich insisted, similar success rates could be expected for the Old Reich. When Göring enquired how such an expensive process would be paid for, Heydrich pointed out that the wealthier Jews could cover the expenses for the less well-off emigrants through compulsory contributions. The envisaged time-frame for the complete emigration of German Jews was 'at least ten years'. Göring approved Heydrich's proposal.[63]

The fact that his suggestion of an organized expulsion of German Jews met with general approval at this meeting was the decisive enabling factor for Heydrich's future role as *the* leading figure in Nazi Germany's anti-Jewish policies. The comprehensive expulsion programme developed by the SD's Jewish department over the preceding years now became the official policy of the Nazi regime, sanctioned by Hitler himself.[64] Göring would continue to claim overall responsibility for the Jewish question, but the power to act had effectively been handed over to Heydrich's Security Police and SD apparatus.

On 24 January 1939, Göring ordered that the emigration of the Jews from the Reich, particularly of poor Jews, should be advanced by every possible means. A Reich Central Office for Jewish Emigration, based on the Vienna model, was to be established under Heydrich's leadership. Only a few days later, on 31 January, Heydrich directed that, with the exception of a few particularly 'dangerous' left-wing intellectuals, Jews held in protective custody should be released *provided* that they were willing to leave Germany for ever.[65]

In late January, Heydrich successively informed the heads of all German ministries that the Reich Central Office for Jewish Emigration had now been set up and asked for co-operation and consultation in all matters relating to the issue of Jewish emigration from Germany.[66] Simultaneously, he proposed the creation of a new umbrella organization for all Jewish societies and associations, the *Reichsvereinigung der Juden in Deutschland* (Reich Association of Jews in Germany), whose main task it would be to co-operate with the Central Office in ensuring an orderly emigration of Jews from Germany.[67] From 4 July 1939 onwards, all Jews living in Germany had to become members of the Reich Association, thus ensuring comprehensive records on each and every Jew in the country. This allowed Heydrich the direct supervision of all Jewish organizations in Germany, while enabling him to keep a closer watch on the Jews them-selves and also to bring about a remarkable simplification of the adminis-tration and processing of Jewish assets.[68]

Although he had not initiated it, the pogrom of November 1938 thus proved to be a major turning point in Heydrich's career, resulting in considerably more power for him and the police apparatus he controlled.[69] Goebbels, who had instigated the pogrom on the evening of 9 November, had hoped that this action would allow him once again to set the tone with regard to Jewish policies. But the initiative backfired. It resulted in millions of Reichsmarks of damage to the economy, severe international criticism and a negative response from large sections of the German population.[70] Göring, like Himmler and Heydrich an opponent of the pogrom, openly confessed to leaders of the party at the beginning of December that he was 'extremely angry about the whole affair'.[71] Heydrich agreed – partly out of conviction and partly for tactical reasons. In December 1938, during a speech to Wehrmacht officers, he maintained that the pogrom constituted 'the worst blow to state and party' since the Röhm 'revolt' of 1934.[72]

The pogrom of November 1938 was followed by a further wave of anti-Semitic laws: Jews were widely excluded from economic life in Germany, their companies were forcibly Aryanized and the insurance pay-outs for the damage they suffered in the pogroms were confiscated. In a particularly cynical move, they were forced to pay a 'redemption fee' of 1 billion Reichsmarks for the damage caused during Kristallnacht.[73]

Already during the meeting of 12 November, Goebbels and Heydrich had argued in favour of further measures to exclude German Jews from the rest of society. New discriminating legislation was to ban them from theatres, cinemas, public swimming pools and 'German forests'; to separate Jews from Aryans in hospitals and railway carriages; and to confiscate privately owned cars. Most of these suggestions were implemented over the following months, either by national laws, by police orders or on the initiative of local communities.[74] Although arguing against 'ghettoization', Heydrich further proposed that in order to 'assist their identification' Jews should wear a distinguishing mark on their clothing: a yellow star. His suggestion was turned down by Hitler in light of both public opinion and the 'predictable recurrent excesses' against Jews. Although disappointed by his failure to secure Hitler's backing, Heydrich would return to his proposals for the introduction of the yellow star during the Second World War.[75]

Kristallnacht and the increasingly threatening chicanery that followed in its wake had a profound impact on Germany's Jewish community. The panic unleashed by the November pogrom and the loosening of immigration regulations in several countries persuaded more and more Jews to leave the Reich: in 1938 alone, 33,000–40,000 escaped Nazi Germany, and in 1939 a further 75,000–80,000 German Jews left the country. Despite the often extraordinary hardships that they experienced during their exodus, future developments would show that they were right to leave while they still had the opportunity to do so.[76]

The Death of Czechoslovakia

Following the Anschluss of Austria in March 1938, Hitler turned his attention to the Sudetenland, giving increasingly inflammatory speeches and demanding that the largest ethnic minority in Czechoslovakia, the roughly 3.1 million Sudeten Germans living in the western, north-western and south-western border areas of the country, should be reunited with their homeland. The success of the Anschluss had made Hitler confident that he could go further in his expansionist policies. After the feeble reaction of the western European powers to the remilitarization of the Rhineland and the annexation of Austria there seemed no reason why the takeover of the Sudetenland should not go ahead.[77]

Heydrich and his staff accordingly began feverishly preparing an operation plan for the Sipo and the SD in the future occupied areas. The plan envisaged that 'where possible, the SD will follow directly behind the

invading troops and secure, analogously to its duties in the Reich, all
aspects of political life.' In order to fulfil this task, they immediately set up
an arrest list for German emigrants and Czech 'enemies of the state',
notably Communists, Social Democrats, Jews, politicizing priests, saboteurs and members of Otto Strasser's Black Front – a revolutionary and
anti-capitalist splinter group formed after Strasser's expulsion from the
Nazi Party in 1930.[78]

By the late summer of 1938, war between Germany and Czechoslovakia
seemed imminent and both governments initiated a general mobilization.
In September, Heydrich approved the formation of two task forces
(*Einsatzgruppen*), subdivided into eleven *Einsatzkommandos*, to be
deployed from Dresden and Vienna in order to 'safeguard' the newly
conquered territories by arresting those deemed politically dangerous.[79]

War was narrowly avoided at the end of September 1938 when – much
to the horror of most Czechs and their government under Edvard Beneš
– Britain, France and Italy agreed to Germany's annexation of the
Sudetenland in return for Hitler's assurances that he would go no further.
The Czechoslovak government was not consulted on the matter, but had to
capitulate to international pressure, leaving Beneš no other option but to
resign in protest.[80] Simultaneously, Heydrich instructed the *Einsatzgruppen*
that their brief for the arrest of 'undesirables' would apply only to the
Sudetenland, although future deployment in the rest of Czechoslovakia
remained a possibility.[81]

On 1 October, only one day after Edouard Daladier, Neville
Chamberlain, Benito Mussolini and Adolf Hitler had signed the Munich
Agreement, the Wehrmacht marched across the border into Czechoslovakia
and annexed the Sudetenland, where cheering crowds of ethnic Germans
greeted the advancing troops.[82] The two SS *Einsatzgruppen*, 863 men
in total, participated in the campaign as planned. Political opponents,
whose names were collected on a 'special arrest list', were to be detained
immediately. At the same time, Heydrich, referring to previous experiences in Austria, called for 'the strictest discipline', allowing for 'no harassment', 'abuse' or 'unnecessary killings'. It was important that his police
units 'act forcefully and with clear objectives' but 'in a decent manner'.[83]

Just what Heydrich meant by 'decent' became evident over the following
weeks, as the Gestapo and the fanatical volunteers of the Sudeten German
Freikorps arrested between 10,000 and 20,000 vaguely defined Czech
and German 'enemies of the Reich' and expelled numerous Czechs across
the new German border. Some 7,000 of those arrested were sent to
concentration camps in the Reich, notably to Dachau where 2,500 Czechs
and German émigrés were interned. Although the majority of the
internees were released over the coming months, Heydrich explicitly

excluded Communists and other radical opponents of the Nazi state from release.[84]

Knowing what fate would await them under German rule, many people fled the Sudetenland while they still could. An estimated 20,000–30,000 Jews, the vast majority of the Jewish community in the Sudetenland, rushed to the remaining Czechoslovak territories, along with more than 160,000 Czechs and thousands of German anti-fascists.[85] The fate of those who remained showed that the others had been wise to leave: in November 1938, the violence of the Kristallnacht pogrom spread to the Sudetenland, and those Jews who remained were subjected to beatings and looting of their property. By May 1939, the number of Jews in the Sudetenland had declined to fewer than 2,000.[86]

The predominantly German-speaking areas of western and northern Bohemia, northern Moravia and southern Silesia – now renamed as the Reichsgau Sudetenland – were added to the Greater German Reich. While the Western Allies grossly misinterpreted the Munich Agreement as, in the famous words of Chamberlain, a chance for 'peace for our time', the Nazi leadership regarded Munich as no more than a temporary setback to their plans for invading the rest of Czechoslovakia.[87] Occupying the rest of the Czechoslovak state would provide Nazi Germany with additional strategic bases in the north of Bohemia from which to attack Hitler's next victim, Poland, and would also bring major economic resources into the Reich. Furthermore, the Czechoslovak army's large stocks of advanced military equipment would help alleviate bottlenecks in German military supplies.[88]

The opportunity to make good the enforced compromises of the Munich Agreement was provided by the rapid deterioration of relations between Czechs and Slovaks over the issue of financial resources. On 14 March 1939 the Slovak parliament proclaimed the country's independence. Confronted with the imminent dissolution of his state, the President of Czechoslovakia, Emil Hácha, a conservative Catholic and former Supreme Court judge, who had become president following Edvard Beneš's resignation, travelled to Berlin to meet Hitler.[89] Ruthlessly bullied by the Führer and threatened with an imminent attack of German bombers on Prague, the elderly, sick Czech President agreed to the establishment of a German protectorate over his country.[90]

Only two hours later, at six in the morning of 15 March, German troops crossed the Czech border and reached Prague by nine, despite heavy snowfalls. The Czech army, demoralized and under orders not to interfere, remained in its barracks. On the evening of the invasion, Hitler arrived in Prague. Heydrich was with him when the swastika was raised over Hradschin Castle. The following morning, Ribbentrop announced on

Prague radio a decree drafted by the State Secretary of the Ministry of the Interior, Dr Wilhelm Stuckart, which declared that the newly conquered Czech lands were henceforth to be known as the Reich Protectorate of Bohemia and Moravia.[91]

The new leaders quickly established their rule and ensured domestic peace, thanks to the by now well-rehearsed SS-engineered political terror that once again aimed to eliminate existing and potential enemies while frightening the rest of the population into submission. Heydrich once again mobilized two *Einsatzgruppen*, which had already gathered on the German–Czech border on 13 March, before the meeting between Hácha and Hitler had even taken place. Immediately after the German invasion, a curfew was imposed in Prague. As the diplomat George Kennan, watching from the American Embassy, observed that night, 'Prague's streets, usually so animated, are now completely empty and deserted. Tomorrow, to be sure, they would fill with life again, but it would not be the same life that had filled them before; and we were all acutely conscious that in this case, the curfew had indeed tolled the knell of a long and distinctly tragic day.'[92]

While Kennan bemoaned the death of democratic Czechoslovakia, Heydrich's men were already busy confiscating files in the occupied territory. Shortly thereafter, within the framework of the so-called *Aktion Gitter* (Operation Grid), they began arresting hundreds of Communists and German émigrés. By May they had detained a total of some 6,000 political enemies, around 1,500 of whom the Gestapo deported to concentration camps within the Reich. It would not be until 1 September that the Security Police's legal status in the Protectorate of Bohemia and Moravia was established by law. In the meantime, Heydrich's men exercised an unrestricted tyranny for nearly six months.[93]

By the summer of 1938, Heydrich had every reason to be confident about the future. Not only had he set up a highly successful repression apparatus in the previous years and assumed the leading role in the persecution of Jews in Nazi Germany. The Anschluss of Austria, the annexation of the Sudetenland and the occupation of Bohemia and Moravia had also demonstrated his ability to master new challenges outside the territory of the Reich. As his responsibilities increased further over the coming months, so too would his determination to carry them out with ruthless energy and extreme violence.

Tannenberg

Following the occupation of Austria, the Sudetenland, Bohemia and Moravia, Nazi Germany began to send more conciliatory signals to

London, but behind the rhetoric of peace, German preparations for war accelerated. The formerly German Baltic town of Danzig – a free city under international administration since the conclusion of the 1919 Paris Peace accords – had been a bone of German–Polish contention ever since, and bilateral relations deteriorated further in the late 1930s. As intended, the occupation of Bohemia and Moravia had bolstered Germany's military capabilities and provided the Wehrmacht with important military bases for the planned attack on Poland. Furthermore, by the last week of August, the signing of the Hitler–Stalin Pact, with its secret protocol dividing Eastern Europe into German and Soviet spheres of influence, smoothed the way for the Nazi invasion of western Poland. Despite his militant anti-Communism, Heydrich welcomed the pact, because he wrongly believed that it would now be impossible for Britain to enter into a conflict with Nazi Germany without also having to declare war on the Soviet Union, which would occupy the eastern half of Poland.[94]

Heydrich's Gestapo and SD had prepared for war against Poland since the spring of 1939. In early May, Heydrich received orders from Hitler via Himmler for his forthcoming tasks in Poland. The Security Police would 'neutralize' centres of potential resistance and destroy those classes of society thought to be carriers of Polish nationalism. In the SD Main Office, a special desk was set up to process all matters relating to 'Germandom in Poland' and to establish a card index carrying the names of those who should be targeted once war broke out.[95] The card index was used to compile a 'special arrest list', which carried the names of some 61,000 Poles to be arrested or killed immediately. It included the names of Poles who had fought in one way or another against ethnic German Poles during the troubles in Upper Silesia after the First World War, nationalist politicians, Communists, Freemasons, Jews and leading Catholic clerics. Heydrich insisted on being personally informed of new developments on a daily basis.[96]

The codename for the operation was Tannenberg – a name that curiously invoked memories of both the fifteenth-century defeat of the Teutonic Knights at the hands of Polish and Lithuanian troops and the German victory over Russian armies in the Battle of Tannenberg in August 1914. Rather than celebrating the Teutonic Knights' defeat, the name reflected a romanticized reading of the medieval past: inspired by a mythologised past, the Nazis saw themselves *re*conquering land that the German knights had won, settled and lost many centuries before. Only this time their motivation would be guided not by Christian missionary zeal but by an eminently modern idea: the commitment to the 'science' of race.[97]

Exhausted by his exertions in the preceding month, Heydrich took a holiday and headed for Fehmarn. Private film footage from these days shows a seemingly untroubled Heydrich relaxing by playing sports and gardening.[98] While he was enjoying the fresh air of the Baltic Sea, his deputy in Berlin, Werner Best, selected the leaders of the individual *Einsatzkommandos* from the ranks of the Security Police and the SD.[99] Before Heydrich left for his holiday, he had convened a meeting in his Berlin home with his closest staff members – Werner Best, Heinrich Müller, Heinz Jost, Walter Schellenberg and Helmut Knochen – in order to discuss 'the most fundamental questions' of the impending attack on Poland, during which the deployment of 2,000 men in four equally sized task forces was agreed.[100]

The men appointed to lead the task forces and their various sub-units, the *Einsatzkommandos*, were senior SD and Security Police officers, mostly well-educated, middle-class men in their late twenties to mid-thirties who had turned to the far right during the Weimar Republic. Heydrich insisted on appointing individuals who possessed the 'relevant experience and faultless military bearing'.[101] Many of the more senior commanders such as Emanuel Schäfer, Lothar Beutel, Josef Meisinger and Heydrich's friend from the early SS days in Hamburg, Bruno Streckenbach, had served in the violent Freikorps campaigns of the early 1920s. Many of them could also build on practical experiences gathered during the annex-ation of Austria and Czechoslovakia. Heydrich by no means regarded their deployment in the field as a punishment but rather as an opportunity to prove the value of the SS's 'fighting administration' under fire.[102]

Even though the assembly of the SS task forces proceeded without problems during Heydrich's holiday, the nature of the working relation-ship between the *Einsatzgruppen* and the Wehrmacht remained unclear. The Wehrmacht commanders had been informed of the planned deploy-ment of SS units during the forthcoming Polish campaign in the spring of 1939. Yet the escalation of SS violence during the conquest of Austria, Bohemia and Moravia had raised concerns within the army leadership about an all too independent SS acting on its own initiative in the occupied territories.[103]

In order to clarify the command relations between the army and the Einsatzgruppen during the forthcoming campaign, Heydrich and Best met with the chief of staff of the army's General Quartermaster, Eduard Wagner, on 29 August. As Wagner noted in his diary after the meeting: 'We came to a quick agreement. Both rather inscrutable types. Heydrich particularly disagreeable.'[104] According to the agreement, Security Police commanders were required to maintain close working relationships with all local military commanders, the heads of the civil administration and

Kurt Daluege's Order Police. A liaison officer from each *Einsatzgruppe* was to be named to ensure 'frictionless communications' with the relevant military and police officials.[105]

According to the 'Guidelines for the Foreign Operations of the Sipo and SD' drafted by Werner Best and signed by Heydrich on 31 July, the *Einsatzgruppen* were instructed to 'render impotent' the 'leading stratum of the population of Poland' and to 'combat all elements in enemy territory to the rear of the fighting troops who are hostile to the Reich and the German people'.[106] These tasks were part of a concerted effort to 'neutralize' centres of real and potential resistance. The lack of clarity as to what exactly was meant by 'neutralization' and who was to be subjected to it would give individual commanders in the field considerable leeway in interpreting their brief – a characteristic element of Heydrich's leadership style and one that encouraged his men to show initiative. At the same time, the SD was to establish an intelligence network in the field, made up of members of the German minority, and to collect and confiscate material pertaining to Jews, Freemasons and Catholic clergymen in Poland.[107]

In terms of content, the regulations contained in these directives provided little that was new: the sections dealing with the tasks of the *Einsatzgruppen* and their relationship with the Wehrmacht were largely identical to the instructions sent to the task forces during the invasion of the Sudetenland. One of the few differences was that this time the instructions contained a section on racial hygiene, forbidding all sexual relations with women of non-German origin as a 'sin against one's own blood', and threatening that 'violations' of this order would be 'severely punished'. At the same time, the guidelines contained regulations that stood in profound contrast to the subsequent actions of the *Einsatzgruppen*. For example, they stated that 'the mistreatment or killing of detained persons is strictly prohibited and, to the extent that it is undertaken by other persons, it is to be prevented. Force may be used only to break up resistance.'[108]

Although the formulations contained in these guidelines appear relatively innocuous when compared to the reality of the invasion, neither Heydrich nor the Wehrmacht leadership had any illusions about the radical nature of the approaching war against Poland. At a meeting with some fifty senior army commanders at the Berghof on 22 August 1939, Hitler talked of the 'destruction of Poland' and 'brutal approaches'.[109] On 29 August, the day of the meeting between Heydrich and Wagner, the latter informed the Chief of the Army General Staff, General Franz Halder, that the *Einsatzgruppen* would arrest some 30,000 Poles and deport them to concentration camps.[110]

In mid-August, at a conference in Berlin, leading members of the *Einsatzgruppen* received further oral instructions from Heydrich and Best, instructions which even by Heydrich's standards were 'extraordinarily radical' and which included a 'liquidation order for various circles of the Polish leadership' affecting 'thousands'.[111] According to post-war trial testimonies of leading task-force officers present that day, Heydrich opened the meeting by informing the men of the atrocities being committed against ethnic Germans in Poland, noting that he expected heavy partisan resistance against the German invasion. It was the responsibility of the *Einsatzgruppen* to 'neutralize' these threats – particularly those posed by saboteurs, partisans, Jews and the Polish intelligentsia – in areas conquered by the German army, and to punish individuals who had committed crimes against Poland's ethnic Germans in the preceding weeks. Although carefully guarded in his language, Heydrich insisted that in carrying out their difficult tasks, 'everything was allowed'.[112]

Heydrich's SD was also assigned the role of staging armed border violations immediately prior to the planned attack, which could then be blamed on the Polish side and used to justify the start of the war. Hitler had announced to his generals at the Berghof on 22 August that he would give 'a propagandistic reason for starting the war, no matter whether it is plausible or not'. Heydrich managed this top-secret operation himself and in mid-August he personally showed Himmler the border sections he had in mind. The co-ordination of the mission was left in the capable hands of Herbert Mehlhorn, the SD lawyer who had advised Heydrich in his family disputes over the Halle Conservatory in the mid-1930s.[113]

On 31 August, small SS units under the command of Alfred Naujocks, dressed in Polish uniforms, attacked the radio station in Gleiwitz, a customs house and a forestry lodge along the German–Polish border in order to stage, as Hitler called it the following day, Polish 'frontier violations of a nature no longer tolerable for a great power'. The men proceeded to broadcast declarations in German and Polish through the Gleiwitz station. They left behind a number of dead concentration-camp prisoners who had been murdered and stuck into Polish uniforms.[114]

That same night in Berlin, Heydrich wrote his testament, drafted as a private letter to his wife and signed at 2 a.m. on 1 September 1939, less than three hours before the beginning of the German invasion of Poland. Heydrich instructed his staff to keep this letter in the safe of his office and to hand it to his wife only 'when I am no longer alive'.

Dearest Lina, my beloved Children! I hope that this letter will never leave my safe. However, both as a soldier of the Führer and as a good husband and father I have to consider all possibilities. The Führer of our Greater Germany, Adolf Hitler, whose handshake earlier this evening continues to burn in my hand, has already made the great decision: tomorrow morning at 4.45 a.m. the German armies will march into Poland; the Reichstag will convene at 10 a.m. I do not believe that anything will happen to me. But if fate chooses differently then all my worldly possessions shall be yours ... Dearest Lina, I believe that even though the past weeks have been impossibly difficult for both of us (notably your lack of faith in me has, due to its unclear foundation, profoundly hurt me), they have nevertheless deepened and strengthened our relationship. Educate our children to become firm believers in the Führer and Germany; to be true to the ideas of the Nazi movement. [Make sure] that they strictly adhere to the eternal laws of the SS, that they are hard towards themselves, kind and generous towards our own people and Germany and merciless towards all internal and external enemies of the Reich ... My dearest Lina, I am not without faults. I have made mistakes, both professional and human, both in thought and in deed, but my love for you and my children is boundless. Please remember our life together with respect and fondness. And once time has healed the wounds, you must give our children a new father. But he has to be a real man *[ein Kerl]*, the kind of man I aspired to be. In endless love, Heil Hitler, Reinhard[115]

Heydrich's deeply personal letter, written exclusively for his wife's consumption, illustrates how far he had developed since he entered the SS in 1931. He had successfully reinvented himself as a model Nazi and firmly believed in his new identity. The mention of the Führer's 'burning' handshake, the precise instructions given for the upbringing of his children and his insistence that Lina remarry a 'real man' in the true Nazi spirit, all testify to a rare certainty of purpose and ideological commitment that was largely a result of formative experiences within the SS.

For Heydrich, the outbreak of the Second World War represented an unprecedented opportunity. He had spent the first six years of the Third Reich as Himmler's first lieutenant, developing an ever-expanding political police apparatus that was intricately linked with the SS. Now, against the background of the war, intoxicating new possibilities arose. Neither Heydrich nor anyone else in the Nazi leadership had a blueprint for the future of Eastern Europe, but it was clear from the start that Poland – unlike the racially allied Austria and the economically vital Protectorate of Bohemia and Moravia – would become some sort of laboratory for Nazi experiments in racial imperialism and ethnic engineering. The kind of utopia that Hitler, Himmler and Heydrich intended to implement in the yet to be occupied territories remained blurry and unspecified. What was clear was that its implementation would not be limited by the same kind of 'restraint' imposed on the SS during the military campaigns of 1938. The German attack on Poland, launched in the early morning hours of 1 September, was to become a watershed for the Third Reich's war of annihilation against the 'lesser races' of the East.[116]

CHAPTER VI

◆

Experiments with Mass Murder

The Invasion of Poland

INVADED FROM THREE SIDES, UNAIDED BY ITS WESTERN ALLIES AND confronted with a militarily superior German army, the poorly prepared Polish troops were in a hopeless situation. Although the defenders put up a valiant fight, staging a counter-attack at Kutno on 9 September 1939 and inflicting unexpectedly heavy losses on the invading Germans, the Wehrmacht quickly advanced on Warsaw. On 17 September, the day the Red Army marched into Eastern Poland in accordance with the secret clause of the Hitler–Stalin Pact, the Polish government fled to Romania. Warsaw fell at the end of the month and the last Polish troops surrendered on 6 October.[1]

Behind the regular troops, Heydrich's five – later seven – SS task forces swiftly moved across the border and descended on Poland's civilian population, informing Heydrich personally of the 'progress' of their work through daily reports. The conquest of Poland, widely perceived by the Nazis as a racially inferior country, significantly expanded conceptions of what was possible and permissible. The SS-engineered terror unleashed in the first days of the invasion far exceeded Heydrich's previous campaigns of violence, persecution and discrimination in the Reich itself after 1933 and in Austria, Bohemia and Moravia after 1938.[2]

The task forces in Poland liberally interpreted their brief to eliminate the 'enemies of the state' behind German lines, and to shoot 'hostages' or 'partisans' in retaliation for any sign of hostility towards the invaders. SS units rounded up politically undesirable Poles, professionals and intelligentsia, either shooting them on the spot or putting them in concentration camps, and thus following Heydrich's insistence that a comprehensive strike against Poland's broadly defined elites should be carried out swiftly and be completed by the beginning of November.[3]

Polish atrocities against ethnic Germans offered a welcome pretext for SS retaliation. In the first week of the war, Polish soldiers and civilians, reacting to real or alleged cases of sabotage by the German minority, arrested some 10,000–15,000 ethnic Germans and force-marched them eastwards. Attacked by Polish neighbours and soldiers, between 4,500 and 6,000 ethnic German civilians were killed during the first days of the campaign, some as a result of maltreatment during the forced marches, others through mass shootings by regular Polish troops.[4]

Rumours of ethnic German civilian snipers firing on retreating Polish troops also exacerbated an already tense atmosphere. Simultaneously, an almost neurotic fear of partisans or 'Francs-Tireurs' operating in the rear of the rapidly advancing German troops, coupled with widely held anti-Polish sentiments, spread among the army leadership, creating a climate in which harsh 'policing actions' seemed not only acceptable but desirable. 'A difficult battle with [Polish] insurgents has erupted,' the army's General Quartermaster, Eduard Wagner, noted as early as 3 September, emphasizing that this form of resistance 'can be broken only through the use of draconian measures'. Three days later, both Wagner and the Chief of the General Staff, Franz Halder, demanded an increase of special police forces for the army's rear to combat partisans.[5]

The general atmosphere of nervousness and fear worked in the SS leadership's favour. When, on 3 September, two days after the beginning of the German invasion, more than one hundred local ethnic German Poles were murdered and mutilated in the Pomeranian city of Bromberg (Bydgoszcz), Heydrich and Himmler recognized the massacre as a welcome opportunity for an intensification of their activities. Not only did the atrocities against German civilians in Bromberg seem to justify violent transgressions by the *Einsatzgruppen*, but, in Heydrich's and Himmler's view, they also called for an extension of the task forces' 'anti-partisan' mission, as outlined in the agreement between the army and the SS prior to the outbreak of war, as well as for greater autonomy from a Wehrmacht leadership allegedly unable or unwilling to 'pacify' the rearward areas of newly occupied Poland.[6]

On the very day of 'Bromberg's Bloody Sunday', Himmler authorized the formation of an additional *Einsatzgruppe*, the 'Special Purpose task force' under the command of Udo von Woyrsch – a notoriously radical member of the Lower Silesian nobility – to 'safeguard' Upper Silesia's industrial areas, and issued his infamous order to 'radically suppress' the 'uprising' with 'all means available', calling for all 'insurgents' to be 'shot on the spot' without trial. One week later, on 10 September, Himmler ordered *Einsatzgruppe* IV to arrest 500 Polish hostages in Bromberg, preferably intellectuals and Communists, who were to be 'ruthlessly shot at the slightest sign of upheaval or resistance attempts'.[7]

In order to make sure that their men were fulfilling their tasks as intended, Himmler and Heydrich embarked on an inspection tour of the task forces in western Poland between 3 and 13 September, leaving Werner Best to take over Heydrich's responsibilities as head of the Security Police during his absence.[8] Their presence had a distinctly radicalizing effect on the task forces. On 11 September, Heydrich met two of his *Einsatzgruppen* commanders, Bruno Streckenbach and Udo von Woyrsch, in the recently conquered city of Kraków (Krakau). Heydrich reiterated that the harshest possible measures were to be taken against insurgents. Jews in particular were to be 'induced' to flee across the German–Soviet demarcation line. Woyrsch was well qualified to carry out this task, having overseen some of the worst anti-Jewish massacres of the Polish campaign over the previous days when his task force embarked on a killing spree in East Upper Silesia, resulting in the death of some 500 Jews in Katowice (Kattowitz), Będzin (Bendzin) and Sosnowiec (Sasnowitz). As a direct result of the meeting with Heydrich in Kraków, Woyrsch's task force doubled its efforts to terrorize the Jewish population into flight, burning a group of Jews alive in a synagogue in Dynów and carrying out mass shootings in a variety of locations across the countryside.[9]

Although Hitler had indicated to his most senior generals, Walther von Brauchitsch and Willhelm Keitel, that his plans called for the 'physical annihilation' of Poland's intellectual, social and political elites, the army commanders in the field were given no explicit instructions regarding Hitler's mandate for shootings and expulsions. Over the first weeks of the Polish campaign, Himmler and Heydrich consciously left the army leadership in the dark about the 'extraordinarily radical' order they had received from Hitler, and in so doing they proved their loyalty to the Führer. Even if they were 'wrongly' accused by the army of committing 'random' and 'brutal' acts of violence – so Heydrich explained in a letter to the head of the Order Police, Kurt Daluege – they were willing to accept sole responsibility for these acts, thus protecting Hitler from any criticism for authorizing atrocities.[10]

Yet while a great number of army leaders, concerned by what they considered serious lapses in military discipline, frowned upon the violent excesses of the SS and some even sought to have men like Udo von Woyrsch court-martialled, the initial response to Heydrich's harsh 'policing actions' was not uniformly negative: many junior military commanders on the ground actively supported the SS's cleansing campaign. In the days that followed the massacre of ethnic Germans in Bromberg, for example, the army turned over 500 prisoners to the SS for execution, and a sweep of one of the neighbourhoods of the city netted another 900 prisoners, of whom 120 were immediately shot in nearby woods and fields. In addition, fifty pupils from a local school were executed after one of them fired at a German officer, while the army itself shot another fifty civilian hostages, most of them priests, teachers or civil servants. In all, it is estimated that at least 1,300 Polish civilians were killed in Bromberg between 5 and 12 September by members of Einsatzgruppe IV, with as many as 5,000 deaths estimated in the wider region.[11]

German atrocities were by no means confined to Bromberg and were not only carried out by the *Einsatzgruppen*. Ordinary army units, military police and ethnic German militias were also involved. More than 12,000 executions were carried out in September alone, with a further 4,200 taking place in October. At the same time, the *Einsatzgruppen* undertook more than 10,000 arrests in fulfilment of their assignment to 'neutralize' potential anti-German elements of the population. All in all, more than 40,000 Poles fell victim to the mass killings between September and December 1939.[12]

In fulfilling their gruesome tasks, the *Einsatzgruppen* were also actively supported by the so-called *Volksdeutscher Selbstschutz*, a civilian militia formed in early September and composed of ethnic German Poles. Having lived under Polish rule for nearly twenty years, many of these ethnic Germans had been subjected to acts of violence in the weeks immediately before and after the outbreak of the war. Suddenly thrust into a position of power and intoxicated by the opportunity to settle old scores, those who joined the *Selbstschutz* went on a rampage of violence, killing thousands of Polish civilians, most notably in West Prussia where ethnic conflict had a long-standing tradition and racial hatred had been intensified by Nazi agitation in the months leading up to the war. Under the leadership of Himmler's personal adjutant, Ludolf von Alvensleben, the West Prussian *Selbstschutz* soon acquired particular notoriety, killing more than 4,000 Poles by 5 October.[13]

Heydrich, always critical of *unsystematic* terror, considered some of the Selbstschutz's atrocities 'impossible', not so much because of the ethnic Germans' 'understandable' rage, but because he feared that they were 'uncontrollable' and easily exploitable by enemy propaganda. More specifically, he objected to the widespread theft and plunder that went hand in hand with the *Selbstschutz's* activities. In line with his twisted understanding of decent and indecent behaviour, Heydrich condoned and even demanded the murder of 'suspect' Jews and Poles, but abhorred crimes committed against property, including the plundering of Jewish-owned shops. He frequently initiated internal investigations against SS men suspected of such crimes.[14]

Heydrich's attitude to theft warrants further explanation. In his view, theft – unlike the killing of political enemies – was a crime committed out

of inferior motives. Furthermore, given that the property of Jewish expellees would be confiscated, that property now no longer belonged to
the Jews but to the German people. In other words: his men were
stealing from their own people and that could not be tolerated under any
circumstances.[15]

During his inspection tour of south-western Poland, Heydrich was thus
pressing for more systematic and less random cleansing operations,
leading to the targeted but comprehensive liquidation of previously identified 'enemy groups' deemed especially dangerous to pacification. At the
same time, he felt that the conservative army leadership was hindering
that task. On 8 September, in a conversation with the head of military
intelligence, Wilhelm Canaris, his former naval superior, Berlin neighbour
and occasional riding companion, Heydrich complained bitterly about the
army's lack of understanding regarding the SS enforcement of pressing
'security measures' behind the lines. He also expressed his dissatisfaction
over the German military courts' apparent reluctance to sentence Polish
partisans to death. The 200 executions per day currently enforced by the
military courts were absolutely insufficient, he argued in a fit of anger, and
if he had his way, the time-consuming practice of holding military tribu-
nals for suspects would be abandoned altogether. Enemies of the Reich,
he concluded, should 'be shot or hanged immediately without trial. We
can show mercy to the common people, but the nobility, the Catholic
clergy and the Jews must be killed.' As soon as Warsaw was conquered, a
new agreement with the army would have to be reached on 'how we
should squeeze out all of these elements'.[16]

Canaris was appalled and reported Heydrich's comments to Lieutenant
General Carl-Heinrich von Stülpnagel, who in turn transmitted the
information to General Halder. Halder already knew about the atrocities
committed by Heydrich's *Einsatzgruppen*, telling the general staff office
Lieutenant Colonel Helmuth Groscurth on 9 September that 'the
butchery of Poles behind the front was intensifying at such a rapid pace
that the army would probably have to take measures against these acts
soon'. Halder admitted that it was Hitler's and Göring's intention 'to
destroy and exterminate the Polish people'. The rest of what Halder told
him, Groscurth noted in his diary, was so horrible it 'could not be
committed to paper'.[17]

When, on 12 September, Canaris drew the attention of the chief of the
German army's High Command, General Wilhelm Keitel, to Heydrich's
plans for large-scale executions, stressing that 'the nobility and clergy will be
exterminated' and warning him that 'the world will hold the Wehrmacht
responsible' for allowing these atrocities to happen, Keitel answered that this
matter had 'already been decided by the Führer'. Hitler had made it clear to

him that he aimed to destroy Poland's intellectual and political elite, and that he had ordered the shootings as part of the 'political cleansing' of newly conquered Polish territory. If the army did not wish to have anything to do with the 'ethnic exterminations', it would have to accept that the SS and civilian militias would carry out the liquidations independently.[18]

Hitler's endorsement of SS policies was hardly surprising. Even before the German invasion, on 22 August, he had announced to German generals that the military campaign against Poland required a 'brutal approach' and the 'greatest toughness', a stance that was further radicalized by the subsequent attacks on ethnic Germans in Poland.[19] Shortly after the Bromberg massacre, on 11 September, the Army High Command officially notified General Adolf Strauss, commander of the Fourth Army, that Hitler had authorized Himmler to arrest 500 hostages in Bromberg and that summary executions were to be carried out until the city was 'pacified'. The army was explicitly ordered not to hinder the *Einsatzgruppen* in carrying out their task. Receiving this order, Strauss was less concerned about the mass killings themselves than by the apparent loss of the army's executive powers to the *Einsatzgruppen*, complaining to the Army High Command that the order would lead to a 'total reversal of responsibilities'.[20]

By the time Heydrich had returned to Berlin from his inspection tour of the task forces in the field, the smouldering conflict between the Wehrmacht and the SS over executive competences in occupied Poland was threatening to escalate. On 18 September, Brauchitsch reminded the army commanders in the field that the Wehrmacht was the sole executive authority in the occupied territories and that orders from any party agency affecting the judicial autonomy of the military courts were to be ignored. This was a scarcely concealed blow against SS ambitions. On the very same day, Himmler reiterated his earlier order to the Security Police commanders in the operational area that 'all members of Polish insurgent groups are to be shot'. The military commanders in Poland were once again not informed of this order.[21]

In view of the mounting tensions between the SS and the army leadership, Heydrich and Wagner met again on 19 September and engaged in 'a highly important, necessary and open' conversation about the rapidly deteriorating relationship between the Wehrmacht and the *Einsatzgruppen*. Wagner insisted that the army be informed of the *Einsatzgruppen*'s exact tasks. In response, Heydrich confirmed that the task assigned to him by Hitler was the 'fundamental cleansing' of Jews, clergy and nobility from Poland. Wagner did not object to the planned liquidations as such, but he was keen to keep the army dissociated from them. In particular, he and Heydrich agreed that the 'ground sweeping' operation should only be carried out after the military administration over Poland had come to an end.[22]

Although the terms of the agreement necessitated a delay in what he considered to be pressing policing actions, Heydrich was nonetheless pleased with the outcome of the meeting. That same afternoon, he informed his senior staff that 'a highly advantageous result' had been achieved. Even if the *Einsatzgruppen* would continue to be formally subordinate to the army commanders, they would nonetheless receive their orders directly from him.[23]

The following day, Hitler authorized the agreement that had been reached between Heydrich and Wagner. In a meeting with Heydrich, Himmler and Brauchitsch, the Führer reassured an uneasy Brauchitsch that major ethnic cleansing campaigns would begin only after executive power had been handed over by the army to a civilian administration. Adjusting to these new realities, Brauchitsch informed his army commanders on 21 September that the *Einsatzgruppen* had been ordered by the Führer 'to carry out certain ethnic tasks in the occupied territory'. He chose not to elaborate on the nature of these tasks, but insisted that their execution would lie 'outside the responsibilities' of the army commanders. Close consultation with the Security Police was to continue to ensure that police activities would not hinder army operations.[24]

That Brauchitsch was not happy with this turn of events became clear in a subsequent meeting with Heydrich the following day. Brauchitsch again insisted that the army should be informed of all orders given to the *Einsatzgruppen* and also made it clear that he wanted Himmler's order to shoot 'insurgents' without trial rescinded. Heydrich agreed to have the order withdrawn and to provide the army leadership with continuous information about *Einsatzgruppen* activities. At the same time, he reiterated his criticism of the apparently slow pace of the court-martial process. Brauchitsch refused to concede the point, but stated that in order to expedite the trials he had authorized the establishment of additional military courts. He did not articulate any reservations about future ethnic-cleansing policies and shootings, provided that the implementation of these policies were postponed until after the military administration of Poland had ended, thus avoiding a situation in which the armies' reputation abroad would be tarnished or its position as the executive power in Poland undermined by the SS.[25]

After Brauchitsch had left, Wagner succeeded in extracting from Heydrich the assurance that the most notorious *Einsatzgruppe*, under the command of Woyrsch, would be withdrawn from Poland. Heydrich was deeply dissatisfied. Wagner, on the other hand, was jubilant. In a letter to his wife he wrote that he had dealt 'a great blow to invisible forces'.[26]

Brauchitsch and Wagner had successfully wrung concessions from Heydrich, but if the Army High Command believed that Heydrich intended to play according to their rules, they were wrong. Although he officially reminded the *Einsatzgruppen* commanders in September that military operations in Poland should not be disturbed and ordered that the shooting of insurgents was to be carried out only 'in cases of emergency', Heydrich also ordered his men to 'overburden' the military courts systematically to the extent 'that they can no longer function properly'. He further demanded that a record be kept of all sentences handed out by the army's courts so that he would be aware of any judgements that did not call for the death penalty. Presumably he intended to keep these records both as incriminating proof of the military courts' inefficiency and for future reference in the next rounds of killings.[27]

Since Brauchitsch never communicated any details of Hitler's decision to wage ethnic warfare in Poland to his military commanders in the field, many among the officer corps objected both to the randomness of the *Einsatzgruppen* violence and to what they perceived as an SS challenge to their role as the sole executive power in the newly occupied territories. Unease about SS methods turned into unmistakable and open criticism when the military commander-in-chief in Poland, Colonel General Johannes Blaskowitz, condemned them as 'criminal atrocities, maltreatment and plundering' and signs of the SS's 'animal and pathological instincts'.[28]

When Blaskowitz's report was passed on to Führer headquarters on 27 November 1939, a furious Hitler expressed his frustration over the Wehrmacht's 'maudlin sentimentality', and responded to Blaskowitz's criticism by offering an amnesty for all those who had committed atrocities against Poland's civilian population during the invasion and by ending the military courts' jurisdiction over the SS. If anything, the Wehrmacht's complaints reinforced Hitler's determination that the emerging German civil administration in Poland should be an instrument of, rather than an obstacle to, Nazi racial policy.[29]

Building a New Racial Order

Long before the beginning of the military campaign in September 1939, it had been clear to Heydrich that Poland would be treated differently from the previous two areas of Nazi expansion, Austria and Czechoslovakia. Throughout the summer, Hitler had repeatedly asserted that the war against Poland would entail a 'harsh racial struggle'. Unlike many Wehrmacht commanders who deluded themselves about the true nature of the conflict ahead of them, Heydrich had immediately understood the implications and opportunities of Hitler's exhortations. The task that lay ahead of him required both energetic ruthlessness in combating Germany's enemies and the development of substantial policy plans to implement

Hitler's vague ideological pronouncements. Heydrich also understood better than some of the Wehrmacht's senior officers that those implementing the policies most attuned to Hitler's wishes would be rewarded with enhanced powers to enforce them.

Yet plans for what was going to happen to the majority of Poles remained uncertain. As Heydrich explained during a meeting with senior SS officers in Berlin on 7 September, a general consensus existed within the Nazi leadership on a break-up of independent Poland and a 'neutralization' of anti-German elements through mass arrests and shootings. Apart from that, Hitler had decided on very few concrete policies. All that was certain at this point was that the 'primitive population' not immediately affected by the current cleansing operations would 'receive no special education' and would be 'suppressed in some way'.[30]

On 20 September, in the euphoria of an imminent victory over Poland, Hitler approved SS proposals for the future of Poland. As Heydrich informed his senior staff and *Einsatzgruppen* commanders in Berlin the following day and again on 29 September, it had been decided that Poland would effectively disappear from the map. The Polish territory now under Nazi control would be divided into three ethnically homogenized zones: one German, one Polish and a small Jewish 'reservation'. The formerly German border areas of West Prussia, the Warthegau region around Poznań (Posen) and the extended province of Upper Silesia were to become purely German through the expulsion of all Poles, Jews and Gypsies, as well as through the resettlement of ethnic Germans from those territories in Eastern Europe that had recently come under Soviet control in fulfilment of the secret terms of the 1939 Hitler–Stalin Pact. That task in itself was enormous: in the territories to be brought into the Reich lived 8.9 million Poles, 603,000 Jews and a mere 600,000 ethnic Germans. An 'Eastern Wall', a fortified ring of German settlements, would surround these new German provinces, shielding them from the 'foreign-speaking' Polish and Jewish zones, the latter of which was to be established in the furthest, most eastern part of the now Nazi-controlled area.[31]

Heydrich had every reason to see Hitler's decision for a fourth partition as a green light for further harshness in pursuing the SS's policies of ethnic 'unweaving' in Poland. His apparatus accordingly began preparations for the large-scale deportation of Poles from the incorporated territories, to be carried out as soon as the military administration had been passed into civilian hands.[32] As a preliminary step towards the 'solution of the Polish problem', the *Einsatzgruppen* were to draw up further lists of significant leaders to be sent to concentration camps, as well as lists of various professional and middle-class groups to be expelled into the

Polish 'rump territory' soon to be known as the General Government. The remaining 'primitive Poles' were to be gradually deported from West Prussia to the 'foreign-speaking *Gau*' in the Kraków region, while 'adolescent Polish elements' were to be exploited as seasonal migrant workers.[33]

On 6 October, the day after his triumphant visit to recently conquered Warsaw, Hitler publicly referred to these decisions when he declared in a speech before the Reichstag that the 'most important task' resulting from Poland's collapse was the 'ethnic reordering' of East-Central Europe.[34] The day after his speech, he formally assigned to Himmler the enormous task of organizing this ethnic reordering by appointing him Reich Commissar for the Strengthening of Germandom (RKFDV), thus giving the SS a second power base – in addition to the police – in Polish territory. Hitler set Himmler two interrelated tasks: to keep Poles and Jews under surveillance in order to 'eliminate' their 'harmful influence' and, by deporting hundreds of thousands of them from their homes in Western Poland, to create the precondition for the second task: the 'repatriation' of hundreds of thousands of ethnic Germans scattered across Eastern-Central Europe, the Baltic States and Russia, to the newly annexed territories of Western Poland.[35]

The decision to place the SS leadership in charge of the ethnic unweaving of the conquered territories was both surprising and momentous. For ideological reasons, Himmler and Heydrich had long shown interest in the so-called *Volksdeutsche* – people of German descent living outside the Reich's borders, often as a result of the redrawing of maps in the aftermath of the First World War. But, until 1939, the SS had had no experience in practical settlement work. Just as in 1933–4, when the two men acquired control over the political police in the German states without any prior experience in police work, Heydrich and Himmler had to improvise. What secured Himmler's appointment as RKFDV was primarily his ideological reliability, which seemed to guarantee a speedy implementation of Hitler's wishes.

The need to resettle ethnic Germans from the now Soviet-occupied Baltic States went hand in hand with Hitler's far-reaching decision in the autumn of 1939 to annex the Western Polish territories now under German occupation and to transform them permanently into German living space. The two newly created *Reichsgaue*, Danzig-West Prussia and Wartheland, were to be ethnically cleansed of Poles and Jews, who were to be deported to Central Poland – the so-called General Government – before being replaced by ethnic German settlers from the Soviet Union and South-Eastern Europe. This was nothing short of an order for a revolutionary unweaving and reordering of Central and Eastern European ethnicities, affecting hundreds of thousands of people.

For Heydrich, too, the new task of unleashing a violent wave of ethnic engineering significantly expanded his responsibilities. The intended resettlement of hundreds of thousands of people necessitated the creation of a sizeable new apparatus under Heydrich's control. On Himmler's orders, a Central Office for Immigration (*Einwandererzentralstelle* or EWZ) was established in mid-December, with branch offices in Posen (Poznań), Litzmannstadt (Łódź) and Gotenhafen (Gdyna). With the help of racial experts from the Race and Settlement Main Office, the agency was to undertake racial tests of ethnic Germans and to decide where to resettle them. Its counterpart, also based in Posen with subsidiary offices in other Polish cities, was the Central Office for Emigration (Umwandererzentralstelle or UWZ), which was responsible for the racial screening and expulsion of Poles and Jews from the annexed territories. The main tools of terror and resettlement – the Security Police, the *Einsatzgruppen*, the UWZ and the EWZ – were now all concentrated in the hands of the SS leadership.[36]

While the scale of the task ahead may have been historically unprecedented, the policies employed by Himmler and Heydrich were not. More or less co-ordinated waves of ethnic or religious 'unmixing', deportations and murder had already occurred on a massive scale in South-eastern Europe between the Eastern Crisis of the 1870s, during which large-scale anti-Ottoman violence errupted in the Caucasus and the Balkans, and the immediate aftermath of the First World War, a period during which hundreds of thousands of the Ottoman Empire's Muslims, Christian Armenians and Orthodox Greeks were expelled or murdered. The genuinely modern idea of creating ethnically homogeneous nation-states through the suppression, expulsion and often murder of 'suspect' minorities was by no means a Nazi invention. Instead it followed a logic of Social Darwinism and sociological positivism – the idea that human society could be perfected through scientific quantification, ethnic categorization and, if necessary, violent unmixing. A similar logic had already guided the Turkish perpetrators of the Armenian genocide and the Bolshevik approach to class enemies. The main difference from these precedents was that the Nazi project of social and ethnic engineering was not based on the somewhat firmer categories of religion or class. Rather it was founded on the slippery concept of race that left ample room for different interpretations. While Heydrich and the SS leadership in general insisted on the rigid application of supposedly objective criteria for racial segregation, some of the civilian authorities in occupied Europe took a more lax stance. The Gauleiter of Danzig – West Prussia, Albert Forster, for example, defied SS population policy by applying his own rather unique interpretation of Hitler's Germanization mandate.

Rather than assiduously measuring the Polish population of Danzig-West Prussia against racial criteria, he simply took at their word Poles claiming German ancestry and declared them citizens of the Reich, thus Germanizing his fiefdom with great speed and minimal effort, but creating a continuous source of conflict with the SS and Heydrich in particular, who considered Forster's approach a severe danger to the racial health of the German people.[37]

Fearing that the civil administration due to replace the military occupation regime on 25 October might limit his freedom of action, on 14 October Heydrich reiterated his earlier order that the 'liquidation of the Polish leadership' in Western Poland should be completed within the next two weeks.[38] In accordance with these orders, the *Einsatzgruppen* carried out a second wave of arrests and mass shootings in West Prussia, again targeting Polish teachers, academics, ex-officers and members of nationalist organizations as well as so-called Congress Poles, that is Poles who had moved to West Prussia from the East since 1919. The total number of victims of this second round of murders and deportations in West Prussia is unclear, but SS men in the field believed that 'approximately 20,000' Poles were 'destroyed' that autumn. A further 87,000 people were deported from Danzig-West Prussia by February 1940.[39]

The terror and ethnic cleansing in south-east Prussia began somewhat later, notably after the arrival of Heydrich's trusted associate, Otto Rasch, in Königsberg in November. Born in 1891, he had studied law, philosophy and political science before the Great War. Rasch had extensive experience in violently persecuting 'enemies of the Reich'. After the war, he had volunteered for the Freikorps campaigns of the early 1920s against Polish insurgents. Known as Dr Dr Rasch because he had completed two PhDs, he joined the SS and the SD in the early 1930s where, thanks to Heydrich's protection, his star rose rapidly. He quickly became head of the Gestapo in Frankfurt. Heydrich recognized his 'talents' as a man in the field and insisted on his participation in the SD campaigns in Austria, Czechoslovakia and Poland, where he acted as deputy of Udo von Woyrsch. After his arrival in Königsberg in the autumn of 1939, Rasch immediately suggested the execution of large numbers of Polish prisoners, mostly drawn from the intelligentsia. Heydrich happily approved, but insisted that the liquidations were to be 'unobtrusive', an order implemented by Rasch by means of secret executions of prisoners in the shady forests along the former East Prussian–Polish border and in the now deserted former Polish army barracks in the town of Soldau.[40]

Systematic murders were not confined to the incorporated territories. What began in West Prussia and the Warthegau in the autumn of 1939, and passed through south-east Prussia in the winter, reached the General Government in the spring of 1940. The targeted liquidation of Poles noted for their education, nationalism or social status demonstrated that the Nazis were capable of and committed to murdering by the thousands. Complementary to this aim was the 'resettlement' of hundreds of thousands, eventually even millions of people. The expulsion of 'undesired elements' to the East and the restitution of 'valuable German stock' in their place would provide the basis for the new German *Lebensraum*.

Although the Poles were the main victims of the first wave of murders and deportations in Eastern Europe, the outbreak of war also impacted dramatically on the fate of the Jews now living under Nazi rule. As Hitler had pointed out in his triumphant Reichstag speech of 6 October, the ethnic reordering of Poland would involve a concerted effort to 'settle and regulate the Jewish problem' once and for all.[41]

But how was this to be achieved? Heydrich was painfully aware that, as a result of the recent German conquests, the scale of the 'Jewish problem' had increased many times over. At the beginning of the German invasion, Poland contained almost 3.5 million Jews, by far the largest number of Jews living in any European state. More than three-quarters of them lived in Poland's towns and cities, with 350,000 in Warsaw alone. All in all, over 2 million Jews lived in the German-controlled territories of Poland in September 1939, of whom 300,000 fled eastwards during the German invasion. But the differences were not just quantitative. The Orthodox Polish Jews whom German troops encountered seemed to conform to the anti-Semitic imagery, with a traditional garb and way of life. Unlike the mostly assimilated Jews of Germany, Orthodox Polish Jews were easily identifiable, spoke a different language and had no protection from German friends or relatives. Furthermore, Germany was now at war and the 'restraints' under which radical Nazis had operated since 1933 no longer applied. Ever since the beginning of the German invasion, Polish Orthodox Jews had routinely been singled out for public humiliation and violent attacks. Of the 16,000 Polish civilians killed during the first six weeks of the war, 5,000 were Jews. Jewish shops and homes were specifically targeted by both the SS and regular German troops as they passed through Polish towns and villages.[42]

Despite the continuous efforts to step up Jewish emigration from Germany since 1938, neither Heydrich nor anyone else in the Nazi leadership had entered the war with a clear conception of what they were going to do with the Jews of Poland. Up to September 1939, Heydrich's forced-emigration policies had led to a drop in the Jewish population of the Reich by more than half – from just over 500,000 to 215,000. Although the conquests of 1938 and 1939 had brought new Jewish communities under Nazi control – 180,000 Jews in Austria and 85,000 in Bohemia and Moravia – the same policy had worked there, too. By the outbreak of war in September 1939, around half of the Austrian and Czech Jews had fled or been forced to emigrate as a result of Eichmann's operations. Poland changed the equation completely. Heydrich now found himself nominally responsible for an additional 1.7 million Polish Jews, a community nearly ten times larger than that in the Old Reich in 1939.[43]

Having been hit by this problem without any predetermined solution, Heydrich wanted to make it go away as quickly as possible. As early as 7 September, he suggested to his subordinates in the Gestapo headquarters in Berlin that SS Jewish policy in Poland would have to include a combination of forced expulsion into the Soviet-occupied zone and the resettlement of Jews within a specially established district, possibly in Galicia. The remaining 'Polish Jews' living in Germany, including those with German citizenship, were also to be expelled eastwards as quickly as possible. Immediately after this meeting, the Security Police were ordered to implement this policy by arresting and confiscating the property of all male Polish Jews still living in Germany. These orders noted that 'in as far as it is possible, detained Jews who formerly held Polish citizenship will be at some point pushed into the non-occupied regions of Poland'.[44]

More concrete and far-reaching proposals emerged over the following two weeks. In a meeting with his senior staff on 14 September, Heydrich reported that Hitler was currently considering SS proposals regarding 'the Jewish problem in Poland'.[45] Central to these proposals remained Heydrich's plan for the establishment of a reservation in Poland for all the Jews under German control, an idea that was further discussed by Heydrich and Göring two days later.[46] On 20 September, during a meeting with Himmler, Heydrich, and the Gauleiter of Danzig, Albert Forster, Hitler approved the proposals.[47] The following day, Heydrich was consequently able to report to his senior officers that the Führer had made a decision on the issue. Polish Jews were to be concentrated in urban ghettos, facilitating their future deportation to a yet unknown destination, while an unspecified number were to be deported immediately across the new German–Soviet demarcation line into Soviet-occupied Eastern Poland. Once these immediate aims had been achieved, Heydrich hoped to commence the deportation of Germany's Jews and Gypsies into Poland, a process he believed could be achieved within one year.[48]

Heydrich's meeting with the *Einsatzgruppen* leaders on 21 September marked the starting point of more systematic Nazi anti-Jewish policies in Poland, policies that differed from the random killings of the previous weeks of the war. Heydrich's idea of concentrating Jews in ghettos in larger cities for the purpose of subsequent deportation was to become a crucial component of Nazi anti-Jewish policy. Yet he never gave much thought to how Jewish life in the envisaged urban ghettos was to be organized. He noted that the 'concentrations of Jews in the cities for general reasons of security will probably bring about orders forbidding Jews from entering certain quarters of the cities altogether, and that – in view of economic necessity – they cannot for instance leave the ghetto, they cannot go out after designated hours, etc'. But these were suggestions, not explicit orders. 'Obviously the tasks at hand cannot be laid out in detail from here,' he conceded in a statement that would hold true not only for ghettoization but also for many other future measures of Nazi anti-Jewish policy.[49]

Heydrich's lack of interest in the implementation details of this policy partly stemmed from the fact that ghettoization was never intended to be a permanent solution. It was merely a precondition to facilitate the future deportations of Jews to an as yet undetermined territory on the furthest extremity of the German sphere of influence. At the same time, Heydrich did not care enough for the victims of the deportations to be encumbered by the 'petty details' of ghettoization. He preferred to think in grand terms and to leave the implementation of policies to his eager underlings or the local authorities.

On the same day, in an attempt to document the SS's active implementation of Hitler's anti-Jewish visions, Heydrich sent a courier letter expanding on the meeting's most important decisions to all task-force commanders as well as to several central agencies of the Third Reich, including Göring's Office of the Four-Year Plan, the Ministry of the Interior, the Army High Command and the designated heads of the civil administration in occupied Poland. In his letter, Heydrich clearly distinguished between 'short-term measures', notably the concentration of Polish Jews, and the 'long-term goal': the deportation and expulsion of all Jews in the region. Short-term measures meant that the Sipo would group together Jews into ghettos in the 'fewest possible numbers of towns' along main railway lines in order to facilitate future deportations. For the time being, each community was to set up 'councils of Jewish Elders' composed of twenty-four men in each community, who were to be held 'fully responsible' for the execution of German orders. All measures were to be carried out in close agreement with the army and local German authorities. The 'final goal' was to be kept 'strictly secret'.[50]

Although Heydrich's letter did not specify what this 'final aim' might be, he made clear to his closest associates that he was planning the deportation of all Jews from the Greater German Reich into a Jewish reservation and, eventually, their expulsion into Eastern Poland.[51] Danzig-West Prussia, Posen (Poznań) and East Upper Silesia were to be 'cleared of Jews' as soon as possible, while in the rest of occupied Poland, not yet needed for German settlement, 'cruder' measures would suffice. To be excluded from these orders was the area east of Kraków, an area which Heydrich at this point believed to be the location for the future Jewish reservation.[52]

The hastily drafted orders of September 1939 illustrate both continuities and new departures in Heydrich's thinking about the Jewish problem. On the one hand, emigration from Germany and deportation from its newly occupied territories, not systematic mass murder, remained the overall policy line. On the other hand, under the impact of war, Heydrich was increasingly prepared to tolerate, and even encourage, the murder of individual Polish Jews if it served to frighten or terrorize others into flight across the German–Soviet demarcation line. But it quickly became clear that piecemeal expulsions were no longer adequate to deal with the huge numbers of Polish Jews with which Heydrich was confronted. By late September 1939, the 'final aim' of SS anti-Jewish policy entailed a combination of ghettoization and deportations into a future 'Jewish state under German administration'.[53]

As the implementation of this goal was largely dependent on factors beyond Heydrich's control – from foreign policy considerations to the extensive and jealously guarded powers given by Hitler to the new civilian administrations in Poland – the following months entailed countless setbacks and adjustments of SS plans to new realities. If, for example, Heydrich had still envisaged the area east of Kraków as the future Jewish reservation on 22 September, his plans had to be modified following German–Soviet negotiations about the future borders between both states. When on 25 September Stalin offered to transfer control over the area around the city of Lublin (then east of the German–Soviet demarcation line) to Germany in exchange for Soviet control over Lithuania, he opened up the prospect of creating a Jewish reservation on Germany's new border with the Soviet Union. Moreover, it was agreed that ethnic Germans in the Soviet sphere would be repatriated to German territory.[54]

On 29 September, only one day after the formal ratification of the German–Soviet Boundary and Friendship Treaty, Heydrich explained to his closest subordinates in Berlin that plans for a Jewish district in Galicia had been abandoned in favour of a new idea: the establishment of a Reich Ghetto in the Lublin district. The Reich Ghetto was to become the new home for 'undesirable' Poles and 'all political and Jewish elements'.[55] Heydrich's revised plan constituted an immediate translation of Hitler's wishes, the Führer having explained that same day to the head of the Nazi Party's Foreign Policy Office, Alfred Rosenberg, that the newly conquered territories should be divided into three zones: the Jews were to be settled along with other 'unreliable elements' between the rivers Vistula and Bug on the new German–Soviet demarcation line, with an Eastern Wall on the Vistula 'protecting' the areas further west. In Western Poland, along the former German–Polish border, he wished to establish a broad area of German colonization and settlement. An as yet undefined Polish state in the territory in between was to become the General Government.[56]

Although authorized by Hitler, the deportation and settlement plans remained difficult to implement as long as the army was the sole executive authority in the occupied territories, and as long as Brauchitsch objected to a swift removal of the Jews 'for economic reasons'. In reality, Heydrich's *Einsatzgruppen* tended to ignore the army leadership's objections, but army intervention often meant that they could not carry out his orders as quickly as they would have liked.[57] Thousands of Polish Jews were nonetheless forcibly expelled over the San river into Soviet-occupied territory before the end of the military administration, often with the active support of local army commanders. The deportations ended only in November, after repeated complaints from the Soviet authorities, who now made the emigration of ethnic German settlers dependent on the end of Jewish deportations into their territory.[58]

On 30 September parallel talks were held between Himmler and Brauchitsch, on the one hand, and Heydrich and the army's Chief of Staff, Franz Halder, on the other. Both Halder and Brauchitsch complained about continuous disruptions caused by the rapid deportation of Polish Jews into cities.[59] Heydrich bowed to army pressure and reiterated his orders of 21 September in another letter to his *Einsatzgruppen* commanders: all measures were to be taken in closest co-operation with the local military authorities. The decision over the timing and the intensity of the deportation and concentration of Jews still remained in the hands of the *Einsatzgruppen* commanders, but they had to be 'unobtrusive'.[60]

Although these concessions merely affected the time-frame of the planned ethnic reordering of Poland and not the policies as such, Heydrich was deeply dissatisfied. On 3 October, he spoke to his *Einsatzgruppen* commanders of the 'old army–SD problem' which had 're-emerged in all its seriousness'.[61] Three days later, a more important issue arose. On 6 October, Heydrich's apparatus received orders from Hitler that the first major wave of deportations – the expulsion of the Jews of Kattowitz (Katowice) in East Upper Silesia – should begin immediately. That same day, Adolf Eichmann, then Director of the Central Office for Jewish Emigration in Prague, was ordered to prepare the eastward expulsion of up to 80,000 Jews from East Upper Silesia over the Vistula river. Jews from nearby Moravia-Ostrava, a town in the eastern corner of the Protectorate, were to be included in the deportations.[62]

The deportation of the Jews of East Upper Silesia was intended only as a trial run for a much larger deportation scheme. In a conversation with a colleague in Vienna on 7 October, and again two days later during a meeting with the Silesian Gauleiter, Josef Wagner, Eichmann reported that Hitler had a made a decision in principle to deport 300,000 Jews from the Old Reich and Austria. Eichmann had been ordered, or so he told Wagner, to prepare a report for Heydrich on the first experimental deportations from Silesia. On the basis of that report Hitler would then issue a definitive order for a large-scale 'general removal' of the Jews from the Reich.[63]

Before this massive deportation plan could be implemented, Eichmann had to find a suitable location for his 'transit camp'. On 12 October, he and the commander of the Security Police in the Protectorate, Walter Stahlecker, drove eastwards from Warsaw in search of an appropriate location. Three days later, Eichmann reported back to Berlin that they had found it on the western border of the Lublin district, around the little town of Nisko on the River San.[64]

On 17 October the first transport with nearly 1,000 Jews left Moravia-Ostrava for Nisko. Two days later the first train from Vienna arrived carrying 912 Austrian Jews, followed by a second transport from the former Austrian capital with 672 deportees. Two further trainloads of Jews from Kattowitz and another transport from Moravia-Ostrava followed over the coming days. Between 20 and 28 October a total of 4,700 Jews were deported to Nisko.[65]

When the first transport arrived, chaos ensued. The transit camp in Nisko did not even exist at this point. The first deportees to arrive were marched out of Nisko across the San river into a swampy meadow near the village of Zarzecze where they started to erect basic barracks. The following morning, the best workers were selected from the group, while the rest were marched away eastwards and told never to return. The following transports were treated similarly.[66] This treatment of the deportees, which involved a ready acceptance of the death of many in the largely inhospitable meadows around Nisko, was entirely in line with Nazi plans: Nisko was never intended to become a permanent home for the Jews of Central Europe, but was rather a transit camp from which the expelled Jews of Kattowitz, Vienna and Moravia-Ostrava were to be brought into the Jewish reservation around Lublin.[67]

Despite some limited success, the deportation programme ended as quickly as it had begun. On 20 October, Eichmann was notified by Heydrich's office in Berlin that the deportations were to be stopped immediately. Military considerations for a future attack on the Soviet Union may have played some role in this decision-making process.[68] More importantly, however, it was Himmler's gigantic resettlement programme, which began to take shape in early October, that hampered plans for a Jewish reservation near Lublin. Anti-Jewish deportation policies were thus stymied by the wider consideration of ethnic German resettlement in occupied Poland.[69]

After entering into a series of agreements with foreign powers to resettle ethnic Germans 'living abroad', the first trainloads with Baltic German settlers arrived in Danzig on 15 October. Himmler and Heydrich hoped to settle many of these new arrivals in West Prussia and the Warthegau and finding lodgings and livelihoods for them took priority over the deportation of Jews from the Reich. Polish farms in the areas designated for German settlement were to be expropriated and handed over to the settlers, with the farmers themselves shoved over the border into the General Government. The scope for deportations of Jews from Germany into the remaining parts of Poland was now extremely limited. Eichmann's deportations, which were focused on the northern Protectorate and Vienna, did not create space for German settlers where Himmler and Heydrich most needed it. For the time being, therefore, priority over the solution of the Jewish question was given to the consolidation of the newly acquired living space in Western Poland through German resettlement.[70]

Although Heydrich's initial deportation plans had failed, he did not waste time in adjusting to the new situation. On 28 November, he presented his first 'short-term plan' (*Nahplan*) as well as a 'long-term plan' (*Fernplan*). According to the short-term plan, to be applied only to the Warthegau as the key target area for ethnic Germans resettled from Eastern Europe, 'enough Poles and Jews are to be deported to provide housing for the incoming Baltic Germans'. In order to achieve this aim as quickly as possible, 5,000 people per day were to be expelled.[71] The long-term plan continued to emphasize as its overall aim the deportation of all Jews and politically 'unreliable' Poles into the General Government, followed by the 'racial screening' and subsequent gradual deportation of the remaining Polish population from the annexed territories.[72]

Even if the removal of unwanted Poles and their replacement with German settlers was the key target of his short-term plan, Heydrich had in no way forgotten about the Jewish question either in Poland or at home. On 21 December he announced that he had decided to appoint Eichmann as his special adviser on the 'preparation of Security Police matters in carrying out evacuations in the east'. Despite the failure of the Nisko plan, he obviously felt that Eichmann had the necessary expertise and drive to bring this important project to a successful conclusion.[73] That same day, Heydrich issued a revised version of his short-term plan, which outlined more clearly those against whom the aforementioned Security Police matters would primarily be directed: within the first few months of 1940, Eichmann was to ensure that 600,000 Jews from the annexed territories, 'without regard to age and gender', were deported into the General Government. No deferments were to be granted for employer claims of economic indispensability.[74]

Only a few weeks later, Heydrich put a new idea on the table: chairing a top-level meeting with senior police officials from the East in Berlin, he noted that between 800,000 and 1 million Polish agricultural workers (in addition to the Polish prisoners of war) were needed as temporary land labourers in the Reich. The General Government, already cramped with deportees, was to receive another 40,000 Jews and Poles from the annexed territories to make room for more Baltic Germans. This would be followed by 'another improvised clearing' of 120,000 Poles to provide space for the Volhynian Germans. Since Himmler had forbidden the deportation of any Poles who might be of German origin, only Congress Poles were to be affected. A racial screening of those Poles deemed capable of Germanization would follow in the future. After the deportation of a total of 160,000 Poles for the Baltic and Volhynian Germans, Heydrich explained, the 'evacuation' to the General Government of all Jews and Gypsies from the newly annexed eastern territories and the Old Reich would begin, presumably in the late spring or early summer of 1940.[75]

In reality, Heydrich's ambitious attempts to find a final solution to the Jewish question through expulsions into Polish territory had made little progress. Since Hitler's statement to Rosenberg in late September that all Jews, including those in the Old Reich, were to be sent to the region between the Vistula and the Bug, and Himmler's orders of 30 October to deport all Jews from the annexed territories by the end of February 1940, very little had been accomplished. The deportation of Jews from the Old Reich had been postponed to an as yet unknown date, and priority was given to the deportation of Poles and Jews from the incorporated territories where space for new German settlers was badly needed.[76]

But even here a key problem remained: the officials in the receiving areas, most notably the General Government's powerful ruler, Hans Frank, continued to oppose large-scale resettlement schemes into their own fief-doms. Frank refused to administer a social 'refuse tip', and aspired instead to create a model German colony, an ambition that required the *expulsion* of Jews from the General Government. Partly for prestige and racial reasons and partly because his General Government was already over-populated, he lobbied vigorously for an end to the deportations. Heydrich tried to brush such objections aside, arguing that several hundreds of thou-sands of Jews could be put in labour camps to build the Eastern Wall.[77]

In February 1940, Frank sought help from a powerful ally: Hermann Göring. During a meeting with Himmler at Göring's country estate,

Carinhall, Frank argued that the SS leadership's drive for resettlement was leading to chaos, maintaining that the food supplies of the province were visibly threatened and that the General Government's economy was in tatters. These arguments, rooted in a more realistic assessment of the actual situation on the ground than that of Heydrich and Himmler, were successful. The first priority, Göring believed, was to strengthen the Reich's war potential and Himmler grudgingly had to concede that further deportations would be carried out only with Frank's agreement. The very same day, however, Heydrich's men in Stettin rounded up 1,200 German Jews, some over eighty years old, and transported them to the General Government. The ensuing complaints from the district governor of Lublin prompted a quick response. On 12 March 1940, Hitler declared that the Jewish question was one of space and that he had none at his disposal. Less than two weeks later, on 24 March, Göring officially forbade any further deportations to the General Government.[78]

The situation was deeply frustrating for Heydrich, who attempted to cover up this fresh defeat by stepping up once more the process of Jewish emigration from the Reich. Deprived of the option of immediately deporting Jews into the General Government, Heydrich's RSHA issued a decree on 24 April 1940 announcing that emigration of German Jews was 'to be intensified during the war'.[79]

Six months after the invasion of Poland, Heydrich had few reasons to be content. On the one hand, the SS had emerged as the key player in the policing and racial reorganization of the newly occupied Polish territories. Yet the progress made was more than outweighed by the setbacks that Heydrich had experienced in the autumn and winter of 1939. The Wehrmacht successfully used the Polish atrocities as an argument against any SS involvement on the Western Front. Moreover, the solution of the Jewish question in the Old Reich had made little progress and the problem of finding a reception area for deportees from the annexed Polish territories remained unresolved. If anything, the experiences in Poland taught Heydrich that while his powers on paper were vast and growing, the implementation of SS policies often faltered in the face of wartime realities and opposition from powerful Nazi Gauleiters and military agencies which carefully guarded their own interests. Heydrich's experiences in Poland confirmed his suspicion that both the army leadership and the Old Fighters now in charge of the civilian administration lacked the necessary commitment to an uncompromising implementation of Nazi ideology as he understood it. They were not to be trusted. For the time being, however, political realities forced him grudgingly to do what he most disliked: to compromise.

Terror on the Home Front

From the beginning of the Second World War, Heydrich envisaged the conflict ahead as a battle on two fronts: a merciless struggle against alien races and nations on the battlefield and a ruthless fight against all internal enemies at home. His obsession with the home front dated from 1918 and the November Revolution, which he had experienced as a teenager in Halle. Immediately after the seizure of power in Bavaria in March 1933, he had confiscated and studied the extensive police files on the Munich Council Republic of 1919. They reinforced his conviction that Imperial Germany had been fatally undermined by defeatism, poor morale and political opposition on the home front. To eliminate the potential for revolution, Heydrich argued, meant to strengthen Germany's ability to win the war. This time, there would be no stab in the back and no surrender.[80]

As soon as war broke out, Hitler charged Himmler with the maintenance of order in Germany 'at all costs'. On the same day, 3 September 1939, Heydrich issued his 'Principles of Inner State Security during the War', a directive he had been working on for some time in anticipation of the military onslaught against Poland. Heydrich's orders were designed to ensure the 'co-ordinated deployment' of all security forces against 'every disruption and subversion' of the German war effort.[81]

Without the rigorous implementation of this task, Heydrich insisted, the Führer's overall aims and objectives could not be realized. A 'ruthless' approach towards the threat of defeatism was necessary: 'Any attempt to subvert the unity and the will to combat of the German people must be ruthlessly suppressed. It is particularly essential to arrest immediately any person who expresses doubts about the victory of the German people or who challenges the just cause of the war.' Yet Heydrich also called for leniency in cases where Germans who had lost family members on the front or who had other 'understandable' causes for personal distress made critical statements about the regime. In such cases, where offences were a singular event, a personal warning or other form of 'intimidation' would be sufficient to reintegrate the offender into the people's community or *Volksgemeinschaft*. At the same time, the person in question was to be left in no doubt that he or she could expect worse if found repeating such behaviour. Repeat offenders, habitual criminals and persons acting out of ideological conviction should not expect mercy. Local police commanders were ordered to bring these cases to Heydrich's immediate attention so that he could personally order their 'brutal liquidation' if necessary.[82]

The institution created by Heydrich in order to co-ordinate terror on the home front and in the occupied territories over the years to come was the Reich Security Main Office (RSHA), formally established on 27 September after many months of preparation. This was brought about by combining the Sipo (the Gestapo and criminal police) with the SD. The RSHA constituted a new type of institution: a merger between the political police, a traditional organ of state repression that had already existed during the Weimar Republic, and a newer party agency of persecution, the SD. In contrast to a conventional police apparatus, the purpose of the RSHA was not merely to persecute criminals, but also preventively to cleanse state and society of political and racial enemies, and thus to act as a key tool for the creation of a utopian New Order.[83]

The creation of the RSHA was largely motivated by two considerations that had ripened in Heydrich's and Himmler's minds over the preceding years: first it would bring the SS one step closer to the establishment of a fully integrated terror agency, a state protection corps, comprising the Gestapo, the criminal police and the SD. Secondly, the creation of a new state agency would resolve the old problem of financing the ever-growing SD. Since 1931 the Nazi Party's treasury had paid its salaries and running costs only erratically. Heydrich was fully aware that independence from party funding meant independence from party intervention, and therefore increased power. By including the SD in the new RSHA, he hoped to finance the SD from exchequer resources, thereby making it possible to expand the scale of its operations and rendering it less dependent on the Nazi Party's administration.[84]

The official launch of the RSHA in the autumn of 1939 was preceded by considerable internal conflict. Back in February 1939, Heydrich had ordered Walter Schellenberg, the young rising star of the SD, to develop a concept for an institutional reorganization of the Security Police and the SD – a project on which Heydrich's deputy as head of the Security Police, Werner Best, had been working for some time. Schellenberg was seven years younger than Best but no less ambitious, and they were widely perceived as competitors within Heydrich's apparatus. Born in Saarbrücken close to the German–French border in 1910 as the last of seven children of a wealthy piano manufacturer, Schellenberg had spent his childhood in Luxembourg. He returned to Germany in the second half of the 1920s, where he studied medicine and law in Marburg and Bonn. During his time in Bonn, Schellenberg was approached by two of his professors who acted as recruitment officers for the SD. Schellenberg jumped at the opportunity. Handsome, bright and praised by his SD superiors as energetic and visionary, he was soon noticed by Heydrich who assigned him two tasks of particular importance: in 1938, Schellenberg accompanied Himmler and Heydrich to

Vienna in order to confiscate Austrian secret service material; the following
year he was put in charge of the politically sensitive mission of abducting
two British secret agents from the neutral Netherlands. It was therefore no
surprise – though perhaps perceived as an insult by Werner Best – that
Heydrich asked Schellenberg to prepare a conceptual paper on the future
merger between the SD and the Security Police.[85] On 5 July Schellenberg
presented Heydrich with a comprehensive policy paper, in which he argued
that the SD's responsibilities should remain clearly separated and autonomous from those of the political police: in contrast to the Security Police
and its case-by-case approach to the persecution of criminals, the SD was
to focus on anticipating crime before it occurred, notably by the surveillance
of all potential opponents of Nazism, both within and outside the Reich's
borders. In essence, Schellenberg's paper was aimed at preventing the
absorption of the SD by the Security Police, while simultaneously arguing
for an improvement of the organization's financial position, which depended
on party subsidies rather than more reliable payments from the state
treasury.[86] In a further memorandum of February 1939, Schellenberg reiterated this point, arguing that the police should be absorbed into the party
institution of the SD 'and not the other way around' – an argument directed
against Werner Best.[87]

Best's response came quickly. Only a few days later, he presented
Heydrich and Schellenberg with a counter-proposal diametrically opposed
to Schellenberg's idea: the SD, Best insisted, should be integrated into a
German Security Police, which would amount to a *de facto* takeover of the
SD by the Gestapo. Even more controversial from Schellenberg's point of
view was Best's insistence on a uniform training system for the Security
Police's future leadership corps, a training system in which a university
degree in law – the traditional qualification for the German higher civil
service – would be compulsory. Dismissing Schellenberg's argument that
the ideological commitment of the police leadership was more important
than its legal training as 'the high-handedness and short-sightedness of a
self-centred Praetorian Guard', Best insisted on formal qualifications as a
precondition for leadership positions in the future RSHA, a stance that led
to extreme tensions with the SD. Unlike Best, who had been a judge in the
Weimar Republic, many of the SD's leaders were not lawyers by training
(although they were often university graduates in other disciplines such as
history, philosophy or literature), and Schellenberg rightly interpreted
Best's description of the SD leadership as an attack on himself.[88]

Heydrich sided with Schellenberg and noted in the margin of Best's
draft that practice-oriented training, not legal studies, should form the
core of the future Security Police leadership's training.[89] He left no doubt
that he did not want lawyers and bureaucrats to run Nazi Germany's

Security Police. As he explained to the head of the Order Police, Kurt Daluege, he had always insisted on 'pushing the lawyers back to where they belong, namely into the role of formal legal advisers'.[90] It was the ideologically committed and politically radical SD that should lead the Security Police, as the struggle against racial and ideological enemies had to rest in reliable hands. Administrative concerns and legal reservations could only hamper the regime's fight against its enemies.[91]

In essence, the internal conflicts of 1938–9 revolved around the issue of whether the future leadership of the Nazi repression apparatus should rest with lawyers or 'political warriors'.[92] After Heydrich's rejection of his proposals, Best did not hesitate to make the internal conflict public – a grave strategic mistake that would seriously strain his relationship with Heydrich. In two articles, published in *Deutsches Recht* and in the *Deutsche Allgemeine Zeitung*, Best reiterated his view that lawyers should be at the top of the future German Security Police.[93]

Heydrich was infuriated by Best's decision to make their internal dispute public, and the affair would ultimately lead to the termination of their shared career path: in the summer of 1940, Best left the RSHA and went to Paris where he became head of the Wehrmacht's civil administration. Their paths would only cross once again, in May 1942, and, even then Best would realize that Heydrich had neither forgotten nor forgiven him.[94]

Based in the Gestapo headquarters in Berlin's Prinz-Albrecht-Strasse, the RSHA consisted of six (and, from March 1941 onwards, seven) sizeable departments. The administrative heart of the RSHA was Department I (*Organisation, Verwaltung, Recht*), run by Werner Best until his departure from Berlin in 1940, and the only department in which former Gestapo and SD personnel worked side by side.[95]

Department II (*Gegnerforschung*) was primarily focused on the 'scientific' exploration of ideological enemy groups within and outside the Reich. Heydrich had long been convinced that a fundamental understanding of the internal structures, political convictions and work methods of enemy groups was an essential precondition for fighting them. Department II mirrored that conviction. Its staff analysed confiscated documents and provided memoranda on the origins, composition and aims of broadly defined enemy groups. Under the leadership of the sociology professor Franz Alfred Six, a man who continued his research and publication career throughout the Second World War, it also exerted significant influence on university appointments and the recruitment of new SD leadership personnel with academic backgrounds.[96]

Department III (*Deutsche Lebensgebiete*) was largely identical with the SD Inland, Heydrich's office for the co-ordination of domestic espionage. Under the leadership of Otto Ohlendorf, it was now divided into four sub-departments responsible for collating intelligence on questions of ethnicity, law, culture and economy. Most importantly, Ohlendorf's department compiled the regular 'Meldungen aus dem Reich', detailed reports on the general mood of the German population, resistance activities and other potential dangers to domestic peace, which served as an important source of information for the Nazi leadership.[97]

While Departments II and III primarily served as think-tanks within Heydrich's terror apparatus, Departments IV (*Gegnerbekämpfung*) and V (*Kriminalpolizei*) acted as its executive arms. Department IV, the Gestapo, continued its operational work under the leadership of Heinrich Müller and played a central role within the RSHA. Responsible for actively fighting political enemies through arrests, it was divided into five sub-departments: political enemies (A); religious denominations, Jews, Freemasons, emigrants, pacificists (B); protective custody (C); occupied territories (D); and a special desk for co-ordination with the military intelligence organization, the Abwehr (E). Alongside the department's responsibility for protective custody (the commitment of 'criminals' to concentration camps), a separate desk, Eichmann's desk B4, dealt with matters of Jewish expulsions and, later in the war, their extermination.[98]

Its clearly defined task of persecuting political and racial enemies of the Nazi regime provided Department IV with a clear advantage vis-à-vis the SD and the understaffed Department V, the former Reich Criminal Police Office under Arthur Nebe, which was responsible for matters of 'crime prevention' and the the arrest of 'ordinary' criminals, although the increasingly biological interpretation of criminals blurred the areas of responsibility between the Gestapo and the criminal police.[99]

With a total of thirty-eight desks, Department VI (*SD Ausland*), responsible for foreign intelligence gathering, was the largest – but by no means the most powerful – department within the RSHA. First under the leadership of the young ex-lawyer Heinz Jost, then under Walter Schellenberg, the department was remarkably amateurish, with limited experience in espionage and enjoying very little success. Although espionage networks were set up in neutral countries such as Switzerland, Sweden, Spain and Portugal, as well as South-eastern Europe, its impact in Great Britain, the United States and the Soviet Union was barely noticeable. In a desperate attempt to chalk up some success, Department VI even set up a brothel in Berlin, the Salon Kitty, where foreign diplomats and suspected spies within the Nazi bureaucracy were hooked up with prostitutes and their conversations secretly recorded. Nothing sensational was ever exposed.[100]

The structure of the RSHA reflected Heydrich's attempt to avoid the duplication of responsibilities between individual departments that had led to various rivalries and conflicts in the past, most notably between the Gestapo and the criminal police, but also between the Security Police and the SD. While the Gestapo now primarily concentrated on matters of political persecution (directed against both Germans and foreigners living in the Reich), the criminal police gained responsibility for policy areas such as economic crimes and the combating of abortions and homosexuality. 'Preventive' measures against asocials and criminals were now also among the responsibilities of the criminal police.[101]

The RSHA became the central organization of the Nazi terror during the Second World War, but measured against Heydrich's original ambitions of merging the SD, the Gestapo and the criminal police into a tightly integrated state protection corps it was a heterogeneous institution: legally trained police officials worked alongside SD leaders, but the SD continued to be financed by the party treasury whereas the Security Police were funded by the state. This RSHA was not the tightly knit and uniformly organized apparatus for which Heydrich had hoped, but rather an institutional roof for the various agencies of the Nazi persecution apparatus, albeit one run by a single administration and under the unifying command of Heydrich.[102]

With a total of 3,000 employees, including secretaries and lower officials, and a leadership corps of some 400 men (and one woman) as heads of individual desks or departments, the RSHA was not a huge institution, but it was one that differed fundamentally from the traditional administration in terms of purpose, institutional ethos and staff composition: 77 per cent of its leadership corps were born after 1900, most were from middle-class families, two-thirds had completed a university education and one-third had a doctoral degree, mostly in law, but also in literature, history, theology and philology. The RSHA was thus an institution for social climbers, not social failures. However, despite Heydrich's preference for well-educated members of staff, he was also consciously anti-intellectual. Scholarship had to be political. Ideas could be proven only through deeds. What Heydrich wanted was the creation of an ideologically committed vanguard or 'fighting administration', an elite which would not only devise new policies but also implement them. Deeds, not words, were what mattered. Most of the members of the RSHA leadership corps, for example, served both in senior administrative functions in Berlin and as heads of the *Einsatzkommandos* in the course of the war. In that sense, the RSHA was a flexible organization, constantly modifying and reorganizing its departments, as well as a mobile institution, whose staff were frequently ordered to fulfil different tasks, from administration jobs in Berlin to participation in fighting and mass killings in the field.[103]

The RSHA's imperfect organizational structure in no way diminished the radicalism of its employees. On the contrary, the loose administrative structure created room for competition between individual desks and departments, leading to increasingly radical initiatives. Heydrich publicly prided himself on having created a police apparatus which was composed of 'ideologically committed Nazis', 'political soldiers' of the 'hidden front', an institution that united under one roof political problem analysis, operational organization and implementation.[104]

Shortly after the establishment of the RSHA, Heydrich's restructured terror apparatus was confronted with its first major challenge. On the evening of 8 November 1939, at 9.20, a bomb exploded in Munich's Bürgerbräukeller, the venue for Hitler's annual commemoration speeches on the anniversary of his failed 1923 putsch. The explosion, set off shortly after the Führer had left the building, killed eight people and wounded dozens. If Hitler, concerned about the bad weather, had not curtailed his speech in order to take an earlier return flight to Berlin, he, too, would have been killed in the explosion. The man responsible for the assassination attempt was caught that same night: Georg Elser, a thirty-eight-year-old cabinet-maker, was arrested while trying to cross the German–Swiss border. In view of the political sensitivity of the case, Heydrich and Himmler personally took charge of the investigations.[105]

Although during the interrogations Elser insisted that he had planned and carried out the assassination attempt without any assistance, Heydrich and the Gestapo officers investigating the case at first doubted his claims. Instead, they believed that it was a plot against Hitler orchestrated by the British Secret Intelligence Service.[106] Coincidentally, the following day, an SD commando under Walter Schellenberg abducted two British SIS agents, Sigismund Payne Best and Richard Stevens, from the Dutch border town of Venlo and brought them to Berlin for interrogation. Heydrich wrongly assumed that the SD had penetrated a British secret operation with the aim of eliminating Hitler – an assumption that reflected his penchant for spy stories and conspiracy theories and that was not supported by any solid evidence.[107]

Elser was taken to Sachsenhausen concentration camp where he was murdered in early 1945, shortly before the Red Army liberated the camp. His fate was shared by a growing number of people. Between August 1939 and the spring of 1942, the number of inmates in concentration camps (excluding those in the death camps constructed further east from late 1941 onwards) rose from about 21,000 to just under 80,000, with most of the new arrivals being non-Germans.[108]

In order to cope with this new influx, four new concentration camps – Auschwitz, Neuengamme, Gross-Rosen and Natzweiler – were built between the outbreak of war and the spring of 1941, in addition to the six camps that had already existed within the Greater German Reich before September 1939: Sachsenhausen, Dachau, Mauthausen, Flossenbürg, Buchenwald and the women's camp at Ravensbrück. Living conditions in these increasingly overcrowded camps deteriorated quickly: food rations decreased substantially, maltreatment became more widespread and mortality rates in the prisoners' barracks rose steadily.[109]

Although he continued to be in charge 'only' of the internment and release of prisoners, and not of camp life itself (which remained the responsibility of Theodor Eicke), Heydrich was heavily involved in the question of how enemies of the state should be treated once imprisoned. In January 1941, he established three categories of concentration camps, which were meant to reflect both 'the personality of the prisoners and the degree of danger they represent for the state'. The so-called 'lesser compromised' prisoners whom Heydrich considered 'capable of improvement' were sent to Dachau, Sachsenhausen and Auschwitz, of which the latter initially served as a 'category I' concentration camp and became a fully operational extermination camp only in early 1942. The more 'seriously compromised' inmates whose re-education would take longer were to be sent to 'category II' camps, namely Buchenwald, Flossenbürg and Neuengamme. The only 'category III' camp, Mauthausen, was reserved for 'seriously compromised' prisoners who were unlikely to be capable of reintegration into the people's community. Mauthausen indeed proved to be the camp within the German Reich with the harshest living conditions for inmates and the highest mortality rates.[110]

Concentration camps were not the only penal institutions for those arrested by Heydrich's men or Kurt Daluege's Order Police. Throughout the history of the Third Reich, the number of inmates in normal prisons remained substantially higher than those in concentration camps, rising from over 108,000 inmates in the summer of 1939 to over 180,000 at the time of Heydrich's death in the summer of 1942. These figures included ordinary criminals such as murderers, rapists and thieves, but after 1939 the definition of what constituted criminal behaviour was cast ever wider to include people deemed work-shy or defeatist, all of whom were now also considered enemies of the state.[111]

Harsh treatment was also issued to 'deviant youths', notably the famous 'Swing Kids' who formed an illegal counter-culture to the Hitler Youth by secretly listening to jazz and organizing dance parties at which they played 'degenerate' English or American music. With strongholds in larger cities such as Hamburg or Berlin, the largely apolitical Swing Kids' crime consisted of defying the military culture that permeated the Hitler Youth and cultivating a musical taste that the Nazis considered inappropriate for

German youth. Himmler urged Heydrich not to show any leniency towards their rebellious behaviour and asked him to 'radically eradicate' the 'whole evil'. The 'ringleaders', Himmler insisted, were to be sent to a concentration camp where they 'will have to be beaten before undergoing rigorous exercising and engaging in hard labour'. Their internment was to last no less than two years. Heydrich happily complied: after a first round of arrests in August 1941, the Gestapo broadened its operations in early 1942 and sent several ringleaders to concentration camps throughout the Reich.[112]

Others fared even worse. According to Heydrich's guidelines of 3 September, his terror apparatus was authorized to execute people without trial, even for minor crimes. This 'special treatment', as it was generally termed, was carried out in concentration camps, ordinary prisons and labour camps.[113] In implementing this policy, secrecy was of the essence, both in view of popular opinion and with respect to the Reich's new diplomatic relations with the Soviet Union after the conclusion of the Hitler–Stalin Pact in August 1939. As Heydrich pointed out in February 1940, the pact had created a 'completely new situation' as far as foreign policy was concerned, even though on the domestic front the Communists remained the enemy above all others.[114]

Within the Third Reich, special treatment was particularly aimed at one 'opposition group', which would grow exponentially over the course of the Nazi conquest of Europe: foreign labourers living in Germany. From late 1939 onwards, various state agencies dealt intensively with the issue of how to segregate from the German population the vast number of Polish prisoners of war and workers who had streamed into the Reich. In March 1940, the question was comprehensively regulated through Hermann Göring's so-called Polish decrees. Gestapo agencies were authorized to punish 'transgressions' committed by Polish labourers – 'chronic careless working', work stoppages or acts of sabotage – without reference to any other institution, such as the courts of law. The measures that could be adopted included internment in labour or concentration camps and, in serious cases, execution. Sexual relations between Polish workers and Germans were to be punished by shooting the Polish worker without trial and the deportation of the German partner, whether male or female, to a concentration camp.[115]

Apart from Polish slave labourers, one other 'enemy group' within wartime Germany was targeted by Heydrich's apparatus with particular rigour: the Jews. Surveillance of Jews living in the Third Reich intensified drastically after the start of the war. From September 1939 onwards, the RSHA reinforced its control over the Reich Association of Jews, which had been created in 1939 as an umbrella organization for all

1 Only a few months after the Nazis' seizure of power, Heydrich as head of the Bavarian Political Police where he and Himmler used their powers to incarcerate political opponents of the new regime in Dachau concentration camp.

2 Heydrich's demolished car after the assassination. The bomb struck the rear wheel of Heydrich's Mercedes convertible causing metal splinters and horse-hair from the upholstering to enter Heydrich's body. He died of blood-poisoning a few days later.

a)   b)

3 a) and b) The Heydrich assassins: Josef Gabčík and Jan Kubiš volunteered for a mission to be parachuted into the Nazi-occupied territories in 1941. After the assassination, both were betrayed and killed during the SS siege of their hide-out.

4 Reinhard's father, Bruno Heydrich, was an accomplished musician and composer, whose Conservatory in Halle was a flourishing family business until the First World War.

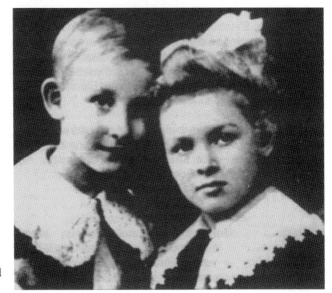

5 Young Reinhard and his sister Maria, c. 1910. The three Heydrich children – Reinhard, Maria and Heinz Siegfried – enjoyed a privileged childhood. Later in life, Reinhard and Maria had a falling out as he treated his family with disdain.

6 Heydrich as a naval officer cadet, 1924. During his time in the German navy Heydrich remained an outsider, but his career seemed to thrive until, in 1931, he was dismissed from military service due to a broken engagement promise and arrogant behaviour towards the military court of honour.

7 The Heydrich wedding, 1931. By the time Reinhard Heydrich married his fiancée, Lina von Osten, he had embarked on a new career path in the SS. Lina had a crucial influence on his decision to join the SS.

8 Heinrich Himmler looks on as Heydrich and Himmler's personal adjutant, Karl Wolff, depart after a birthday party at Himmler's Bavarian home in Waltrudering. No other figure except his wife had a greater impact on Heydrich's career than the Reich Leader SS, Heinrich Himmler. Their personal relationship was close and Heydrich rose steadily in Himmler's shadow.

9 The Hunters: Himmler, Heydrich and the chief of the uniformed German Order Police, Kurt Daluege, shared a passion for deer-hunting. The three men represent the key institutions in charge of repression and mass murder in the Third Reich: the SS, the SD, the Gestapo, and the Order Police.

10 Heydrich (second from left with his back to the camera) explains the exhibits in the SS Freemason Museum in Berlin to a delegation of German industrialists, *c.* 1935. In the first years of the Third Reich, Heydrich perceived the Freemasons as one of the Nazis' key enemies. By 1935, he considered the problem resolved and established a museum for this 'vanished cult' close to Gestapo headquarters in Berlin.

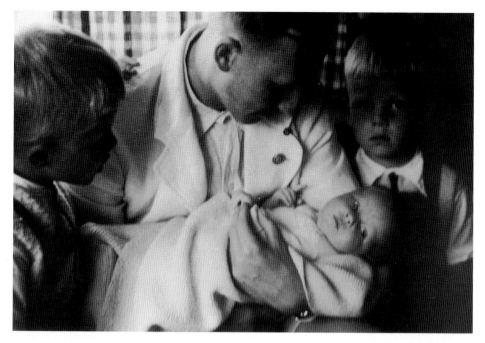

11 Heydrich, his sons and his new-born daughter Silke on the eve of the Second World War. Although he was never really a family man, he felt particular affection for his first-born daughter who worked as a fashion model after the end of the Second World War.

12 Heydrich looks on as Hitler observes the front line in Poland, 1939. During the German attack on Poland Heydrich repeatedly visited the front line, encouraging his SS *Einsatzgruppen* to speed up the process of murdering the Polish elites in the rear of the advancing German armies.

13 Heydrich in pilot gear during the Battle of Britain, 1940. He often indicated that he felt deprived of the possibility to fight on the front and repeatedly participated in combat missions as a fighter pilot, often without Himmler's knowledge.

14 Himmler, Heydrich, and the chief of the Criminal Police, Arthur Nebe, confer after Georg Elser's failed attempt on Hitler's life in 1939. Although they first suspected a British conspiracy, it soon turned out that Elser had no foreign assistance.

15 Heydrich takes a break during a fencing tournament in Berlin, *c.* 1941. Throughout the 1930s and the early stages of the Second World War, Heydrich kept up an ambitious training schedule to keep physically fit and participated in a number of fencing tournaments.

16 Heydrich and Göring at the latter's birthday reception in January 1941. Göring and Heydrich had a troubled relationship at first, but became close collaborators on Nazi anti-Semitic policies after Kristallnacht. It was Göring who authorised Heydrich to prepare a 'total solution of the Jewish question'.

17 Rudolf Hess, Himmler (first and second left) and Heydrich (centre) listen attentively as Professor Konrad Meyer explains his plans for German settlement in the East, March 1941. Meyer's General Plan East was designed to provide a road-map for the ethnic reordering of Eastern and Central Europe and played a major role in Heydrich's thinking on Germanization policies.

18 Heydrich saltues the SS flag as it is raised over Prague Castle on his arrival in September 1941. As acting Reich Protector of Bohemia and Moravia, Heydrich successfully suppressed the Czech opposition through rigorous persecution and instigated racial policies designed to Germanize the Protectorate of Bohemia and Moravia

19 Heydrich greets his former adjutant, Carl Albrecht Oberg, on his arrival in Paris where he installs him as the new higher SS and police leader in France, May 1942. Oberg was the first higher SS leader in France, marking a major breakthrough for the SS whose power had previously been largely confined to Germany and the occupied East. This was Heydrich's last journey. One month later, he was dead.

20 An emotional Himmler speaks at Heydrich's funeral in Berlin. It was the largest state funeral held in Nazi Germany during the war and attended by Hitler and virtually every influential figure in the Third Reich.

remaining Jewish organizations in Germany. In the first months after the outbreak of war, Heydrich and his RSHA further perfected mechanisms for excluding the Jews from German society. On 12 September 1939, for example, Heydrich banned Jews from shopping in all but a few select food shops. Less than two weeks later, he ordered all radio sets in the possession of Jews to be confiscated throughout the Reich.[116]

Polish slave labourers and German Jews were the chief victims of Heydrich's terror on the home front. But the outbreak of war also changed the destiny of other groups that the Nazi leadership considered racially inferior or unfit. Just prior to the outbreak of the war, on 1 September, Hitler authorized a special euthanasia programme, the so-called T4 Aktion. Run by the party Chancellery and Hitler's personal physician, Dr Karl Brandt, but aided by the RSHA's technical staff, T4 was designed to select and kill physically or mentally handicapped children and adults. Until August 1941, approximately 70,000 disabled Germans were murdered, providing Heydrich's technical staff with an expertise in mass killings that they would put to use against Russian POWs and Jewish civilians over the following years. Concern about potential unrest on the home front led to the official halt of the euthanasia killings in August 1941, although the murder of disabled people continued in a more covert way throughout the war.[117]

The outbreak of war also impacted profoundly on the fate of Germany's roughly 26,000 Gypsies. Suspect because of their lifestyle, they had been subjected to constant harassment and social exclusion ever since the Nazis came to power. In the second half of the 1930s, anti-Gypsy policies escalated further, leading to mass arrests in 1938 and to Heydrich's announcement that further measures would be introduced shortly to guarantee the 'racial separation of the Gypsies from the German people'.[118]

On the outbreak of war, Heydrich banned Gypsies from plying their itinerant trades, thus deliberately undermining their sole means of making a living. In pursuit of a 'final solution' to the 'Gypsy Question', Heydrich informed his senior staff on 21 September 1939, and again at the end of January 1941, that the Gypsies would be deported alongside the Jews from Germany to Eastern Poland. This order was swiftly implemented: by late April 1940, some 2,500 Gypsies had been sent to the General Government.[119]

The murders, expulsions and arrests that were carried out by Heydrich's men both in Germany and in the newly occupied territories during the early months of the Second World War testified to the radicalizing impact of war on Nazi policies of persecution. For Heydrich and his closest collaborators, the increasing brutality with which enemies of the state were suppressed, expelled and often murdered was necessitated and justified by the historic battle with Germany's internal and external enemies on which the Nazis had just embarked. Even if systematic mass murder remained the exception rather than the rule in Heydrich's handling of political and ethnic enemies in late 1939 and early 1940, he and the Nazi leadership as a whole had crossed an important line on the slippery path to genocide.

CHAPTER VII

At War with the World

Into the West

ON 9 APRIL 1940, AFTER MORE THAN SIX MONTHS OF INACTIVITY ON the Western Front, the Wehrmacht staged a surprise attack on neutral Denmark and Norway. It did so primarily in order to pre-empt a much feared British military intervention in Scandinavia, as well as to secure coastal ports for German submarine operations and the ice-free harbour of Narvik for vital iron-ore transports from Sweden. Both Copenhagen and Oslo fell into German hands that same day. Unlike the Danish, however, who surrendered within two hours of the German invasion, the Norwegians fought back staunchly until they were eventually forced to surrender two months later.[1]

From the very beginning of the military attacks, it was clear to the SS leadership that these campaigns would differ substantially from the war against Poland. The people of Northern Europe, both Hitler and Alfred Rosenberg emphasized in their writings and speeches, were to play an important role in the future Germanic Empire. A regime of sheer terror would be detrimental to these interests. While Himmler and Heydrich shared these beliefs, they were nonetheless disappointed to learn that in Western Europe – unlike in Poland – the army would be allowed to run a more traditional military occupation regime, which would necessarily undermine vital SS interests.[2] The excessive violence of Heydrich's *Einsatzgruppen* and the *Selbstschutz* during the Polish campaign was at the heart of the army's refusal to accept any SS involvement during the military assault on Western Europe. Heydrich noted in an uncharacteristically understated letter to Kurt Daluege that regarding 'fundamental issues pertaining to the combating of enemies of the state' an 'entirely different opinion' prevailed among the 'senior commanders of the army' from that held within the RSHA.[3] By late March, a frustrated Heydrich told his senior staff members that the planned participation of *Einsatzkommandos* in the western campaigns had been 'called off'.[4]

Seemingly deprived of the ability to play an active role in the invasion of Western Europe, Heydrich opted for a 'heroic' gesture and asked Himmler for permission temporarily to join the Luftwaffe on the Norwegian front. Heydrich had been passionate about flying long before the outbreak of war. From 1935 onwards, he had trained as a sports pilot and repeatedly participated in aerobatic flight shows. But his ambitions went further. During the summer of 1939, usually at dawn before work, he trained to become a fighter pilot at the pilot school in Werneuchen near Berlin and then at Staaken airport until he successfully passed his examination. On 12 September 1939, he carried out his first combat mission as a turret gunner over Poland. [5]

Both in private and in public, Heydrich had repeatedly expressed his frustration that as 'political soldiers' on the home front he and his men were deprived of the 'good fortune' to serve and die for Germany.[6] He must have been insistent in his pleas to join the fighting, for contrary to earlier orders forbidding him to endanger his life by flying planes Himmler gave his permission and on 14 April 1940 Heydrich arrived in Oslo as a vaguely disguised air force captain. He stayed with Fighter Squadron 77 for a total of four weeks, flying attacks on retreating Norwegian troops, socializing with his fellow officers, and playing card games until late at night. For Heydrich, who had grown up in a world permeated by heroic tales of bloodshed and had spent the better part of the 1920s in the German navy without ever witnessing any real fighting, the front experience was the fulfilment of a long-held adventurous dream that had previously been denied to him twice: first by his late birth in 1904 and then again by his dismissal from the navy in 1931.[7]

On 5 May, he reported to Himmler that he was well and that the front experience was both 'interesting and instructive'. Himmler quickly responded, expressing his fatherly concern: 'I think of you often and hope that you are well and again wish you much luck and all the best! Let me hear from you on a daily basis if at all possible.' Himmler's concern was not unfounded: on 13 May 1940 Heydrich's Messerschmitt 109 overshot the runway at Stavanger on takeoff. While Heydrich suffered only a minor hand injury, the plane itself was completely destroyed. The following day, he returned to his desk in Berlin sporting a front-line bar in bronze – awarded after twenty combat missions – and an Iron Cross second class.[8]

The real purpose of Heydrich's visit to Norway, however, was not to indulge his passion for flying, but rather to orchestrate the first wave of arrests of political opponents in Oslo and other Norwegian cities. On 20 April, shortly before Hitler's appointment of Josef Terboven as Reich commissioner for Norway, Himmler received Hitler's consent to install a higher SS and police leader in Norway and to send an SS task force into the country.[9] Heydrich, jubilant over Hitler's unexpected change of mind, ordered the immediate dispatch of an *Einsatzgruppe* under Dr Franz Walter Stahlecker, one of his most trusted men who had previously been in charge of the Security Police in Prague.[10]

Stahlecker arrived in Oslo on 29 April with around 200 Security Police and SD men who were subsequently sent to Norway's larger cities: Oslo, Bergen, Trondheim, Kristiansand and Stavanger. Heydrich instructed the commando leaders that the mission ahead of them was *not* an expedition into 'enemy territory'. He emphasized instead that Norway 'has been placed under the protection of the German Reich, and it can expect that all measures taken by the Security Police will remain solely within a framework that is absolutely essential for securing the war effort'. While enemies of the Reich were to be neutralized, he continued, this task was to be carried out 'with the utmost skilfulness and tact'. Both officers and NCOs would be 'ruthlessly and strictly prosecuted' should they act in violatation of these instructions.[11]

While Heydrich was still recovering from his minor injury received when his plane overshot the runway at Stavanger, the Wehrmacht had already launched its large-scale attack on France and the Benelux countries. Success was anything but certain. Memories of the protracted stalemate on the Western Front during the Great War were still vivid, and Germany's opponents substantially outnumbered the Wehrmacht in troops and equipment. Yet thanks to poorly marshalled opposition, some inspired strategic decisions, high morale and luck, German troops delivered a crushing blow. The Netherlands surrendered in only four days; Belgium in eighteen. France lasted scarcely a month.

Heydrich, in common with most German generals, was surprised by the swiftness of the military advance and quickly realized that immediate action was of the essence if his SD was to play any role whatsoever in the occupation regimes in Western Europe. Following Hitler's hasty appointment of the Austrian Nazi politician Arthur Seyss-Inquart as Reich commissioner of the occupied Netherlands on 18 May, Himmler managed to appoint a higher SS and police leader: the Austrian Heimwehr veteran Hanns Albin Rauter. Hans Nockemann, who had arrived in Amsterdam immediately after the Dutch surrender, became Heydrich's commander of the Security Police and the SD in the Netherlands.[12]

Heydrich was nevertheless dissatisfied. The instalment of Rauter and Nockemann in late May 1940 had occurred 'too late' to combat political opponents and émigrés effectively in the occupied territories of the West, since the military Abwehr had 'failed to obtain relevant information on the political émigrés'. Had the State Police been deployed during the campaign, documents of relevance could have been secured that were now presumably lost for ever.[13]

The situation in Belgium, Heydrich quickly realized, was even less favourable. Although Himmler had pleaded with Hitler to install a civilian Reich commissioner rather than a military occupation regime, Hitler ignored his wishes and the Wehrmacht managed to stay in charge of the occupation for almost the entire war. The military administration in Brussels was also responsible for Luxembourg and northern France (Pas de Calais and Nord). The whole territory, with a population of some 12 million people, was run by a conservative general, Baron Alexander von Falkenhausen, whose close relations with members of the German resistance would subsequently lead to his arrest in July 1944. In the first weeks of the occupation, Falkenhausen and the energetic chief of the military administration, Eggert Reeder, successfully managed to fend off the SS leadership's advances into their sphere of influence. Despite his honorific SS membership, Reeder permitted Heydrich only a tiny foothold in Brussels where Heydrich's protégé, Max Thomas, was installed as head of the Security Police and the SD for Belgium and France. Thomas struggled to exert much influence on German occupation policies in Belgium in the face of opposition from the military administration.[14]

In France, the most significant prize of the Wehrmacht's Western campaign, the situation was no different. The military administration that was set up after the French defeat in the summer of 1940 was unwilling to grant the RSHA any influence on occupation policy. Following the armistice on 22 June, a small Security Police and SD contingent under the command of the thirty-year-old Dr Helmut Knochen – Heydrich spoke of a 'pitiful' little group of fifteen men whom he managed to dispatch with Göring's blessing – was sent to Paris in order to monitor the activities of 'Jews, Communists, émigrés, lodges and Churches'. The group consisted of highly ambitious young men, but until May 1942, when Heydrich's former personal adjutant Carl Albrecht Oberg was installed as higher SS and police leader in Paris, their actions were restricted by the overall authority of the military administration under the arch-conservative Prussian General Otto von Stülpnagel.[15]

From Heydrich's personal point of view, matters were further complicated by the fact that Werner Best, who had left the RSHA after his falling-out with Heydrich, was appointed head of the civil administration in occupied France. Although Heydrich had no reason to doubt Best's firm ideological commitment to SS policies, he knew that, in implementing these policies,

Best would largely rely on his own apparatus rather than on Heydrich's agents. Given that Heydrich had no intention of reconciling with Best, it would be difficult to exert any direct influence on German occupation policies in France for the foreseeable future.[16]

Nazi Germany's victorious campaigns in Western Europe thus constituted a setback for Heydrich. He had not been able to use the conquests of the spring of 1940 – the occupation of Norway, Denmark, the Netherlands, Belgium and Luxembourg – in the same way as the campaign against Poland. But he was not ready to despair completely. Distrustful of the military Abwehr, led by Canaris, and confident that Germany would emerge victorious from the now imminent Battle of Britain, he instructed his staff to compile arrest lists for the soon-to-be conquered British Isles. Franz Six, head of Department II in Heydrich's RSHA, was put in charge of *Einsatzgruppen* operations in the United Kingdom while Heydrich himself prepared for flight operations over the Channel. His actual involvement in the Battle of Britain, however, amounted to no more than a handful of patrol flights over the North Sea island of Wangerooge – a perfect way of being involved in the battle without running the risk of actually getting killed.[17]

Based on the interrogations of the abducted British MI6 agents Best and Stevens and on his own preconceptions, Walter Schellenberg compiled a handbook on Britain for Gestapo use after a successful invasion. Schellenberg's classified *Informationsheft GB* offers a glimpse of his and Heydrich's perception of Britain as a country supposedly run by Freemasons, Jews and a small public-school-trained elite. 'Democratic freedom in Britain' was described as a sham, while the Archbishop of Canterbury and the Church of England Council on Foreign Relations were held responsible for anti-German propaganda. At the end of the document, the 'Special Search List GB' ('Sonderfahndungsliste GB') listed 2,820 individuals for special Gestapo attention, of whom thirty were to be arrested immediately after the invasion. Had the Nazis ever conquered Britain, the Gestapo would have arrested not only Winston Churchill and the leader of the Labour Party, Clement Attlee, but also pacifists like Norman Angell, writers such as H. G. Wells and German émigrés such as the novelist Stefan Zweig.[18]

The 'Special Search List GB' quickly disappeared in the archives of the RSHA. In the autumn of 1940, after a series of bombing raids that left more than 20,000 civilians dead, the Luftwaffe abandoned the Battle of Britain and the navy shelved its plan for Operation Sea Lion, the invasion of England. Hitler instead decided to attack the Soviet Union the following year as an indirect means of putting pressure on Britain.[19]

Madagascar

In the intoxicating summer of 1940, when Germany seemed to have won the war and influential elements in the British government were at least secretly considering the option of a negotiated peace, Heydrich's thoughts turned to the future. While the military conquest of Western Europe had brought him more frustrations than successes, the fall of France promised to open up new avenues for the solution of the Jewish question. The euphoria of victory in June 1940 provided the perfect moment for a renewed attempt to implement sweeping plans for the total removal of all Jews and Poles from the now massively expanded Third Reich. Following the French defeat, earlier plans to push the Jews into a reservation in Poland were replaced with another project for the territorial solution of the Jewish problem: the Madagascar plan.

The idea of creating a large Jewish reservation on Madagascar, a French colonial island off the African coast, was hardly original. Since the late nineteenth century, it had been promoted in various anti-Semitic pamphlets about the future of European Jewry, not only in Germany, but also in France, Britain and the Netherlands. The Polish, French and British governments of the late 1930s all toyed with the idea of resettling at least some of 'their' Jews on Madagascar, although none of these plans ever materialized.[20]

Heydrich's SD, too, had been contemplating the possibility of transforming some inhospitable territory abroad into a future Jewish state ever since the early 1930s, but practical planning was slow.[21] By 1937 internal discussions had proceeded only to the point where the SD's Jewish experts could present Heydrich with a memorandum that envisaged achieving the 'de-Judification of Germany' through the emigration of German Jews into countries with a 'low cultural level', thus preventing the emergence of 'new world conspiracy centres' in more advanced countries. Alongside Madagascar, the territories of Ecuador, Colombia and Palestine were advocated as possible areas for future Jewish settlement.[22] In early March of the following year, the director of the SD's Jewish desk, Herbert Hagen, ordered his subordinate, Adolf Eichmann, to prepare for Heydrich a memorandum on the foreign-policy implications of the Jewish question.[23]

In the early summer of 1940 such previously abstract plans suddenly seemed feasible and Heydrich quickly grasped their relevance as a potential sinecure to his numerically increasing Jewish problem. If the concentration of East European Jews around Lublin was an idea that had proved impossible to realize, the concept of shipping all European Jews to Madagascar seemed like a panacea to Germany's frustrated demographic engineers. Inspired by the sudden availability of France's colonial possessions, Heydrich quickly informed Himmler of the new possibilities.

Himmler in turn presented Hitler with a memorandum on the 'treatment of alien populations in the East'. Within the broader context of ethnic engineering in Eastern Europe, Himmler speculated on the future fate of the Jews. He envisaged that through 'large-scale emigration of all Jews to Africa or to some other colony I hope to see the term Jew completely extinguished'. Although Himmler, out of 'inner conviction', rejected 'the Bolshevik methods of physical annihilation of a people as unGerman and impossible', he advocated forced migration as a possible non-genocidal solution. Implicit in his suggestions, however, was the subtext that any colonial setting was likely to lack the basic conditions necessary for the survival of all of the deported Jews. Hitler commented that the memorandum was 'very good and correct' and repeatedly referred to the Madagascar project over the coming weeks.[24]

The earliest concrete plan for Jewish resettlement on Madagascar was worked out not by the RSHA but by the Foreign Office's newly appointed Jewish expert, Franz Rademacher, a young career diplomat who had recently returned from his first post in Montevideo. Rademacher presented a first memorandum on the Madagascar project to his boss, Under Secretary Martin Luther, on 3 June 1940, less than three weeks before the official French surrender at Compiègne.[25] Rademacher's proposed solution to the Jewish problem – 'all Jews out of Europe' – envisaged that Madagascar would be 'placed under the administration of a German police governor who will be subordinated to the administration of the Reich Leader SS. In this territory the Jews will be granted self-administration.' By adopting this strategy the Jews would remain 'in German hands' to guarantee 'the future good behaviour of their racial comrades in America'. The Madagascar project (just like the Jewish reservation project in Poland that preceded it) was thus intended as a form of hostage taking.[26]

Heydrich quickly got wind of the Foreign Office's plans. Although he, too, believed that a unique opportunity had arrived to solve the Jewish question, he was dismayed that the Foreign Office had dared to venture into an area he perceived as his own jurisdiction. Convinced that only his apparatus had the necessary expertise to deal with the Jewish problem, he acted swiftly. On 24 June, only two days after France had signed the armistice, he wrote a letter to Foreign Minister von Ribbentrop, reminding him that in January 1939 Göring had placed *him* in charge of co-ordinating Jewish emigration and demanding to be included in all future deliberations about the planned 'territorial solution'. Heydrich also reminded Ribbentrop that his forced emigration policies up until September 1939 had been highly successful, indicating that he, not the Foreign Office, was ideally placed to orchestrate the now necessary 'territorial final solution'. This 'solution' would tackle the 'whole problem' of some 3.25 million Jews *presently* under German control'.[27]

Heydrich did not wait for Ribbentrop's reply. Preparations for a comprehensive deportation plan were begun by the RSHA immediately, even though Heydrich intended to see the plan implemented only after the anticipated end of the war in 1942. On Heydrich's orders, Eichmann and his team of Jewish experts began to collate climatic and geographic information on Madagascar from the German Tropical Institute in Hamburg and the French Colonial Ministry. Eichmann also consulted with representatives of the two major German shipping lines, Hapag and Norddeutsche Lloyd, for their views on how to solve transportation issues.[28] Fantastical as it may seem, the Madagascar project was taken very seriously by Heydrich, both because it promised a major breakthrough regarding the Jewish problem and because it offered a way out of the long-standing conflict with the powerful ruler of the General Government, Hans Frank. Frank, delighted to hear that the deportations from Germany would no longer affect the General Government, took note of the Madagascar plan with 'colossal relief'.[29]

In response to Heydrich's letter of 24 June, Ribbentrop conceded Heydrich's jurisdiction in the administration of a potential Jewish 'super-ghetto' on Madagascar and instructed Rademacher to proceed with his preparations in 'closest agreement' with the RSHA. In his 'Plan for the Solution of the Jewish Question' of 2 July 1940, Rademacher envisaged the establishment of a 'police state' on Madagascar in which the 4 million Jews of Europe currently under German control would live under an autono-mous (but SS-controlled) jurisdiction with its own police and postal administration, a move, he believed, that would underline Germany's 'generosity'. The real power, however, would lie in the hands of Heydrich's Security Police, the only agency with 'the necessary experience in this area: it has the means to prevent escapes from the island, and it also has the experience to take those suitable punitive measures which may become necessary on account of hostile actions against Germany by Jews in the United States'. The Jews would be held financially liable for the entire resettlement process to Madagascar and all their European assets would be administered by a special European bank for that purpose.[30]

Despite the far-reaching responsibilities offered to the Security Police by the Foreign Office, Heydrich was not impressed. Two weeks later, on 15 August, he transmitted the RSHA's own extensive proposals for the Madagascar project to Ribbentrop. The entire project, from the logistical planning stage to the management of a police state on the island, was to be the responsibility of Heydrich, whose empowerment in matters of Jewish emigration by Göring was once more reiterated.[31]

Although much more detailed than Rademacher's original plan, it deviated from it in only a few important respects: the RSHA plan contained no vacuous rhetoric about demonstrating Germany's 'generosity' to the world by granting Jewish autonomy. Heydrich and his advisers envisaged that after the war had been brought to a triumphant conclusion, several million Jews were to be shipped off to Madagascar within the next five years. The first shipments of Jewish deportees would mainly consist of farmers, builders, craftsmen, workers and doctors up to the age of forty-five, who would immediately begin to make the inhospitable areas of the island habitable. Unlike Rademacher, Heydrich envisaged a much more limited form of Jewish self-government, confined to the creation of special Jewish organizations for carrying out selected tasks that would be given to them by the SS.[32]

The notion that millions of European Jews could be transported to the inhospitable island of Madagascar testifies to a further radicalization in Heydrich's inner circle. As Peter Longerich has argued convincingly, the project clearly anticipated a huge death toll among the deportees and possibly even entailed a conscious attempt at physical extermination, even if such an outcome could theoretically be prevented by 'good behaviour' on the part of the United States. The planning for the final solution within the RSHA was gradually evolving toward the 'eradication' – if still 'only' through neglect – that Himmler had rejected only three months earlier.[33]

The Madagascar plan remained on Heydrich's mind over the following weeks. In a circular to all Security Police headquarters in Germany on 30 October 1940, he described the 'plans for the resettlement' of all Jews within the German sphere of influence that would be implemented 'after the conclusion of peace' as an 'evacuation overseas'.[34] Even more than a month later, in December 1940, Eichmann told the Interior Ministry's racial expert, Bernhard Lösener, that the Madagascar plan was still sitting on Heydrich's desk, awaiting his approval.[35] By that stage, however, it had become highly unlikely that the plan would be implemented in the near future. From the start, its implementation had depended not only on the defeat of France, but also on an expected peace settlement with Britain, which would have enabled the Germans to use the British merchant fleet for the envisaged deportations. After the failure of the Luftwaffe to secure victory over the RAF in the Battle of Britain and the abandonment of the German invasion plan, the Madagascar plan was dropped, primarily because the sea routes from Europe to the Indian Ocean could not be secured.

Heydrich's frustration grew immeasurably in the autumn of 1940. After the Nisko disaster, the Madagascar plan was the second major territorial solution that had been devised and abandoned within only a few months.

Yet, despite the failure of the plan, Heydrich remained firmly committed to the idea of expelling the Jews to the furthest extremity of the German sphere of influence. If Madagascar was no longer an option, another territory would have to be found. 'Decimation' of the deported in significant numbers had been part of Heydrich's thinking ever since the invasion of Poland, but there is no evidence or indication that he had yet developed any comprehensive plan for the systematic mass murder of all Jews within the German sphere of influence.

Throughout the autumn of 1940 and the spring of 1941, piecemeal deportations of Jews and other undesirables from the borderlands of the Reich into the General Government continued. Following the French defeat and the annexation of Alsace-Lorraine, the SS immediately began to expel the region's Jews, Gypsies, asocials and French nationalists. Between the summer and winter of 1940, the Germans had deported more than 47,000 people from Lorraine and another 24,000 from Alsace. A further 71,000 people who had fled the region during the invasion were barred from returning.[36]

In the neighbouring German *Gaue* of Baden and Saarpfalz, local authorities used the opportunity to rid themselves of 'their' Jews, proposing to Himmler and Heydrich that they could be deported to unoccupied Vichy France. Heydrich jumped at the opportunity and on 22 October police squads descended upon the Jews in every village in Baden and Saarpfalz. With merely two hours' notice, the deportees were ordered to pack no more than fifty kilograms of luggage before being put on trains to France. On 22 and 23 October, nine trains, two from Saarpfalz and seven from Baden, departed with more than 6,000 German Jews for Vichy France. To Heydrich's satisfaction, the round-ups proceeded 'without friction or incident' and were 'barely noticed by the population'.[37] However, the Vichy authorities, having no desire to be treated as a dumping ground for German Jews, interned them on the French–Spanish border and complained to the Foreign Office, which was unaware of the deportations. Heydrich conceded to Luther that the deportations had been carried out without prior consultation. However, he emphasized that he had acted on the basis of a Führer order. Ribbentrop fell into line and ordered that the French complaint be treated 'dilatorily'.[38] From Heydrich's point of view (and that of many regional Nazi Gauleiters in the Reich), these small-scale successes and deportations were hardly satisfying. A 'total solution' of the Jewish question had yet to be found.

In November or December 1940, roughly at the same time that Hitler made a decision in principle to attack the Soviet Union the following year, Heydrich received the order from Hitler (via Göring) to prepare a first draft for a 'final solution project' to be implemented after the war's end.

Although the exact wording of Heydrich's proposal – presented to Göring during a two-hour meeting on 24 January 1941 – is unknown, it is possible to reconstruct its content.[39] An Eichmann memorandum of 4 December sheds some light on how Heydrich and his inner circle saw the 'solution to the Jewish question' at this time. Madagascar was no longer mentioned. Instead Eichmann referred to the 'resettlement of the Jews' from German-controlled Europe into a 'territory yet to be determined'. Eichmann calculated that this project would affect 'some 5.8 million Jews', a significant increase when compared to the figure of 4 million Jews cited in the RSHA's Madagascar plan of the previous summer. The Jews targeted for deportation now included those of Germany's South-east European allies and puppet states as well as those living in the French colonies.[40]

A second memorandum, written by Heydrich's Jewish expert in Paris, Theodor Dannecker, in January 1941, likewise indicates how far plans had developed since the summer of 1940:

> In accordance with the will of the Führer, the Jewish question within the German-dominated or -controlled part of Europe must be brought to a final solution after the war's end. The head of the Security Police and the SD [Heydrich] has already received ... orders from the Führer to prepare a plan for the final solution project. – Thanks to the extensive existing experiences of the Sipo and the SD in the treatment of Jews and the long-standing preparatory works in this area the main points of the project have already been mapped out. It has been presented to the Führer and the Reichsmarschall [Göring] ... [The plan entails] total expulsion of the Jews on the basis of previous plans and a detailed settlement programme in a territory yet to be determined.[41]

The question remained as to where the Jews were going to be deported. Given that Hitler had by now made a decision to attack the Soviet Union, it is almost certain that Heydrich began to view the General Government as merely a collection point for large-scale deportations into the soon-to-be conquered areas of the Soviet Union. Since Hitler's plan to invade the Soviet Union the following summer could not be mentioned openly without compromising the secrecy surrounding the preparations for Operation Barbarossa, Heydrich's correspondence with other decision-makers in the Nazi bureaucracy during these months referred to a 'territory yet to be determined' or 'the country that will be chosen later'.[42]

When, on 26 March, Heydrich met Göring to discuss both his proposals of January 1941 and his future jurisdiction in the yet to be conquered Soviet territories, Göring approved his suggestions 'with one amendment concerning the jurisdiction of Rosenberg'. The reference to Alfred Rosenberg – the designated Minister for the Occupied Eastern Territories – indicates yet again that the 'territory yet to be determined' was the Soviet Union.[43] Heydrich resubmitted his revised draft on the solution of the Jewish question on 31 July 1941 when Göring formally entrusted him with the task of undertaking 'preparations in organizational, technical and material respects for the complete solution to the Jewish question in the German area of influence in Europe'.[44]

So far as the Nazi solution to the Jewish question was concerned, the era of mass expulsions ended when military preparations for Operation Barbarossa brought the last deportation transports to Poland to a halt in mid-March 1941. Still, in the summer of 1941, Heydrich continued to envisage the final solution in terms of forced resettlement to the furthest extremity of the German sphere of influence. In the context of these forced resettlements, countless expellees would die of thirst, hunger and exhaustion – a side-effect to which Heydrich was largely indifferent. His task, as he understood it, was to remove the Jews to the furthest part of the German sphere of influence, not to murder them, but if some of them died in the course of these expulsions, then it was no concern of his. Although inherently destructive and murderous, he had not, as yet, begun to think of the final solution in terms of the systematic murder of every Jew in Europe, irrespective of age and gender.[45]

Between 1939 and 1941, Heydrich primarily advocated two anti-Jewish policies: ghettoization and expulsion, with the former intended as a short-term measure to facilitate the latter, longer-term goal. Expulsion to the furthest extremity of the German Empire, not systematic, indiscriminate murder, was Heydrich's solution to the Jewish problem in this period. The relentless search for a reception area – first east of Kraków, then around Lublin, in Madagascar and then again in the General Government – characterized Heydrich's anti-Jewish thinking in these months. The gradual transition to genocide would follow only after the German attack on the Soviet Union in 1941.

Preparing for Total War

Following his swift rise in the SS hierarchy after 1931, Heydrich had experienced a number of serious setbacks since the outbreak of war in September 1939. The atrocities committed by his *Einsatzgruppen* in Poland had greatly strained relations with the Wehrmacht to the extent that the Sipo and the SD were granted scarcely any role in the occupation of Western Europe. Moreover, both Himmler's ambitious settlement plans and Heydrich's own proposals for a territorial solution to the Jewish question had not achieved any great success. It was in these circumstances that a new opportunity arose following Hitler's decision to attack the Soviet Union. Heydrich was determined not let this opportunity pass him by.

In the spring of 1941, Hitler's plans for a military confrontation with the Soviet Union took firm shape and Heydrich was well aware that Operation Barbarossa was to be fought as a war of destruction. When, on 30 March, Hitler assembled the supreme commanders of the armed forces in the New Reich Chancellery, he emphasized that the impending war with the Soviet Union would be a fight to the death between two irreconcilable ideologies, a war that left no room for outdated notions of chivalry. The supporters of the Bolshevik cause, including members of the secret police and political commissars, were to be killed on the spot.[46] Unlike in the case of Western Europe, Himmler would now be 'granted special responsibilities on behalf of the Führer' in the rear area of the army where the SS would act 'independently' and on its 'own responsibility'. In this way, the Wehrmacht leadership believed it could keep its distance from the mass murders that were expected to occur on an even larger scale than had been the case in Poland.[47]

Negotiations between Heydrich and the General Quartermaster of the army, Eduard Wagner, about the exact nature of SS and Wehrmacht collaboration in the forthcoming campaign against the Soviet Union began in February 1941 and intensified in mid-March when Heydrich returned from a brief holiday on the Baltic coast. The atmosphere was far more cordial than during their previous discussions in the lead-up to the Polish campaign of 1939. The draft agreement of late March 1941 specified that the 'implementation of certain security policy tasks' required the 'deployment of special commandos of the Security Police' in the operational area.[48]

The exact task of these special units was only vaguely described: in the rear operational areas near the front, the task forces would be in charge of the 'identification and combating of subversive activities against the Reich'. The *Einsatzkommandos* were to fulfil their tasks 'on their own responsibility', receiving their orders for 'executive measures against the civilian population' directly from Heydrich. At the same time, they were subject to the army's authority in all matters of 'transport, supply and lodging'. Phrased differently, Heydrich and Wagner had agreed that the intended mass liquidations of Communist functionaries in the army's rear would be the sole responsibility of the *Einsatzgruppen*, which, in turn, could rely on the Wehrmacht's logistical support. Close co-operation with the army was to be ensured through an SS task-force liaison officer on the staff of each army. The military would be kept informed of all of Heydrich's orders and instructions to the *Einsatzgruppen*.[49]

On the same day, 26 March, Göring asked Heydrich to produce a brief memorandum for the army, informing them of the 'dangerous nature' of the Soviet Union's political commissars, secret police and Jews, so that they would 'understand who they will be putting up against the wall'.[50]

The negotiations between the SS and the army were still under way when unexpected events occurred in South-eastern Europe. On 27 March the pro-German Yugoslav government under Dragiša Cvetković was toppled by a military coup, giving rise to fears in Berlin that the new rulers in Belgrade would join the Allied war effort against Nazi Germany. Both the army and the SS leadership hurriedly made preparations for an improvised attack on Yugoslavia. Simultaneously, Hitler decided to invade Greece, which was already at war with Germany's ally, Italy, and had successfully resisted the Italian advance with the aid of its British ally. On 6 April the Wehrmacht marched into Yugoslavia, which capitulated less than two weeks later. Greece was occupied by German troops by the end of April. Heydrich hastily requested Himmler's permission to join the advancing armed forces and briefly participated in the attack as a fighter pilot, but the swiftness of the German victory prevented him from having any major involvement in combat.[51]

Two *Einsatzgruppen* of the Security Police and the SD followed the advancing German troops into the Balkans – one in Yugoslavia, the other in Greece. The question of what role Heydrich's Security Police and SD should play in this improvised war was handled pragmatically on the basis of the draft agreement that Heydrich and Wagner had worked out in late March, although with one small but highly significant modification: the list of persons whom Heydrich's men were to arrest included not only 'emigrés, saboteurs and terrorists', but also the far less delimited group of 'Communists and Jews'. From Heydrich's point of view, the deployment of SS *Einsatzgruppen* in the Balkan campaign was a major improvement when compared to the setbacks experienced the previous year during the occupation of Denmark, France, Belgium and the Netherlands.[52]

On 16 April, one day before the surrender of Yugoslavia, Heydrich and Himmler met with Wagner in a hotel room in the Austrian city of Graz. On the basis of the draft of 26 March, they reached final agreement on a 'regulation of the deployment of the Security Police and the SD within the framework of the army' for the impending war against the Soviet Union. Although 'Communists and Jews' were not expressly mentioned in the final document, all of the participants in the meeting were fully aware would be the main target of the conflict ahead.[53]

Heydrich had not waited for the conclusion of this agreement to start his own preparations for the war against the Soviet Union. Throughout

March, he and his chief of personnel, Bruno Streckenbach, selected leading officers for the originally envisaged three *Einsatzgruppen*, each of which was to follow one army group into the Soviet Union. Eventually, a fourth task force was added for the Romanian front. Task Force A, led by Dr Franz Walter Stahlecker, was to follow Army Group North through the Baltic States. Task Force B, under the command of Arthur Nebe, was instructed to advance with Army Group Centre through Belorussia and central Russia all the way to Moscow. Task Forces C and D, under the command of Dr Dr Otto Rasch and Dr Otto Ohlendorf, were to operate in the Ukraine, Romania and the Crimea. Each of the task forces was, in turn, subdivided into two special commandos operating directly behind the front and two task force commandos operating in their rear. Compared with the 3 million Wehrmacht soldiers that were about to plunge into Soviet territory, Heydrich's *Einsatzgruppen* were almost insignificant in size: in total, the four task forces numbered only 3,000 to 3,200 men, composed of members of the SD and the Security Police, and also of ordinary policemen and members of the Waffen-SS.[54]

As in previous campaigns, the leadership of the *Einsatzgruppen* was dominated by highly educated Nazis from Heydrich's RSHA empire, most of them under the age of forty. Of the seventeen leading officers of Einsatzgruppe A, for example, eleven were lawyers, nine of them with doctoral degrees. Thirteen of the men had been members of the Nazi Party or one of its affiliated organizations before 1933 and all of them had been long-standing members of the SS and police apparatus prior to the outbreak of war in 1939. Whatever their previous postings, many of the leading officers of the *Einsatzgruppen* had risen through Heydrich's SD and presumably impressed him not just because of their widely shared ideological views on Jews, Bolsheviks and Slavs, but because they exemplified the RSHA's dominant ethos of energetic ruthlessness, initiative and activism. Throughout May and early June, those assigned to the task forces assembled in the border police training schools in Pretzsch and the neighbouring towns of Düben and Bad Schmiedeberg in Saxony where Heydrich repeatedly visited them before the invasion.[55]

Himmler and Heydrich met several times in late May and early June to finalize their preparations for Operation Barbarossa.[56] No detailed records of these meetings have survived, but it is likely that they discussed the overall SS strategy for the war against the Soviet Union, which was revealed two days later. On 11 June, Himmler gathered the entire SS leadership – including Heydrich, Daluege, Wolff and the three designated higher SS and police leaders for the occupied Soviet territories, Hans-Adolf Prützmann, Erich von dem Bach-Zelewski and Friedrich Jeckeln – for a four-day conference at the Wewelsburg, a medieval castle near

Paderborn in Westphalia that Himmler wished to develop into the cultural and spiritual centre of the SS.[57]

During this meeting, the SS leadership revelled in the forthcoming possibilities for demographic engineering that would dwarf the experiments of the previous eighteen months. Himmler referred to an estimated death toll of 30 million people among the populations of Eastern Europe. His speech reflected the murderous mood that prevailed within the highest SS leadership in the days and weeks preceding the attack on the Soviet Union. They were entirely aware that they were about to embark on a campaign of historically unprecedented and racially motivated extermination.[58]

These murderous plans of truly genocidal proportions were by no means confined to the top echelons of the SS leadership. Five weeks earlier, on 2 May 1941, the state secretaries of various ministries had met with General Georg Thomas, head of the War Economy and Armaments Office, in order to discuss the economic preparations for the war against the Soviet Union. They agreed that the invading Wehrmacht would have to be supplied with food from within Russia if Germany was to win the war. Furthermore, agricultural products essential for the provision of the home front such as oil and grain would have to be shipped back to Germany. 'In so doing', the meeting's protocol laconically stated, 'x million people' in the conquered Soviet Union 'will doubtless starve to death'. Three weeks later the target group of potential victims of the so-called hunger plan was further specified to include 'many tens of millions' of Soviet citizens.[59]

It is likely, though impossible to prove, that the abstract figure of 'tens of millions' of people who would have to die to secure Germany's victory entered Himmler's and Heydrich's mindset through one of the key figures present at the May conference: Herbert Backe. Born in 1896 to German parents in Georgia, then part of the Russian Empire, Backe was interned as an enemy alien in 1914 before moving to Germany at the end of the Great War. In the 1920s, Backe studied for a diploma (and later a doctorate) in agriculture, first at the University of Göttingen, then in Hanover. In his doctoral thesis Backe explained the inevitable decline of Soviet Russia as a result of racial inferiority and argued that Germany had a natural right to occupy the uncultivated Slavic lands in the East. Some of Backe's published articles caught the attention of Walther Darré, the future Nazi Minister for Food and Agriculture. He invited Backe to join the Nazi Party, which he did in 1931. Three years after the Nazis' seizure of power, Backe was recommended to Göring, who was looking for an agriculture expert for his office of the Four-Year Plan, a position that put Backe in direct competition with his former mentor. Darré. It was at that time that Heydrich and Backe met. The former was particularly impressed with and inspired by Backe's unreserved radicalism. Heydrich and Backe became close friends and they frequently met for dinner at their houses in Berlin.[60] Backe had been working on the hunger plan in his capacity as state secretary in the Reich Food Ministry since the beginning of 1941 and was also responsible for drafting the so-called Twelve Commandments for future administrators in the occupied East. Backe emphasized that 'we wish not to convert the Russians to National Socialism but to make them our tools ... The Russian has stood poverty, hunger and austerity for centuries. His stomach is flexible; hence no false pity!'[61]

Two days after the meeting of the SS leadership at Wewelsburg Castle, Heydrich briefed the commanding officers of his SS task forces, first at a conference in Berlin on 17 June and then again at the closing ceremony at the border police training school in Pretzsch shortly before the German attack on the Soviet Union. According to the post-war testimonies of several *Einsatzgruppen* members present at these gatherings, Heydrich spoke of a mission that demanded 'unprecedented severity'.[62] As the commander of Task Force D, Otto Ohlendorf, recalled after the war, Heydrich explicitly ordered that Communist functionaries and Jews, who in Heydrich's mind had amalgamated into a single enemy, were to be executed.[63]

After the meeting in Berlin on 17 June, one of the designated *Einsatzkommando* leaders, wanting to make sure he had understood his orders correctly, asked: 'Are we supposed to shoot the Jews?' Heydrich allegedly assured him that the answer to his question was obvious.[64] Another witness among the *Einsatzgruppen* officers, Erwin Schulz, testified that Heydrich spoke in more general terms, while implying that the Jews in particular had to be dealt with 'severely'.[65]

Even if we take into account the consideration that the post-war testimonies of many *Einsatzgruppen* members were driven by the desire to whitewash their own direct responsibility for the mass atrocities committed in the Soviet Union by pointing to a comprehensive killing order that they had to obey, it seems plausible that Heydrich did indeed give general orders along these lines. Shortly after the beginning of the German invasion, he summarized his oral instructions of 17 June in two written orders to the *Einsatzgruppen* commanders and the higher SS and police leaders for the newly occupied territories.[66] Reminding his men in the field that their immediate task of 'politically pacifying' the occupied Soviet Union demanded 'ruthless severity', he reiterated that 'all Jews in the service of the [Communist] Party and the state' should be 'eliminated', along with 'officials of the Comintern (together with professional Communist politicians in general), top- and medium-level officials and radical lower-level officials of the party, the Central Committees and district and sub-district committees, people's commissars', as well as 'other radical elements (saboteurs, propagandists, snipers, assassins, demagogues etc)'.[67]

The target group of people to be executed was deliberately kept vague but it was clear that the formulation 'all Jews in the service of the party and the state' was merely a coded reference for an order to kill a nebulously defined Jewish upper class.[68] It would be largely left to the commando leaders themselves to decide who precisely would be included in this class – an approach that was once more highly characteristic of Heydrich's leadership style, which called for intitiative without specifying exact aims, and which would contribute significantly to the rapid escalation of mass murder over the following weeks.[69]

Barbarossa

On 22 June 1941, a historically unprecedented invasion army of 3 million German soldiers and more than 600,000 Italian, Hungarian and Finnish troops plunged into the Soviet Union on an extended battle-front of 1,500 kilometres. The speed of the Wehrmacht's advance was extraordinary. Within two days of launching the invasion, Army Group North had captured the Baltic cities of Grodno, Vilnius and Kaunas. By the end of June, Lvov had fallen, too. Army Group Centre pushed eastwards, taking Smolensk in mid-July, while Army Group South drove deep into the southern Ukraine. By late autumn, the Wehrmacht had captured more than 3 million Soviet soldiers, the vast majority of whom would perish in German POW camps due to starvation, typhus and other infectious diseases.[70]

Heydrich's *Einsatzgruppen* followed in the armies' rear, grimly determined to excel in carrying out their orders. Although Heydrich was to be informed of their progress through daily incident reports, he and Himmler quickly decided that they would monitor their work first hand.[71] Eight days after the beginning of Operation Barbarossa, on 30 June, they travelled from Hitler's headquarters in East Prussia to Grodno in the former Soviet-occupied part of Poland and Augustowo in recently conquered Lithuania, home to the largest Jewish community of the Baltic States. In Grodno, Heydrich was dismayed to find that, even though the town had already been captured a week earlier, not a single representative of the Security Police or the SD was on hand. He issued a reprimand and a warning to the commando leader in charge of the area, ordering him to show 'greater flexibility in tactical operations' and 'to keep pace with military advances'. The commander of Einsatzgruppe B, Arthur Nebe, responded with an apology: although 'only ninety-six Jews were liquidated' in the first days of the occupation of Grodno and Lida, he assured

Heydrich that he had given orders 'that this must be greatly intensified'. The 'implementation of the necessary liquidations' was 'guaranteed under all circumstances'.[72]

Meanwhile in Augustowo, Heydrich and Himmler caught up with the *Einsatzkommando Tilsit* under the command of Hans-Joachim Böhme. Over the previous week, Böhme and his men had engaged in various shootings of civilians and had come to Augustowo in order to initiate further 'punitive actions' in the rear of the quickly advancing Wehrmacht. Both Himmler and Heydrich approved of these mass shootings 'in their entirety'. Encouraged by the endorsement of their superiors, the *Einsatzkommando Tilsit* shot more than 300 civilians the following day, most of them Jewish men between the ages of seventeen and forty-five. By 18 July, Böhme's unit claimed to have murdered a total of 3,302 victims.[73]

On 11 July, Heydrich and Himmler returned to Grodno to view the progress of the *Einsatzgruppen's* extermination campaign. Both could see for themselves that the murder squads had overcome the 'passivity' for which they had been criticized on 30 June: when they arrived, mass shootings of civilians took place in Grodno, Oschmiany and Vilnius.[74] In between these visits, Heydrich found distraction and solace in daily fencing exercises, preparing himself for the German National Fencing Championships in Bad Kreuznach in August 1941 (where he came fifth).[75]

Heydrich's inspection tour to Grodno, and the subsequent radicalization of pacification measures that followed it, was indicative of a more general pattern: throughout the first weeks of the war against Soviet Russia, Himmler, Heydrich and other senior SS officers frequently visited their men in the field and their inspection tours usually preceded or co-incided with an increase in the number of atrocities. While there is no hard evidence that either of them called directly for the killing of unarmed civilians irrespective of age and gender, Himmler's and Heydrich's mere presence appears to have led to an upsurge in the mass murders of Jewish civilians in the formerly Soviet-occupied territories. By approving what had happened already and by encouraging their men to show more initiative, they made a decisive contribution to the swift escalation of mass murder. Radicalism and initiative were sure to receive praise, a lesson that was quickly learned by *Einsatzgruppen* officers along the Eastern Front.[76]

The killings consequently intensified over the course of the summer. From late June onwards, nearly all *Einsatzkommandos* as well as a range of German police battalions along the entire front line began to shoot indiscriminately Jewish men of military age, often hundreds or even thousands at a time. These executions took place under a variety of pretexts, ranging from 'retribution' for atrocities committed by the Soviet secret service, the NKVD, to the punishment of 'looters' and the combating of 'partisans'.[77]

With memories of clashes between the SS and the army in occupied Poland still fresh, Heydrich had been concerned that tensions over the executions might re-emerge and instructed the leaders of advance units to show 'the necessary political sensitivity' in carrying out their tasks. His fears proved to be unfounded. Co-operation with the Wehrmacht was 'excellent', the first activity report of the *Einsatzgruppen* noted.[78] Individual complaints continued to be submitted to army commanders, but no widespread outrage similar to that in Poland occurred. When, in August 1941, partisan activities behind the vastly overstretched German front began to burgeon, the Wehrmacht's willingness to tolerate and participate in atrocities further increased. Manpower shortages on a rapidly overextended front went hand in hand with growing fears of partisan warfare. The response to this dilemma was greater 'pre-emptive' violence against potential as well as real enemies.

Mass murder was not, however, restricted to the SS task forces. In numerous newly occupied territories, the SS succeeded in unleashing pogroms carried out by local populations. On 29 June, presumably in response to the horrific pogrom which took place in Kaunas in late June and which cost the lives of some 3,800 Jews, Heydrich reminded task-force commanders that 'self-cleansing efforts of anti-Communist or anti-Jewish groups' in the occupied Soviet territories 'are not to be hindered'. On the contrary, they were to be actively encouraged and incited 'without leaving a trace' of German involvement so that they would look like spontaneous outbursts of anti-Jewish rage.[79] In the areas occupied by the Red Army from 1939 onwards, there is evidence of anti-Jewish pogroms in at least sixty towns, particularly in Lithuania, Latvia and the western Ukraine. Although estimates of victims vary, at least 12,000 and possibly as many as 24,000 Jews fell victim to these pogroms.[80]

Despite his eagerness to use pogroms as an indicator of local hatred towards 'Jewish Bolsheviks', Heydrich was also aware of the dangers inherent in this policy. Given the complex mix of nationalistic, opportunistic and anti-Semitic motives at work, pogroms contained an element of unpredictability that ran counter to any systematic anti-Jewish policy. The basic ingredients recommended by the RSHA – instigating pogroms and making use of local collaborators without officially sanctioning their auxiliary function – did not strike army commanders in the field as a recipe for efficient occupation policy. On 1 July, following an enquiry from the Seventeenth Army under General Carl-Heinrich von Stülpnagel, Heydrich elaborated on his previous order regarding the 'non-prevention of self-cleansing measures by anti-Communist and anti-Jewish circles', partly to prevent an uncontrollable mushrooming of violence by non-Germans and partly to avoid clashes with the army. Heydrich called it 'self-evident that the cleansing actions have to be directed primarily against Bolshevists and Jews'. Poles, on the other hand, were to be exempted for the time being, as Heydrich believed them to be sufficiently anti-Semitic to be 'of special importance as initiators of pogroms'.[81] Their long-term fate was to be decided at a later stage.

The fate of Bolshevik commissars, by contrast, was straightforward: when captured, they were to be shot immediately, although Heydrich managed to convince the army that, whenever possible, they should be interrogated by SD and Abwehr officers before their execution. Their statements, usually given after sustained periods of torture, helped Heydrich to gain a clearer picture of the organizational structure and operational methods of the NKVD.[82]

For Heydrich, the German attack against the Soviet Union thus marked the end of a highly unsatisfactory period of stagnation in terms of both ideological fulfilment and career ambitions. Between the invasion of Poland and the beginning of Operation Barbarossa, he had failed to advance the influence of the SD and the Security Police in the occupied territories of Western Europe. Simultaneously, both the Germanization of Western Poland and the Jewish question remained unresolved. Operation Barbarossa offered him a potential exit strategy from this stalemate.

Fateful Decisions

Following the lightning German advances into Soviet territory in June and early July 1941, which led Heydrich to issue detailed instructions for the role of the Security Police in the capture of Moscow, a jubilant Hitler announced to a number of top Nazi officials his plans for the future of the occupied East. Until this point, there had been considerable uncertainty about what would happen with the conquered territories in the mysterious hazy realm that the Germans called 'the East' – a supposedly uncultivated wilderness of swamps, impenetrable forests and marshes between the Baltic and the Black Sea.[83] In a speech of 16 July Hitler offered some clarity: the East was to become Germany's 'Garden of Eden' and the realization of this utopia was to be achieved by using 'all necessary measures – shootings, resettlements, etc'. As usual, Hitler did not give any explicit orders for systematic mass murder, but his fundamental message was unmistakable: there was no space for Communists, Jews and other undesirables in the German Garden of Eden. His subordinates, particularly Himmler and Heydrich, were eager not to disappoint their Führer.[84]

Characteristically, Hitler remained uncommitted to any concrete vision for the territories formerly ruled by the Soviet Union, but decided, much to Himmler's and Heydrich's disappointment, that at the end of military operations in the Soviet Union the occupied territories would be administered by civilian authorities under the overall authority of the newly appointed Minister for the Occupied Eastern Territories, Alfred Rosenberg. Rosenberg was a Baltic German, born in 1893, who had studied in Moscow and became head of the Nazi Party's Foreign Policy Office in 1933. If Heydrich had hoped that Hitler would give Himmler political control over the newly occupied territories – thus allowing the SS to co-ordinate Germanization policies beyond Poland – his hopes were dashed. For the time being, Hitler limited SS authority to policing matters in the newly conquered territories. Heydrich was to serve as the liaison between Rosenberg and the SS, and was thereby, in his own words, 'responsible to the Reich Leader SS for political matters in the occupied territories'.[85]

The potential for future conflict was clear from the start: Rosenberg wished ultimately to divide the newly occupied territory into four civilian Reich Commissariats: Ukraine, Ostland (the Nazi term for the territories comprising the Baltic States and Belorussia), the Caucasus and Russia proper. Only two of these, the Reich Commissariat Ukraine (under Erich Koch) and the Reich Commissariat Ostland (under Hinrich Lohse), were ever created in reality. Heydrich, by contrast, saw the Reich commissioners as natural rivals and interpreted his policing mission as an inherently *political* task that should be carried out without any interference from civilian administrators. As he pointed out in a letter to Kurt Daluege, '90% of all matters in the East are of a primarily political nature and therefore of major interest to my own apparatus.'[86] Unsurprisingly, Heydrich requested in a letter to the chief of the Reich Chancellery, Hans Lammers that the Sipo be granted the right to issue orders in policing matters to the civilian administration in the occupied East, a request that immediately prompted Rosenberg's sharpest objections.[87]

Heydrich's attitude towards Rosenberg's administrations and the civilian authorities in the East was partly influenced by his enduring dislike of the Old Fighters who were appointed to key positions in the East simply for being long-serving party veterans. Neither Lohse nor the grossly overweight Erich Koch was exactly what Heydrich considered an appropriate type for the creation of a new German Garden of Eden. An additional key figure in the new administration, the Governor of White Ruthenia (the part of Ostland carved out of pre-1939 Eastern Poland and Soviet Belorussia) was Wilhelm Kube, another Old Fighter of the Nazi movement against whom Heydrich had instigated a police investigation in December 1935, leading to Kube's conviction for embezzlement and his temporary loss of all party functions.[88] Vain and corrupt, Kube held a grudge against Heydrich, and future dealings with him would be very difficult indeed. Furthermore Rosenberg advocated an anti-Bolshevik wartime alliance with local Eastern European nationalists, an idea that Heydrich considered inherently flawed and potentially dangerous. A racial war could not be won by relying on lesser races, but only by permanently subduing them.[89]

Hitler's refusal to grant Himmler overall political responsibility for the racial reorganization of the occupied East was yet another bitter setback for the ambitious SS leadership. However, the lesson Himmler and Heydrich drew from this defeat was characteristic: instead of scaling down their ambitions, they decided to unleash a policy of systematic ethnic cleansing of the former Soviet territories *before* the civilian administrations were properly installed and not, as originally planned, *after* the defeat of the Soviet Union.[90] It was in this context of increasing radicalism, mixed with the euphoria of an apparently imminent victory, that Heydrich proposed to Himmler on 20 October 1941 that Leningrad and Moscow, the two major 'symbols of Judaeo-Bolshevism', should be razed to the ground. The most remarkable thing about this proposition was not its radicalism, but its privileging of ideological objectives over military necessities.[91]

If the overall aim of the SS leadership was to unleash an unparalleled programme of expulsions and exterminations in the former territories of the Soviet Union, a genocidal onslaught which – according to the estimates discussed at the start of the war – would kill some 30 million former Soviet subjects, the implementation of such a vast extermination programme aimed at the entire native population of Eastern Europe remained utterly utopian in the summer of 1941. It was simply impossible to raze major Russian cities to the ground, to shoot 30 million people or to cut off their food supply and let them starve without running the risk of serious unrest in the affected areas. However, from Heydrich's point of view, these concerns did not apply to the much smaller group of Soviet Jews. As a first step towards the elimination of all alien population elements in the East, the SS would render entire regions 'Jew-free' through a combination of mass executions in the shadow of war and the ghettoization of those who could still be exploited as forced labourers.

By eliminating the Jews of Soviet Russia *during* the war, Himmler and Heydrich could demonstrate that they, rather than Rosenberg or any other civilian or military authorities, possessed the ideological determination and experience necessary to implement Hitler's plans for the racial reordering of Eastern Europe. By putting into effect anti-Jewish policies, the SS leadership would demonstrate how German rule in the East could be efficiently implemented and managed.[92]

Such considerations were not merely cynical and strategic, but very much in line with Heydrich's own unshakeable ideological convictions. The war against the Soviet Union, perceived by Heydrich as a life-and-death struggle between two irreconcilable political ideologies, led to an intensification of the moral paradigm shift that had already manifested itself during the Polish campaign. In Heydrich's eyes the SS had to prove its dedication to Hitler's racial fantasies and to display hardness against the broadly defined enemies of the German people.

As the ideological shock troops of Nazism, the SS would fulfil Hitler's orders unconditionally, a task that was difficult but historic. According to this twisted logic, the killing of tens of thousands, ultimately millions, of undesirables was a task without alternative and anyone who did *not* murder the racial-ideological enemies of the Reich effectively committed a crime against future generations of Germans. This task was to be carried out with 'decency', not to enrich the perpetrators or to give them sadistic pleasure, but in full consciousness of the historic sacrifice that had been made in order to create a better world. The perpetrators were the victims of an indecent world in which such tasks had been brought upon them. Just like Himmler, Heydrich convinced himself that the bloody task ahead of the SS was without alternative, describing himself on occasions as the 'chief garbage collector of the Third Reich' – carrying out an unpleasant and dirty task that nonetheless needed to be done for the sanitary health of the body politic and the future of the German nation.[93]

Shortly after Hitler's Garden of Eden speech, Heydrich substantially increased the number of men attached to SS *Einsatzgruppen* on the Eastern Front. At the same time, Himmler assigned police reserve battalions and SS cavalry to the higher SS and police leaders in the Soviet Union and charged them with the task of cleansing the area of partisans and other loosely defined enemies. Local Lithuanians, Latvians, Estonians, Belorussians and Ukrainians, agitated by their experience of Soviet occupation and the killing of thousands of their countrymen by the NKVD before the Red Army's retreat, were also recruited into police auxiliary units in order to bulk up the killing squads. Some of the *Einsatzgruppen* leaders in the field received further personal encouragement from Himmler, who travelled through much of the occupied East over the following weeks. Others, such as Otto Ohlendorf, received their orders directly from Heydrich.[94]

Heydrich decided to visit Ohlendorf's *Einsatzgruppe* D in late July and combined his inspection tour with a brief excursion to the front. Caught up in the general euphoria of imminent victory, he did not want to miss out on fighting before the war was over. It was time for another heroic gesture. On 20 July 1941, around four weeks after the start of the German campaign, Heydrich interrupted his work in Berlin for a three-day trip to the southern Russian front, near Jampol, where he rejoined Fighter Squadron 77 with which he had already flown in air raids over Norway the previous year.[95]

Heydrich's excursion had not been authorized by Himmler. It was, as Himmler stated later 'with proud joy', the 'only secret in the eleven years of our shared path'.[96] Heydrich arrived in his own plane, a Messerschmidt 109, which he had apparently borrowed from Air Force general Ernst Udet in exchange for a special police permit to drive through Berlin at night and during air raids. As in Norway, Heydrich enjoyed his 'adventure trip', drinking wine and playing card games with both ordinary soldiers and fellow officers until late at night, while flying a number of attacks on retreating Russian troops during the day.[97]

The fighter squadron's mission was to secure a strategically vital bridge over the Dniestr river. The pilots were instructed to prevent the bridge's destruction by the retreating Red Army, so that the German soldiers could cross the river unhindered. On 22 July, shortly after 2 p.m., the squadron encountered heavy Russian flak. Heydrich's aeroplane was hit and the engine malfunctioned. An emergency landing left the pilot stranded in the Olshanka District – behind Russian lines. Back at the Luftwaffe base, panic spread and the commander feared that Heydrich was either dead or – even worse – in the hands of the NKVD. Only a few hours later, an infantry officer called to report that an advance patrol had rescued a downed pilot. The pilot of the plane was seemingly uninjured, but had clearly suffered some brain damage since he kept insisting he was the head of the Reich Security Main Office.[98]

Once safely back in Berlin, Heydrich prepared himself for an important meeting with Hermann Göring that took place in the early evening of 31 July 1941. It was here that Heydrich obtained Göring's signature on a deceptively simple document of a mere three sentences, a document that presumably originated from Heydrich himself. Extending the powers entrusted to Heydrich on 24 January 1939 to organize a solution to the Jewish question within the (by then substantially enlarged) German Reich through emigration, Göring now authorized Heydrich to make 'all necessary preparations' for a 'total solution of the Jewish question in the German sphere of influence in Europe'. Furthermore, he empowered Heydrich to co-ordinate the participation of those organizations whose jurisdiction was affected and to submit a 'comprehensive draft' of a plan for the 'final solution to the Jewish question'.[99]

The question remains as to how Heydrich at this point envisaged the final solution. Did he still view it as the mass expulsion of European Jewry from the German sphere of influence into the inhospitable regions of Siberia where they would be decimated by the climatic conditions and forced labour, as he had in the spring of 1941? Or was the term 'final solution' already imply the intention to murder each and every Jew in Europe? [100]

Some historians have interpreted Heydrich's authorization of 31 July as an order for a 'feasibility study' for the mass murder of European Jews.[101] But there are other ways of interpreting this mandate. Clearly, Heydrich's mind turned from a solution primarily focused on Germany, Poland and the Soviet Union to Nazi-controlled Europe as a whole. However, his actions and orders over the next few months do not indicate a fundamental policy change. He clearly recognized that as a result of the conquest of the Soviet Union the scope of the Jewish problem had substantially expanded. As German armies raced eastwards, the number of Jews that came under Nazi control multiplied daily. Yet at this point he still believed in an overall solution that involved two components. The systematic murder of Soviet Jews and those living in the reception areas for German settlers and deportees from the Reich was one of them. The second continued to be the idea of deporting the Jews from other parts of the German sphere of influence to the Soviet Union as soon as the military situation allowed him to do so.

If, during the first weeks of the war, there were reservations about killing Jewish women and children in the conquered Soviet territories, these reservations were quickly overcome, even though the point in time at which individual task forces widened the scope of their killing varied considerably. *Einsatzkommando* 9 under Alfred Filbert was the first to murder Jewish women and children systematically, in Belorussia from the end of July onwards, apparently on explicit orders from Heydrich.[102]

The extension of mass murders in the Soviet Union followed an inverted logic that had ripened in Heydrich's and Himmler's minds and was shared by many of their officers in the field: they saw themselves as acting in self-defence against their past (and potentially future) victimizers. The children, if allowed to survive, would take revenge. The women would bear more children. The elderly would tell the tale. Germany's past misfortunes – allegedly created by the Jews in the first place – could end only by means of a terrible final reckoning, a harsh but definitive solution that would also be 'kind' to the next generation of Germans, who would no longer have to deal with either the Jewish problem in its current form or a future 'generation of avengers'.[103]

Heydrich left no documents or letters indicating that he ever felt moral ambiguity about his central role in the murderous escalation of anti-Jewish policies. Those close to him, like Himmler or Lina, did however suggest that he was conscious that his actions constituted a radical breach of the norms of Western civilization and the values cultivated in his paternal home. At Heydrich's funeral in June 1942, Himmler insisted:

'From my countless discussions with Heydrich I know what it cost this man to be so hard and severe despite the softness of his heart; to make tough decisions in order to act always in accordance with the law of the SS which binds us to spare neither our own blood nor that of others when the life of the nation demands it.'[104] His wife, too, claimed that Heydrich 'was fully aware of his role as hangman but knew how to justify it positively': by convincing himself that in order to be kind to future generations of Germans, and to bring about Hitler's utopia, he and his men had to be hard in the present conflict.[105]

The rate at which the *Einsatzgruppen* killed depended not only on Heydrich's orders or those of individual task-force commanders, but also on the speed with which their army group advanced, the density of the Jewish population they encountered, the degree of help they received from the local population and the relevance of the local Jews as slave labourers for the German war effort. In Lithuania, for example, where the genocide of local Jews escalated notably earlier than in other parts of the conquered territories, the economic concerns that long prevented the wholesale murder of Jews in the General Government did not apply and the food shortages that became evident in the autumn of 1941 made it even more pressing to get rid of 'useless mouths'. *Einsatzgruppe* A under Stahlecker, responsible for the destruction of the sizeable Jewish communities of Lithuania and Latvia, proved to be particularly efficient in fulfilling its murderous brief.[106]

The result of the gradual increase of violence was staggering: by the end of 1941, Germans and their local helpers had murdered between 500,000 and 800,000 Jewish men, women and children in the former Soviet territories, often between 2,700 and 4,200 per day, with most of the deaths resulting from shootings at close quarters. Local helpers, agitated by hatred against 'Judaeo-Bolshevism', sometimes resorted to clubs and pick-axes against a largely defenceless Jewish population.[107]

By the late summer of 1941, both Himmler and Heydrich became concerned that the face-to-face killings carried out by *Einsatzgruppen* threatened the mental health of their men. Ever since attending an execution of Jews in Minsk in mid-August 1941, Himmler had been worried about creating sadistic, psychologically deranged killers who would be difficult to reintegrate into German post-war society, a problem that was also apparent to Heydrich who was regularly confronted with frequent reports of alcohol abuse and mental breakdowns among the men assigned to his task forces.[108]

Suggestions on how to solve these self-inflicted problems came from different directions. One of the earliest proposals for using gas to accelerate and 'humanize' the murder of those Jews 'incapable of work' came from Rolf Heinz Höppner, a local official in the General Government. On 16 July, Höppner wrote to Eichmann suggesting that a 'quick-acting agent' should be used to rid Łódź of useless Jewish mouths. On the central Russian front, too, *Einsatzgruppe* commander Arthur Nebe explored the possibility of gassing in meetings with chemical experts from Berlin in mid-September.[109]

Inspired by these suggestions and experiments, Heydrich instructed the head of his office for technical affairs within the RSHA, Walter Rauff, to investigate new means of mass murder. Rauff, whose jurisdiction included the 4,000 motor vehicles of the Security Police, turned to his staff to develop a 'more humane method of execution' for the *Einsatzgruppen* on the Eastern Front.[110]

In late October, the proposed solution – in the form of mobile gas vans – was first tested in Sachsenhausen concentration camp near Berlin, where forty naked Russian POWs were killed in the back of a van with exhaust gas. Thirty more of these gas vans were ordered and sent to the East, where they were used in Minsk and Mogilev, then in the Warthegau and in Serbia. Heydrich considered this means of killing more humane for the perpetrators, but the gas vans never really caught on. Asphyxiation by carbon monoxide in medium-sized vans was simply too slow and ultimately no less disturbing than the shootings. The perpetrators had to wait for their screaming victims to die inside the vans, which often took more than fifteen minutes, before removing the bodies from the vehicles. While experiments with more 'efficient' stationary gassing facilities began in Poland, notably in Belzec, execution by hand continued to be the dominant practice in the German-occupied territories of the Soviet Union.[111]

Simultaneously, experiments with Zyklon B, a powerful chemical fumigant, began in Auschwitz in September when Russian POWs were gassed in a series of test runs. Neither Heydrich's vans nor the Zyklon B experiments in Auschwitz were initially intended to be used for the systematic murder of all of Europe's Jews. They were conceived first and foremost to facilitate the killing operations on the Eastern Front and in order to create space in the General Government for incoming deportees from the Reich.

Word of the massacres on the Russian front quickly filtered through German society. Soldiers in the East who had witnessed, participated in or merely heard of mass executions relayed the information back to their friends and relatives at home. A future member of the military resistance against Hitler, Philipp von Boeselager, for example, heard about the mass executions of Jews from a fellow officer who had shared a railway carriage with some drunken SD men, who had boasted that they had murdered 250,000 Jews in the rear areas of Army Group South in 1941. Such incidents were no exception, and by September 1941 rumours about large-scale atrocities on the Eastern Front were recorded by the SD in nearly every German city.[112]

The rumours created anxiety and caused Heydrich to urge his men to exercise greater caution and secrecy in carrying out their tasks. 'The Führer', he explained to his subordinates in early September, 'has repeatedly stressed that all enemies of the Reich use – just like during the [First] World War – every opportunity to sow disunity among the German people. It is thus urgently necessary to abstain from all measures that can affect the uniform mood of the people.' Presumably in order to avoid both unnecessary rumours in Germany and further tensions between SS units in the field and the civilian administration, Heydrich ordered that his personal approval be sought 'before taking any especially drastic measures', but left a loophole in cases of 'imminent danger'.[113]

No such caution or secrecy was necessary vis-à-vis the Nazi leadership. The regular reports from the *Einsatzgruppen* were edited in Heydrich's RSHA and distributed to other government agencies in order to inform them about – and adapt them to – the course of events in the occupied East. The number of recipients of these reports constantly increased and by late October Heydrich was flooding the German bureaucracy with *Einsatzgruppen* reports. SS officers at the periphery could thus expect their reports to be read by a large and influential circle of Nazi officials. For the purpose of presenting it to Hitler, the RSHA also gathered 'illustrative material', notably photographs, which documented the murderous work of the task forces in the East.[114]

The gradual expansion of the mass executions in the Soviet Union and the constant inclusion of new victim groups in the mass shootings were unlikely to attract any criticism from the top Nazi leadership. Quite the opposite. Heydrich's orders merely anticipated what Hitler had already intended for the period following the end of the war: the physical destruction of the Soviet Jews, regardless of the form that it might take.

Hitler was more cautious when it came to the German Jews. When, in late July or early August 1941, Heydrich proposed the complete and immediate evacuation of German Jews from the Reich, Hitler was hesitant and rejected the idea.[115] Murdering Soviet Jews hundreds of kilometres away from the home front was one thing, but removing German Jews, including decorated war veterans, from their homes was quite another matter. Public opinion mattered and was not to be unnecessarily antagonized at a decisive moment of the war. However, when US involvement in the Allied war effort – allegedly the result of Jewish propaganda – became increasingly likely from mid-August onwards, Hitler changed his mind. Germany was now no longer engaged in a struggle merely against Jewish Bolshevism, embodied by the Soviet Union, but also against an all-encompassing 'Jewish world conspiracy', which bound the emerging coalition of Communism and capitalism together.

In this context, the regime further intensified the persecution of German Jews. Not only did German Jews have to endure new discriminatory measures from September onwards, but following a decision by Hitler on 18 August they were also subject to mandatory identification through the wearing of the yellow star (which had already been compulsory in the General Government and the Warthegau for two years), thus making them visible as 'internal enemies' and further facilitating their envisaged future deportation to the East, which Hitler continued to refuse to authorize.[116] Heydrich was delighted by Hitler's decision to mark the Jews, having already made a similar proposal after the November pogroms of 1938. Back then, Hitler had rejected this initiative, but the idea continued to resurface over the following years, most notably in the spring of 1941 when Goebbels urged Hitler to reconsider the possibility of marking the Jews.[117]

Deteriorating morale on the home front in the summer of 1941 was closely connected with the revival of the marking plans. Although the Wehrmacht advanced swiftly into Soviet territory after the invasion of 22 June 1941 and achieved some remarkable early victories over its surprised Red Army adversary, many Germans feared that, this time, Hitler had gone too far. Starting that July the SD noted a clear decline in confidence, along with fears that the campaign against the Soviet Union could develop into an extended conflict of indefinite duration and heavy losses. These pessimistic assessments were aggravated by the worsening supply situation and repeated British bombing raids on western German cities.[118] As Goebbels noted in his diary on 12 August, he and other Nazi leaders were convinced that the Jews were responsible for the deteriorating morale by spreading rumours and acting as 'mood spoilers'. By making them visible as Jews, Goebbels hoped to render it impossible for them 'to speak in the name of the German people'.[119]

Three days after this diary entry, on 15 August, a conference was held at the Propaganda Ministry concerning the marking issue. Eichmann participated in the conference as Heydrich's representative and confirmed that his boss was seeking a direct decision on the matter by the Führer. Eichmann also told the other delegates that the RSHA was already working on a 'partial evacuation' of Jews from large cities in the Old Reich.[120]

Hitler's approval of the marking proposal on 18 August was a decision influenced less by Goebbels's personal intervention than by the Führer's general change of mind on the issue of deporting German Jews from the Reich.[121] Word of Hitler's approval spread fast in Berlin. As the Foreign Office's Jewish expert, Franz Rademacher, recorded in a note for his boss Luther on 21 August, Eichmann had 'informed me confidentially that . . .

Hey[drich] had received a telex from the Führer's headquarters according to which the Führer had approved the marking of Jews in Germany'.[122]

Eichmann's phone call was a deliberate attempt to demonstrate to the Foreign Office that Heydrich and his Jewish experts were already working on the implementation of Hitler's order. While the Reich Interior Ministry was still contemplating potential exceptions from the marking decree, such as Jews living in 'privileged mixed marriages', Heydrich's RSHA processed the marking regulations with extraordinary speed. Already on 1 September, scarcely two weeks after Hitler's decision, Heydrich signed the 'police regulation on the marking of Jews'.[123] Heydrich's order not only stigmatized all German Jews over the age of six by forcing them to wear a clearly visible yellow star with the word 'Jew' printed on it, but also included regulations on 'no-go areas' for Jews and prohibited them from leaving their places of residence without police permission.[124]

More detailed instructions from Heydrich followed over the next few weeks, and he personally informed the representatives of the Reich's remaining Jewish organizations of the coming measures.[125] On 8 September, Paul Eppstein from the Reich Association of Jews in Germany and Josef Löwenherz from the Israelite Congregation of Vienna were summoned to the RSHA to be acquainted with the details relating to the distribution of the 'Jewish stars'. They were given three days to complete their task of distributing the badges at a price of 10 pfennigs per piece.[126] Yet although he had approved the marking of German Jews in August, Hitler remained reluctant to authorize their deportation. In September, encouraged by the Wehrmacht's successes on the Eastern Front, which would soon lead to the encirclement of Leningrad and Kiev, he was prepared to revise his position on this issue and to make a number of decisions that were far-reaching both for the further escalation of Nazi genocidal policies and for Heydrich's personal and professional life.[127]

Crucially, in response to the rise of resistance activities in the Protectorate and as a result of his expressed wish to make Prague one of the first 'Jew free' cities in the Greater German Empire, Hitler decided, in late September, to replace his 'weak' representative in Prague, Baron von Neurath, with Heydrich. Back in 1939, Neurath, an arch-conservative but well-mannered and internationally respected Swabian aristocrat and career-diplomat, had been a strategic appointment, a choice driven by Hitler's desire to appease London, where Neurath had once served as an ambassador to the court of St James's. Heydrich's appointment, by contrast, was dictated by the necessities of total war. As intended by Hitler, Heydrich's appointment as acting Reich Protector had immediate ramifications for the Jews of Bohemia and Moravia. Beginning on 1 October 1941, less than a week after his arrival in Prague, the Protectorate's Office for Jewish Emigration ordered the Jewish Religious Congregation of Prague, by now terrorized into complete compliance, to begin the process of registering anew every Jew in the Protectorate. Heydrich did not trust the figures produced under the 'lax' regime of Neurath, whom he suspected of having little understanding of racial matters. In Prague alone thirty-seven members of the Jewish congregation worked almost ceaselessly and under the threat of deportation, at times registering 2,000 people per day. Denunciations from the German and Czech population were actively encouraged and proved crucial in identifying Jews.[128]

On 10 October, Heydrich chaired a meeting in Prague with Eichmann and other race and settlement experts in attendance. According to the transcript, the purpose of the meeting was to discuss ways in which the Jewish problem in the Protectorate and the Reich could be resolved. Heydrich announced that Hitler demanded that 'all Jews be removed from this German space by the end of the year' and noted that 'all pending questions [regarding the Jewish policy] must be solved immediately. Even the transportation question must not present any problems.' Following their concentration in 'temporary collection camps', notably in Theresienstadt (Terezín), the Jews of the Protectorate were to be deported to Łódź. In view of predictable objections from the local authorities in Łódź, however, 50,000 of the 'most burdensome' Jews – those least capable of work – were to be shipped to Minsk and Riga. The leaders of Einsatzgruppen B and C, Nebe and Rasch, would make space for some of these Jews and others from the Reich 'in the camps for Communist prisoners'. An additional 5,000 Gypsies were to be sent from Austria to Riga.[129]

In a press announcement issued the following day, Heydrich summarized the results of the meeting: the 'final aim', he stated, was not merely to exclude Jewry from social and economic life, but to 'resettle them outside Europe' and to do so 'as quickly as possible.' Four days later, on 15 October, the deportations from Prague began with daily transports carrying 1,000 people each.[130]

Heydrich clearly envisaged the deportation of the Central European Jews as no more than a first step towards a pan-European solution, a plan which, as he underlined in a meeting with representatives of Rosenberg's Ministry for the Occupied Eastern Territories on 4 October and again in a letter to the army's Quartermaster General of 6 November, would ultimately lead to the 'total evacuation of Jews from Europe'.[131]

Shortly after the beginning of the deportations of Jews from the Protectorate and the Reich, all exit possibilities from German-controlled Europe were closed. When on 13 October the Spanish Foreign Office proposed to expel 2,000 Spanish Jews residing in France to Spanish Morocco, Heydrich rejected the proposal on two grounds. First, he believed that the Spanish government had neither the will nor the determination to guard the Jews effectively in Morocco. Secondly, 'these Jews would also be too much out of the direct reach of the measures for a basic solution to the Jewish question to be enacted after the war'.[132]

Emigration was clearly no longer part of Heydrich's solution to the Jewish question. On 18 October, one day after he had informed Luther in the Foreign Office of his objection to the Spanish government's proposal, he and Himmler took a more general decision on the issue of Jewish emigration. 'No emigration by Jews to overseas', Himmler noted in his diary after a telephone conversation with Heydrich.[133] On 23 October, the emigration gates were officially closed. All of Europe's Jews were now to be included in the final-solution project.

Yet the implementation of even the limited deportation programme authorized by Hitler continued to pose practical problems. One of the most pressing issues – the question of reception areas – remained unresolved; and if Heydrich hoped that the deportees from the Reich could be temporarily lodged in occupied Poland before being sent into the Soviet Union after the German victory, local officials on the ground took a very different view. In early October, Friedrich Uebelhoer, the District President of Łódź, lodged a vehement protest against the intended transfer of 60,000 German Jews to the already overcrowded Łódź ghetto.[134] An infuriated Heydrich, appalled by Uebelhoer's 'oppositional attitude', threatened to draw 'appropriate conclusions' should he not change his 'hostile manner'.[135] In the end, Heydrich had to settle for a compromise and the number of deportees sent to Łódź was subsequently scaled down to 20,000 Jews and 5,000 Gypsies. As an immediate alternative solution, Heydrich advised Himmler that the ghettos of Riga and Minsk would have to accommodate 50,000 additional Jews, predominantly from the Protectorate.[136]

While unfriendly letters were still being exchanged between Himmler, Heydrich and Uebelhoer, Heydrich met with high-ranking officials from Rosenberg's Ministry for the Occupied Eastern Territories in order to address a second problem: the issue of overlapping competences in the Eastern territories. Ever since Hitler had declared that Himmler's jurisdiction as Reich commissioner for the strengthening of Germandom, previously confined to Poland, was to be extended to the newly occupied territories of the Soviet Union, clashes between Rosenberg and Himmler had become the norm.[137]

Heydrich now suggested that a co-ordinated approach to the Jewish question would be useful, especially in preventing pseudo-economic considerations from jeopardizing any 'plan of a total resettlement of the Jews from the territory occupied by us'. He complained bitterly that many businesses in Germany claimed Jewish labourers as 'indispensable' instead of trying to employ other foreign labourers. He also expressed his dissatisfaction with Rosenberg's apparently 'uncooperative' attitude and stressed that 'the implementation of the treatment of Jews' would lie 'in every respect in the hands of the Security Police'.[138]

On the same day, Heydrich managed to convince the Foreign Office that the Jewish problem in Serbia, where partisan activities were causing serious disruptions, required an urgent solution. Heydrich and Under Secretary Martin Luther agreed to send their Jewish experts to Belgrade the following week. Their presence spurred on both the SD commander on the ground, Wilhelm Fuchs, and the chief administrative officer of the military occupation regime in Serbia, Harald Turner, to speed up the killing of Jewish men.[139] As Browning has rightly argued, the mass murder of the male Jews of Serbia was not consciously part of a Europe-wide final solution to the Jewish question: 'The killing of the male Jews emerged primarily out of local factors related to the partisan war and the army's reprisal policy. The victims, both Jews and Gypsies, were considered 'expendable' groups whose execution would satisfy the required reprisal quotas without producing undesired political repercussions and aggravating the anti-partisan struggle. The army did not operate with the avowed aim of exterminating the entire Jewish population, and thus the women, the children and the elderly were not killed'.[140]

The most pressing issue for the moment remained the question of reception areas for the Jews from the Reich. On the one hand, there was mounting pressure for the complete removal of all Jews from the Reich and Protectorate. On the other hand, there was no obvious viable destination for them. A radical solution was put forward by Himmler's SS and Police Leader in the Lublin district, Odilo Globocnik, a notoriously fanatical and abrasive Austrian bound to Himmler in unswerving loyalty for rescuing his career after being sacked as Gauleiter of Vienna on charges of corruption in 1939. In a meeting with Himmler on 13 October, 'Globus' – as he was affectionately known in the SS – proposed the construction of a gas chamber at Belzec, originally intended 'only' for the murder of non-able-bodied Jews living in the Lublin district.[141] Himmler was very receptive to the idea, and construction works in Belzec, the first purpose-built extermination camp, began two weeks later on 1 November, the day Heydrich and Lina set off for their holiday lodge near Nauen for a pleasant long weekend of deer-hunting.[142]

Heydrich and Himmler were increasingly determined to mitigate the overcrowding of reception areas by substantially reducing the existing Jewish population in the ghettos of occupied Poland through systematic mass murder.[143] It was around the same time, in October or November

1941, that they opened negotiations with Gauleiter Arthur Greiser regarding the possibility of sending large numbers of German Jews into the Warthegau. Greiser declared his willingness to accept deportations from the Reich. In return, Heydrich and Himmler promised to have no fewer than 100,000 Jews from Greiser's Warthegau murdered within a few months.[144] The site chosen was a deserted manor house surrounded by a fence and trees outside the village of Chelmno, about fifty-five kilometres from Łódź, where ultimately 150,000 Jews would be murdered. While authorization for this mass murder came from the centre, the initiative came from the local authorities: the goal was the solution of a local 'problem' rather than a comprehensive programme.[145]

Only one day after Globocnik's visit to Berlin, on 14 October, Heydrich and Himmler had a five-hour meeting, presumably to discuss both the imminent first wave of deportations of Jews from the Reich to Łódź, Riga and Minsk and Globocnik's proposal to create space in the reception areas by murdering the Jews currently living there. Two further opportunities to exchange ideas on these issues arose in late October, first on the occasion of a joint visit to Hitler on 25 October, and again four days later during Himmler's visit to Prague.[146]

Some historians have argued that by late October 1941 the Nazi regime had moved away from its previous anti-Jewish policy of violent expulsions and piecemeal murder to the systematic physical destruction of the entire European Jewry.[147] In recent years, a new consensus has emerged to view the plan to construct extermination camps in Belzec and Mogilev as localized solutions, designed to create space for the large numbers of deportees from the Reich rather than the beginning of the systematic mass murder of every Jew in Europe. As Peter Longerich has convincingly argued, 'a concrete plan for the short-term, systematic murder' of all Jews living in the German sphere of influence did not exist in the autumn of 1941 when 'the murder of hundreds of thousands, but not millions of human beings was being prepared'.[148]

In the euphoria of imminent victory and under increasing pressure from various German Gauleiters to deport 'their' Jews, Hitler had made the fateful decision to allow for a limited deportation programme from the Reich and the Protectorate, while simultaneously extending Himmler's jurisdiction as Reich commissioner for the strengthening of Germandom to the Soviet territories and appointing Heydrich as acting Reich Protector of Bohemia and Moravia, one of the areas for which deportations had been approved. At the same time, scarce food supplies and a rise in resistance activities in the conquered territories led to an intensification of mass murder of Soviet Jews and the spatial expansion of the extermination campaign beyond the occupied Soviet territories (to encompass certain regions of Eastern and Central Europe, particularly Serbia). Finally, the problem of reception areas for Jewish deportees from the Reich led to the planning and construction of mass extermination centres near the target areas for deportees. In the autumn of 1941, the SS had begun constructing stationary gassing facilities with the purpose of killing Jews 'incapable of working' near the target ghettos for the first waves of deportees from the Reich: Riga, Łódź (Chelmno), Lublin (Belzec) and Minsk (Mogilev). The deportation of Central European Jews into these areas was still considered to be a temporary solution, leading to deportations further east the following spring. This latter plan was genocidal in nature, as anticipated survival rates among the deportees would be very low. Yet there was no plan as yet to solve the Jewish question by systematically shooting or gassing every single Jew on the European continent. [149]

Impulses for mass murder came from both the centre and the peripheries of the Nazi empire. In the newly occupied Eastern territories, local civilian authorities, military commanders and SS *Einsatzgruppen* leaders searched for their own solutions to the Jewish problem, partly in response to the 'impossible situations' that had been created by the Nazis in the first place: deportees were sent to ghettos in the General Government that were already overcrowded, to camps that did not yet exist and to areas that had actually been intended for the resettlement of ethnic Germans from the East. Heydrich's role in the deliberate creation of these 'impossible situations' calling for 'radical solutions' is difficult to overestimate: he encouraged task-force commanders to compete for radical solutions; his office oversaw many of the expulsions and resettlements; and his team of Jewish experts co-ordinated the deportations.[150]

It was at this critical juncture that military fortunes began to turn against Nazi Germany. The second week of December was one of the most dramatic of the entire war. On 7 December, Pearl Harbor was attacked by Japanese forces. Four days later, Germany declared war on the United States. Hitler regarded this undertaking as risk-free since the American armed forces would be tied up in the Pacific for at least another year, during which time he would be able to end his European war victoriously and simultaneously attack American maritime transports to Europe without any restrictions. At a special session of the Reichstag on 11 December, he formally announced Germany's entry into the war on the side of Japan. The members of the Reichstag, with Heydrich among them, greeted this announcement with frenetic applause.[151]

On 12 December, one day after his Reichstag speech, Hitler invited various Nazi dignitaries to his private quarters in the Reich Chancellery. Emphasizing that the world war now upon Germany was a struggle of life and death in which all means were justified, the Führer returned to his 'prophecy' of 30 January 1939. 'As regards the Jewish question', Goebbels noted in his diary,

the Führer has decided to make a clean sweep. He prophesied to the Jews that, if they ever started a world war again, it would mean their annihilation. This was not mere phrasemaking. The world war is upon us; the extermination of the Jews must be the necessary consequence. This question should be regarded without any sentimentality. We are not here to sympathize with the Jews but to sympathize with our German people. With the German people having once more sacrificed 160,000 dead in the campaign in the East, the original agents of this bloody conflict must pay for it with their lives.[152]

As radical as these statements appear, they were not fundamentally different in tone and substance from similar threats made previously by Hitler and Goebbels.[153] Hitler's statement of 12 December was indicative not so much of a fundamental radicalization of Nazi policies towards the Jews than as an of intensification and extension of the process of mass murder that was already well on its way.[154] When Himmler met with Hitler on 18 December, his diary contained an ominous reference to the 'Jewish question'. Next to these words, apparently as a result of his meeting with Hitler, he noted: 'to be eliminated as partisans'.[155] Given that Jews had been murdered on a massive scale since the summer under the pretext of anti-partisan activities, it is likely, as Peter Longerich has suggested, that Himmler merely wanted to have this practice endorsed by Nazi Germany's supreme authority.[156]

Since the summer and autumn of 1941 the challenges involved in finding a comprehensive solution to the Jewish question had multiplied. The simultaneous implementation of the murder of the Jews in the occupied Soviet Union and the deportation of the Jews from the Reich necessitated further co-ordination between Heydrich's RSHA and other ministerial authorities with vested interests in the Jewish question. For this purpose, Heydrich ordered Eichmann to convene a meeting at the state secretary level, a meeting that had originally been planned for mid-December but, due to Germany's declaration of war on the United States, was postponed to January 1942: the Wannsee Conference.

Wannsee

On 20 January 1942, a snowy Tuesday morning, Heydrich gathered fourteen senior Nazi civil servants, party officials and high-ranking SS officers in a former industrialist's villa on the shores of Berlin's Lake Wannsee.[157]

As Heydrich indicated in his invitation letter of late November 1941, the purpose of the meeting was to establish 'a common position among the central authorities' in regard to the final solution. Heydrich even referred to the eastward 'evacuation' of Jews from the Reich and the Protectorate as the reason why co-ordination with other central agencies of Nazi Germany had become necessary.[158]

Heydrich's guests were important and, for the most part, well-educated men (over half of them had a doctorate, mainly in law). Many of them were of equivalent status to Heydrich, although none had equivalent powers. The largest group around the table comprised the representatives of ministries with responsibilities for the Jewish question: Dr Wilhelm Stuckart (Interior), Dr Roland Freisler (Justice), Erich Neumann (Four-Year Plan Organization), Friedrich-Wilhelm Kritzinger (Reich Chancellery) and Dr Martin Luther (Foreign Ministry). The two representatives of the Ministry for the Occupied Eastern Territories, Dr Alfred Meyer and Dr Georg Leibbrandt, fell into this category, but, together with Hans Frank's State Secretary in the General Government, Dr Josef Bühler, they formed a second group, namely German agencies with responsibilities for the civilian administration of occupied territories in the East. Then there were the officials from the SS and party with a special interest in race questions: Gerhard Klopfer (Party Chancellery) and Otto Hofmann (director of the SS Race and Settlement Office). In addition, Heydrich had instructed officials from his own apparatus to attend. The most senior of them was Heinrich Müller, head of the Gestapo, and, below him, Adolf Eichmann, Heydrich's Jewish expert. From the field there was Dr Karl Eberhard Schöngarth, head of the Security Police and SD in the General Government, and Dr Rudolf Lange, the regional Security Police chief in Latvia, where he had been responsible for the mass shootings of Jews in Riga at the end of November 1941.[159]

Heydrich opened the meeting by reminding his guests that Göring had entrusted *him* with the task of resolving the Jewish question in Europe. The purpose of the present meeting, he declared, was therefore only to establish clarity on fundamental questions and to co-ordinate a 'parallelization of policies'. What followed was directed against the representatives of the General Government and the Ministry for the Occupied Eastern Territories: 'Centralized control in the handling of the final solution' now lay 'irrespective of geographical boundaries', with the SS.[160]

Heydrich deliberately chose the words 'irrespective of geographical boundaries' in order to underline that neither Rosenberg as minister for the occupied Eastern territories nor the General Governor, Hans Frank, would be able to make independent decisions regarding Jewish policy in their respective fiefdoms. This was by no means uncontroversial. The matter of whether the Jewish question should be treated as a 'policing issue', thus falling into Heydrich's area of responsibility, or a political issue, thus remaining within Rosenberg's jurisdiction, remained highly contested. In the winter of 1941, Rosenberg had repeatedly tried to impose tighter control over SS representatives in the former Soviet Union, causing Heydrich to insist in a letter to him of 10 January 1942 that Nazi Jewish policies in the East were a policing matter outside Rosenberg's jurisdiction.[161]

Heydrich's words were also aimed at Bühler, Hans Frank's deputy, whose relationship with Heydrich had been overshadowed by a conflict over executive competences in the General Government ever since the autumn of 1939.[162] In the months and weeks before the Wannsee Conference, Himmler and Heydrich had repeatedly clashed with civilian agencies in Poland over issues of competence in relation to Jewish matters.[163] In late November 1941, for example, Himmler's representative in the General Government complained to Heydrich that Frank wished to take control of the 'handling of the Jewish problem' in the General Government himself. Shortly after this meeting, Bühler was added to the list of invitees, presumably to settle the matter of competences over Jewish policies once and for all.[164]

After reasserting his unquestionable authority in all matters concerning the Jewish question, Heydrich recapitulated the previous stages and past achievements in the Nazis' struggle against Jewry. The principal aim since 1933 had been to remove the Jews from all sectors of German society and then from German soil. The only solution available at that time had been to accelerate Jewish emigration, a policy that had led to the creation of the Reich Central Office for Jewish Emigration. The disadvantages of the policy of emigration were clear to all those involved, but in the absence of alternatives the policy was tolerated, at least initially. With pride, Heydrich recalled that between January 1933 and 31 October 1941, a total of 537,000 Jews had been 'induced to emigrate' from Germany, Austria and the Protectorate.

Since the outbreak of war with the Soviet Union, however, the situation had changed entirely. Emigration from Germany was no longer an option and had indeed been forbidden altogether by Himmler in the autumn of 1941. Instead, Heydrich suggested, 'new possibilities in the East' offered 'a further possible solution' which had recently been approved by Hitler: 'the evacuation of the Jews to the East'. The small-scale deportations from the Reich and the Protectorate to Łódź, Minsk and Riga that had commenced in October 1941 had provided important 'practical experiences', which would be 'of great significance for the coming final solution to the Jewish question'. Unfortunately, he continued, regional discrepancies in the treatment of Jews persisted. Inconsistencies regarding the destination of the transports and the fate of the deportees made it clear that the central agencies involved were struggling to adopt a coherent approach regarding the Jews to be deported from the Reich. These were the persisting problems that Heydrich hoped to resolve at the Wannsee Conference.[165]

Following his brief general introduction, Heydrich outlined the scale of the task that lay ahead of them. Roughly 11 million Jews – including those living under German occupation, the Jews of neutral European states such as Turkey, Ireland and Sweden and those living in states still at war with Nazi Germany, such as Great Britain – would be affected by the final solution. This figure, Heydrich added disapprovingly, was an estimate based on statistics of religious rather than racial affiliation 'since some countries still do not have a definition of the Jew according to racial principles'.[166] The full implementation of the final solution could thus occur only after a victorious conclusion of the war, but Heydrich was confident that Germany would soon be in a position to put sufficient pressure on the neutral countries to surrender their Jews to the Nazis.

Heydrich then informed his guests of the fate he envisaged for those Jews already under German control: 'Under appropriate leadership, the Jews should be put to work in the East in the context of the final solution. In large, single-sex labour columns, Jews fit to work will work their way eastwards constructing roads. Doubtless the large majority will be eliminated by natural causes.' Any 'final remnants that survive will no doubt consist of the most resistant elements'. These 'elements' would 'have to be dealt with appropriately' in order to avoid, as the 'experience of history' confirmed, the formation of 'the germ cell [*Keimzelle*] of a new Jewish revival'. The fate of the millions of Jews deemed unable to work in the first place, most notably the elderly and the sick, was much more straightforward. It was so obvious that it did not even need to be discussed.[167]

Heydrich's reference to Jewish slave labour in the East has generated considerable debate among historians of the Holocaust. Spurred on by Eichmann's admission during his trial in Jerusalem, some scholars have argued that the coded language used at the Wannsee Conference ultimately concealed a coherent plan to murder systematically all Jews in the German sphere of influence. Others, however, have suggested that Heydrich's forced-labour programme was not pure camouflage but rather one of many elements making up his plan for the final solution. Since the construction of the extermination camps in the Warthegau and in the General Government was only progressing slowly and as Jewish forced labour had great significance for the German war economy, the latter argument appears to be more plausible.[168]

Germany and the Protectorate, Heydrich said, would be cleared of Jews first. Only then would Europe be combed from west to east. The Jews would be brought to 'transit ghettos' and then sent further east, although he conceded that Jews should not be removed from essential enterprises in the wartime economy unless foreign replacement labour could be provided. Even Heydrich could not ignore wartime economic needs at a time when Nazi Germany was confronted with manpower shortages on a dangerous scale. He attempted to balance recognition of current labour scarcities with a desire to eliminate all Jews, although his determination to kill all 'resilient' surviving Jewish labourers shows that he privileged ideology over economic concerns and military necessities.[169]

Heydrich then identified some key prerequisites for the deportations. There had to be clarity about who was going to be deported. Jews over sixty-five and decorated war veterans would be sent to the 'old-age ghetto' of Theresienstadt, primarily to obviate the numerous predictable interventions from German neighbours or friends on their behalf. In relation to other considerations, Heydrich remained notably vague about how he hoped to implement his murderous concept of deportation, extermination and annihilation through labour. After emphasizing once more that the speed of the deportations would largely depend on the military situation over the next few months, he suggested that concrete implementation plans would be discussed at a follow-up conference of middle-rank experts from the ministries and agencies involved in anti-Jewish policies.[170]

Heydrich's position on the Jewish question at Wannsee was not entirely new. As in early 1941, he continued to assume that the comprehensive solution to the Jewish question would take place *after* the end of the war through a combination of forced labour and mass murder. More immediately, the systematic mass killing of Jews that had already begun in the Soviet Union during the previous summer could be intensified and extended to occupied Poland.[171]

Frank's deputy, Bühler, accordingly suggested to Heydrich that the final solution should begin in the General Government since 'the transport problem does not play a significant role here' and most of the Jews living in this area were already incapable of working anyway. The solution of the Jewish question in the General Government could and should therefore begin as quickly as possible. The representative of the Ministry for the Occupied Eastern Territories, Meyer, also pleaded that 'certain preparatory measures in the context of the final solution' should be conducted immediately. Given that 'various types of solution possibilities' (in other words, different means of mass murder) were discussed at Wannsee, Meyer's reference to 'preparatory measures' can only have meant one thing: the creation of further extermination camps based on the model of the Belzec camp, which was already under construction.[172]

Bühler and Meyer thus placed an alternative on the table that rendered Heydrich's envisaged deportation programme largely superfluous. It was a surprising turn of events, but a proposal that Heydrich endorsed because it promised a speedy solution of the Jewish problem in the General Government, a territory with the largest concentration of Jews in German-occupied Europe. Himmler and Heydrich would take up Bühler's suggestion in the ensuing months and develop it further, as the focal point of the Europe-wide final solution shifted from the formerly Soviet territories to occupied Poland.[173]

The remainder of the Wannsee Conference was devoted to a lengthy discussion of whether half-Jews and Jews in 'privileged' mixed marriages should be included in the final solution, an issue of high priority for Heydrich. Ever since the Nuremberg Laws of 1935, SS racial experts had demanded further measures to address the alleged threat of racial decomposition of the German *Volk* posed by the so-called *Mischlinge* or mixed breeds.[174] They had been bitterly disappointed by the second Nuremberg Law of 1935, the Law for the Protection of German Blood, which treated as Jews only persons with three or four Jewish grandparents, thus allowing most people with two or fewer Jewish ancestors to be considered as Germans. Although Hitler favoured a more radical stance, he hesitated to impose laws that would antagonize the countless German relatives of the half-Jews in question. The compromise solution was a new legal category, the *Mischling*, defined by a disparate muddle of religious and racial criteria. Quarter-Jews were termed *Mischlinge* but were allowed to marry other Germans, although not other *Mischlinge* or Jews. Half-Jews were also considered *Mischlinge* unless they were members of a synagogue or had married a Jew, in which case they were considered full Jews (the so-called *Geltungsjuden*).[175]

In 1941 party radicals renewed efforts to extend their definitional power, remove the protected categories and have the *Mischlinge* legally equated with full Jews. Heydrich, too, began to take a more active interest in the question, particularly once it became important to define which groups should be deported from the Reich. By the summer of 1941, he decided that the time had come to revise the protection of the *Mischlinge* and to mount a frontal attack on the compromises established by the Nuremberg Laws.[176]

The numbers at stake were comparatively small. In 1939, there were 64,000 first-degree and around 43,000 second-degree *Mischlinge* in the Old Reich, Austria and the Protectorate. Nonetheless, Heydrich spent considerable time outlining his own narrow definition of the *Mischlinge*.

First-degree *Mischlinge* or half-Jews, he suggested, should be considered Jews (and consequently be deported) unless they were either married to 'persons of German blood' *and* the marriage had resulted in children *or* if they had received an exemption permit from a top Nazi authority. In return for being spared from deportation, the first-degree *Mischling* would have to submit to 'voluntary' sterilization if he or she was to remain in the Reich. A second-degree *Mischling* or quarter-Jew was to be considered a Jew if any of the following three criteria applied: if both parents were *Mischlinge*; if he or she had an 'exceptionally poor racial appearance' that distinguished him or her as a Jew; or if he or she 'feels and behaves like a Jew'.[177]

Heydrich's proposals did not encounter much opposition from the other delegates. Stuckart's only concern was that the proposed measures involved 'endless administrative work'. He therefore suggested as an alternative the complete sterilization of the *Mischlinge* population, a suggestion supported by the director of the Race and Settlement Office, Otto Hofmann.[178]

As far as German Jews in mixed marriages were concerned, of which there were fewer than 20,000 at this point, Heydrich also suggested a radical solution: all fully Jewish partners of German spouses should be deported. The primary decision that remained to be made was whether the Jewish partner should be evacuated to the East (that is, murdered) or, in view of the psychological impact of such measures on German relatives, be sent to an old-age ghetto. The only exception to this rule, Heydrich believed, should be cases where there were children deemed to be second-degree *Mischlinge*. In these cases the Jewish parent could stay for the foreseeable future.[179]

Once again, the purpose of Heydrich's suggestion seems to have been to assert the SS's total definitional power in all aspects of the Jewish question. The Nuremberg Laws, though banning future unions between Jews and non-Jews, had little to say about existing mixed marriages. At the end of 1938, after consulting Hitler, Göring drew up guidelines distinguishing between so-called privileged mixed marriages and others. The privileged marriages were those where the man was non-Jewish, with the exception of marriages where there were 'Jewishly educated' children. Marriages in which the husband was Jewish were not privileged, with the exception of those marriages in which there were Christian children. At Wannsee, it was once again Stuckart who made a radical suggestion for how to solve the issue of mixed marriages. He called for a straightforward legislative act that would dissolve all existing mixed marriages, paving the way for the deportation of the Jewish spouses.[180]

No consensus on this issue was reached at Wannsee, but it was agreed that SS racial experts and other Nazi officials should discuss the fate of the

Mischlinge and of Jews in mixed marriages at the mid-level conferences and meetings that would follow the Wannsee Conference in the summer and autumn of 1942.[181]

After a further request for future co-operation in carrying out the final solution, Heydrich closed the meeting. All in all, it had lasted no longer than an hour and a half. If Heydrich had expected 'considerable stumbling blocks and difficulties' prior to the meeting, he must have been pleasantly surprised by the amicable nature of the negotiations. According to Eichmann, Heydrich was visibly satisfied with the results of the meeting, and invited him and Müller to stay behind for 'a glass or two or three of cognac'.[182]

Heydrich's satisfaction was not unfounded. He had hoped to achieve three things at the gathering. First, he sought official endorsement from civil authorities of the deportation process, as well as of the extent of the planned comprehensive solution to the Jewish question. Secondly, he wanted to emphasize his sole responsibility for the solution of the Jewish question against all resistance from those civilian authorities, which, over the previous months, had sought to protect their waning influence from further incursions by the RSHA. Thirdly, he wanted to reach a consensus on the groups of people that were to be deported.

At least two of these aims were fulfilled. Wannsee had unambiguously affirmed Heydrich's overall authority in relation to the final solution. The Ministry of the Interior, the General Government and the Ministry for the Occupied Eastern Territories had all fallen into line, and had even occasionally proposed more radical solutions than Heydrich had initially deemed acceptable. The long-standing conflict with the civil authorities in the General Government also seemed to be resolved. Reducing the number of Jews in the General Government, rather than dumping them on the region, was something on which Heydrich and Frank's representative at Wannsee could agree. Disputes would continue after January 1942, but the 'basic line', Heydrich confidently stated in a letter to Luther, had been established.[183]

However, if Heydrich believed that he had carried the day on the *Mischling* question, he was soon to be disappointed. If, as originally planned, the Wannsee Conference had taken place after a successful capture of Moscow, it is not unlikely that his attempt to include the *Mischlinge* in the deportations would have succeeded. Nazi racial policy usually radicalized at times of German military success, as the euphoria of victory tempted an elated Hitler to dare ever more drastic policies.[184] But there were no military successes in the winter of 1941–2 and, even in the following months, the SS leadership found it difficult to push its line on the *Mischlinge*. During the mid-level follow-up meetings to Wannsee in 1942, Eichmann pressed for radical solutions along the lines of Stuckart's or Heydrich's suggestions, but such policies were never implemented. Both the Ministry of Propaganda and the Justice Ministry were concerned about the implications of compulsory divorce. In October 1943, Justice Minister Otto Georg Thierack and Himmler agreed not to deport *Mischlinge* for the duration of the war.[185]

Similar obstacles remained with respect to mixed marriages. The regime feared the effects on public morale if the partners of Aryan men and women were deported. When, in the spring of 1943, for example, hundreds of non-Jewish women in Berlin publicly protested against the threatened deportation of their Jewish husbands, the Nazis backed off and released the men. These so-called Rosenstrasse protests of 1943 demonstrated that the regime was prepared to revise its policies when it encountered determined popular resistance.[186] For the most part, however, Jews in privileged mixed marriages would be saved. Only after the death of their Aryan husbands were some Jewish widows in formerly privileged marriages deported after December 1943. Wannsee had thus failed to provide the decisive breakthrough on this issue for which Heydrich had hoped.[187]

Nor was Wannsee the moment at which a fundamental decision was made to turn the already murderous anti-Jewish policies in the East into an all-encompassing genocide of all European Jews. Nobody at the conference, not even Heydrich, was able to make that decision without Hitler's explicit consent. The discussions at Wannsee rather testified to the gradually increasing radicalism with which the central authorities of Nazi Germany viewed the Jewish question. Decisions that would turn 1942 into the most astounding year of murder in the Holocaust, indeed one of the most horrifying years of systematic mass killings in the history of mankind, were yet to follow.[188]

The day after the Wannsee Conference, Heydrich telephoned Himmler to inform him of the meeting's results, before boarding a plane that would bring him back to Prague, where, in his capacity as acting Reich Protector of Bohemia and Moravia, he had spent the past three months installing a regime based uncompromisingly on terror.[189]

CHAPTER VIII

Reich Protector

The Protectorate of Bohemia and Moravia

OF THE NUMEROUS TERRITORIES OCCUPIED AND ADMINISTERED BY NAZI Germany over the course of the Second World War, the Protectorate of Bohemia and Moravia was one of the more curious. With a size of roughly 49,000 square kilometres and an overall population of 7.5 million inhabitants (245,000 of whom were ethnic Germans), the Protectorate was by no means the largest of the Nazi-occupied territories. However, it played a special role in occupied Europe, both because the Nazis perceived Bohemia and Moravia as an integral part of the future Greater German Reich, and because of its crucial geo-strategic location and economic importance for Germany's war effort.[1]

Established on 16 March 1939, the day after the German occupation of the western half of Czechoslovakia, the Protectorate was to become a German colony presided over by an appointed Reich Protector, a viceroy directly responsible to Hitler. Yet while the colonial rhetoric employed by leading Nazis in order to describe the future of the Protectorate was striking, it concealed more than it revealed: the new constitutional structure imposed on the country was merely a wartime solution which would eventually give way to the full political, economic and racial integration of Bohemia and Moravia into the Greater German Reich. After Germany's victory in the Second World War, the Czechs would either become Germans or they would have to disappear in one way or another.[2]

For the time being, however, the Czech inhabitants of the Protectorate retained their own autonomous government (at least in theory), while the Sudeten Germans were granted full citizenship of the Reich. All democratic remnants of the Czechoslovak Republic, including the parliament, were abolished. Existing political parties were dissolved and reorganized under the umbrella of the so-called National Solidarity Movement. All that remained of the once thriving democratic system was a nominal Czech administration, headed by Emil Hácha as president, with an appointed fifty-member Committee of National Solidarity chaired by Prime Minister Alois Eliáš. Some 400,000 Czech state employees and civil servants remained in their posts after 1939, alongside, or rather subordinate to, some 11,000 German civilian administrators. This peculiar form of administration imposed on the Protectorate differed significantly from those introduced elsewhere in Nazi-occupied Europe and it reflected the Nazi leadership's recognition that the Protectorate's advanced economy was too precious to be upset by a brutal occupation regime of the sort inflicted on Poland, Belorussia and Ukraine.[3]

With a major armaments industry in Brünn (Brno) and other Protectorate cities, including one of Europe's leading arms manufacturers, the Škoda works in Pilsen (Plzeň), as well as a large number of skilled labourers, the Protectorate's importance for Hitler's war is difficult to overestimate. From the beginning of the occupation, German special units had seized huge quantities of military equipment, arms and ammunition, and Jewish assets were transferred to the German authorities.[4] Native industry, however, was left to get on with things under nominal German direction. Czech-owned international companies such as the Bata shoe empire brought in valuable profits and high tax returns, and were not seriously restricted by the German occupiers.[5]

Until the outbreak of the Second World War, the first Reich Protector, Konstantin von Neurath, ran a remarkably lenient regime compared to that in occupied Poland. An old-fashioned conservative rather than a radical Nazi, Neurath had spent more than twenty years in the diplomatic service, crowning his career by becoming the first Foreign Minister in Hitler's coalition government of 1933, before being assigned to Bohemia and Moravia in 1938. Compared to his successor, Neurath was not a man of heavy-handed occupation policies. Although he had enthusiastically supported the remilitarization of the Rhineland in 1939 and the annexation of Austria in 1938, he was privately dismissive of Hitler's ideas about German *Lebensraum* in the East. He was also, however, respected abroad for being well mannered and cultured, which was the key reason why Hitler appointed him Reich Protector in the spring of 1939 against objections from other senior Nazis.[6]

The priority of the German occupiers was initially to gain control over the country's resources and to suppress any open resistance to German rule. After the outbreak of the Second World War on 1 September 1939 and Czech mass demonstrations the following month, the Nazi grip on

Czech society began to tighten. The predicament of Jews, in particular, deteriorated rapidly. Their persecution had begun immediately after the German invasion, when the Nuremberg Laws were applied to Protectorate Jews. Until September 1939 Czech Jews had still been able to emigrate, but the outbreak of war closed all doors for Jewish émigrés. More repressive laws followed in a process that was overseen by Heydrich's Jewish expert in Prague, Adolf Eichmann: as of 1940 Jewish identification cards were stamped with a 'J'; and in late August 1941 Neurath issued an order that from 1 September that year onwards all Jews in the Protectorate over the age of six had to wear a yellow star. Mirroring regulations introduced earlier in the General Government, the star was to be sewn on the left front of their clothing. Only Jews in privileged mixed marriages were exempt.[7]

Alterations to German occupation policy affected the rest of society, too. As soon as the war began, newspapers and posters across the Protectorate announced that any act of resistance would result in a death sentence. In November 1939, following a number of violent demonstrations in Prague and other cities, the Nazis responded with the arrest of student protesters and the closure of Czech universities, initially for a period of three years. The wave of arrests swept up thousands of intellectuals, priests, Communists Social Democrats and Jewish community leaders.[8]

The second year of the Nazi occupation thus constituted a radical break from the comparatively lenient regime of 1939. It also marked a turning point for the Czech resistance. Previously, resistance had been highly fragmented. Apart from the Communist underground composed of the remnants of the KSČ (the Communist Party of Czechoslovakia), three democratic resistance groups formed shortly after the German invasion: the Political Centre (Politické Ústředí or PÚ), the Committee of the Petition 'We Remain Faithful!' (Petiční výbor 'Věrni zůstaneme!' or PVVZ), and the Nation's Defence (Obrana národa or ON). In addition, sizeable sports associations such as the Sokol served as a reservoir for recruitment into the underground resistance.[9] Under the pressure generated by the mass arrests in the autumn of 1939 and the spring of 1940, the three major non-Communist resistance organisations – PÚ, PVVZ and ON – consolidated their ranks under the Central Leadership of Home Resistance (Ústřední vedení odboje domácího or ÚVOD), which served as the principal clandestine intermediary between the London-based Czechoslovak government-in-exile and the resistance within the Protectorate.[10]

It was only after the German attack on the Soviet Union on 22 June 1941 that resistance activities in the Protectorate, as in many other countries under Nazi rule, began to develop on a noticeable scale, as Neurath had to admit in a report to Hitler.[11] In early September, resistance activities in the Protectorate culminated in a number of strikes and 'work slowly' campaigns that triggered an average fall of 18 per cent in the Protectorate's industrial production. Telephone wires across Bohemia and Moravia were cut, railway carriages set on fire, and the resistance organized a successful one-week boycott of the German-controlled Protectorate press. Simultaneously, the number of Communist underground leaflets distributed across the Protectorate rose dramatically from 377 in June 1941 to 3,797 in July, peaking at 10,727 in October.[12]

The leaflet campaign showed that the Communist resistance, most adept at underground work, had overcome the involuntary paralysis induced by the Hitler–Stalin Pact of August 1939. As a wave of strikes, sabotage actions and assassinations of German military personnel swept across various occupied countries in the late summer and autumn of 1941, Hitler was convinced that only draconian punishment would prevent opposition to German rule from spreading further. On 16 September he called for 'the most drastic means' to be employed against any provocation, while Keitel demanded that fifty to a hundred Communist hostages be shot for every German soldier killed by partisans. Although military commanders in Serbia, France, Belgium and Norway responded with mass arrests, the shooting of hostages and other reprisals, acts of resistance nonetheless continued on a worrying scale.[13]

From the beginning of Operation Barbarossa in the summer of 1941, Heydrich had been one of the most outspoken advocates of a 'tough' response to the challenge posed by indigenous resistance, ordering local Sipo commanders to use 'intensified interrogation methods' (that is, torture) to obtain information about 'wire-pullers'. Simultaneously, he issued an order that 'hostile Czechs and Poles as well as Communists and other scumbags must be transferred to a concentration camp for longer periods of time'. In early September 1941, Heydrich flew to Norway, where a strike wave had reached alarming proportions. He met with Reich Commissioner Terboven, who shortly afterwards – on 10 September – took his advice and imposed martial law in Oslo.[14]

In the Netherlands the commander of the Security Police, Wilhelm Harster, also acted on Heydrich's orders and undertook mass arrests following the German attack on the Soviet Union. In September, he had the conservative former Dutch Prime Minister Hendrikus Colijn arrested on a charge of espionage.[15] Also in September, Heydrich ordered the arrest and shooting of members of the Ukrainian Organization of Nationalists, whom, despite their firmly anti-Bolshevik stance, he considered to be a potential source of unrest in the rear of the rapidly advancing Wehrmacht.[16]

The noticeable increase in resistance activities confirmed Heydrich's belief that the time was ripe for a more comprehensive assertion of SS authority in the running of German-controlled Europe. On 18 September, the same day that he and Himmler embarked on a three-day inspection tour of the conquered Baltic territories, he submitted a far-reaching proposal to Lammers, reminding him 'that the securing of the Reich, the protection of its frontiers ... the combating of espionage and political subversion, as well as the struggle against international crime' were of 'decisive importance'. For this reason, he included a draft Führer order granting the SS further police competences in the General Government and the Protectorate, as well as in the territories of Western Europe under civil administration (Lorraine, Alsace, Luxembourg, the Netherlands and Norway). The SS and police should henceforth assume responsibility for all matters of 'internal political security' within the Nazi Empire, not merely for matters of 'police security'.[17]

Although the proposal was never put to Hitler for fear of provoking severe conflict between the SS, Rosenberg and the heads of the civil and military administrations in the occupied territories, it offers a revealing glimpse into Heydrich's strategic thinking. From very early on in his SS career, Heydrich had realized that the best way of increasing his personal powers and those of the SS more generally was to paint an overly dramatic picture of the strength of opposition with which Nazism was confronted. In 1932, he had deliberately used the exaggerated notion of a Nazi movement undermined by spies and traitors to build up his SD; in the mid-1930s, when the Communist movement in Germany was largely suppressed, he developed the idea of largely invisible enemies of Nazism whose power could be broken only by a significant SS police formation with extra-legal means. After the outbreak of the Second World War, he instrumentalized the widespread fear of partisans to extend continuously his brief of fighting an illusive network of broadly defined enemies. Now that concern about the intensification of resistance in the occupied territories was growing within the Nazi leadership and among senior military figures, he used the same argument: only the SS had the experience and determination to fight resistance activities effectively before they could escalate on a truly threatening scale. Heydrich's track-record in combating the enemies of the Reich both at home and abroad undoubtedly contributed to the decision of Martin Bormann, a party hardliner who had emerged as head of the Party Chancellery after Rudolf Hess's flight to Scotland in May 1941, to recommend him to the Führer as an appropriate candidate to serve as acting Reich Protector in Bohemia and Moravia where strikes and 'work slowly' campaigns had begun to undermine the German war effort.

Heydrich was well informed about the deteriorating situation in the Protectorate through the regular reports he received from the Gestapo and SD offices in Bohemia and Moravia. The information gathered by his agents and transmitted to Berlin, where it was summarized and collated for the Nazi leadership, helped to create the impression that Neurath was no longer in control of the situation. Although there is no hard evidence to suggest that Heydrich actively pursued Neurath's replacement and his own nomination as Reich Protector, he certainly pressed for a considerable extension of SS responsibilities in the Protectorate, thus, in effect, undermining Neurath's position.[18]

Concerned about the declining productivity of the Czech armaments industry and the resistance activities outlined in the SD reports, Hitler decided to replace Neurath in late September 1941. On Bormann's recommendation, the Führer ordered Neurath, the Higher SS and Police Leader in the Protectorate, Karl Hermann Frank, and Heydrich to join him at his military headquarters, the Wolf's Lair near Rastenburg in East Prussia. Here he disclosed his decision that Neurath would be sent on indefinite 'sick leave' and Heydrich would be dispatched to Prague in his stead. Hitler's decision implied more than an exchange of personnel: it reflected his determination to replace Neurath's restraint and 'unsuccessful' occupation policy in the Protectorate with a campaign of terror.[19]

The second, and in many ways related, reason for Heydrich's appointment was Hitler's reversal on the issue of Jewish deportations from the Reich. As late as mid-August 1941, he had made it clear that these deportations could take place only after the defeat of the Soviet Union. However, from the second week of September, and presumably encouraged by major Wehrmacht breakthroughs on the Eastern Front that would soon lead to the encirclement of Leningrad and the fall of Kiev, the Führer was prepared to revise his decision.[20]

After Hitler had turned down Heydrich's proposal for the complete deportation of Jews from the Reich and the Protectorate in August, the RSHA began to work on a proposal for a partial evacuation during the war – a wave of deportations that would primarily affect those Jews living in the larger cities.[21] Such a proposal was more agreeable to Hitler in mid-September, when military advances on the Russian front made the eastward deportations possible and when increasing pressure from the Reich's Gauleiters to turn their fiefdom's into 'Jew free' zones, thus easing the housing problem created by Allied bombings of German cities, also made deportations politically desirable. On 18 September Himmler informed Arthur Greiser in the Warthegau that it was Hitler's expressed wish 'that the Old Reich and the Protectorate be emptied and freed of Jews from west to east as quickly as possible'. As a 'first step', Himmler continued, the Jews would be deported into occupied Poland before moving them 'further east next spring'. Some 60,000 Jews from the Old Reich and the Protectorate would thus have to be interned in the Łódź ghetto, in the annexed Warthegau, over the winter.[22]

When Heydrich met with Goebbels at the Führer headquarters on the day of his appointment as acting Reich Protector, Goebbels expressed similar sentiments and emphasized that 'in the end' the Jews of the Reich would be 'transported into the camps that have been erected by the Bolsheviks. These camps were built by the Jews, so what could be more fitting than populating them with Jews?' Goebbels also confirmed in his diary on the same day that the 'Führer is of the opinion that the Jews are to be removed from Germany step by step. The first cities to be cleared of Jews are Berlin, Vienna and Prague.'[23]

That Heydrich was installed as acting Reich Protector of Bohemia and Moravia at precisely the time that the Nazi leadership decided on a further radicalization of anti-Jewish policies was hardly coincidental. Now that Hitler had selected Prague, alongside Berlin and Vienna, as one of the first major cities to be rendered 'Jew-free', Heydrich must have seemed to be the obvious choice to guarantee a swift implementation of his wishes.

Heydrich's arrival in Prague thus coincided with the very moment when Hitler and Himmler, prompted by the rapid advance of the German armies into the Soviet Union, began to think about the racial reordering of the conquered territories, and the creation of Germany's Garden of Eden in the East. Heydrich's policies in the Protectorate over the following months suggest that he was sent to Prague not only to restore order – a task that could have been undertaken by a less prominent SS officer such as the Protectorate's higher SS and police leader, Karl Hermann Frank – but also to initiate and oversee the next radical steps in the Nazis' racial policies. These involved the beginning of deportations of all Jews from Germany and the Protectorate, and the commencement of preparations for the full racial integration of Bohemia and Moravia into the Reich, thus testing anti-Semitic policies that were soon to be employed in the entire Reich as well as even more far-reaching policies of ethnic engineering that Hitler and Himmler intended to carry out in all border regions considered to be Germanizable after the war's end.

For Hitler, Himmler, Heydrich and Goebbels in particular, the simultaneous intensification of repressive measures against the various resistance movements in occupied Europe, the escalation of the systematic murder of Jews in the Soviet Union and the deportation of Jews from the Reich were logically connected. Since they assumed that Communism and Jewry were largely identical, they were convinced that the Jews were also the key engineers of anti-German resistance movements in the occupied territories. To some extent, this logic became a self-fulfilling prophecy. With few other options for survival available, many Jews in the Baltic States and in Belorussia gravitated towards the Communist partisans active in the forests of the occupied territories.[24]

Heydrich must nonetheless have been ambivalent about Hitler's decision to appoint him acting Reich Protector. He was keen to see his influence on Protectorate policies increase, but that could have been achieved by extending SS powers over policing matters under the command of one of his trusted associates. The idea of leaving Berlin, the centre of power in Nazi Germany, at a time when military victory over the Soviet Union seemed imminent, may have made Heydrich suspicious that ulterior motives were behind his new appointment. But the pill was sweetened in various ways. In true Nazi style, Heydrich took on the new responsibilities not instead of but in addition to the offices he had already accumulated. He also knew that this new task would allow him to implement SS policies without having to take into consideration the objections of reluctant administrators or Nazi Party Gauleiters. A promotion to SS-*Obergruppenführer* and general of the police also came with his new assignment, but most importantly, perhaps, the new position opened up direct access to Hitler, since the Reich Protector was answerable only to the Führer himself.

It has often been maintained that this appointment and Heydrich's growing independence from the Reich Leader SS created tensions between Heydrich and Himmler, but there is no concrete evidence to suggest that their relationship deteriorated after September 1941. Quite the opposite: over the following months, their collaboration on Germanization policies, anti-Jewish persecution and policing in the occupied territories further developed, and there is no indication that Heydrich's loyalty towards his mentor was ever in question.[25]

After a long conversation with Himmler at the Wolf's Lair on 24 September, Heydrich called his wife from Rastenburg to report the 'extraordinary news' of his appointment as acting Reich Protector. When he told Lina that, for the time being, she and their three children would remain in Berlin and that he would he would go to Prague alone, his wife was anything but excited. Already infuriated by his constant absences and his neglect of family matters, she expressed her deep frustration. His assurances that he would be in Berlin for many of the weeks ahead did not improve the situation.[26]

Early in the afternoon of 27 September, Heydrich arrived at Prague's Ruzyně airport, where he was welcomed by the Higher SS and Police Leader in the Protectorate, Karl Hermann Frank. Born in 1889 to a family of Sudeten Germans in Karlsbad, Frank had served in the Austrian army during the Great War and spent a year studying law in Prague before leaving university to work at a number of small, badly paid jobs. He joined Konrad Henlein's Sudeten German movement in 1933 and quickly rose to become Henlein's party deputy, a post he was to keep until the German occupation when he became higher SS and police leader in the Protectorate. Frank had been a close collaborator of Heydrich's for several years and even if he was disappointed at not having been appointed Reich Protector himself, he remained a most loyal servant.[27]

After a brief sight-seeing tour of the city, Heydrich moved into his new lodgings in the left wing of Černín Palace. The following morning, after reviewing a guard of honour in front of the castle, he officially assumed his new post and the black flag of the SS was raised over the turrets and spires of the city.[28]

Pacifying the Czechs

Less than a week after his arrival in Prague, on 2 October 1941, Heydrich addressed a gathering of senior Protectorate officials and Nazi party functionaries at the Černín Palace. He normally dreaded giving public speeches, repeatedly rehearsing them in front of his wife who then commented on his performance, but this time was different.[29] As he walked into the Černín Palace's reception hall, resplendent in his new SS general's uniform and surrounded by obsequious aides, Heydrich had every reason to be confident. By the autumn of 1941, Germany occupied almost one-third of the European continent and ruled nearly half its inhabitants. The stunning victories of the Wehrmacht in the first week of October, which brought the German army close to the outskirts of Moscow, made him confident that the Soviet Union's surrender was only a matter of days.

In his speech, Heydrich emphasized that his approach to the internal affairs of the Protectorate would differ fundamentally from that of his predecessor. Unlike Neurath, he would build on his long-standing experience in fighting enemies of the Reich. The task set for him by the Führer was a clearly defined 'combat task' for the SS, not a diplomatic mission. His most pressing short-term goal in Prague, Heydrich explained, was therefore the 'pacification' of the Protectorate in order to safeguard Germany's vital economic and security interests in the area. Industrial sabotage and other resistance activities were to be brought to an immediate end. Heydrich urged his audience always to bear in mind that 'the Czech is a Slav' who 'interprets any form of kindness as weakness'. For that reason, his first move would be to 'show them who is the master in this house'. According to one witness, Heydrich added that anyone who disapproved of his measures would be issued with a one-way ticket to Germany or the Eastern Front.[30]

When Heydrich spoke on 2 October, the first phase of his programme of pacification had, in fact, already been in operation for several days. On the very day of his arrival in Prague, he proclaimed martial law over the Protectorate in order to demonstrate his determination to act upon the promise that 'treason at the rear of the front will be punished most severely'.[31] Martial law allowed for the establishment of summary courts which, staffed with members of the SD and the Sipo, could pass only three possible verdicts: the death sentence, shipment to a concentration camp or release. Within days of his arrival, buildings across the Protectorate were splattered with red posters listing the names of people sentenced to death by the new courts. In the first three days of Heydrich's rule, ninety-two defendants were sentenced to death. On 30 September alone, fifty-eight people were executed and 256 sent to Gestapo prisons. Only one person accused and put on trial was found innocent.[32]

The official death sentences represented only a small proportion of those arrested. For 'psychological reasons', Heydrich wished the number of official executions to decline gradually, creating the impression that calm had been restored and encouraging popular co-operation.[33] This was nothing more than propaganda: all in all, between Heydrich's arrival in Prague and the end of November 1941, a total of 404 official death sentences were carried out (the vast majority against members of the Czech resistance) and some 6,000 arrests were made. All domestic resistance groups suffered dramatic losses, in terms both of human lives and of equipment. Hundreds of people disappeared in the Gestapo cellars below the Pecek Palace. In identifying and arresting enemies of the state, Heydrich could draw on a substantial apparatus in the Protectorate. That autumn 1,841 Gestapo officers operated in Bohemia and Moravia to monitor a population of 10.3 million people. Each Gestapo officer was therefore responsible for 5,600 Czechs, a density of political supervision that was not as high as Communist surveillance levels in the Soviet Union, but was twice as high as that in the Old Reich.[34]

Many of the Czechs convicted but not immediately executed boarded one of five transports to the Mauthausen concentration camp in the winter of 1941–2. Of the 1,299 Czech people sent to Mauthausen, only 4 per cent survived the war. In addition, 1,487 Czechs accused of political crimes were sent to Auschwitz. Few of them returned.[35] More than 1,500 of Heydrich's victims had belonged to nationalist organizations, such as the popular patriotic sports organization Sokol, which was dissolved on 11 October 1941 and whose considerable assets worth 1.12 billion Czech crowns were confiscated. In addition, within the first four months of

Heydrich's rule, more than ninety illegal wireless transmitters were confiscated – a great success for the German security forces as they severed all radio links between London and the Czech underground. These sweeps nearly wiped out all organized resistance in the Protectorate.[36]

In late March 1942, after deciphering coded messages from arrested Czech paratroopers, Heydrich's Gestapo chalked up another important success in arresting Paul Thümmel, a double agent who worked for both the German Abwehr and, under the codename A-54, for Beneš's government-in-exile. Heydrich took a strong personal interest in the Thümmel case. As a senior Abwehr officer and an Old Fighter in the Nazi movement with strong resentments against political latecomers like Heydrich, Thümmel combined two characteristics that Heydrich despised. Proving Thümmel's guilt was useful not only in the continuing quarrel with the Abwehr and the army, but also in the power struggle with party representatives over political supremacy in the occupied East. It helped to discredit these rivals and prove to Hitler that the SS was the only reliable pillar of the New Order. After his arrest, Thümmel was held in the Theresienstadt concentration camp, where he was murdered by SS guards on 27 April 1945, only twelve days before the end of the Second World War.[37]

With its leaders arrested and its radio networks destroyed, ÚVOD essentially ceased to exist. As the Prague SD observed with bitterness, only the Communist resistance survived, although it, too, suffered a large number of arrests. Strikes and work slowdowns disappeared. Isolated acts of sabotage continued, but few managed to hit vital targets such as telephone and telegraph lines or armaments factories.[38] A whole array of Czech and German police organizations guarded railway lines. Heydrich made it perfectly clear to the Protectorate government that he would respond 'drastically' to all future acts of sabotage against railway lines or telecommunications facilities and that he would make the entire population of the affected area 'liable with their heads'.[39]

The arrests which followed Heydrich's arrival did not spare the Protectorate government, long regarded by the Gestapo as a nest of traitors and spies for the British. Heydrich's lesson to the Czechs began at the top with the arrest of the Prime Minister, Alois Eliáš, who had indeed served as ÚVOD's principal contact in the Protectorate government. Heydrich had known of Eliáš's communications with the underground movement for some time, but Hitler had decided that 'the reckoning with the resistance movement and the compromised Czech leaders' would have to wait until after Germany's immininent victory in the war against the Soviet Union.[40]

Eliáš's arrest was one of the most visible indicators of a radical reversal of German occupation policy under Heydrich. The German People's Court, hastily summoned from Berlin to Prague, wasted little time in sentencing him and Prague's mayor, Otakar Klapka, to death. Heydrich proudly reported to Bormann that he had staged a 'fair' trial and had forced Eliáš to sign a declaration condemning resistance activities. More importantly, Eliáš's declaration, published on the front pages of the collaborationist press throughout the Protectorate, culminated in an unlikely rejection of Czech claims to an independent state and nationhood: 'I think it is impossible for political, economic, and social reasons that our small people of 7½ million, surrounded by German living space, will ever be able to exist as an independent state.'[41]

After the trial, president Hácha pleaded with Heydrich to spare Eliáš's life. Heydrich rejected this request and repeatedly urged Hitler to have Eliáš executed as soon as possible. Hitler decided otherwise: for the time being, Eliáš was to remain in prison as a hostage in order to keep Hácha and the rest of the Czech government under control.[42] With ÚVOD's leaders arrested and Eliáš a hostage, Hácha had two options: to resign in protest or to remain in office, thereby acknowledging Heydrich's terror regime as legitimate. On the day of Eliáš's arrest, Hácha prepared a letter of resignation. Heydrich had anticipated Hácha's move and met with him in the afternoon of 28 September. Fearing that Hácha's resignation would further encourage the resistance, Heydrich professed to regret the repressive measures he had been forced to introduce 'with a bleeding heart' and assured the elderly President that Czech autonomy would remain untouched.[43] Hácha stayed in office and embarked on a policy of collaboration designed to spare the Czech people further bloodshed. Driven by the desire to prevent greater evil, on 4 December he denounced Beneš on Prague radio, accusing the exiled President of stirring up trouble at a safe distance with no thought of the consequences. Czechoslovak BBC broadcasts from London responded by calling Hácha a traitor, to which the beleaguered President replied: 'Mr Beneš does not see, as I do, the tears of the mothers and wives who address their desperate pleas to me because their sons and husbands fell into disaster after having been seduced by deceptive radio broadcasts. He is in a position to permit himself illusions, to build castles in the air, and to paint alluring pictures of the future ... For us, there is no way but to face reality with resolution and to act soberly in accordance with bare facts.'[44] Heydrich was jubilant. The Protectorate government, he remarked joyfully in a speech to Nazi leaders, had finally burned all bridges between Prague and London.[45]

Heydrich's emergency measures were aimed not only against the Protectorate government and Czech underground, but also against black-marketeers, who were officially held responsible for the food shortages which plagued the Protectorate. Heydrich tried to capitalize on public resentment of the black market to discredit the resistance. The under-

ground and black-marketeers – the 'hyenas of the home front' – were
accordingly designated 'enemies of the Czech people'. Of the 404 death
sentences handed down by the martial law courts in the first few months
of Heydrich's rule, 169 were for alleged economic crimes. In pursuit of
illegal traders, Heyrich executed ethnic Germans as well as Czechs. This
apparent even-handedness concealed his real aim, which was to increase
Czech agricultural production for the Nazi war effort. The attack on the
black market was accompanied by a recount of grain and livestock, which
successfully relied on the impact of the terror to produce an accurate
return. Farmers were promised amnesty for past evasions, but faced death
or deportation for further cheating.[46]

Although paling in comparison to events in Poland, the speed and
viciousness of Heydrich's new regime of terror and repression were
unprecedented in the history of Bohemia and Moravia. Heydrich
considered his terror measures to be unavoidable: as a Slav, 'the Czech ...
is more dangerous and must be handled differently' from Aryan peoples.
'The Nordic, Germanic man can be either convinced or broken – the
Czech, Slavic man is very difficult to convince ... And the consequence of
this is that we must constantly keep our thumb on him so that he always
remains bent, so that he will obey us and co-operate.'[47]

In late October 1941, however, the first wave of terror officially subsided
for 'optical reasons'. In order to give the outward impression of the
Protectorate's complete pacification, the summary courts temporarily
ceased to impose death penalties, although the SS secretly continued
to carry out executions at Mauthausen concentration camp.[48] On
29 November Heydrich went further in his propagandistic policy of
'postive gestures' by suspending the state of emergency in all regional
districts of the Protectorate with the exception of Prague and Brünn.
Between 30 November 1941 and 27 May 1942, Nazi authorities announced
only thirty-three executions. Still, as one London informant reported,
'people [kept] clear of any public actions, associational life, discussions and
conversations, and the majority [avoided] relations altogether ... [All
Czechs are] gritting their teeth.'[49]

Governing a State

Between 1939 and 1941, Heydrich was primarily concerned with policing
the newly conquered territories under German control rather than with
the problem of how they were to be governed. He had come to Prague as
a political novice, well versed in the in-fighting of competing Nazi agencies, but with a merely theoretical knowledge of the challenges involved in
running an occupied territory.

To be sure, the SS leadership more generally had given increasing thought to the future of the German Empire after the invasion of the Soviet Union. A 1941 *Festschrift* for Heinrich Himmler, for example, sheds some light on the possible future governance of the Nazi Empire. The most intellectually sophisticated contribution to the volume was an essay written by Heydrich's former deputy Dr Werner Best, now in charge of the civil administration of occupied France. Best proposed four ways of administering the diverse territories of occupied Europe in accordance with Nazi principles: one was what he called 'co-operative', with Denmark being the best case study of a 'racially valuable' country run without much interference from the Foreign Ministry. A second category was 'supervisory'. The examples here were France, Belgium and the Netherlands, where German officials were currently working through the existing national civil service, while maintaining a strong military presence. The third was a 'ruling' occupation, as in the Protectorate of Bohemia and Moravia, where the German reshaping of the local bureaucracy was much greater and Nazi police agencies had to remain more watchful for threats to German interests. Best's fourth and final category was 'colonial': the General Government and the territories further east served as key examples for communities where the 'inferior' civilization level of the inhabitants required the occupiers to take up the burden of government for the sake of 'order and health'.[50]

From Heydrich's point of view, Best's proposals had two serious flaws. First, by arguing that some non-Germans should essentially be allowed to police themselves, it gave the SS – the key agency concerned with policing and security – no entry-point into Western Europe. This was something with which Heydrich could most definitely not agree. Secondly, Best had merely proposed a theoretical framework for German occupation regimes after the war's end and offered no advice on the actual running of the Protectorate. Heydrich therefore had to improvise. The learning curve was steep, but, characteristically, he immersed himself in his new task with relentless energy, usually working more than fifteen hours a day and hiring and firing three adjutants within his first week in Prague for being unable to keep up with his demands.[51]

During his first three months in Prague, Lina hardly saw her husband, who returned only infrequently to Berlin.[52] Whatever precious time he had left outside the office, he invested in sport, one of his great passions. Even in Prague, he kept up his ambitious training schedule. In September 1941, he commenced training for an international sabre-fencing competition between Germany and its ally, Hungary, which took place in early December. The Hungarian team, internationally dominant throughout the 1930s, was almost impossible to beat and the German team had been substantially weakened: the 1940 national champion, Georg Frass, had fallen on the Eastern Front, and the leading German sabre fencer of the time, Josef Losert, could not be released from the Russian campaign. Heydrich volunteered to step into the breach. As expected the Hungarians won the competition with great ease, but obviously had no desire to offend the head of Nazi Germany's terror apparatus: Heydrich won all three of his bouts.[53]

Heydrich's family life improved when, in early January 1942, Lina and their children moved to Prague. As wife of the acting Reich Protector, Lina could now live the kind of lifestyle she had always considered her due. Food was more plentiful than in Berlin and she had an army of servants at her command, but she never warmed to the idea of living in Prague Castle with its ornamental rooms and impersonal furnishings. After three months, she grew tired of living in a 'museum' and urged Reinhard to find her a more family-friendly home that offered more privacy. There was 'too much history' surrounding her in Prague Castle, she complained.[54]

At Easter 1942, the Heydrich family moved to the luxurious manor house of Jungfern-Breschan (Panenské Břežany), some twenty kilometres north of the capital. The white neo-classical mansion had thirty rooms and was surrounded by a seven-hectare garden, leading to 125 hectares of dense, shady forest and a little village. The property had been confiscated from its Jewish owner, the sugar manufacturer and renowned art collector Ferdinand Bloch-Bauer, shortly after the German invasion. As the summer residence of Heydrich's predecessor in Prague, the building had been completely redecorated and refurbished. When the Heydrichs decided to use the house as their primary residence, central heating was installed to allow the family to stay in the manor house during the winter, and slave labourers from Theresienstadt concentration camp were brought in to build a swimming pool in the garden. Lina was delighted with the result and felt that Reinhard had finally provided his 'princess' with an appropriate home.[55]

But Heydrich was rarely home. Apart from his commitment to sport, his responsibilities as head of the Reich Security Main Office and his co-ordination of the final solution, he was now involved in all matters of governance in Prague: from increases in ministerial salaries of members of the Protectorate government and the appointment of individual chairs at the German University in Prague to the renovations and excavations at Prague Castle, and the question of the political reliability of individual engineers working at the Škoda factories.[56]

To fulfil his responsibilities, Heydrich commuted between Berlin and Prague by train or plane, at least twice and often three times a week.[57] He used the frequent trips to Berlin not only to preside over important

RSHA meetings, but also to maintain close contact with Goebbels and other powerful Nazis.[58] Of these contacts, the most influential in relation to Heydrich's occupation policies was Dr Herbert Backe, the State Secretary in the Reich Ministry of Economics and, from May 1942 onwards, Minister of Food. Backe, who had come to Germany as a refugee in the wake of the Russian Revolution, was one of the few people with whom Heydrich entertained a close personal friendship. As so often in Heydrich's life, this friendship was based less on strong mutual sympathy than on shared ideological beliefs and the conviction that compromises on ideology were a sign of cowardice. Their children often played together while the adults frequently invited each other for dinner parties at their homes in Berlin. The close family ties would even outlast the violent deaths of Heydrich and Backe in 1942 and 1947 respectively. When Heydrich's son, Heider, studied engineering in Hanover in the early 1950s, he lived with Backe's widow, Ursula.[59]

Backe profoundly shaped Heydrich's thinking about the economic dimension of German occupation policy. For both men, economic reorganization was inseparably intertwined with the question of race. The 'lesser' races of Europe were to be subjugated to Germany's needs. More than anyone else, Backe was conscious of the disparity between Germany's growing need for food supplies to feed the home population, the army and a vast number of POWs and forced labourers, and the increasingly scarce resources at its disposal. He played a key role in devising the so-called hunger plan in the spring of 1941; that is, the plan to engineer an extraordinary mass famine in Eastern Europe with the aim of killing off the entire urban population of the western Soviet Union, thereby removing up to 30 million 'useless mouths' from the food chain. Backe's ideas for the East were entirely compatible with those of the SS leadership, articulated in the General Plan East of the same year, which envisaged massive ethnic cleansing and resettlements in the occupied territories, coupled with an extensive slave-labour programme through which Jews and Soviet POWs would be worked to death in the construction of new infrastructure in the East.[60]

For the rest of Europe, Backe envisaged a German-dominated *Grossraumwirtschaft*, a multinational self-sufficient European economy with Germany at its heart. The gold standard and the liberal free-market economies of the post-Versailles order were to be replaced by barter trade and production planning on a continental scale in an extension of the German trade policy of the 1930s. The geo-political idea of a broad, German-led economic sphere in Central Europe was not new, and had been promoted by Friedrich Neumann and other liberal nationalists in the early 1900s, as well as by Carl Schmitt, the leading right-wing constitutional theorist of the 1930s. But men like Backe merged this older idea with the modern theory of race, giving the call for German economic superiority a new justification and purpose.[61]

To achieve his aims, Backe advocated the creation of a tariff-free zone in the occupied and 'affiliated' territories, including the Balkans, where German economic penetration had intensified throughout the 1930s. Trade agreements were negotiated in 1939 and 1940 with Romania and Hungary, which brought vital raw materials under the control of the Third Reich. Economic plans for the Balkans were to be the first step in an even more ambitious plan to set up the entire European continent as a single market which would be able to compete with the United States and Japan in the post-war global order.[62]

Such ideas impacted strongly on Heydrich's thinking about the economic imperatives of occupation policy in the Protectorate as well as German-controlled Europe more generally. The New Order, as Heydrich and other leading Nazis envisaged it, demanded a stronger economic integration of the Protectorate into the Greater German sphere of influence, involving a division of labour with Germany. Czech industry was to be encouraged to export to South-east Europe, while the German exports would focus on the West. Economic imperialism was thus a crucial element of Nazi empire-building. For this purpose, on 17 December 1941, Heydrich convened the first international economic conference of the German Südost-Europa-Gesellschaft, a Vienna-based society founded by the city's Gauleiter, Baldur von Schirach. It engaged in economic research on Eastern Europe with the long-term objective of forcibly integrating the South-eastern European economies into the German power bloc. Heydrich liked to think of himself as a 'mediator between the Reich and the south-eastern regions' of Europe, and made sure that he was perceived as such in the Reich.[63]

In the presence of the Reich Economics Minister, Walther Funk, Heydrich highlighted the urgent necessity of designing the future economic order of a 'united Europe': 'In assessing the tasks of the Bohemian-Moravian economy as part of the economy of the Reich, one arrives at the conclusion that this space meets the best possible requirements both for the cultivation of relations with the south-eastern regions and the development of the New East.' The Protectorate was to serve as an 'important bridge between the Reich and the south-east' – an idea that had been promoted by Sudeten German leaders since the mid-1930s. 'For the first time in the history of Europe,' Heydrich continued, 'the vast resources of the East, which have previously served only as a tool of destruction, will now be utilized positively and for the good of the New Europe.' No concrete policies were agreed on at the conference and, like most other plans for the future of Europe, the implementation of major initiatives was postponed until after the war's end.[64]

If, publicly, Heydrich talked about European reconstruction, German pragmatism and the economic wellbeing of the entire European continent, his immediate concerns lay elsewhere, namely in how best to exploit occupied Europe's economic potential for winning the war. Throughout his time in Prague, he remained mindful of wartime needs and the special role of Bohemia's armaments industry for the German war effort, although at times leading Nazis in Berlin worried that he would prioritize ideology over pragmatic considerations. Göring, for example, felt obliged to remind Heydrich that he considered the weapons produced by Škoda to be 'the very best and at times superior to our own'. Regardless of all 'necessary actions against the management of the Škoda factories', he urged Heydrich not to forget their vital importance for the German war effort.[65]

Heydrich did take economic necessities into consideration. The vital importance of increasing production dictated his relations with the Czech working classes. Shortly after his arrival in Prague, he told Nazi officials in the Protectorate that he was determined to 'give the Czech worker the chow he needs' in order to undertake work for the German war effort. After all, he insisted, 'there is no point in me bludgeoning the Czech and using all efforts and police power to make him go to work if he does not ... have the physical strength required to do his work'. Heydrich announced on 2 October that the Führer had approved his proposal for 'an increase in the fat rations for Czech workers by around 400 grams' – an 'impressive amount'. He insisted, however, that the increase in food rations had to be coupled with an unambivalent message to the Czech population: 'you stay quiet – or otherwise it may well happen that your rations are reduced again. These are things one has to deal with in a psychologically appropriate way.'[66]

In keeping with this directive, the Protectorate press credited Heydrich with the increase in fat rations for workers introduced on 27 October 1941, but emphasized that the Reich Protector's gesture of 'good faith' had yet to be matched by any signs of Czech loyalty.[67] Three days before, on 24 October, Heydrich received a trade-union delegation at Prague Castle and expressed his 'sincere' interest in the Czech workers' needs by promising to improve living standards. This was matched by a carefully orchestrated shop-floor campaign in more than 500 Czech factories during which pre-selected labour representatives were encouraged to voice their economic grievances. In the following weeks, fat and tobacco rations were increased for certain categories of labourers and 200,000 pairs of shoes were distributed free through works councils. As Heydrich admitted to his staff, the aim was 'the depoliticization of the Czech population', a policy which aimed to encourage the individual to focus 'on his job and his material needs'.[68]

The compliance with workers' demands – from improved working conditions to increased rations of food and tobacco – was portrayed by the Nazi propaganda machine as a form of serious and well-intended rapprochement, a gesture of Heydrich's good faith and his determination to fight black-marketeers and war profiteers on behalf of the ordinary Czech worker. On the day of Heydrich's meeting with carefully chosen labour representatives, for example, food confiscated from black-marketeers was distributed in the canteens of armaments factories.[69] The results that Heydrich reported back to Berlin after these measures had been carried through seemed impressive: gross industrial production during his rule over the Protectorate rose by 23 per cent. Moreover, his 'grain action' of late autumn 1941 – a large-scale police operation against the black market – resulted in the late reporting of 560,000 previously concealed pigs and 250,000 tonnes of grain.[70]

Other measures adopted by Heydrich to pacify the Protectorate were deliberately aimed at politically dividing the Czech population by corrupting some of them into compliance.[71] Free entrance to football matches was offered on May Day 1942. Furthermore, Heydrich redesigned the formerly Czech-run National Union of Employees to mirror the German Labour Front. Its 'Strength through Joy' campaign, using equipment and property confiscated from the Sokol, organized sports events, movies, plays, concerts and musicals in order to boost their work ethic.[72]

Further propaganda measures introduced by Heydrich were intended to convince the Czech population that they were living through a time of decisive struggle, in which they had to decide between a Bolshevik Europe and a National Socialist Europe. To facilitate that decision, Heydrich brought to Prague from Vienna the exhibition 'Soviet Paradise', which opened on 28 February 1942.[73] Displaying photographs taken during the early months of Operation Barbarossa, the exhibition portrayed the appalling living conditions in the Soviet Union and the apparent misery that Bolshevism had brought to the peoples of Eastern Europe. The message was unambiguous, as an article in the collaborationist newspaper *Der Neue Tag* noted: 'The Czech labour representatives have been given the opportunity to see the sad state of affairs in the Bolshevik "Workers' Paradise" with their own eyes. They can now see for themselves just how fortunate Bohemia and Moravia are to have been protected from the horrors of Bolshevism by the intervention of the German Wehrmacht.'[74] During the four-week showing of the exhibition, it was visited by approximately half a million people including Emil Hácha, the Minister of Education, Emanuel Moravec, and indeed Heydrich's future assassins, Josef Gabčík and Jan Kubiš, who had been parachuted into the Protectorate in December and now spent their days wandering around the Czech capital.[75]

Another of the key challenges for Heydrich was to step up the recruitment of Czech slave labourers, desperately needed to alleviate the increasingly serious bottlenecks created by the conscription of almost every able-bodied German man into the armed forces, without depriving the Protectorate economy of its potential to continue its vital contributions to the German war effort. From the beginning of the Second World War, the Germans had begun to step up the conscription of labour in the occupied territories. Some thirty thousand Czech workers signed up to go to the Old Reich within the first month of the occupation. Far more were needed and coercion became increasingly likely after the outbreak of war in September 1939.[76]

By the summer of 1941, there were indeed some 1.7 million forced civilian labourers and 1.3 million POWs living in the Third Reich. After the invasion of the Soviet Union, the swift capture of some 3 million POWs, as well as the acquisition of vast territories with huge labour reserves, produced both major economic opportunities and corresponding risks for Germany. As the regime believed that the apparently imminent victory would ensure access to as many foreign workers as it required, it made no plans to use Russian POWs as labourers. Indeed Hitler actively blocked their deployment in the Reich. The end of the war was expected to bring a rapid demobilization of the Wehrmacht, easing Germany's labour shortages once and for all. But this was a risky policy. Should the war not go as predicted, Germany would face enormous difficulties: the mobilization for Operation Barbarossa had already left a record number of unfilled vacancies in the home economy and the increasing number of military deaths required further workers to be sent to the front. Between May 1938 and May 1942, conscription caused the civilian workforce to shrink by 7.8 million. Only in October 1941 did Hitler finally relent and authorize the comprehensive exploitation of Soviet POWs inside Germany, by which time for most of them it was far too late. Having killed 2 million Russian POWs through calculated neglect in the winter of 1941–2, the Nazis now began to feel a desperate need for forced labourers.[77]

Following Heydrich's arrival in Prague, the recruitment of Czech slave labourers, thus increased dramatically, not so much because Heydrich was keen to see more 'foreigners' of 'questionable racial stock' in the Old Reich as because, by the autumn of 1941, army commanders, economic planners and other top Nazi leaders realized that Soviet defeat would not come as quickly as they had hoped. The domestic economy required more labourers to allow the German war effort to function at even higher capacity.[78]

In December 1941 Albert Speer, the soon-to-be Reich Minister for Armaments and Munitions, visited Prague and obtained from Heydrich a promise to send an additional 15,000 Czech construction workers to the Reich. Despite Heydrich's 'reputation for cruelty and unpredictability', Speer was pleasantly surprised by his host, noting that he was 'very polite, not all arrogant in his manner, and above all very self-assured and practical'. It was the latter quality above all others that impressed Speer.[79] But ideology, Heydrich insisted, could not be abandoned altogether. He hated the idea that Germany's reliance on foreign workers might become permanent. War had produced an absurd situation: Germany, fighting for economic autarky and racial purity, had become more ethnically diverse in terms of its labour force than it had ever been before (or has been since). Heydrich hoped that ultimately Germany's labour needs could be satisfied by 'Germanic peoples' and the assimilation of those 'fit for Germanization'. Just before Speer's visit to Prague, he presided over a Reich Security Main Office meeting in Berlin that laid out plans for the segregation and policing of foreign workers in Germany, noting that 'While all agree that the economic aspects are relevant and pressing, we must resist any attempt to defer racial and *völkisch*-political questions until after the war has ended, since it is uncertain how long the war may continue.'[80]

Despite Heydrich's insistence on the primacy of ideology over pragmatism, the pressure for Czech labourers continued to increase. In late March 1942, Hitler named the Gauleiter of Thuringia, Fritz Sauckel, plenipotentiary-general for the mobilization of foreign workers, a role complementary to that of Speer's and designed to feed the ever-growing manpower needs of Speer's factories. Although privately sceptical about the racial value of many of the foreign labourers that were to be forcibly recruited, Heydrich fell into line. In May 1942, he announced the introduction of compulsory labour service for all Czech men, and a Protectorate decree of the same month made all able-bodied Protectorate inhabitants over the age of fourteen subject to labour mobilization and assignment to factories in Germany. In the next four months, 40,000 names were added to the rolls.[81] 'In Prague,' an informer reported to London in late May 1942, 'the once crowded cafés are almost empty; in the restaurants, people gobble up their meals and hurry away as quickly as they can. The growing lack of manpower in Germany has led to systematic raids on such places: all visitors, especially women, who are unable to prove that they are fully employed in war work, are taken immediately to Gestapo headquarters and sent to forced labour camps in Germany.'[82]

Apart from pursuing his dual short-term aim of eradicating the resistance and exploiting the Protectorate's economic potential through a combination of terror, forced recruitment of labourers, incentives and propaganda, Heydrich was also determined to increase the efficiency of the German occupation regime. He wanted a small but effective bureaucracy, run by a combination of reliable Reich and Sudeten Germans and their Czech underlings, that was able to strengthen the Nazis' control over every aspect of socio-economic, political and cultural life in the Protectorate. Hácha and his government, Heydrich insisted, had to understand that the Germans were here to stay and that their future fate was inextricably linked to the Third Reich. Heydrich wanted to force them to acknowledge this 'fact' through 'actions' rather than through rhetorical assurances of loyalty from possible 'traitors' and 'saboteurs' within the ranks of the Protectorate government.[83] To that end, a November decree allowed Heydrich to discharge or transfer 'politically unreliable' civil servants, regardless of age. He also began personally to censor Hácha's public speeches. In only a matter of months Hácha and those around him had become little more than Czech-speaking executors of Nazi policies.[84]

Heydrich wanted to go even further. He intended to restructure the Protectorate government in such a way as to give him total control over all of its actions. While planning for the administrative reform began in the Reich Protector's Office, the Heydrichs spent the Christmas of 1941 at their hunting lodge in Stolpshof near Nauen, less than forty kilometres west of Berlin, spending the nights deer-stalking. Heydrich's mind was elsewhere. Too many tasks were awaiting him in the new year and he was anxious to return to work: he even worked on the restructuring of ministerial salaries on Christmas Eve 1941.[85]

On 19 January 1942, after months of intensive planning, a new Protectorate government was put in place. Following instructions that Heydrich had received from Hitler during their meeting at the Wolf's Lair in October 1941 and further discussed with the head of the Reich Chancellery, Hans Lammers, during a meeting in Munich on 9 November, the number of Czech ministries was reduced to seven, each of which became directly responsible to the Reich Protector's Office. The role of the council of ministers, headed by Jaroslav Krejčí as minister president, was confined to the practical implementation of Heydrich's orders.[86]

Much to the dismay of his Czech colleagues, SS-Oberführer Walter Bertsch was appointed head of the newly created Ministry of Economy and Labour. Bertsch served – in Heydrich's own words – as his 'informer within the government'. Since Bertsch was a Reich German who pretended to speak no Czech, government dealings had henceforth to be conducted in German.[87] Another important innovation was the establishment of the Office for People's Enlightenment, responsible for the press, theatre, literature, art and film. This office was subordinate to the newly named Minister of Education, Emanuel Moravec, a former Czech legionnaire and political pragmatist, who was frequently referred to by the government-in-exile as the 'Czech Quisling' and who was known for his weekly pro-Nazi radio addresses. Moravec was not an admirer of Heydrich or his methods, but he was astute and opportunistic enough to recognize that his future career depended on Heydrich's goodwill.[88] Heydrich in turn considered Moravec's appointment vital since he believed that the Czechs would be more receptive to Nazi propaganda if it came from one of their fellow citizens. Leaving nothing to chance, he nonetheless kept a tight control over Moravec's activities.[89]

In his address to the newly established Protectorate government on 19 January 1942, one day before flying to Berlin to chair the Wannsee Conference, Heydrich prided himself on having 'made up with a firm hand for what the Czech government has failed to do in 2½ years'. He also stated that the future work of the Protectorate government would be reduced to two principal tasks: the day-to-day running of the Protectorate administration and, perhaps more importantly, 'the difficult task' of introducing a 'correct and unambivalent education of [the Czech] youth' in the spirit of Germanization. Heydrich concluded by stressing that the era of autonomous 'ministerial decisions, which hinder practical, active governance and leadership, is definitively over'.[90]

Two of Heydrich's most important short-term objectives in the Protectorate had thus been achieved: Bohemia and Moravia had been pacified and the Protectorate government had been brought into line. In return for the new government's pledges of loyalty, Heydrich lifted martial law in Prague and Brünn and released some Czech students from the concentration camps in which they had been incarcerated since 1939. The Czechs were shown that collaboration paid.

Heydrich's administrative reforms constituted a radical reorganization of German occupation policy in the Protectorate, a reorganization that explicitly aimed at the 'disempowerment' of the Protectorate government while at the same time retaining the façade of Czech autonomy that Hitler had guaranteed in March 1939. Since the Führer had insisted in private conversations with Heydrich that this façade should be upheld, Heydrich opted for a strategy of 'liquidating the autonomy from within'.[91] As he explained to senior members of his staff in Prague, this would not happen overnight. Instead, he aimed for 'a gradual and inconspicuous dismantlement of Czech autonomy', which would avoid any unnecessary outrage among the civilian population.[92] In the meantime, Heydrich told Bormann, he would 'order the Czechs to carry out all measures that could incite bitterness, while transferring the implementation of those measures that will have a positive impact to the Germans'.[93]

Heydrich's plans to undermine Czech autonomy were to be kept 'strictly confidential'.[94] Instead, Nazi propaganda and the collaborationist press were instructed to represent his administrative reform as an important correction to the misguided historical path which the 'egotistical and ambitious class' of Czech intellectuals, spurred on by the Western 'plutocratic powers and – in the guise of so-called pan-Slavism – the Bolshevik forces' of the East, had followed between 1918 and 1938. The Protectorate press followed Heydrich's instructions and depicted the administrative reform as an attempt to *strengthen* Czech autonomy.[95]

Heydrich also moved energetically to eliminate administrative drag in the Protectorate in an attempt to introduce a more efficient administration. The administration of the Protectorate, he quickly realized, clearly required too much manpower: one Reich official for every 790 Czechs. In France, by contrast, the ratio was 1:15,000. Reducing the number of German officials would have two positive side-effects: first it would free up a large number of German administrators for military service on the Eastern Front, and second, since Heydrich was to decide who would stay and who would leave, he could reshape the administration according to his own preferences.[96]

In executing his powers, Neurath had relied both on the vast number of staff in his office as well as on thirty-five (from 1941 onwards, fifteen) *Oberlandräte* who were responsible for the local German administration, the German police, citizenship registration and Czech–German relations within their respective fiefdoms.[97] Heydrich believed that the parallel German and Czech administrations were far too big, thus hindering rather than speeding up decision-making processes. He curbed the independence of the *Oberlandräte* by assigning each of them an SS officer. He also shut eight of their offices down, reducing the number of *Oberlandräte* to seven, while hoping to get rid of them altogether at a later stage.[98] One-sixth of the Protectorate's German civil servants, some 50,000 men, Heydrich claimed in a self-congratulatory report for Hitler, would soon be 'freed up for military service'.[99] Even close associates such as Heydrich's State Under Secretary, Kurt von Burgsdorff, were released from their duties in March 1942 and sent off to the Eastern Front. Before Heydrich's tenure had begun, 9,362 Germans worked in the Reich Protector's Office and a further 4,706 were assigned to Czech agencies. According to Heydrich's plans, following the conclusion of the reform only 1,100 Germans would remain in the Protectorate administration and 700 in the offices of the Reich Protector and the *Oberlandräte*.[100] Heydrich told his staff that the Office of the Reich Protector would 'finally become what it must be: a leadership apparatus with a small number of outstanding personnel'.[101]

Heydrich's reforms and his ability to pacify the Protectorate were noted with great approval in Berlin. 'The policy that Heydrich has pursued in the Protectorate', an impressed Goebbels noted in his diary, 'can be described as nothing short of exemplary. He has mastered the crisis there with ease and the result is that the Protectorate is now in the best of spirits, in great contrast to other occupied and annexed areas.'[102] Hitler, too, expressed his satisfaction. In a rambling after-dinner monologue in January 1942, he praised the German occupation policy in Prague as 'pitiless and brutal'.[103] Four months later, on 20 May, the Führer added:

> The right and, indeed for the German Reich, the obvious policy is firstly to purge the country of all dangerous elements, and then to treat the Czechs with friendly consideration. If we pursue a policy of this sort, all the Czechs will follow the lead of President Hácha. In any case ... the fear of being compelled to evacuate their homes as the result of the transfer of population we are undertaking will persuade them that it will be in their best interests to emerge as zealous co-operators with the Reich. It is this fear which besets them that explains why the Czechs at the moment – and particularly at the war factories – are working to our complete satisfaction.[104]

In reality, things on the ground were much less rosy than Heydrich was willing to admit in his regular reports to Berlin. Although some workers (most notably those in the armaments industry) received increased food and tobacco rations, better welfare services, free shoes, paid holidays and, for a time, Saturdays off, the situation for the majority of workers did not improve.[105] Heydrich's propaganda campaigns and his perks for selected labourers in the armaments industry could not conceal the fact that during the eight months of his rule in Prague the food-supply situation had got worse, not better. After January 1942, largely due to the military situation in the East, butter allocation declined to 73 per cent of the level it had been before Heydrich's arrival in Prague while meat rations in the Protectorate decreased from a total of more than 12,000 tonnes in September 1941 to 7,826 tonnes in March 1942. By the spring of 1942, SD agents noted widespread grumbling among workers, but the growing dissatisfaction did not translate into any significant decreases in productivity.[106]

In the meantime, Heydrich was busy fending off the repeated attempts of other Nazi agencies to interfere in his sphere of influence. In the Protectorate, just as in the Old Reich and other occupied territories, a variety of agencies – from the army to party officials – vied for power and influence. Heydrich particularly despised the Protectorate's four Party Gauleiters (of Sudetenland, Oberdonau, Niederdonau and Bayerische Ostmark), repeatedly commenting on the mediocrity of party function-aries whose physical appearance and intellectual potential contrasted sharply with his own idea of leadership personalities.[107]

Heydrich's scepticism about the party's ability to rule the new German Empire was no secret. According to his wife, he was deeply concerned about the calibre of the party officials dispatched to subdue the Slavs, privately condemning these 'golden pheasants' of the East as corrupt and inefficient. Senior posts in the Eastern administrations were indeed often reserved for Old Fighters or long-standing members of the Nazi Party, many with close personal ties to Hitler. Their only qualification for administering occupied territories was the length of their party membership and they, in turn, brought with them trusted party followers as administration staff, many of whom were poorly trained, corrupt and therefore unsuitable for service in Western Europe.[108]

Heydrich was nonetheless well aware that the four Gauleiters continued to retain influential contacts in Berlin.[109] Conscious that his powers in Prague would not remain unchallenged if he did not assert his own authority, he asked for Bormann's renewed assurances that he was bound to follow only the orders of the Führer himself, and not those of party representatives.[110] There was to be no more nonsense and interference from party hacks in the implementation of SS policies. 'With four different methods working beneath mine,' he stated to the Gauleiters after receiving Bormann's positive response, 'I cannot rule the Czechs.' In that same speech he singled out the Reich Protector Office's most determined rival, the Gauleiter of Niederdonau, Hugo Jury, for disrupting his plans. Other uncooperative Nazi Party officials were simply removed from their posts.[111]

In May 1942, however, Heydrich had privately to acknowledge that the Czech resistance movement, which he had considered to be crushed, had regenerated and that incidents of sabotage were on the rise again. Having informed Hitler in early October 1941 that the resistance was finally broken and that the Czech workers had quietly accepted the liquidation of resistance fighters, Heydrich did not want to admit that the situation might once again get out of control. He repeatedly assured Berlin that there was no cause for alarm.[112]

All of this was part of a cunning communication strategy designed to present his activity in Prague in a positive light. In order to prevent the discrepancy between his often sugar-coated reports and the reality on the ground from leaking back to Berlin, Heydrich monopolized reports on the situation in the Protectorate. He put an end to the daily and monthly intelligence reports on the Protectorate and made sure that the SD reports, *Meldungen aus dem Reich*, contained virtually no information on his fiefdom from October 1941 onwards.[113]

During his eight months in Prague, Heydrich instead sent a total of twenty-one reports on his activities in the Protectorate directly to Martin

Bormann, insisting that the Führer be informed of their content. The reports primarily served as a means of preserving his position in the Third Reich's power elite and presented developments in the Protectorate in a triumphal light. They were not without success. On 15 February 1942, Goebbels noted in his diary:

> I had a long discussion with Heydrich about the situation in the Protectorate. The situation there has been stabilized. Heydrich's measures show good results . . . the danger of the Czechs threatening German security in the Protectorate has been completely overcome. Heydrich has been successful. He is playing cat-and-mouse with the Czechs and they swallow everything he tells them. He has taken a series of extraordinarily popular measures, including the almost complete elimination of the black market . . . He emphasizes that the Slavs cannot be ruled in the same way one rules a Germanic people; one must break them or constantly bend them. He is apparently pursuing the second path, and with success. Our task in the Protectorate is absolutely clear. Neurath completely misunderstood it, and that is what led to the crisis in Prague in the first place.[114]

Four months after his arrival at Prague Castle, Heydrich took stock of the situation in the Protectorate: setting the stage for an appraisal of his own achievements, he started by sharply criticizing the 'fundamental errors' of German occupation policy in the Protectorate under Neurath, who had treated 'the Czechs and the Czech government as if this was an independent state and as if the Reich Protector's Office was merely an enhanced delegation to a foreign president'. Neurath had also committed tactical errors: 'One cannot lead the Czech man and the Czech population to the Reich by believing that it is possible to maintain influence over the population through good social contacts with the Czech aristocracy.' His own track-record, by contrast, was impressive, or so Heydrich suggested. The short-term objectives of crushing the Czech resistance, of stimulating the Protectorate's war economy and of reorganizing the occupation system had been achieved. Now, he said, it was time to pursue the 'real objective' or the 'final aim' of the German occupation which, 'if not otherwise possible', should be implemented through 'violent means': the Germanization of the Protectorate.[115]

Germanizing the Protectorate

The Germanization of the conquered territories and border regions – their complete cultural, socio-economic, political and, above all, racial assimilation

into the Greater German Empire – remained at the very heart of SS population policy throughout the Second World War. In essence, Germanization,
as Heydrich understood it, aimed at total control over the conquered populations, the obliteration of their former national character and the extermination of all elements that could not be reconciled with Nazi ideology. The
utopia of an ethnically cleansed Greater German Empire in which racially
suitable members of the conquered populations would be merged with the
German *Volk* was to be created through the identification of 'valuable' racial
stock among non-German populations, and the parallel expulsion and
murder of those deemed 'racially unsuitable'.[116]

The war in the East, Himmler told Heydrich and others in June 1941,
would be 'a racial struggle of pitiless severity, in the course of which twenty
to thirty million Slavs and Jews will perish through military actions and a
crisis of food supply'. By the spring of 1942, more than 2 million Soviet
soldiers in German captivity, along with countless Jewish and non-Jewish
non-combatants, had been killed. A further 1 million civilians and prisoners
of war in or from the Reichskommisariat Ukraine lost their lives. And in
Belorussia, a territory home to 10.6 million inhabitants in 1939, a total of
2.2 million civilians and prisoners of war perished during the German occupation.[117] But what exactly was to happen to the surviving populations? In
order to gain a complete picture of the 'racial stock' of the newly occupied
territories, from the end of 1939 onwards SS racial experts of the Race and
Settlement Main Office (RuSHA) carried out 'racial screenings' of millions
of ethnic Germans and non-Germans across occupied Eastern Europe, the
results of which would determine the individual's' fate.[118]

Similar procedures were applied to Alsace, Lorraine and the Protectorate
of Bohemia and Moravia. In April 1940 the Reich Protector's Office
decreed that all mixed Czech–German marriages would require the
approval of the local *Oberlandrat* while marriages between party members
and Czechs, Poles and Magyars fell under the jurisdiction of the local
Gauleiter. Local medical officers, party officials, government bureaucrats
and police submitted their own reports for the *Oberlandrat*'s consideration.
To co-ordinate the myriad approaches to the Germanization of the
Protectorate, a conference was held in Neurath's office on 9 October 1940.
Three possible strategies were discussed: first, a large-scale population
transfer of all Czechs living in Moravia to Bohemia, thereby creating
living space for German settlers from the East; secondly and most radically, the complete deportation of all Czechs from the Protectorate to an
unknown destination; and thirdly, the 'assimilation' of approximately half
of the Czech population and the 'resettlement' of the remaining half.[119]

Hitler decided in favour of the third option: Germanization efforts in
the Protectorate should be reinforced by the Reich Protector while

simultaneously maintaining the façade of Czech autonomy for the duration of the war.[120] At Himmler's request, Karl Hermann Frank and the
head of the Prague SD, Horst Böhme, made preparations for testing
Czech schoolchildren in January 1941. In February they were joined by
SS-Sturmbahnführer Erwin Künzel, who had previously established the
Race and Settlement Office in Posen and Litzmannstadt and now began
to set up similar offices in the Protectorate.[121]

As German troops invaded the Soviet Union in the summer of 1941,
health experts from the Reich Protector's Office gathered German
medical officers and their assistants for lessons in the science of racial
selection. Unlike in Poland, however, very few people in the Protectorate
were actually subjected to racial tests before Heydrich's arrival in Prague.
The main concern of the Reich Protector's Office was the containment of
underground resistance movements and industrial sabotage. Moreover,
Germanization measures involving large-scale expulsion and settlement
had few devoted proponents within the Protectorate. As in occupied
Poland, the Protectorate's four Nazi Gauleiters objected to large-scale
racial testing in order to prevent the political or economic destabilization
of their respective fiefdoms.[122]

Unlike Neurath and the Gauleiters of the Protectorate, however, Heydrich
was genuinely determined to realize the complete Germanization of
Bohemia and Moravia, reminding his subordinates on various occasions
that 'all short-term tasks have to be carried out in a way that does
not compromise the faultless execution of the final aim'.[123] A narrow
focus on Heydrich's role in the appeasement of the Protectorate therefore
misses the crucial point that his pragmatic terror campaign, sweetened
by incentives for collaboration, was merely a short-term strategy that
would ultimately give way to the long-term project of politically, culturally
and racially integrating the Protectorate into the Greater German
Reich.[124]

In his first official speech in Prague on 2 October 1941, Heydrich elaborated on his long-term policy aims for the Protectorate and Europe more
generally. The fact that by the end of 1941 the land masses controlled by
Nazi Germany stretched from the Arctic Ocean to the fringes of the Sahara
desert, from the Atlantic to the Ukraine, made him confident enough to
speculate publicly about Europe's future. Asserting that the German occupation of Europe 'will not be temporary, but permanent', he raised the
crucial question of what the future post-war European order would
look like. With an 'iciness' that stunned even some of the senior
Nazi Party representatives in the audience, Heydrich talked about ethnic
cleansing programmes on a historically unprecedented scale.[125] The ultimate
aim was the creation of a German *Lebensraum* in the middle of Europe

that would incorporate all Germanizable inhabitants: 'The future of the Reich after the war's end depends on the ability of the Reich and the ability of the people of the Reich to hold, to rule and if necessary to fuse these [newly acquired] areas with the Reich. It also depends upon the means ... [with which we] deal with, lead and fuse with these people.' 'These people' included the Norwegians, Dutch, Flemish, Danes and Swedes, who thanks to 'bad political leadership and the influence of Jews' had forgotten their Germanic roots, but who would eventually be assimilated into the Greater German Reich by being treated like Germans. In the lands further east, Germans would rule over the indigenous populations and exploit the regions' raw materials. A third space, which included incorporated Western Poland, would form an Eastern Wall facing the Slavic world. Germans must inhabit the lands behind this wall, while 'piece by piece, step by step, the Polish element [will be] tossed away'.[126]

The Protectorate was included behind this Eastern Wall and would thus fall within the German Empire. 'The final solution' of the Czech question, Heydrich told his audience, 'must be the following: that this space will once and for all be settled by Germans.' Historically, Bohemia and Moravia had always been a part of the German sphere of influence, forming a 'bulwark of Germandom' and a 'sentry facing east'. Heydrich therefore demanded his subordinates to produce – through various forms of systematic pseudo-scientific racial testing – a 'total picture' that would allow him to 'get a feel for the racial and *völkisch* character of the entire population' as well as an inventory of 'people from this space who are Germanizable'.[127]

It has become popular among some historians to interpret the Third Reich's war of conquest in the East in general and Nazi Germanization policies more specifically as a German form of colonialism.[128] Such ideas have been inspired by statements made by Himmler and the Führer, most famously perhaps Hitler's statement of September 1941 that 'the Russian space is our India, and just as the English have ruled it with a handful of men, so will we rule this colonial space of ours'.[129]

Yet such quotations are misleading. The actual policies employed by the Nazis in the governance of the occupied territories bore little resemblance to British or French colonial techniques, and in fact underlined how limited the Nazis' knowledge of Western blue-water colonialism really was. Nowhere in occupied Eastern Europe, for example, did the Nazis employ 'indirect rule' – a characteristic feature of early twentieth-century British imperialism. The Nazi leadership's frequent references to Western colonialism may have reflected its admiration for Britain's ability to rule the world's largest empire with a handful of colonial officers, or, alternatively, they may have been an attempt to justify Germany's violent expansion by pointing to the misdeeds of other European nations, but they hardly amount to proof that the Nazis ever treated or intended to treat the populations of Eastern Europe in the same manner as the British treated the Indians.[130]

If British colonialism in the early twentieth century was characterized by a combination of development and force, with the aim of creating new commercial markets, the 'development' of Poland, Belorussia, the Ukraine and indeed the Protectorate involved the physical annihilation of the indigenous elite, the expulsion and possibly death of some 30 million people and the complete eradication of all indigenous culture. No member of the indigenous elites of Eastern Europe would ever be allowed to follow the example of Nehru or Gandhi by studying law at the best universities of the colonial motherland. Moreover, the policy of expelling or murdering 'racially inferior' populations was not a means to bring the war to a triumphant end or to 'restore order', as was often enough the case in the colonial wars fought by Britain and France, but rather an end in itself. Mass murder, expulsion and exploitation, coupled with the aim of turning the remaining population of East-Central Europe into Germans or slaves, constituted the very purpose of Operation Barbarossa and the General Plan East of July 1941.

More directly relevant to SS population policies than Western colonialism were the models established by Imperial Germany and Habsburg Austria. In relation to their Eastern European neighbours and ethnic minorities, both Germany and Austria-Hungary had indeed shown a colonial attitude long before 1933. The idea of a 'civilizing mission' had also been part of Imperial Germany's and Habsburg Austria's policy towards their own Slavic minorities. For Heydrich and the racial experts in the SS, however, Prussia's attitude towards the Poles and the Habsburgs' policies towards the Czechs were prime examples of how *not* to pursue a policy of empire-building. Both states, Heydrich insisted, had never fully grasped the importance of race, which he and his closest associates considered the sole criterion for the reordering of Europe. Neither had they tried to identify Germanizable population groups.[131] Leaving behind what he saw as a misguided, outdated and half-hearted nationalities policy, Heydrich wanted to turn race and biology into the guiding principle for administration. This commitment to the ethnic homogeneity of the states of East-Central Europe was not confined to Nazi Germany, having under very different auspices also guided Woodrow Wilson's Fourteen Points at the end of the First World War and most notably his concept of 'national self-determination'. What was different about the implementation of such homogeneity by the SS was its unshakeable adherence to biological racism and its determination to resolve the 'unweaving of peoples' in a violent way.

Heydrich was therefore highly dismissive of the Habsburgs' pre-1914 population policies: the 'old ways' of 'turning this Czech garbage into Germans' had failed, he insisted in his speech of October 1941. Now it was time to be guided solely by the 'objective' criterion of race. Heydrich promised to act on this idea without further ado: 'When [Germanization] happens is a question the Führer must decide. But the planning and collection of raw data can begin immediately.'[132]

Heydrich's speech, praised by Goebbels as 'refreshingly clear' and 'exemplary for the occupied territories', drew on the latest ideas on the reordering of Europe within the Nazi leadership, most notably those articulated in the General Plan East of July 1941.[133] In late June 1941, Himmler, in his capacity as Reich commissar for the strengthening of Germandom, had ordered one of his chief demographic planners, Professor Konrad Meyer, to produce a comprehensive expulsion and resettlement plan for occupied Poland. Meyer had been the principal organizer of the exhibition 'Construction and Planning in the East', which Himmler and Heydrich had visited in Berlin on 20 March 1941. Both were so impressed by Meyer's model villages for German settlers that Himmler commissioned him to develop a grand design for the future of the conquered territory: the General Plan East.[134]

On 15 July, just three weeks after receiving Himmler's order, Meyer presented the first version of his General Plan East, which called for the Germanization of Poland's and its western border regions. In the meantime, however, German troops had already invaded the Soviet Union, advancing so quickly that the plan no longer seemed ambitious enough: only one day after Meyer's first submission, Hitler demanded the creation of a Garden of Eden in the East, a vast settlement area for Germans in the Baltics, Belorussia, Ukraine and the Crimea. Himmler consequently ordered Meyer to extend his planning to the Soviet Union. Its designs, to be implemented over the next twenty to thirty years, envisaged that large numbers of ethnic Germans would be transplanted to the occupied East where they would live in a neo-feudal system of farms and model villages, interspersed with heavily armed SS outposts along two main communication routes leading to Leningrad and the Crimea respectively. The great majority of the local population were to be expelled while a small minority would be retained as helots. On the most eastern border of the new Germanic Empire, along the Urals, warrior villages would protect the frontier against the barbarian hordes of the East.[135]

Heydrich's speech in the Černín Palace was therefore informed by the latest ideas emanating from Hitler, Himmler and various SS racial experts, including a number of prominent Prague-based academics such as Karl Valentin Müller and Hans Joachim Beyer.[136] Müller, a social anthropologist with expertise in eugenics and excellent connections in the RSHA, had a particularly strong influence on Heydrich's perception of the Germanization problem in the Protectorate. Shortly after Heydrich's arrival in Bohemia and Moravia, on 6 November 1941, Müller was appointed to a newly created chair of social anthropology in Prague where he devoted most of his time to the pursuit of questions of 'ethnic re-engineering [*Umvolkung*]' and Germanization, the results of which were of 'greatest interest to the Reich Protector'.[137]

Müller maintained that a substantial proportion of the Czech population were originally of German origin, but that their blood had been mixed with and contaminated by Slavic influences. To regain and cultivate this German blood, Müller argued, was imperative for the overall Germanization process.[138] He expanded on this line of thought in two memoranda which he submitted to the head of the Prague SD, Horst Böhme, in the autumn of 1941, arguing that roughly 50 per cent of the Czech population contained valuable German blood – a figure that Heydrich immediately picked up from the report.[139]

Hans Joachim Beyer was the second demographer to have a major impact on Heydrich's thinking. Born near Hamburg in 1908, Beyer had studied history, law and anthropology and joined the SA, in timely fashion, in July 1933. By 1935, he had published his first book, in which he argued that Bohemia had traditionally been an area of German settlement. Only after the devastations brought about by the early fifteenth-century Bohemian Wars against and among the followers of Jan Hus had the Czechs begun to outnumber the German settlers. To revise that historical aberration, Beyer suggested, was of critical importance.[140]

Over the following years, Beyer continued to work on his dual concept of 'depopulation' and 'repopulation', arguing among other things that ethnic Germans should disassimilate themselves from their Slavic neighbours, that racially mixed marriages should be entered into only with partners of 'related' blood, and that the peoples of Eastern Europe should be ranked according to their degree of German genetic influences.[141] The Czechs, he insisted, had the largest proportion of German blood which needed to be 'regained'.[142] Such radical ideas quickly captured the attention of SS population planners and in 1938 Beyer was recruited into the SD. His memoranda also kick-started his academic career. In 1940, at the age of thirty-two, he was given a prestigious chair at Berlin's Friedrich-Wilhelms-Universität, although he continued to work simultaneously for Heydrich's RSHA. In 1941, as an ethno-political advisor to SS *Einsatzgruppe* C, he marched into Lemberg, where Polish intellectuals whose names had been added to an arrest list compiled by Beyer himself were murdered. His own experiences and impressions of Galicia formed the empirical basis of his next academic publications in which he described the Polish leadership, 'contaminated' by Jewish blood, as a group of people outside the margins of European society, who should never be allowed to play a part in the continent's history again.[143]

After a brief stint at the Reich University in Posen in September 1941, Heydrich insisted on Beyer's transfer to the German University in Prague where he acted as Heydrich's chief demographic adviser and director of the Institute for European Anthropology and Peoples' Psychology within the newly founded Reinhard Heydrich Foundation, an umbrella organization for all academic institutions in Prague with a focus on the anthropological and demographic study of Eastern and South-eastern Europe.[144]

Armed with the pseudo-scientific knowledge gathered in Müller's and Beyer's memoranda as well as in Meyer's General Plan East, Heydrich confidently talked about racial hierarchies in the newly conquered territories, hierarchies in which the Poles, East Ukrainians and Belorussians, who had been 'contaminated' by mixing with various Soviet peoples and Bolshevik ideas, assumed the lowest positions. Some of the neighbouring Baltic peoples were racially less inferior than others. 'The best racial elements are found among the Estonians,' Heydrich stated with absolute certainty, 'because of the Swedish influence, then come the Latvians with the Lithuanians being the worst of them all.'[145]

For the Protectorate, too, Heydrich imagined categories into which individuals might be placed. 'Racially good' and 'well-intentioned' Czechs, he announced, would certainly become Germans. 'Racially bad' and 'ill-intentioned' Czechs would be 'removed' to the 'wide spaces' of the East. Racially inferior Czechs with good intentions would be sterilized and then resettled in the Old Reich where they would be exploited as slave labourers. 'Ill-intentioned' but 'racially good' Czechs, the 'most dangerous of them all', would be 'put up against the wall'. Two-thirds of the population would immediately fall into one category or another. The remaining, less easily labelled people in the middle would be sorted out in a few years' time.[146]

Here again, Heydrich drew on racial categories and policies that had first been implemented in Nazi-occupied Poland in 1939 and 1940. Confronted with the mind-boggling ethnic complexity of East-Central Europe, Himmler and the race experts of the RuSHA had created four categories of racial value corresponding to those that had previously been applied to SS candidates: the categories were 'racially top', 'good or average', 'borderline cases' and 'racially unfit and alien blood'. This categorization of persons as 'desirable' or 'undesirable' was to guide Nazi population policy and the entire ethnic reconstruction of Europe.[147]

In addition, on 30 September 1941, Himmler had decreed that 'border-line case' candidates who had previously acquired German citizenship through a place on the so-called People's List (the *Volksliste*, first intro-duced by Arthur Greiser, the Gauleiter of Wartheland, as a means of regis-tering German citizens in his fiefdom) on the grounds of 'political merit', social qualities or language skills were to be re-examined according to racial criteria. All persons with 'uncertain' German roots – totalling more than 1 million people – were to be screened from late 1941 onwards, and the results were to be entered on the individual's racial identity card (*Kennkarte*).[148] Heydrich, whose RSHA oversaw the activities of both the Central Office for Emigration (UWZ), responsible for expulsion and the collection of racial data, and the Central Office for Immigration (EWZ), in charge of naturalizing ethnic Germans from formerly non-German territories, was familiar with the underlying issues of 'ethnic engineering'.[149] In early February 1942, encouraged by a meeting with Hitler less than a week before, Heydrich once again pointed to Germanization as the overall aim of Nazi rule in the Protectorate:[150]

> I would like to underline clearly as our internal principle that Germanization is intended, but only for those who are genuinely Germanizable. This requires that we shall now covertly proceed to undertake a racial inventory. It is entirely clear: if I want to Germanize, I have to know first who is Germanizable. I still reckon with a figure between forty and sixty per cent. This racial inventory will now proceed by means of an identity card ... By using identity-card checks, we will probably be able to sift out around a third of those who are not Germanizable to begin with, and perhaps we can identify another third of those whom we consider to be superficially Germanizable. That will leave roughly one-third of the population who will still have to be tested in a first brief examination. This means that we can reduce the time needed for the racial inventory from three years to one, which is both practical and desirable.[151]

Heydrich did not specify exactly how racial experts would place Czechs into one of these racial categories. Unlike the labelling of Jews and Gypsies, comparatively small minorities after all, testing for Germanizability involved the entire Czech population. The matter was further complicated by the fact that there was no unambiguous definition of what constituted a Slav or a German.[152] Heydrich argued that real or potential Germans could be spotted by their blue eyes, pleasing bodies, height and well-shaped heads. Yet he was also surprisingly open to a non-biological understanding of Germanness: often, he argued, it was non-physical characteristics that betrayed a German heritage. Clean houses, virility, sexual morality and social behaviour were criteria for membership. The most willing Germans among the Czechs, those 'unprincipled scoundrels' and 'rubbish', were the least suitable candidates. Ironically, Heydrich felt that it was the Czech patriots dedicated to their cause, healthy and independent, who would make the best Germans.[153]

As Heydrich pointed out on various occasions, the situation in the Protectorate was particularly complicated since all of the most prominent Czechs had some German blood. The mother of Alois Eliáš, he told Hitler, seemed from her outward appearance to be a German.[154] Jaroslav Krejčí's 'beautiful blue eyes', Heydrich decided, meant that the newly appointed Czech Minister of Justice certainly had a German background. Hácha, on the other hand, was considered 'incapable of Germanization' by Heydrich because he 'is always sick, arrives with a trembling voice and attempts to evoke a pity that demands our mercy'. As Heydrich made clear, behaviour, mental disposition, and physiognomy, could be key indicators of someone's 'racial core'.[155]

As the only leading SS officer occupying key positions at both the centre of the Nazi Empire and its territorial periphery, Heydrich's ability to drive and contour Nazi Germanization policies was unparalleled in Europe. No other administration in Nazi-controlled Europe – with the possible exception of Greiser's Warthegau – ever attempted so ambitious a policy of racial classification and separation in so short a time. Under Heydrich's rule in Prague, the testing and registration process intensified dramatically. In the autumn of 1941, his office announced plans to have experts from the Race and Settlement Office examine Czech women who had married Germans before the occupation. Also to be examined were children born out of wedlock to Czech–German partners. In May Heydrich reported to Bormann that Race and Settlement Office experts had fanned out across the Protectorate. Their aim was to produce a racially ordered cross-section of society, all done under the cover of a Protectorate-wide campaign against tuberculosis.[156]

Although aimed at facilitating the distant goal of Germanization, Heydrich's testing and registration schemes had immediate consequences for Protectorate inhabitants. A 'racially unsuitable' Czech man who had had sexual intercourse with a German woman was sent to a concentration camp. If a marriage was approved, the male candidate was identified as a German, in the eyes of both his compatriots and the state, and was therefore treated differently. Czech mothers married to Germans were required to raise their children as Germans. Failure to do so meant having their children put up for adoption. Anyone not carrying a new identity card, the *Kennkarte*, was immediately arrested, allowing police authorities more easily to track down parachutists, partisans, and Jews in hiding.[157]

Another important tool of Heydrich's Germanization policies in the Protectorate was the so-called Land Office (*Bodenamt*), an SS-controlled property administration in charge of identifying and confiscating Czech property targeted for Germanization.[158] Already on 17 October 1941 Heydrich had announced to senior members of his staff in Prague that the Land Office was 'the only appropriate agency' for the 'gradual Germanization of the East'.[159] His idea to create 'islands of Germandom' in densely populated Slavic areas through the confiscation of Czech property provided an inspiration for the extensive settlement projects implemented by Himmler in the Ukraine, notably in the region around Zhytomyr, in the summer of 1942.[160]

Heydrich quickly appointed his director of choice, the radical Sudeten German SS officer Ferdinand Fischer, who had served in the Prague SD office since 1939.[161] Fischer spent the following months expelling the owners of targeted properties – not only Jews, but also beneficiaries of the Czech land reforms of the 1920s and 1930s, as well as aristocrats who had declared their loyalty to the Czech Republic on 17 September 1938 – making room for some 6,000 German settlers, particularly from Bessarabia, the Bukovina, Dobruja, Transylvania, South Tyrol and the Sudetenland.[162] By the spring of 1942, the Land Office in Prague administered almost eighty confiscated estates with 46,000 hectares of land. Over 11,000 hectares of land were to be added in the next eighteen months. By May 1942, more than 15,000 Protectorate inhabitants had been displaced from their homes.[163]

Heydrich's settlement policies illustrate the unrealistic and even fantastical nature of Nazi Germanization plans: the SS expropriated huge amounts of land, but finding Germans willing to farm it was a far greater challenge. In October 1940, Germans made up just 3.5 per cent of the Protectorate's population and few wished to join them. Instead of the 150,000 ethnic Germans Heydrich hoped to resettle in the Protectorate, fewer than 6,000 actually decided to move there during the Second World War.[164] Heydrich and Himmler had set out to address the largely imagined problem that Germany was a 'people without space', but what they effectively did was to create spaces without people. Heydrich, however, was not easily deterred: conscious that Germany did not have the necessary population surplus to populate the vast conquered territories, he argued that, for the time being, it would suffice to have a German 'master class' to supervise the otherwise 'leaderless workers' of Czech origin.[165]

In order to further his aim of Germanization, Heydrich put trusted SS men in charge of research centres in Prague, many of whom had influenced or directly participated in racial testing in Poland and regions further east.[166] His racial experts descended, almost unimpeded, upon forced labourers, schoolchildren and, finally, the general population. One of his first acts as

Reich Protector was to correct 'shocking mistakes' in the Protectorate's previous Germanization policies. Neurath and the *Oberlandräte*, Heydrich fumed, had allowed 'racially imperfect and asocial elements' to become Germans, pointing to the roughly 20,000 Czechs – 6,000 in Prague alone – who had suddenly 'remembered' their German heritage when the Nazi occupation began. The legal German community was full of what Heydrich called 'margarine Germans': people whose sole reason for changing citizenship was to obtain higher food rations and other privileges.[167]

Appalled by the 'fact' that a high percentage of Czech 'riff-raff' had obtained German citizenship, Heydrich ordered his racial experts to retest *all* previously successful candidates for German citizenship in April 1942. Men in white coats were to rerun classification panels to decide which of the Czechs they stripped and measured were 're-Germanizable'. Persons deemed 'incapable of re-Germanization' were to have their citizenship revoked. Even before then, Race and Settlement Office officials had begun to review 'questionable' citizenship applications in October, and in the spring of the next year Heydrich ordered that the agency's racial experts resolve all cases not yet decided – 12,368 in total at the end of 1941. As in incorporated Poland, however, inconsistency, bureaucratic rivalries and individual intransigence remained. In Iglau only 10 per cent of the applicants received German citizenship following the SS's intervention; in Pilsen 78 per cent passed into Germandom.[168]

In February 1942, two weeks after the Wannsee Conference, Heydrich announced to Protectorate officials a 'new way' of advancing the Germanization process: seventeen- and eighteen-year-old Czechs would be gathered into labour camps where they would be subjected to racial tests.[169] Inspired by policies implemented in occupied Poland in 1939 and 1940, he insisted that those 'capable of becoming Germans' would be assigned to work in the Old Reich where they would be 're-educated' as Germans. This would have the added benefit of providing German industry and agriculture with cheap labourers who – unlike other slave labourers of more questionable racial stock – would pose no 'racial danger' to the German *Volk*. The unGermanizable youth, and perhaps their families, would be shipped to Siberia, where they could serve as 'supervisors for the eleven million Jews of Europe'. In order to avoid an 'unnecessary rocking of the boat' for the duration of the war, Heydrich proposed 'for the time being' a 'non-brutal, non-violent' way of implementing his Germanization policy in the Protectorate: he would allow the deportees to bring their families with them, thus accelerating the speed of the region's ethnic cleansing.[170]

Although Heydrich remained very conscious of wartime demands, he insisted that the imperative of racial ideology would guide Nazi policies in the Protectorate as soon as the military situation allowed for the deportation of racially undesirable Czechs. While the Jews were marked for immediate extermination, other racially undesirable Czechs would suffer deportation as soon as possible. Following Heydrich's comments to their logical conclusion, the Czechs may well have been just months away from the type of deportations Europe's Jews were facing in the spring of 1942.[171] Heydrich's solution to the 'Czech question' was thus part of a wider Nazi discourse on what to do with unGermanizable Slavs across Eastern Europe. According to SS population planners' estimates, at least 40 million people inhabited the target regions for Germanization, more than 30 million of whom were considered racially undesirable. This included a staggering 80 per cent of the Polish population, 64 per cent of Belorussians, 75 per cent of Ukrainians and half of the Czechs. Even within the inner circle of SS population planners, the exact fate of these unwanted Slavic populations remained uncertain. In early September 1941, the head of the Central Resettlement Office in Posen, Rolf Heinz Höppner, wrote to Adolf Eichmann enquiring about the fate of those who were not Germanizable. He noted that 'it is essential that we are totally clear from the outset about what is to be done in the end with those displaced populations that are undesirable for the Greater German settlement areas. Is the goal to secure for them permanently some sort of subsistence, or should they be totally eradicated?'[172] Heydrich clearly favoured the latter option, hoping to eradicate all undesirable populations from the German *Lebensraum* at any cost, but neither he nor Himmler had the power to make such a far-reaching decision without consulting the highest authority in Nazi Germany. On the crucial question about the fate of millions of non-Germans in Eastern Europe, Heydrich and Himmler were still keenly awaiting Hitler's final decision.

Holocaust

Whereas, according to Heydrich, roughly half of the Czech population would emerge from the ethnic engineering process of the coming years as Germans, the ultimate aim for the Protectorate's Jewish population was fundamentally different: the goal of Nazi anti-Jewish policies was immediate exclusion, then deportation and, ultimately, extermination.

Unsurprisingly, Heydrich's arrival in Prague led to a decisive radicalization of anti-Jewish policies in the Protectorate. As of 29 September 1941, Jews in mixed marriages with Czech partners, who had previously been exempted from wearing the yellow star, had this exemption revoked. All synagogues were closed and non-Jews who continued to interact socially with Jews were threatened with protective custody.[173] At one of his first

press conferences at Prague Castle, Heydrich told the assembled journalists of his 'fundamental belief' that:

'Judaism poses a racial and spiritual danger to the peoples. The experiences of Germany and, for those who are reasonable, the experiences of
the Protectorate as well, confirm this view. The Reich's objective will and
must be not only to eliminate the influence of Judaism within the
peoples of Europe but, to the extent to which this is possible, to resettle
them outside of Europe. All other measures are . . . stages on the path to
this final aim. I have decided to pursue these stages in the Protectorate
as consistently and as quickly as possible. The first step in the immediate
future will be the concentration of Jewry in a town or in part of a
town . . . as a collection point and transitional solution for the already
initiated evacuation. The first 5,000 Jews will leave the Protectorate over
the course of the coming weeks. It goes without saying that the Jews
who have parasitically engaged in black-marketeering, illegal butchering
etc will be led to work in an orderly way that serves the community . . .
For those who, for oppositional reasons or due to a lack of understanding, believe that they must continue to have open or secret dealings
with the Jews or express sympathy for them, I reserve the right to apply
the previously outlined measures to them as well.[174]

The next day, 6 October, Heydrich demanded that the Protectorate
government immediately dismiss or retire all 'Jewish half-breeds and
public officials with Jewish relatives' who had previously been exempted
from persecution. Exceptions, such as Jewish *Mischlinge* who had already
been public officials before 1914 and had served in the First World War,
required the explicit approval of Heydrich himself.[175]

In the spring of 1942, Heydrich further extended his policies
against the 'half-breeds', ordering that all *Mischlinge* who had obtained
Reich citizenship under Neurath's 'lax' regime were to undergo 'proper'
racial testing. Another decree prohibited Protectorate nationals from
marrying Jews, while first-degree *Mischlinge* could marry Czechs
only with the permission of the Ministry of the Interior. The Protectorate,
under Heydrich's aegis, was therefore among the first of the
occupied territories to screen Jewish *Mischling* and to revoke their
German citizenship if they were considered an 'unwanted population
addition'.[176]

On Heydrich's orders, the director of the Central Office for Jewish
Emigration in Prague, Hans Günther, presented a statistical survey on the
preparations for the 'final solution of the Jewish question' in the Protectorate
in early October 1941. According to this report, just over 118,000 Jews (as

defined by the Nuremberg Laws) had been living in the Protectorate at the beginning of the German occupation in March 1939. Of this number, nearly 26,000 had emigrated by 1 October 1941. Due to the low birthrate in the same period, only 88,105 Jews were still living in the Protectorate at the time of Heydrich's arrival in Prague.[177]

Between late 1941 and the autumn of 1944, the German authorities deported almost 74,000 Jews from the Protectorate to Theresienstadt, sixty kilometres north-west of Prague. Theresienstadt served as a transit camp for Protectorate Jews on their way to various killing sites in Eastern Europe, particularly, from 1942 onwards, to Auschwitz. Of the 82,309 Jews deported from the Protectorate during the war, the Germans and their Ukrainian, Baltic and Russian collaborators killed approximately 77,000 men, women and children. Only 14,000 Protectorate Jews survived the end of the Second World War.[178]

Heydrich was determined to solve the Protectorate's 'Gypsy problem' in a similar fashion. In the months leading up to his arrival in Prague, police had rounded up hundreds of 'wandering Gypsies' or 'tramps', suggesting that 'Gypsy' was still primarily considered a criminal, rather than racial, category that included a whole array of asocials. Upon his arrival, Heydrich inserted racial criteria into the definition of 'Gypsy', hence widening the net for persecution. In October 1941, Heydrich noted that he wished to 'evacuate' all Gypsies living in Bohemia and Moravia.[179] The following spring he ordered that their identification cards be marked with a 'Z' for *Zigeuner*, the German word for 'Gypsy'. In total, 6,500 people in the Protectorate fell into this category. At least 3,000 of them were murdered in the Gypsy camp at Auschwitz-Birkenau, and a further 533 died in special camps in Lety and Hodonín in the Protectorate.[180] Yet Heydrich's energetic drive for the total extermination of the Protectorate's Gypsies was the exception rather than the rule in Nazi-occupied Europe. Right up to the end of the war, it remained uncertain whether all Gypsies within the German sphere of influence would be murdered. In the summer of 1942, for example, Himmler gave an explicit order that in the case of Gypsies with permanent homes in the General Government 'police intervention' was unnecessary.[181]

The accelerated speed of the implementation of Nazi anti-Gypsy and anti-Jewish policies was largely due to Heydrich's own activism, spurred on by Hitler's decision, in mid-September 1941, 'to make the Old Reich as well as the Protectorate, from east to west, as Jew-free as soon as possible'. However, Hitler insisted that the progress of deportations be dependent on the further development of the military situation.[182] Heydrich nonetheless hoped to be able to resettle the Jews from the Old Reich and the Protectorate temporarily in the former Polish territories, particularly in the Łódź ghetto, and then more permanently further east as soon as the military situation allowed them to do so.[183]

In view of the hopeless overcrowding of the ghetto and strong protests from the local German authorities, only 20,000 Jews and 5,000 Gypsies from the Protectorate, Berlin and Vienna were actually deported to Łódź in the second half of October. During the following three months, 30,000 more Jews were deported to Minsk and Riga. What happened to them was extremely variable. Those sent to Łódź were interned in the ghetto where living conditions were appalling, but inmates were not immediately murdered. The Jews dispatched to Riga, on the other hand, arrived before the ghetto construction was completed. The five transports were therefore sent on to Kaunas in Lithuania where all of the deportees were murdered on arrival in the infamous Fort IX.[184]

At a meeting of the Protectorate's leading SS representatives on 10 October 1941, further measures for the solution of the Jewish question were discussed. Under Heydrich's chairmanship and in the presence of his chief adviser on Jewish matters, Eichmann, the meeting established that roughly 88,000 Jews were still living in the Protectorate, roughly half of them in Prague. At this stage Heydrich still thought that he could evacuate 50,000 of the Protectorate's most 'burdensome' Jews – those least capable of work – to Riga and Minsk. He further believed that Arthur Nebe and Otto Rasch, the heads of two of the four *Einsatzgruppen* operating in occupied Soviet territory, could concentrate some of the deported Jews 'in the camps for Communist prisoners in the operational area'. For Jews not on the first deportation lists, Heydrich planned to create separate ghettos for those able to work and those dependent on relief (*Versorgungslager*). He clearly anticipated very low survival rates, envisaging that the remaining Jewish communities would suffer high mortality rates even before they eventually boarded the trains to the East.[185]

One week later, on 17 October, Heydrich first introduced the idea of converting the garrison town of Theresienstadt into a temporary collection point and transit camp for deported Jews, demanding that 'under no circumstances should even the smallest detail' of this plan become known to the general public.[186] The barracks of the town would be evacuated and its civilian population resettled. Heydrich confidently expected that the evacuation of the Jews from the Protectorate to Theresienstadt would happen quickly. Every day, two or three trains would depart for the camp each carrying 1,000 Jewish deportees. Heydrich assumed that Theresienstadt would be able 'comfortably' to accommodate 50,000 to 60,000 Jews, but by the end of the year only 7,350 persons were 'resettled' in Theresienstadt. Aside from the Jews who had been deported to Łódź, only a single transport – from Brünn to Minsk – could be dispatched.[187]

Before the first Jewish deportees arrived in Theresienstadt on 24 November, another idea regarding the future function of this ghetto had begun to take shape in Heydrich's mind. As Goebbels noted on 18 November 1941, following a meeting with him in Berlin, the Reich Protector planned to establish Theresienstadt as an 'old-age ghetto' for German Jews whose deportation continued to pose 'unforeseen difficulties'.[188]

The Wannsee Conference of January 1942 confirmed this role for Theresienstadt. German and Austrian Jews aged over sixty-five years, Jewish war invalids and decorated Jewish veterans from the First World War would not be 'evacuated' to the East but rather 'transferred' to the old-age ghetto in Theresienstadt. This solution would solve the foreseeable problem of interventions and objections from within the German population. Furthermore, the establishment of an old-age ghetto would deceive the inmates of Theresienstadt about their future fate. Theresienstadt was still intended only as a transit camp from which prisoners would be deported to the East in order to murder them or use them as forced labour. Indeed, the first transport eastward from Theresienstadt had left on 9 January 1942. Of the nearly 87,000 Theresienstadt inmates deported to the East, roughly 84,000 died before the end of the war.[189]

Shortly after the beginning of deportations from Theresienstadt, the Nazis' extermination policy against the Jews escalated further. Up to this point, systematic and indiscriminate mass murders of Jews had been restricted to certain geographical areas, particularly to Serbia and the territories of the Soviet Union, where, by the end of 1941, between 500,000 and 800,000 Jews of all ages and both sexes had been murdered by the Germans and their local helpers.[190]

In the spring of 1942, the pan-European implementation of the Holocaust began to take shape. Heydrich and Himmler are likely to have sought Hitler's authorization for a 'third wave' of deportations from the Reich into the Lublin district during their meeting with the Führer on 30 January 1942. No record of this meeting has survived, but only one day after the meeting, in an express letter to all Gestapo branch offices, Adolf Eichmann announced that 'the recent evacuations of Jews from individual areas to the East' marked 'the beginning of the final solution to the Jewish question' in the Reich and the Protectorate.[191]

By early March, Eichmann had refined the plans for these deportations. During a meeting at Gestapo headquarters in Berlin on 9 March, he explained that over the course of the next few months 55,000 Jews would be deported from the Reich and the Protectorate to a number of ghettos in the Lublin district. He also announced that most of the remaining, elderly German Jews would be deported from the Reich to Theresienstadt over the course of the summer or the autumn of 1942.[192] Heydrich, who had just returned from a relaxing skiing holiday with his family in the Bavarian Alps, was happy with the progress made in his absence.[193] On 11, 12, and 13 March, he and Himmler discussed the progress of the solution to the Jewish problem. Just before the deportation trains arrived, the SS and Police Leader in the Lublin district, Odilo Globocnik, cleared the Lublin ghetto of its inhabitants, shooting thousands of Polish Jews on the spot between 16 March and 20 April and deporting a further 30,000 to Belzec where they were gassed.[194]

The miserable living conditions in the ghettos around Lublin – in Izbica, Piaska, Zamocs and Trawniki – meant that a great majority of the German, Austrian and Slovak deportees died within a few months of their arrival. Those Jews who had been deported to Łódź from the Reich during the previous autumn, and had survived the devastating conditions in the Łódź ghetto – almost 11,000 people in total – were deported to Chelmno between 4 and 15 May and murdered in stationary gas vans.[195] Heydrich, in the meantime, decided to begin the clearing of the Theresienstadt ghetto, primarily to create space for new arrivals.[196]

In March 1942, the deportations were also extended to Slovakia and France. According to the terms of an agreement with Slovakia, some 4,500 young Jews 'fit to work' were deported to Majdanek in the Lublin district and an additional four trainloads of young women were sent to Auschwitz between 26 March and 7 April.[197] On 10 April, Heydrich travelled to Bratislava to meet with the Slovak Prime Minister, Vojtech Tuka, who declared his government's willingness to deport *all* of Slovakia's more than 70,000 Jews. The deportations from Slovakia began the following day – a significant event as Slovakia was the first state outside direct German control to agree to the deportation of its Jewish citizens. By 20 June, seven trains from Slovakia had arrived at Auschwitz where the deportees were used as slave labourers. A further thirty-four transports were sent to ghettos in the district of Lublin where the Slovakian deportees replaced those Jewish inhabitants who had previously been sent to the extermination camps of Sobibor and Belzec. As Heydrich explained to Tuka during his visit to Bratislava, the deportation of Jews from Slovakia was only part of a much wider programme of resettlement that would affect not only Slovakia, the Reich and the Protectorate but also Western Europe, including the Netherlands, Belgium and France.[198]

In France, from where 1,000 Jewish hostages were deported to Auschwitz on 30 March in retaliation for bombing attacks by the French Resistance, Heydrich pressed his Jewish expert, Theodor Dannecker, to step up the pace. While still negotiating with the German military administration over the eastward deportation of Jewish hostages in early March

1942, Dannecker recorded Heydrich's determination to have 'further Jews deported in the course of 1942'.[199]

These major pan-European waves of deportations coincided with the completion of construction works on various extermination sites in the General Government. By mid-March 1942, camp officials at Auschwitz-Birkenau had converted a former peasant hut into a gas chamber and started to murder Jews incapable of work that summer with Zyklon B. In May, the extermination camp Sobibor was opened, while the first extermination camp, Belzec, underwent construction work that summer to extend its killing capacity. At the same time, in the district of Warsaw, construction work began on a further extermination camp, Treblinka.[200]

Simultaneously, in May 1942, Heydrich's *Einsatzgruppen* in the Soviet Union resumed the mass murders of Soviet Jews, which had begun in the summer of the previous year. This was particularly the case in Ukraine and Belorussia, where Heydrich's brief visit to Minsk in April and his announcement that those deported from the Reich were to be liquidated upon arrival appear to have triggered a renewed wave of mass shootings with more than 15,000 Jewish victims.[201] But this was merely the tip of the iceberg. Heydrich's *Einsatzgruppen* and special SS 'anti-partisan' units shot at least 360,000 Jews in the Ukraine and Belorussia during the spring and summer of 1942.[202]

The decision-making process that led to this further escalation of anti-Jewish extermination policies and the beginning of a full-blown, pan-European genocide is difficult to pin down with any certainty. At the Wannsee Conference of 20 January 1942, two proposals had been made for solving the Jewish question on a European scale. Apart from Heydrich's older notion of deporting European Jews to the occupied Soviet territories, where they would be decimated by a combination of forced labour and 'special treatment', a new option had been discussed: the systematic murder of those Jews incapable of work in the General Government which was, with 1.7 million people, by far the largest community of Jews under German control. This was to be achieved through gassing facilities in Belzec and Auschwitz, which were completed and fully operational by the spring of 1942.

The idea of systematically murdering the Jews in occupied Poland gained further impetus when, in March 1942, the SS managed to gain complete control over anti-Jewish policies in the General Government. Compromised by a serious corruption scandal in the spring of that year, General Governor Hans Frank conceded complete authority over all policing matters and questions of Germanization in the General Government to the local higher SS and police leader, Friedrich-Wilhelm Krüger, thus strengthening the hand of the SS vis-à-vis the civilian authorities. Himmler, Heydrich and their men on the ground – Krüger and Globocnik – would use their new powers to include Jews from all parts of occupied Poland in the killing process.[203]

Shortly before the murders were decisively extended at the beginning of May 1942, Heydrich and Himmler met seven times in three different places within the space of a week: their first meetings took place in Berlin on 25, 26 and 27 April, followed by long conversations in Munich on 28 and 30 April, and then in Prague on 2 May, a meeting for which Himmler made a special journey. This series of intense discussions was framed by two longer meetings between Himmler and Hitler, which took place on 23 April and 3 May. No records of these meetings have survived the war, but the chronology of the events of the following weeks suggests that it was during these meetings that Hitler, Himmler and Heydrich decided on the framework for the implementation of a pan-Europan programme of systematic destruction that was to be carried out from May 1942 onwards.[204]

Cultural Imperialism

If the realization of the Nazis' Germanization project was based on a historically unprecedented programme of racial stock-taking, theft, expulsion and murder, Germanization, as understood by Heydrich, meant far more than racial tests and extermination. Murder and resettlement were only the preconditions for the creation of a racially 'purified' utopia, a German empire that would dominate the New Europe for the next thousand years. As Heydrich pointed out in mid-December 1941: 'While under the blows of Germany and her allies a degenerate world is being crushed, perishing in the chaos which it has created, a New Order is appearing behind the fronts of our soldiers, an order whose structures are already becoming clearly visible.'[205]

The full integration of the Protectorate into this New Order required the complete Germanization of the Protectorate's cultural life and the eradication of indigenous Czech and Jewish culture. This was the task of Department IV of the Reich Protector's Office, a department designed to co-ordinate and direct the Protectorate's cultural life, from theatres and cinemas to radio programmes and the press.[206] The aim of Department IV, under the leadership of Baron Dr Karl von Gregory, was thus the indoctrination of the Protectorate's Czech population in order to create a suitably pro-German atmosphere. In theory, these developments should have enabled the administration to dominate the Protectorate's cultural economy through the imposition of censorship and propaganda. In practice, inter-agency disputes, personality clashes and a chronic shortage of personnel meant that these policies were never coherently enforced and cultural resistance within the Czech population persisted. Until Heydrich's arrival in Prague, Department IV had subordinated cultural Germanization to the smooth flow of war-related production.[207] Once Heydrich took charge, this policy changed abruptly. Accusing Gregory of being unable to implement a comprehensive cultural Germanization plan for the Protectorate, Heydrich replaced him with one of his trusted associates, SS-Sturmbannführer Martin Paul Wolf, a former high-school teacher and a close friend of Heydrich's favourite academic in Prague, Karl Valentin Müller.[208]

Heydrich's cultural imperialism was a fundamental assault on the fertile cultural world of late Habsburg and interwar Prague, a world of high international standing in literature, music and the arts. Before the German invasion, the multicultural city, with its diverse German, Jewish and Czech influences, had been associated with such acclaimed artists as the expressionist Oskar Kokoschka (who lived in Prague between 1934 and 1938), the composer Leoš Janáček (1854–1928), and the novelists Franz Kafka (1883–1924) and Max Brod (1884–1968), all of whom the Nazis considered to be prime examples of 'degenerate' art. The purging of Prague's cultural diversity was a key component of Heydrich's Germanization strategy, a strategy that aimed, in Goebbels's words, at the *Verreichlichung* (incorporation into and adaptation to the Reich) of cultural life in the Protectorate. Shortly after Heydrich's arrival in Prague, he and Goebbels began to negotiate the cultural and propaganda policies in the Protectorate with the aim of formulating a coherent strategy, while at the same time securing Heydrich's right to a final decision on all cultural matters in the Protectorate.[209] Within two weeks, a comprehensive eighteen-page agreement had been elaborated, outlining new initiatives to guarantee total German control over radio programmes, movie theatres and film production companies, as well as a gradual increase of German-speaking programmes on Czech radio. All of these measures were to be achieved through the expropriation of the few remaining cultural facilities in Czech hands as well as by strengthening centralized control by Heydrich's office in Prague.[210] Furthermore, Heydrich hoped that by conducting cultural and political affairs exclusively in German, the Czech language would be 'reduced to the private sphere' before eventually becoming extinct.[211]

One of his most important tasks in the Protectorate, Heydrich believed, was to revive German cultural traditions that had been 'suppressed' in the 'Jewified' Czechoslovak Republic since its foundation after the Great War. In order to underscore the idea of Bohemia and Moravia's historical affiliation with the Reich, he mined the quarry of the past to 'prove' that the region had enjoyed peace and prosperity only when it aligned with Germany against the barbarian hordes of the East. One of the historical reference points most favoured by Heydrich was St Wenceslas, patron saint of the Czechs, who, he claimed, had turned against the Slav world and recognized 'the historical destiny of this area and its eternal involvement with the Reich'. In his inaugural speech at Prague Castle, Heydrich argued that the Nazis should 'increasingly emphasize the idea of St Wenceslas' who 'must not be depicted as a patron saint of the Czechs', but as 'the man who recognized that the Czech people could exist only within the German space'. He urged his associates to convey this message from 'the right psychological angle': 'When the Czechs celebrate St Wenzel, then they are demonstrating that he was right. That is what we can exploit historically.'[212] Nazi propaganda, assisted by a large number of collaborationist newspapers, constantly reiterated the centuries-old connections and interdependencies between Bohemia and the Reich.[213]

The visit that Heydrich and Hácha paid to the Bohemian Crown Jewels on 19 November 1941 was very much in line with this policy of historical appropriation. Soon after his arrival in Prague, Heydrich demanded that Hácha formally acknowledge that the Protectorate was now an 'integral part' of the Reich through a historically symbolic gesture. The ceremony took place in the Wenceslas Chapel inside the Cathedral of St Vitus at Prague Castle, where Hácha handed Heydrich the seven keys to the Coronation Chamber on a velvet cushion. 'The Coronation Insignia', Hácha declared, 'are the symbol of Bohemia and Moravia's loyalty to the Reich.' Heydrich accepted the gift and returned three of the seven keys to Hácha as a 'token of trust and a reminder of your responsibilty' as 'guarantor of Bohemia's loyalty'.[214]

Heydrich believed that the symbolically charged event in St Vitus' Cathedral 'ended centuries-old uncertainties'. After being exposed to influences and population transfers from both the Slavic and the Germanic worlds, 'Wenceslas, recognizing historical necessity, had once and for all thrown in his lot with the Reich and turned against the East. The rebels who, under the leadership of his brother Boleslav, took up arms against the statesmanlike policy of Wenceslas, failed to recognize the historical destiny of this area and its eternal involvement with the Reich. They overthrew Wenceslas and his policy, murdered the king and attempted to establish this space as a bastion against the West.' But Bohemia's German destiny, Heydrich maintained, could not be altered. Hácha's acceptance of the establishment of the Protectorate of Bohemia and Moravia was therefore 'a decision in the true spirit of the Wenceslas tradition'.[215]

Heydrich's efforts at rewriting history did not go unnoticed in London, where intelligence reports commented on his 'extremely clever historical argument, purporting to prove that the Czech nation has always been most prosperous at periods when the German influence was strongest, and that the Protectorate owing to its geographical position cannot exist otherwise than as an integral part of the German living space'.[216] Heydrich also claimed that his actions against the Czech resistance were in line with the Wenceslas tradition: 'The rebels against the Reich during the days of September and October of this year were brought to justice because they failed to grasp the Wenceslas tradition and reverted to ancient Eastern habits by stabbing the Reich in the back in order to convert a bastion against the East once more into a bastion against the West.' What they had overlooked, Heydrich argued, was that the leadership of the Reich and indeed the larger part of the Protectorate's inhabitants had learned 'the lessons of history'. 'The Wenceslas tradition', he concluded, was therefore a permanent reminder that 'Bohemia and Moravia will only ever be strong with the Reich, and that it will remain forever weak without it.'[217] The 'stab in the back' myth was a recurrent theme in Heydrich's speeches. Time and again, he claimed that the Bohemian heartland of the Reich had 'plunged a knife into the back' of German unity – a tradition that had begun with Marbod, who had refused to participate in Arminius' 'war of liberation' against the Romans in AD 9, and which had continued through to the Defenestration of Prague and the Thirty Years' War in the seventeenth century up until the present day when some Czechs, engaged in illegal resistance activities, were trying 'to attack the Reich from behind during its decisive fateful battle against Bolshevism'.[218] Only 'on the day when the banner of the new Reich was raised on the roof of this house', Heydrich declared elsewhere, 'was the baneful development that ensued in the days of the Prague defenestration overcome for all time. We are now entering an era of construction, leaving the centuries that stood in the shadow of Münster and Osnabrück [the treaties that ended the Thirty Years' War] behind us like a bad dream ... Through the events of 1938 and 1939 the terrible condition into which Central Europe had fallen has been eliminated.'[219]

Although obviously important from a political point of view, these historical interpretations were more than propaganda for Heydrich. He firmly believed that Bohemia and Moravia were historically part of the Reich – a conviction that he shared with the German deputy mayor of Prague, Josef Pfitzner, a former professor of medieval and Eastern European history at the German University of Prague, whose arguments about Bohemia and Moravia's long-standing historical 'connections' with the Reich, put forward in his widely read book *Das tausendjährige Prag* (1940), profoundly influenced Heydrich's historical perceptions.[220]

Indeed, Heyrich developed a new passion for the history of Bohemia, often reading popular history books, historical novels and biographies on his sofa in Jungfern-Breschan until the small hours of the morning.[221] Apart from Wenceslas, he was particularly interested in Albrecht von Wallenstein (1583–1634), the supreme commander of the Imperial army until 1634, reading a constant stream of historical literature on the subject. Wallenstein's refusal to join the rebellious Bohemian and Moravian nobility during the Thirty Years' War and his decision to serve Emperor Ferdinand II instead provided a model for Bohemia's loyalty to the Reich. On Sundays, Heydrich made several trips to Friedland, Wallenstein's duchy. He also visited Mělník, where he saw the grave of St Ludmila (Wenceslas's grandmother) and showed great interest in the excavations at Prague Castle which were carried out by the staff of the German University of Prague.[222]

Heydrich regarded the repression of indigenous cultures in occupied Europe as an essential precondition for the creation of a flourishing German culture in the East. This included a policy of 'intellectual sterilization', permitting the local population no more than basic vocational training. According to Heydrich, vocational experience and cultural Germanization had to be the goals of the Czech education system. In the autumn of 1941, he ordered that Czech history lessons at school were to be cancelled in favour of German classes.[223]

Heydrich's 'educational policy' was very much in line with Himmler's view, articulated in May 1940, that schooling for the local population in the occupied territories should be reduced to 'simple arithmetic up to 500 at most; writing one's name; a doctrine that it is divine law to obey the Germans and to be honest, industrious and good'.[224] In February 1942, Heydrich further announced that he intended to 'strike violently' at the heart of the Czech teaching establishment, which he saw as the 'training corps of the opposition', and threatened that he would drastically reduce the number of Czech secondary schools. Czech youth, he noted bitterly, had for too long been misled by its 'thoroughly chauvinistic teachers'.[225]

The collaborationist press echoed the view that education was an unnecessary luxury for the majority of the Czech population. On 1 May 1942, Labour Day, the widely circulated paper Česke slovo commented: 'The fact that we have at present 70,000 secondary school pupils is economically unbearable.' Boys in secondary education, the paper argued, should leave school immediately in order to become apprentices and attend professional schools after training.[226] The aim of these measures, as a British Intelligence Report pointedly remarked, was to turn Czech youths 'into a race of slaves which the Herrenvolk system requires'.[227]

Heydrich pursued a similar policy line towards the universities. He announced that the Czech University in Prague, which according to the University Act of 1920 had assumed the sole legal succession of the former Charles University and had been 'temporarily' closed after student unrest in 1939 during which nine students had been shot and 1,200 arrested, would never reopen. Henceforth, the German University of Prague, 73 per cent of whose academic staff consisted of Nazi Party members, would be the only remaining university in Prague. 'The oldest university of the Reich' should, Heydrich insisted, 'not only maintain a status worthy of its historical tradition' but also serve as a 'pathbreaking' institution for a new form of academia that 'infuses scholarship with the *völkisch* necessities' of the New Age.[228]

In institutional terms, the university was to work closely with a new and independent educational foundation, later called the Reinhard Heydrich Foundation. The purpose of the foundation was to undertake research on the '*völkisch*, cultural, political and economic conditions of Bohemia and Moravia as well as the peoples in the Eastern and South-eastern European region'.[229] Overall, the Heydrich Foundation comprised eight institutes occupying the buildings of the dissolved Czech University. The directors of the institutes simultaneously served as professors at the German Charles University so that a close link between the university and the foundation could be guaranteed.[230]

The foundation was a key element of Heydrich's long-term vision for the Protectorate's place in Nazi Germany's academic landscape, which he outlined to Bormann in May 1942. He flagged two principal political tasks for future academic scholarship in the Protectorate: first, to conduct research into the history of Bohemia and Moravia; and secondly, actively to pursue scholarship on the re-Germanization of South-eastern Europe more generally.[231] In essence, the Reinhard Heydrich Foundation was to conduct scientific studies that would facilitate the Germanization of the region. With regard to the intended denationalization and depoliticization of the population, so-called *tschechenkundliche* (Czechological) studies were conducted in order to demonstrate the centuries-old positive German influence on the region.[232]

But Heydrich's cultural imperialism, aimed at undermining and eventually eradicating Czech culture, was by no means limited to academia. It was also to be applied to the field of architecture. When, on 4 December 1941, Albert Speer visited Heydrich in Prague in order to negotiate future contingents of Czech slave labourers to be sent to the Old Reich, they also discussed the architectural future of Prague. One of Heydrich's aims was to turn Prague into a thriving German city, the gateway of the New Nazi Empire into the Balkans and the occupied East. After a two-hour sight-seeing tour of the city, Heydrich and Speer contemplated a variety of architectural plans for the post-war rebuilding of Prague as a German city, including the construction of new German university buildings and a German opera house as well as a new German government complex around the castle. Furthermore, the city was to be encircled by a major ring road that would link up with the German autobahn system. In architectural matters, too, Speer found Heydrich to be refreshingly straight forward:

> There was no comparison with all those Gauleiters, who indulged in their hobby-horses, plans that were technically or architecturally impossible, perhaps an old dream from their youth or their wives' fantasies, which they obstinately stuck to ... By contrast, Heydrich was uncomplicated. He had only a few objections to my suggestions, all of which showed his sensible approach to the problem. If his objections were impractical for technical reasons, he was prepared to be convinced of this instantly.[233]

While he attempted to undermine and eventually eradicate Czech culture and national identity, Heydrich emerged as a patron of German arts. Particularly in the field of music, he energetically pushed for cultural Germanization. Under the aegis of Heydrich, Prague celebrated the 150th anniversary of Mozart's death on 5 December 1941 with considerable pomp – including the renaming of Smetana Square as Mozart Platz, a number of elaborate Mozart exhibitions and guest performances by the Vienna State Opera.[234] Heydrich also planned the establishment of a permanent opera in Prague in 1943–4, a plan supported by Goebbels but which, despite personal discussions between Heydrich and the Reich Finance Minister, had to be postponed for war-related reasons.[235]

In October 1941, Heydrich became patron of the German Philharmonic Orchestra and reopened the German Concert Hall in Prague, the Rudolfinum, founded in the nineteenth century, but converted into the Czech Chamber of Deputies after the Great War. At the festive opening of the newly renovated Rudolfinum on 16 October, to which Heydrich had invited the Berlin Philharmonic Orchestra to perform Beethoven's Ninth Symphony, he reiterated his firm conviction that culture and politics were inseparably intertwined, a point he sought to underline by pointing to the history of the Rudolfinum itself. Heydrich recalled that Anton Bruckner had played the organ here, but noted sadly that after 1918 musical life had become 'Czechified' and had therefore 'degenerated'. After twenty years of darkness, the Rudolfinum was now once more a 'site of German art'.[236]

The opening of the Rudolfinum gave Heydrich an opportunity to reflect on his cultural policies in the Protectorate. After urging those engaged in cultural work 'always to act as German artists in the spirit of the Reich', he pledged that, as a professed admirer of the arts, he would provide German artists with all 'the inspirational and material conditions they need for their work'. He then reminded his audience of the close interconnection between 'art and politics, race and character' and the particular relevance of the arts for 'the soul and the heart of our people'. 'Historical periods of true greatness and true inner meaning', he observed, 'have always prompted a flourishing of true art and genuine ability.' Times of 'cultural and ideological decline', on the other hand, were historical periods in which Jewry thrived. It was the Jews, Heydrich insisted, who had 'injected the Czech people with the madness of independent statehood and made it blind to . . . their self-evident belonging to the Reich'.[237]

Heydrich also wanted to start a new cultural tradition by establishing Prague's 'Cultural Week' as 'a festive manifestation of German power'. This was to be a week-long display of German cultural achievements, particularly in the field of music, which he considered a source of spiritual recreation 'in great times of struggle'. He firmly believed that such a display of cultural superiority, coupled with the political message of abandoning Slavic influences in the Protectorate, would have 'the greatest impact on the Slav; it testifies to our power and culture and eases the integration of the racially desired part of the [Czech] population'.[238] As patron of the festival, Heydrich opened the first concert on 15 May 1942: Bruckner's Eighth Symphony performed by the German Philharmonic Orchestra of Prague and their head conductor Joseph Keilberth, with whom Heydrich occasionally played 'house music' in his country mansion. Shortly thereafter, he and Lina attended a concert given by the famous Leipzig Thomaner-Choir, during which the choirboys, much to their delight, sang Bach's motets in Hitler Youth uniforms.[239]

On the evening of 26 May 1942, the night before his assassination, an event of special emotional relevance to Heydrich was staged in the Wallenstein Palace: a violin concerto composed by Heydrich's father, Bruno. As a special tribute to his father – whom he had treated rather disdainfully and unsympathetically between 1931 and his death in 1938 – he had engaged a quartet of former employees of the Halle Conservatory who played those pieces from Bruno's opera *Amen* that celebrated its hero figure, Reinhard. One of the opera's more memorable pieces, 'Reinhard's Crime', was wisely omitted by the musicians. Visibly touched by the event, Heydrich displayed his softer side: he invited the *Oberlandräte* and several senior civil servants and their wives to join him for a surprise banquet at the fashionable Hotel Avalon where he greeted his guests with unusual friendliness, kissing the ladies' hands and presenting himself as a 'master of etiquette, entertaining, interested in everyone, a charming conversationalist'.[240]

The Rise of Resistance

The winter of 1941–2 marked the end of the German Blitzkrieg strategy in the East, the United States' entry into the war and a general rise in resistance activity in the occupied territories. At this point, Heydrich was forced to acknowledge that the realization of his Germanization goals had receded into the distant future. As he admitted in a report to Hitler in mid-May 1942, the situation in the Protectorate had 'stiffened' as a result of recent reductions in rations, British air strikes against Pilsen and the infiltration of a growing number of enemy agents. He also conceded that the 'military successes of the Reich' were viewed 'with scepticism' by the Czech population, but assured the Führer that there was no cause for serious concerns, adding that he was merely waiting for an 'appropriate moment to strike swiftly, thus underscoring the fact that the Reich is still able to strike and that my clemency is not a sign of weakness'.[241]

Heydrich repeated this threat during a press conference in Prague on 26 May, one day before his assassination: 'I sense and see that foreign propaganda and defeatist anti-German rumours in this space are on the rise again ... Small acts of sabotage, too, which do less damage but rather aim to demonstrate an oppositional attitude, have increased. You must know that despite my patience I shall not hesitate to strike outrageously hard if I should gain the impression that the Reich is considered to be weak and that my generous concessions to you are misinterpreted as softness.'[242]

Heydrich's concerns were not unfounded. There was indeed mounting evidence of increasing resistance activities, not only in the Protectorate but throughout Nazi-occupied Europe. On 23 March, one of Heydrich's closest associates, Franz Walter Stahlecker, the commander of *Einsatzgruppe* A, had been killed by partisans near Krasnogvardeysk in Russia. Similar attacks on German military personnel and installations across Europe had almost become part of the daily routine – a problem that Heydrich believed could be resolved only by intensifying terror and mass shootings.[243]

In Western Europe, too, resistance activities increased significantly and Heydrich acknowledged that the problem here was more complex due to the racial value of some Western European populations and the impor-tance of their economies for the German war effort. Even in Denmark, previously a haven of co-operative calm, illegal Communist leaflets against German rule were distributed in ever larger numbers, prompting Heydrich to urge Foreign Minister von Ribbentrop to allow the Gestapo to arrest anyone suspected of orchestrating the campaign and, more generally, to 'act firmly' against any emerging potential unrest.[244]

Although concerned about the impact of partisan activities on the Wehrmacht's ability to achieve a swift victory over the Soviet Union, Heydrich also saw the rise in resistance as an opportunity to increase SS influence over Western Europe by preaching the virtues of a centrally co-ordinated approach to resistance activities. This was nowhere more evident than in France where, until the spring of 1942, the Wehrmacht had successfully fended off SS interference. Even in the face of growing resistance activity, the military commander in Paris, General Otto von Stülpnagel, argued strongly that reprisals for partisan attacks should be calibrated so as not to jeopardize good relations with the majority of the French population who were working on behalf of the German war effort.[245]

The already tense relationship between Heydrich's SD office in Paris and the German military administration in France deteriorated massively after an incident in the autumn of 1941: during the night of 2–3 October seven synagogues in Paris were bombed and, even though the SD officially claimed that French anti-Semitic nationalists had carried out the attacks, it was clear who had pulled the wires. Heydrich had grown increasingly impatient with the Wehrmacht's 'half-hearted' implementation of anti-Jewish policies and authorized the covert operation. When an investigation by the German military police revealed that Heydrich's men in Paris were behind the attacks, and General von Stülpnagel demanded the immediate dismissal and trial of the SD perpetrators, Heydrich candidly admitted full responsibility. The bombing attacks, he argued in a letter to the army leadership, had targeted Jews 'as the culpable incendiary in Europe . . . which must definitely disappear from Europe'. The bombings had therefore sent a clear signal to international Jewry 'that the Jews are no longer safe in their former European headquarters'.[246]

Heydrich's conflict with the army in France was paralleled by renewed tensions between the SS and the military Abwehr under Canaris. In the winter of 1941–2 Heydrich demanded further concessions from military intelligence in the field of foreign espionage and counter-espionage. He insisted that the Sipo should obtain control over the Secret Military Police (Geheime Feldpolizei), thereby attempting to revise the 'Ten Commandments' of 1935, which had previously regulated the division of labour between Canaris's Abwehr and Heydrich's Security Police apparatus, in favour of the SS. Heydrich and Canaris discussed the matter over the Christmas holidays, which, despite their mounting professional disagreements, they spent together at the Heydrichs' hunting lodge in Stolpshof near Berlin. At first, it seemed that Canaris was prepared to bow to Heydrich's wishes. However, the deteriorating relationship between the SS and the Wehrmacht in France prompted him to change his mind and to argue that the Wehrmacht leadership should not concede any further powers to the SS. On 5 February 1942, a disgruntled Heydrich wrote to Canaris expressing his 'deepest disappointment' over Canaris's change of heart, which threatened to end a relationship that had previously been characterized by 'true openness and honesty in every respect'.[247]

Canaris responded three days later with a letter in which he maintained that 'the human disappointment is all mine. I had never thought that after so many years of comradely collaboration you would be willing to end our relationship so easily.' At the same time, Canaris underlined his determination to end their dispute: 'We both must be absolutely clear about one thing: that both of us – each in his own area of responsibility – serve one and the same cause. In that I demand the same trust in me as I place in you. Then all questions relating to our two offices will be easy to resolve.'[248]

In early March, Heydrich and Canaris came to a written understanding that largely conceded Heydrich's demands: among other things, it placed the Secret Military Police under Heydrich's control – an important step towards SS mastery over policing matters in Western Europe. Simultaneously, the agreement announced a joint conference of some 300 senior Abwehr and Security Police officials in Prague where the first experiences of the new collaboration were to be discussed.[249] On 18 May, Canaris arrived in Prague for the intelligence conference in the splendour of Prague Castle, accompanied by his senior staff. As a gesture of goodwill and a sign of future amicable collaboration, Canaris and his wife stayed in the Heydrich home.[250]

The renewed professional tensions between Canaris and Heydrich do not seem to have impacted on their personal friendship, as Canaris was deeply shaken by Heydrich's death a few weeks later. He attended the funeral in Berlin in June 1942 'with tears in his eyes' and told the SD officer Walter Huppenkothen – who would, in April 1945, act as prosecutor at the court-martial that sentenced Canaris to death for allegedly supporting the 1944 attempt on Hitler's life – how he had 'respected and admired' Heydrich as a 'great man'.[251] To Lina Heydrich, Canaris wrote a few days later: 'Please be assured: I have lost a true friend.'[252]

The agreement between the two men of March 1942 was not the only success for Heydrich in the spring of 1942. In early March, confronted with a new wave of resistance activities in France, Hitler changed his mind on occupation policy and authorized the installation of a higher SS and police leader in Paris, a major breakthrough for the SS leadership's attempt to get their hands on occupied Western Europe.[253] On 5 May, Heydrich flew from Prague to Paris with the new Higher SS and Police Leader in occupied France, his former personal adjutant Carl Albrecht Oberg. Heydrich's visit was not merely a symbolic gesture. As he put it in a letter to Bormann, he hoped to make recommendations for combating the French resistance and on the reorganization of the occupation system 'on the basis of my experiences in the Protectorate'.[254]

By spring 1942, the RSHA was also actively pursuing the complete deportation of all European Jews within German-controlled Europe, including occupied France. During a conference of Heydrich's Jewish experts in Berlin on 4 March, Eichmann announced the immediate deportation of 1,000 French Jews to Auschwitz and assumed that another 5,000 deportees would be transported eastwards before the end of that year. At the same time, Heydrich announced far more extensive deportations from France for the following year.[255]

Against this background, the leading representatives of the German occupation regime in France expected Heydrich to make suggestions on how to combat the resistance and to expand on the solution of the Jewish question in France. On 6 May he did offer some thoughts on both subjects. Acts of retaliation for resistance attacks on German personnel in France had to be handled differently from the situation in Eastern Europe. The shooting of hostages, he assured a sceptical German officer corps in the Hôtel Majestic, was inappropriate for Western Europe.[256]

Within a smaller circle that evening, Heydrich reported on the progress that had been made in solving the Jewish question. After a briefing on the results of the Wannsee Conference, he mentioned the use of gassing vans in the East, a procedure which – much to his 'regret' – had proven 'technically insufficient' to deliver the desired results. Instead, Heydrich added confidently, 'bigger, more perfect and numerically more productive solutions' had been developed. A 'death sentence' had been passed on the 'entirety of European Jews', including those living in France whose eastward deportation would begin over the coming weeks.[257]

On a more personal note, Heydrich's trip to Paris also meant that he would have to meet with his former deputy in the RSHA, Dr Werner Best, with whom he had not spoken since Best's resignation in June 1940. Best was fully aware that the introduction of a higher SS and police leader in France would deprive him of control over the French police. Learning of Heydrich's imminent visit, he sought a personal audience with his former boss in order to improve their strained relationship. In a letter to Heydrich, he wrote that he had always wished to be more that his 'closest member of staff', namely a 'true friend'. But Heydrich had 'never wanted that friend. You wanted a subordinate.' Heydrich, he insisted, had misinterpreted his subsequent disappointment and reserve as jealous ambition and had treated him with undue suspicion and public humiliation. While Best had hoped 'that our separation would have been sufficient to reduce our past misundertandings and tensions', he accepted that this was not the case. He therefore proposed a personal meeting in Paris to restore a relationship which had previously been distinguished by seven years of 'positive and constructive collaboration'.[258]

Heydrich's reaction was characteristic. Best's insinuation that they were equally to blame for their falling out seemed outrageous to him. He also knew from his contacts in Berlin that Best had recently written an emotional letter to Himmler's personal adjutant, Karl Wolff, complaining that he was denied any access to Himmler, whose impression of him had been clouded by false reports.[259] Although his name was not mentioned, Heydrich was well aware to whom Best was referring and immediately intervened with Himmler. He also rejected Best's subsequent offer of reconciliation, arguing that Best had complained to Himmler about him.[260] Best panicked. Fearing that his career in the SS was now once and for all compromised, he wrote a series of apologetic letters to Wolff and Heydrich, suggesting that the tone of his letter to Wolff, his 'bitter words', was the result of his constant state of depression since leaving the RSHA.[261] Despite Best's humiliating attempt at reconciliation, Heydrich chose to ignore his request. Although their professional encounters in Paris were 'frictionless' and Best attempted to 'serve the interests of the SS and Obergruppenführer Heydrich in every conceivable way', their meetings remained 'without any personal touch'. Heydrich and Best would never talk or meet again.[262]

Like so much else in the life of Reinhard Heydrich, his trip to Paris has inspired the imaginations of many historians. Referring to a letter of 7 May from Heydrich to Frank's personnel officer, Robert Gies, the historian Čestmír Amort (and, in his wake, many other Heydrich biographers) has claimed that Hitler intended to appoint Heydrich head of the civilian administration of northern France and Belgium and protector of Vichy France.[263] This appointment would, for the first time, have given the SS dominance over a Western European (former) great power, a bastion in the West to match the growing SS influence in the East. However, the letter upon which this speculation is based was probably never written.[264]

It is true that in mid-May 1942, against the backdrop of a resurgence of primarily Communist-led resistance activities across occupied Europe, Heydrich promised both Bormann and Himmler that he would soon present the Führer with a clear and concise dossier which would both summarize his experiences in the reorganization of German occupation policy in the Protectorate and include policy suggestions for other occupied territories in Eastern and Western Europe. Of central importance was Heydrich's conviction that the partisan activities in Western and Eastern Europe were intrinsically connected and that they therefore required a co-ordinated approach – obviously under the auspices of the

SS. A few days later, Heydrich was summoned to the Führer's headquarters. It is not known whether it was on this occasion that he intended to present the Führer with a general policy document on the future of the German occupation of Europe, since the documents that he may have carried with him when he left for Rastenburg on 27 May have disappeared, probably for ever.[265]

Despite his obsession with matters of policing, Heydrich carelessly neglected his own security in Prague, even though there were strong indications of a threat against his life. In March 1942, the Gestapo arrested a musician during a routine patrol at Warsaw's central railway station. Although his papers were in order and showed him to be a 'German musician' on his way to Prague, his over-sized, brand-new suitcase aroused suspicion. In a secret compartment, the Gestapo agents found a sniper's gun equipped with telescopic sights and a silencer. After days of brutal interrogations, the man cracked and confessed to being a Russian agent sent by Moscow to assassinate Heydrich.[266]

This was not the only warning. An SD report of 18 April 1942 which, as usual, was sent to Heydrich and other leading figures of the occupation regime, recorded rumours about 'parachutists who have already landed in the Protectorate and have already committed acts of sabotage, strikes in large factories, an assassination attempt on the acting Reich Protector himself etc.'[267]

Even if Heydrich had not heard of the Warsaw incident or read the alarming report, it seems unlikely that none of his subordinates would have alerted him to the rumours of a potential assassination threat. Heydrich must have been warned, but he failed to respond adequately to the threats with enhanced security measures. Although he began to wear a bullet-proof vest, he continued, much to the dismay of his wife and Himmler, to drive through Prague in an open car without a security escort.[268]

Albert Speer, when he visited Heydrich in Prague in December 1941, had been surprised by Heydrich's lack of interest in his personal safety: 'Heydrich, whose entire house in Berlin was linked by alarm bells (even in the toilet) to the surrounding police stations' and whose cars were 'equipped with replacement number plates, with pistols in front of each seat and sub-machine guns in front of those riding in the rear seats – that same Heydrich was travelling in contravention of the regulations he had himself drawn up for the protection of leading personalities of state and party'.[269] As acting Reich Protector Heydrich regarded his personal security as a political matter. He categorically refused an escort on the grounds that it would damage German prestige and create the impression that he feared the Czechs. As long as he retained the psychological initiative, he would not be attacked – a fateful miscalculation, as it turned out. On the morning of 27 May 1942, Heydrich set out on his trip to visit Hitler. He would never get further then the hairpin curve in Liběn where his assassins were already waiting for him.

CHAPTER IX

✦

Legacies of Destruction

On 9 June 1942, the body of Reinhard Heydrich was laid to rest in one of the most elaborate funeral ceremonies ever staged in the Third Reich. Over the previous two days, his coffin had been exhibited in the courtyard of Prague Castle, where tens of thousands of ethnic German and Czech civilians – some voluntarily, some 'encouraged' by the Nazi authorities – filed past to pay their final respects. The coffin was then transported to the Mosaic Room of the New Reich Chancellery in Berlin, where, to the solemn notes of the Funeral March from Richard Wagner's *Twilight of the Gods*, the entire leadership of the Third Reich bid a final farewell to Heydrich.[1]

The spectacle was carefully stage-managed by Goebbels's Propaganda Ministry in an attempt to portray Heydrich as the 'ideal Nazi', a heroic martyr of the Nazi cause whose qualities offered an example to all Germans. Press reports about the funeral and the deceased were subjected to strict censorship and prescribed terminology, emphasizing his death as the ultimate sacrifice in a life-and-death struggle for the Greater German Reich. In accordance with these instructions, Nazi papers praised Heydrich as a 'Nordic man' of the 'finest racial quality' – a member of the new racial 'aristocracy of the nation', who had fallen 'victim to those dark forces that flourish only in the twilight of the ambush'. His death, it was said, 'is an admonition and an obligation. We honour his memory by living and acting in the way we may assume he would have wanted us to.'[2]

Himmler himself, in his funeral speech of 9 June, set the tone for how Heydrich was to be remembered: as a Nazi martyr and an impeccable SS man, 'an ideal always to be emulated, but perhaps never again to be achieved'. With his 'healthy, simple and disciplined lifestyle', his 'unbending spirit' and his 'noble' and 'decent' character, Heydrich was a role model who would 'inspire future generations'. As a man of 'irreplaceable, unique abilities, combined with a character of the rarest purity and a mind of penetrating logic and clarity', he had been rightly

> feared by the sub-humans, hated and slandered by Jews and other criminals ... whatever measures and actions he took, he always approached them as a National Socialist and as an SS man. From the deepest reaches of his heart and his blood, he felt, understood and realized the worldview of Adolf Hitler. He seized all the tasks he was charged with from his fundamental comprehension of a genuine racial worldview and from the knowledge that the purity, security and defence of our blood is the supreme law.[3]

Following Himmler's eulogy, a visibly moved Hitler mounted the stage and added his authority to the celebration of an exemplary Nazi life: 'He was one of the best National Socialists, one of the strongest defenders of the German Reich, one of the greatest opponents of all enemies of the Empire. He has died as a martyr for the preservation and protection of the Reich.' Hitler then posthumously decorated Heydrich 'with the highest award in my gift, the highest stage of the German Order', an honour specially created for those who had rendered exceptional service to party and Fatherland.[4]

As Hitler left the funeral ceremony, gently patting the cheeks of Heydrich's two sons on his way, the coffin was transported from the New Reich Chancellery to the Invaliden cemetery, originally founded in the nineteenth century as a resting place for Prussia's military elite. Heydrich's body was buried alongside the graves of Scharnhorst, Moltke and other eminent generals from Germany's past.[5]

But Heydrich was by no means forgotten after 9 June. On the contrary: it was only after his assassination, and as a result of the extensive news coverage of his state funeral, that he became a household name both in the Reich and internationally. On the day of his death, Hitler added Heydrich to the 'honorary list of the Fallen of the Nazi Movement' and arranged for the 6th SS Infantry Division, currently fighting the Red Army on the Eastern Front, to be named after him. In the Protectorate, a special-issue postage stamp bearing a picture of Heydrich's death mask was released on the first anniversary of his assassination. Streets and squares in eighteen Protectorate cities and towns were renamed in his honour. Heydrich's light was to shine beyond Germany, as the *Germanische Leithefte*, the journal for non-German SS volunteers, demonstrated when it celebrated Heydrich as a reincarnation of the legendary Norwegian king Sverre Sigurdsson, who had led a successful anti-Church rebellion in the late twelfth century. The journal even advocated the inscription of a rune-shrine commemorating Sigurdsson for use on Heydrich's grave: 'Here he lies who was the ornament of kings, the pillar of faith, courage and honour, example and paragon, invincible heroic spirit, defender of the Fatherland, guardian of the national heritage, the terror of his foes, his people's fame and glory.'[6]

Heydrich's elevation to a martyr in the Nazi pantheon of fallen heroes was the culmination point of the by then well-established Nazi cult of the dead, which exalted death for party and Fatherland as the logical end to a fulfilled and meaningful life. The purpose of the Nazis' cult of the fallen warrior was to unite the German *Volksgemeinschaft* in an unshakeable determination to fight on. The SS in particular saw death as an ongoing obligation for the living, an obligation to continue the struggles of the fallen. The violent death of a hero was never in vain, but rather a model for the wider SS community to emulate. As Heydrich's former deputy in Prague, Karl Hermann Frank, declared, Heydrich had set an example in more ways than one: he had shown the world both 'how to live and how to die' as a German hero, the latter of which was to become increasingly important during the last two years of the Second World War.[7]

While Heydrich's body was being laid to rest in Berlin, the Nazi leadership sought revenge for what Goebbels described in his diary as the 'irreplaceable' loss of 'the most radical and most successful persecutor of all enemies of the state'.[8] The atmosphere in Berlin can only be described as murderous. 'Nothing can prevent me from deporting millions of Czechs if they do not wish for peaceful coexistence,' an infuriated Hitler screamed at Czech President Hácha after the funeral. Wartime needs no longer concerned him. The assassins had to be found immediately or the Czech population would face unprecedented consequences.[9] Immediately after his meeting with Hitler on 9 June, Karl Hermann Frank telephoned Horst Böhme, head of the Security Police and SD in the Protectorate, to convey the Führer's order for an immediate act of retaliation: the complete annihilation of the Bohemian village of Lidice, including the murder of all of its male inhabitants and the deportation of all women to a concentration camp. The children – if Germanizable – were to be sent to foster-parents in the Reich.[10] Böhme could hardly have been surprised by this order, for he was the one who had suggested Lidice as a possible target for retaliation in the first place. On the day of Heydrich's funeral, he had phoned Himmler in Berlin to report that the assassins had allegedly received support from the village's inhabitants. Himmler, in turn, informed Hitler, who decided that Lidice was to be razed to the ground.[11]

Lidice, a small village with around 500 inhabitants located north-west of Prague in the industrial district of Kladno, had first aroused the suspicion of the Gestapo in late autumn 1941, when a captured Czech parachutist testified that two families living in Lidice, the Horáks and Stříbrnýs, had served as contact points for resistance fighters dropped into the Protectorate. The story was probably made up, but the Gestapo chose to believe it, partly because two of the sons of these families, Josef Horák and Josef Stříbrný, had fled the country in 1939 and joined the Czech Brigade in Britain.[12]

In early June 1942, while Heydrich was still in hospital and his fate uncertain, Lidice appeared again on the radar of the German authorities when a suspicious letter fell into the Gestapo's hands. Václav Říha, a married man from a small dwelling near Lidice, had sent a message to his young lover, Anna Maruščáková, calling off their affair under the pretext of having to 'disappear' for a while. The reason was deliberately elided, but he gave the impression that he knew Josef Horák from Lidice and had received a message from him. Desperate for any possible lead that might aid the search for Heydrich's assassins, the Gestapo arrested both Říha and Maruščáková. Although it quickly became clear that Říha had never met Josef Horák and that he had no connection to the Czech resistance whatsoever, he and Anna Maruščáková were deported to Mauthausen, where they were gassed alongside 261 other Czech camp inmates in October 1942.[13]

Despite the fact that the allegations had proved to be false, Böhme continued to regard Lidice as suspicious, and, on the day of Heydrich's death, Gestapo men from Kladno arrested fifteen members of the Horák and Stříbrný families. Worse was yet to come: just a few hours after Hitler's destruction order of 9 June, German police units surrounded the village. Male inhabitants were herded on to the farm of the Horák family where they were successively shot in groups of ten. All in all, 172 men between the ages of fourteen and eighty-four were murdered in Lidice on 9 June. The shootings were still under way when the first houses were set on fire. By ten in the morning, every house in Lidice had been burned down and their ruins blown up with explosives or bulldozed to the ground.[14] The women of Lidice were deported to Ravensbrück concentration camp while their children underwent racial screening. Only nine of the children of Lidice were deemed Germanizable and given new German names and identification papers before being assigned to German foster-parents. The majority were murdered.[15]

Gestapo officers further tracked down eleven men from Lidice who had been working the night shift in a nearby factory, a miner from the village who was recovering from a broken leg in the regional hospital and another villager who had hidden in the woods for three days. All of them, as well as those remaining members of the Horák and Stříbrný families who were not living in Lidice, were shot in the next few days. All in all, 199 men from Lidice were executed, a massacre which, as Goebbels noted with satisfaction in his diary, 'will not fail in its cooling effect on the remnants of the underground movement in the Protectorate'.[16]

The Lidice killings, broadcast with pride by German propaganda, made the front pages of newspapers around the world.[17] Long before Auschwitz, Lidice became, as the British War Office succinctly remarked, the 'symbol of the German policy of *Schrecklichkeit* [terror] ... a symbol of all the Lidices in all the countries touched by German hate'. Of all the sites of brutal German reprisals in the Second World War – from Oradour, Marzabotto, Kraguljevac, Distomo to Kalavryta and other villages – Lidice possessed the greatest propagandistic value to the Allied cause, precisely because the Germans were gleefully reporting its destruction in news-reels and propaganda speeches. As the War Office report suggested, 'each time it is remembered, mankind becomes a little more determined that the thing which tried to kill Lidice shall itself be killed, shall be driven from the earth so that no Lidice will ever die again'.[18]

Shortly after the destruction of the village, several communities in the United States, Mexico, Peru and Brazil renamed their villages and towns 'Lidice', making Heydrich known throughout the world. In his Californian exile, Heinrich Mann wrote the novel *Lidice* (1943), director Humphrey Jennings filmed *The Silent Village* (1943) and Bertolt Brecht and Fritz Lang collaborated on the Hollywood blockbuster *Hangmen Also Die* (1943). Cecil Day Lewis and Edna St Vincent Millay wrote elegies to the village, and US war posters called on Americans to 'Remember Pearl Harbor and Lidice'. 'The Nazis are stupid beasts,' the most famous German writer-in-exile, Nobel Laureate Thomas Mann, remarked from the United States: 'They wanted to consign the name of Lidice to eternal oblivion, and they have engraved it forever into the memory of man by their atrocious deed. Hardly anyone knew this name before they murdered the entire population of the settlement and razed it to the ground; now it is world famous.'[19]

Mann, whose Munich home had been raided on Heydrich's orders by the Bavarian Political Police in 1933, also commented on the Reich Protector's assassination on the famous German-language BBC radio broadcast *Deutsche Hörer!* in June 1942:

> Since the violent death of Heydrich, the most natural death that a bloodhound can die, terror is raging everywhere, in a more sickly, unrestrained fashion than ever before. It is absurd, and once more our disgust is aroused by this mixture of brutality and shrieking whininess that has always been a hallmark of Nazism ... Wherever this killer went, blood flowed in rivers. Everywhere, even in Germany, he was simply called: the Hangman ... Now he has been murdered. And how are the Nazis reacting? They are getting cramps. They are literally behaving as if the most inconceivable misdeed has been committed, as if the highest level of humanity has been attacked ... Thousands must die – men and

women. An entire town, that supposedly sheltered the perpetrators, is massacred and razed. The surviving population of Prague must line the streets as the saint's funeral procession passes by. At home, a pompous state funeral is commanded, and another butcher [Himmler] says at his grave that he had been a pure soul and a man of profound humanity. All of this is insane . . . to say that Heydrich was a noble person one needs power – absolute power to prescribe what is truth and what is idiocy.[20]

In the midst of the international outrage over the Lidice killings, one person could search for a ray of light: the Czech President-in-exile, Edvard Beneš. 'What the Germans are doing is horrible,' he assured the Czech home resistance, the vast majority of whom would be arrested and murdered over the following days and weeks, 'but from a political point of view they gave us one certainty: under no circumstances can anyone doubt Czechoslovakia's national integrity and her right to independence.'[21] As Beneš had hoped and anticipated, the Allies rewarded him for backing the Heydrich assassination. On 5 August 1942, Anthony Eden officially repudiated the Munich Agreement of 1938 and secretly assured Beneš that, after the war's successful conclusion, the problem of ethnic diversity in a restored Czechoslovakia would be resolved once and for all, thus paving the way for the eventual expulsion of almost 2 million ethnic Germans from the Sudetenland after May 1945.[22]

In the Protectorate, the response of the West to the massacre in Lidice radicalized an already tense atmosphere. Karl Hermann Frank noted that 'the genuinely American fad of naming towns after Lidice' would not prevent him 'for one second from continuing to proceed against the enemies of the Reich with even harsher measures'.[23] Meanwhile, the Gestapo had failed to achieve its most pressing objective: the capture of Heydrich's assassins. While martial law courts continued to pass an ever-growing number of death sentences, the Protectorate authorities promised an increased reward for anyone who knew of the assassins' location. At the same time, they announced drastic measures if the assassins were not handed over by 18 June. As the date approached, the tensions came to a climax. Rumours spread that the Nazis would execute every tenth non-German in the Protectorate, and many Czechs, either out of fear for their lives or in exchange for money, offered information to the Germans. None of it, however, delivered a real lead on the assassins. The investigation seemed to have reached a stalemate.[24]

Then, on 16 June, two days before the deadline, Karel Čurda, a parachutist dropped into the Protectorate in late March 1942, walked into the Gestapo headquarters in Prague's Peček Palace – not a place many Czechs entered voluntarily. To save his life and protect his family, Čurda was willing to sacrifice those of others. He did not know Gabčík's and Kubiš's current location, but he did betray those who had provided safe houses since their arrival in December 1941, including that of the Moravec family in the Žižkov district of Prague, who had sheltered Heydrich's assassins for several weeks.[25]

A wave of arrests followed. On 17 June, before daybreak, the Moravec apartment was raided. The mother of the family, Marie Moravec, killed herself with a cyanide capsule when the Gestapo officers arrived. Her husband, Alois Moravec, oblivious to his family's involvement with the resistance, was taken to the cellars of Peček Palace alongside his teenage son, Vlastimil. After withstanding nearly twenty-four hours of brutal interrogation, Vlastimil cracked when the Germans showed him his mother's severed head in a fish tank and threatened to place his father's beside it. Vlastimil told the Gestapo that the assassins had taken shelter in the Orthodox Church of St Cyril and Methodius in central Prague. His forced confession was not rewarded. Both Vlastimil Moravec and his father Alois were deported to Mauthausen concentration camp and executed.[26]

In the early hours of 18 June, 800 SS men surrounded the Orthodox Church. Their orders were to take the assassins alive, allowing for further interrogations regarding their confederates in the Protectorate. The unsuspecting Kubiš and two fellow parachutists, Adolf Opálka and Jaroslav Švarc, had the night watch as the Germans burst into the church. From the choirstalls the parachutists opened fire and managed to keep the attackers at bay for nearly two hours. By 7 a.m., the first Czech was dead; the other two, including Kubiš, were seriously wounded and captured. Kubiš was carried out of the church alive and brought to the SS military hospital, but died there without regaining consciousness.[27]

Initially, the Germans were unaware that there were four additional parachutists hiding in the crypt, but on searching the choirstall they found items of clothing that clearly did not belong to any of the dead men. The Gestapo searched the building more thoroughly and found a trapdoor to the catacombs. Under pressure, the resident priest, Vladimír Petřek, admitted that four more parachutists – including Heydrich's second assassin, Gabčík – were hiding there. Petřek and Čurda tried to persuade the men to surrender, but they refused. Over the following four hours, the SS desperately tried to find a way into the catacombs. Tear gas and water were pumped into the cellar in an attempt to force the parachutists out. When the SS finally used dynamite to enlarge the narrow entrance to the catacombs and prepared to raid the cellar, the four parachutists – knowing that their fate was decided and that torture could be avoided only through suicide – shot themselves in the head.[28]

The death of Heydrich's assassins was greeted with great relief and joy in Berlin, but the reprisals nonetheless continued. On 1 September, the spiritual leader of the Orthodox community in Prague, Bishop Gorazd, who had accepted full responsibility for the events in the Church of St Cyril and Methodius, was sentenced to death, alongside Father Petřek, and two other Orthodox priests who had sheltered the assassins. Their sentence was carried out three days later. Over the next few weeks, 236 other supporters and providers of safe houses for the parachutists were taken to Mauthausen concentration camp and murdered.[29]

Nazi reprisals continued throughout the summer. With the help of local informants, Gestapo agents rounded up most of the surviving members of the Communist resistance and ÚVOD, including its entire Central Committee. The Czech underground was almost completely wiped out and was never to recover from the blows it suffered in the weeks after Heydrich's death. In Prague, Alois Eliáš, the former Prime Minister of the Protectorate government, who had been arrested immediately after Heydrich's arrival in Prague, was executed. Hitler had no more use for him. More innocent people fell victim in the village of Ležáky, where Gestapo agents found the transmitter of the underground radio team Silver A that had been parachuted into the Protectorate alongside Gabčík and Kubiš. All of the village's adult inhabitants – thirty-three in total – were shot. The children were handed over to the German authorities and the village's buildings reduced to rubble. Alfréd Bartoš himself, the leader of Silver A, who had repeatedly warned Beneš about the potential reper- cussions of an attempted Heydrich assassination, was fatally wounded when his hide-out was discovered by the Gestapo.[30] Excluding those killed in Lidice and Ležáky, 3,188 Czechs were arrested and 1,327 were sentenced to death during the reprisals that summer, 477 of them for simply approving of the assassination. Up to 4,000 people with relatives among the exiles were rounded up and placed in concentration camps or ordinary prisons.[31]

The terrifying memory of the *Heydrichiáda*, as the wave of terror that followed the assassination was soon to be known in Czechoslovakia, served as a powerful deterrent to a revival of active resistance. Contrary to Beneš's intentions, the War Office in London noted a 'dying enthusiasm' for further resistance within the Czech population. The Czech armaments industry remained one of the strongest and most reliable pillars of the German war effort until the Wehrmacht's unconditional surrender in the spring of 1945. Through his death, Heydrich had inadvertently fulfilled one of his short-term missions in Prague: the complete and lasting 'paci- fication' of the Protectorate.[32]

If Heydrich's assassination triggered an unprecedented wave of retaliation against the Czech population, it also prompted the Nazi leadership in Berlin to a further radicalization of its policies towards its main perceived enemy: international Jewry. Although the Nazis' genocidal campaign of systematically murdering Europe's Jews was well advanced by early June 1942, Heydrich's death added extra ferocity to the Nazi crusade. In Heydrich, Himmler had lost his closest and most important collaborator, and he was more determined than ever that the vast majority of European Jews would have to die before the year was over. As Himmler proclaimed in a secret speech to senior SS officers in Berlin immediately after Heydrich's funeral: 'It is our sacred obligation to avenge his death, to take over his mission and to destroy without mercy and weakness, now more than ever, the enemies of our people.' Himmler also ordered his subordinates to be more careful of their personal safety in the future – 'after all we want to kill our enemies; our enemies are not supposed to kill us' – and made it very clear that the programme of mass extermination was to be completed as soon as possible: 'The migration of the Jewish people will be completed within a year. Then no more of them will be migrating. Now we shall make a clean sweep [*jetzt muss eben reiner Tisch gemacht werden*].'[33]

That responsibility for Heydrich's death should first and foremost be pinned on 'the Jews' was, in the twisted logic of the Nazis, perfectly obvious. Ever since the German attack on the Soviet Union and America's entry into the war, Nazi Germany had been at 'war with the Jews' and the assassination of the head of the Nazi security apparatus constituted an act of hostility that could be fully avenged only through the destruction of the Jewish enemy allegedly responsible for that act. Himmler kept his word. At the time of Heydrich's death, about three-fourths of the 6 million Jews whom the Nazis and their accomplices would murder over the course of the Second World War were still alive. Nine months later, there were 4.5 million Jewish victims.[34] It is likely that Himmler sought and received Hitler's approval for this further extension of the mass murders during their frequent meetings in late May and early June 1942. On 19 July, Himmler visited Lublin, where he told the higher SS and police leader East, Friedrich-Wilhelm Krüger, that, with few exceptions, all Jews living in the General Government should be killed before the end of the year. Three days later, on 22 July, the most murderous phase of the final solution began with mass deportations from the Warsaw ghetto to the Treblinka extermination camp.[35]

In 'honour' of Heydrich, the extermination programme in the General Government was given the operational name 'Aktion Reinhardt'.[36] When Aktion Reinhardt tailed off in the autumn of 1943, some 2 million people – the vast majority of them Jews – had been murdered.[37]

The transition to full-blown genocide was not confined to the General Government, but increasingly affected the rest of Nazi-controlled Europe and indeed the Reich itself. Under the influence of Heydrich's assassination, Goebbels immediately stepped up the persecution of Berlin Jews:

> In Berlin I am having the planned arrest of 500 Jews carried out and I have told the Jewish community leaders that for every attack or for every Jewish attempt at insurrection 100 or 150 of the Jews in our hands will be shot. As a result of the Heydrich assassination, a whole range of incriminated Jews have been shot in Sachsenhausen. The more of this filth is swept away, the better for the security of the Reich.

Deportations from the Reich now increasingly included those who had previously been exempted such as older Jews and decorated war veterans and their families. Between June and October 1942, approximately 45,000 German Jews were deported to Theresienstadt, which continued officially to serve, as Heydrich had intended, as an old-age ghetto, thus concealing its real purpose as a transit camp for Jews on their way to the extermination sites in occupied Poland.[38]

In the case of the destruction of the Protectorate's Jewish community, no such precautions were necessary. In the months after Heydrich's death, some twenty-nine trains brought almost 30,000 additional Protectorate Jews to the killing factories of Auschwitz and Bergen-Belsen. In June 1943, the last transport of full Jews left Prague, carrying the remaining 4,000 members of the now dissolved Jewish Congregation of Prague and their families. By the end of the war, only 424 members of Prague's once substantial Jewish community had managed to survive the occupation in hiding.[39]

The fate of the German and Czech Jews reflected a wider European pattern. In the summer of 1942, the RSHA demanded that Germany's allies – Croatia, Romania, Hungary and Italy – surrender their Jews to the Nazi authorities, a move that underlined Himmler's determination to realize the threat made on the day of Heydrich's funeral that 'Jewish migration' in Europe would end in 1942. Furthermore, in mid-June that year the deportation of 15,000 Dutch, 10,000 Belgian and 100,000 French Jews was negotiated by the RSHA's Jewish experts. Between July and November 1942 alone, thirty-three transports carrying 1,000 Jews each left France for Auschwitz.[40]

The Slavic population of Eastern Europe also remained in danger of mass deportations. Immediately after Heydrich's assassination, Hitler had threatened to deport 'millions of Czechs' – 'if necessary during the war'.[41] Himmler, too, had pledged on the occasion of Heydrich's funeral that that his death would not put an end to the Germanization of the Protectorate.[42]

Others echoed these sentiments. On 6 June 1942, the Gauleiter of Vienna and head of the Hitler Youth, Baldur von Schirach, declared openly: 'This autumn we will celebrate a Jew-free Vienna. Then we shall turn towards the solution of the Czech question. For the bullets that have killed our comrade Heydrich have injured us, too. As Gauleiter of Vienna, I therefore give order to deport all Czechs from this city as soon as the Jews have been evacuated. Just as I will make this city Jew-free, I will also make it Czech-free.'[43] Hitler, suddenly concerned about morale in the Czech armaments industry, immediately banned all further public discussion about the future treatment of the Czechs, but it was too late: for a brief moment, members of the inner Nazi leadership circle had publicly spoken their minds on what the Czechs could expect if Germany won the war.[44]

Fortunately, none of the dystopian fantasies for the Germanization of Eastern Europe was ever implemented. Germanization plans in the Protectorate and Eastern Europe more generally faltered at the very moment when the murder of Europe's Jews reached its climax.[45]

Instead of focusing on the distant goal of Germanization, Nazi leaders turned to other, more immediate concerns of which winning the war was the most vital. After a string of Wehrmacht losses in the Soviet Union and Africa in the winter of 1942–3, victory on the battlefield became a more pressing issue than the bloody unweaving of ethnicities. Heydrich's short-term goals of maintaining domestic peace and industrial productivity became paramount, not just in the Protectorate, but throughout all of Hitler's Europe.[46]

How this was to be achieved remained a bone of contention between the army, the SS, and the various German civilian administrations operating throughout Nazi-occupied Europe. The administrators, population planners, and racial hygienists who operated in every corner of German-controlled territory never had time to develop a coherent and consistently applied approach to their self-imposed problems in governing populations several times larger than that of the Reich itself. As military fortunes turned against Germany in late 1942, even Himmler was forced to make concessions, be it by recruiting Eastern European and even Muslim volunteers for the SS (whom he would have previously regarded as 'racially unsuitable'), or by abandoning his ambitious settlement projects in Ukraine and Poland. With respect to Bohemia and Moravia, Germany's military misfortunes, its transport shortages and dependence on the Czech arms industry provided a saving grace for the local population and a stumbling block for those who hoped to resolve the 'Czech question' in a radical way. Even Heydrich – had he lived – could not have ignored these new realities. [47]

While pressure on the Czechs to become Germans decreased after Heydrich's death, little changed in the persecution of political enemies on the home front after June 1942. If anything, the Nazi terror apparatus under Heydrich's successors as head of the RSHA – Heinrich Himmler and, from January 1943 onwards, Ernst Kaltenbrunner – tightened its grip on German society, fearing a repetition of the 1918 'stab in the back' and a collapse of the home front that suffered increasingly from the Allied bombing attacks. Kaltenbrunner may have lacked Heydrich's organizational ability and ferocious energy, but the Security Police apparatus remained a powerful institution. Yet the brutal persecution of the inner German opposition after the failed attempt on Hitler's life on 20 July 1944 could not conceal the fact that the RSHA had not been able to uncover the plot in time. The organization had little more than half a year left before the Third Reich collapsed.[48]

The end of the Third Reich marked a decisive caesura for the Heydrich family, whose good fortunes had steadily eroded since June 1942. Heydrich's widow, Lina, was thirty-one years old and heavily pregnant when her husband was assassinated in Prague. She was left so distraught by his death that she could not bear to attend the funeral in Berlin. In the early hours of 23 July 1942, their fourth child and second daughter, Marte, was born. In recognition of her late husband's contribution to Nazism, Hitler gave his widow the country estate of Jungfern-Breschan as a gift to be kept in the Heydrich family in perpetuity. In the autumn of 1942, Lina sold the family home in Berlin and gave up their hunting lodge near Nauen.[49]

To ease her transition into a permanent life in rural Bohemia, Himmler arranged for some thirty Jewish forced labourers to work on her estate. Unsurprisingly, given Lina's long-held anti-Semitic beliefs, the forced labourers were treated with contempt. According to post-war testimonies given by Jewish survivors who worked on the Heydrich estate, Lina frequently observed the workers with a telescope from her veranda, ordering the whipping of those who worked too slowly and displaying 'no emotions whatsoever' when prisoners were maltreated. On one occasion, she had 'the SS man Ilmer beat our comrade Adolf Neumann ... until his back drew blood, only because Neumann was unable to run with his fully laden trolly'. Jewish slave labourers who failed to show adequate respect were spat at or beaten by Lina. In January 1944, the Jewish forced labourers were deported to extermination camps and replaced by fifteen female Jehovah's Witnesses from the women's camp in Ravensbrück.[50]

The Heydrichs' eldest son, Klaus, died in a car accident in 1943 and was buried in the garden of the country estate.[51] More blows were to follow: in December 1944, Heydrich's younger brother, Heinz Siegfried, who worked for the army propaganda journal *Panzerfaust* on the Eastern Front, committed suicide under mysterious circumstances. It is possible that his suicide was partly triggered by his knowledge of his brother's crimes, and by his fear that the Gestapo might discover his own involvement in helping Jews to escape from the Third Reich. There are at least two confirmed cases in 1943–4 in which Heinz Siegfried prevented the deportation of Jews personally known to him by providing them with forged exit visas.[52] In reality, however, the main reason for his suicide appears to have been significantly less heroic: Heydrich's only surviving son, Heider, maintained after the war that Heinz Siegfried decided to commit suicide because he was facing a court martial for theft and corruption.[53]

Lina and her children continued to live in Jungfern-Breschan until April 1945, when they shared the fate of hundreds of thousands of ethnic German refugees fleeing from both the advancing Red Army and the much feared retribution of their long-suppressed non-German neighbours. Hard-pressed for time, Lina had to leave behind nearly all of her possessions, but she did rescue her husband's blood-stained SS uniform which has remained in the hands of her son until now. The Heydrich family escaped to rural Bavaria only days before the end of German rule over the Protectorate.[54] Reinhard Heydrich's mother, Elisabeth, who had moved in with the Heydrichs after her son's death, also left Jungfern-Breschan in the spring of 1945 and escaped to her native town of Dresden, where she was caught up with thousands of other refugees in the Allied bombings of 13–15 February, which turned the city into smouldering rubble. She survived the firestorms, but, deprived of any family assistance, the once prosperous and proud Elisabeth Heydrich met an end similar to that of many other helpless elderly refugees: she starved to death in the final days of the Third Reich.[55]

While the world around her was collapsing, Lina was more fortunate than others. Shortly after Germany's unconditional surrender, which the Heydrich family experienced as refugees in Bavaria, Lina moved back to her native island of Fehmarn on the Baltic coast, where her parents were able to offer her shelter. An attempt by the Beneš government in 1947 to have her extradited from the British occupation zone in Germany and tried in Prague was rejected by the British military administration. By now, the logic of the early Cold War dictated that good relations with the emerging West German state were of greater relevance in the fight against international Communism than the demands of a former Czech ally about to be absorbed into Stalin's Eastern European empire.[56]

The German authorities, too, turned a blind eye to the Heydrich case. Lina never stood trial for the maltreatment of her slave labourers in Jungfern-Breschan. On the contrary, in the context of the so-called de-Nazification process, she was officially cleared and allowed to retake possession of her financial assets and house on Fehmarn, which had been temporarily confiscated by the British army in 1945. It was here that Lina ran a small pension and restaurant, the Imbria Parva, in which former SS officers frequently met for reunions and exchanged memories of the 'good old days'. In 1956 and 1959, Lina also won a series of court cases against the Federal Republic that had previously denied her pension rights. After the trial, and despite extensive evidence about her late husband's role in the Holocaust, the Federal Republic was forced to pay her the widow's pension of a German general killed in action, roughly equivalent to that of a retired minister president.[57] Well subsidized by the German taxpayer, Lina never expressed regret or remorse for her husband's deeds and publicly declared that she dreamed of him 'almost every night'.[58] As if to mock the state prosecutor and the left-wing press, which had strongly criticized the court's verdict, she entitled her memoirs, published in the 1970s, *My Life with a War Criminal*. She died in August 1985, full of disgust for a society that failed to acknowledge her family's sacrifices for the cause of German greatness.

Throughout the later stages of her life, Lina denied her husband's responsibility for the brutal persecution of Nazi Germany's political enemies, his crucial involvement in the Holocaust and his deep commitment to the bloody unweaving of Europe's ethnicities. Reinhard Heydrich, so she claimed, was a victim of historical circumstances, of a life conditioned by violence and wars, in which men like him were forced to make difficult decisions in order to serve their country. Lina may have been right in stressing that Heydrich was a product of specific historical circumstances, of political and cultural structures that were larger than him. But to argue that he was a victim was an insult to the millions of people directly afftected – often in the most cruel ways imaginable – by the deliberate decisions Heydrich, Himmler and Hitler took out of deep ideological conviction. It also unduly downplays individual agency and responsibility within the polyocratic jungle that was the Third Reich. Hitler's dictatorship was backed by millions of Germans who often enthusiastically supported the Nazis' dystopian fantasy of a Jew-free, German-dominated Europe, but few – if any – made a more direct and personal contribution to its murderous implementation than Reinhard Heydrich. It was Heydrich who – in close co-ordination with Hitler, Himmler and Göring – devised Nazi Germany's operative policies of persecution against the Jews between 1938 and 1942, a murderous task which, once achieved, was to be followed by the even more extensive project of Germanizing the conquered territories.

Yet Heydrich's path to virtually unlimited power in persecuting and murdering Nazi Germany's enemies in the Reich and its occupied territories was anything but straightforward. His youth in the shadow of war and revolution, his family's social decline and his first career in the staunchly nationalist Weimar navy many have made him susceptible to right-wing politics, but his conversion to Nazism came only in 1931, after the abrupt and unexpected end of his military career. Without the existential crisis prompted by his dismissal from the navy and the simultaneously growing influence of his fiancée and her family of committed Nazis, Heydrich may never have joined the SS as a staff officer.

But if desperation for a second career in uniform and a desire to please his fiancée and her family were dominating factors in Heydrich's decision to apply for a position in the SS, he quickly came to endorse Nazism in its most extreme form. In order to succeed in a new working environment in which radicalism was rewarded, he fully subscribed to the SS's ethos of ruthless efficiency and decisiveness. His determination to make up for the serious 'imperfections' of his earlier life – such as his belated conversion to Nazism and the persistent rumours about his Jewish ancestry that led to a humiliating party investigation in 1932 – also helps to explain his swift transformation into a model SS man.

By the mid-1930s, Heydrich had successfully reinvented himself as one of the most radical proponents of Nazi ideology and its implementation through rigid and increasingly extensive policies of persecution. He was never a man of ideas – he was no dystopian visionary like Hitler or Himmler – but he was a highly talented organizer of terror, who combined a rare perceptiveness of human weakness with an ability to surround himself with very capable technical and administrative staff who compensated for his own lack of experience in police and intelligence work. By rewarding initiative and penalizing those who showed insufficient commitment, he created a terror apparatus whose radicalized staff and work ethos differed fundamentally from that of other Nazi and state institutions in its ideological drive and commitment.

Increasingly, Heydrich's mentality or worldview was unimpeded by the moral standards of bourgeois European society. The only ethical criteria that should influence conduct – or so he convinced himself – pertained to the welfare of the Aryan people and the good of the future Greater German Reich. The fate of non-Aryans was simply not a factor to be taken into consideration when making or implementing policy. The realization of Hitler's utopian society, so he firmly believed, required the ruthless and violent exclusion of those elements deemed dangerous to German society, a task that could best be carried out by the SS as the uncompromising executioner of Hitler's will. Only by cleansing German society of all that was alien, sick and hostile could a new 'national community' and 'better world' emerge – a world dominated by a racially purified German people.

Heydrich's willingness to use violence in realizing this vision was partly a result of his personal circumstances. Ever since the First World War, he had lived in a world surrounded by, and suffused with, violence: he had experienced war and revolution as a teenager, only to enter the military and subsequently join the SS, whose primary purpose consisted in violently suppressing political enemies. Nonetheless, the cleansing mechanisms envisaged by Heydrich radicalized dramatically between 1933 and 1942, partly in response to new political circumstances after the outbreak and escalation of war in 1939 and partly as a result of his rapid ascent in the SS hierarchy and the intoxicating sense of historic opportunity that gripped him after the outbreak of the Second World War. While the mass extermination of Jews seemed inconceivable even to Heydrich before the outbreak of war in 1939, his views on the matter altered significantly over the following two and a half years. A combination of wartime brutalization, frustration over failed expulsion schemes, pressures from local German administrators in the occupied East and an ideologically motivated determination to solve the Jewish problem once and for all led to a situation in which he perceived systematic mass murder to be both feasible and desirable.

It is of course a matter of speculation how Heydrich's career would have progressed had he survived the assassination attempt of May 1942. There is little doubt that, for the short time the Third Reich had left, the mounting pressure of resistance in occupied Europe strengthened those within the Nazi movement who, like Heydrich, advocated a tough and radical response to resistance organizations. There is similarly no question that he would have wholeheartedly supported the further escalation of genocidal policies in the occupied East and the violent suppression of the German resistance in July 1944. Yet, as was the case with his rise, his fall, too, would have been conditioned by developments and events beyond his control. Had he survived the assassination attempt of May 1942, Heydrich's life would have ended either in suicide in 1945 or at the War Criminals' Tribunal in Nuremberg, where his conviction as a mass murderer and perpetrator of crimes against humanity is beyond doubt.

Such a verdict would have reflected the fact that Heydrich was far more than a career-orientated desk perpetrator in the Nazi dictatorship. He played a decisive role in developing and promoting the notion of an illusive conglomerate of political and racial enemies that could be defeated only by an ever-expanding terror apparatus that was unconfined by any laws. As the executor of Nazi terror policies and the final solution until 1942, he was intimately involved in all crucial decision-making processes that led to the destruction of European Jewry and the murder of hundreds of thousands of Poles, Ukrainians, Russians, Czechs and Germans deemed politically or racially dangerous. Heydrich's central role in devising these policies, and his degree of 'success' in implementing them, makes him one of the key figures of the Third Reich and its murderous policies of persecution. This alone demands an effort to understand the events and forces that shaped his life, from its origins in a highly cultured and stable bourgeois household to its violent ending at one of the darkest moments in Europe's history.

Notes

Abbreviations

AMV   Archive of the Ministry of the Interior
DÖW   Dokumentationsarchiv des Österreichischen Widerstandes, Vienna
GStA   Geheimes Staatsarchiv, Berlin
IfZ   Institut für Zeitgeschichte, Munich
IMT   *International Military Tribunal, Nuremberg*, 42 vols (Nuremberg, 1947–9)
OA   Osoby Archive
PAAA   Politisches Archiv des Auswärtigen Amtes, Berlin
StaH   Stadtarchiv Halle
USHMMA   United States Holocaust Memorial Museum Archive
VfZ   *Vierteljahrshefte für Zeitgeschichte*

Introduction

1. The most widely known popular accounts of the Heydrich assassination are Callum MacDonald, *The Killing of SS Obergruppenführer Reinhard Heydrich: 27 May 1942* (London, 1992); Hellmut Haasis, *Tod in Prag. Das Attentat auf Reinhard Heydrich* (Reinbek, 2002); Miroslav Ivanov, *Der Henker von Prag. Das Attentat auf Heydrich* (Berlin, 1993); Jiří Fiedler, *Atentát 1942* (Brno, 2002); Michal Burian, Aleš Knížek, Jiří Rajlich and Eduard Stehlík, *Assassination: Operation Anthropoid 1941–1942* (Prague, 2002). For a helpful survey of the extensive Czech literature on the assassination up until 1991, see Zdeněk Jelínek, 'K problematice atentátu na Reinharda Heydricha', *Historie a vojenství* 40 (1991), 65–101.
2. On Himmler, see Peter Longerich, *Heinrich Himmler. Biographie* (Munich, 2008); Richard Breitman, *The Architect of Genocide: Himmler and the Final Solution* (New York, 1991); Peter R. Black, *Ernst Kaltenbrunner: Ideological Soldier of the Third Reich* (Princeton, NJ, 1984); on Best, Ulrich Herbert, *Best. Biographische Studien über Radikalismus, Weltanschauung und Vernunft, 1903–1989* (Bonn, 1996); on Eichmann, David Cesarani, *Becoming Eichmann: Rethinking the Life, Crimes and Trial of a Desk Murderer* (Cambridge, MA, 2006).
3. Shlomo Aronson, 'Heydrich und die Anfänge des SD und der Gestapo, 1931–1935', PhD thesis, FU Berlin, 1967; subsequently published as Shlomo Aronson, *Reinhard Heydrich und die Frühgeschichte von Gestapo und SD* (Stuttgart, 1971). See, too, the shorter essays of Charles Sydnor, 'Reinhard Heydrich. Der "ideale Nationalsozialist"', in Ronald Smelser and Enrico Syring (eds), *Die SS. Elite unter dem Totenkopf. 30 Lebensläufe* (Paderborn, 2000), 208–19; idem, 'Executive Instinct: Reinhard Heydrich and the Planning for the Final Solution', in Michael Berenbaum and Abraham Peck (eds), *The Holocaust and History: The Known, the Unknown, the Disputed and the Re-examined* (Bloomington, IN, 1998), 159–86.

4. Charles Whiting, *Heydrich: Henchman of Death* (Barnsley, 1999); Charles Wighton, *Heydrich: Hitler's Most Evil Henchman* (London, 1962); Günther Deschner, *Heydrich: The Pursuit of Total Power* (London, 1981); Edouard Calic, *Reinhard Heydrich: The Chilling Story of the Man Who Masterminded the Nazi Death Camps* (New York, 1985); Mario Dederichs, *Heydrich: The Face of Evil* (London, 2006); Joachim Fest, 'The Successor', in idem, *The Face of the Third Reich: Portraits of the Nazi Leadership* (New York, 1970), 98–114.

5. Carl Jacob Burckhardt, *Meine Danziger Mission, 1937–1939* (Munich, 1960), 57.

6. Statement on Heydrich by Dr Werner Best, 1 October 1959: IfZ, ZS 207/2.

7. Wolff's post-war testimony: IfZ, ZS 317, ff. 34f.; Walter Schellenberg, *The Labyrinth: The Memoirs of Hitler's Secret Service Chief* (London, 1956), 36. For a similar account, see Walter Hagen (alias Wilhelm Höttl), *Die geheime Front. Organisation, Personen und Aktionen des deutschen Geheimdienstes* (Linz and Vienna, 1950), 27; on Höttl and his account, see Thorsten Querg, 'Wilhelm Höttl – Vom Informanten zum Sturmbannführer im Sicherheitsdienst der SS', in Barbara Danckwortt, Thorsten Querg and Claudia Schöningh (eds), *Historische Rassismusforschung. Ideologie – Täter – Opfer* (Hamburg and Berlin, 1995), 208–30.

8. Hagen, *Geheime Front*, 21.

9. Felix Kersten, *Totenkopf und Treue – Heinrich Himmler ohne Uniform* (Hamburg, 1952), 128. See, too, the memoirs of Hans Bernd Gisevius, *Bis zum bitteren Ende. Bericht eines Augenzeugen aus den Machtzentren des Dritten Reiches* (Hamburg, 1954), 118.

10. Hugh Trevor-Roper, 'Introduction', Felix Kersten, *The Kersten Memoirs, 1940–1945*, ed. Hugh Trevor-Roper (London, 1957); Fest, 'Successor', 139ff.; Karl Dietrich Bracher, *The German Dictatorship: The Origins, Structure, and Consequences of National Socialism* (New York, 1970), 60. The myth of Heydrich's alleged Jewish family background continues to resurface periodically. See Dederichs, *Heydrich*, 69; Michael Puntenius, 'Das Gesicht des Terrors. Reinhard Heydrich (1904–1942)', in idem, *Gelehrte, Weltanschauer, auch Poeten. Literarische Porträts berühmter Hallenser* (Halle, 2006), 199–201, here 200; and Paula Diehl, *Macht – Mythos – Utopie. Die Körperbilder der SS-Männer* (Berlin, 2005), 163, n. 51. The myth of Heydrich's Jewish descent has been convincingly disproved by Aronson, *Frühgeschichte*, 18f., 24, 63f.; and Karin Flachowsky, 'Neue Quellen zur Abstammung Reinhard Heydrichs', *VfZ* 48 (2000), 319–27.

11. Fest, 'Successor', 139. On the idea that Heydrich wanted to succeed Hitler, see, too, Horst Naudé, *Erlebnisse und Erkenntnisse als politischer Beamter im Protektorat Böhmen und Mähren* (Berlin, 1975), 145; and Gisevius, *Bis zum bitteren Ende*, 264.

12. Hannah Arendt, *Eichmann in Jerusalem: A Report on the Banality of Evil* (London, 1963).

13. The most influential interpretation along these lines was Raul Hilberg, *The Destruction of the European Jews* (London, 1961).

14. Cesarani, *Eichmann*, 4; the best known example is Zygmunt Baumann, *Modernity and the Holocaust* (Ithaca, NY, 1989).

15. Deschner, *Heydrich*. The myth of Heydrich's lack of ideological conviction originated in Werner Best's post-war statement on Heydrich of 1 October 1959: IfZ, ZS 207/2.

16. Jens Banach, *Heydrichs Elite. Das Führerkorps der Sicherheitspolizei und des SD, 1936–1945* (Paderborn, 1996); George C. Browder, *Hitler's Enforcers: The Gestapo and the SS Security Service in the Nazi Revolution* (New York, 1996); Friedrich Wilhelm, *Die Polizei im NS-Staat. Die Geschichte ihrer Organisation im Überblick* (2nd edn, Paderborn, 1999); Herbert, *Best*; Klaus-Michael Mallmann and Gerhard Paul (eds), *Karrieren der Gewalt. Nationalsozialistische Täterbiographien* (Darmstadt, 2004); Michael Wildt, *Generation des Unbedingten. Das Führungskorps des Reichssicherheitshauptamtes* (Hamburg, 2002); Cesarani, *Eichmann*; Götz Aly and Susanne Heim, *Vordenker der Vernichtung. Auschwitz und die deutschen Pläne für eine europäische Ordnung* (Frankfurt am Main, 1993); Harald Welzer, *Täter. Wie aus ganz normalen Menschen Massenmörder werden* (Frankfurt am Main, 2005).

17. Edouard Calic, *Reinhard Heydrich. Schlüsselfigur des Dritten Reiches* (Düsseldorf, 1982).

18. Peter Hüttenberger, 'Nationalsozialistische Polykratie', *Geschichte und Gesellschaft* 2 (1976), 417–42; Hans Mommsen, 'The Realization of the Unthinkable: The "Final Solution of the Jewish Question" in the Third Reich', in Gerhard Hirschfeld (ed.), *The Policies of Genocide: Jews and Soviet Prisoners of War in Nazi Germany* (London, 1986); Martin Broszat, 'Hitler und die "Endlösung". Aus Anlass der Thesen von David Irving', *VfZ* 25 (1977), 739–75; Ian

Kershaw, '"Working towards the Führer": Reflections on the Nature of the Hitler Dictatorship', *Contemporary European History* 2 (1993), 103–18.

19. For clear and carefully argued syntheses, see Christopher R. Browning, *The Origins of the Final Solution: The Evolution of Nazi Jewish Policy, September 1939–March 1942* (Lincoln, NB, 2004); Peter Longerich, *Politik der Vernichtung. Eine Gesamtdarstellung der nationalsozialistischen Judenverfolgung* (Munich and Zurich, 1998); Saul Friedländer, *Nazi Germany and the Jews*, vol. 1: *The Years of Persecution, 1933–1939*, and vol. 2: *The Years of Extermination, 1939–1945* (New York, 1997 and 2007); Donald Bloxham, *The Final Solution: A Genocide* (Oxford, 2009).

20. Cesarani, *Eichmann*, 5.

21. Aly and Heim, *Vordenker*; Karl Heinz Roth, 'Konrad Meyers erster "Generalplan Ost" (April/Mai 1940)', *Mitteilungen der Dokumentationsstelle zur NS-Sozialpolitik* 1 (1985), 45–52; Isabel Heinemann, '*Rasse, Siedlung, deutsches Blut'. Das Rasse- und Siedlungshauptamt der SS und die rassenpolitische Neuordnung Europas* (Göttingen, 2003).

22. Longerich, *Himmler*, 766.

Chapter I: Death in Prague

1. Deschner, *Heydrich*, 240.

2. MacDonald, *Killing*; Haasis, *Tod*; Ivanov, *Henker*; Burian et al., *Assassination*; Fiedler, *Atentát 1942*; Chad Bryant, *Prague in Black: Nazi Rule and Czech Nationalism* (Cambridge, MA, 2007), 167ff.

3. Extensive material on the planning of the assassination issue can be found in SOE's 'Detailed Report on Operation Anthropoid' (30 May 1942), in National Archives, Kew, HS 4/39, as well as in the German Criminal Police's own extensive investigative report of 1942, in BAB, R 58/336.

4. National Archives, Kew, HS 4/79.

5. Frantisek Moravec, *Master of Spies: The Memoirs of General Frantisek Moravec* (Garden City, NY, 1975), 196. On Beneš, see Zbyněk Zeman, *The Life of Edvard Beneš 1884–1948: Czechoslovakia in Peace and War* (Oxford, 1997).

6. On Beneš's post-war ambitions, see Richard J. Crampton, 'Edvard Beneš', in Steven Casey and Jonathan Wright (eds), *Mental Maps in the Era of the Two World Wars* (Basingstoke, 2008), 135–56.

7. IfZ, OKW T-77/1050, 6526169–70, NA.

8. MacDonald, *Killing*, 97, 118ff., 142f.; Detlef Brandes, *Die Tschechen unter deutschem Protektorat*, 2 vols (Munich, 1969 and 1975), vol. 1, 251ff. See, too, Václav Kural, *Vlastenci proti okupaci. Ústřední vedení odboje domácího 1940–1943* (Prague, 1997); Jan Němeček, 'Německá okupační politika v protektorátu a český protiněmecký odpor', in *Historické, právní a mezinárodní souvislosti Dekretů prezidenta republiky* (Prague, 2003), 21–40.

9. Hugh Dalton, *The Second World War Diary of Hugh Dalton 1940–1945*, ed. Ben Pimlott (London, 1986), 329.

10. Stephen Twigge, Edward Hampshire and Graham Macklin, *British Intelligence: Secrets, Spies and Sources* (Kew, 2008), 167–210.

11. National Archives, Kew, HS 4/79. On the SOE in Czechoslovakia, see Michael R. D. Foot, *SOE: An Outline History of the Special Operations Executive, 1940–1946* (London, 1984), 199–202; Twigge et al., *British Intelligence*, 167–210.

12. National Archives, Kew, HS 4/79; Lieutenant Colonel Peter Wilkinson, Staff Officer, Czech–Polish Section, SOE HQ, London, as quoted in Roderick Bailey, *Forgotten Voices of the Secret War: An Inside History of Special Operations during the Second World War* (London, 2008), 111.

13. Hansjürgen Köhler, *Inside the Gestapo: Hitler's Shadow over Europe* (London, 1941), extracts in Heydrich's SOE file, National Archives, Kew, WO 208/4472.

14. National Archives, Kew, HS 4/39.

15. Peter Wilkinson (MX) to Colin Gubbins (M), and Peter Wilkinson (MX) to AD/P, 25 July 1942, in National Archives, Kew, HS 4/39; and National Archives, Kew, HS 4/79.

16. Whiting, *Henchman*, 268.

17. Their 'last wills' are reprinted in Burian et al., *Assassination*, 44.

18. The arrival of the parachutists was subsequently reconstructed by the German Criminal Police in minute detail. See their final report on the assassination, in BAB, R 58/336.
19. Bryant, *Prague in Black*, 167f.
20. 'Totenbuch des SS-Standortarztes Mauthausen', 24 October 1942, in KZ-Gedenkstätte Mauthausen, AMM Y/46.
21. MacDonald, *Killing*, 142f.; Ladislav Vaněk, *Atentát na Heydricha* (Prague, 1962).
22. Bartoš to Czech government-in-exile, report of 3 February 1942, in National Archives, Kew, HS 4/39. Bryant, *Prague*, 168. On Silver A, Silver B and other missions, see Zdeněk Jelínek, *Operace Silver A* (Prague, 1992); Jan Břećka, *Silver B neodpovídá. Historie čs. paraskupiny z Velké Británie v letech 2. světové války* (Brno, 2004); Marie Matušů, *Muži pro speciální operace* (Prague, 2004).
23. Brandes, *Tschechen*, vol. 1, 247ff.; MacDonald, *Killing*, 146f., 199; Bryant, *Prague*, 168.
24. MacDonald, *Killing*, 155.
25. Vojtech Mastny, *The Czechs under Nazi Rule: The Failure of National Resistance, 1939–42* (New York, 1971), 156; Brandes, *Tschechen*, vol. 1, 252.
26. ÚVOD to Czech government-in-exile, transmitted on 11 May 1942, in National Archives, Kew, HS 4/39. The message was intercepted by the Gestapo, but obviously not taken seriously enough to implement additional security measures for Heydrich.
27. Beneš to ÚVOD, 15 May 1942, as quoted in Mastny, *Czechs*, 209.
28. Dossier for SOE leadership and War Office, 4 March 1942, in National Archives, Kew, HS 4/79.
29. Ivanov, *Henker*, 229f.
30. The German Criminal Police undertook a thorough investigation of the case after Heydrich's death and established a detailed reconstruction of the events of 27 May 1942. See Stanislav F. Berton, 'Das Attentat auf Reinhard Heydrich vom 27. Mai 1942. Ein Bericht des Kriminalrats Heinz Pannwitz', *VfZ* 33 (1985), 668–706.
31. Ibid., 690f.
32. MacDonald, *Killing*, 166–7, 171–3; Burian et al., *Assassination*, 65. See, too, Hans-Ulrich Stoldt, 'Operation Anthropoid', in Stephan Burgdorff (ed.), *Der Zweite Weltkrieg. Wendepunkte der deutschen Geschichte* (Munich, 2005), 171–5; Peter Witte et al. (eds), *Der Dienstkalender Heinrich Himmlers 1941/42* (Hamburg, 1999), 27 May 1942, p. 438. Over the following days, Gebhardt delivered daily telephone reports on Heydrich's condition to Himmler: Witte et al. (eds), *Dienstkalender*, 438ff.
33. SD report 'Meldungen aus dem Reich' no. 287, 28 May 1942, ff. 4ff., and report no. 288 of 1 June 1942, 3ff. in: BAB, R58/172. See, too: Mastny, *Czechs*, 215; Brandes, *Tschechen*, vol. 1, 256.
34. *Völkischer Beobachter*, 27 May 1942.
35. Joseph Goebbels, *Die Tagebücher von Joseph Goebbels*, ed. Elke Fröhlich (Munich, 1995), part II, vol. 4, 386.
36. IfZ, Ed 450; Himmler's telegram to Frank, 27 May 1942, in Miroslav Kárný, Jaroslava Milotová and Margita Kárná (eds), *Deutsche Politik im 'Protektorat Böhmen und Mähren' unter Reinhard Heydrich 1941–1942* (Berlin, 1997), doc. 104, p. 280. See, too, Brandes, *Tschechen*, vol. 1, 254f.
37. See Karl Hermann Frank's protocol of his meeting with Hitler on 28 May 1945, in Kárný et al. (eds), *Deutsche Politik*, doc. 106, pp. 282–90, here pp. 283–5.
38. *Verordnungsblatt des Reichsprotektors in Böhmen und Mähren* 19 (28 May 1942), 123f.; Brandes, *Tschechen*, vol. 1, 254f. The reward is mentioned in Goebbels's diary. See *Tagebücher*, part II, vol. 4, 386.
39. See the official announcement of 29 May 1942, in National Archives, Prague, Úřad říšského protektora (Office of the Reich Protector), supplement 1, carton 53.
40. See the final report on the police operation by Dr Geschke, 24 June 1942, in Archive of the Ministry of the Interior, Prague, 301-5-4. See, too, Berton, 'Attentat', 683.
41. See the long list of informers and sums paid to them in exchange for information in Archive of the Ministry of the Interior, Prague, 315-194-30.
42. Beneš to Bartoš, as quoted in Brandes, *Tschechen*, vol. 1, 254. See, too, Beneš's public declaration of 29 May 1942, in National Archives, Kew, HS 4/79.
43. Witte et al. (eds), *Dienstkalender*, 440ff. (reports by Prof. Gebhardt and entry for 31 May 1941). See, too, Lina Heydrich, *Leben mit einem Kriegsverbrecher* (Pfaffenhofen, 1976), 6.

44. Goebbels, *Tagebücher*, part II, vol. 4, 432.
45. Military intelligence report of 27 May 1942, in National Archives, Kew, WO 208/4472.
46. See the post-mortem protocol by Prof. Weyrich (17 June 1942), in Archive of the Institute for Judicial Medicine, Prague. See, too, Witte et al. (eds), *Dienstkalender*, 3 June 1942, p. 448; Thomas Mann, 'Nachruf auf einen Henker' (June 1942), in: Thomas Mann, *Essays*, vol. 5: *Deutschland und die Deutschen 1938–1945*, ed. Hermann Kurzke and Stephan Stachorski (Frankfurt am Main, 1997), 185f and 373f.

Chapter II: Young Reinhard

1. The birth was publicly announced in the local newspaper, *Hallescher Central-Anzeiger*, on 10 March 1904.
2. Baptismal register, 1904, St Franziskus und Elisabeth Kirche, Halle, p. 356, entry no. 154. A copy of the baptism certificate can be found in StaH, Handschriftenabteilung J 36. See, too, Aronson, *Frühgeschichte*, 320.
3. Perceptions of Wilhelmine Germany have changed dramatically since the late 1990s. For an account focusing on its dark sides, see Volker Ullrich, *Die nervöse Grossmacht. Aufstieg und Untergang des Kaiserreiches, 1871–1918* (3rd edn, 2007). For subsequent accounts emphasizing Imperial Germany's modernity, see Sven Oliver Müller and Cornelius Torp (eds), *Imperial Germany Revisited: Continuing Debates and New Perspectives* (Oxford and New York, 2010); Dominik Geppert and Robert Gerwarth (eds), *Wilhelmine Germany and Edwardian Britain: Essays on Cultural Affinity* (Oxford, 2008).
4. 'Gutachten über die rassische Herkunft des Oberleutnant z. See a.D. Reinhardt Heydrich', 22 June 1932, in BAB, BDC, SSO Reinhard Heydrich. See, too, Flachowsky, 'Abstammung', 325.
5. Bruno Heydrich, 'Bericht zum zehnjährigen Bestehen von Bruno Heydrichs Konservatorium für Musik und Theater, I. Hallesches Konservatorium', 1909, in StaH, Akten der Schulverwaltung, 118, vol. II; Flachowsky, 'Abstammung', 325.
6. Heydrich, 'Bericht', in StaH, Akten der Schulverwaltung, 118, vol. II.
7. Heydrich, *Kriegsverbrecher*, 6.
8. Ibid., 7f. and 17. On Cosima Wagner, see Oliver Hilmes, *Herrin des Hügels. Das Leben der Cosima Wagner* (Munich, 2007).
9. Aronson, *Frühgeschichte*, 30.
10. Bruno Walter, *Thema und Variationen. Erinnerungen und Gedanken* (Stockholm, 1947), 117.
11. Quotations from Dr Otto Reitzel, Cöln am Rhein and Prof. Bulthaupt, Bremen, in 'Pressstimmen über meine Thätigkeit als Sänger, Componist, Dirigent', in StaH, Akten der Schulverwaltung, 118, vol. I.
12. Hans Pfitzner, *Reden, Schriften, Briefe. Unveröffentlichtes und bisher Verstreutes* (Berlin, 1955), 240. On Pfitzner's role in the Third Reich, see Sabine Busch, *Hans Pfitzner und der Nationalsozialismus* (Stuttgart, 2001). On his relationship with Bruno Heydrich, see John W. Klein, 'Hans Pfitzner and the Two Heydrichs', *Music Review* 26 (1965), 308–17.
13. See, for example, the comments of Carl Wolff, 22 September 1895, in StaH, Akten der Schulverwaltung, 118, vol. I.
14. Heydrich, *Kriegsverbrecher*, 15–19; see, too, the anonymous letter of a schoolfriend of Reinhard Heydrich, written to publisher W. Ludwig, in response to the publication of Lina Heydrich's memoirs, in IfZ, Ed 450.
15. SS-Ahnentafel Heinz Siegfried Heydrichs, in BAB, (BDC), RS (Rasse- und-Siedlungshauptamt); see, too, Aronson, *Frühgeschichte*, 15f.
16. All quotations from the brochure *Grosser populärer Erfolg von 'Frieden', Oper (Elegie) in 3 Akten (4 Bildern)* (Halle, 1907), in StaH, Akten der Schulverwaltung, 118, vol. I.
17. '13., 14. und 15. Jahresbericht von Bruno Heydrichs Konservatorium für Musik und Theater, Halle 1915', in StaH, Akten der Schulverwaltung, 118, vol. II. See, too, Aronson, *Frühgeschichte*, 21; Hugo Riemann, *Riemanns Musik-Lexikon* (8th edn, Berlin and Leipzig, 1916), vol. 1.
18. On the general population trend, see Hans-Ulrich Wehler, *Deutsche Gesellschaftsgeschichte*, vol. 3: *Von der deutschen Doppelrevolution bis zum Beginn des Ersten Weltkrieges, 1849–1914* (2nd edn, Munich, 2007), 724ff.; Jürgen Reulecke, *Geschichte der Urbanisierung in*

Deutschland (Frankfurt am Main, 1985), 68ff. On Halle more specifically, see Werner Freitag, Katrin Minner and Andreas Ranft (eds), *Geschichte der Stadt Halle*, vol. 2: *Halle im 19. und 20. Jahrhundert* (Halle an der Saale, 2006), 18f., 33f., Mathias Tullner, *Halle 1806 bis 2006. Industriezentrum, Regierungssitz, Bezirksstadt. Eine Einführung in die Stadtgeschichte* (Halle an der Salle, 2007), 40ff.

19. On the general trend, see Matthew Jefferies, *Imperial Culture in Germany, 1871–1918* (Basingstoke and New York, 2003); Carl Dahlhaus, *Nineteenth-Century Music* (Berkeley, CA, 1989); Walter Frisch, *German Modernism: Music and the Arts* (Berkeley, CA., 2005); Celia Applegate, 'Culture and the Arts', in James Retallack, *Imperial Germany, 1871–1918* (Oxford, 2008), 106–27. On Halle more specifically Andrea Hauser, *Halle wird Grossstadt. Stadtplanung, Grossstadtleben und Raumerfahrungen in Halle an der Saale 1870 bis 1914* (Halle an der Saale, 2006), 21; Tullner, *Halle*, 51.

20. Konrad Sasse, 'Aus Halles Musikleben von der Mitte des 19. Jahrhunderts bis 1945', in Rat der Stadt Halle (ed.), *Halle als Musikstadt* (Halle an der Saale, 1954), 40–52, here 44.

21. Aronson, *Frühgeschichte*, 16.

22. Freitag et al., *Halle*, 46; Aronson, *Frühgeschichte*, 20 and 259, n. 44. On the Masonic Lodge of the Three Sabres, see Gustav Friedrich Hertzberg, *Geschichte der Freimaurerloge zu den drei Degen im Orient von Halle* (Halle, 1893, reprint 1907). '11. und 12. Jahresbericht des Konservatoriums von Bruno Heydrich', 1., in StaH, Akten der Schulverwaltung, 118, vol. I.

23. Freitag et al. (eds), *Halle*, 46; Aronson, *Frühgeschichte*, 16 and 20, n. 45. 'Bericht zum 10jährigen Bestehen von Bruno Heydrichs Konservatorium für Musik und Theater (1909)', 9, vol. II, and '11. und 12. Jahresbericht des Konservatoriums von Bruno Heydrich (1911)', 3f., in StaH, Akten der Schulverwaltung, 118, vol. I.

24. Aronson, *Frühgeschichte*, 15f. and 25. On Luckner, see Norbert von Frankenstein, *'Seeteufel' Felix Graf Luckner. Wahrheit und Legende* (Hamburg, 1997).

25. Ute Frevert, *Women in German History: From Bourgeois Emancipation to Sexual Liberation* (Oxford and Washington, DC, 1990) and the brief overview provided by Angelika Schaser, 'Gendered Germany', in Retallack (ed.), *Imperial Germany*, 128–50; Christian Berg, 'Familie, Kindheit, Jugend', in *Handbuch der deutschen Bildungsgeschichte*, vol. IV, 91–139, here 99ff.

26. Hauser, *Halle*, 22f.; 'Bericht zum 10jährigen Bestehen von Bruno Heydrichs Konservatorium für Musik und Theater, 1. Hallesches Konservatorium (1909)', in StaH, Akten der Schulverwaltung, 118, vol. I.

27. Heydrich, *Kriegsverbrecher*, 113; Aronson, *Frühgeschichte*, 32.

28. Christopher Clark, 'Religion and Confessional Conflict', in Retallack (ed.), *Imperial Germany*, 83–105.

29. Chris Clark, 'Religion and confessional conflict' in Retallack, *Imperial Germany*, 83–105; Olaf Blaschke and Frank-Michael Kuhlemann (eds), *Religion im Kaiserreich. Milieus – Mentalitäten – Krisen* (Gütersloh, 1996).

30. Heydrich, *Kriegsverbrecher*, 56.

31. Heinrich Silbergleit (ed.), *Preussens Städte. Denkschrift zum 100jährigen Jubiläum der Städteordnung vom 19. November 1808* (Berlin, 1908), 61.

32. Dederichs, *Heydrich*, 33; Aronson, *Frühgeschichte*, 16 and 20; Herbert Edler von Daniels, 'Reinhard Heydrich als nationalsozialistischer Leibeserzieher', *Leibesübungen und körperliche Erziehung* 61 (1942), 114–17; Heydrich, *Kriegsverbrecher*, 24; Berno Bahro, 'Reinhard Heydrich und Hermann Fegelein. Sportler – Soldaten – Helden', *Stadion. Internationale Zeitschrift für Geschichte des Sports* 31 (2007), 111–30.

33. Lina later maintained that these experiences captured young Reinhard's imagination to the extent that he decided to become a naval officer. See Heydrich, *Kriegsverbrecher*, 22f.

34. 'Bericht zum 10jährigen Bestehen von Bruno Heydrichs Konservatorium für Musik und Theater (1909)', in StaH, Akten der Schulverwaltung, 118, vol. I, f. 18.

35. '11. und 12. Jahresbericht des Konservatoriums von Bruno Heydrich (1911)', 3–4, in StaH, Akten der Schulverwaltung, 118, vol. I.

36. Anonymous letter of a schoolfriend of Reinhard Heydrich, written to publisher W. Ludwig, in response to the publication of Lina Heydrich's memoirs, in IfZ, Ed 450. See, too, Lina Heydrich to Peter Schneiders (Amsterdam), 12 January 1962, in NIOD, doc. I, 691A. On the house's location, see Steffen Mikolajczyk, 'Eine aufstrebende Industriestadt huldigt der Monarchie. Der Kaiserbesuch 1903', in Werner Freitag and Katrin Minner (eds), *Vergnügen*

und Inszenierung. Stationen städtischer Festkultur in Halle (Halle an der Saale, 2004), 206–13; Hauser, *Halle*, 105ff.

37. 'Bericht zum 10jährigen Bestehen von Bruno Heydrichs Konservatorium für Musik und Theater, 1. Hallesches Konservatorium (Staatl. Genehmigte Anstalt)' (Halle, 1909), 17, in StaH, Akten der Schulverwaltung, 118, vol. I, f. 13.

38. Andrew Donson, *Youth in the Fatherless Land: War Pedagogy, Nationalism and Authority in Germany, 1914–1918* (Cambridge, MA, 2010), 22f.

39. Angelika Schaser, 'Gendered Germany', in Retallack, *Imperial Germany*, 128–50, here 133f.

40. Deschner, *Heydrich*, 26; Maria Heydrich's post-war testimony, according to which her brother read only adventure books, including spy and crime novels. See Aronson, *Frühgeschichte*, 19.

41. On German public opinion in August 1914, see Jeffrey Verhey, *The Spirit of 1914: Militarism, Myth and Mobilization in Germany* (Cambridge, 2000); Steffen Bruendel, *Volksgemeinschaft oder Volksstaat. Die 'Ideen von 1914' und die Neuordnung Deutschlands im Ersten Weltkrieg* (Berlin, 2003).

42. On the 'war youth generation', see Donson, *Youth*; Herbert, *Best*, particularly pp. 42ff.; Wildt, *Generation*. One of the best and earliest descriptions of the wartime children's games can be found in Sebastian Haffner, *Geschichte eines Deutschen. Die Erinnerungen 1914–1933* (4th edn, Stuttgart, 2000), 22. Haffner was the first to make the important observation that the male wartime generation itself produced fewer radical Nazis than the war youth generation.

43. '13., 14. und 15. Jahresbericht des Konservatoriums von Bruno Heydrich' (Halle, 1915), 4ff., in StaH, Akten der Schulverwaltung, 118, vol. II. On knitting as a widespread female expression of patriotism, see Donson, *Youth*, 85.

44. Donson, *Youth*, 125.

45. Deschner, *Heydrich*, 23f. (based on Erich Schulze's post-war testimony).

46. Alexander Rehding, *Hugo Riemann and the Birth of Modern Musical Thought* (Cambridge, 2003).

47. Aronson, *Frühgeschichte*, 18.

48. Ibid., 15.

49. Post-war testimony of Heydrich's sister-in-law, Gertrude Heydrich, as quoted in ibid., 19 and 15, n. 21; see, too, Deschner, *Heydrich*, 22 and 74.

50. Dederichs, *Heydrich*, 45. On the Jewish population of Halle in 1910, see Heinrich Silbergleit, *Die Bevölkerungs- und Berufsverhältnisse der Juden im Deutschen Reich* (Berlin, 1930), 24.

51. The literature on this subject is unsurprisingly vast. As a classic overview, see Peter G. Pulzer, *Die Entstehung des politischen Antisemitismus in Deutschland und Österreich 1867–1914* (2nd edn, Göttingen, 2004); Stefan Scheil, *Die Entwicklung des politischen Antisemitismus in Deutschland zwischen 1881 und 1912* (Berlin, 1999); Massimo Ferrari Zumbini, *Die Wurzeln des Bösen. Gründerjahre des Antisemitismus. Von der Bismarckzeit zu Hitler* (Frankfurt am Main, 2003); Olaf Blaschke, *Katholizismus und Antisemitismus im Deutschen Kaiserreich* (Göttingen, 1997).

52. On propaganda during the war, see David Welch, *Germany, Propaganda and Total War, 1914–1918* (New Brunswick, NJ, 2000). On its effects on youths, see Donson, *Youth*, 176ff.

53. Heinrich August Winkler, 'Die Revolution von 1918/19 und das Problem der Kontinuität in der deutschen Geschichte', *Historische Zeitschrift* 250 (1990), 303–19. Fritz Klein, 'Between Compiègne and Versailles: The Germans on the Way from a Misunderstood Defeat to an Unwanted Peace', in Manfred F. Boemeke, Gerald D. Feldman and Elisabeth Glaser (eds), *The Treaty of Versailles: A Reassessment after 75 Years* (New York, 1998), 203–20. On the role of returning soldiers, see Scott Stevenson, *The Final Battle: Soldiers of the Western Front and the German Revolution of 1918* (Cambridge, 2009).

54. Georg Maercker, *Vom Kaiserheer zur Reichswehr. Geschichte des freiwilligen Landesjägerkorps. Ein Beitrag zur Geschichte der deutschen Revolution* (Leipzig, 1921).

55. Robert Gerwarth, 'The Central European Counter-Revolution: Paramilitary Violence in Germany, Austria and Hungary after the Great War', *Past and Present* 200 (2008), 175–209.

56. See Maercker's memoirs, *Vom Kaiserheer zur Reichswehr*.

57. Hans-Walter Schmuhl, 'Halle in der Weimarer Republik und im Nationalsozialismus', in Freitag et al. (eds), *Halle*, vol. 2, 237–302, here 237–48; see, too, the report of Halle's mayor, Oberbürgermeister Rive, of 11 April 1919, in StaH, Centralbüro Kap. I, Abt. B, no. 12, vol. I.

58. An identity card issued on 6 March 1919 shows that Heydrich was in the service of the 3rd Division of the Volunteer Landesjäger Regiment and the Halle citizens' militia. See BAB, R 58, annexe 21; BAB, BDC, SSO Reinhard Heydrich. See, too, Aronson, *Frühgeschichte*, 23ff., and Heydrich, *Kriegsverbrecher*, 23.

59. Gerwarth, 'Counter-Revolution'; Hagen Schulze, *Freikorps und Republik* (Boppard, 1968); Dirk Schumann, *Politische Gewalt in der Weimarer Republik. Kampf um die Strasse und Furcht vor dem Bürgerkrieg* (Essen, 2001).

60. Robert Waite, *Vanguard of Nazism: The Free Corps Movement in Postwar Germany, 1918–23* (Cambridge, MA, 1952).

61. Longerich, *Himmler*, 34.

62. Deschner, *Heydrich*, 22. On general responses of the war youth generation to the German defeat, see Donson, *Youth*, 239.

63. *Hallesche Nachrichten*, 30 March 1920, particularly the supplement 'Die Schreckenstage in Halle vom 13. bis 26. März 1920'; on the context, see Heinrich August Winkler, *Von der Revolution zur Stabilisierung. Arbeiter und Arbeiterbewegung in der Weimarer Republik 1918 bis 1924* (Berlin and Bonn, 1984), 515–20.

64. Aronson, *Frühgeschichte*, 23 and 259, n. 57.

65. Heydrich made this claim in his SS officer's file: BAB, BDC, SSO Reinhard Heydrich. On the League, see Stefan Breuer, *Die Völkischen in Deutschland. Kaiserreich und Weimarer Republik* (Darmstadt, 2008), 150–60.

66. BAB, BDC, SSO Reinhard Heydrich.

67. BAB, R 58, annexe 21. On the 'Deutsche Orden', see Uwe Puschner, *Die völkische Bewegung im wilhelminischen Kaiserreich. Sprache, Rasse, Religion* (Darmstadt, 2001), 237.

68. Helmut Kerstingjohänner, *Die deutsche Inflation, 1919–23. Politik und Ökonomie* (Frankfurt am Main, 2004); Gerald D. Feldman, *The Great Disorder: Politics, Economics and Society in the German Inflation 1914–1924* (Oxford, 1993); Evans, *The Coming of the Third Reich*, 103ff. Martin H. Geyer, *Verkehrte Welt. Revolution, Inflation und Moderne, München 1914–1924* (Göttingen, 1998); Aronson, *Frühgeschichte*, 12.

69. Anonymous letter of a schoolfriend of Reinhard Heydrich, written to publisher W. Ludwig, in response to the publication of Lina Heydrich's memoirs, in IfZ, Ed 450.

70. Bruno Heydrich's letter to the magistrate of the city of Halle, 6 July 1922, in StaH, Akten der Schulverwaltung, 118, vol. II. On the technological advances and cultural changes that Bruno Heydrich was referring to, see Elisabeth Harvey, 'Culture and Society in Weimar Germany: The Impact of Modernism and Mass Culture', in Mary Fulbrook (ed.), *Twentieth-Century Germany: Politics, Culture, and Society 1918–1990* (London, 2001), 279–97; Lynn Abrams, 'From Control to Commercialization: The Triumph of Mass Entertainment in Germany 1900–1925', *German History* 8 (1990), 278–93; Corey Ross, *Media and the Making of Modern Germany: Mass Communications, Society and Politics from the Empire to the Third Reich* (Oxford, 2008).

71. Aronson, *Frühgeschichte*, 23ff.; Deschner, *Heydrich*, 26f.

72. Heydrich, *Kriegsverbrecher*, 22f.; Aronson, *Frühgeschichte*, 25; Deschner, *Heydrich*, 27.

73. Aronson, *Frühgeschichte*, 25; Deschner, *Heydrich*, 27; Dederichs, *Heydrich*, 39f.

74. Deschner, *Heydrich*, 27 and 333, n. 3.

75. Heinz Lemmermann, *Kriegserziehung im Kaiserreich. Studien zur politischen Funktion von Schule und Schulmusik 1890–1918*, 2 vols (Liliental bei Bremen, 1984), vol. 2, 671; Donson, *Youth*, 54f.

76. Richard Bessel, 'The "Front Generation" and the Politics of Weimar Germany', in Mark Roseman (ed.), *Generations in Conflict: Youth Revolt and Generation Formation in Germany, 1770–1968* (Cambridge, 2003), 121–36.

77. On the 'shame' of 1918 and Scapa Flow, see Andreas Krause, *Scapa Flow. Die Selbstversenkung der wilhelminischen Flotte* (Berlin, 1999). On the Weimar navy, see Keith W. Bird, *Weimar, the German Naval Officer Corps and the Rise of National Socialism* (Amsterdam, 1977); Michael Salewski, *Die Deutschen und die See. Studien zur deutschen Marinegeschichte des 19. und 20. Jahrhunderts*, 2 vols (Stuttgart, 1998 and 2002), vol. 2, 102–14. On the image of German officers, see Ursula Breymayer and Bernd Ulrich (eds), *Willensmenschen. Über deutsche Offiziere* (Frankfurt am Main, 1999).

78. Aronson, *Frühgeschichte*, 25; Deschner, *Heydrich*, 27.

79. 'Deutsche Dienststelle für die Benachrichtigung der nächsten Angehörigen von Gefallenen der ehemaligen deutschen Wehrmacht (WASt)', 8 July 2009. See, too, Aronson, *Frühgeschichte*, 25, 27 and 259, n. 65; Deschner, *Heydrich*, 27; Dederichs, *Heydrich*, 40. On Mürwick Naval College, see Jörg Hillmann and Reinhard Scheiblich, *Das rote Schloss am Meer. Die Marineschule Mürwik seit ihrer Gründung* (Hamburg, 2002).

80. Post-war testimonies of Hans Rehm and Hans Heinrich Lebram, as quoted in Aronson, *Frühgeschichte*, 26f.; see, too, Deschner, *Heydrich*, 28. While Rehm described his own antipathy towards Heydrich as part of a general mood within their cadet group, Lina Heydrich suggested that Rehm was the only 'openly hostile' cadet in Heydrich's 'Crew 22'. Heydrich, *Kriegsverbrecher*, 23.

81. Beucke as quoted in Aronson, *Frühgeschichte*, 27f.; see, too, Deschner, *Heydrich*, 28.

82. Deschner, *Heydrich*, 29.

83. BAB, R 58, annexe 21; Lina Heydrich to Peter Schneiders (Amsterdam), 12 January 1962, NIOD, doc. I, 691A; Deschner, *Heydrich*, 30; Heydrich, *Kriegsverbrecher*, 22.

84. Heydrich, *Kriegsverbrecher*, 23.

85. Deschner, *Heydrich*, 28f.; Heydrich, *Kriegsverbrecher*, 23f.

86. Rehm's post-war testimony according to Aronson, *Frühgeschichte*, 26ff. and 260, n. 71. According to Dederichs and Calic, Heydrich was 'indoctrinated' by Canaris; see Dederichs, *Heydrich*, 42; Calic, *Heydrich*, 32–40, particularly 38.

87. Lina Heydrich as quoted in Aronson, *Frühgeschichte*, 34.

88. Aronson, *Frühgeschichte*, 28f.

89. Deschner, *Heydrich*, 30; see, too, Michael Müller, *Canaris. Hitlers Abwehrchef. Biographie* (Berlin, 2006), 123; Heinz Höhne, *Canaris. Patriot im Zwielicht* (Munich, 1976), 91; André Brissaud, *Canaris. Fürst des deutschen Geheimdienstes oder Meister des Doppelspiels?* (Frankfurt am Main, 1976), 26f.; Heydrich, *Kriegsverbrecher*, 24.

90. Lehmann-Jottkowitz, as quoted in Aronson, *Frühgeschichte*, 32.

91. Lebram's post-war testimony as quoted in ibid., 31; see, too, Deschner, *Heydrich*, 32f. Lebram's post-war account of Heydrich's lack of manners are somewhat unconvincing and are contradicted by other accounts. See, for example, the post-war account of his childhood friend Günther Gereke, as quoted in Calic, *Schlüsselfigur*, 48, and that of his fellow crew member Heinrich Beucke in Aronson, *Frühgeschichte*, 32 and 260, n. 80.

92. 'Deutsche Dienststelle für die Benachrichtigung der nächsten Angehörigen von Gefallenen der ehemaligen deutschen Wehrmacht (WASt)', 8 July 2009; see, too, Aronson, *Frühgeschichte*, 31.

93. Beucke, as quoted in Aronson, *Frühgeschichte*, 32.

94. Schultze as quoted in Deschner, *Heydrich*, 35.

95. Aronson, *Frühgeschichte*, 33; and the more 'colourful' description in Calic, *Heydrich*, 38.

96. Aronson, *Frühgeschichte*, 32 and 260, n. 80. Lebram and Lina Heydrich confirmed this assessment in their own post-war recollections. See Lebram's testimony in Aronson, *Frühgeschichte*, 33, and Heydrich, *Kriegsverbrecher*, 24.

97. Beucke, as quoted in Aronson, *Frühgeschichte*, 32 and 260, n. 80. See, too, Deschner, *Heydrich*, 34.

98. Christine Eisenberg, 'Massensport in der Weimarer Republik. Ein statistischer Überblick', *Archiv für Sozialgeschichte* 33 (1993), 137–77, here 147.

99. Calic, *Heydrich*, 35; Dederichs, *Heydrich*, 44.

100. Gustav Kleikamp's letter in *Der Spiegel*, 9/1950 (2 March 1950), 42.

101. Beucke, as quoted in Aronson, *Frühgeschichte*, 32 and 260, n. 80.

102. Lebram, as quoted in ibid., 49.

103. Beucke, as quoted in ibid., 32 and 260, n. 80.

104. Ibid., 53.

105. Ibid., 34; Heydrich, *Kriegsverbrecher*, 12ff.

106. Heydrich, *Kriegsverbrecher*, 7f.; Dederichs, *Heydrich*, 30f.

107. Heydrich, *Kriegsverbrecher*, 9; Dederichs, *Heydrich*, 49.

108. Heydrich, *Kriegsverbrecher*, 10f.; Deschner, *Heydrich*, 37; Dederichs, *Heydrich*, 50.

109. Reinhard Heydrich to Lina von Osten, 18 December 1930, in IfZ, Ed 450.

110. Aronson, *Frühgeschichte*, 34; Deschner, *Heydrich*, 37. On the social decline and political radicalization of the German aristocracy, see Stephan Malinowski, *Vom König zum Führer. Deutscher Adel und Nationalsozialismus* (Frankfurt am Main, 2003).

111. Lina Heydrich as quoted in Aronson, *Frühgeschichte*, 54.
112. Lina Heydrich as quoted in Aronson, *Frühgeschichte*, 35.
113. Aronson, *Frühgeschichte*, 34; Deschner, *Heydrich*, 37f.; Heydrich, *Kriegsverbrecher*, 42f.
114 Evans, *Coming of the Third Reich*, 76.
115. Richard J. Evans, 'The Emergence of Nazi Ideology', in Jane Caplan (ed.), *Nazi Germany* (Oxford, 2008), 26–47.
116. Jürgen Falter, Thomas Lindenberger and Siegfried Schumann, *Wahlen und Abstimmungen in der Weimarer Republik. Materialien zum Wahlverhalten 1919–1933* (Munich, 1986), 41.
117. Heydrich, *Kriegsverbrecher*, 12f. and 19; Dederichs, *Heydrich*, 50.
118. Reinhard Heydrich to Lina von Osten's parents, 3 January 1931, in IfZ, Ed 450.
119. Heydrich, *Kriegsverbrecher*, 20; Aronson, *Frühgeschichte*, 34; Dederichs, *Heydrich*, 50f.; Deschner, *Heydrich*, 38; Calic, *Heydrich*, 45.
120. Deschner, *Heydrich*, 39; Dederichs, *Heydrich*, 51; Aronson *Frühgeschichte*, 35; Deschner, *Heydrich*, 39; Gustav Kleikamp, *Der Spiegel*, 9/1950 (2 March 1950), 42; Heydrich, *Kriegsverbrecher*, 21.
121. Beucke, as quoted in Aronson, *Frühgeschichte*, 35. This version of events was backed up by one of the members of the honour court, Vice Admiral Gustav Kleikamp. See *Der Spiegel*, 2 March 1950, 42f.
122. Kleikamp in *Der Spiegel*, 2 March 1950.
123. Kleikamp in *Der Spiegel*, 2 March 1950. See, too, Aronson, *Frühgeschichte*, 35; Deschner, *Heydrich*, 40; Dederichs, *Heydrich*, 51.
124. Notice of Heydrich's discharge, in *Marineverordnungsblatt*, 1 May 1931; Heydrich, *Kriegsverbrecher*, 25.
125. Heydrich, *Kriegsverbrecher*, 21 and 26f.; Aronson, *Frühgeschichte*, 35; Deschner, *Heydrich*, 40.
126. Unemployment figures according to Falter et al., *Wahlen*, 38. On the origins and consequences of the Great Depression, see Milton Friedman and Anna Jacobson Schwartz, *The Great Contraction, 1929–1933* (Princeton, NJ, 2008); Patricia Clavin, *The Great Depression in Europe, 1929–1939* (Basingstoke, 2000).
127. Deschner, *Heydrich*, 40; Heydrich, *Kriegsverbrecher*, 20f.; Aronson, *Frühgeschichte*, 35.
128. Heydrich, *Kriegsverbrecher*, 21; Aronson, *Frühgeschichte*, 36.
129. 'Abschrift des Berichts aus dem September 1931 über die Besichtigung des Heydrichschen Musikseminars', StaH, Akten der Schulverwaltung, 118, vol. II; see, too, Aronson, *Frühgeschichte*, 36; Heydrich, *Kriegsverbrecher*, 21f.
130. Heydrich, *Kriegsverbrecher*, 25.
131. A copy is reprinted in ibid., 32.
132. Deschner, *Heydrich*, 41; Dederichs, *Heydrich*, 54; Heydrich, *Kriegsverbrecher*, 25.
133. Heydrich, *Kriegsverbrecher*, 26; Aronson, *Frühgeschichte*, 36.
134. Deschner, *Heydrich*, 41; Heydrich, *Kriegsverbrecher*, 22; Aronson, *Frühgeschichte*, 37.
135. Aronson, *Frühgeschichte*, 33.
136. Post-war trial testimony of Karl von Eberstein, 15 October 1965, in Eberstein Papers, Bayerisches Hauptstaatsarchiv, Munich.
137. Aronson, *Frühgeschichte*, 37; Dederichs, *Heydrich*, 54; Heydrich, *Kriegsverbrecher*, 25; Deschner, *Heydrich*, 42.
138. Aronson, *Frühgeschichte*, 37.
139. BAB, BDC, SSO Reinhard Heydrich; Eberstein's letter of reference, in National Archives, Kew, WO 219/5283, 5.
140. Warzecha's letter of reference, in National Archives, Kew, WO 219/5283, 5–6.
141. George C. Browder, *Foundations of the Nazi Police State: The Formation of Sipo and SD* (Lexington, KY, 1990), 21.
142. Heydrich, *Kriegsverbrecher*, 26; Aronson, *Frühgeschichte*, 37; Deschner, *Heydrich*, 43ff.

Chapter III: Becoming Heydrich

1. Heydrich, *Kriegsverbrecher*, 26.
2. See, for example, Breitman, *Architect*, 87; Heinrich Fraenkel and Roger Manvell, *Himmler. Kleinbürger und Massenmörder* (Frankfurt am Main, 1965), 80; affidavit of Wilhelm Höttl,

in *IMT*, vol. 11, 259; testimony Kaltenbrunner of 12 April 1946, in *IMT*, vol. 11, 337f.; Fest, 'Successor', 143, 146f., and 151f.; Andreas Schulz and Gundula Grebner, *Generationswechsel und historischer Wandel* (Munich, 2003); Schellenberg, *Labyrinth*, 228 and 256f.; Deschner, *Heydrich*, 10 and 282.

3. Kersten, *Totenkopf*, 130. See, too, the post-war testimony of Wilhelm Wanek, a senior official in the SD-Ausland, in IfZ, ZS 1579. This interpretation was popularized by Fest, 'Successor', 139ff.

4. Longerich, *Himmler*; Breitman, *Architect*; on his early years, see, too, Bradley F. Smith, *Heinrich Himmler: A Nazi in the Making, 1900–1921* (Stanford, CA, 1974).

5. Diehl, *Körperbilder*; Sven Reichardt, 'Gewalt, Körper, Politik. Paradoxien in der Kulturgeschichte der Zwischenkriegszeit', in Wolfgang Hardtwig (ed.), *Politische Kulturgeschichte der Zwischenkriegszeit 1918–1939* (Göttingen, 2005), 205–39.

6. Deschner, *Heydrich*, 45f.; Dederichs, *Heydrich*, 55; Shlomo Aronson and Richard Breitman, 'Eine unbekannte Himmler-Rede vom Januar 1943', *VfZ* 38 (1990), 337–48, here 343.

7. Wildt, *Generation*, 241.

8. Heydrich, *Kriegsverbrecher*, 27; Aronson and Breitman, 'Rede', 343f., suggest that the salary was even lower: 120 Reichsmarks per month. For these and other comparative salaries in 1931, see Dietmar Petzina, Werner Abelschauser and Anselm Faust (eds), *Materialien zur Statistik des Deutschen Reiches 1914–1945* (Munich, 1978), 100ff.

9. See the post-war testimony of Erich Schultze, as quoted in Deschner, *Heydrich*, 46.

10. Himmler's funeral speech as printed in Walter Wannenmacher (ed.), *Reinhard Heydrich. Ein Leben der Tat* (Prague, 1944), 81ff.

11. BAB, BDC, SSO Reinhard Heydrich; Heinz Höhne, *Der Orden unter dem Totenkopf. Die Geschichte der SS* (Munich, 1984), 23ff.

12. Höhne, *Orden*, 56.

13. Inspekteur für Statistik to Himmler, 1 March 1943, as quoted in Bernd Wegner, *Hitlers politische Soldaten. Die Waffen-SS 1933–1945. Leitbild, Struktur und Funktion einer national-sozialistischen Elite* (Paderborn, 1997), 80. See, too, Adrian Weale, *The SS: A New History* (London, 2010), 19ff.; on aristocrats in the SS, see Malinowski, *Führer*; on the SA see Peter Longerich, *Die braunen Bataillone. Geschichte der SA* (Munich, 1989), 111. Heydrich's SS membership number was 10,120. See BAB, BDC, SSO Reinhard Heydrich.

14. Sven Reichardt, *Faschistische Kampfbünde. Gewalt und Gemeinschaft im italienischen Squadrismus und in der deutschen SA* (Cologne, 2002), 166ff.

15. BAB, BDC, SSO Streckenbach; Michael Wildt, 'Der Hamburger Gestapochef Bruno Streckenbach. Eine nationalsozialistische Karriere', in Frank Bajohr and Joachim Szodrzynski (eds), *Hamburg in der NS-Zeit: Ergebnisse neuerer Forschungen* (Hamburg, 1995), 93–123.

16. On Heydrich's apolitical stance in 1931, see Heydrich, *Kriegsverbrecher*, 27 and 63; Aronson and Breitman, 'Rede', 344; on Hamburg in this period, see Anthony McElligott, *Contested City: Municipal Politics and the Rise of Nazism in Altona, 1917–1937* (Ann Arbor, MI, 1998), 163ff.; Ursula Büttner, 'Der Aufstieg der NSDAP', in Forschungsstelle für Zeitgeschichte in Hamburg (ed.), *Hamburg im Dritten Reich* (Göttingen, 2005), 27–68.

17. Calic, *Heydrich*, 58f. To be sure, such stories have to be taken with a pinch of salt. It is strange that Nazi propaganda never mentioned Heydrich's time in Hamburg after 1942 when a violent confrontation with an ideological opponent, perhaps even an injury received during an attack, would have increased Heydrich's nimbus as a 'man of deed'.

18. On Streckenbach, see Wildt, 'Streckenbach'.

19. Aronson, *Frühgeschichte*, 55ff.; Browder, *Enforcers*, 105ff.; Lawrence D. Stokes, 'The Sicherheitsdienst (SD) of the Reichsführer SS and German Public Opinion, September 1939–June 1941', unpublished PhD thesis, Johns Hopkins University, 1972, 28.

20. BAB, BDC, SSO Hildebrandt; Aronson, *Frühgeschichte*, 56; Deschner, *Heydrich*, 51.

21. Reinhard Heydrich to Mathilde von Osten, 11 August 1931, in IfZ, Ed 450.

22. Reinhard Heydrich to Mathilde von Osten, 22 August 1931, in IfZ, Ed 450.

23. Aronson, *Frühgeschichte*, doc. 7, pp. 317f. See Wolff's post-war testimony, in IfZ, ZS 317, ff. 34f.

24. Himmler's order in Aronson, *Frühgeschichte*, 55 and (as doc. 8) 318.

25. Aronson, *Frühgeschichte*, 56; Deschner, *Heydrich*, 55; Heydrich, *Kriegsverbrecher*, 27.

26. Wildt, *Generation*, 242; Browder, *Enforcers*, 107ff.

27. Browder, *Foundations*, 23.

28. Heydrich, *Kriegsverbrecher*, 28f.
29. Heydrich, *Kriegsverbrecher*, 29; see the promotion documents of 11 and 18 December 1931 (signed by Himmler), in IfZ, Ed 450. For comparative salaries, see Petzina et al. (eds), *Materialien*, 100ff.
30. Himmler's 'Verlobungs- und Heiratsbefehl', 31 December 1931, BAB, NS 2/174; see, too, Gudrun Schwarz, *Eine Frau an seiner Seite. Ehefrauen in der SS-Sippengemeinschaft* (Hamburg, 1997), 24ff.; Isabel Heinemann, '"Another Type of Perpetrator": The SS Racial Experts and Forced Population Movements in the Occupied Regions', *Holocaust and Genocide Studies* 15 (2001), 387–411.
31. Schwarz, *Frau an seiner Seite*.
32. Richard Walther Darré, *Neuadel aus Blut und Boden* (Munich, 1930), 127–200; Josef Ackermann, *Heinrich Himmler als Ideologe* (Göttingen, 1970), 103f.; Alexandra Gerstner, *Neuer Adel. Aristokratische Elitekonzeptionen zwischen Jahrhundertwende und Nationalsozialismus* (Darmstadt, 2008); Eckart Conze, 'Adel unter dem Totenkopf. Die Idee eines Neuadels in den Gesellschaftsvorstellungen der SS', in idem and Monika Wienfort (eds), *Adel und Moderne. Deutschland im europäischen Vergleich im 19. und 20. Jahrhundert* (Cologne, 2004), 151–76.
33. Ulrich Herbert, 'Traditionen des Rassismus', in idem, *Arbeit, Volkstum, Weltanschauung. Über Fremde und Deutsche im 20. Jahrhundert* (Frankfurt am Main, 1995), 11–29, particularly 22–6; Ludolf Herbst, *Das nationalsozialistische Deutschland, 1933–1945. Die Entfesselung der Gewalt. Rassismus und Krieg* (Frankfurt am Main, 1996), 37–58, particularly 54ff.; Stefan Kühl, *Die Internationale der Rassisten. Aufstieg und Niedergang der internationalen Bewegung für Eugenetik und Rassenhygiene im 20. Jahrhundert* (Frankfurt am Main and New York, 1997), 122f.; Peter Weingart, Jürgen Kroll and Kurt Bayertz, *Rasse, Blut und Gene. Geschichte der Eugenik und Rassenhygiene in Deutschland* (Frankfurt am Main 1988), 367ff.
34. Richard Weikart, *From Darwin to Hitler: Evolutionary Ethics, Eugenics, and Racism in Germany* (Basingstoke, 2004); Mike Hawkins, *Social Darwinism in European and American Thought, 1860–1945* (Cambridge, 1997); Heydrich, *Kriegsverbrecher*.
35. Heydrich, *Kriegsverbrecher*, 29 and 34; membership card of the football club Lochhausen, 1 June 1932, in BAB, R 58, annexe 21.
36. Reinhard Heydrich to Lina's parents, 6 January 1932, in IfZ, Ed 450.
37. Lina Heydrich on Margarete Himmler, in *Der Spiegel*, 9 February 1950, 24–8, here 24. See, too, Heydrich, *Kriegsverbrecher*, 30.
38. Aronson, *Frühgeschichte*, 57; Dederichs, *Heydrich*, 66.
39. Aronson, *Frühgeschichte*, 57f.
40. Ibid., 43ff. and 57; see, too, Heydrich, *Kriegsverbrecher*, 33.
41. Aronson, *Frühgeschichte*, 60; Yad Vashem Archive, 97–210 F I.
42. Heydrich, *Kriegsverbrecher*, 34; on the bloody election campaigns, see Reichardt, *Kampfbünde*, 579ff.
43. Jordan to Strasser, 6 June 1932, in BAB, PK E0071.
44. Aronson, *Frühgeschichte*, 63 and 260, n. 72.
45. Gercke to Reichsorganisationsleitung der NSDAP, 22 June 1932, in BAB, PK E71. A copy of Gercke's letter was also sent to Himmler. See Aronson, *Frühgeschichte*, 63; a copy of the letter is reprinted as doc. 4 on pp. 312f.
46. Post-war testimony of Ernst Hoffmann, 9 March 1971, in IfZ, Ed 450. See, too, Flachowsky, 'Abstammung', 317ff.; Wolfgang Heindorf's letter to Heydrich of 30 November 1935, reporting on progress in the private investigations into the alleged Jewish heritage of Bruno Heydrich, in BAB, R 58, annexe 22.
47. Deschner, *Heydrich*, 62.
48. See the post-war testimony of Paul Leffler, one of the few salaried full-time SD employees in 1932, as quoted in Aronson, *Heydrich*, 61; on Heydrich's ambition to copy the British secret service, see Heydrich, *Kriegsverbrecher*, 33.
49. Wildt, *Generation*, 243; on the number of SD employees, see George Browder, 'The Numerical Strength of the Sicherheitsdienst des RFSS', *Historical Social Research* 28 (1983), 30–41.
50. Aronson, *Frühgeschichte*, 62; Heydrich, *Kriegsverbrecher*, 35f.
51. For a detailed account of these events, see Ian Kershaw, *Hitler 1889–1936: Hubris* (London, 1998), 413ff.
52. Henry Ashby Turner, *Hitler's Thirty Days to Power: January 1933* (London, 1997); Heydrich, *Kriegsverbrecher*, 38.

53. On the role of terror in the early phase of the Third Reich, see Klaus Drobisch und Günther Wieland, *System der NS-Konzentrationslager 1933–1939* (Berlin, 1993), 11ff.; Browder, *Foundations*, 50ff.; Richard Bessel, 'The Nazi Capture of Power', *Journal of Contemporary History* 39 (2004), 169–88.

54. On the different types of early concentration camps in 1933–4, see Johannes Tuchel, *Konzentrationslager. Organisationsgeschichte und Funktion der 'Inspektion der Konzentrationslager' 1934–1938* (Boppard, 1991), 38ff.; Nikolaus Wachsmann, 'The Dynamics of Destruction: The Development of the Concentration Camps, 1933–1945', in Jane Caplan and idem (eds), *Concentration Camps in Nazi Germany: The New Histories* (London, 2009), 17–43.

55. Evans, 'Coercion and Consent'; see, too, Richard Bessel, *Political Violence and the Rise of Nazism: The Storm Troopers in Eastern Germany 1925–1934* (New Haven, CT, 1984), 97ff.; Eric G. Reiche, *The Development of the SA in Nürnberg, 1922–1934* (Cambridge, 1986), 173ff.; Longerich, *SA*, 165ff.

56. Bessel, 'Capture of Power', 169ff; Evans, 'Coercion and Consent'.

57. Browder, *Foundations*, 50f.; Tuchel, *Konzentrationslager*, 47ff.; Aronson, *Frühgeschichte*, 75ff.

58. Heydrich to Daluege, 5 March 1933, in IfZ, Ed 450. See, too, Johannes Tuchel and Reinold Schattenfroh, *Zentrale des Terrors. Prinz-Albrecht-Str. 8. Das Hauptquartier der Gestapo* (Berlin, 1987), 63f.; Wildt, *Generation*, 244; Aronson, *Frühgeschichte*, 107.

59. Deschner, *Heydrich*, 84f.; Dederichs, *Heydrich*, 73f.; Heydrich, *Kriegsverbrecher*, 38f.; Aronson, *Frühgeschichte*, 107.

60. On the seizure of power in Bavaria, see Jochen Klenner, *Verhältnis von Partei und Staat 1933–1945, dargestellt am Beispiel Bayerns* (Munich, 1974), 44ff.; Robert Gellately, *The Gestapo and German Society: Enforcing Racial Policy 1933–1945* (Oxford, 1990), 53f.; Ortwin Domröse, *Der NS-Staat in Bayern von der Machtergreifung bis zum Röhm-Putsch* (Munich, 1974), 80ff.; Tuchel, *Konzentrationslager*, 121ff.; Aronson, *Frühgeschichte*, 98ff.; Heydrich's appointment went hand in hand with another promotion, this time to *SS-Oberführer*. See Yad Vashem Archive, 97–210 F I.

61. Lina Heydrich to her parents, 13 March 1933, in IfZ, Ed 450.

62. Martin Broszat and Hartmut Mehringer (eds), *Bayern in der NS-Zeit*, vol. 5: *Die Parteien KPD, SPD, BVP in Verfolgung und Widerstand* (Munich, 1983); Aronson, *Frühgeschichte*, 117ff.

63. Doris Seidel, 'Die jüdische Gemeinde Münchens 1933–1945', in Angelika Baumann and Andreas Heussler (eds), *München arisiert. Entrechtung und Enteignung der Juden in der NS-Zeit* (Munich, 2004), 31–53, here 34; Douglas Bokovoy, 'Verfolgung und Vernichtung', in idem and Stefan Meining (eds), *Versagte Heimat. Jüdisches Leben in Münchens Isarvorstadt* (Munich, 1994), 223–60, here 223; Baruch Z. Ophir and Falk Wiesemann, *Die jüdischen Gemeinden in Bayern 1918–1945* (Munich 1979), 43f. Reinhard Weber, *Das Schicksal der jüdischen Rechtsanwälte in Bayern nach 1933* (Munich, 2006), 50.

64. On Müller, see Joachim Bornschein, *Gestapochef Heinrich Müller. Technokrat des Terrors* (Leipzig, 2004); see, too, Andreas Seeger, *'Gestapo-Müller'. Die Karriere eines Schreibtischtäters* (Berlin, 1996).

65. Reinhard Heydrich, *Wandlungen unseres Kampfes* (Munich and Berlin, 1936), 19.

66. On the triangular system of SS, political police and concentration camps, see Browder, *Foundations*, 66ff.; on the early camps, see Jane Caplan, 'Political Detention and the Origin of the Concentration Camps in Nazi Germany, 1933–1935/6', in Neil Gregor (ed.), *Nazism, War and Genocide: New Perspectives on the History of the Third Reich* (Exeter, 2008), 22–41; Drobisch and Wieland, *System*, 27ff.

67. Longerich, *Himmler*, 160f.; on Dachau, see Barbara Distel and Ruth Jakusch, *Konzentrationslager Dachau, 1933–1945* (Brussels, 1978); Anne Bernou-Fieseler and Fabien Théofilakis (eds), *Das Konzentrationslager Dachau. Erlebnis, Erinnerung, Geschichte. Deutsch–Französisches Kolloquium zum 60. Jahrestag der Befreiung des Konzentrationslagers Dachau* (Munich, 2006); Hans-Günter Richardi, *Schule der Gewalt. Die Anfänge des Konzentrationslagers Dachau 1933–1934. Ein dokumentarischer Bericht* (Munich, 1983).

68. Tuchel, *Konzentrationslager*, 125f.; Richardi, *Schule*, 55ff. and 88ff.; Christopher Dillon, 'We'll Meet Again in Dachau': The Early Dachau SS and the Narrative of Civil War', *Journal of Contemporary History* 45 (2010), 535–54.

69. Both letters from Heydrich to Wagner of 5 August 1933 and 1 January 1934 are reprinted in Aronson, *Frühgeschichte*, 325, docs 17 and 17a. On the figures, see Stanislav Zámečník,

'Dachau-Stammlager', in Wolfgang Benz and Barbara Distel (eds), *Der Ort des Terrors* (Munich, 2005–9), vol. 2, 233–74, here 234.

70. Zámečník, 'Dachau-Stammlager', 235.
71. See Best's post-war statement on Heydrich in IfZ, ZS 207/2.
72. BAB, BDC, SSO Eicke.
73. On the 'Dachau model', see Tuchel, *Konzentrationslager*, 141ff.; Richardi, *Schule*, 119ff.
74. Heydrich to Gestapo branch offices, 29 October 1934, in BAB, R 58/264, f. 69. See, too, Browder, *Foundations*, 157.
75. On life in the early camps, see Caplan and Wachsmann (eds), *Concentration Camps*.
76. Paul Egon Hübinger, 'Thomas Mann und Reinhard Heydrich in den Akten des Reichsstatthalters von Epp', *VfZ* 28 (1980), 111–43.
77. Ibid., quotation on pp. 136ff.
78. Hartmut Mehringer, 'Die KPD in Bayern 1919–1945. Vorgeschichte, Verfolgung und Widerstand', in Broszat and idem (eds), *Bayern in der NS-Zeit*, vol. 5: *Die Parteien KPD, SPD, BVP in Verfolgung und Widerstand*, 1–286, here 73ff.; see, too, Tuchel, *Konzentrationslager*, 53ff.
79. On Hamburg, see Browder, *Foundations*, 100ff.; Wildt, 'Streckenbach', 93ff.; Ludwig Eiber, 'Unter Führung des NSDAP-Gauleiters. Die Hamburger Staatspolizei (1933–1937)', in Gerhard Paul and Klaus-Michael Mallmann (eds), *Die Gestapo. Mythos und Realität* (Darmstadt, 1995), 101–17. On Lübeck, Mecklenburg and Württemberg, see Browder, *Foundations*, 104ff. On Baden, see Michael Stolle, *Die Geheime Staatspolizei in Baden. Personal, Organisation, Wirkung und Nachwirken einer regionalen Verfolgungsbehörde im Dritten Reich* (Konstanz, 2001), 85ff. On Bremen, see Inge Marssolek and René Ott, *Bremen im 'Dritten Reich'. Anpassung – Widerstand – Verfolgung* (Bremen, 1986), 121ff. and 176ff. On Anhalt, Hessen, Thüringen, Saxony and Lippe, see Browder, *Foundations*, 109ff. On Brunswick, see Gerhard Wysocki, *Die Gehemeine Staatspolizei im Land Braunschweig. Polizeirecht und Polizeipraxis im Nationalsozialismus* (Frankfurt am Main and New York, 1997), 58f.
80. Wildt, *Generation*, 247; Browder, *Foundations*, 100f.; Alwin Ramme, *Der Sicherheitsdienst der SS. Zu seiner Funktion im faschistischen Machtapparat und im Besatzungsregime des sogenannten Generalgouvernements* (East Berlin, 1970), 33ff.; Aronson, *Frühgeschichte*, 156ff.
81. Herbert, *Best*, 133ff.
82. Statement on Heydrich by Dr Werner Best, 1 October 1959, in Copenhagen, in IfZ, ZS 207/2, p. 3. For a similar account, see Schellenberg, *Labyrinth*, 36; and the post-war testimony of Anatol von der Milwe (26 June 1949), in IfZ, ZS 106.
83. Statement on Heydrich by Dr Werner Best, 1 October 1959, in Copenhagen, in IfZ, ZS 207/2, p. 13.
84. Herbert, *Best*, 91ff.
85. Stefan Breuer, *Ordnungen der Ungleichheit. Die deutsche Rechte im Widerstreit ihrer Ideen, 1871–1945* (Darmstadt, 2001).
86. Helmut Lethen, *Cool Conduct: The Culture of Distance in Weimar Germany* (Berkeley, CA, 2002); see, too, Moritz Bassler and Ewout van der Knaap (eds), *Die (k)alte Sachlichkeit. Herkunft und Wirkungen eines Konzepts* (Würzburg, 2004).
87. Longerich, *Himmler*, 265ff.
88. See the post-war testimony of Walter Wanek, a senior official in the SD-Ausland, in IfZ, ZS 1579.
89. The most insightful of these is the post-war account of Werner Best, in IfZ (Munich), ZS 207/2. Arthur Nebe wrote after the war that Heydrich's presence alone caused him 'physical shaking'. See Arthur Nebe, 'Das Spiel ist aus. Glanz und Elend der deutschen Kriminalpolizei', in *Der Spiegel*, 22 December 1949, 27. In a similar post-war statement, the head of SD-Inland, Franz Alfred Six, maintained that 'everyone was afraid of Heydrich'. Post-war testimony of Franz Alfred Six as quoted in *Frankfurter Allgemeine Zeitung*, 25 October 1963, p. 7. See, too, the post-war testimony of Walter Wanek, a senior official in the SD-Ausland, in IfZ, ZS 1579.
90. See the post-war testimony of Heydrich's personal adjutant Hans-Hendrik Neumann in IfZ, ZS 1260; see, too, Heydrich, *Wandlungen*, 19f. From 1937 onwards, Heydrich personally supervised the regular physical exercise of his men as *SS Inspekteur für Leibesüberungen*. See Heydrich's orders of 9 May 1937 and 16 December 1940, in IfZ, Ed 450; see, too, Daniels, 'Leibeserzieher', *Leibesübungen und körperliche Erziehung* 61 (1942), 114–17; Ulrich Popplow,

'Reinhard Heydrich oder die Aufnordung durch den Sport', *Olympisches Feuer. Zeitschrift der deutschen Olympischen Gesellschaft* 8 (1963), 14–20.

91. See Heydrich's orders of 18 May 1940, 26 July 1940 and 6 January 1942, on 'Dienstliche Körperschulung im Reichssicherheitshauptamt', in IfZ, MA-445. From 1941 onwards, RSHA employees could choose between fencing, handball, football, boxing, athletics and swimming. The fencing lessons, in which Heydrich participated himself, took place on Thursdays between 6 p.m. and 9 p.m. in the RSHA's own gym. See Heydrich's order of 23 April 1941, in IfZ, MA 445.

92. See Lina Heydrich to Peter Schneiders, 12 June 1962, NIOD, doc. I, 691A; Dieter Rebentisch and Karl Teppe (eds), *Verwaltung contra Menschenführung im Staate Hitlers. Studien zum politisch-administrativen System* (Göttingen, 1986).

93. George C. Browder, 'Die Anfänge des SD. Dokumente aus der Organisationsgeschichte des Sicherheitsdienstes des Reichsführers SS', VfZ 27 (1979), 299–324; Banach, *Elite*, 95f.

94. On the war youth generation and its leadership role in the SS, see Wildt, *Generation*; Ulrich Herbert, 'Ideological Legitimization and Political Practice of the Leadership of the National Socialist Secret Police', in Hans Mommsen (ed.), *The Third Reich between Vision and Reality: New Perspectives on German History, 1918–1945* (Oxford, 2001), 99–108; Herbert, *Best*, 187.

95. Post-war testimony of Werner Best, in IfZ, ZS 207/2, pp. 3–5.

96. BAB, BDC, SSO Hans-Achim Ploetz. He fell, in the late summer of 1944, on the Eastern Front.

97. Banach, *Elite*, 19.

98. Tuchel and Schattenfroh, *Zentrale*, 63f.; Tuchel, 'Gestapa und Reichssicherheitshauptamt. Die Berliner Zentralinstitutionen der Gestapo', in Paul and Mallmann (eds), *Gestapo. Mythos und Realität*, 84–100, here 86; Wildt, *Generation*, 217; Browder, *Foundations*, 89f.; Wilhelm, *Polizei*, 42; Gellately, *Gestapo*, 46; Christoph Graf, *Politische Polizei zwischen Demokratie und Diktatur. Die Entwicklung der preussischen Politischen Polizei vom Staatsschutzorgan der Weimarer Republik zum Geheimen Staatspolizeiamt des Dritten Reiches* (Berlin, 1983), 139ff.

99. Tuchel, *Konzentrationslager*, 46; Graf, *Politische Polizei*, 179ff.; Browder, *Foundations*, 87.

100. Wildt, *Generation*, 219f.; Tuchel, 'Gestapa', 88f.; Longerich, *Himmler*, 178.

101. Heydrich to Göring, 9 July 1934, Geheimes Preussisches Staatsarchiv, I HA Rep. 90 P 8H2; see, too, Banach, *Elite*, 283; Tuchel, 'Gestapa', 90; Wildt, *Generation*, 222; Rudolf Diels, *Lucifer ante Portas. Es spricht der erste Chef der Gestapo* (Stuttgart, 1950), 415f.

102. Tuchel and Schattenfroh, *Zentrale*, 80; Hans Buchheim, 'Die SS – Das Herrschaftsinstrument', in idem, Martin Broszat, Hans-Adolf Jacobsen and Helmut Krausnick, *Anatomie des SS-Staates* (3rd edn, Munich, 1994), vol. 1, 113–36; Tuchel, 'Gestapa', 90; Wildt, *Generation*, 222; Browder, *Foundations*, 115; Longerich, *Himmler*, 184.

103. Elisabeth Kohlhaas, 'Die Mitarbeiter der regionalen Staatspolizeistellen. Quantitative und qualitative Befunde zur Personalausstattung der Gestapo', in Paul and Mallmann (eds), *Gestapo. Mythos und Realität*, 219–35; Browder, *Foundations*, 56.

104. Walter Otto Weyrauch, *Gestapo V-Leute. Tatsachen und Theorie des Geheimdienstes. Untersuchungen zur Geheimen Staatspolizei während der nationalsozialistischen Herschaft* (Frankfurt am Main, 1989); on the block warden, see Detlef Schmiechen-Ackermann, 'Der "Blockwart". Die unteren Parteifunktionen im nationalsozialistischen Terror- und Überwachungsapparat', VfZ 48 (2000), 575–602; Gisela Diewald-Kerkmann, *Politische Denunziation im NS-Regime oder die kleine Macht der 'Volksgenossen'* (Bonn, 1995).

105. Howard Smith as quoted in Roger Moorhouse, *Berlin at War: Life and Death in Hitler's Capital, 1939–45* (London, 2010), 227.

106. Gellately, *Gestapo*; Eric A. Johnson, *Nazi Terror: The Gestapo, Jews, and Ordinary Germans* (New York, 1999), 392ff.; Reinhard Mann, *Protest und Kontrolle im Dritten Reich. Nationalsozialistische Herrschaft im Alltag einer rheinischen Grossstadt* (Frankfurt am Main, 1987); Stolle, *Geheime Staatspolizei*, 252ff.; Wildt, *Generation*, 214–62; Richard J. Evans, 'Coercion and Consent in Nazi Germany', *Proceedings of the British Academy* 151 (2007), 53–81, here 74.

107. Moorhouse, *Berlin*, 224.

108. The image of the Gestapo as an omnipresent and universally intrusive institution was challenged by Robert Gellately, 'Allwissend und allgegenwärtig? Entstehung, Funktion und

Wandel des Gestapo-Mythos', in Paul and Mallmann (eds), *Gestapo. Mythos und Realität*, 47–70. See, too, idem, *Hingeschaut und weggesehen. Hitler und sein Volk* (Munich, 2002), 67ff.; Carsten Dams and Michael Stolle, *Die Gestapo. Herrschaft und Terror im Dritten Reich* (Munich, 2008); on Heydrich as a 'propagandist of terror', see Mallmann, Klaus-Michael and Paul, Gerhard, *Herrschaft und Alltag. Ein Industrierevier im Dritten Reich* (Bonn, 1991), 164; and Heydrich's speech on the occasion of the 1941 Day of the German Police, as quoted in *Völkischer Beobachter*, 17 February 1941; idem, 'Die deutsche Sicherheitspolizei. Zum Tag der Deutschen Polizei', *Völkischer Beobachter*, 28 January 1939.

109. Longerich, *SA*, 184 and 206f.
110. Heinz Höhne, *Mordsache Röhm. Hitlers Durchbruch zur Alleinherrschaft, 1933–1934* (Reinbek bei Hamburg, 1984), 224ff.; Longerich, *SA*, 204ff.; Herbert, *Best*, 141f. After the purges, the Security Police continued to collect 'evidence' to prove the homosexuality of leading SA members killed during the Night of the Long Knives. See Hamburg Police to Heydrich, 29 July 1934, in IfZ, Fa 108.
111. Edmund Forschbach, *Edgar J. Jung. Ein Konservativer Revolutionär, 30. Juni 1934* (Pfullingen, 1984), 154ff.
112. Kershaw, *Hitler: Hubris*, 505–17.
113. See the trial testimonies of Karl Wolff (7–8 September) and Werner Best (1 October 1951), and the case against Sepp Dietrich (Munich, July 1956 and May 1957), as quoted in Browder, *Foundations*, 289, n. 4. For different interpretations, see Höhne, *Orden*, 97–112; Bessel, *Political Violence*, 132f.
114. Post-war testimony of Dr Werner Best (18 June 1951), in IfZ, ZS 207; see, too, Wolfgang Sauer, *Die Mobilmachung der Gewalt* (Cologne, 1974), 955. On the context, see Höhne, *Mordsache Röhm*, 228f.
115. Aronson, *Frühgeschichte*, 193; Herbert, *Best*, 143f.
116. Evans, 'Coercion', 64; Höhne, *Mordsache Röhm*, 247ff.; Richard J. Evans, *The Third Reich in Power* (London, 2005), 31ff.
117. Yad Vashem Archive, 97–210 F I; Herbert, *Best*, 156.
118. The decline of the family business is documented in Heydrich's correspondence of the early 1930s. See BAB, R 58/9319 (formerly 'Anhang 22'); see, too, Heydrich, *Kriegsverbrecher*, 21f. On the general trends in the music industry, see Tim Blanning, *The Triumph of Music: Composers, Musicians, and their Audiences, 1700 to the Present* (London, 2008), 202.
119. See copies of the letter exchange in BAB, R 58/9319 (formerly annexe 22). Two receipts for payments of 50 Reichsmarks each, paid on 21 and 23 November 1933, have survived in Heydrich's personal papers. See BAB, R 58/9318. On Wolfgang Heindorf's SD employment, see Aronson, *Frühgeschichte*, 62.
120. BAB, R 58/9319 (formerly annexe 22).
121. On Maria's party membership, see Bruno Heydrich to the magistrate of Halle, 7 July 1933, in StaH, Akten der Schulverwaltung, 118, vol. II. The letter can be found in BAB, R 58/9319.
122. BAB, BDC, SSO Mehlhorn; on Herbert Mehlhorn and the SD in Saxony, see, too, Carsten Schreiber, *Elite im Verborgenen. Ideologie und regionale Herrschaftspraxis des Sicherheitsdienstes der SS und seines Netzwerks am Beispiel Sachsen* (Munich, 2008), 417f.
123. Mehlhorn to Heydrich, 18 December 1933, in BAB, R 58/9319.
124. Reinhard Heydrich to his mother Elisabeth, 29 January 1934, in BAB, R 58/9318; Heydrich, *Kriegsverbrecher*, 38 and 44.
125. Reinhard Heydrich to his mother, Elisabeth, 29 January 1934, in BAB, R 58/9318.
126. StaH, FA 2571.
127. Heydrich, *Kriegsverbrecher*, 43ff. and 63.

Chapter IV: Fighting the Enemies of the Reich

1. Browder, *Foundations*, 180ff.
2. Walter Nicolai, *Geheime Mächte. Internationale Spionage und ihre Bekämpfung im Weltkrieg und Heute* (Leipzig, 1923).

3. Browder, *Foundations*, 180ff.

4. Reinhard Heydrich, 'Vergiftung des Verhältnisses zwischen Waffenträger der Nation und Träger der Weltanschauung in Staat und Partei', January 1935, in IfZ, MA 438, ff. 2374ff.

5. Müller, *Canaris*, 162ff.

6. Heydrich, *Kriegsverbrecher*, 63.

7. See the file collection on Abwehr–Gestapo/SD collaboration in BAB, R 58/242; Browder, *Foundations*, 180ff.

8. Browder, *Foundations*, 148ff.; Horst Duhnke, *Die KPD von 1933 bis 1945* (Cologne, 1972), 194; Stolle, *Geheime Staatspolizei*, 222f.; Johnson, *Terror*, 19ff.; Norbert Frei, 'Zwischen Terror und Integration. Zur Funktion der politischen Polizei im Nationalsozialismus', in Christoph Dipper, Rainer Hudemann and Jens Petersen (eds), *Faschismus und Faschismen im Vergleich. Wolfgang Schieder zum 60. Geburtstag* (Cologne, 1998), 217–28.

9. Browder, *Foundations*, 163ff.

10. Longerich, *Himmler*, 209f.; Buchheim et al., *SS*, 52; Tuchel, 'Gestapa', 84.

11. Gellately, *Gestapo*, 59; Browder, *Foundations*, 231ff.

12. Heydrich, *Wandlungen*, 5; Longerich, *Himmler*, 211ff.

13. Heydrich, *Wandlungen*, 14ff; Longerich, *Himmler*, 205.

14. *Wandlungen*, 18 and 20; Heydrich held on to this belief throughout his career. Still in October 1941, half a year before his assassination, he described the role of the SS as that of an ideological 'shock troop' of the party and its supreme leader. See Heydrich's speech in Černín Palace on 2 October 1941, in National Archives, Prague, 114-6-4, carton 22.

15. Heydrich, *Wandlungen*, 3.

16. Ibid., 6, 18f.

17. Heydrich, as quoted in Burckhardt, *Danziger Mission*, 56.

18. Longerich, *Himmler*, 217.

19. Heydrich, *Wandlungen*, 18ff.

20. Heydrich, 'Die Bekämpfung der Staatsfeinde', *Deutsches Recht* 6 (1936), 121–3. See, too, Banach, *Elite*, 283.

21. Heydrich to Taubert, 4 March 1940, in BAB, BDC, SSO Walter Fentz; see, too, Banach, *Elite*, 283.

22. Heydrich, 'Aufgaben und Aufbau der Sicherheitspolizei im Dritten Reich', in Hans Pfundtner (ed.), *Dr. Wilhelm Frick und sein Ministerium* (Munich, 1937), 153.

23. Himmler in Wannenmacher, *Leben der Tat*, 81ff.

24. Heydrich, 'Aufgaben', 149; see, too, Wildt, *Generation*, 254.

25. Heydrich, 'Bekämpfung der Staatsfeinde', 121ff.; on the notion of the 'Wehrmacht within', see Werner Best, 'Der Reichsführer SS und Chef der Deutschen Polizei', *Deutsches Recht* 6 (1936), 257f.; Longerich, *Himmler*, 205f. and 824; Wegner, *Politische Soldaten*, 110ff. See, too, Andreas Schwegel, *Der Polizeibegriff im NS-Staat. Polizeirecht, juristische Publizistik und Judikative 1931–1944* (Tübingen, 2005), 208.

26. Heydrich to Hanke, 26 November 1936, in IfZ, Fa 199/37. See, too, Reinhard Heydrich, 'Der Anteil der Sicherheitspolizei und des SD an den Ordnungsmassnahmen im mitteleuropäischen Raum', *Böhmen und Mähren* 25 (1941), 176–8, here 177.

27. Heydrich's order of 1 July 1937, in BAB, R 58/239, ff. 198–202. See, too, Wildt, *Generation*, 254f.; Longerich, *Himmler*, 221; Buchheim et al., *SS*, 201ff.; Höhne, *Orden*, 136f.

28. Heydrich's order of 15 December 1936, USHMMA, 11.001 M01, reel 1, folder 25.

29. On the SD after 1936, see Browder, *Enforcers*, 210ff.; idem, 'Numerical Strength', 30–41; Wildt, *Generation*, 378ff.

30. Evans, *Third Reich in Power*, 536f.

31. Longerich, *Politik*, 26ff.; Avraham Barkai, *Vom Boykott zur 'Entjudung'. Der wirtschaftliche Existenzkampf der Juden im Dritten Reich, 1933–1943* (Frankfurt, 1988), 23ff.; Friedländer, *Persecution*, 36ff.

32. Michael Wildt, 'Before the "Final Solution": The Judenpolitik of the SD, 1935–1938', *Leo Baeck Institute Year Book* (1998), 245f.; see, too, the post-war testimony of Dieter Wisliceny, 18 November 1946, in Fa 64 IfZ, Fa 64, and the vast body of SD files on Communist and Socialist organizations (1932–4) in OA Moscow, 500/1/88–134.

33. Graf, *Politische Polizei*, 238.

34. Heydrich, *Kriegsverbrecher*, 97.
35. Jeffrey Herf, *The Jewish Enemy: Nazi Propaganda during World War II and the Holocaust* (Cambridge, MA, 2006).
36. The literature on this subject is vast. For a competent survey, see Walter Laqueur, *The Changing Face of Antisemitism: From Ancient Times to the Present Day* (Oxford, 2006).
37. Post-war statement on Heydrich by Dr Werner Best, 1 October 1959, in Copenhagen, in IfZ, ZS 207/2, p. 12.
38. On Himmler and the Jews, see Longerich, *Himmler*, 224ff.
39. Heydrich, *Wandlungen*, 13.
40. Ibid.
41. Holger Berschel, *Bürokratie und Terror. Das Judenreferat der Gestapo Düsseldorf 1935–1945* (Essen, 2001), 171.
42. See Heydrich's orders of 28 January and 6 March, in BAB, R 58/269. For a further order of 9 March 1935, see National Archives Prague, 114, supplement I, carton 89. See, too, Berschel, *Bürokratie*, 275ff.
43. Uwe Dietrich Adam, *Judenpolitik im Dritten Reich* (Düsseldorf, 1972), 155; see, too, Joseph Walk (ed.), *Das Sonderrecht für die Juden im NS-Staat. Eine Sammlung der gesetzlichen Massnahmen und Richtlinien. Inhalt und Bedeutung* (2nd edn, Heidelberg, 1996), vol. 1, 516ff.
44. Göring's order of 4 July 1937, in BAB, R 43II/357. Heydrich would make extensive use of his new competences. See, for example, his orders of 27 November and 3 December 1941 ('Verfügungsbeschränkungen über das bewegliche Vermögen für Juden' and 'Massnahmen zur Verhinderung von Veräusserung jüdischen Vermögens') in IfZ, Eich 739 and MA 445, pp. 7845–53.
45. Longerich, *Himmler*, 589.
46. Internal SD memorandum for Heydrich, 24 May 1934, as printed in Michael Wildt (ed.), *Die Judenpolitik des SD 1935 bis 1938. Eine Dokumentation* (Munich, 1995), 66ff. See, too, the Gestapo report 'Gegenwärtiger Stand der Judenfrage', 2 November 1934, in OA Moscow, 501/1/18, ff. 49–56; reprinted in Otto Dov Kulka and Eberhard Jäckel (eds), *Die Juden in den geheimen NS-Stimmungsberichten 1933–1945* (Düsseldorf, 2004), doc. 48, pp. 90ff.
47. Michael Wildt, 'Before the "Final Solution": The Judenpolitik of the SD, 1935–1938', *Leo Baeck Institute Year Book* (1998), 241–69.
48. Heydrich's order of 20 March 1934 is reprinted in Hans Mommsen, 'Der nationalsozialistische Polizeistaat und die Judenverfolgung vor 1938', *VfZ* 10 (1962), 68–87, here 77f. On the Reichsbund, see Ulrich Dunker, *Der Reichsbund jüdischer Frontsoldaten 1919–1938* (Düsseldorf, 1977), 113ff.
49. Heydrich to all State Police Offices, 17 January 1935, in IfZ, MA 172. Four weeks later, on 10 February 1935, Heydrich ordered the closing down of all Jewish gatherings advocating that Jews should remain in Germany. Heydrich to all State Police Offices, 10 February 1935, in IfZ, MA 172.
50. Heydrich, *Wandlungen*, 10ff.
51. Heydrich to Lammers, 16 July 1935, quoted in Werner Jochmann, *Gesellschaftskrise und Judenfeindschaft in Deutschland 1870–1945* (Hamburg, 1988), 236–54, here 245f.
52. SD Report of 17 August 1935, in OA Moscow, 500/3/316, ff. 1–3; reprinted in Wildt (ed.), *Judenpolitik*, 69–70.
53. Gestapo report on the meeting of 20 August 1935, in OA Moscow 500/1/379, ff. 75–85; as quoted in Wildt, 'Before the "Final Solution"', 249. On Schacht's role, see Albert Fischer, *Hjalmar Schacht und Deutschlands 'Judenfrage'. Der 'Wirtschaftsdiktator' und die Vertreibung der Juden aus der deutschen Wirtschaft* (Cologne, 1995), 208.
54. Heydrich on 9 September 1935, in OA Moscow, 500/1/379, ff. 115–20; reprinted in Wildt (ed.), *Judenpolitik*, 70–3.
55. Heydrich's letter to the participants of the top-level meeting in the Reich Economics Ministry, 9 September 1935, in OA Moscow, 500/1/379, ff. 115–20; reprinted in Wildt, (ed.), *Judenpolitik*, 70–3.
56. Bernhard Lösener, 'Als Rassereferent im Reichsministerium des Innern', *VfZ* 9 (1961), 261–313; Adam, *Judenpolitik*, 125. For a critical assessment of Lösener's view, see Reinhard Rürup, 'Das Ende der Emanzipation. Die antijüdische Politik in Deutschland von der "Machtergreifung" bis zum Zweiten Weltkrieg', in Arnold Paucker, Sylvia Gilchrist and

Barbara Suchy (eds), *Die Juden im nationalsozialistischen Deutschland, 1933–1943* (Tübingen, 1986), 97–114; and Jochmann, 'Judenpolitik', 247.

57. Hilberg, *Destruction*, vol. 1, 72 and 434–47. On the Nuremberg Laws, see Cornelia Essner, *Die 'Nürnberger Gesetze' oder die Verwaltung des Rassewahns, 1933–1945* (Paderborn, 2002); Otto Dov Kulka, 'Die Nürnberger Rassegesetze und die deutsche Bevölkerung im Lichte geheimer NS Lage- und Stimmungsberichte', *VfZ* 32 (1984), 582–624; Lothar Gruchmann, '"Blutschutzgesetz" und Justiz. Zur Entstehung und Auswirkung des Nürnberger Gesetzes vom 15. September 1935', *VfZ* 31 (1983), 418–42.

58. See Chapter VII of this book.

59. Wildt (ed.), *Judenpolitik*, 38. On their ideological commitment to anti-Semitism: Yaacov Lozowick, *Hitlers Bürokraten. Eichmann, seine willigen Vollstrecker und die Banalität des Bösen* (Zurich, 2000).

60. Herbert A. Strauss, 'Jewish Emigration from Germany: Nazi Policies and Jewish Responses (II)', *Leo Baeck Institute Year Book* 26 (1981), 343–7; Francis R. Nicosia, 'The End of Emancipation and the Illusion of Preferential Treatment: German Zionism, 1933–1938', *Leo Baeck Institute Year Book* 36 (1991), 243–65; idem, 'Ein nützlicher Feind. Zionismus im nationalsozialistischen Deutschland 1933–1939', *VfZ*, 37 (1989), 367–400; Yehuda Bauer, *Jews for Sale? Nazi–Jewish Negotiations 1933–1945* (New Haven and London, 1994).

61. Wisliceny, 'Was wird aus Palastina?', 15 July 1937, reprinted in Serge Klarsfeld (ed.), *Centre de Documentation Juive Contemporaine, Recueil de Documents du Service des Affaires Juives, le II-112, du Sicherheitsdienst SD (1937–1949)* (New York, 1980), 76–84. See, too, Nicosia, *Nützlicher Feind*, 388f.

62. Hagen's report on Polkes's visit for Heydrich, 17 June 1937, in BAB, R 58/954, ff. 42–6. See, too, Adam, *Judenpolitik*, 200.

63. Cesarani, *Eichmann*, 18–60; on Kaltenbrunner, see Black, *Kaltenbrunner*.

64. Memo Six, 4 September 1937, BAB, R 58/623.

65. Eichmann's report of 4 November 1937, in BAB, R 58/954, ff. 11–64.

66. Bauer, *Jews for Sale?*, 27; Nicosia, *Nützlicher Feind*, 392f.

67. Nicosia, *Nützlicher Feind*, 392.

68. Friedländer, *Persecution*, 282; Longerich, *Politik*, 121ff.

69. On Himmler's hostility towards the Churches, see Longerich, *Himmler*, 227ff.; Ackermann, *Himmler*, 88ff.

70. Heydrich, *Wandlungen*, 7ff.; on Heydrich's attitude towards non-institutionalized religion and spirituality, see Heydrich, *Kriegsverbrecher*, 96.

71. Clark, 'Religion', 97.

72. Heydrich, *Kriegsverbrecher*, 85. on the figures quoted above, see Longerich, *Himmler*, 229. On Nazi attitudes towards Chritianity more generally, see Richard Steigmann-Gall, *The Holy Reich: Nazi Conceptions of Christianity, 1919–1945* (Cambridge, 2003).

73. Wolfgang Dierker, *Himmlers Glaubenskrieger. Der Sicherheitsdienst der SS und seine Religionspolitik 1933–1941* (Paderborn, 2002), 192ff.; Doris Bergen, *Twisted Cross: The German Christian Movement in the Third Reich* (Chapel Hill, NC, 1996); Manfred Gailus, *Protestantismus und Nationalsozialismus. Studien zur Durchdringung des protestantischen Sozialmilieus in Berlin* (Cologne, 2001); Kurt Meier, *Kreuz und Hakenkreuz. Die evangelische Kirche im Dritten Reich* (Munich, 1992); on the Confessing Church as an example of Protestant defiance, see Victoria Barnett, *For the Soul of the People: Protestant Protest against Hitler* (New York, 1992).

74. John S. Conway, *The Nazi Persecution of the Churches, 1933–45* (London, 1968).

75. Heydrich's order of 18 March 1934, reiterating earlier orders of July 1933, in IfZ, Fa 183/1; Aronson, *Frühgeschichte*, 118–20.

76. Dierker, *Glaubenskrieger*, 96ff.

77. Petra Madeleine Rapp, *Die Devisenprozesse gegen katholische Ordensangehörige und Geistliche im Dritten Reich* (Bonn, 1981); on the involvement of the SD, see Dierker, *Glaubenskrieger*, 178ff.

78. Hans Günter Hockerts, *Die Sittlichkeitsprozesse gegen katholische Ordensangehörige und Priester 1936/1937. Eine Studie zur nationalsozialistischen Herrschaftstechnik und zum Kirchenkampf* (Mainz, 1971), 4ff., 12ff., 63ff.; Dierker, *Glaubenskrieger*, 178ff., 185ff.

79. Dierker, *Glaubenskrieger*, 335ff.; Friedrich Zipfel, *Kirchenkampf in Deutschland 1933–1945. Religionsverfolgung und Selbstbehauptung der Kirchen in der nationalsozialistischen Zeit* (Berlin, 1965), 458ff.; on Hitler's views, see Goebbels, *Tagebücher*, part I, vol. 3/2, 376.

80. Heydrich to Hitler, 27 May 1937, in National Archives, Kew, GFM 33/4830; Heydrich to Lammers, 15 July 1938, in National Archives, Kew, GFM 33/4830; Hitler in a monologue in his field headquarters, 13 December 1941, in Adolf Hitler, *Adolf Hitlers Monologe im Führerhauptquartier 1941–1944. Die Aufzeichnungen Heinrich Heims*, ed. Werner Jochmann (Munich, 1982), 32; Ian Kershaw, *Hitler 1936–1945: Nemesis* (London, 2000), 424.

81. On the persecution of Jehovah's Witnesses, see Detlef Garbe, *Zwischen Widerstand und Martyrium. Die Zeugen Jehovas im 'Dritten Reich'* (Munich, 1993); Richard Steigmann-Gall, 'Religion and the Churches', in Jane Caplan (ed.), *Nazi Germany* (Oxford, 2008), 146–67, here 146ff.; Hans Hesse (ed.), *Persecution and Resistance of Jehovah's Witnesses during the Nazi Regime, 1933–1945* (Bremen 2001); James Penton, *Jehovah's Witnesses and the Third Reich: Sectarian Politics under Persecution* (Toronto, 2004).

82. Garbe, *Zeugen*, 234ff. and 247ff.

83. Heydrich, *Wandlungen*, 12.

84. See OA Moscow, 500/4/261 and 500/1/154.

85. Helmut Neuberger, *Freimaurerei und Nationalsozialismus. Die Verfolgung der deutschen Freimaurerei durch völkische Bewegung und Nationalsozialismus 1918–1945*, 2 vols (Hamburg, 1980), vol. 2, 16ff., 101f., 119f.

86. Heydrich's order of 1 July 1937 (Gemeinsame Anordnung für den Sicherheitsdienst des Reichsführer-SS und die Geheime Staatspolizei), in BAB, R 58/239, ff. 198–202; reprinted in Wildt, *Judenpolitik*, 118–20. See, too, Wildt, *Generation*, 254f.; Longerich, *Himmler*, 221; Buchheim et al., *SS*, 62.

87. On the Central Jewish Museum, see Jan Björn Potthast, *Das jüdische Zentralmuseum der SS in Prag. Gegnerforschung und Völkermord im Nationalsozialismus* (Frankfurt am Main, 2002).

88. Neuberger, *Freimaurerei*, vol. 2, 45f. and 108; Burckhardt, *Danziger Mission*, 55.

89. Burckhardt, *Danziger Mission*, 57f.

90. Heydrich, 'Aufgaben', 149ff.; idem., 'Bekämpfung der Staatsfeinde', 121ff.

91. Browder, *Foundations*, 152; Detlef J. K. Peukert, *Inside Nazi Germany: Conformity, Opposition, and Racism in Everyday Life* (New Haven and London, 1987), 264f.; Burkhard Jellonek, *Homosexuelle unter dem Hakenkreuz. Die Verfolgung von Homosexuellen im Dritten Reich* (Paderborn, 1990), 95ff.

92. OA Moscow, 500/1/261. 'At least' is underlined in the original. See, too, Wolfgang Ayass, '"Ein Gebot der nationalen Arbeitsdisziplin". Die "Aktion Arbeitsscheu Reich" 1938', *Beiträge zur nationalsozialistischen Gesundheits- und Sozialpolitik* 6 (1988), 43–74; idem, *'Asoziale' im Nationalsozialismus* (Stuttgart, 1995).

93. Patrick Wagner, *Volksgemeinschaft ohne Verbrecher. Konzeptionen und Praxis der Kriminalpolizei in der Zeit der Weimarer Republik und des Nationalsozialismus* (Hamburg, 1996), 292ff.

94. Nikolaus Wachsmann, *Hitler's Prisons: Legal Terror in Nazi Germay* (New Haven and London, 2004), 165–83; Evans, *Third Reich in Power*, 85ff.

95. Karin Orth, *Das System der nationalsozialistischen Konzentrationslager. Eine politische Organisationsgeschichte* (Hamburg, 1999), 32 and 38f.; Ulrich Herbert, Karin Orth and Christoph Dieckmann, 'Die nationalsozialistischen Konzentrationslager. Geschichte, Erinnerung, Forschung', in Ulrich Herbert, Karin Orth and Christoph Dieckmann (eds), *Die nationalsozialistischen Konzentrationslager. Entwicklung und Struktur*, 2 vols (Frankfurt, 2002), vol. 1, 117–42.

96. Orth, *System*, 35ff.; Tuchel, *Konzentrationslager*, 326ff. On Sachsenhausen, see Hermann Kaienburg, 'Sachsenhausen-Stammlager', in Benz and Distel (eds), *Ort des Terrors*, vol. 3, 17–72; Günter Morsch (ed.), *Mord und Massenmord im Konzentrationslager Sachsenhausen 1936–1945* (Berlin, 2005). On Buchenwald: Harry Stein, 'Buchenwald-Stammlager', in Benz and Distel (eds), *Ort des Terrors*, vol. 3, 301–56. On Flossenbürg: Jörg Skriebeleit, 'Flossenbürg-Stammlager', in Benz and Distel (eds), *Ort des Terrors*, vol. 4, 17–66. On Mauthausen: Florian Freund and Bertrand Perz, 'Mauthausen-Stammlager', in Benz and Distel (eds), *Ort des Terrors*, vol. 3, 293–346. On Neuengamme: Hermann Kaienburg, *Das Konzentrationslager Neuengamme 1938–1945* (Berlin, 1997). On Ravensbrück: Bernhard Strebel, *Das KZ Ravensbrück. Geschichte eines Lagerkomplexes* (Paderborn, 2003).

97. Prützmann to Heydrich, 30 November 1938 (with a reference to the dinner in Dachau), in USHMMA, RG 11.001 M.24, reel 94, folder 1525.

98. On Gustav Rall, see BAB, BDC, SSO Gustav Rall; see, too, Johannes Tuchel, 'Reinhard Heydrich und die "Stiftung Nordhav". Die Aktivitäten der SS-Führung auf Fehmarn', *Zeitschrift der Gesellschaft für Schleswig-Holsteinische Geschichte* 117 (1992), 199–225, here 201, n. 8.

99. Heydrich, *Kriegsverbrecher*, 50 and 88f. On the camp in Nauen/Stolpshof, see Wolfgang Weigelt, 'Nauen/Stolpshof', in Benz and Distel (eds), *Ort des Terrors*, vol. 3, 231f.

100. Heydrich, *Kriegsverbrecher*, 59f.; Speer as quoted in Callum MacDonald, *Heydrich. Anatomie eines Attentats* (Munich, 1990), 148f.

101. Heydrich, *Kriegsverbrecher*, 60.

102. Heydrich's tax declaration for 1935, 1936 and 1937, in IfZ, Ed 450. On comparative salaries, see Browder, *Foundations*, 129.

103. Heydrich, *Kriegsverbrecher*, 60f.; Heydrich's tax declaration for 1938, in IfZ, Ed 450.

104. Heydrich, *Kriegsverbrecher*, 57f.; post-war testimony of Heydrich's personal adjutant Hans-Hendrik Neumann, in IfZ, ZS 1260; Joachim Lilla, *Der Preussische Staatsrat 1921–1933. Ein biographisches Handbuch* (Düsseldorf, 2005), no. 2.39; idem, *Statisten in Uniform. Die Mitglieder des Reichstags 1933–1945. Ein biographisches Handbuch* (Düsseldorf, 2004), 237. For the additional salary, see BAB, NS 19/3454.

105. Heydrich, *Kriegsverbrecher*, 54.

106. Arthur Nebe, 'Das Spiel ist aus', *Spiegel*, 9 February 1950, 24f. 58.

107. Lina Heydrich, *Kriegsverbrecher*, 82 and 84.

108. Lina Heydrich to Peter Schneiders, NIOD, doc. I, 69/A; Heydrich, *Kriegsverbrecher*, 63.

109. Jochen von Lang, *Der Adjutant Karl Wolff. Der Mann zwischen Hitler und Himmler* (Munich, 1985), 65ff. See, too, Schwarz, *Ehefrauen*.

110. Interview with Lina Heydrich, *Jasmin* 4/1969, pp. 70ff.; Schellenberg, *Labyrinth*, 41.

111. Schellenberg, *Labyrinth*, 17; Kersten, *Totenkopf*, 120.

112. *Der Spiegel* 6/1950, 9 February 1950, 25.

113. Lina Heydrich to Peter Schneiders, 30 January 1962, in IfZ, ZS 3092; Schellenberg, *Labyrinth*, 14; Reinhard Doerries, *Hitler's Last Chief of Foreign Intelligence: Allied Interrogations of Walter Schellenberg* (London, 2003), 73.

114. Heydrich, *Kriegsverbrecher*, 77.

115. Heydrich's speech on 17 March 1942, in National Archives, Prague, 114, carton 8.

116. Matthew Stibbe, *Women in the Third Reich* (London, 2003), 88f. On the 'New Woman' in the Weimar Republic, see, for example, Gesa Kessemeier, *Sportlich, sachlich, männlich. Das Bild der 'Neuen Frau' in den Zwanziger Jahren* (Dortmund, 2000).

117. See the various letter exchanges, SD reports and employers' complaints in BAB, R 58/9319.

118. Ibid.

119. Maria Heindorf (née Heydrich) to Reinhard Heydrich, 30 June 1939, in National Archives, Kew, WO 219/5283.

120. Heinz Pomme to Maria Heindorf, 19 July 1939, in National Archives, Kew, WO 219/5283. On Pomme, see BAB, BDC, SSO Kurt Pomme. On the subsequent correspondence, see BAB, R58/9319.

Chapter V: Rehearsals for War

1. The speech was recorded in the Hossbach protocol, in *IMT*, vol. 25, doc. 386-PS, pp. 402ff. See, too, Kershaw, *Hitler: Nemesis*, 63ff. Longerich, *Himmler*, 411ff.

2. Kirstin A. Schäfer, *Werner von Blomberg. Hitlers erster Field marshall* (Paderborn, 2006), 180ff.; Klaus-Jürgen Müller, *Das Heer und Hitler. Aimee und nationalsozialistischos Regime, 1933–1940* (Stuttgart, 1969), 255ff.; Karl-Heinz Janssen and Fritz Tobias, *Der Sturz der Generäle. Hitler und die Blomberg–Fritsch–Krise 1938* (Munich, 1997). *Third Reich in Power*, 649. 22–81 (on Blomberg) and 83–195 (on Fritsch); Longerich, *Himmler*, 412ff.

3. Janssen and Tobias, *Sturz*, 92. See, too, post-war testimony of Himmler's adjutant, Karl Wolff, in IfZ, ZS 317.

4. Kershaw, *Hitler: Nemesis*, 63ff.

5. Janssen and Tobias, *Sturz*, 159ff.

6. Ibid., 166 and 181f.

7. Herbert, *Best*, 185; Wolfgang Foerster, *Generaloberst Ludwig Beck. Sein Kampf gegen den Krieg. Aus den nachgelassenen Papieren des Generalstabschefs* (Munich, 1953), 92; Müller, *Heer*, doc. 34, pp. 639f.; Schellenberg, *Labyrinth*, 40f.

8. Conrad Patzig (10 November 1953), as quoted in: Müller, *Canaris*, 171.

9. Müller, *Canaris*, 162ff.

10. Janssen and Tobias, *Sturz*, 191.

11. Evans, *Third Reich in Power*, 664; Kershaw, *Hitler: Nemesis*, 63ff.; G. E. R Gedye, *Fallen Bastions: The Central European Tragedy* (London, 1939), 144–216.

12. Evans, *Third Reich in Power*, 649. Kershaw, *Hitler: Nemesis*, 70ff.; Gedye, *Fallen Bastions*, 217ff.; Erwin A. Schmidl, *März 38. Der deutsche Einmarsch in Österreich* (Vienna, 1987), 31ff.

13. Hans-Joachim Neufeld, Jürgen Huck and Georg Tessin, *Zur Geschichte der Ordnungspolizei, 1936–1945* (Koblenz, 1957), 9ff.

14. Evans, *Third Reich in Power*, 650f. Barbara Jelavich, *Modern Austria: Empire and Republic, 1815–1986* (Cambridge, 1987), 218ff.; Gedye, *Fallen Bastions*, 236ff.

15. Evans, *Third Reich in Power*, 652. Kershaw, *Hitler: Nemesis*, 76ff.; Schmidl, *März 38*, 111ff.

16. *Neue Freie Presse*, 15 March 1938. See, too, Gerhard Botz, *Nationalsozialismus in Wien. Machtübernahme, Herrschaftssicherung, Radikalisierung* (rev. edn, Vienna, 2008), 72.

17. See Himmler's '"Sonderauftrag Österreich", 11 March 1938', in BAB, R 19/401.

18. *Neue Freie Presse*, evening edition, 15 March 1938; *Neue Freie Presse*, morning edition, 16 March 1938. One day earlier, Heydrich had given orders for the new organizational structure of the Security Police in Austria, which was largely based on the German example. See his order of 15 March 1938, in DÖW, E 20.530. On Kaltenbrunner, see Black, *Kaltenbrunner*.

19. Franz Weisz, 'Personell vor allem ein "ständestaatlicher" Polizeikörper. Die Gestapo in Österreich', in Paul and Mallmann (eds), *Gestapo im Zweiten Weltkrieg*, 439–62. Evans, *Third Reich in Power*, 656.

20. Heydrich subsequently refused to hand these files over to the Ministry of Justice. See the letter exchange between Dr Hueber (Reich Ministry of Justice) and Heydrich, 21 June–26 July 1938, in DÖW, 01905.

21. Botz, *Wien*, 55ff.; Schmidl, *März 38*, 232–7; Freund and Perz, 'Mauthausen-Stammlager', 254ff.

22. See the daily reports of the Stapoleitstelle in Vienna, July–December 1938, in IfZ, MA 145/1. The figures of arrests quoted in the literature range from 10,000 to 70,000. Heydrich himself mentioned the figure of 10,000 people arrested to Ernst von Weizsäcker. See Weizsäcker's notes on the conversation of 5 July 1938, in *Akten zur deutschen auswärtigen Politik 1918–1945* (Baden-Baden, 1950–95), series D, vol. 1, doc. 405, pp. 509–10. On Heydrich's express orders not to release anyone without his explicit consent, see his order to the Stapoleitstelle in Vienna on 16 March 1938, in DÖW, 9413.

23. Heydrich to Bürckel, 16 March 1938, in DÖW, Bürckel 2020.

24. See Heydrich's letter exchange with the Stapoleitstelle in Vienna about the arrests of leading Communists, 27 and 30 September 1938, in DÖW, 01575, and Heydrich's dossier on Habsburg royalists, in DÖW, 22124; and Heydrich to all Gestapo Offices, 16 March 1938, in DÖW, 21058/20.

25. Botz, *Wien*, 55ff.; Schmidl, *März 38*, 232ff.; Freund and Perz, 'Mauthausen-Stammlager', 254ff.

26. Heydrich to Ernst von Weizsäcker, 5 July 1938, *Akten zur deutschen auswärtigen Politik*, series D, vol. 1, doc. 405, pp. 509–10.

27. Heydrich to Stapoleitstelle Vienna, BAB, R 581/256, f. 90. See, too, Erwin A Schmidl, *Der 'Anschluss' Österreichs. Der deutsche Einmarsch im März 1938* (Vienna, 1994), 236. On the Stapoleitstelle in Vienna, see Thomas Mang, *Gestapo – Leitstelle Wien – Mein Name ist Huber* (Münster, 2004). On the Ketteler affair, see Lutz Hachmeister, *Der Gegnerforscher. Die Karriere des SS-Führers Franz Alfred Six* (Munich, 1998), 10ff.

28. Goebbels' diary entry of 26 March 1938, in Goebbels, *Tagebücher*, part I, vol. 5, 231.

29. Evans, *Third Reich in Power*, 657ff. Hans Safrian and Hans Witek (eds), *Und keiner war dabei. Dokumente des alltäglichen Antisemitismus in Wien 1938* (Vienna, 1988); Eckart Früh, 'Terror und Selbstmord in Wien nach der Annexion Östereichs', in Felix Kreissler (ed.), *Fünfzig Jahre danach. Der Anschluss von innen und aussen gesehen* (Vienna and Zurich, 1989), 216–23; Herbert Rosenkranz, 'Entrechtung, Verfolgung und Selbsthilfe der Juden in

Österreich', in Gerald Stourzh and Birgitta Zaar (eds), *Österreich, Deutschland und die Mächte. Internationale und Österreichische Aspekte des 'Anschlusses' vom März 1938* (Vienna, 1990), 367–417, here 376–7.

30. Carl Zuckmayer, *Als wär's ein Stück von mir* (2nd edn, Hamburg, 1977), 88.

31. BAB, R 58/991, ff. 106–21.

32. *Völkischer Beobachter*, 17 March 1938.

33. Heydrich to Bürckel, 17 March 1938, Dokumentationsarchiv des Österreichischen Widerstandes, 15.909, reprinted in Dokumentationsarchiv des Österreichischen Widerstandes (ed.), *'Anschluss' 1938. Eine Dokumentation* (Vienna, 1988), 440.

34. Order for the 'SS-Oberabschnitt Österreich' of 5 April 1938, in BAB, NS 31/236. See, too, Schmidl, *'Anschluss' Österreichs*, 236.

35. Heydrich's order of 14 April 1938, in IfZ, MA 444/2.

36. Heydrich's order of 17 March 1938, in IfZ, MA 445, ff. 8207–8; and 8218–21.

37. Courier letter of Dr Werner Best, 22 March 1938, in IfZ, MA 438.

38. Otmar Jung, *Plebiszit und Diktatur. Die Volksabstimmungen der Nationalsozialisten. Die Fälle 'Austritt aus dem Völkerbund' (1933), 'Staatsoberhaupt' (1934) und 'Anschluss Österreichs' (1938)* (Tübingen, 1995); Evans, *Third Reich in Power*, 655.

39. Evans, *Third Reich in Power*, 657f.; Friedländer, *Persecution*, 241ff.

40. Evans, *Third Reich in Power*, 659. Peter F. Hoerz, *Jüdische Kultur im Burgenland. Historische Fragmente – volkskundliche Analysen* (Vienna, 2006).

41. Botz, *Wien*, 143; Evans, *Third Reich in Power*, 659.

42. See the extensive files on the Viennese Central Office in USHMMA, RG 11.001 M, reel 8, 625; see, too, Botz, *Wien*, 332; Jonny Moser, 'Die Zentralstelle für jüdische Auswanderung in Wien', in Kurt Schmid and Robert Streibel (eds), *Der Pogrom 1938. Judenverfolgung in Österreich und Deutschland* (Vienna, 1990); also Hans Safrian, *Die Eichmann-Männer* (Vienna, 1993), 36ff.; Friedländer, *Persecution*, 241ff.

43. Heydrich during the meeting convened by Göring on 12 November 1938, in *IMT*, vol. 28, doc. 1816-PS, pp. 499ff.

44. Evans, *Third Reich in Power*, 661f. Doron Rabinovici, *Instanzen der Ohnmacht. Wien 1938–1945. Der Weg zum Judenrat* (Frankfurt, 2000); Hans Safrian, 'Expediting Expropriation and Expulsion: The Impact of the "Vienna Model" on Anti-Jewish Policies in Nazi Germany, 1938', *Holocaust and Genocide Studies* 14 (2000), 390–414; Gabriele Anderl and Dirk Rupnow, *Die Zentralstelle für jüdische Auswanderung als Beraubungsinstitution* (Vienna, 2004); Friedländer, *Persecution*, 243ff.

45. Evans, *Third Reich in Power*, 661.

46. Adam, *Judenpolitik*, 201. Heydrich closely observed the proceedings at Evian and sent regular reports on the conference discussions to Himmler, Göring and Ribbentrop. See copies of the reports in USHMMA, RG 11.001 M, reel 9, 649.

47. 'Aufenthaltsverbot für Juden mit polnischer Staatsangehörigkeit', 26 October 1938, in BAB, R 58, 276; reprinted in Walk (ed.), *Sonderrecht*, II/569, p. 247; see, too, Sybil H. Milton, 'The Expulsion of Polish Jews from Germany, October 1938 to July 1939: A Documentation', *Leo Baeck Institute Yearbook* 29 (1984), 169–74.

48. Alan E. Steinweis, *Kristallnacht 1938* (Cambridge, MA, 2009), 17.

49. Bradley F. Smith, Agnes F. Peterson and Joachim Fest (eds), *Heinrich Himmler: Geheimreden, 1933 bis 1945 und andere Ansprachen* (Frankfurt am Main, 1974), 25ff. (8 November 1938); Longerich, *Himmler*, 424.

50. No copy of Goebbels's speech exists, but it can be reconstructed on the basis of his own diary entry and the testimony of several people present at the gathering. The most important account remains: 'Bericht des Obersten Parteirichters der NSDAP, Reichsleiter Walter Buch über die Vorgänge und parteigerichtlichen Verfahren im Zusammenhang mit den antisemitischen Kundgebungen vom 9. November 1938', in: Michaelis and Schaepler (eds.) *Ursachen und Folgen*, vol. 12, 582. Christian T. Barth, *Goebbels und die Juden* (Paderborn, 2003), 132ff.; Hermann Graml, *Reichskristallnacht. Antisemitismus und Judenverfolgung im Dritten Reich* (Munich, 1998), 17ff.; Martin Gilbert, *Kristallnacht: Prelude to Disaster* (London, 2006); Angela Hermann, 'Hitler und sein Stosstrupp in der "Reichskristallnacht"', *VfZ* 56 (2008), 603ff; Peter Longerich, *Joseph Goebbels. Biographie* (Munich, 2010), 393.

51. Rudolf Jordan, *Erlebt und erlitten. Weg eines Gauleiters von München bis Moskau* (Leoni, 1971), 181f.; see, too, Barth, *Goebbels*, 135.

52. Dieter Obst, *'Reichskristallnacht'. Ursachen und Verlauf des antisemitischen Pogroms vom November 1938* (Frankfurt, 1991); Hans-Jürgen Döscher, *Reichskristallnacht. Die Novemberpogrome* (Munich, 2000), Longerich, *Himmler*, S. 424.

53. Müller to all Stapoleitstellen, 9 November 1938 (11.55 p.m.), in BAB, R 58/276, f. 124; see, too, Döscher, *Reichskristallnacht* 98. See, too, the post-war account of Werner Best (1 October 1959), in IfZ, ZS 207/2, f. 4.

54. Heydrich's telegram from Munich, 10 November 1938, 1.20 a.m., as reprinted in *IMT*, vol. 31, doc. 3051-PS, pp. 516–18.

55. Heydrich's telegram of 10 November 1938 (no time given), in BAB, R 58/276, f. 129, reprinted in *IMT*, vol. 31, doc. 3051-PS, pp. 518f.

56. On the mass arrests, see Heiko Pollmeier, 'Inhaftierung und Lagererfahrung deutscher Juden im November 1938', *Jahrbuch für Antisemitismusforschung* 8 (1999), 107–30; Harry Stein, 'Das Sonderlager im Konzentrationslager Buchenwald nach den Pogromen 1938', in Monica Kingreen (ed.), *Nach der Kristallnacht. Jüdisches Leben und antijüdische Politik in Frankfurt am Main 1938–1945* (Frankfurt, 1999), 19–54.

57. Botz, *Wien*, 397–411. On anti-Jewish violence in the Sudetenland, see Jörg Osterloh, *Nationalsozialistische Judenverfolgung im Reichsgau Böhmen und Sudetenland, 1938–1945* (Munich, 2006), 185ff; see, too: Evans, *Third Reich in Power*, 661.

58. Peter Longerich, *'Davon haben wir nichts gewusst!' Die Deutschen und die Judenverfolgung 1933–1945* (Munich, 2006), 129ff.

59. International newspaper reports on German anti-Jewish policies were closely monitored by the SD. See the collection of press clippings in USHMMA, RG 11.001 M, reel 9, folder 645.

60. Herbert Hagen, 'Bericht über die Zentralstelle für jüdische Auswanderung in Wien', November 1938, as printed in Wildt (ed.), *Judenpolitik*, 193f.

61. Heydrich to Göring, 11 November 1938, in IfZ, Eich 1503.

62. Minutes of the meeting of 12 November 1938, in *IMT*, vol. 28, doc. 1816-PS, pp. 499ff.; on emigration figures, see Jonny Moser, 'Österreich', in Benz (ed.), *Dimension des Völlkermords*, 67–93, here 68; Jacob Toury, 'Ein Auftakt zur "Endlösung". Judenaustreibungen über nichtslawische Reichsgrenzen 1933–1939', in Ursula Büttner, Werner Johe and Angelika Voss (eds), *Das Unrechtsregime. Internationale Forschung über den Nationalszoialismus* (Hamburg, 1986), vol. 2, 164–9.

63. Minutes of the meeting of 12 November 1938, in *IMT*, vol. 27, doc. 1816-PS, pp. 499ff.; see, too, Longerich, *Politik*, 208f.

64. Göring confirmed this at another meeting with regional party chiefs on 6 December 1938. See Göring's speech of 6 December 1938, as quoted in Götz Aly and Susanne Heim, 'Staatliche Ordnung und "organische Lösung". Die Rede Hermann Görings "Über die Judenfrage" vom 6. Dezember 1938', *Jahrbuch für Antisemitismusforschung* 2 (1992), 378–404, here 384. For Hitler's instructions following the November Pogrom see also Adam, *Judenpolitik*, 216ff.

65. Heydrich to Stapoleitstellen, 31 January 1939, in IfZ, Fa 183/1.

66. Heydrich to Ribbentrop, 30 January 1939, in IfZ, Eich 1368. See, too, Gabriele Anderl, 'Die "Zentralstellen für jüdische Auswanderung" in Wien, Berlin und Prag. Ein Vergleich', *Tel Aviver Jahrbuch für Deutsche Geschichte* 23 (1994), 275–99.

67. Göring to Frick, 24 January 1939, in BAB, R 58/276, ff. 195f.; and Heydrich's circular letter of 11 February 1939, informing the ministries of the completion of preparations for the Reich Central Office, in, IfZ, MA 445, ff. 7828–9.

68. Wolf Gruner, 'Poverty and Persecution: The Reichsvereinigung, the Jewish Population, and anti-Jewish Policy in the Nazi State, 1939–1945', *Yad Vashem Studies* 27 (1999), 23–60; Esriel Hildesheimer, *Jüdische Selbstverwaltung unter dem NS-Regime. Der Existenzkampf der Reichsvertretung und Reichsvereinigung der Juden in Deutschland* (Tübingen, 1994), 79ff.

69. See Ulrich Herbert, 'Von der "Reichkristallnacht" zum "Holocaust": Der 9. November und das Ende des "Radauantisemitismus"', in idem, *Arbeit, Volkstum, Weltanschauung. Über Fremde und Deutsche im 20. Jahrhundert* (Frankfurt am Main, 1995), 59–77.

70. David Bankier, *The Germans and the Final Solution: Public Opinion under Nazism* (Oxford, 1992), 85ff.

71. Göring's speech of 6 December 1938, reprinted in Aly and Heim, 'Staatliche Ordnung', 395.

72. Helmuth Groscurth, *Tagebücher eines Abwehroffiziers 1938–1940*, ed. Helmut Krausnick and Harold C. Deutsch (Stuttgart, 1970), 162.

73. Adam, *Judenpolitik*, 213ff.

74. Minutes of the meeting of 12 November 1938, in *IMT*, vol. 27, doc. 1816-PS, pp. 499ff.; see, too, Adam, *Judenpolitik*, 210ff.

75. Minutes of the meeting of 12 November 1938, in *IMT*, vol. 27, doc. 1816-PS, pp. 499ff. An extended proposal for the marking, including five drafts of the marks, is to be found in USHMMA, RG 11.001 M, reel 9, folder 659. Karl A. Schleunes (ed.), *Legislating the Holocaust: The Bernhard Loesener Memoirs and Supporting Documents*, trans. Carol Scherer (Boulder, CO, 2001), 88ff. Göring communicated Hitler's decision against Heydrich's proposal during the Gauleiter meeting of 6 December 1938.

76. Strauss, 'Jewish Emigration', 313ff.; Arndt and Boberach, 'Deutsches Reich', 34.

77. On Czechoslovakia and the Sudeten German problem see Jürgen Tampke, *Czech–German Relations and the Politics of Central Europe: From Bohemia to the EU* (London, 2003), 25ff.; Mark Cornwall, '"A Leap into Ice-Cold Water": The Manoeuvres of the Henlein Movement in Czechoslovakia, 1933–8', in idem and R. J. W. Evans (eds), *Czechoslovakia in a Nationalist and Fascist Europe, 1918–1948* (Oxford, 2007), 123–42; Jörg Kracik, *Die Politik des deutschen Aktivismus in der Tschechoslowakei 1920–1938* (Frankfurt am Main, 1999); Jörg K. Hoensch and Dušan Kováć (eds), *Das Scheitern der Verständigung. Tschechen, Deutsche und Slowaken in der Ersten Republik* (Essen, 1994); Kershaw, *Hitler: Nemesis*, 90f.

78. On the organization of the SD task forces and Gestapo units in the Protectorate, see 'Einsatz des SD im Falle CSR', June 1938, in *IMT*, vol. 39, doc. 509-USSR, pp. 537ff. On the arrest lists, see Tuchel and Schattenfroh, *Zentrale*, 127ff.; Herbert, *Best*, 235f.; Oldrich Sládek, 'Standrecht und Standgericht. Die Gestapo in Böhmen und Mähren', in Mallmann and Paul (eds), *Gestapo im Zweiten Weltkrieg*, 317–39.

79. Heydrich, 'Der Anteil der Sicherheitspolizei und des SD an den Ordnungsma nahmen im mitteleuropäischen Raum', *Böhmen und Mähren* 2 (1941), 176; and 'Einsatz des SD im Falle CSR'. Schellenberg added in a note that Heydrich had personally approved the composition of the *Einsatzgruppen*. On Stahlecker, see Jürgen Schuhladen-Krämer, 'Die Exekutoren des Terrors', in Michael Kissener and Joachim Scholtyseck (eds), *Die Führer der Provinz, NS-Biographien aus Baden und Württemberg* (Konstanz, 1997), 405–43.

80. Gerhard L. Weinberg, *Hitler's Foreign Policy 1933–1939: The Road to World War II* (New York, 2005), 699–777; Igor Lukeš and Eric Goldstein (eds), *The Munich Crisis, 1938: Prelude to World War II* (London, 1999).

81. Heydrich to Best, 22 September 1938, as quoted in Sládek, 'Standrecht', 319.

82. Volker Zimmermann, *Die Sudetendeutschen im NS-Staat. Politik und Stimmung der Bevölkerung im Reichsgau Sudetenland (1938–1945)* (Essen, 1999), 71ff.

83. 'Richtlinien für die Tätigkeit der Einsatzkommandos der Geheimen Staatspolizei in den sudetendeutschen Gebieten', BAB, R 58/291; on the Order Police, see Neufeld et al., *Ordnungspolizei*, 11.

84. Sládek, 'Standrecht', 317ff. On the Sudeten German Freikorps, see Werner Röhr, 'Das Sudetendeutsche Freikorps – Diversionsinstrument der Hitler-Regierung bei der Zerschlagung der Tschechoslowakei', *Militärgeschichtliche Mitteilungen* 52 (1993), 35–66. Heydrich to Stapoleitstellen, 24 December 1938, in IfZ, Fa 183/1.

85. See Jan Gebhart, 'Migrace ćeského obyvatelstva v letech 1938–1939', *Český Časopis Historický* 3 (1998), 561–73; Peter Heumos, *Die Emigration aus der Tschechoslowakei nach Westeuropa und dem Nahen Osten* (Munich, 1989), 21.

86. Evans, *Third Reich in Power*, 678f. Tampke, *Relations*, 57; Zimmermann, *Sudetenland*, 79ff.

87. Kershaw, *Hitler: Nemesis*, 164f. and 169; Evans, *Third Reich in Power*, 681.

88. Miroslav Kárný, 'Die Logik von München. Das Protektorat Böhmen und Mähren', in Dietrich Eichholtz and Kurt Pätzold (eds), *Der Weg in den Krieg* (Berlin, 1989), 279–308; Kershaw, *Hitler: Nemesis*, 157ff; Evans, *Third Reich in Power*, 681.

89. Theodor Procházka, *The Second Republic: The Disintegration of Post-Munich Czechoslovakia, October 1938–March 1939* (Boulder, CO, 1981), 69. On Beneš, see Zeman, *Beneš*. On Hácha, see Tomáš Pasák, *Emil Hácha (1938–1945)* (Prague, 1997). On Slovakia, see Tatjana Tönsmeyer, *Das Dritte Reich und die Slowakei 1939–1945. Politischer Alltag zwischen Kooperation und Eigensinn* (Paderborn, 2003).

90. *Akten zur deutschen auswärtigen Politik*, series D, vol. 4, doc. 228; Donald Cameron Watt, *How War Came: The Immediate Origins of the Second World War, 1938–1939* (London, 1989), 141ff.; Weinberg, *Foreign Policy*, 465ff.

91. Mastny, *Czechs*, 45ff.; Bryant, *Prague*, 32ff.

92. George Kennan, as quoted in Bryant, *Prague*, 1.

93. 'Verordnung über den Aufbau der Verwaltung und der Deutschen Sicherheitspolizei im Protektorat', *Reichsgesetzblatt* 1939, I, 1682f.; the RSHA draft of this document in IfZ, MA 433, ff. 728354f.; Sládek, 'Standrecht', 323ff.; Helmut Krausnick, 'Die Einsatzgruppen vom Anschluss Österreichs bis zum Feldzug gegen die Sowjetunion. Entwicklung und Verhältnis zur Wehrmacht', in idem and Hans-Heinrich Wilhelm, *Die Truppe des Weltanschauungskrieges. Die Einsatzgruppen der Sicherheitspolizei und des SD, 1938–1942* (Stuttgart, 1981), 13–278, here 25f.; Brandes, *Tschechen*, vol. 1, 37f.

94. Heydrich during the meeting with his senior staff and Einsatzgruppen commanders in Berlin, 27 September 1939, in IfZ, Eich 983. See, too, the internal RSHA report on Communist activities inside and outside the Soviet Union since August 1939, 20 August 1940, in BAB, R 58/18.

95. 'Vermerk aus dem Sicherheitshauptamt', 22 April 1939, in BAB DH (Dahlwitz-Hoppegarten), ZR 521 A9, ff. 36/7–9. See, too, Dorothee Weitbrecht, 'Ermächtigung zur Vernichtung. Die Einsatzgruppen in Polen im Herbst 1939', in Klaus-Michael Mallmann and Bogdan Musial (eds), *Genesis des Genozids. Polen 1939–1941* (Darmstadt, 2004), 57–70, here 57; Wildt, *Generation*, 421f.; Klaus-Michael Mallmann, Jochen Böhler and Jürgen Matthäus, *Einsatzgruppen in Polen. Darstellung und Dokumentation* (Darmstadt, 2008), 15.

96. Wildt, *Generation*, 422. Figure according to Wodzimierz Borodziej, *Terror und Politik. Die deutsche Polizei und die polnische Widerstandsbewegung im Generalgouvernement 1939–1944* (Mainz, 1999), 29; and Dorothee Weitbrecht, *Der Exekutionsauftrag der Einsatzgruppen in Polen* (Filderstadt, 2001), 9.

97. On the recurrent theme of Germany's medieval drive to the East in Hitler's speeches and writings, see Neil Gregor, 'Hitler', in Casey and Wright (eds), *Mental Maps*, 177–202.

98. See the extensive video coverage in BAB Filmarchiv (Berlin), DW 615/26/1942.

99. Mallmann et al., *Einsatzgruppen*, 16.

100. See Helmut Knochen's protocol of the meeting, in BAB DH, ZR 512 A9, ff. 36/10–12. See, too, Krausnick and Wilhelm, *Truppe*, 33 and 41, n. 52.

101. Schellenberg to Jost, 22 July 1939, in USHMMA, RG 11.001 M.01, reel 1, folder 20.

102. Michael Wildt, 'Das Reichssicherheitshauptamt. Radikalisierung und Selbstradikalisierung einer Institution', *Mittelweg* 36 (1998), 33–40, here 22; Evans, *Third Reich at War*, 17.

103. See Keitel's post-war testimony of 29 March 1946, in *IMT*, vol. 10, 376ff. (doc. Keitel-12), here 378; see, too, Christian Hartmann and Sergej Slutsch, 'Franz Halder und die Kriegsvorbereitungen im Frühjahr 1939. Eine Ansprache des Generalstabschefs des Heeres', *VfZ* 45 (1997), 467–95, here 493.

104. Eduard Wagner, *Der Generalquartiermeister. Briefe und Tagebuchaufzeichnungen des Generalquartiermeisters des Heeres General der Artillerie Eduard Wagner*, ed. Elisabeth Wagner (Munich and Vienna, 1963), 103.

105. 'Richtlinien für den auswärtigen Einsatz der Sicherheitspolizei und des SD, 31 July 1939', BAB, R 58/241, f. 169; see, too, Mallmann et al., *Einsatzgruppen*, 16; Wildt, *Generation*, 426.

106. 'Richtlinien', BAB, R 58/241.

107. On this, see, too, Wildt, *Generation*, 427.

108. 'Richtlinien', BAB, R 58/241, ff. 169–71.

109. Hitler's speech of 22 August 1939, in *Akten zur deutschen auswärtigen Politik*, series D, vol. 7, 172; see, too, Kershaw, *Hitler: Nemesis*, 208f.

110. Hans-Adolf Jacobsen (ed.), *Generaloberst Halder: Kriegstagebuch*, vol. 1: *Vom Polenfeldzug bis zum Ende der Westoffensive* (Stuttgart, 1962), 44; Wildt, *Generation*, 427.

111. Heydrich to Daluege, 2 July 1940, in BAB, R 19/395; see the commentary by Helmut Krausnick, 'Hitler und die Morde in Polen. Ein Beitrag zum Konflikt zwischen Heer und SS um die Verwaltung der besetzten Gebiete', *VfZ* 11 (1963), 196–209, here 207.

112. Testimonies of Lothar Beutel (20 July 1965) and Ernst Gerke (2 November 1966) in Bundesarchiv Ludwigsburg, B 162/Vorl. Dok. Slg. Einsatzgruppen in Polen II; Beutel's

testimony is reprinted in Mallmann et al., *Einsatzgruppen*, 121f. See, too, Wetbrecht, 'Ermächtigung', 59ff.
113. Hitler's speech of 22 August 1939, in *Akten zur deutschen auswärtigen Politik*, series D, vol. 7, 172; post-war testimony of Emanuel Schäfer, 13 June 1952, in IfZ, ZS 573; Longerich, *Himmler*, 490ff.
114. Post-war testimony of Erwin Lahousen, 6 June 1950, in IfZ, ZS 658. See, too, Alfred Spiess and Heiner Lichtenstein, *Unternehmen Tannenberg. Der Anlass zum Zweiten Weltkrieg* (2nd rev. edn, Frankfurt am Main and Berlin, 1989), 26ff., quotation on p. 30. See, too, Jürgen Runzheimer, 'Die Grenzzwischenfälle am Abend vor dem Angriff auf Polen', in Wolfgang Benz and Hermann Graml (eds), *Sommer 1939. Die Grossmächte und der Europäische Krieg* (Stuttgart, 1979), 107–47; Höhne, *Orden*, 240ff.; post-war testimony of Alfred Naujocks, 19 November 1945, in *IMT*, vol. 31, doc. 2751-PS, pp. 90ff. Hitler's Reichstag speech of 1 September 1939 in Adolf Hitler, *Reden und Proklamationen*, ed. Max Domarus, 2 vols (Würzburg, 1962–3), vol. 2, 1312ff., quotation on p. 1315.
115. Reinhard Heydrich to Lina Heydrich, 1 September 1939, in IfZ, Ed 450; see, too, Heydrich, *Kriegsverbrecher*, 119.
116. Browning, *Origins*, 12ff.

Chapter VI: Experiments with Mass Murder

1. A detailed account of the military campaign is provided by Horst Rohde, 'Hitler's First Blitzkrieg and its Consequences for North-Eastern Europe', in Militärgeschichtliches Forschungsamt (ed.), *Germany and the Second World War*, 10 vols (Oxford 1990–), vol. 2, 67–150.
2. The activities of the SS task forces in Poland are recorded in the daily 'Tannenberg reports' (forty-five in total), which were submitted to Heydrich by the Security Police commanders in the field. Their usefulness as historical evidence is, however, undermined by the subsequent alterations made to these reports as well as by the coded language used to describe mass killings. See the reports in BAB, R 58/1082. See, too, Mallmann et al., *Einsatzgruppen*, 116ff.; Wildt, *Generation*, 481; Czeslaw Madajczyk, *Die Okkupationspolitik Nazideutschlands in Polen 1939–1945* (Cologne, 1988), 14ff., 186ff.
3. 'Protokoll der Amtschefbesprechung', 7 September 1939, in BAB, R 58/825, and 'Protokoll der Amtschefbesprechung', 14 October 1939, in BAB, R 58/825.
4. The lower figure is quoted in Christian Jansen and Arno Weckbecker, *Der 'Volksdeutsche Selbstschutz' in Polen 1939/40* (Munich, 1992), 28; the higher figure is quoted in Browning, *Origins*, 31.
5. Wagner, *Generalquartiermeister*, 123; Jacobsen, *Halder: Kriegstagebuch*, vol. 1, 57 and 62. See, too, Mallmann et al., *Einsatzgruppen*, 18.
6. Włodzimierz Jastrzębski, *Der Bromberger Blutsonntag. Legende und Wirklichkeit* (Poznán, 1990); Weitbrecht, 'Ermächtigung', 61; Wildt, *Generation*, 438ff.
7. See Alexander B. Rossino, 'Nazi Anti-Jewish Policy during the Polish Campaign: The Case of the Einsatzgruppe von Woyrsch', *German Studies Review* 24 (2001), 35–53; idem, *Hitler Strikes Poland: Blitzkrieg, Ideology and Atrocity* (Lawrence, KS, 2003), 77 and 159; Weitbrecht, 'Ermächtigung', 60; Mallmann et al., *Einsatzgruppen*, 19; Wildt, *Generation*, 433ff. and 448; Tannenberg report of 11 September 1939, BAB, R 58/1082, ff. 51f.; Edward B. Westermann, *Hitler's Police Battalions: Enforcing Racial War in the East* (Lawrence, KS, 2005), 127ff; Longerich, *Himmler*, 445.
8. Heydrich to all departmental heads of Sipo and SD, 1 September 1939, Yad Vashem Archives, 97-210-FI; Wildt, *Generation*, 452; Mallmann et al., *Einsatzgruppen*, 54 and 59. Heydrich's own report about his experiences in Poland to departmental heads of the RSHA on 14 September is very vague. See the transcript of the meeting in BAB, R 58/825.
9. See Streckenbach's post-war testimony of 25 November 1966, in BA Ludwigsburg, 201 AR-Z 76/59, vol. 2, p. 42. See, too, the post-war testimony of Jakub Gasecki (a former resident in Dynów), in BA Ludwigsburg, B 162/Vorl. AR-Z 302/67, vol. 3., ff. 498f., partly reprinted in Mallmann et al., *Einsatzgruppen*, doc. 27, pp. 133f.; see, too, Rossino, *Poland,* 88ff.; Jacobsen, *Halder: Kriegstagebuch*, vol. 1, 67 (10 September 1939).

10. Heydrich to Daluege, 2 July 1940, in BAB, R 19/395. See, too, Mallmann et al., *Einsatzgruppen*, 59.
11. Wildt, *Generation*, 444ff.; Weitbrecht, 'Ermächtigung', 61; Rossino, *Poland*, 69ff.
12. Browning, *Origins*, 29; Hans Umbreit, *Deutsche Militärverwaltungen 1938/39. Die militärische Besetzung der Tschechoslowakei und Polens* (Stuttgart, 1977), 166. According to Wodzimierz Borodziej, 30,000 people were killed in Danzig-West Prussia, 10,000 in the Wartheland, 1,500 in Eastern Upper Silesia and 1,000 in the Zichenau district. See Borodziej, *Terror*, 29. No concrete figures have been established for how many of these victims were killed by the task forces as opposed to the Selbstschutz. See Mallmann et al., *Einsatzgruppen*, 87f. See, too, Volker Riess, *Die Anfänge der Vernichtung 'lebensunwerten Lebens' in den Reichsgauen Danzig-Westpreussen und Wartheland 1939/40* (Frankfurt am Main, 1995), 173ff.
13. On the Selbstschutz: Christian Jansen and Arno Weckbecker, 'Eine Miliz im "Weltanschuungskrieg". Der "Volksdeutsche Selbstschutz" in Polen 1939/40', in Wolfgang Michalka (ed.), *Der Zweite Weltkrieg. Analysen, Grundzüge, Forschungsbilanz* (Weyarn, 1997), 482–500. On the participation of ordinary Wehrmacht soldiers in the atrocities, see Joachim Böhler, *Auftakt zum Vernichtungskrieg. Die Wehrmacht in Polen 1939* (Frankfurt am Main, 2006); Rossino, *Poland*, 90f. and 99. On Alvensleben, see BAB, BDC, SSO Alvensleben; see, too, Dieter Schenk, *Hitlers Mann in Danzig. Albert Forster und die NS-Verbrechen in Danzig-Westpreussen* (Bonn, 2000), 157, n. 12.
14. Heydrich to Daluege, 2 July 1940, BAB, R 19/395; Müller to Eicke, 10 October 1939, informing Eicke that Heydrich was investigating incidents of plunder in Wloclawek, in USHMMA, RG 48.004 M, reel 3, folder 300041. See, too, Rossino, *Poland*, 102; Mallmann et al., *Einsatzgruppen*, 59.
15. Heydrich shared this attitude with Himmler, who, in his infamous Posen speech of 4 October 1943, explicitly threatened personal enrichment from Jewish property with the death penalty – an almost absurd twist of logic in light of the mass theft organized by the Nazi state. For Himmler's speech, see *IMT*, vol. 29, doc. 1919-PS, pp. 110–73, here p. 146.
16. Groscurth's diary entry of 8 September 1939, in Groscurth, *Tagebücher*, 201. Heydrich repeated the same sentiments in a conversation with Eduard Wagner some days later. See Jacobsen, *Halder: Kriegstagebuch*, vol. 1, 79 (19 September 1939).
17. Groscurth, *Tagebücher*, 201f.
18. 'Vermerk Oberstleutnant Lahousen vom 14.9.1939. Besprechung im Führerzug in Illnau am 12.9.1939', in IfZ, Nbg. Dok. PS-3047.
19. *Akten zur deutschen auswärtigen Politik*, series D, vol. 7, doc. 193. On Hitler's response to the massacres of ethnic Germans, see Kershaw, *Hitler: Hubris*, 242.
20. OKH to AOK 4, 11 September 1939 as quoted in Krausnick and Wilhelm, *Truppe des Weltanschauungskrieges*, 33 and 57; Böhler, *Auftakt*, 205ff. See, too, Groscurth, *Tagebücher*, 360.
21. Brauchitsch to army commanders, 18 September 1939, Bundesarchiv Militärarchiv (Freiburg), RH 1/58; Groscurth, *Tagebücher*, 206.
22. Wagner, *Generalquartiermeister*, 134; Jacobsen, *Halder: Kriegstagebuch*, vol. 1, 79 (19 September 1939).
23. BAB, R 58/825.
24. Jacobsen, *Halder: Kriegstagebuch*, vol. 1, 82 (20 September 1939); Brauchitsch's order 'Tätigkeit und Aufgaben der Polizei-EG im Operationsgebiet' of 21 September 1939, in BA-MA, RH 20–14/178.
25. Groscurth, *Tagebücher*, 361–2; BA Ludwigsburg, 'Einsatzgruppen in Polen', vol. 1, 129ff.; see, too, Browning, *Origins*, 19.
26. Groscurth, *Tagebücher*, 209 and 362; Wagner, *Generalquartiermeister*, 135.
27. Protocol of the RSHA meeting of departmental heads and task-force commanders in September, in IfZ, Eich 983; see, too, Wildt, *Generation*, 460; Rossino, *Poland*, 118. Heydrich's order appears to have been a direct result of a meeting between Himmler and Brauchitsch earlier that day. See Mallmann et al., *Einsatzgruppen*, 64.
28. Blaskowitz to OKH, 27 November 1939, as quoted in Kershaw, *Hitler*, vol. 2, 342. Similar complaints were made by General Walter Petzel, General Wilhelm Ulex and Lieutenant General Fedor von Bock; see Evans, *Third Reich at War*, 25f. See, too, Krausnick, 'Einsatzgruppen', 80ff.

29. Browning, *Origins*, 17; Catherine Epstein, *Model Nazi: Arthur Greiser and the Occupation of Western Poland* (Oxford, 2010), 124ff.; Umbreit, *Militärverwaltungen*, 154f.; Rossino, *Poland*, 116f.; Gerhard Engel, *At the Heart of the Reich: The Secret Diary of Hitler's Army Adjutant* (London, 2005), 79 (entries for 15 October and 18 November 1939). On army jurisdiction, see Heydrich's comments during the RSHA meeting of 21 September, in BAB, R 58/825. Martin Broszat, *Nationalsozialistische Polenpolitik (1939–1945)* (Stuttgart, 1961), 34f.

30. 'Protokoll der Amtschefbesprechung', 7 September 1939, in BAB, R 58/825. Similar sentiments were expressed in Himmler's memorandum on the 'treatment of alien peoples in the East' which he submitted to an approving Hitler in the spring of 1940. See *VfZ* 5 (1957), 195ff.

31. 'Protokoll der Amtschefbesprechung', 21 September 1939, in BAB, R 58/825, and 29 September 1939, in IfZ, Eich 983. Hitler referred to the idea of an Eastern Wall in a conversation with Rosenberg one week later. See Hans-Günther Seraphim (ed.), *Das politische Tagebuch Alfred Rosenbergs 1934/35 und 1939/40* (Munich, 1956), 98.

32. 'Protokolle der Amtschefbesprechung', 29 September, 3 October, 10 October and 14 October 1939, all in BAB, R 58/825. The term 'unweaving' was coined by Bloxham, *Final Solution*, 59ff.

33. 'Protokoll der Amtschefbesprechung', 21 September 1939, in BAB, R 58/825; 'Rundbrief Heydrich an Chef der Zivilverwaltung in Polen und Einsatzgruppen', 30 September 1939, in IfZ, MA 682, ff. 797f.

34. *Verhandlungen des Reichstages*, vol. 460, 51ff.

35. 'Erlass des Führers und Reichskanzlers zur Festigung des deutschen Volkstums', in *IMT*, vol. 26, doc. 686-PS, pp. 255f.; see, too, Phillip Terrell Rutherford, *Prelude to the Final Solution: The Nazi Program for Deporting Ethnic Poles 1939–1941* (Lawrence, KS, 2007), 55. Heydrich had already announced Himmler's imminent appointment as RKFDV to his departmental heads and the *Einsatzgruppen* commanders on 21 September. See 'Protokoll der Amtschefbesprechung', 21 September 1939, in BAB, R 58/825.

36. Heydrich's order of 13 October 1939 and 22 December 1939, in USHMMA, RG 15.007 M, 8/101/13; see, too, Heinemann, *Rasse*, 195ff. and 232ff.; and Aly and Heim, *Vordenker*, 152.

37. A good general discussion of these themes can be found in Bloxham, *Final Solution*, 58ff.

38. 'Protokoll der Amtschefbesprechung', 14 October 1939, in BAB, R 58/825.

39. Jansen, *'Selbstschutz'*, 154ff., 212ff.; Browning, *Origins*, 32ff.

40. Friedländer, *Extermination*, 40.

41. *Verhandlungen des Reichstages*, vol. 460, 51ff.

42. Bogdan Musial, *Deutsche Zivilverwaltung und Judenverfolgung im Generalgouvernement. Eine Fallstudie zum Distrikt Lublin 1939–1944* (Wiesbaden, 1999), 183ff.; Rossino, *Poland*, 88ff.

43. Longerich, *Politik*, 224 and 251f.; Browning, *Origins*, 12.

44. 'Protokoll der Amtschefbesprechung', 7 September 1939, in BAB, R 58/825; and order to Stapoleitstellen in the Reich, 8 September 1939, in IfZ, Eich 1633.

45. 'Protokoll der Amtschefbesprechung', 14 September 1939, in BAB, R 58/825.

46. 'Protokoll der Sitzung des Ministerrats für die Reichsverteidigung', 19 September 1939, in *IMT*, vol. 31, 230–2. See, too, Wildt, *Generation*, 457.

47. Broszat, *Polenpolitik*, 20.

48. 'Protokoll der Amtschefbesprechung', 21 September 1939, in BAB, R 58/825.

49. Heydrich's courier letter of 21 September 1939, in BAB, R 58/276. See, too, Broszat, *Polenpolitik*, 21f.; Dan Michman, 'Why Did Heydrich Write the "Schnellbrief"? A Remark on the Reason and on its Significance', *Yad Vashem Studies* 32 (2004), 433–47; Browning, *Origins*, 111f.

50. Heydrich's courier letter of 21 September 1939, in BAB, R 58/276; see, too, Michman, 'Schnellbrief'; Hans Mommsen, *Auschwitz: 17. Juli 1942* (Munich, 2002), 97.

51. Protocol of the RSHA Amtsleiter and task-force commander meeting of 29 September 1939, in IfZ, Eich 983. See, too, Longerich, *Himmler*, 456.

52. Heydrich's courier letter to all *Einsatzgruppen* commanders, 21 September 1939, in BAB, R 58/276. Heydrich told Brauchitsch on 22 September that the area around Kraków had been chosen as the location for the future 'Jewish state'. See Groscurth, *Tagebücher*, 361.

53. Heydrich to Brauchitsch, in Groscurth, *Tagebücher*, 361f.

54. Rutherford, *Prelude*, 258.

55. 'Protokoll der Amtschefbesprechung', 29 September 1939, in BAB, R 58/825.
56. Rosenberg, *Tagebuch*, 98.
57. Mallmann et al., *Einsatzgruppen*, 63f.
58. Wildt, *Generation*, 464f.
59. Browning, *Origins*, 27; Mallmann et al., *Einsatzgruppen*, 64.
60. Schnellbrief, 30 September 1939, in BAB, R 58/276.
61. 'Protokoll der Einsatzgruppenleitertagung', 3 October 1939, in BAB, R 58/825; see, too, Mallmann et al., *Einsatzgruppen*, 64.
62. Müller to Eichmann, 6 October 1939, Akten der Gestapo Mährisch-Ostrau, Yad Vashem Archives, 0–53/93/283. See, too, Seev Goshen, 'Eichmann und die Nisko-Aktion im Oktober 1939. Eine Fallstudie zur NS-Judenpolitik in der letzten Etappe vor der Endlösung', *VfZ* 29 (1981), 74–96; Longerich, *Politik*, 256ff.; Wildt, *Generation*, 468ff.; Cesarani, *Eichmann*, 78.
63. On Eichmann's conversation with Wagner see Longerich, *Himmler*, 456–7; on Eichmann's conversation with Bürckel's Jewish expert, Becker, on 7 October 1939, see Longerich, *Politik*, 257.
64. On the 'Nisko project', see Miroslav Kárný, 'Nisko in der Geschichte der Endlösung', *Judaica Bohemiae* 23 (1987), 69–84; Goshen, 'Nisko-Aktion', 74ff.; Jonny Moser, 'Nisko: The First Experiment in Deportation', *Simon Wiesenthal Center Annual* 2 (1985), 1–30; Ludmila Nesládková (ed.), *The Case Nisko in the History of the Final Solution of the Jewish Problem* (Ostrava, 1995).
65. Goshen, 'Nisko-Aktion', 89ff.; Safrian, *Eichmann-Männer*, 77ff.; see, too, Lukáš Přibye, 'Das Schicksal des dritten Transports aus dem Protektorat nach Nisko', *Theresienstädter Studien und Dokumente* 7 (2000), 297–342.
66. Browning, *Origins*, 40f.
67. Longerich, *Himmler*, 457.
68. 'Fernschreiben SD-Hauptamt an Sipo und SD Donau, Mährisch-Ostrau vom 19.10.1939', Yad Vashem Archives, 053/87. See, too, Himmler's letter to Bürckel of 9 November 1939, as quoted in Gerhard Botz, *Wohnungspolitik und Judendeportation in Wien 1928–1945* (Vienna, 1975), 196. See, too, Longerich, *Politik*, 259.
69. Wildt, *Generation*, 471, n. 176.
70. Browning, *Origins*, 42.
71. Heydrich to the HSSPF in Krakau (Krüger) and Posen (Koppe) and to the Sipo commanders in both districts (Streckenbach and Damzog), 28 November 1939, in DÖW, 21732/62.
72. Although no copy of the finalized 'long-term plan' seems to have survived the war, an undated draft can be found in BAB, R 69/1146.
73. Heydrich to Sipo Krakau, Breslau, Posen, Danzig and Königsberg, 21 December 1939, in BAB, R 58/276.
74. '2. Nahplan', 21 December 1939, USHMMA, RG 15.015 M, 2/97/1–7. See, too, Götz Aly, *'Final Solution': Nazi Population Policy and the Murder of the European Jews* (London and New York, 1999), 73ff.; Longerich, *Politik*, 266.
75. Protocol of the meeting with representatives of the General Government in Berlin of 8 January 1940, in IfZ, MA 225; BAB, R 58/1032, protocol of the RSHA meeting of 30 January 1940. See, too, Browning, *Origins*, 59–60.
76. Longerich, *Himmler*, 461; Aly, *'Final Solution'*, 157; Sybille Steinbacher, *'Musterstadt' Auschwitz. Germanisierungspolitik und Judenmord in Ostoberschlesien* (Munich, 2000), 133f.
77. On the problems of implementing the short-term plan, see the report of Albert Rapp, head of the UWZ in Posen, 26 January 1940, in DÖW, 21732/62.
78. Adam, *Judenpolitik*, 254; Longerich, *Politik*, S. 267.
79. RSHA order of 24 April 1940, as quoted in Hans Günther Adler, *Der Verwaltete Mensch. Studien zur Deportation der Juden aus Deutschland* (Tübingen, 1974), 27.
80. See, for example, Reinhard Heydrich, 'Kripo und Gestapo', in *Düsseldorfer Nachrichten*, 29 January 1939; Timothy W. Mason, 'Die Erbschaft der Novemberrevolution für den Nationalsozialismus', in idem, *Sozialpolitik im Dritten Reich. Arbeiterklasse und Volksgemeinschaft* (Opladen, 1977), 15–41, here 21.
81. Heydrich to all Security Police Head Offices, 3 September 1939 ('Grundsätze der inneren Staatssicherung während des Krieges'), in IfZ, MA 444/2.

82. Ibid.
83. See Himmler's official order for the creation of the RSHA of 27 September 1939, in BAB, R 58/240, ff. 1f. On the RSHA more generally, see Wildt, *Generation*, 283ff.; and idem, 'Reichssicherheitshauptamt', 33ff.
84. Wildt, *Generation*, 259ff.; Banach, *Elite*, 287ff.
85. Wildt, *Generation*, 263f.
86. 'Vermerk Schellenberg', 5 July 1938, in BAB, R 58/827, ff. 13–17. See, too, Dierker, *Glaubenskrieger*, 318; Banach, *Elite*, 288; Wildt, *Generation*, 264.
87. Memorandum Schellenberg 'Reorganisation des Sicherheitsdienstes des Reichsführers SS im Hinblick auf eine organisatorische und personelle Angleichung mit der Sicherheitspolizei', 24 February 1939, in BAB, R 58/8262–30; memorandum Schellenberg 'Laufbahnrichtlinien und Dienstanweisung für die Inspekteure der Sicherheitspolizei', 22 February 1939, in BAB, R 58/826, ff. 31–40; memorandum Ploetz 'Die Laufbahnen im Sicherheitsdienst', in BAB, R 58/827, ff. 27–40; see, too, Dierker, *Glaubenskrieger*, 318f.; Wildt, *Generation*, 267.
88. Memorandum Best 'Grundzüge der Ausbildung und der Laufbahn der Führer (leitenden Beamten) der Deutschen Sicherheitspolizei', 1 March 1939, in BAB, R 58/827, ff. 53ff.; see, too, Banach, *Elite*, 291; Wildt, *Generation*, 269f.; Dierker, *Glaubenskrieger*, 320.
89. Wildt, *Generation*, 270.
90. Heydrich to Daluege, 30 October 1941, in IfZ, MA 325/8591. See, too, Wilhelm, *Polizei*, 170.
91. Michael Wildt, 'Radikalisierung und Selbstradikalisierung 1939. Die Geburt des Reichssicherheitshauptamtes aus dem Geist des völkischen Massenmordes', in Paul and Mallmann (eds), *Gestapo im Zweiten Weltkrieg*, 11–41, here 15.
92. See BAB, R 58/826: 'Vermerk Schellenberg vom 4. April 1939'; BAB, R 58/137: 'Besprechung bei Heydrich am 15. April 1939 betr. Neugestaltung von Sipo und SD'; BAB, R 58/137: 'Vermerk Schellenberg vom 25. April 1939 betr. Kritik an Bests Position'; BAB, R 58/826: 'Runderlass Heydrichs vom 5. Juli 1939'; see, too, Wildt, *Generation*, 265; Dierker, *Glaubenskrieger*, 318.
93. Werner Best, 'Apologie des Juristen', *Deutsches Recht* 9 (1939), 196–9; idem, 'Der "politischste" Beruf', *Deutsche Allgemeine Zeitung*, 12 April 1939; on this, see in greater detail Herbert, *Best*, 231ff. Heydrich held back Schellenberg's aggressive response because he was concerned about his apparatus's public image. See Schellenberg's comments on Best's articles in BAB, R 58/827, ff. 111f.; Banach, *Elite*, 292.
94. Statement on Heydrich by Dr Werner Best, 1 October 1959, in Copenhagen, in IfZ, ZS 207/2; see, too, Wildt, *Generation*, 93; Wilhelm, *Polizei*, 121; Herbert, *Best*, 228ff.
95. Heydrich's order of 5 July 1939, in BAB, R 58/826; Himmler's order of 27 September 1939, in BAB, R 58/240, p. 1. See, too, Reinhard Rürup, *Topographie des Terrors. Gestapo, SS und Reichssicherheitshauptamt auf dem 'Prinz-Albrecht-Gelände'. Eine Dokumentation* (Berlin, 1987), 71; Gerhard Paul, '"Kämpfende Verwaltung". Das Amt IV des Reichssicherheitshauptamtes als Führungsinstanz der Gestapo', in idem and Mallmann (eds), *Gestapo im Zweiten Weltkrieg*, 42–81, here 47.
96. Hachmeister, *Gegnerforscher*; Dierker, *Glaubenskrieger*, 331ff.; Wildt, *Generation*, 364ff.; Banach, *Elite*, 366f.
97. Wilhelm, *Polizei*, 119f.; Wildt, *Generation*, 378ff.; Heinz Boberach (ed.), *Meldungen aus dem Reich 1938–1945. Die geheimen Lageberichte des Sicherheitsdienstes der SS*, 18 vols (Herrsching, 1984–5).
98. Wildt, *Generation*, 335ff. and 352ff.; Paul, '"Kämpfende Verwaltung"', 42ff.
99. Patrick Wagner, *Hitlers Kriminalisten. Die deutsche Kriminalpolizei und der Nationalsozialismus* (Munich, 2002), 76; Wildt, *Generation*, 301ff.
100. Thorsten J. Querg, *Spionage und terror. Das Amt VI des Reichssicherheitshauptamtes 1939–1945*. Phil. Diss., Freie Universität Berlin, Berlin, 1997., 165 and 183ff.; Wildt, *Generation*, 391ff.; Schellenberg, *Labyrinth*, 41.
101. Heydrich's order 'Entlastung der Geheimen Staatspolizei', 31 September 1939, in BAB, R 58/239; see, too, Wagner, *Volksgemeinschaft*, 330ff.
102. Tuchel, 'Gestapa', 97.
103. Michael Wildt, 'The Spirit of the Reich Security Main Office (RSHA)', *Totalitarian Movements and Political Religions* 6 (2005), 333–49. Heydrich used the term 'fighting

administration' in a speech in Prague in September 1941. See Kárný et al. (eds), *Deutsche Politik*, 108.

104. Wildt, *Generation*, 209ff. and 230ff.; Paul, ' "Kämpfende Verwaltung" ', 46. Quotation from Heydrich's speech on the occasion of the 1941 Day of the German Police, as printed in *Völkischer Beobachter*, 17 February 1941.

105. On Elser's assassination attempt, see Anton Hoch and Lothar Gruchmann, *Georg Elser. Der Attentäter aus dem Volke. Der Anschlag auf Hitler im Münchner Bürgerbräu 1939* (Frankfurt, 1980); Roger Moorhouse, *Killing Hitler: The Third Reich and the Plots against the Führer* (London, 2006), 36ff.; RSHA directive, 9 November 1939, in USHMM, RG 11.001 M.01, reel 13/21; Longerich, *Himmler*, S. 488f.

106. See the post-war account of Dr Albrecht Böhme, head of the Bavarian Criminal Police at the time of Elser's assassination attempt, in IfZ, ZS 1939.

107. Schellenberg, *Labyrinth*, 82ff.; Höhne, *Orden*, 263ff.; Querg, *Spionage*, 224ff.; Wildt, *Generation*, 399f.; see, too, the post-war testimony of Walter Huppenkothen (Reg. Dir. RSHA/IV), in IfZ, ZS 249, ff. 16f.

108. Orth, *System*, 97ff.

109. Orth, *System*, 37ff., 86ff. and 109ff.

110. Heydrich's order of 2 January 1941, in IfZ, PS-1063; on Mauthausen, see Orth, *System*, 86f.

111. Heydrich to Frick, 4 October 1939, in IfZ, MA 145/1; on the context, Nikolaus Wachsmann, *Hitler's Prisons: Legal Terror in Nazi Germany* (New Haven and London, 2004), 194ff. and 394f.

112. Himmler to Heydrich, 16 January 1942, in BAB, NS 19/219. On the persecution of 'deviant youths', see, too, Alfons Kenmann, 'Störfaktor and der "Heimatfront". Jugendliche Nonkonformität und die Gestapo', in Mallmann and Paul (eds), *Gestapo im Zweiten Weltkrieg*, 179–200.

113. Heydrich to all Security Police Head Offices, 3 September 1939 ('Grundsätze der inneren Staatssicherung während des Krieges'), in IfZ, MA 444/2. The first written usage of the word *Sonderbehandlung* can be found in Heydrich's order of 20 September 1939, in BAB, R 58/243. See, too, Gerd Wysocki, 'Lizenz zum Töten. Die "Sonderbehandlungs"-Praxis der Stapo-Stelle Braunschweig', in Paul and Mallmann (eds), *Gestapo im Zweiten Weltkrieg*, 237–54.

114. Heydrich to Lammers, 22 January 1940, in National Archives, Kew, GFM 33/4830; Heydrich to all Stapoleitstellen, 5 February 1940 and 12 March 1940, DÖW 20752/93b.

115. Ulrich Herbert, *Hitler's Foreign Workers: Enforced Foreign Labor in Germany under the Third Reich* (Cambridge and New York, 1997), 87ff.

116. Heydrich's order of 12 September 1939, in Walk (ed.), *Sonderrecht*, IV/2. On Heydrich's order of 21 September 1939, see Adam, *Judenpolitik*, 260; Barkai, *Boykott*, 183ff.; Walk (ed.), *Sonderrecht*, 303ff.; Wildt, *Generation*, 132ff. and 153ff.

117. On T4, see Götz Aly (ed.), *Aktion T4 1939–1945. Die 'Euthanasie'-Zentrale in der Tiergartenstrasse 4* (2nd edn, Berlin, 1989); Ulf Schmidt, 'Reassessing the Beginning of the "Euthanasia" Programme', *German History* 17 (1999), 543–50. Aly, *'Final Solution'*, 70ff.; Eugen Kogon, Hermann Langbein and Adalbert Rückert, *Nationalsozialistische Massentötungen durch Giftgas* (Frankfurt, 1983), 62ff.; Heike Bernhardt, ' "Euthanasie" und Kriegsbeginn. Die frühen Morde an Patienten aus Pommern', *Zeitschrift für Geschichtswissenschaft* 9 (1996), 773–88; Henry Friedländer, *The Origins of Nazi Genocide. From Euthanasia to the Final Solution* (Chapel Hill, NC, 1995); Michael Burleigh, *Death and Deliverance: 'Euthanasia' in Germany, c.1900–1945* (Cambridge, 1994); Hans-Walter Schmuhl, *Rassenhygiene, Nationalsozialismus, Euthanasie. Von der Verhütung zur Vernichtung 'lebensunwerten Lebens' 1890–1945* (Göttingen, 1987), 190ff.

118. Heydrich's order of 1 March 1939 in *Mitteilungsblatt des Reichskriminalamtes* 2/4 (April 1939), 58–61; see, too, Guenter Lewy, *The Nazi Persecution of the Gypsies* (Oxford, 2001), particularly 54.

119. See Heydrich's orders of 17 October 1939 and 27 April 1940, in IfZ, Fa 506/3; see, too, Michael Zimmermann, *Rassenutopie und Genozid. Die nationalsozialistische 'Lösung der Zigeunerfrage'* (Hamburg, 1996); Sybil H. Milton, ' "Gypsies" as Social Outsiders in Nazi Germany', in Robert Gellately and Nathan Stoltzfus (eds), *Social Outsiders in Nazi Germany* (Princeton, NJ, 2001), 212–32.

Chapter VII: At War with the World

1. Hans-Martin Ottmer, *'Weserübung'. Der deutsche Angriff auf Dänemark und Norwegen im April 1940* (Munich, 1994); Richard J. Evans, *The Third Reich at War* (London, 2008), 117ff. See, too, Hans-Dietrich Loock, *Quisling, Rosenberg und Terboven. Zur Vorgeschichte und Geschichte der nationalsozialistischen Revolution in Norwegen* (Stuttgart, 1970), 277ff.; Robert Bohn, *Reichskommissariat Norwegen. 'Nationalsozialistische Neuordnung' und Kriegswirtschaft* (Munich, 2000), 31ff.

2. Hitler's decision in favour of a military occupation regime in Western Europe was noted with relief by the Army High Command: BA-MA, RW 4/v. 581 ('Vortragsnotiz OKW', 20 January 1940), See, too, Bernhard R. Kroener, Rolf-Dieter Müller and Hans Umbreit, *Das Deutsche Reich und der Zweite Weltkrieg*, vol. 5/1: *Kriegsverwaltung, Wirtschaft, und personelle Resourcen* (Stuttgart, 1988), 57, n. 178.

3. Heydrich to Daluege, 2 July 1940, in BAB, R 19/395.

4. 'Aktenvermerk über Besprechung bei Amtschef I', 2 April 1940, in BAB DH, ZR 277, ff. 8–9. Less than a week earlier, on 26 and 28 March, Heydrich had approved the formation of two *Einsatzkommandos*, one for the Netherlands and one for Belgium. He also ordered that no internal SD or Sipo documents should be passed on to the Wehrmacht. See IfZ (Munich), FA-228/2, ff. 205f.

5. See Stefan Semerdjiev, 'Reinhard Heydrich. Der deutsche Polizeichef als Jagdflieger', *Deutsche Militärzeitschrift* 41 (2004), 36–8; Deschner, *Heydrich*, 141f.

6. Heydrich, *Kriegsverbrecher, 72*; see, too, Heydrich's article in *Völkischer Beobachter*, 17 February 1941.

7. On 27 May 1937, Himmler had explicitly forbidden Heydrich to fly: IfZ, Ed 450. On Heydrich's time in Stavanger, see the reports of Frank-Werner Rott, Karl Holland and Berthold Jung, in Jochen Prien, *Geschichte des Jagdgeschwaders 77*, vol. 1: *1934–1941* (Eutin, 1992), 209.

8. Heydrich to Himmler, 5 May 1940; the postcard is reprinted in Max Williams, *Reinhard Heydrich: The Biography*, 2 vols (Church Stretton, 2001 and 2003), vol. 2, 30; Himmler to Heydrich, 15 May 1940, in Helmut Heiber (ed.), *Reichsführer! . . . Briefe an und von Himmler* (Stuttgart, 1968), doc. 66, p. 80; Prien, *Jagdgeschwaders 77*, vol. 1, 209.

9. Robert Bohn, 'Die Errichtung des Reichskommissariats Norwegen' in idem (ed.), *Neutralität und totalitäre Aggression. Nordeuropa und die Grossmächte im Zweiten Weltkrieg* (Stuttgart, 1991), 129–47; Loock, *Quisling*, 277ff.; Longerich, *Himmler*, 508.

10. See Werner Best's notes on the meeting of the RSHA's departmental heads of 20 April 1940, in BA Dahlwitz-Hoppegarten, ZR 277.

11. On the role of the Security Police in Norway, see Robert Bohn, '"Ein solches Spiel kennt keine Regeln". Gestapo und Bevölkerung in Norwegen und Dänemark', in Paul and Mallmann (eds), *Gestapo im Zweiten Weltkrieg*, 463ff.; Heydrich's order of 14 April 1940, as quoted in Bohn, *Reichskommissariat*, 77.

12. Konrad Kwiet, *Reichskommissariat Niederlande. Versuch und Scheitern nationalsozialistischer Neuordnung* (Stuttgart, 1968), 83ff.; Guus Meershoek, 'Machtentfaltung und Scheitern. Sicherheitspolizei und SD in den Niederlanden', in Paul and Mallmann, *Gestapo im Zweiten Weltkrieg*, 383–402, here 387ff.

13. Heydrich to Daluege, 2 July 1940, in BAB, R 19/395.

14. Werner Warmbrunn, *The German Occupation of Belgium, 1940–1944* (New York, 1993), 110ff.; Wolfram Weber, *Die innere Sicherheit im besetzten Belgien und Nordfrankreich 1940–1944. Ein Beitrag zur Geschichte der Besatzungsverwaltungen* (Düsseldorf, 1978); Jay H. Geller, 'The Role of the Military Administration in German-Occupied Belgium, 1940–1944', *Journal of Military History* 63 (1999), 99–125. On the Sipo in Belgium, see Wildt, *Generation*, 522ff. On Reeder, Falkenhausen and their relationship with the SS, see, too, the post-war testimony of Erwin Brunner, 'Entwicklung des Verhältnisses zwischen Wehrmacht und SS in Belgien', in IfZ, ZS 1718, ff. 1–16.

15. Bernd Kasten, *'Gute Franzosen'. Die französische Polizei und die deutsche Besatzungsmacht im besetzten Frankreich 1940–1944* (Sigmaringen, 1993), 22f. On the role of the Sipo and SD in the first phase of the occupation, see Ahlrich Meyer, *Die deutsche Besatzung in Frankreich 1940–1944. Widerstandsbekämpfung und Judenverfolgung* (Darmstadt, 2000), 13ff.; and

Wildt, *Generation*, 514ff.; Heydrich to Daluege, 2 July 1940, in BAB, R 19/395; Heydrich to RSHA Amtschefs, 24 August 1940, in BAB, R 58/241. Claudia Steur, *Theodor Dannnecker. Ein Funktionär der 'Endlösung'* (Essen, 1997), 48.

16. Herbert, *Best*, 251ff.
17. Walter Schellenberg, *Invasion 1940: The Nazi Invasion Plan for Britain* (London, 2000); see, too, Heydrich's memorandum of 5 May 1939, in IfZ, MA 451.
18. Ibid. See, too: Mazower, *Empire*, 112 f.
19 Mazower, *Empire*, 113.
20 On the evolution of the Madagascar plan, see Magnus Brechtken, *'Madagascar für die Juden'. Antisemitische Idee und politische Praxis 1885–1945* (Munich, 1997); Browning, *Origins*, 81ff.; Hans Jansen, *Der Madagaskar-Plan. Die beabsichtigte Deportation der europäischen Juden nach Madagascar* (Munich, 1997), particularly 320ff.; Leni Yahill, 'Madagascar, Phantom of a Solution for the Jewish Question', in Bela Vago and George L. Mosse (eds), *Jews and Non-Jews in Eastern Europe, 1918–1945* (New York, 1974), 315–34.
21. 'Memorandum des SD-Amtes IV/2 an Heydrich vom 24.5.1934', in OA Moscow, 501–1–18, ff. 18–20; reprinted in Michael Wildt (ed.), *Die Judenpolitik des SD 1935 bis 1938. Eine Dokumentation* (Munich, 1995), 66–9.
22. Memorandum in BAB, R 58/956, ff. 2–19; see, too, Wildt, *Generation*, 501.
23. Hagen to Eichmann, 5 March 1938, in BAB, R 58/956, f. 47. See, too, Jansen, *Madagaskar-Plan*, 228; Brechtken, *'Madagaskar für die Juden'*, 142ff. The plan was taken up again after the Kristallnacht pogroms of November 1938. See *IMT*, vol. 28, doc. 1816-PS, pp. 499ff.; see, too, Browning, *Origins*, 82.
24. The document is published in *VfZ* 5 (1957), 194–8. See, too, Longerich, *Politik*, 273f. Hitler informed Mussolini during a meeting in Munich in mid-June 1940 of his intention to use Madagascar as a Jewish reservation. On Hitler's comments to Mussolini, see Browning, *Origins*, 83. Hitler also mentioned the plan to the navy's Commander-in-Chief, Admiral Raeder. See Gerhard Wagner (ed.), *Lagevorträge Oberbefehlshabers der Kriegsmarine vor Hitler, 1939–45* (Munich, 1972), 106ff.
25. PAAA, Inland II A/B 347/3. See, too, Brechtken, *'Madagaskar für die Juden'*, 226f.
26. PAAA, Inland II A/B 347/3; Longerich, *Himmler*, 525.
27. Heydrich to Ribbentrop, 24 June 1940, in IfZ, Eich 464 ('presently' is underlined in the original); see, too, Jansen, *Madagaskar-Plan*, 327.
28. Cesarani, *Eichmann*, 87; Brechtken, *'Madagaskar für die Juden'*, 234f.; Jansen, *Madagaskar-Plan*, 332; Claudia Steur, 'Eichmanns Emissäre. Die "Judenberater" in Hitlers Europa', in Paul and Mallmann (eds), *Gestapo im Zweiten Weltkrieg*, 403–36. 'Protokoll der Abteilungsleitersitzung vom 12.7.1940', printed in Werner Präg and Wolfgang Jacobmeyer (eds), *Das Diensttagebuch des deutschen Generalgouverneurs in Polen 1939–45* (Stuttgart, 1975), 261.
29. Brechtken, *'Madagaskar für die Juden'*, 239; Jansen, *Madagaskar-Plan*, 335.
30. Rademacher's plan of 2 July, in PAAA, Inland IIg 177. See, too, Jansen, *Madagaskar-Plan*, 327ff.
31. On the RSHA's plan, compiled by Eichmann and his assistants Theodor Dannecker and Erich Rajakowitsch, see PAAA, Inland IIg 177, ff. 197–221. See, too, Dannecker to Rademacher, 15 August 1940, in Jansen, *Madagaskar-Plan*, 341ff; Christopher R. Browning, *The Final Solution and the German Foreign Office: A Study of Referat DIII of Abteilung Deutschland 1940–43* (New York and London, 1978), 40f.
32. PAAA, Inland IIg 177, ff. 197–221.
33. Longerich, *Himmler*, 526.
34. Heydrich's circular of 30 October 1940, in USHMMA, RG 15.015 M, reel 3/168/8–14.
35. Browning, *Origins*, 88.
36. Ibid., 90ff.
37. Heydrich to Luther, 29 October 1940, in PAAA, Inland IIg 189. See, too, Jacob Toury, 'Die Entstehungsgeschichte des Austreibungsbefehls gegen die Juden der Saarpfalz und Badens', *Jahrbuch des Instituts für Deutsche Geschichte* 15 (1986), 431–64; Browning, *Origins*, 89ff.
38. Heydrich to Luther, 29 October 1940, in PAAA, Inland IIg 189.
39. On the preparations for Operation Barbarossa see Hitler's orders of 12 November 1940 (no. 18) and 18 December 1940 (no. 21), reprinted in Walther Hubatsch (ed.), *Hitlers Weisungen für die Kriegsführung 1939–1945. Dokumente des Oberkommandos der Wehrmacht* (2nd rev.

edn, Koblenz, 1983), 67ff. and 84ff. On Hitler's orders to Heydrich, see Longerich, *Politik*, 287f. On 21 January 1941, Theodor Dannecker in a note for Eichmann referred explicitly to Heydrich's 'mandate from the Führer' to 'submit a proposal for a final solution project'. Dannecker to Eichmann, 21 January 1941, reprinted in Serge Klarsfeld, *Vichy – Auschwitz. Die Zusammenarbeit der deutschen und französischen Behörden bei der 'Endlösung der Judenfrage' in Frankreich* (Nördlingen, 1989), 361ff. Göring's appointment book, entry for 24 January 1941, in IfZ, Ed 180/5. That same day, Heydrich met Himmler, presumably to discuss the same subject. Witte et al. (eds), *Dienstkalender*, 24 January 1941, p. 112.

40. BAB, NS 19/3979. See, too, Wildt, *Generation*, 535; Longerich, *Himmler*, 528.

41. Memorandum Dannecker, 21 January 1941, as printed in Klarsfeld, *Vichy – Auschwitz*, 361f.

42. See, for example, Heydrich to Luther, 5 February 1941, in PAAA, Inland II AB 80–41 Sdh. III, vol. 1. See, too, Browning, *Origins*, 101ff.

43. Heydrich's memorandum of 26 March 1941, in OA Moscow, 500/3/795; see, too, Aly, *'Final Solution'*, 172.

44. Heydrich to head of SS Personnel Main Office, SS-Gruppenführer Schmitt, 25 January 1942, with annexed letter from Göring dated 31 July 1941, in *IMT*, vol. 26, doc. 710–PS. See, too, Browning, *Origins*, 315.

45. This contradicts Edouard Husson's recent argument that a comprehensive genocide of Europe's Jews was already planned by Heydrich in January 1941. See Edouard Husson, 'Die Entscheidung zur Vernichtung aller europäischen Juden. Versuch einer Neuinterpretation', in Klaus Hildebrand, Udo Wengst and Andreas Wirsching (eds), *Geschichtswissenschaft und Zeiterkenntnis. Von der Aufklärung bis zur Gegenwart. Festschrift für Horst Möller* (Munich, 2008), 277–89, particularly 284ff., and, more comprehensively, idem, *Heydrich et la solution finale* (Paris, 2008).

46. Halder, *Kriegstagebuch*, vol. 2, 335f., and vol. 1, 341f. See, too, Evans, *Third Reich at War*, 170ff. Peter Jahn and Reinhard Rürup (eds), *Erobern und Vernichten. Der Krieg gegen die Sowjetunion 1941–1945* (Berlin, 1991); Christian Hartmann, *Wehrmacht im Ostkrieg. Front und militärisches Hinterland 1941/42* (Munich, 2009).

47. 'Richtlinien auf Sondergebieten zur Weisung Nr. 21 (Fall Barbarossa)', reprinted in Hans-Adolf Jacobsen, 'Kommissarbefehl und Massenexekution sowjetischer Kriegsgefangener', in Buchheim et al., *SS*, doc. 1, pp. 449–544.

48. Christian Gerlach, *Kalkulierte Morde. Die deutsche Wirtschafts- und Vernichtungspolitik in Weissrussland 1941 bis 1944* (Hamburg, 1999), 71 and 81; Breitman, *Architect*, 148. Heydrich reported back to duty after his holiday on 7 March; see Witte et al. (eds), *Dienstkalender*, 7 March 1941. Heydrich and Himmler met again on 10 and 15 March, presumably to discuss the SS position in the ongoing negotiations: Witte et al. (eds), *Dienstkalender*, 10 and 15 March. First draft of the agreement of 26 March 1941, reprinted in Jacobsen, 'Kommissarbefehl', doc. 2, pp. 202 ff.

49. Krausnick and Wilhelm, *Truppe*, 117; Andrej Angrick, *Besatzungspolitik und Massenmord. Die Einsatzgruppe D in der südlichen Sowjetunion 1941–1943* (Hamburg, 2003), 45, n. 48.

50. Heydrich's notes of 26 March 1941 on a meeting with Göring, as quoted in Aly, *'Final Solution'*, 270.

51. On the German military campaign in the Balkans see Klaus Olshausen, *Zwischenspiel auf dem Balkan. Die deutsche Politik gegenüber Jugoslawien und Griechenland von März bis Juli 1941* (Stuttgart, 1973); Walter Manoschek, *'Serbien ist judenfrei'. Militärische Besatzungspolitik und Judenvernichtung in Serbien 1941/42* (Munich, 1993); Stevan Pavlowitch, *Hitler's New Disorder: The Second World War in Yugoslavia* (London, 2008); Karl-Heinz Golla, *Der Fall Griechenlands 1941* (Hamburg, 2007); Mark Mazower, *Inside Hitler's Greece: The Experience of Occupation, 1941–1944* (New Haven, 1993), 1ff.; Anestis Nessou, *Griechenland 1941–1944* (Osnabrück, 2009). Himmler, Heydrich and Daluege held an emergency meeting on 27 March 1941: Witte et al. (eds), *Dienstkalender*, 27 March 1941. On 8 April, Heydrich received Himmler's permission to fly: *Dienstkalender*, 8 April 1941.

52. Longerich, *Himmler*, 536. See, too, Roland G. Förster (ed.), *'Unternehmen Barbarossa'. Zum historischen Ort der deutsch-sowjetischen Beziehungen von 1933 bis Herbst 1941* (Munich, 1993), 507f.; Manoschek, *'Serbien ist judenfrei'*, 41f.

53. Witte et al. (eds), *Dienstkalender*, 16 April 1941. Longerich, *Himmler*, 536. A detailed account of the negotiations can be found in Angrick, *Besatzungspolitik*, 41ff.

54. Krausnick and Wilhelm, *Truppe*, 281ff.; Peter Klein (ed.), *Die Einsatzgruppen in der besetzten Sowjetunion, 1941/42: Die Tätigkeits- und Lageberichte des Chefs der Sicherheitspolizei und des SD* (Berlin, 1997).

55. Hans-Heinrich Wilhelm, *Die Einsatzgruppe A der Sicherheitspolizei und des SD 1941/42* (Frankfurt am Main, 1996), 281ff.; Wildt, *Generation*, 538ff.

56. Witte et al. (eds), *Dienstkalender*, 19, 26, 29 May and 9 June 1941.

57. Ibid., 11–15 June 1941; on the Wewelsburg, see Karl Hüser, *Wewelsburg 1933 bis 1945 – Kult- und Terrorstätte der SS. Eine Dokumentation* (2nd edn, Paderborn, 1987); and, more recently, Jan Erik Schulte (ed.), *Die SS, Himmler und die Wewelsburg* (Paderborn, 2009).

58. Longerich, *Himmler*, 540; Angrick, *Besatzungspolitik*, 108, n. 240.

59. Memorandum of the meeting of 2 May 1941, in *IMT*, vol. 31, doc. 2718-PS, pp. 84–5; and economic policy guidelines for the East, 23 May 1941, in *IMT*, vol. 36, doc. 126-EC 135–57, here 145; see, too, Alex J. Kay, 'Germany's Staatssekretäre, Mass Starvation, and the Meeting of 2 May 1941', *Journal of Contemporary History* 41 (2006), 685–700; idem, *Exploitation, Resettlement, Mass Murder: Political and Economic Planning for German Occupation Policy in the Soviet Union, 1940–1941* (New York and Oxford, 2006); Gerlach, *Kalkulierte Morde*, 46f.

60. Heydrich, *Kriegsverbrecher*, 86ff. See, too: Lizzie Collingham, *The Taste of War: World War Two and the Battle for Food* (London, 2011), 33.

61. Backe as quoted in Alexander Dallin, *German Rule in Russia, 1941–1945: A Study of Occupation Policies* (rev. edn, Boulder, CO, 1981), 39f. No serious biography of Backe exists to date. For brief biographical sketches, see Joachim Lehmann, 'Herbert Backe – Technokrat und Agrarideologe', in Ronald Smelser (ed.), *Die braune Elite* (Darmstadt, 1993), vol. 2, 1–12; Gesine Gerhard, 'Food and Genocide: Nazi Agrarian Politics in the Occupied Territories of the Soviet Union', *Contemporary European History* 18 (2009), 45–65; Joachim Lehmann, 'Verantwortung für Überleben, Hunger und Tod. Zur Stellung von Staatssekretär Herbert Backe im Entscheidungsgefüge von Ernährungs- und Landwirtschaft, Agrar- und Agressionspolitik in Deutschland während des Zweiten Weltkrieges sowie deren Voraussetzungen', in Ernst Münch (ed.), *Festschrift für Gerhard Heitz zum 75. Geburtstag* (Rostock, 2000), 509–26.

62. Post-war testimony of task-force commando 7a leader Dr Walter Blume, in IfZ, ZS 2389; and post-war testimony of Dr Erhard Kröger in Angrick, *Besatzungspolitik*, 109.

63. Ohlendorf's post-war trial testimony of 31 January 1946, in *IMT*, vol. 4, doc. 2348-PS 344ff., here 350.

64. Wildt, *Generation*, 557.

65. Ralf Ogorreck, *Die Einsatzgruppen und die 'Genesis der Endlösung'* (Berlin, 1996), 83, 98.

66. Heydrich to all *Einsatzgruppen* commanders, 29 June 1941, in BAB, R 70 SU/32, and Heydrich to HSSPF, 2 July 1941, in BAB, R 70 SU/31, reprinted in Peter Longerich (ed.), *Die Ermordung der europäischen Juden. Eine umfassende Dokumentation des Holocaust 1941–1945* (Munich, 1989), 116ff.

67. Heydrich to HSSPFs, 2 July 1941, in BAB, R 70 SU/31, reprinted in Longerich, *Ermordung*, 116ff. See, too, Yitzhak Arad, Yisrael Gutman and Abraham Margaliot (eds), *Documents on the Holocaust: Selected Sources on the Destruction of the Jews of Germany and Austria, Poland, and the Soviet Union* (Yad Vashem, 1981), doc. 171, pp. 377f.

68. Longerich, *Himmler*, 541.

69. When, in mid-July, Heydrich issued guidelines for the screening of Soviet POW camps calling for the identification 'of all Jews', he again left it to the recipients of this order to decide what was to be done with Jewish POWs once they had been identified. Heydrich's 'Einsatzbefehl no. 8', 17 July 1941, reprinted in Klein, *Einsatzgruppen*, 331ff.

70. Christian Hartmann, *Wehrmacht im Ostkrieg. Front und militärisches Hinterland 1941–42* (Munich, 2009); Dieter Pohl, *Die Herrschaft der Wehrmacht. Deutsche Militärbesetzung und einheimische Bevölkerung in der Sowjetunion 1941–1944* (Munich, 2008); Christian Streit, *Keine Kameraden. Die Wehrmacht und die sowjetischen Kriegsgefangenen 1941–1945* (Stuttgart, 1978), 128; Timothy Snyder, *Bloodlands: Europe Between Hitler and Stalin* (London, 2010), 182.

71. See the daily 'incident reports' of the *Einsatzgruppen* for the period between 23 June 1941 and 24 April 1942, in BAB, R 58/214–21. See, too, Ronald Headland, *Messages of Murder: A Study of the Reports of the Einsatzgruppen of the Security Police and the Security Service* (Rutherford, NJ, 1992).

72. Witte et al. (eds), *Dienstkalender*, 30 June 1941; Heydrich's 'Einsatzbefehl no. 3', 1 July 1941, in BAB, R 70 SU/32; Incident Report no. 21, 13 July 1941, in BAB, R 58/214–21.

73. Report of Stapostelle Tilsit, 1 July 1941, OA Moscow, 500/1/758; 'Incident Report USSR no. 19', 11 July 1941, and 'Incident Report USSR, no. 26', 18 July 1941, both in BAB, R 58/214.

74. Witte et al. (eds), *Dienstkalender*, 11 July 1941; Diary Bach-Zelewski, entry for 12 July 1941, in BAB, R 20/45b, f. 3; Gerlach, *Kalkulierte Morde*, 544f; Longerich, *Himmler*, 544.

75. Popplow, 'Aufnordung', 15.

76. Browning, *Origins*, 256ff.

77. Headland, *Messages*, 211ff; Longerich, *Himmler*, 544.

78. See Klein, *Einsatzgruppen*, 113.

79. Heydrich to *Einsatzgruppen* commanders, 29 June 1941, in BAB, R 70 SU/32. Browning, *Origins*, 258ff

80. Andrzej Zbikowski, 'Local Anti-Jewish Pogroms in the Occupied Territories of Eastern Poland, June–July 1941', in Lucjan Dobroszycki and Jeffrey S. Gurock (eds), *The Holocaust in the Soviet Union: Studies and Sources on the Destruction of the Jews in the Nazi-Occupied Territories of the USSR, 1941–1945* (Armonk, NY, 1993), 173–9; Aharon Weiss, 'The Holocaust and the Ukrainian Victims', in Michael Berenbaum (ed.), *A Mosaic of Victims: Non-Jews Persecuted and Murdered by the Nazis* (New York, 1990), 109–15; Bogdan Musial, 'Konterrevolutionäre Elemente sind zu erschiessen'. *Die Brutalisierung des deutsch–sowjetischen Krieges im Sommer 1941* (Berlin and Moscow, 2000), 172.

81. Heydrich to *Einsatzgruppen*, 1 July 1941 BAB, R70 SU/32; Klein, *Einsatzgruppen*, S. 320.

82. A comprehensive dossier on the NKVD, based on this extorted information, was sent by Heydrich to all higher SS and police leaders as well as to the Sipo and SD commanders on 2 April 1942. See National Archives, Kew, WO 208/1858, 324795.

83. Vejas Gabriel Liulevicius, *The German Myth of the East: 1800 to the Present* (Oxford, 2009); idem, 'Der Osten als apokalyptische Raum. Deutsche Fronterfahrungen im und nach dem Ersten Weltkrieg', in Gregor Thum (ed.), *Traumland Osten. Deutsche Bilder vom östlichen Europa im 20. Jahrhundert* (Göttingen, 2006), 47–65; David Blackbourn, *The Conquest of Nature: Water and the Making of Modern German Landscapes* (London, 2005), 251ff.

84. On the 'Garden of Eden' speech, see Martin Bormann's notes, in *IMT*, vol. 38, doc. 221-L, pp. 86–94. See, too, Browning, *Origins*, 309f.

85. See 'Erlass des Führers über die Verwaltung in den neu besetzten Ostgebieten', 17 July 1941, in *IMT*, vol. 38, doc. L-221, pp. 86ff.; Longerich, *Himmler*, 545ff.; Witte et al. (eds), *Dienstkalender*, 24 June 1941. On Rosenberg, see Ernst Piper, *Alfred Rosenberg. Hitlers Chefideologe* (Munich, 2005). Quotation: Heydrich to Berger, 4 November 1941, in Buchheim et al., *SS*, 100.

86. Heydrich to Daluege, 30 October 1941, as quoted in Buchheim et al., *SS*, 100.

87. See the correspondence between Heydrich and Lammers, 18 July–23 October 1941, in IfZ, Fa 199/41, ff. 165–75.

88. On Heydrich's search warrant for Kube's house, see the letter exchange between Kube and Himmler of March 1936, in BAB, BDC, Wilhelm Kube.

89. Mark Mazower, *Hitler's Empire: Nazi Rule in Occupied Europe* (London, 2008), 144ff. On Heydrich's scepticism towards the mobilization of Slavic populations for the German war effort, see Christoph Dieckmann, Babette Quinkert and Tatjana Tönsmeyer (eds), *Kooperation und Verbrechen. Formen der 'Kollaboration' im östlichen Europa 1939–1945* (Göttingen, 2003), 171.

90. Longerich, *Himmler*, 545ff.

91. Heydrich to Himmler, 20 October 1941, in IfZ, MA 328, f. 30.

92. Longerich, *Himmler*, 545ff.

93. Heydrich in *Völkischer Beobachter*, 17 February 1941. See, too, Heydrich, 'Der Anteil der Sicherheitspolizei und des SD in Böhmen und Mähren', *Böhmen und Mähren* 2 (1941), 176.

94. Browning, *Origins*, 310ff. On Ohlendorf's visit to Berlin in late August, see Ogorrek, *Einsatzgruppen*, 208f.

95. Prien, *Jagdgeschwaders 77*, vol. 2, 704f.

96. Himmler's funeral speech of 9 June as printed in Reichssicherheitshauptamt (ed.), *Reinhard Heydrich, 7. März 1904–4. Juni 1942. Meine Ehre heisst Treue* (Berlin, 1942), 14–22, here 19.

97. Report Georg Schirmböck, in Prien, *Jagdgeschwaders 77*, vol. 2, 704.

98. See the reports of Georg Schirmböck and Joachim Deicke, in ibid., 704ff.; Semerdjiev, 'Jagdflieger', 36f.; Deschner, *Heydrich*, 141f.

99. *IMT*, vol. 26, doc. 710-PS, pp. 266–7.

100. Browning, *Origins*, 315.

101. Browning, *Origins*, 315f.

102. On Einsatzkommando 9, see Gerlach, *Kalkulierte Morde*, 545f.; on Einsatzkommando 3, which adopted the same approach in early August, see the 'Jäger report' of 1 December 1941, in OA Moscow, 500/1/25, reprinted in Vincas Bartusevičius, Joachim Tauber and Wolfram Wette (eds), *Holocaust in Litauen. Krieg, Judenmorde und Kollaboration im Jahre 1941* (Cologne, 2003), 303ff.

103. This was openly articulated in Himmler's infamous Posen speech of 1943. See, too, Omer Bartov, 'Defining Enemies, Making Victims: Germans, Jews, and the Holocaust', in Amir Weiner (ed.), *Landscaping the Human Garden: Twentieth-Century Population Management in a Comparative Framework* (Stanford, CA, 2003), 135–47.

104. Himmler's funeral speech as printed in Wannenmacher (ed.), *Leben der Tat*, 81ff.

105. Heydrich, *Kriegsverbrecher*, 48.

106. By mid-October 1941, Einsatzgruppe A claimed to have killed 125,000 Jews, 80,000 of them in Lithuania alone. See Stahlecker's activity report of 15 October 1941, in *IMT*, vol. 37, doc. L-180, pp. 670–17; see, too Krausnick, Helmut, *Einsatzgruppen: Die Truppen des Weltanschauungskrieges 1938–1942* (Frankfurt, 1989), 606; Konrad Kwiet, 'Rehearsing for Murder: The Beginning of the Final Solution in Lithuania in June 1941', *Holocaust and Genocide Studies* 12 (1998), 3–26.

107. Figures as quoted in Browning, *Origins*, 244. On collaboration, see Katrin Reichelt, 'Kollaboration und Holocaust in Lettland, 1941–1945', in Wolf Kaiser (ed.), *Täter im Vernichtungskrieg. Der Überfall auf die Sowjetunion und der Völkermord und den Juden* (Munich, 2002). On the particularly early escalation of genocidal policies in Lithuania, see Christoph Dieckmann, 'The War and the Killing of the Lithuanian Jews', in Ulrich Herbert (ed.), *National Socialist Extermination Policies: Contemporary German Perspectives and Controversies* (New York and Oxford, 2000), 240–75.

108. Longerich, *Himmler*, 565; Browning, *Origins*, 410–14.

109. Longerich, *Ermordung*, 74f. Browning, *Origins*, 354f.

110. Ibid., 355.

111. Gerlach, *Kalkulierte Morde*, 648; Alfred Gottwald and Diana Schulle, *Die 'Judendeportationen' aus dem Deutschen Reich von 1941–1945. Eine kommentierte Chronologie* (Wiesbaden, 2005), 52ff.; on Serbia, see Manoschek, '*Serbien ist judenfrei*', 169ff.

112. Moorhouse, *Berlin at War*, 172ff.

113. Heydrich to Sipo commanders, 3 September 1941, printed in Wolfgang Benz, Konrad Kwiet and Jürgen Matthäus (eds), *Einsatz im 'Reichskommissariat Ostland'. Dokumente zum Völkermord im Baltikum und in Weissrussland, 1941–1944* (Berlin, 1998), 67ff.

114. Browning, *Origins*, 263.

115. Lösener, 'Rassereferent', 303; Kershaw, *Hitler: Nemesis*, 473.

116. Adam, *Judenpolitik*, 254f.; Adler, *Verwaltete Mensch*, 47f.; Goebbels's diary entry of 19 August 1941, in *Tagebücher*, part II, vol. 2/1, 265f.; Longerich, '*Davon haben wir nichts gewusst*', 159ff.

117. Friedländer, *Extermination*, 305; Hilberg, *Destruction*, 130; Longerich, *Politik*, 214; Adam, *Judenpolitik*, 334; Notes of Walter Tiessler, 21 April 1941, in IfZ, MA 423; see, too, Adler, *Verwaltete Mensch*, 48; and Willi A. Boelcke, *Kriegspropaganda 1939–1945. Geheime Ministerkonferenzen im Reichspropagandaministerium* (Stuttgart, 1955), 695.

118. Longerich, '*Davon haben wir nichts gewusst*', 161f.

119. Goebbels, *Tagebücher*, part II, vol. 1 (entry for 12 August 1941), 218.

120. Lösener, 'Rassereferent', 303f.

121. Goebbels, *Tagebücher*, part II, vol. 1 (entry for 19 August 1941), 265f.; on the conversation between Goebbels and Hitler on 18 August 1941, see, too, Friedländer, *Extermination*, 267; Longerich, *Politik*, 427.

122. Adler, *Verwaltete Mensch*, 49.

123. *Reichsgesetzblatt* 1941, part I, 547; Lösener, 'Rassereferent', 307. See, too, IfZ, Eich 1064; and MA 445, ff. 7854–60.

124. *Reichsgesetzblatt* 1941, part I, 547.
125. Heydrich's letter of 15 September 1941, in BAB, R 58/276; as well as Heydrich's orders of 30 September and 16 October 1941, in ibid.
126. Printed in Konrad Kwiet, 'Die Kennzeichnung mit dem Judenstern im Herbst 1941', in Wolfgang Benz (ed.), *Die Juden in Deutschland 1933–1945. Leben unter nationalsozialistischer Herrschaft* (Munich, 1988), 614–31, here 615ff.
127. On Hitler's change of mind, see Heydrich to Ribbentrop, 24 September 1941, explaining the new police directive on the marking of Jews, in IfZ, Eich 949.
128. On the renewed registration process, see 'Evidenz der Juden. Registrierung. Transporte', reproduced in Helena Krejćová, Jana Svobodová and Anna Hyndráková (eds), *Židé v Protektorátu. Hlašení Židovské náboženské obce v roce 1942. Dokumenty* (Prague, 1997), doc. 10, pp. 167–8; Livia Rothkirchen, *The Jews of Bohemia and Moravia: Facing the Holocaust* (Lincoln, NB, 2005), 126. Anti-Jewish measures were widely publicized throughout the Protectorate. See, for example, *Der Neue Tag*, 6 October 1941.
129. Senior staff meeting in the Reich Protector's Office, 10 October 1941, in National Archives, Prague, 114–2–56, reprinted in Kárný et al. (eds), *Deutsche Politik*, doc. 29, pp. 137–41.
130. Heydrich at a press conference in Prague on 11 October 1941, as quoted in Eva Schmidt-Hartmann, 'Tschechoslowakei', in Wolfgang Benz (ed.), *Dimension des Völkermords. Die Zahl der jüdischen Opfer des Nationalsozialismus* (Munich, 1991), 353–80, here 361 n. 28; Heydrich to Himmler, 19 October 1941 on 'Movement of Jews from the Old Reich into the Litzmannstadt Ghetto', BAB, NS 19/2655.
131. Protocol of the meeting of 4 October 1941, in BAB, NS 19/1734; Heydrich's letter to the General Quartermaster of 6 November 1941, as quoted in Klarsfeld, *Vichy*, 369f.
132. Luther memoranda of 13 and 17 October 1941, as quoted in Browning, *Origins*, 368–9.
133. Witte et al. (eds), *Dienstkalender*, 18 October 1941, p. 238.
134. Uebelhoer to Himmler, 4 and 9 October 1941 and Heydrich to Himmler, 8 October 1941, all in BAB, NS 19/2655.
135. Heydrich to Himmler, 19 October 1941, in BAB, NS 19/2655. See, too, Browning, *Origins*, 332.
136. Heydrich to Himmler, 8 October 1941, BAB, NS 19/2655. Heydrich quoted this figure again during a meeting with senior SS staff members in Prague on 10 October 1941, in Kárný et al. (eds), *Deutsche Politik*, doc. 29, pp. 137ff.
137. Lammers to Rosenberg, 6 September 1941, in BAB, R 43II/684a. See, too, Longerich, *Himmler*, 557.
138. RSHA memorandum on the meeting between Heydrich and Rosenberg's deputy, Alfred Meyer, 4 October 1941, in BAB, NS 19/1734; see, too, Gerlach, *Kalkulierte Morde*, 580f.
139. Manoschek, *'Serbien ist judenfrei'*, 105ff.; Browning, *Foreign Office*, 56ff.
140. Browning, *Origins*, 346ff.
141. Longerich, *Himmler*, 565f.
142. No written record of the meeting exists, but most scholars agree that the construction of the Belzec extermination camp can be traced back to Globocnik's initiative. See Dieter Pohl, 'Die grossen Zwangsarbeiterlager der SS- und Polizeiführer für Juden im Generalgouvernement 1942–1945', in Herbert et al. (eds), *Die nationalsozialistischen Konzentrationslager*, vol. 1, 415–38; Musial, *Zivilverwaltung*, 265; Browning, *Origins*, 359ff.; Michael Tregenza, 'Belzec Death Camps', *Wiener Library Bulletin* 30 (1977), 8–25. On Heydrich in Nauen, see Witte et al. (eds), *Dienstkalender*, 253.
143. Browning, *Origins*, 333f.
144. Epstein, *Model Nazi*, 188f.
145. Ian Kershaw, 'Improvised Genocide? The Emergence of the "Final Solution" in the Warthegau', *Transactions of the Royal Historical Society*, 6th series (1992), 51–98.
146. Witte et al. (eds), *Dienstkalender*, 14, 25 and 29 October; see, too, Longerich, *Himmler*, 556.
147. Browning, *Origins*, 373.
148. Longerich, *Politik*, 440, 448, 456.
149. Ibid.
150. Longerich, *Himmler*, 569; Dieter Pohl, *Nationalsozialistische Judenverfolgung in Ostgalizien 1941–1944. Organisation und Durchführung eines staatlichen Massenverbrechens* (Munich, 1996), 405. On the role of local actors in committing the atrocities, see Martin Dean,

Collaboration in the Holocaust: Crimes of the Local Police in Belorussia and Ukraine, 1941–44 (New York, 2000); Bernhard Chiari, *Alltag hinter der Front. Besatzung, Kollaboration und Widerstand in Weissrussland 1941–1944* (Düsseldorf, 1998), 96ff.

151. Hitler's Reichstag speech of 11 December 1941, in Hitler, *Reden und Proklamationen*, vol. 2, 1794ff. On Heydrich and Himmler attending the Reichstag session together, see Witte et al. (eds), *Dienstkalender*, 11 December 1941, p. 288.

152. See Goebbels's diary entry of 13 December 1941, in *Tagebücher*, vol. II, vol. 2, 487ff.

153. Longerich, *Himmler*, 570.

154. Christian Gerlach in particular has argued that Hitler's statement of 12 December indicated a principle decision, after the declaration of war on the United States, to murder all European Jews. Christian Gerlach, 'Die Wannsee-Konferenz, das Schicksal der deutschen Juden und Hitlers politische Grundsatzentscheidung, alle Juden Europas zu ermorden', *WerkstattGeschichte* 6 (1997), 7–44.

155. Witte et al. (eds), *Dienstkalender*, 18 December 1941.

156. Longerich, *Himmler*, 570f.

157. See Heydrich to Luther, 29 November 1941, in PAAA, (Inland IIg 177) R 100857, f. 188. See, too, Mark Roseman, *The Villa, the Lake, the Meeting: Wannsee and the Final Solution* (London and New York, 2002), 56f.; Johannes Tuchel, *Am Grossen Wannsee 56–58: Von der Villa Minoux zum Haus der Wannsee-Konferenz* (Berlin, 1992).

158. Heydrich to Luther, 29 November 1941, PAAA, (Inland IIg 177) R 100857, f. 188. See, too, Wildt, *Generation*, 630.

159. Roseman, *Wannsee*, 57f; On the participants, see Wolf Kaiser, 'Die Wannsee-Konferenz. SS-Führer und Ministerialbeamte im Einvernehmen über die Ermordung der europäischen Juden', in Heiner Lichtenstein and Otto R. Romberg (eds), *Täter – Opfer – Folgen. Der Holocaust in Geschichte und Gegenwart* (2nd edn, Bonn, 1997), 24–37.

160. The following quotations are based on the only surviving copy of the protocol, in PAAA, (Inland IIg 177) R 100857, ff. 166–180, here f. 168. See, too, the reprint: 'Besprechungsprotokoll der Wannsee-Konferenz vom 20. Januar 1942', in Kurt Patzold and Erika Schwarz (eds), *Tagesordnung. Judenmord. Die Wannsee Konferenz am 20. Januar 1942. Eine Dokumentation zur Organisation der 'Endlösung'* (Berlin, 1992), 102–12.

161. Heydrich to Rosenberg, 10 January 1942, Yad Vashem Archives, M9/584.

162. On this conflict, see Longerich, *Himmler*, 453.

163. Roseman, *Villa*, 85.

164. Friedländer, *Extermination*, 367; Wildt, *Generation*, 636, n. 89; Eichmann memorandum of 1 December 1941, as printed in Pätzold and Schwarz (eds), *Tagesordnung*, 90ff.; Yehoshua Büchler, 'A Preparatory Document for the Wannsee Conference', *Holocaust and Genocide Studies* 9 (1995), 121–9.

165. PAAA, (Inland IIg 177) R 100857, f. 170; see, too, Wildt, *Generation*, 628.

166. The estimates were based on statistics that Eichmann had begun to compile in early November 1941. See Cesarani, *Eichmann*, 112.

167. PAAA, (Inland IIg 177) R 100857, ff. 172–3; Friedländer, *Extermination*, 371.

168. The strongest proponent of the first position is Gerlach, 'Wannsee-Konferenz', 33ff. Peter Longerich and Saul Friedländer, by contrast, pointed out that 'road construction' was not merely a codeword for murder: Friedländer, *Extermination*, 370; Longerich, *Politik*, 470f. See Eichmann's testimony of 24 July 1961, in Longerich, *Ermordung*, 92. See, too, Cesarani, *Eichmann*, 237ff.; Roseman, *Villa*, 72.

169. PAAA, (Inland IIg 177) R 100857, f. 179f.; John A. S. Grenville, 'Die "Endlösung" und die "Judenmischlinge" im Dritten Reich', in Ursula Büttner, Werner Johe and Angelika Voss (eds), *Das Unrechtsregime. Internationale Forschung über den Nationalsozialismus* (Hamburg, 1986), vol. 2, 91–21.

170. PAAA, (Inland IIg 177) R 100857, f. 174.

171. Longerich, *Himmler*, 575.

172. PAAA, (Inland IIg 177) R 100857, ff. 179f; Longerich, *Himmler*, 575.

173. Longerich, *Himmler*, 576.

174. On Nazi policies towards the *Judenmischlinge*, see Essner, '*Nürnberger Gesetze*', 410ff.; Jeremy Noakes, 'The Development of Nazi Policy towards the German "Mischlinge", 1933–1945', *Leo Baeck Institute Yearbook* 34 (1989), 291–354. A detailed study of the fate

of Hamburg's Jewish *Mischlinge* is Beate Meyer, *'Jüdische Mischlinge'. Rassenpolitik und Verfolgungserfahrung 1933–1945* (Hamburg, 1999); and Claudia Koonz, *The Nazi Conscience* (Cambridge, MA, 2003), 163–89. On the discussion about *Mischlinge* at Wannsee in particular, see Pätzold and Schwarz, *Tagesordnung*, 109–111.

175. Noakes, 'Development', 69.
176. Roseman, *Villa*, 82. The propositions made by Heydrich at the Wannsee Conference were not *per se* new. On 21 August 1941, Eichmann had convened a meeting at which the party Chancellery, the Race and Settlement Office and the RSHA co-ordinated their demands. The demands raised were almost identical with those Heydrich put on the table at Wannsee. See Noakes, 'Development', 339; Lösener, 'Rassereferent', 297.
177. PAAA, Inland IIg 177, f. 179; Hilberg, *Destruction*, vol. 2, 418.
178. PAAA, Inland IIg 177, f. 179.
179. Meyer, *Mischlinge*, 25.
180. Noakes, 'Development', 337; Meyer, *Mischlinge*, 30f.
181. On the two follow-up conferences on the treatment of *Mischlinge* and mixed marriages in 1942, see Hilberg, *Destruction*, vol. 2, 436ff. See, too, the protocol of the RSHA meeting of 5 March 1942, in IfZ, Eich 119.
182. Cesarani, *Eichmann*, 114.
183. Heydrich to Luther, 26 February 1942, in PAAA, (Inland IIg 177) R 100857, p. 156; see, too, Hilberg, *Destruction*, 491.
184. Noakes, 'Development', 341; Pätzold and Schwarz, *Tagesordnung*, 158.
185. For the minutes of the meetings, see Robert Kempner, *Eichmann und Komplizen* (Zurich, Stuttgart, Vienna, 1961), 165–80 (March), and 255–67 (October); Roseman, *Villa*, 101; Meyer, *'Mischlinge'*, 12.
186. Wolf Gruner, 'The Factory Action and the Events at the Rosenstrasse in Berlin: Facts and Fictions about 27 February 1943 – Sixty Years Later', *Central European History* 36 (2003), 178–208.
187. Adler, *Verwaltete Mensch*, 202ff., 280f.
188. Wolfgang Benz, 'Die Dimension des Völkermordes', in idem. (ed.), *Dimension des Völkermordes*, 1–23, here 17; Streit, *Keine Kameraden*, 142ff.
189. Witte et al. (eds), *Dienstkalender*, 21 January 1942, p. 331.

Chapter VIII: Reich Protector

1. For the latest analysis of the Nazi occupation of Bohemia and Moravia, see Bryant, *Prague in Black*.
2. The 'viceroy' analogy to British India was first used by the State Secretary of the Interior, Wilhelm Stuckart, who devised the Protectorate's civil administration structure. See Miroslav Kárný and Jaroslava Milotová (eds), *Anatomie okupační politiky hitlerovského Německa v 'Protektorátu Čechy a Morava'. Dokumenty z období říšského protektora Konstantina von Neuratha* (Prague, 1987), doc. 2, p. 7.
3. Alice Teichová, 'The Protectorate of Bohemia and Moravia (1939–1945): The Economic Dimension', in Mikulas Teich (ed.), *Bohemia in History* (Cambridge, 1998), 267–305; Brandes, *Tschechen*, 166; Eva Drdácková, *Správní uspořádání protektorátu do Heydrichovy správní reformy (1939–1942)* (Plzeň, 2004).
4. Eduard Kubů and Drahomír Jančík, *'Arizace' a arizátoři. Drobný a střední židovský majetek v úvěrech Kreditanstalt der Deutschen (1939–45)* (Prague, 2005); Evans, *Third Reich in Power*, 686f; Drahomír Jančík, Eduard Kubů and Jan Kuklík (eds), *Arizace a restituce židovského majetku v českých zemích (1939–2000)* (Prague, 2003).
5. Teichová, 'Protectorate', 274f.; Evans, *Third Reich*, vol. 2, 665ff. Heydrich's 17th report for Bormann (30 December 1941), in Kárný et al. (eds), *Deutsche Politik*, 201ff.
6. John L. Heinemann, *Hitler's First Foreign Minister: Constantin Freiherr von Neurath, Diplomat and Statesman* (Berkeley, CA, 1979), esp. 3, 9–16, 86–166; Mastny, *Czechs*, 60; Richard Overy, *Interrogations: The Nazi Elite in Allied Hands, 1945* (New York, 2001), 82.
7. John G. Lexa, 'Anti-Jewish Laws and Regulations in the Protectorate of Bohemia and Moravia', in Avigdor Dagan (ed.), *The Jews of Czechoslovakia*, 4 vols (Philadelphia,

1968–84), vol. 3, 77–103. See, too, the collection of policy documents and internal documents in 'Befehlshaber der Sicherheitspolizei und des SD. Zentralamt für die Regelung der Judenfrage in Böhmen und Mähren', in Yad Vashem Archives, 051/204.

8. Brandes, *Tschechen*, vol. 1, 83ff.

9. On the Czech resistance, see Jaroslav Čvaćara, *Někomu život, někomu smrt. Československý odboj a nacistická okupační moc 1939–1941* (Prague, 2002); Radomír Luža, *V Hitlerově objetí. Kapitoly z českého odboje* (Prague, 2006); on the German Communists in the Sudetenland, see Mark Cornwall, 'Stirring Resistance from Moscow: The German Communists of Czechoslovakia and Wireless Propaganda in the Sudetenland, 1941–1945', *German History* 24 (2006), 212–42.

10. Brandes, *Tschechen*, vol. 1, 171ff.

11. Neurath's report to Bormann and Hitler of 15 September 1941, in Kárný et al. (eds), *Deutsche Politik*, doc. 1, pp. 77ff.

12. See Brandes, *Tschechen*, vol. 1, 196; Sládek, 'Standrecht', 330f.

13. On Hitler's order (31a) of 16 September, see Hubatsch (ed.), *Hitlers Weisungen*, 149; Keitel's order of the same day, in BA-MA, RH 26, 104/14. On Serbia, see Manoschek, *'Serbien ist judenfrei'*, 43ff. On Western Europe, Guus Meershoeck et. al. (eds), *Repression und Kriegsverbrechen. Die Bekämpfung von Widerstands- und Partisanenbewegungen gegen die deutsche Besatzung in West- und Südosteuropa* (Berlin and Göttingen, 1997); Weber, *Sicherheit*, 59ff.

14. Heydrich to Stapoleitstellen, 27 August 1941, in BAB, R 58/1027, f. 205; Bohn, *Reichskommissariat*, 81f. and 92ff.

15. Guus Meershoek, 'Machtentfaltung und Scheitern. Sicherheitspolizei und SD in den Niederlanden', in Paul and Mallmann (eds), *Gestapo im Zweiten Weltkrieg*, 383–402.

16. John A. Armstrong, *Ukrainian Nationalism, 1935–1949* (2nd edn, New York, 1963), 69f.

17. Heydrich to Lammers, 18 September 1941, BAB, R 43 II/396. Heydrich and Himmler flew to Riga, and drove on to Mitau and Reval (Tallinn) the next day, and from there to Dorpat and Pleskau. On 21 September, they arrived at the Führer headquarters near Rastenburg in the Masurian Forests where they dined with Hitler and discussed the situation in the Protectorate and Heydrich's appointment to the post of acting Reich Protector. Witte et al. (eds), *Dienstkalender*, 18–21 September 1941, pp. 214f. On the meeting with Hitler, see, too, Koeppen, report no. 35 of 22 September 1941, BAB, R 6/34a, f. 24.

18. See, for example, the report from the Stapoleitstelle in Prague of 19 September 1941, in Kárný et al. (eds), *Deutsche Politik*, doc. 6, p. 86; Detlef Brandes, 'Nationalsozialistische Tschechenpolitik', in idem and Václav Kural (eds), *Der Weg in die Katastrophe. Deutsch–tschechoslowakische Beziehungen 1938–1947* (Essen, 2004), 39–50, here 46.

19. Kershaw, *Hitler*, vol 2, 641; *Dienstkalender*, 217ff.

20. On the reasons for Hitler's change of mind on this issue, see Friedländer, *Extermination*, 291f. See, too, Browning, *Origins*, 326; Kershaw, *Hitler: Nemesis*, 477.

21. See Lösener's memorandum for Frick of 18 August 1941, in Lösener, 'Rassereferent', 303. The issue was also discussed between Himmler and Heydrich on 2 September. See Witte et al. (eds), *Dienstkalender*, 203.

22. Himmler to Greiser, 18 September 1941, in BAB, NS 19/2655, f. 3; reprinted in Peter Witte, 'Two Decisions Concerning the "Final Solution of the Jewish Question": Deportations to Lodz and the Mass Murder in Chelmno', *Holocaust and Genocide Studies* 9 (1995) 318–45. A copy of the letter was sent to Heydrich.

23. Goebbels's diary entry of 24 September 1941, in *Tagebücher*, part II, vol. 1, 480ff.

24. Yet, despite the existence of Jewish partisan brigades, Jews made up less than 5 per cent of the overall partisan strength in the occupied territories. See Leonid Smilovitsky, 'Righteous Gentiles, the Partisans and Jewish Survival in Belorussia, 1941–44', *Holocaust and Genocide Studies* 11 (1997), 301–29.

25. On Heydrich's emotional response to the appointment, see Schellenberg, *Labyrinth*, 225; Heydrich, *Kriegsverbrecher*, 56. On the relationship with Himmler after 1941, see Longerich, *Himmler*, 589.

26. Heydrich, *Kriegsverbrecher*, 98f.; Witte et al. (eds), *Dienstkalender*, 24 September 1941, p. 217.

27. On Frank, see BAB, BDC, SSO Karl Hermann Frank; Miloslav Moulis and Dušan Tomášek, *K. H. Frank. Vzestup a pád karloovarského knihkupce* (Prague, 2003), 12ff.; Ralf

Gebel, *'Heim ins Reich'. Konrad Henlein und der Reichsgau Sudetenland (1938–1945)* (Munich, 1999), 43ff.

28. Heydrich, *Kriegsverbrecher*, 102. Heydrich to Bormann, 27 September 1941, in Kárný et al. (eds), *Deutsche Politik*, doc. 11, p. 93. See, too, the description of the mood in Prague as described by Naudé, *Politischer Beamter*, 116; and Wilhelm Dennler, *Die böhmische Passion* (Freiburg, 1953), 55.

29. Heydrich, *Kriegsverbrecher*, 104.

30. Heydrich's speech in Černín Palace on 2 October 1941, in National Archives, Prague, 114–6–4, carton 22. Naudé, *Politischer Beamter*, 124. Similar sentiments were expressed in Heydrich's speech of 4 February 1942, in National Archives, Prague, 114–22, f. 56.

31. See Heydrich's Declaration of the State of Emergency of 27–28 September 1942 and the version for press dissemination in National Archives, Prague, 114, carton 1140. See also the second (more detailed) Declaration of the State of Emergency of 1 October 1941, in ibid. The quotation is from Heydrich's speech to Protectorate journalists on 10 October 1941, National Archives, Prague, 114–2–47, carton 8.

32. Kural, *Vlastenci proti okupaci*, 156ff. On the number of people brought before summary courts, see Brandes, *Tschechen*, vol. 1, 212. On the verdicts of 30 September, see Gregory's report to Heydrich of 20 September 1941, in National Archive, Prague, 114, carton 1140. See, too, Martin Hořák and Tomáš Jelínek, *Nacistická perzekuce obyvatel českých zemí* (Prague, 2006).

33. Heydrich to Bormann, 1 October 1941, in Kárný et al. (eds), *Deutsche Politik*, doc. 20, p. 105; and protocol of the senior staff meeting in the Reich Protector's Office, 17 October 1941, in National Archives, Prague, 114–2–26.

34. Sládek, 'Standrecht', 326.

35. Brandes, 'Nationalsozialistische Tschechenpolitik', 45; Hans Maršálek, *Die Geschichte des Konzentrationslagers Mauthausen* (Vienna, 1980), 122; on the number of prisoners sent to Auschwitz, see Miroslav Kárný, 'Introduction', in idem et al. (eds), *Deutsche Politik*, 41.

36. See Heydrich's decree as published in *Der Neue Tag*, 12 October 1941. See, too, Mark Dimond, 'The Sokol and Czech Nationalism, 1918–48', in Mark Cornwall and R. J. W. Evans (eds), *Czechoslovakia in a Nationalist and Fascist Europe, 1918–1948* (Oxford, 2007), 185–206. Report of the Foreign Office representative in the Reich Protector's Office, Gerstberger, of 2 October 1941, in PAAA, R 101109, vol. 2.

37. Heydrich to Bormann, 16 May 1942, in Kárný et al. (eds), *Deutsche Politik*, docs 96 and 97, pp. 259f. and 262f. See, too, Jaroslav Kokoška and Stanislav Kokoška, *Spor o agenta A-54* (Prague, 1994).

38. Stapo Leitstelle Prague, report on arrests of resistance members, 10 November 1942, in Kárný et al. (eds), *Deutsche Politik*, doc. 47, pp. 177–81. On the fate of the democratic resistance, see Brandes, *Tschechen*, vol. 1, 217ff.

39. Heydrich to Hácha, 9 October 1941, in National Archives, Prague, 109–4–16.

40. Hitler as quoted in Kárný et al. (eds), *Deutsche Politik*, 11.

41. See the trial proceedings in BAB, R 22/4070; and Helmut Heiber, 'Zur Justiz im Dritten Reich. Der Fall Eliáš', *VfZ* 3 (1955), 275–396. Eliáš as quoted in Heydrich's letter to Bormann of 1 October 1941, in Kárný et al. (eds), *Deutsche Politik*, doc. 20, p. 103. He had previously reported the news to Himmler over the phone on 28 September; see Witte et al. (eds), *Dienstkalender*, 221. For the published declaration, see, for example, *Der Neue Tag*, 2 October 1941; *České slovo*, 2 October 1941; *Venkov*, 2 October 1941; *Národní politika*, 2 October 1941. On collaboration in the Protectorate more generally, see Detlef Brandes, 'Kolaborace v Protektorátu Čechy a Morava', *Dějiny a současnost* 16 (1994), 25–9; Jiří Frajdl, *Protektorátní kolaborantské a fašistické organizace, 1939–1945* (Prague, 2003).

42. Heydrich to Bormann, 30 December 1941, in Kárný et al. (eds), *Deutsche Politik*, doc. 65, p. 202, and Heydrich to Bormann, 3 January 1942, ibid., doc. 66, p. 208. See, too, Gustav von Schmoller, 'Heydrich im Protektorat Böhmen und Mähren', *VfZ* 27 (1979), 626–45. Brandes, *Tschechen*, vol. 1, 213ff.; Mastny, *Czechs*, 187ff.

43. Mastny, *The Czechs*, 200.

44. Hácha on 4 December 1941, as quoted in Mastny, *Czechs*, 197ff. See, too, Kural, *Vlastenci proti okupaci*, 156f.

45. Heydrich's speech in Prague Castle, 4 February 1942, in National Archives, Prague, 114–6–2, carton 22, p. 10.

46. Brandes, *Tschechen*, vol. 1, 225–7.

47. Heydrich's speech in Prague Castle, 4 February 1942, National Archives, Prague, 114–6–2, carton 22, pp. 1–2. Similar sentiments were articulated in Heydrich's telegram to Lammers of 9 October 1941, BAB, R 43II/1326.

48. See the eyewitness report in Lisl Urban, *Ein ganz gewöhnliches Leben* (Leipzig, 2006), 113. On Heydrich's strategy, see Heydrich to Bormann, 1 October 1941, in Kárný et al. (eds), *Deutsche Politik*, doc. 20, p. 105, and protocol of senior staff meeting in the Reich Protector's Office, 17 October 1941, in National Archives, Prague, 114–2–26. On the continuation of executions: SS-Sturmbannführer Illmer, President of the Prague summary court, to Frank, 6 November 1941, in Kárný et al. (eds), *Deutsche Politik*, doc. 46, pp. 176–7. It is likely that this strategy was discussed between Himmler and Heydrich during a five-hour meeting in Berlin on 14 October. See Witte et al. (eds), *Dienstkalender*, 234f.

49. Intelligence Report as quoted in Bryant, *Prague in Black*, 144. See, too, Brandes, *Tschechen*, vol. 1, 212.

50. Werner Best, 'Grundfragen einer deutschen Grossraum-Verwaltung', in *Festgabe für Heinrich Himmler* (Darmstadt, 1941), 33–60; see, too, Herbert, *Best*, 275ff.; Mazower, *Hitler's Empire*, 235ff.

51. Heydrich, *Kriegsverbrecher*, 100; Naudé, *Politischer Beamter*, 122.

52. Lina Heydrich to Peter Schneiders, 12 January 1962, NIOD, doc. I, 69 A.

53. *Völkischer Beobachter*, 3 December 1941 and 16 December 1941. See, too, Daniels, 'Leibeserzieher', 116; Bahro, 'Sportler', 118.

54. Heydrich, *Kriegsverbrecher*, 10 and 100ff.

55. On Panenské Břežany, see: http://www.panenskebrezany.cz/view.php?cisloclanku= 2007110002. Heydrich, *Kriegsverbrecher*, 108 and 112.

56. On these areas of interest, see Heydrich to Hácha, 24 December 1941, in National Archives, Prague, 114–6–2, carton 22; Heydrich to Hácha, 4 May 1942, in National Archives, Prague, 114–5–15, carton 19; Heydrich's notes of 22 April 1942, in National Archives, Prague, 114–5–15, carton 19; Heydrich to Göring, 27 December 1941, in National Archives, Prague, 114–6–2.

57. Heydrich, *Kriegsverbrecher*, 106.

58. Lina Heydrich to Peter Schneider (Amsterdam), 12 January 1962, NIOD, doc. I 691 A.

59. Heydrich, *Kriegsverbrecher*, 86ff.; see, too, Heydrich to Backe, 6 December 1941, in National Archives, Prague, 114–5–15, carton 19. Interview with Heider Heydrich, March 2009.

60. Adam Tooze, *Wages of Destruction: The Making and Breaking of the Nazi Economy* (London, 2006), 477ff. Kay, 'Staatssekretäre', 685–700.

61. Richard Overy, 'Business in the "Grossraumwirtschaft": Eastern Europe, 1938–1945', in Harold James (ed.), *Enterprise in the Period of Fascism in Europe* (Burlington, VT, 2002), 151–77; Václav Kural, 'Von Masaryks "Neuem Europa" zu den Grossraumplänen Hitler-Deutschlands', in Richard Plaschka (ed.), *Mitteleuropa-Konzeptionen in der ersten Hälfte des 20. Jahrhunderts* (Vienna, 1995), 351–7; Horst Kahrs, 'Von der "Grossraumwirtschaft" zur "Neuen Ordnung". Zur strategischen Orientierung der deutschen Eliten 1932–1943', in Götz Aly (ed.), *Modelle für ein deutsches Europa. Ökonomie und Herrschaft im Grosswirtschaftsraum* (Berlin, 1992), 9–28.

62. Werner Daitz, Walther Funk and Hermann Göring, in Jeremy Noakes and Geoffrey Pridham (eds), *Nazism, 1919–1945. A Documentary Reader*, 4 vols (Exeter, 1995–8), vol. 3, 884–900; see, too, Paolo Fonzi, 'Nazionalsocialismo e nuovo ordine europeo: la discussione sulla "Grossraumwirtschaft"', *Studi Storici* 45 (2004), 313–65.

63. Mastny, *Czechs*, 80ff.; correspondence Heydrich and Reich Press Chief Dr Dietrich of 9 December 1941, in National Archives, Prague, 114-5-15, carton 19.

64. Heydrich's opening speech at the economic forum of the South-Eastern Europe Society in Prague, 17 December 1941, National Archives, Prague, 114-5-15, carton 8. He had discussed the event with Himmler over the phone on the previous day. See Witte et al. (eds), *Dienstkalender*, 291.

65. Göring to Heydrich, 27 December 1941, in National Archives, Prague, 114-6-2.

66. Heydrich's speech in Černín Palace on 2 October 1941, in National Archives, Prague, 114-6-4, carton 22.

67. Newspaper articles crediting Heydrich personally with the increase in food rations can be found in *České slovo*, 25 October 1941; *Národní politika*, 25 October 1941; *Venkov*, 25 October 1941.

68. Heydrich's speech to union representatives on 24 October 1941, in National Archives, Prague, 114-6-8. See, too, the notes on the event taken by SS-Sturmbannführer Wolf, in National Archives, Prague, 109-4-175. The propaganda gatherings were deemed to be a complete failure by the SD – they had been too overtly propagandistic and were rejected as such by the very same workers whom they sought to convince. See the SD report of 20 October 1941, in Kárný et al. (eds), *Deutsche Politik*, doc. 35, pp. 158–9.

69. *Der Neue Tag*, 25 and 26 October, 30 September and 4 October 1941. See, too, *České slovo*, 3 October 1941; Walter Wannenmacher, 'Reinhard Heydrich', *Böhmen und Mähren* (1942), 188–9.

70. Jaroslav Krejčí, 'The Bohemian-Moravian War Economy', in Michael Charles Kaser and Edward Albert Radice (eds), *The Economic History of Eastern Europe, 1919–1975* (Oxford, 1986), 491, table 19; see, too, Heydrich's speech to Czech agricultural workers' representatives in Prague Castle on 5 December 1941, in National Archives, Prague, 114-6-8.

71. Senior staff meeting in the Reich Protector's Office, 1 November 1941, in National Archives, Prague, 114-2-26. Heydrich's speech in Černín Palace on 2 October 1941, in National Archives, Prague, 114-6-4, carton 22. Similar sentiments are expressed in Heydrich's speech in Prague Castle, 4 February 1942, in National Archives, Prague, 114–22, ff. 30–3. See, too, the post-war interrogations of Walter Jacobi, Archive of the Ministry of the Interior (AMV), Prague, 325-166-3.

72. Vaclav Průcha, *Hospodářské a sociální dějiny Československa 1918–1992, 1. díl období 1918–1945* (Brno, 2004), 427–31; Dana Musilová, 'Problémy sociálně ekonomického vývoje v letech 1939–1945 v protektorátu Čechy a Morava', *Historický obzor* 3 (1992), 149–52.

73. *Der Neue Tag*, 12 February 1942. When the exhibition moved to Berlin, a fire-bomb went off on 18 May 1942. In response, Heydrich had the instigator of the incident, the 'Communist Mischling' Herbert Baum and 154 other Jewish men arrested and sent to Sachsenhausen where they were shot alongside ninety-six other Jewish inmates. See Wolfgang Scheffler, 'Der Brandanschlag im Berliner Lustgarten im Mai 1942 und seine Folgen. Eine quellenkritische Betrachtung', *Berlin in Geschichte und Gegenwart. Jahrbuch des Landesarchivs Berlin* 3 (1984), 91–118, and Witte et al. (eds), *Dienstkalender*, 26 May 1942, p. 437.

74. *Der Neue Tag*, 26 October 1941.

75. Burian et al., *Assassination*, 53. It is difficult to assess how successful this form of propaganda was, but it is likely to have had little bearing on the Czech population at large. Tim Fauth, *Deutsche Kulturpolitik im Protektorat Böhmen und Mähren, 1939–1941* (Göttingen, 2004), 89f.

76. Evans, *Third Reich in Power*, 686f.

77. Mazower, *Hitler's Empire*; Evans, *Third Reich at War*, 346ff; Streit, *Keine Kameraden*, 128.

78. Herbert, *Foreign Workers*, 143ff.; Jaroslava Milotová, ' "Cizorodí" dělníci a jejich pracovní nasazení v nacistickém Německu v letech 1939–1945', in Jana Havlíková (ed.), *Museli pracovat pro Říši. Nucené pracovní nasazení českého obyvatelstva v letech 2. světové války. Doprovodná publikace k výstavě* (Prague, 2004), 26.

79. Speer as quoted in Deschner, *Heydrich*, 322.

80. Havlíková (ed.), *Museli pracovat pro Říši*, 28; Herbert, *Foreign Workers*, 163ff.

81. Heydrich's speech on 26 May 1942, in National Archives, Prague, 114, carton 8. On the May decree see IMT, vol. 26, p. 485; Miroslav Kárný, 'Der "Reichsausgleich" in der deutschen Protektoratspolitik', in Ulrich Herbert (ed.), *Europa und der 'Reichseinsatz'. Ausländische Zivilarbeiter, Kriegsgefangene und KZ-Häftlinge in Deutschland 1938–1945* (Essen, 1991), 26–50, here 38.

82. Intelligence report of 21 May 1942, in National Archives, Kew, HS 4/79.

83. Heydrich to Hácha on 6 November 1941, in National Archives, Prague, 114-5-15, carton 19.

84. Brandes, *Tschechen*, vol. 1, 224–5. See also Heydrich's letter to Bormann of 18 May 1942 in Kárný et al. (eds), *Deutsche Politik*, doc. 98, pp. 262–3. Heydrich's letter to Hácha of 6 November 1941, in National Archives, Prague, 114-5-15, carton 19.

85. Heydrich, *Kriegsverbrecher*, 92f., 99; Heydrich to Hácha, 24 December 1941, in National Archives, Prague, 114-6-2.

86. Senior staff meeting of 1 November 1941 (with Heydrich, Frank, Burgsdorff, Böhme, Fuchs and Maurer in attendance), in National Archives, Prague, 114-2-26. Jaroslava Milotová, 'Výsledky Heydrichovi správní reformy z pohledu okupaćního aparátu', *Paginae historiae* 2 (1994), 161–74. Jaroslava Milotová, 'Personální aspekty tzv. Heydrichovi správní reformy', *Paginae historiae* 1 (1993), 196–218. On the meeting with Lammers in Munich on 9 November 1941, see Heydrich's notes of 11 November 1941, in National Archives, Prague, 114-5-15, carton 19; Heydrich to Bormann on 30 December 1941, in Kárný et al. (eds), *Deutsche Politik*, doc. 65, p. 206.

87. Heydrich's speech in Prague Castle, 4 February 1942, in National Archives, Prague, 114-6-2, p. 19. On the critical response to Bertsch's appointment from his Czech colleagues, see the SD report for Heydrich of 20 January 1942, National Archives, Prague, 114-5-15, carton 19.

88. See, for example the British Intelligence Reports in National Archives, Kew, HS 4/79/324795.

89. See the protocol of Moravec's meeting with Frank of 6 February 1942, in which the latter handed Moravec Heydrich's detailed instructions for propaganda in the Protectorate, in Kárný et al. (eds), *Deutsche Politik*, doc. 78, pp. 234–5. On Moravec, see Jiří Pernes, *Až na dno zrady. Emanuel Moravec* (Prague, 1997).

90. Heydrich's speech to the new Protectorate government, 19 January 1942, in National Archives, Prague, 114-6-8.

91. Heydrich to Bormann, 16 November 1941, in National Archives, Prague, 114-3-17.

92. Protocol of the senior staff meeting in the Reich Protector's Office, 1 November 1941, in National Archives, Prague, 114-2-26.

93. Heydrich to Bormann, 16 November 1941, in National Archives, Prague, 114-3-17.

94. Protocol of the senior staff meeting in the Reich Protector's Office, 1 November 1941, in National Archives, Prague, 114-2-26.

95. Heydrich's speech to the new Protectorate government, 19 January 1942, in National Archives, Prague, 114-6-8; *Der Neue Tag*, 20 January 1942.

96. Figures according to Mazower, *Hitler's Empire*, 238; Heydrich to Bormann, 18 May 1942, in Kárný et al. (eds), *Deutsche Politik*, doc. 98, p. 266.

97. Bryant, *Prague in Black*, 31ff.

98. Heydrich to senior staff members on 1 November 1941, in National Archives, Prague, 114-2-26. By June 1942, the only remaining *Oberlandrat* offices were in Prague, Budweis, Pilsen, Königgrätz, Brünn and Iglau.

99. Heydrich to Bormann, 18 May 1942, in Kárný et al. (eds), *Deutsche Politik*, doc. 98, p. 266. In reality, the number of civil servants 'freed up for military service' was significantly lower, perhaps around 30,000. See Miroslav Kárný, 'Introduction', in idem et al. (eds), *Deutsche Politik*, 53.

100. Mastny, *Czechs*, 201; Brandes, 'Nationalsozialistische Tschechenpolitik', 46.

101. Heydrich's speech of 4 February 1942, in National Archives, Prague, 114–22, 39.

102. Goebbels's diary entry of 21 January 1942, in *Tagebücher*, part II, vol. 3, 161.

103. Hitler on 25 January 1942, Hitler, *Monologe*, 227f.

104. Adolf Hitler, *Hitler's Table Talk 1941–1944*, (London, 1953), 490ff., quotation on p. 494.

105. Brandes, 'Nationalsozialistische Tschechenpolitik', 51. On Heydrich's measures for workers, see Dana Severová, 'Sociální politika nacistů v takzvaném Protektorátu v letech 1939–1945', *Dějiny socialistického Československa* 7 (1985), 184–90; Mastny, *Czechs*, 194f.; Brandes, *Tschechen*, vol. 1, 230f.

106. See Miroslav Kárný, 'Die materiellen Grundlagen der Sozialdemagogie in der Protektoratspolitik Heydrichs', *Historica* 19 (1989), 123–59.

107. Naudé, *Politischer Beamter*, 123.

108. Pohl, *Ostgalizien*; Gerlach, *Kalkulierte Morde*; Wendy Lower, *Nazi Empire-Building and the Holocaust in Ukraine* (Chapel Hill, NC, 2005).

109. Brandes, *Tschechen*, vol. 1, 32ff; Mastny, *Czechs*, 94f.

110. Bormann to Heydrich, in National Archives, Prague, 114-2-26.

111. Heydrich quotation from his speech in Černín Palace of 2 October 1941, in Kárný et al. (eds), *Deutsche Politik*, doc. 22, p. 120. Bryant, *Prague in Black*, 31.

112. Werner Koeppen's report on Heydrich's conversation with Hitler, 2 October 1941, in Kárný et al. (eds), *Deutsche Politik*, doc. 21, p. 107.

113. Kárný, 'Introduction', in ibid., 13–14. On the SD reports, see Boberach (ed.), *Meldungen aus dem Reich*. Heydrich's time in Prague is covered in vols 8 to 10, pp. 2809–3787. The daily and monthly SD reports from the Protectorate ended in October 1941.

114. Goebbels's diary entry of 15 February 1942, in *Tagebücher*, part II, vol. 3, 316.

115. Heydrich's speech in Prague Castle, 4 February 1942, in National Archives, Prague, 114-6-2, carton 22, f. 4.

116. Heinemann, '"Perpetrator"', 387ff.

117. Browning, *Origins*, 240ff.; Gerlach, *Kalkulierte Morde*, 26ff.; Karel C. Berkhoff, *Harvest of Despair: Life and Death in Ukraine under Nazi Rule* (Cambridge, MA, 2004), 35ff.; Dean, *Collaboration*, 110ff.; Streit, *Keine Kameraden*, 128.

118. Heinemann, '"Perpetrator"', 387ff.

119. Memorandum by General Friderici, Plenipotentiary of the Wehrmacht to the Reich Protector of Bohemia and Moravia, on the meeting of 9 October 1940, as printed in Václav Král (ed.), *Die Deutschen in der Tschechoslowakei 1933–1947. Dokumentensammlung* (Prague, 1964), doc. 322a, pp. 427f.

120. Foreign Office memo on Hitler's decision about Czech autonomy and Germanization policies in the Protectorate of 14 October 1940, in ibid., 428.

121. Heinemann, '*Rasse*', 155ff.

122. Bryant, *Prague in Black*, 159. See, too, Isabel Heinemann, '"Deutsches Blut". Die Rasseexperten der SS und die Volksdeutschen', in Jerzy Kochanowski and Maike Sach (eds), *Die 'Volksdeutschen' in Polen, Frankreich, Ungarn und der Tschechoslowakei. Mythos und Realität* (Osnabrück, 2006), 163–82.

123. Heydrich during the senior staff meeting in the Reich Protector's Office on 17 October 1941, in National Archives, Prague, 114-2-26.

124. Deschner, *Heydrich*, 217ff.; Dederichs, *Heydrich*, 155ff.

125. Naudé, *Politischer Beamter*, 124; see, too, Dennler, *Böhmische Passion*, 62f.

126. Heydrich's speech in Černín Palace on 2 October 1941, in National Archives, Prague, 114-6-4, carton 22.

127. Ibid., Bryant, *Prague in Black*, 159.

128. On this debate, see in greater detail Robert Gerwarth and Stephan Malinowski, 'Hannah Arendt's Ghosts: Reflections on the Disputable Path from Windhoek to Auschwitz', *Central European History* 42 (2009), 279–300.

129. Hitler on 17 September 1941, as quoted in Hitler, *Monologe*, 62f.; see, too, 193 and 361.

130. Birthe Kundrus, 'Kontinuitäten, Parallelen, Rezeptionen. Überlegungen zur Kolonialisierung des Nationalsozialismus', *WerkstattGeschichte* 43 (2006), 45–62, here 57f.

131. Reinhard Höhn and Helmut Seydel, 'Der Kampf um die Wiedergewinnung des deutschen Ostens. Erfahrungen der preussischen Ostsiedlung 1866–1914', in *Festgabe für Heinrich Himmler* (Darmstadt, 1941), 61–174, particularly 99ff. On Imperial Germany's 'colonial policies' towards Poland, see Philipp Ther, 'Deutsche Geschichte als imperiale Geschichte. Polen, slawophone Minderheiten und das Kaiserreich als kontinentales Empire', in Sebastian Conrad and Jürgen Osterhammel (eds), *Das Kaiserreich transnational. Deutschland in der Welt, 1871–1914* (Göttingen, 2004), 129–48; Thomas Serrier, *Entre Allemagne et Pologne: Nations et identités frontalières, 1848–1914* (Paris, 2002); Vejas Gabriel Liulevicius, *The German Myth of the East: 1800 to the Present* (Oxford, 2009).

132. Heydrich's speech in Černín Palace on 2 October 1941, in National Archives, Prague, 114-6-4, carton 22.

133. Goebbels had read a draft of the speech and commented on it in writing. See his letter to Heydrich of 28 September 1941, in National Archives, Prague, 114-6-4, carton 1140.

134. Witte et al. (eds), *Dienstkalender*, 20 March 1941; Helmut Heiber, 'Der Generalplan Ost', *VfZ* 6 (1958), 281–325.

135. On the genesis of the Generalplan Ost and the RuSHA's plans, see Heinemann, '*Rasse*', 362ff.; Rutherford, *Prelude*; Czeslaw Madajczyk (ed.), *Vom Generalplan Ost zum Generalsiedlungsplan* (Munich, 1994); Rolf-Dieter Müller, *Hitler's Ostkrieg und die deutsche Siedlungspolitik. Die Zusammenarbeit von Wehrmacht, Wirtschaft und SS* (Frankfurt, 1991); Mechtild Rössler and Sabine Schleiermacher (eds), *Der 'Generalplan Ost'. Hauptlinien der nationalsozialistischen Planungs-und Vernichtungspolitik* (Berlin, 1993).

136. On the context, see Alena Mišková, 'Rassenforschung und Oststudien an der Deutschen (Karls-) Universität in Prag', in Detlef Brandes, Edita Ivaničková and Jiří Pešek (eds), *Erzwungene Trennung. Vertreibungen und Aussiedlungen in und aus der Tschechoslowakei 1938–1947 im Vergleich mit Polen, Ungarn und Jugoslawien* (Essen, 1999). On Karl Valentin Müller, see Eduard Kubů, '"Die Bedeutung des deutschen Blutes im Tschechentum". Der "wissenschaftspädagogische" Beitrag des Soziologen Karl Valentin Müller zur Lösung des Problems der Germanisierung Mitteleuropas', *Bohemia. Zeitschrift für Geschichte und Kultur der böhmischen Länder* 45 (2004), 93–114.

137. Müller's appointment certificate, 6 November 1941, as quoted in Kubů, 'Bedeutung', 98.

138. Martin Paul Wolff to Franz-Alfred Six, with copy of Müller's memorandum 'Die tschechisch–deutsche Frage', in Státní oblastní archiv Praha (Prague State Archive), NSDAP Prag, file collection 'K. V. Müller'. See, too, Kubů, 'Bedeutung', 96ff.

139. Kubů, 'Bedeutung', 96ff.

140. Hans Joachim Beyer, *Aufbau und Entwicklung des ostdeutschen Volksraums* (Berlin, 1935); Karl Heinz Roth, 'Heydrichs Professor. Historiographie des "Volkstums" und der Massenvernichtungen. Der Fall Hans Joachim Beyer', in Peter Schöttler (ed.), *Geschichtsschreibung als Legitimationswissenschaft* (Frankfurt, 1997), 262–342, esp. 307.

141. Alexander Pinwinkler, '"Assimilation" und "Dissimilation" in der Bevölkerungsgeschichte ca. 1918–1960', in Rainer Mackensen (ed.), *Bevölkerungsforschung und Politik in Deutschland im 20. Jahrhundert* (Wiesbaden, 2006), 23–48, here 36.

142. Hans Joachim Beyer, 'Auslese und Assimilation', *Deutsche Monatshefte* 7 (1940), 418; idem, 'Amerikanisches oder bolschewistisches "Volkstum"', *Deutsche Volksforschung in Böhmen und Mähren* 2 (1943), 204ff.; see, too, Roth, 'Heydrichs Professor', 262ff.

143. Hans Joachim Beyer, *Das Schicksal der Polen. Rasse – Volkscharakter – Stammesart* (Leipzig, 1942), 158ff.

144. In 1945, Beyer escaped from Prague to Germany and started a second and rather different career, first as spokesperson of the Protestant Church in Schleswig-Holstein, then, from 1950, as professor of history at the University of Flensburg. Pinnwinkler, '"Assimilation"', 30; Andreas Wiedemann, *Die Reinhard-Heydrich-Stiftung in Prag 1942–1945* (Dresden, 2000); Alena Míškováin, 'Die Deutsche Universität Prag im Vergleich mit anderen deutschen Universitäten der Kriegszeit', in Hans Lemberg (ed.), *Universitäten in nationaler Konkurrenz. Zur Geschichte der Prager Universitäten im 19. und 20. Jahrhundert* (Munich, 2003), 177–94, here 186.

145. Heydrich's speech in Černín Palace on 2 October 1941, in National Archives, Prague, 114-6-4, carton 22. For the SS racial surveys of March 1940 on which Heydrich's opinion was based, see BAB, NS 2/88, 30–8.

146. Heydrich's speech in Černín Palace on 2 October 1941, in National Archives, Prague, 114-6-4, carton 22. On the context, see Boris Čelovský (ed.), *Germanisierung und Genozid. Hitlers Endlösung der tschechischen Frage. Deutsche Dokumente 1933–1945* (Brno and Dresden, 2005).

147. Götz Aly and Karl Heinz Roth, *Die restlose Erfassung. Volkszählen, Identifizieren, Aussondern im Nationalsozialismus* (Frankfurt am Main, 2000); Bartov, 'Defining Enemies', 135ff.; Eric D. Weitz, *A Century of Genocide: Utopias of Race and Nation* (Princeton, NJ, 2003), 113ff.

148. Heinemann, "Perpetrator", 392.

149. For a general discussion of the various agencies involved in the ethnic reconstruction of occupied Europe, see Isabel Heinemann, '"Ethnic Resettlement" and Inter-Agency Cooperation in the Occupied Eastern Territories', in Gerald D. Feldman and Wolfgang Seibel (eds), *Networks of Nazi Persecution: Bureaucracy, Business, and the Organization of the Holocaust* (Oxford and New York, 2004), 213–35.

150. Although no record exists of this conversation, Hitler's lunchtime table talk that day consisted of a monologue on the destruction of the Czech people. Heydrich was present and their conversation about the Protectorate must have taken place either before or after that meal. See Hitler, *Monologe*, 106ff.

151. Heydrich's speech in Prague Castle on 4 February 1942, in National Archives, Prague, 114–22.

152. Bryant, *Prague in Black*, 158. John Connelly, 'Nazis and Slavs: From Racial Theory to Racist Practice', *Central European History* 32 (1999), 1–33, here 16–19; Lothar Kettenacker,

Nationalsozialistische Volkstumspolitik im Elsass (Stuttgart, 1973), 232; Doris Bergen, 'The Nazi Concept of "Volksdeutsche" and the Exacerbation of Anti-Semitism in Eastern Europe, 1939–1945', *Journal of Contemporary History* 29 (1994), 569–82, here 572.

153. Bryant, *Prague in Black,* 158–9.
154. Werner Koeppen's report on the meeting of Heydrich and Hitler of 1–2 October 1941, in Kárný et al. (eds), *Deutsche Politik*, doc. 21, p. 107.
155. Heydrich to Bormann, 30 December 1941, in ibid., doc. 65, p. 206. See, too, Bryant, *Prague in Black,* 158.
156. Heydrich to Bormann, 18 May 1942, in Kárný et al. (eds), *Deutsche Politik*, doc. 98, p. 272.
157. Bryant, *Prague in Black.*
158. On the Bodenamt and land confiscations, see Miloš Hořejš, 'Spolupráce Böhmisch-Mährische Landgesellschaft, Bodenamt für Böhmen und Mähren a Volksdeutsche Mittelstelle na germanizaci české půdy na Mělnicku a Mladoboleslavsku (1939–1945)', *Terezínské listy* 34 (2006), 89–124.
159. Heydrich at senior staff meeting in the Reich Protector's Office, 17 October 1941, in National Archives, Prague, 114-2-26. Heydrich's speech of 4 February 1942, in National Archives, Prague, 114–22, p. 23.
160. Wendy Lower, 'A New Ordering of Space and Race: Nazi Colonial Dreams in Zhytomyr, Ukraine 1941–1944', *German Studies Review* 25 (2002), 227–54; Uwe Mai, *Rasse und Raum. Agrarpolitik, Sozial-und Raumplanung im NS-Staat* (Paderborn, 2002).
161. SD files on members of the Prague Land Office, in National Archives, Prague, 114-5-15, carton 19.
162. Brandes, 'Nationalsozialistische Tschechenpolitik', 53–4.
163. On the number of Czechs expelled from their homes, see Brandes, *Tschechen*, vol. 1, 170; Heinemann, *'Rasse'*, 166–7.
164. Mazower, *Hitler's Empire*, 186.
165. Heydrich's speech in Černín Palace on 2 October 1941, in National Archives, Prague, 114-6-4, carton 22.
166. On Heydrich's racial experts, see Roth, 'Generalplan Ost', 36; Heinemann, *'Rasse'*, 131; Míšková, 'Rassenforschung', 39ff.
167. Brandes, 'Nationalsozialistische Tschechenpolitik', 52; Heydrich, *Kriegsverbrecher*, 101.
168. Heinemann, *'Rasse'* 169ff.; Bryant, *Prague in Black*, 161.
169. Heydrich's speech in Prague Castle of 4 February 1942, in National Archives, Prague, 114–22, 24. For a detailed discussion of Heydrich's youth policy, see Tara Zahra, *Kidnapped Souls: National Indifference and the Battle for Children in the Bohemian Lands, 1900–1948* (Ithaca, NY, and London, 2008), 232ff.
170. Heydrich's speech in Prague Castle of 4 February 1942, in National Archives, Prague, 114–22, 24.
171. Ibid.
172. Höppner to Ehlich and Eichmann, 3 September 1941, as quoted in Michael Alberti, *Die Verfolgung und Vernichtung der Juden im Reichsgau Wartheland* (Wiesbaden, 2006), 375.
173. See Heydrich's order of 29 September 1941, in Kárný et al. (eds), *Deutsche Politik*, doc. 15, pp. 97–8. See, too, *Der Neue Tag*, 6 October 1941.
174. Heydrich at the press conference of 10 October 1941, in National Archives, Prague, 114-2-47, carton 8.
175. Heydrich to Hácha, 6 October 1941, in National Archives, Prague, 114, supplement I, carton 43.
176. Heinemann, *Rasse*, 174; Rothkirchen, *Jews*, 51f.; Nathan Stoltzfus, 'The Limits of Policy: Social Protection of Intermarried German Jews in Nazi Germany', in Robert Gellately and idem (eds), *Social Outsiders in Nazi Germany* (Princeton, NJ, 2001), 117–44. See, too, Heydrich's circular to the district governors on the naturalization of Jewish *Mischlinge* of 28 March 1942, in USHMM RG 48.005 M, reel 2; Report of the Chief of the Racial Office of RuSHA on the activities of RuSHA in Bohemia and Moravia, 25 January 1944, in BAB, NS 2/153.
177. 'Bericht der Zentralstelle für jüdische Auswanderung', 2 October 1941, in Kárný et al. (eds), *Deutsche Politik*, doc. 23, pp. 122–7.

178. Miroslav Kárný, 'Zur Statistik der jüdischen Bevölkerung im sogenannten Protektorat', *Judaica Bohemiae* 23 (1987), 9–19.

179. Zimmermann, *Rassenutopie*, 218ff.

180. On the number of deaths, see Ctibor Nećas, *Holocaust českých Romů* (Prague, 1999), 175.

181. Witte et al. (eds), *Dienstkalender*, 405, n. 60.

182. Werner Koeppen's report on Hitler's table talk of 6 October 1941, in Kárný et al. (eds), *Deutsche Politik*, doc. 25, p. 130.

183. Bryant, *Prague in Black*, 149; Kershaw, *Hitler: Nemesis*, 479.

184. Heydrich to Himmler, 19 October 1941, in IfZ, Eich 1544. On the Łódź Ghetto, see Sascha Feuchert, Erwin Leibfried and Jörg Riecke (eds), *Die Chronik des Ghettos Lodz/Litzmannstadt* (Göttingen, 2006), and Andrea Löw, *Juden im Getto Litzmannstadt. Lebensbedingungen, Selbstwahrnehmung, Verhalten* (Göttingen, 2006). Longerich, *Politik*, 434ff.

185. Senior staff meeting in the Reich Protector's Office, 10 October 1941, in Kárný et al. (eds), *Deutsche Politik*, doc. 29, pp. 137–41.

186. Senior staff meeting in the Reich Protector's Office, 17 October 1941, in National Archives, Prague, 114-2-26. On Theresienstadt, see the reprint of Hans Günther Adler, *Theresienstadt 1941–1945. Das Antlitz einer Zwangsgemeinschaft* (Göttingen, 2005); Vojtěch Blodig, 'Dějiny ghetta Terezín (1941–1945)', in Miloš Pojar (ed.), *Stín šoa nad Evropou* (Prague, 2001), 57–66; Tomáš Fedorovič, 'Zánik města Terezín a jeho přeměna v ghetto', *Terezínské listy* 32 (2004), 15–43.

187. On the number of arrivals at Terezin, see Hilberg, *Destruction*, vol. 2, 455.

188. Goebbels's diary entry of 18 November 1941, in *Tagebücher*, part II, vol. 2, 309.

189. Miroslav Kárný, 'Konečné řešení'. *Genocida českých židů v německé protektorátní politice* (Prague, 1991), 155ff.

190. Browning, *Origins*, 244.

191. Eichmann's courier letter of 31 January 1942, reprinted in Longerich, *Ermordung*, 165f.

192. Transcript of the meeting of 9 March 1942, as reprinted in Longerich, *Ermordung*, 167ff.

193. Private film coverage of Heydrich in the Bavarian Alps shows him relaxed and cheerful. See BA Filmarchiv (Berlin), DW 615/26/1942. See, too; Witte et al. (eds), *Dienstkalender*, 7 March 1942, p. 371.

194. Dieter Pohl, *Von der 'Judenpolitik' zum Judenmord. Der Distrikt Lublin des Generalgouvernements 1939–1944* (Frankfurt am Main, 1993), 13ff.; David Silberklang, 'Die Juden und die ersten Deportationen aus dem Distrikt Lublin', in Bogdan Musial (ed.), *'Aktion Reinhardt'. Der Völkermord an den Juden im Generalgouvernement 1941–1944* (Osnabrück, 2004), 141–64.

195. Witte, 'Two Decisions', 335f.

196. Kárný, 'Konečné řešení', 153f. On Sobibor more generally, see Jules Schelvis, *Vernichtungslager Sobibór. Dokumente – Texte – Materialien* (Berlin, 1998).

197. Witte et al. (eds), *Dienstkalender*, 20 October 1941; Yehoshua Büchler, 'The Deportation of Slovakian Jews to the Lublin District of Poland in 1942', *Holocaust and Genocide Studies* 6 (1991), 151–66.

198. Tuka's memorandum on Heydrich's visit, dated 10 April, in National Archives, Prague, 114-7-300; see, too, Büchler, 'Deportation', 153ff.

199. Note by Dannecker, 10 March 1941, printed in Klarsfeld, *Vichy*, 374f. The deportation of 5,000 French Jews to Auschwitz was carried out between 5 June and 17 July.

200. Yitzhak Arad, *Belzec, Sobibor, Treblinka: The Operation Reinhard Death Camps* (Bloomington, IN, 1987), 36ff and 75; Jürgen Matthäus, ' "Operation Barbarossa" and the Onset of the Holocaust', in Browning, *Origins*, 253–5, here 304.

201. This visit was reconstructed during the trial of the former Gestapo chief in Minsk, Georg Heuser, in 1963. See Irene Sagel-Grande, H. H. Fuchs and C. F. Rüter (eds), *Justiz und NS-Verbrechen. Sammlung deutscher Strafurteile wegen nationalsozialistischer Tötungsverbrechen 1945–1966*, vol. 19: *Die vom 10.01.1963 bis zum 12.04.1964 ergangenen Strafurteile* (Amsterdam, 1978), vol. 19 (Amsterdam, 1987), doc. no. 552 p. 192. On the new round of mass killings, see Gerlach, *Kalkulierte Morde*, 694ff.

202. On the Ukraine, see Dieter Pohl, 'Schauplatz Ukraine. Der Massenmord an den Juden im Militärverwaltungsgebiet und im Reichskommissariat 1941–1943', in Norbert Frei,

Sybille Steinbacher and Bernd C. Wagner (eds), *Ausbeutung, Vernichtung, Öffentlichkeit. Neue Studien zur nationalsozialistischen Lagerpolitik* (Munich, 2000), 135–73, here 159f.

203. Longerich, *Himmler*, 583.
204. Witte et al. (eds), *Dienstkalender*, 410ff.; Longerich, *Himmler*, 582f.
205. Heydrich's speaking notes of 19 Decemeber 1941, in National Archives, Prague, 114–22.
206. On German cultural policies in the Protectorate up until Heydrich's arrival in Prague, see Fauth, *Kulturpolitik*; Jiří Doležal, *Česká kultura za protektorátu* (Prague, 1996); František Červinka, *Česká kultura a okupace* (Prague, 2002).
207. Fauth, *Kulturpolitik*, 88.
208. Heydrich to Goebbels, February 1942, in National Archives, Prague, 109–4–711.
209. Letter, Heydrich to Goebbels, 29 September 1941, and Goebbels's response of 1 October 1941, both in National Archives, Prague, 114, carton 1140. See, too, Goebbels's diary entry of 17 November 1941, in *Tagebücher*, part II, vol. 2, 309.
210. See the 'Protokoll über die Abmachungen mit dem Reichspropagandaministerium über die beabsichtigten Massnahmen auf dem Sektor Kulturpropaganda' of 14 October 1941, in National Archives, Prague, 114, carton 1140.
211. Heydrich's speech in Prague Castle, 4 February 1942, in National Archives, Prague, 114–22, ff. 23 and 50. Himmler warmly approved of these 'very good' ideas. See Himmler to Heydrich, 23 October 1941, in National Archives, Prague, 114, carton 1140.
212. Heydrich's speech in Černín Palace on 2 October 1941, in National Archives, Prague, 114–6–4, carton 22. On the importance of the Wenceslas myth for Heydrich's propaganda, see, too, the post-Second World War interrogations of Walter Jacobi, Archive of the Ministry of the Interior (AMV), Prague, 325–166–3.
213. See, for example, 'Tschechische Betrachtungen zur Wenzelstradition', *Der Neue Tag*, 21 November 1941.
214. Hácha and Heydrich as quoted in *Der Neue Tag*, 19 November 1941.
215. Reinhard Heydrich, 'Die Wenzelstradition', *Der Neue Tag*, 20 November 1941.
216. National Archives, Kew, HS 4/79/324795.
217. Heydrich, 'Die Wenzelstradition'.
218. Heydrich's speech in Černín Palace, 2 October 1941, in National Archives, Prague, 114–6–4, carton 22.
219. Heydrich's notes on the history of Bohemia (undated), in National Archives, Prague, 114–5–15, carton 8. Few of these interpretations originated with Heydrich. He drew heavily on memoranda written by Karl Hermann Frank in 1940, as well on a series of essays published by the Sudeten German law professor Hermann Raschhofer in the Nazi periodical *Böhmen und Mähren*. See Karl Hermann Frank, *Böhmen und Mähren im Reich. Vortrag gehalten am 24. Juni 1941 im Ostinstitut in Krakau* (Prague, 1941). See, too, Himmler to Heydrich, 23 October 1941 (with particular emphasis on the Wenceslas myth), in National Archives, Prague, 114, carton 1140.
220. Hans Lemberg, 'Prag im Zerrspiegel. Die Propagierung des "deutschen Prag" in der Protektoratszeit', in *Magister noster. Sborník statí věnovaných in memoriam Prof. Dr. Janu Havránkovi* (Prague, 2005), 383–94. Vojtěch Šustek, 'Josef Pfitzner a germanizace města Prahy', in *Osm set let pražské samosprávy. Sborník příspěvků z 18. vědecké konference Archivu hlavního města Prahy* (Prague, 2002), 167–81.
221. Heydrich's speech in Prague Castle, 4 February 1942, in National Archives, Prague, 114–22, f. 56. On his genuine passion for the history of Bohemia and Moravia see, too, Heydrich, *Kriegsverbrecher*, 105.
222. On Heydrich's interest in Wallenstein, see Deschner, *Heydrich*, 218. On the excavations, see Heydrich to Hácha, 4 May 1942, in National Archives, Prague, 114–5–15, carton 19.
223. Heydrich to Bormann, 8 May 1942, in National Archives, Prague, 114–3–17; Heydrich to Bormann, 16 November 1941, in ibid.
224. See Himmler's 'Denkschrift über die Behandlung der Fremdvölkischen' of May 1940, reprinted in *VfZ* 5 (1957), 195ff.
225. Heydrich's speech of 4 February 1942, in National Archives, Prague, 114–22, f. 29; Heydrich to Bormann, 22 January 1942, National Archives, Prague, 114–3–17.
226. *České slovo*, 1 May 1942.
227. National Archives, Kew, HS 4/79/324795.

228. Heydrich's speech in Prague Castle, 4 February 1942, in National Archives, Prague, 114–22, f. 28. On the German academics in Prague involved in the Germanization of the academic landscape, see Ota Konrád, 'Die deutschen Hochschullehrer in Prag vor und nach 1938/39. Versuch einer Bestandsaufnahme', in Jerzy Kochanowski and Maike Sach (eds), *Die 'Volksdeutschen' in Polen, Frankreich, Ungarn und der Tschechoslowakei. Mythos und Realität* (Osnabrück, 2006), 147–62; Míšková, 'Rassenforschung'; quotation from Karl Hermann Frank, in Wannenmacher (ed.), *Leben der Tat*, 39.

229. Wiedemann, *Reinhard-Heydrich-Stiftung*, 44; Alan E. Steinweis, 'German Cultural Imperialism in Czechoslovakia and Poland, 1938–1945', *International History Review* 13 (1991), 466–80.

230. Wiedemann, *Reinhard-Heydrich-Stiftung*, 89.

231. Heydrich to Bormann, 18 May 1942, in Kárný et al. (eds), *Deutsche Politik*, doc. 98, pp. 264ff.; Wiedemann, *Reinhard-Heydrich-Stiftung*, 44.

232. The Reinhard Heydrich Foundation was officially launched on 27 May 1943, the first anniversary of Heydrich's death. See Wiedemann, *Reinhard-Heydrich-Stiftung*.

233. Heydrich to Bormann, 30 December 1941, in Kárný et al. (eds), *Deutsche Politik*, doc. 65, pp. 203–4. See, too, Heydrich, *Kriegsverbrecher*, 105. Dinner seating plans modified by Heydrich at Prague Castle on 4 December 1941 (dress code: men in uniform, women in short evening dresses) can be found in Burian et al., *Assassination*, 40. Speer's post-war account of Heydrich as quoted in Deschner, *Heydrich*, 322.

234. *Böhmen und Mähren*, November 1941, 400ff.; *Der Neue Tag*, 29 October 1941. See, too, Vlasta Reittererová, 'Das Mozartjahr 1941 in Prag. Ein Beitrag zur Geschichte des Musiklebens im Protektorat Böhmen und Mähren', in *Přednášky z 47. běhu Letní školy slovanských studií* (Prague, 2004), 184–206.

235. File 'Heydrich und das Deutsche Theater (nur Rohmaterial!)', in National Archives, Prague, 114-2-26. See, too, Karl Hermann Frank, in Wannenmacher (ed.), *Leben der Tat*, 40.

236. Heydrich's speech of 16 October 1941 on the occasion of the reopening of the Rudolfinum, in National Archives, Prague, 114-2-47, carton 8.

237. Ibid.

238. Heydrich, 'Grusswort' for Musical Week, in IfZ, Ed 450; Berndt to Goebbels, 13 January 1941, in BAB, R 55, 20750.

239. Heydrich, *Kriegsverbrecher*, 114.

240. Ibid.; Naudé, *Politischer Beamter*, 127f.; Klein, 'Pfitzner and the Two Heydrichs', 308–17.

241. Heydrich to Bormann, 16 May 1942, in Kárný et al. (eds), *Deutsche Politik*, doc. 96, p. 258. See, too, the daily SD reports of January–May 1942 which highlighted the surge in resistance activities that Heydrich was referring to.

242. Heydrich's speech of 26 May 1942, in National Archives, Prague, 114, carton 8.

243. On Eastern Europe, see the draft 'Verordnung über Kollektivmassnahmen in den besetzen Ostgebieten', sent by Heydrich to Rosenberg on 16 March 1942, in BA-MA, SF-01/28985, ff. 127–9.

244. Heydrich to Ribbentrop, 3 June 1942 (the letter was signed by Heydrich before his assassination, but only posted afterwards), printed in Fritz Petrick, *Die Okkupationspolitik des deutschen Faschismus in Dänemark und Norwegen, 1940–45* (Berlin, 1992), doc. 61, p. 139.

245. Witte et al. (eds), *Dienstkalender*, 28 January 1942, p. 331.

246. Heydrich to General Quartermaster Wagner, 6 November 1941, in IfZ, MA 280; reprinted in Klarsfeld, *Vichy*, 369. See, too, Burrin, *Hitler and the Jews*, 123f. The content of the letter had apparently been approved by Himmler who talked to Heydrich over the phone on the very same day that Heydrich's letter was posted. See Witte et al. (eds), *Dienstkalender*, 21 December 1941, p. 255.

247. Heydrich to Canaris, 5 February 1942, in IfZ, MA 1498. A copy of the letter was sent to Himmler, who discussed the matter with Heydrich on 7 and 10 February. See Witte et al. (eds), *Dienstkalender*, 7 and 10 February 1942, pp. 340 and 343.

248. Canaris to Heydrich, 8 February 1942, in IfZ, MA 1498.

249. 'Grundsätze für die Zusammenarbeit der Sicherheitspolizei und des SD und den Abwehrstellen der Wehrmacht', in BAB, NS 19/3514.

250. On the conference, see BA Hoppegarten, MIA, 35; Archive of the Czech Interior Ministry, 114–3–14/36–7; on Canaris as a house guest in the Heydrich home, see Lina Heydrich to Peter Schneiders (Amsterdam), 12 January 1962, in NIOD, doc. I, 691A.

251. Post-war testimony of Huppenkothen, IfZ, ZS 249, 40.

252. Letter, Canaris to Lina Heydrich, as quoted in: Höhne, *Canaris*, 379.

253. See Hitler's order of 9 March 1942, in BAB, R 70/13, and the previous negotiations between the SS and the Wehrmacht during February 1942, in IfZ, MA 342 ff. 8339–45.

254. Heydrich to Bormann (from Paris), 7 May 1942, in Káraý et al. (eds), *Deutsche Politik*, doc. 93, p. 254.

255. Dannecker to Knochen, 10 March 1942, as quoted in Klarsfeld (ed.), *Endlösung*, doc. 28.

256. Post-war testimony of Hans Boetticher, Chief Justice in the German military administration in France, 29 October 1949, as quoted in Bernhard Brunner, *Der Frankreich-Komplex. Die nationalsozialistischen Verbrechen in Frankreich und die Justiz der Bundesrepublik Deutschland* (Göttingen, 2004), 59.

257. Walter Bargatzky, *Hotel Majestic. Ein Deutscher im besetzten Frankreich* (Freiburg im Breisgau, 1987), 103f.

258. Best to Heydrich, 15 April 1942, in BAB, BDC, Best; see, too, Best's post-war statement on Heydrich (1 October 1959), in IfZ (Munich), ZS 207/2, ff. 6–7; and Herbert, *Best*, 316–19.

259. Best to Wolff, 15 November 1941, in BAB, BDC, Best; see, too, Herbert, *Best*, 316.

260. Heydrich to Wolff, 14 April 1942, in BAB, BDC, Best. On 4 May, Heydrich sent Best's letter to him on to Himmler, adding in the margin that 'I have nothing to add to Best's letter.' Heydrich to Himmler, 4 May 1942, in BAB, BDC, Best.

261. Best to Heydrich, 7 May 1942, in BAB, BDC, Best. The previous day, he had written to Wolff to clarify his position: ibid.

262. Best to Wolff, 13 May 1942, BAB, BDC, Best.

263. Čestmír Amort, *Heydrichiáda* (Prague, 1965), 37; MacDonald, *Killing*, 166; Brandes, *Tschechen*, vol. 1, 263; Deschner, *Heydrich*, 236; Dederichs, *Heydrich*, 139.

264. Miroslav Kárný, 'Heydrichova cesta do Paříže (5.5.1942)', *Historie a vojenství* 41 (1992), 95–108. In Giese's papers there is only a brief note from Böhme to Frank of 4 May 1942, indicating that Heydrich was currently in Paris and that he had ordered that they should pretend that he was in Berlin. Böhme to Frank, 4 May 1942, in National Archives, Prague, 109–4–729.

265. This meeting had also been encouraged by Himmler, who informed Heydrich on 11 May that he had suggested to Hitler that he should meet Heydrich in order to discuss ways of overcoming the wave of resistance throughout Europe. Himmler to Heydrich, 11 May 1942, in IfZ, MA 328. Kárný et al. (eds), *Deutsche Politik*, 74.

266. Post-war testimony of Dr Ludwig Hahn, the Sipo and SD commander in Warsaw, as quoted in Deschner, *Heydrich*, 236f.

267. SD report 58/42, in National Archives, Prague, 114–308–3.

268. Karl Wolff remembered after the war that Himmler had asked Heydrich in May to take greater precautions in the light of recent threats against his life. See Wolff's post-war testimony, in IfZ, ZS 317, ff. 34f. According to the only Czech surgeon present during Heydrich's operation on 27 May, Alois Vincenc Honek, Heydrich wore a bullet-proof vest on the day of the operation. See Dederichs, *Heydrich*, 144.

269. Speer as quoted in MacDonald, *Killing*, 148f.

Chapter IX: Legacies of Destruction

1. Haasis, *Tod*, 116; Axel Huber, '"Du, Reinhard Heydrich, bist ein wahrhaft gutter SS-Mann gewesen": Totenkult und Heldenmythos nach dem Tod von SS-Gruppenführer Reinhard Heydrich', MA thesis, University of Konstanz, 2009. See, too, the detailed programme of and instructions for Heydrich's funeral services in Prague and Berlin, in BAB, BDC, SSO Reinhard Heydrich, and IfZ, Ed 450. See, too, Heydrich, *Kriegsverbrecher*, 6f. and 131; and Witte et al. (eds), *Dienstkalender*, 4 and 7 June 1942, pp. 450 and 455.

2. See the strict guidelines provided by the Ministry of Propaganda as summarized by the Berlin correspondent of *Frankfurter Zeitung*, Fritz Sänger, in Kárný et al. (eds), *Deutsche*

Politik, doc. 107, pp. 291f.; see, too, Volker Ackermann, *Nationale Totenfeiern in Deutschland. Von Wilhelm I. tris Franz Josef Strauss, eine Studie zur politischen Semiotik* (Stuttgart, 1990), 196. Quotations from the obituary in *Der Neue Tag*, 5 June 1942. See, too, *Völkischer Beobachter*, 5 June 1942; 'Ein Leben für das Reich', *Das Schwarze Korps*, 11 June 1942; Herbert von Daniels, 'Synthese Sportler und Soldat. Heydrich bleibt Vorbild für die deutsche Jugend', undated article, in BAB, BDC, SSO Reinhard Heydrich; Fritz Helke, 'Jagdflieger Heydrich', *Königsberger Allgemeine Zeitung*, 9 June 1942.

3. Himmler's funeral speech as printed in Wannenmacher (ed.), *Leben der Tat*, 81–90. The volume was published by the Prague-based publishing house Volk und Reich on the second anniversary of Heydrich's death. On the extensive preparations for the volume, see the correspondence between SS-Standartenführer Gies (Prague) and SS-Standartenführer Brandt (Persönlicher Stab Reichsführer SS), in National Archives, Prague, 110–4–549. See, too, the correspondence between Frank and Himmler on the festive commemoration of Heydrich's death, in National Archives, Prague, 110–4–549.

4. Hitler's speech as printed in Reichssicherheitshauptamt (ed.), *Meine Ehre heisst Treue*, 23.

5. See Himmler's correspondence on this matter, in BAB, NS 19/3454, and the letters written by Wilhelm Petersens to Lina Heydrich, in BAB, R 58, supplement 23. According to Hitler's orders, Heydrich was to be reburied in a newly built Great Hall for Germany's military leaders after the war's end. Bormann to Lammers, 6 June 1942, in BAB, R 45II/1157b. On Heydrich's grave, see Laurenz Demps, *Der Invalidenfreidhof. Denkmal preussisch-deutscher Geschichte in Berlin* (Stuttgart, 1996), 80ff.

6. On Heydrich becoming a household name, see the SD report, no. 290, of 11 June 1942 in BAB, R 58/172; reprinted in Boberach (ed.), *Meldungen aus dem Reich*, vol. 10, 3802ff. See, too, *Wochenschau*, no. 615, 17 June 1942. On Hitler's orders: letter from the NSDAP-Reichsleitung to SS-Obergruppenführer Schmitt, head of the SS Personnel Department, 23 July 1942, in BAB, BDC, SSO Reinhard Heydrich. On the name change of the 6th SS Infantry Standard, see *Völkischer Beobachter*, 7 June 1942, and IfZ, Ed 450. See, too, the letter exchanges between Lina Heydrich and the commanders of the SS infantry regiment 'Reinhard Heydrich', in BAB, R 58 appendix 23. On the special Heydrich stamp, see BAB, NS 19/545. The stamp is reprinted in Deschner, *Heydrich*, 176. On the renaming of streets, see *Der Neue Tag*, 31 May 1943. The quotation is from *Germanische Leithefte*, June 1942, p. 2.

7. Sabine Behrenbeck, *Der Kult um die toten Helden. Nationalsozialistische Mythen, Riten und Symbole 1923 bis 1945* (Cologne, 1996), 595ff.; Daniel Siemens, *Horst Wessel. Tod und Verklärung eines Nationalsozialisten* (Munich, 2009). On SS celebrations of death, see Fritz Weitzel, *Die Gestaltung der Feste im Jahres- und Lebenslauf in der SS-Familie* (Wuppertal, 1942), 38 and 76; Karl Hermann Frank, 18 October 1942, in National Archives, Prague, 114–6–8, carton 22.

8. Goebbels, *Tagebücher*, part II, vol. 4, p. 450 (entry for 4 June 1942).

9. Brandes, *Tschechen*, vol. 1, 261.

10. See Böhme's notes of 12 June 1942, Archive of the Ministry of the Interior, Prague, 114–10–1/II, and Král, *Deutschen*, 480.

11. Brandes, *Tschechen*, vol. 1, 263; Berton, 'Attentat', 690f.

12. Berton, 'Attentat', 668ff.

13. The letter is quoted in length in ibid., 688, n. 15. On the murder of the two suspects, see 'Totenbuch des SS-Standortarztes Mauthausen', 24 October 1942, in KZ-Gedenkstätte Mauthausen, AMM Y/46. On the fact that they were gassed rather than shot, see the confessions of the two SS officers in charge of the killings, Martin Roth and Werner Fassel, in 'Urteil des Landgerichts Hagen', 24 July 1970, 11 KS 1/70, in KZ-Gedenkstätte Mauthausen, AMM P/19/45; and Pierre Serge Choumoff, *Nationalsozialistische Massentötungen durch Giftgas auf österreichischem Gebiet 1940–1945* (Vienna, 2000), 101ff.

14. Brandes, *Tschechen*, vol. 1, 263f.; Mastny, *Czechs*, 215ff. See, too, Peter Steinkamp, 'Lidice 1942', in Gerd R. Ueberschär (ed.), *Orte des Grauens. Verbrechen im Zweiten Weltkrieg* (Darmstadt, 2003), 126–35. See, too, Geschke's final report on the destruction of Lidice, dated 24 June 1942, in Archive of the Ministry of the Interior, Prague, 301–5–4. See, too, Daluege's 'Führerbericht über den Mordanschlag auf SS-Obergruppenführer Heydrich' (29 June 1942), in Archive of the Ministry of the Interior, Prague, 301–5–4. Death figures

as quoted in Wolfgang Benz, *Legenden, Lügen, Vorurteile. Ein Wörterbuch zur Zeitgeschicte* (Munich, 1992), 140. The youngest victim was fourteen-year-old Josef Hroník, the oldest was eighty-four-year-old Emanuel Kovářovský. See, too, Official Statement by the German government, 10 June 1942, as quoted in the British SOE Report, National Archives, Kew, HS 4/79.

15. Archive of the Interior Ministry, Prague, 325–2–2, 325–2–4, 325–2–5. On the 'Lebensborn' project, see Georg Lilienthal, *Der 'Lebensborn e. v.'. Ein Instrument nationalsozialistischer Rassenpolitik* (Frankfurt, 1993), 242ff. See, too, Zahra, *Kidnapped Souls*, 197.

16. Miroslav Kárný, ' "Heydrichiaden": Widerstand und Terror im "Protektorat Böhmen und Mähren"', in Loukia Droulia and Hagen Fleischer (eds), *Von Lidice bis Kalavryta. Widerstand und Besatzungsterror. Studien zur Repressalienpraxis im Zweiten Weltkrieg* (Berlin 1999), 51–63, here 61. For Goebbels's quotation, see his diary entry of 14 June 1942, in *Tagebücher*, part II, vol. 4, 523f.

17. See, for example, *The Times*, 26 June 1942; *New York Times*, 11 June 1942.

18. War Office 'Memorandum on German Occupation of the Protectorate' (12 January 1943), in National Archives, Kew, HS 4/79.

19. See the eulogies in *Lidice: A Tribute by Members of the International P.E.N.* (London 1944), Thomas Mann's quotation on p. 90. On Mann's *Lidice*, originally entitled *Der Protektor*, see Uwe Naumann, *Faschismus als Groteske. Heinrich Manns Roman 'Lidice'* (Worms, 1980). The story of this operation and the subsequent annihilation of Lidice have also inspired countless post-war films, novels, plays and songs. The story of the assassination inspired films such as *Attentat* (1964), *Operation Daybreak* (1975) and *The Assassination of Reinhard Heydrich* (1991), as well as the song 'A Lovely Day Tomorrow' by the British rock band Sea Power.

20. Thomas Mann, *Essays*, vol. 5: *Deutschland und die Deutschen 1938–1945*, ed. Hermann Kurzke and Stephan Stachorski (Frankfurt, 1997), 185f. On the text's dissemination as a propaganda leaflet dropped behind German lines in September and October 1942, see ibid., 373f. On Mann and Heydrich, see Hübinger, 'Mann und Heydrich', 111ff.

21. Beneš to Bartoš, as quoted in Mastny, *Czechs*, 217.

22. Less than two months later, on 29 September 1942, Czechoslovak Foreign Minister Jan Masaryk received written assurance from the French government-in-exile that it, too, considered the Munich Agreement null and void. See Jan Kuklík, 'Oduznání mnichovské dohody za druhé světové války', *Historie a vojenství* 46 (1997), 49–68; Jan Němeček, 'Rok 1942 v československém zahraničním odboji', in *Rok 1942 v českém odboji. Sborník příspěvků z vědecké konference* (Prague, 1999), 19–24.

23. Frank's speech of October 1942, in National Archives, Prague, 114–6–8.

24. Brandes, *Tschechen*, vol. 1, 265; Dennler, *Böhmische Passion*, 78–80. See the long list of informers and sums paid to them in exchange for information in Archive of the Ministry of the Interior, Prague, 315–194–30.

25. MacDonald, *Killing*, 193ff. Čurda was arrested by the Czech authorities in 1945 and, after an unsuccessful suicide attempt, was hanged in 1947 for high treason.

26. Berton 'Attentat', 694, n. 27; 'Totenbuch des SS-Standortarztes Mauthausen', 24 October 1942, in KZ-Gedenkstätte Mauthausen, AMM Y/46.

27. See Daluege's 'Führerbericht über den Mordanschlag auf SS-Obergruppenführer Heydrich' (29 June 1942), in Archive of the Czech Ministry of the Interior, 301–5–4.

28. Berton, 'Attentat', 668ff.; Haasis, *Tod*, 152.

29. 'Totenbuch des SS-Standortarztes Mauthausen', 24 October 1942, in KZ-Gedenkstätte Mauthausen, AMM Y/46.

30. Brandes, *Tschechen*, vol. 1, 265; Mastny, *Czechs*, 220f.; MacDonald, *Killing*, 196; Frantiček Schildberger, *Ležáky* (Hradec Králové, 1982).

31. See Geschke's report on death sentences of 24 June 1942, in Archive of the Ministry of the Interior, Prague, 301–5–4; see, too, Brandes, 'Nationalsozialistische Tschechenpolitik', 47; Sládek, 'Standrecht', 332f.

32. See the report 'Protectorate Background for Operations', 14 August 1942, in National Archives, Kew, HS 4/79. On the productivity of the Czech armaments industry until 1945, see Vladimír Francev, 'Panzerjäger – Program. Nový úkol pro protektorátní průmysl', in *Válečný rok 1944* (Prague, 2002), 320ff.

33. Smith et al., *Himmler: Geheimreden*, 146–61, here 159. That Himmler was deeply shaken by Heydrich's death is confirmed by Wolff's post-war testimony, in IfZ, ZS 317, f. 31. See, too, Longerich, *Himmler*, 586ff. Kurt Daluege argued along similar lines when on 7 June 1942 he wrote in *Völkischer Beobachter* that Heydrich's death had made the SS 'even more determined to exterminate those elements of the European underworld' responsible for the assassination, by which he meant the Jews. *Völkischer Beobachter*, 7 June 1942.

34. Longerich, *Himmler*, 586ff.; Christopher R. Browning, *The Path to Genocide: Essays on Launching the Final Solution* (Cambridge, 1992), 169; see, too, Pohl, *Ostgalizien*.

35. Meetings between Himmler and Hitler took place on 27, 28, 30 and 31 May, as well as on 3, 4 and 5 June 1942. See Witte et al. (eds), *Dienstkalender*, 441–56; and Longerich, *Himmler*, 588ff.; Witte, 'Two Decisions', 333f.; Pohl, *Ostgalizien*, 204f.

36. The odd spelling of Heydrich's first name with a 't' has given rise to the somewhat curious speculation that the genocidal operation in the General Government was not named after the murdered Reich Protector and chief organizer of the 'Final Solution', but after the State Secretary of Finance, Fritz Reinhardt, whose ministry administered the stolen property of the murdered Jews. See: Robert Lewis Koehl, *German Resettlement and Population Policy, 1939–1945: A History of the Reich Commission for the Strengthening of Germandom* (Cambridge MA, 1957), 198. The confusion caused by the existence of both spellings – *Aktion Reinhard* and *Aktion Reinhardt* – is easily explained. Throughout the 1930s, Heydrich himself used both spellings for his first name. See: Peter Witte and Stephen Tyas, 'A New Document on the Deportation and Murder of Jews during 'Einsatz Reinhard' 1942' in *Holocaust and Genocide Studies* 15 (2001), 468–486, here 484, note 41.

37. See Shlomo Aronson and Richard Breitmann, 'Eine unbekannte Himmler-Rede vom Januar 1943', *VfZ* 38 (1990), 337–48. See, too, Peter Black, 'Die Trawniki-Männer und die Aktion Reinhard', in Bogdan Musial (ed.), *'Aktion Reinhardt'. Der Völkermord an den Juden im Generalgouvernement 1941–1944* (Osnabrück, 2004), 309–52; BAB, BDC, SSO Reinhard Heydrich; see, too, the letter exchange between Himmler and Globocnik, 4 and 30 November 1943 and 5 January 1944, in BAB, NS 19/2234, also printed as part of 4024–PS, in *IMT*, vol. 34, 68–71.

38. Goebbels, *Tagebücher*, part II, vol. 4, 432 (diary entry for 2 June 1942); Gottwald and Schulle, *Judendeportationen*, 260ff.

39. Kárný, *Konečné řešení*, 153f. On the number of Jewish survivors, see Adler, *Theresienstadt*, 15.

40. Longerich, *Himmler*, 638f.; Juliane Wetzel, 'Frankreich und Belgien', in Benz (ed.), *Dimensionen des Völkermordes*, 105–35; Klarsfeld, *Vichy*, 379ff.; Longerich, *Himmler*, 590ff.

41. Brandes, *Tschechen*, vol. 1, 261.

42. Smith et al., *Himmler: Geheimreden*, 146–61, here 159. See, too, Heinemann, *'Rasse'*, 167f.

43. Schirach as quoted in Botz, *Wien*, 597f.

44. Bormann to Goebbels, 8 June 1942, in BAB, NS 19/1969.

45. Bryant, *Prague*, 173f. Heinemann, *'Rasse'*, 157.

46. Ibid., 359f., n. 10; Lower, *Nazi Empire-Building*, 177.

47. Heinemann, *'Rasse'*, 162ff.

48. Wildt, *Generation*, 704.

49. Heydrich, *Kriegsverbrecher*, 123.

50. See Lina's correspondence about the camp inmates in BAB, NS 19/18. Testimonies of eyewitnesses and former slave labourers on the Heydrich estate, recorded in Prague after 1945, as quoted in Schwarz, *Frau an seiner Seite*, 211. See, too, Archive of the Ministry of the Interior, Prague, 325–57–3; Jörg Skriebeleit, 'Jungfern-Breschan', in Benz and Distel, *Ort des Terrors*, vol. 4, 164ff.

51. Newspaper clipping with the announcement of Klaus's death, in IfZ, Ed 450.

52. Gitta Sereny, *Das Ringen mit der Wahrheit. Albert Speer und das deutsche Trauma* (Munich, 1995), 381f.; Lili Scholz, *'Bis alles in Scherben fällt'. Tagebuchblätter 1933–1945* (2nd edn, Hamburg, 2007), 415f. See, too, the letter published by Heydrich's commanding officer, Kurt Joachim Fischer, in *Der Spiegel*, 16 March 1950.

53. Interview with the author in March 2009. The theft theory was confirmed by a military court case against Fischer on 28 December 1944. See Generallandesarchiv Halle, Sign. 465a/59/15/7492. I am grateful to Axel Huber for this reference.

54. On expulsions, see Benjamin Frommer, *National Cleansing: Retribution against Nazi Collaborators in Postwar Czechoslovakia* (Cambridge, 2005).
55. The fate of Elisabeth Heydrich according to her grandson, Heider Heydrich, in an interview with the author in March 2009.
56. Heydrich, *Kriegsverbrecher*, 154f.; and Werner Maser's commentary on 201f.
57. See the extensive documentation in IfZ, Ed 450 II. See, too, Uwe Danker, 'NS-Opfer und Täter. Versorgung mit zweierlei Mass. Lina Heydrich und Dr. Norbert L. mit Rentenangelegenheiten vor Gericht', *Demokratische Geschichte. Jahrbuch zur Arbeiterbewegung und Demokratie in Schleswig-Holstein* 10 (1996), 277–305.
58. *Jasmin* 4/69.

Bibliography

Archival Sources
Bundesarchiv Berlin

NS 2 (*Rasse- und Siedlungshauptamt*)
30–8, 88   174

NS 19 (*Persönlicher Stab Reichsführer SS*)
219   1969   3514
545   2234   3979
1757   2655
                       3454

NS 31 (*SS-Hauptamt*)
236

R 19 (*Ordnungspolizei*)
395   401

R 22 (*Reichsjustizministerium*)
4070

R 43II (*Neue Reichskanzlei*)
1326   357

R 45II (*Reichskanzlei*)
1157b

R 58 (*Reichsicherheitshauptamt*)
18   269   956
137   276   991
172   291   1027
239   336   1032
240   623   1082
241   825   9318 (formerly annexe 21)
242   826   9319 (formerly annexe 22)
243   827   9320 (formerly annexe 23)
256   954
264   956

R 55 (*Reichspropagandaministerium*)
20750

R 69 (*Einwanderzentralstelle*)
1146

R 70 (*Besetzte Gebiete*)
13

Files of the former Berlin Document Centre

PK, Heydrich, Reinhard
PK, Best, Werner
SSO, Alvensleben, Ludolf-Hermann von
SSO, Best, Werner
SSO, Eicke, Theodor
SSO, Fentz, Walter
SSO, Frank, Karl Hermann

SSO, Heydrich, Heinz
SSO, Heydrich, Reinhard
SSO, Hildebrandt, Richard
SSO, Mehlhorn, Herbert
SSO, Ploetz, Hans-Achim
SSO, Pomme, Kurt
SSO, Rall, Gustav

Bundesarchiv Berlin, Abteilung Filmarchiv
DW 615/26/1942 (*Deutsche Wochenschau*)

Bundesarchiv Berlin, Dahlwitz-Hoppegarten

MIA, 35
ZR 277

ZR 512 A9
ZR 521 A9

Bundesarchiv Freiburg, Militärarchiv

BA-MA, RH 1/58.
BA-MA, RH 20–14/178

BA-MA, RW 4/v. 581
BA-MA, SF-01/28985

Bundesarchiv Ludwigsburg

201 AR-Z 76/59, vol. 2, p. 42
B 162/Vorl. Dok. Slg. Einsatzgruppen in Polen II

B 162/Vorl. AR-Z 302/67, vol. 3

Archiv der KZ-Gedenkstätte Mauthausen

AMM Y/46

AMM P/19/45

Archive of the Ministry of the Interior, Prague

114-10-1/II
114-3-14 / 36–7
315-194-30

325-166-3
325-2-2
325-2-4

325-2-5
325-57-3
325-166-3 301-5-4

Dokumentationsarchiv des Österreichischen Widerstandes, Vienna

15.909
E20.530
17072a/b
20752/93b

21732/62
01575
01905
21058/20

21732/62
22124
9413
2020

Archiv des Instituts für Zeitgeschichte, Munich

Ed 180/5
Ed 450
Eich 1368
Eich 1503
Eich 1633
Eich 464
Eich 739
Eich 983
Fa 108
Fa 183

Fa 199
Ed 450 II
Fa 506
Fa 64
MA 145/1
MA 172
MA 225
MA 280
MA 325
MA 328

MA 682
MA 1498
PS-3047
OKW T-77/1050
PS 1063
ZS 106
ZS 207
ZS 3092
ZS 249
ZS 317

MA 342	ZS 573
MA 433	ZS 658
MA 438	ZS 1260
MA 444	ZS 1579
MA 445	ZS 1718
MA 451	ZS 1939

National Archives, Kew

GFM 33/4830	HS 4/79	WO 208/4472
HS 4/39	HW 16	WO 219/5283

National Archive, Prague

109-4-16	109-4-711	110-4-549
109-4-175	109-4-729	114, carton 43
114, carton 53	114-2-47, carton 8	114-6-8
114, carton 89	114-308-3	114-6-8, carton 22
114, carton 1140	114-3-17	114-7-300
114, carton 8	114-5-15, carton 19	
114-22	114-5-15, carton 8	
114-22-39	114-6-2	
114-2-26	114-6-2, carton 22	
	114-6-4, carton 22	

Nederlands Instituut voor Oorlogsdocumentatie, Amsterdam

Doc. I, 691 A

Osobyi Archive, Moscow

500/1/154	500/3/795	500/4/261
500/1/261	500/1/88	501/1/18
500/1/379	500/3/316	501/1/18

Politisches Archiv des Auswärtigen Amtes, Berlin

PAAA, Inland II A/B 347/3	PAAA, R 101109
PAAA, Inland IIg 177	PAAA, R 101109
PAAA, Inland IIg 81	PAAA, Inland II AB 80–41 Sdh. III, vol. 1
PAAA, Inland IIg 189	

Stadtarchiv Halle an der Saale

Akten der Schulverwaltung, 118, vol. II, Konservatorium Bruno Heydrich   FA 2571

Prague State Archive

NSDAP Prag, file collection 'K.V. Müller'

United States Holocaust Memorial Museum Archive, Washington, DC

11.001 M, reel 1, folder 25	RG 11.001 M, reel 94, folder 1525
RG 11.001 M, reel 8, 625	RG 11.001 M, reel 9, folder 649
RG 11.001 M, reel 1, folder 20	RG 11.001 M, reel 9, folder 645
RG 15.007 M, reel 8, folder 101	RG 11.001 M, reel 9, folder 659
RG 15.015 M, reel 3, folder 168	RG 11.001 M, reel 13, folder 21
RG 48.004 M, reel 3, folder 300041	RG 48.005 M, reel 2

Yad Vashem Archives, Jerusalem

051/204
053/87
0-53/93/283
97-210 F I
M9/584

Primary Printed Sources

Akten zur deutschen auswärtigen Politik 1918–1945, Series D: *1937–1941*, 8 vols (Baden-Baden, 1950–95).

Arad, Yitzhak, Gutman, Yisrael and Margaliot, Abraham (eds), *Documents on the Holocaust: Selected Sources on the Destruction of the Jews of Germany and Austria, Poland, and the Soviet Union* (Yad Vashem, 1981).

Bargatzky, Walter, *Hotel Majestic. Ein Deutscher im besetzten Frankreich* (Freiburg im Breisgau, 1987).

Benz, Wolfgang, Kwiet, Konrad and Matthäus, Jürgen (eds), *Einsatz im 'Reichskommissariat Ostland'. Dokumente zum Völkermord im Baltikum und in Weissrussland, 1941–1944* (Berlin, 1998).

Best, Werner, 'Apologie des Juristen', *Deutsches Recht* 9 (1939), 196–9.

Best, Werner, 'Der "politischste" Beruf', *Deutsche Allgemeine Zeitung*, 12 April 1939.

Best, Werner, 'Der Reichsführer SS und Chef der Deutschen Polizei', *Deutsches Recht* 6 (1936), 257–8.

Best, Werner, 'Grundfragen einer deutschen Grossraum-Verwaltung', in *Festgabe für Heinrich Himmler* (Darmstadt, 1941), 33–60.

Beyer, Hans Joachim, 'Amerikanisches oder bolschewistisches "Volkstum"', *Deutsche Volksforschung in Böhmen und Mähren* 2 (1943), 204ff.

Beyer, Hans Joachim, *Aufbau und Entwicklung des ostdeutschen Volksraums* (Berlin, 1935).

Beyer, Hans Joachim, 'Auslese und Assimilation', *Deutsche Monatshefte* 7 (1940).

Beyer, Hans Joachim, *Das Schicksal der Polen. Rasse – Volkscharakter – Stammesart* (Leipzig, 1942), 158ff.

Beyer, Hans Joachim, *Umvolkung. Studien zur Frage der Assimilation und Amalgamation in Ostmitteleuropa und Übersee* (Brünn, 1945).

Burckhardt, Carl Jacob, *Meine Danziger Mission, 1937–1939* (Munich, 1960).

Czechoslovak Ministry of Foreign Affairs (ed.), *German Massacres in Occupied Czechoslovakia Following the Attack on Reinhard Heydrich* (London, 1942).

Czechoslovak Ministry of Foreign Affairs (ed.), *Memorandum of the Czechoslovak Government on the Reign of Terror in Bohemia & Moravia under the Regime of Reinhard Heydrich* (London, 1942).

Dalton, Hugh, *The Second World War Diary of Hugh Dalton 1940–1945*, ed. Ben Pimlott (London, 1986).

Daniels, Herbert Edler von, 'Reinhard Heydrich als nationalsozialistischer Leibeserzieher', *Leibesübungen und körperliche Erziehung* 61 (1942), 114–17.

Darré, Richard Walther, *Neuadel aus Blut und Boden* (Munich, 1930).

Dennler, Wilhelm, *Die böhmische Passion* (Freiburg im Breisgau, 1953).

Diels, Rudolf, *Lucifer ante Portas. Es spricht der erste Chef der Gestapo* (Stuttgart, 1950).

Dokumentationsarchiv des Österreichischen Widerstandes (ed.), *'Anschluss' 1938. Eine Dokumentation* (Vienna, 1988).

Engel, Gerhard, *At the Heart of the Reich: The Secret Diary of Hitler's Army Adjutant* (London, 2005).

Foerster, Wolfgang, *Generaloberst Ludwig Beck. Sein Kampf gegen den Krieg. Aus den nachgelassenen Papieren des Generalstabschefs* (Munich, 1953).

Frank, Karl Hermann, *Böhmen und Mähren im Reich. Vortrag gehalten am 24. Juni 1941 im Ostinstitut in Krakau* (Prague, 1941).

Gisevius, Hans Bernd, *Bis zum bitteren Ende. Bericht eines Augenzeugen aus den Machtzentren des Dritten Reiches* (Hamburg, 1954).

Goebbels, Joseph, *Die Tagebücher von Joseph Goebbels*, ed. Elke Fröhlich, 29 vols (Munich, 1993–2005).

Groscurth, Helmuth, *Tagebücher eines Abwehroffiziers 1938–1940*, ed. Helmut Krausnick and Harold C. Deutsch (Stuttgart, 1970).

Haffner, Sebastian, *Geschichte eines Deutschen. Die Erinnerungen 1914–1933* (4th edn, Stuttgart, 2000).

Hagen, Walter (alias Wilhelm Höhl), *Die geheime Front. Organisation, Personen und Aktionen des deutschen Geheimdienstes* (Linz and Vienna, 1950).

Heiber, Helmut (ed.), *Reichsführer! . . . Briefe an und von Himmler* (Stuttgart, 1968).

Hertzberg, Gustav Friedrich, *Geschichte der Freimaurerloge zu den drei Degen im Orient von Halle* (Halle, 1893, reprint 1907).

Heydrich, Lina, *Leben mit einem Kriegsverbrecher* (Pfaffenhofen, 1976).

Heydrich, Reinhard, 'Aufgaben und Aufbau der Sicherheitspolizei im Dritten Reich', in Pfundtner (ed.), *Dr. Wilhelm Frick und sein Ministerium*, 125–30.

Heydrich, Reinhard, 'Der Anteil der Sicherheitspolizei und des SD an den Ordnungsmassnahmen im mitteleuropäischen Raum', *Böhmen und Mähren* 25 (1941), 176–8.

Heydrich, Reinhard, 'Der Anteil der Sicherheitspolizei und des SD in Böhmen und Mähren', *Böhmen und Mähren* 2 (1941), 176–7.

Heydrich, Reinhard, 'Die Bekämpfung der Staatsfeinde', *Deutsches Recht* 6 (1936), 121–3.

Heydrich, Reinhard, 'Kripo und Gestapo', *Düsseldorfer Nachrichten*, 29 January 1939.

Heydrich, Reinhard, *Wandlungen unseres Kampfes* (Munich and Berlin, 1936).

Himmler, Heinrich, 'Denkschrift über die Behandlung der Fremdvölkischen im Osten' (May 1940), reprinted in *VfZ* 5 (1957), 194–8.

Hitler, Adolf, *Adolf Hitlers Monologe im Führerhauptquartier 1941–1944. Die Aufzeichnungen Heinrich Heims*, ed. Werner Jochmann (Munich, 1982).

Hitler, Adolf, *Hitler's Table Talk 1941–1944; with an introductory essay on The Mind of Adolf Hitler by Hugh R. Trevor-Roper* (London, 1953).

Hitler, Adolf, *Reden und Proklamationen*, ed. Max Domarus, 2 vols (Würzburg, 1962–3).

Höhn, Reinhard and Seydel, Helmut, 'Der Kampf um die Wiedergewinnung des deutschen Ostens. Erfahrungen der preussischen Ostsiedlung 1866–1914', in *Festgabe für Heinrich Himmler* (Darmstadt, 1941), 61–174.

Hubatsch, Walther (ed.), *Hitlers Weisungen für die Kriegsführung 1939–1945. Dokumente des Oberkommandos der Wehrmacht* (2nd rev. edn, Koblenz, 1983).

Internationaler Militärgerichtshof Nürnberg (ed.), *Der Prozess gegen die Hauptkriegsverbrecher vor dem Internationalen Militärgerichtshof* (14. November 1945 bis 1. Oktober 1946), 42 vols (Nuremberg, 1947–9).

Jacobsen, Hans-Adolf (ed.), *Generaloberst Halder. Kriegstagebuch*, vol. 1: *Vom Polenfeldzug bis zum Ende der Westoffensive* (14.8.1939–30.6.1940) (Stuttgart, 1962).

Jordan, Rudolf, *Erlebt und erlitten. Weg eines Gauleiters von München bis Moskau* (Leoni, 1971).

Kárný, Miroslav and Milotová, Jaroslava (eds), *Anatomie okupační politiky hitlerovského Německa v 'Protektorátu Čechy a Morava'. Dokumenty z období říšského protektora Konstantina von Neuratha* (Prague, 1987).

Kárný, Miroslav, Milotová, Jaroslava and Kárná, Margita (eds), *Deutsche Politik im 'Protektorat Böhmen und Mähren' unter Reinhard Heydrich 1941–1942* (Berlin, 1997).

Kersten, Felix, *The Kersten Memoirs, 1940–1945*, ed. Hugh Trevor-Roper (London, 1957).

Kersten, Felix, *Totenkopf und Treue – Heinrich Himmler ohne Uniform* (Hamburg, 1952).

Klarsfeld, Serge (ed.), *Centre de Documentation Juive Contemporaine, Recueil de Documents du Service des Affaires Juives, le II-112, du Sicherheitsdienst SD (1937–1949)* (New York, 1980).

Klein, Peter (ed.), *Die Einsatzgruppen in der besetzten Sowjetunion, 1941/42. Die Tätigkeits- und Lageberichte des Chefs der Sicherheitspolizei und des SD* (Berlin, 1997).

Köhler, Hansjürgen, *Inside the Gestapo: Hitler's Shadow over Europe* (London, 1941).

Král, Václav (ed.), *Die Deutschen in der Tschechoslowakei 1933–1947. Dokumentensammlung* (Prague, 1964).

Lidice: A Tribute by Members of the International P.E.N. (London 1944).

Lösener, Bernhard, 'Als Rassereferent im Reichsministerium des Innern', *VfZ* 9 (1961), 261–313.

Maercker, Georg, *Vom Kaiserheer zur Reichswehr. Geschichte des freiwilligen Landesjägerkorps. Ein Beitrag zur Geschichte der deutschen Revolution* (Leipzig, 1921).

Mann, Thomas, *Essays*, vol. 5: *Deutschland und die Deutschen 1938–1945*, ed. Hermann Kurzke and Stephan Stachorski (Frankfurt am Main, 1997).

Matlock, Siegfried (ed.), *Dänemark in Hitlers Hand. Der Bericht des Reichsbevollmächtigten Werner Best über seine Besatzungspolitik in Dänemark mit Studien über Hitler, Göring, Himmler, Heydrich, Ribbentrop, Canaris u. a.* (Husum, 1988).

Michaelis, Herbert and Schraepler, Ernst (eds), *Ursachen und Folgen. Vom deutschen Zusammenbruch 1918 und 1945 bis zur staatlichen Neuordnung Deutschlands in der Gegenwart. Eine Urkunden- und Dokumentensammlung zur Zeitgeschichte*, vol. 12: *Das Dritte Reich* (Munich 1967).

Moravec, Frantisek, *Master of Spies: The Memoirs of General Frantisek Moravec* (Garden City, NY, 1975).

Naudé, Horst, *Erlebnisse und Erkenntnisse als politischer Beamter im Protektorat Böhmen und Mähren 1939–1945* (Berlin, 1975).

Nicolai, Walter, *Geheime Mächte. Internationale Spionage und ihre Bekämpfung im Weltkrieg und Heute* (Leipzig, 1923).

Noakes, Jeremy and Pridham, Geoffrey (eds), *Nazism, 1919–1945: A Documentary Reader*, 4 vols (Exeter, 1995–8).

Petzina, Dietmar, Abelshauser, Werner and Faust, Anselm (eds), *Materialien zur Statistik des Deutschen Reiches 1914–1945* (Munich, 1978).

Pfitzner, Hans, *Reden, Schriften, Briefe. Unveröffentlichtes und bisher Verstreutes* (Berlin, 1955).

Pfundtner, Hans (ed.), *Dr. Wilhelm Frick und sein Ministerium* (Munich, 1937).

Präg, Werner and Jacobmeyer, Wolfgang (eds), *Das Diensttagebuch des deutschen Generalgouverneurs in Polen 1939–45* (Stuttgart, 1975).

Reichssicherheitshauptamt (ed.), *Reinhard Heydrich, 7. März 1904–4. Juni 1942. Meine Ehre heisst Treue* (Berlin, 1942).

Riemann, Hugo (ed.), *Riemanns Musik-Lexikon* (8th edn, Berlin and Leipzig, 1916), vol. 1.

Safrian, Hans and Witek, Hans (eds), *Und keiner war dabei. Dokumente des alltäglichen Antisemitismus in Wien 1938* (Vienna, 1988).

Sagel-Grande, Irene, Fuchs, H. H. and Rüter, C. F. (eds), *Justiz und NS-Verbrechen. Sammlung deutscher Strafurteile wegen nationalsozialistischer Tötungsverbrechen 1945–1966*, vol. 19: *Die vom 10.01.1963 bis zum 12.04.1964 ergangenen Strafurteile* (Amsterdam, 1978).

Sauer, Paul (ed.), *Dokumente über die Verfolgung der jüdischen Bürger in Baden-Württemberg durch das nationalsozialistische Regime 1933–1945* (Stuttgart, 1966).

Schellenberg, Walter, *The Labyrinth: The Memoirs of Hitler's Secret Service Chief* (London, 1956).

Schellenberg, Walter, *Invasion 1940: The Nazi Invasion Plan for Britain* (London, 2000).

Scholz, Lili, *'Bis alles in Scherben fällt'. Tagebuchblätter 1933–1945* (2nd edn, Hamburg, 2007).

Schramm, Percy Ernst and Picker, Henry (eds), *Hitlers Tischgespräche im Führerhauptquartier 1941–1942* (Stuttgart, 1963).

Seraphim, Hans-Günther (ed.), *Das politische Tagebuch Alfred Rosenbergs 1934/35 und 1939/40* (Göttingen, 1956).

Silbergleit, Heinrich, *Die Bevölkerungs- und Berufsverhältnisse der Juden im Deutschen Reich* (Berlin, 1930).

Silbergleit, Heinrich (ed.), *Preussens Städte. Denkschrift zum 100jährigen Jubiläum der Städteordnung vom 19. November 1808* (Berlin, 1908).

Simmert, Johannes and Herrmann, Hans-Walter, *Dokumentation zur Geschichte der jüdischen Bevölkerung in Rheinland-Pfalz und im Saarland von 1800*, vol 6: *Die nationalsozialistische Judenverfolgung in Rheinland-Pfalz 1933–1945. Das Schicksal der Juden im Saarland, 1920–1945* (Koblenz, 1974).

Smith, Bradley F., Peterson, Agnes F. and Fest, Joachim (eds), *Heinrich Himmler. Geheimreden 1933 bis 1945 und andere Ansprachen* (Frankfurt am Main, 1974).

Speer, Albert, *Erinnerungen* (Frankfurt, Berlin and Vienna, 1969).

Urban, Lisl, *Ein ganz gewöhnliches Leben* (Leipzig, 2006).

Verhandlungen des Reichstages. Stenographische Berichte, 4. Wahlperiode 1939–1942, vol. 460.

Wagner, Eduard, *Der Generalquartiermeister. Briefe und Tagebuchaufzeichnungen des Generalquartiermeisters des Heeres General der Artillerie Eduard Wagner*, ed. Elisabeth Wagner (Munich and Vienna, 1963).

Wagner, Gerhard (ed.), *Lagevorträge des Oberbefehlshabers der Kriegsmarine vor Hitler, 1939–1945* (Munich, 1972).

Walk, Joseph (ed.), *Das Sonderrecht für die Juden im NS-Staat. Eine Sammlung der gesetzlichen Massnahmen und Richtlinien. Inhalt und Bedeutung* (2nd edn, Heidelberg, 1996).

Walter, Bruno, *Thema und Variationen. Erinnerungen und Gedanken* (Stockholm, 1947).

Wannenmacher, Walter (ed.), *Reinhard Heydrich. Ein Leben der Tat* (Prague, 1944).

Weitzel, Fritz, *Die Gestaltung der Feste im Jahres- und Lebenslauf in der SS-Familie* (Wuppertal, 1942).

Winiewicz, Józef Marja, *Aims and Failures of the German New Order* (London, 1943).

Witte, Peter et al. (eds), *Der Dienstkalender Heinrich Himmlers 1941/42* (Hamburg, 1999).

Zuckmayer, Carl, *Als wär's ein Stück von mir* (2nd edn, Hamburg, 1977).

Newspapers and Periodicals

České slovo; Deutsches Recht; Frankfurter Allgemeine Zeitung; Hallesche Nachrichten; Hallescher Central-Anzeiger; Jasmin; Königsberger Allgemeine; Mitteilungsblatt des Reichskriminalamtes; Národní politika; Neue Freie Presse; Der Neue Tag; New York Times; Reichsgesetzblatt; Das Schwarze Korps; Der Spiegel; The Times; Venkov; Verordnungsblatt des Reichsprotektors in Böhmen und Mähren; Völkischer Beobachter.

Secondary Printed Sources

Abrams, Lynn, 'From Control to Commercialization: The Triumph of Mass Entertainment in Germany 1900–1925', *German History* 8 (1990), 278–93.

Ackermann, Josef, *Heinrich Himmler als Ideologe* (Göttingen, 1970).

Ackermann, Volker, *Nationale Totenfeiern in Deutschland. Von Wilhelm I. bis Franz Josef Strauss, eine Studie zur politischen Semiotik* (Stuttgart, 1990).

Adam, Uwe Dietrich, 'The Gas Chambers', in François Furet (ed.), *Unanswered Questions: Nazi Germany and the Genocide of the Jews* (New York, 1989), 134–54.

Adam, Uwe Dietrich, *Judenpolitik im Dritten Reich* (Düsseldorf, 1972).

Adler, Hans Günther, *Theresienstadt 1941–1945. Antlitz einer Zwangsgemeinschaft* (Göttingen, 2005).

Adler, Hans Günther, *Der Verwaltete Mensch. Studien zur Deportation der Juden aus Deutschland* (Tübingen, 1974).

Alberti, Michael (ed.), *Die Verfolgung und Vernichtung der Juden im Reichsgau Wartheland* (Wiesbaden, 2006).

Albrecht, Catherine, 'Economic Nationalism in the Sudetenland, 1918–38', in Mark Cornwall and R. J. W. Evans (eds), *Czechoslovakia in a Nationalist and Fascist Europe, 1918–1948* (Oxford, 2007), 89–108.

Aly, Götz (ed.), *Aktion T4 1939–1945. Die 'Euthanasie'-Zentrale in der Tiergartenstrasse 4* (2nd edn, Berlin, 1989).

Aly, Götz, *'Final Solution': Nazi Population Policy and the Murder of the European Jews* (London and New York, 1999).

Aly, Götz, *Hitler's Beneficiaries: Plunder, Racial War, and the Nazi Welfare State* (New York, 2007).

Aly, Götz and Heim, Susanne, 'Staatliche Ordnung und "organische Lösung". Die Rede Hermann Görings "Über die Judenfrage" vom 6. Dezember 1938', *Jahrbuch für Antisemitismusforschung* 2 (1992), 378–404.

Aly, Götz and Heim, Susanne, *Vordenker der Vernichtung. Auschwitz und die deutschen Pläne für eine europäische Ordnung* (Frankfurt am Main, 1993).

Aly, Götz and Roth, Karl Heinz, *Die restlose Erfassung. Volkszählen, Identifizieren, Aussondern im Nationalsozialismus* (Frankfurt am Main, 2000).

Amort, Čestmír, *Heydrichiáda* (Prague, 1965).

Anderl, Gabriele, 'Die "Zentralstellen für jüdische Auswanderung" in Wien, Berlin und Prag: Ein Vergleich', *Tel Aviver Jahrbuch für Deutsche Geschichte* 23 (1994), 275–99.

Anderl, Gabriele and Rupnow, Dirk, *Die Zentralstelle für jüdische Auswanderung als Beraubungsinstitution* (Vienna, 2004).

Angrick, Andrej, *Besatzungspolitik und Massenmord. Die Einsatzgruppe D in der südlichen Sowjetunion 1941–1943* (Hamburg, 2003).

Applegate, Celia, 'Culture and the Arts', in James Retallack, *Imperial Germany, 1871–1918* (Oxford, 2008), 106–27.

Arad, Yitzhak, *Belzec, Sobibor, Treblinka: The Operation Reinhard Death Camps* (Bloomington, IN, 1987).

Arendt, Hannah, *Eichmann in Jerusalem: A Report on the Banality of Evil* (London, 1963).

Armstrong, John A., *Ukrainian Nationalism, 1935–1949* (2nd edn, New York, 1963).

Arndt, Ingo and Boberach, Heinz, 'Deutsches Reich', in Benz (ed.), *Dimension des Völkermords*, 23–65.

Aronson, Shlomo, *Reinhard Heydrich und die Frühgeschichte von Gestapo und SD* (Stuttgart, 1971).

Aronson, Shlomo and Breitman, Richard, 'Eine unbekannte Himmler-Rede vom Januar 1943', *VfZ* 38 (1990), 337–48.

Ayass, Wolfgang, *'Asoziale' im Nationalsozialismus* (Stuttgart, 1995).

Ayass, Wolfgang, '"Ein Gebot der nationalen Arbeitsdisziplin". Die "Aktion Arbeitsscheu Reich" 1938', *Beiträge zur nationalsozialistischen Gesundheits- und Sozialpolitik* 6 (1988), 43–74.

Bahro, Berno, 'Reinhard Heydrich und Hermann Fegelein. Sportler – Soldaten – Helden', *Stadion. Internationale Zeitschrift für Geschichte des Sports* (31) 2007, 111–30.

Bailey, Roderick, *Forgotten Voices of the Secret War: An Inside History of Special Operations during the Second World War* (London, 2008).

Bajohr, Frank, '"Die Zustimmungsdiktatur". Grundzüge nationalsozialistischer Herrschaft in Hamburg', in Forschungsstelle für Zeitgeschichte in Hamburg (ed.), *Hamburg im 'Dritten Reich'* (Göttingen, 2005), 69–131.

Banach, Jens, *Heydrichs Elite. Das Führerkorps der Sicherheitspolizei und des SD 1936–1945* (Paderborn, 1996).

Bankier, David, *The Germans and the Final Solution: Public Opinion under Nazism* (Oxford, 1992).

Barkai, Avraham, *Vom Boykott zur 'Entjudung'. Der wirtschaftliche Existenzkampf der Juden im Dritten Reich, 1933–1943* (Frankfurt, 1988).

Barnett, Victoria, *For the Soul of the People: Protestant Protest against Hitler* (New York, 1992).

Barth, Christian T., *Goebbels und die Juden* (Paderborn, 2003).

Bartov, Omer, 'Defining Enemies, Making Victims: Germans, Jews, and the Holocaust', in Amir Weiner (ed.), *Landscaping the Human Garden: Twentieth-Century Population Management in a Comparative Framework* (Stanford, CA, 2003), 135–47.

Bartusevičius, Vincas, Tauber, Joachim and Wette, Wolfram (eds), *Holocaust in Litauen. Krieg, Judenmorde und Kollaboration im Jahre 1941* (Cologne, 2003).

Bassler, Moritz and van der Knaap, Ewout (eds), *Die (k)alte Sachlichkeit. Herkunft und Wirkungen eines Konzepts* (Würzburg, 2004).

Bauer, Yehuda, *Jews for Sale? Nazi–Jewish Negotiations 1933–1945* (New Haven and London, 1994).

Baumann, Zygmunt, *Modernity and the Holocaust* (Ithaca, NY, 1989).

Behrenbeck, Sabine, *Der Kult um die toten Helden. Nationalsozialistische Mythen, Riten und Symbole 1923 bis 1945* (Cologne, 1996).

Benz, Wolfgang (ed.), *Dimension des Völlkermords. Die Zahl der jüdischen Opfer des Nationalsozialismus* (Munich, 1991).

Benz, Wolfgang, *Legenden, Lügen, Vorurteile. Ein Wörterbuch zur Zeitgeschichte* (Munich, 1992).

Benz, Wolfgang and Distel, Barbara (eds), *Der Ort des Terrors. Geschichte der nationalsozialistischen Konzentrationslager*, 9 vols (Munich, 2005–8).

Berg, Christian, 'Familie, Kindheit, Jugend', in *Handbuch der deutschen Bildungsgeschichte*, vol. IV, 9–39.

Bergen, Doris, 'The Nazi Concept of "Volksdeutsche" and the Exacerbation of Anti-Semitism in Eastern Europe, 1939–1945', *Journal of Contemporary History* 29 (1994), 569–82.

Bergen, Doris, *Twisted Cross: The German Christian Movement in the Third Reich* (Chapel Hill, NC, 1996).

Berghahn, Volker R. and Laessig, Simone (eds), *Biography between Structure and Agency: Central European Lives in International Historiography* (Oxford and New York, 2008).

Berkhoff, Karel C., *Harvest of Despair: Life and Death in Ukraine under Nazi Rule* (Cambridge, MA, 2004).

Bernhardt, Heike, *Anstaltspsychiatrie und Euthanasie in Pommern 1933 bis 1945. Die Krankenmorde an Kindern und Erwachsenen am Beispiel der Landesheilanstalt Ueckermünde* (Frankfurt am Main, 1994).

Bernhardt, Heike, '"Euthanasie" und Kriegsbeginn. Die frühen Morde an Patienten aus Pommern', *Zeitschrift für Geschichtswissenschaft* 9 (1996), 773–88.

Bernou-Fieseler, Anne and Théofilakis, Fabien (eds), *Das Konzentrationslager Dachau. Erlebnis, Erinnerung, Geschichte. Deutsch–Französisches Kolloquium zum 60. Jahrestag der Befreiung des Konzentrationslagers Dachau* (Munich, 2006).

Berschel, Holger, *Bürokratie und Terror. Das Judenreferat der Gestapo Düsseldorf 1935–1945* (Essen, 2001).

Berton, Pierre, *The Great Depression 1929–1939* (Toronto, 1990).

Berton, Stanislav F., 'Das Attentat auf Reinhard Heydrich vom 27. Mai 1942. Ein Bericht des Kriminalrats Heinz Pannwitz', *VfZ* 33 (1985), 668–706.

Bessel, Richard, 'The "Front Generation" and the Politics of Weimar Germany', in Roseman (ed.), *Generations in Conflict*, 121–36.

Bessel, Richard, 'The Nazi Capture of Power', *Journal of Contemporary History* 39 (2004), 169–88.

Bessel, Richard, *Political Violence and the Rise of Nazism: The Storm Troopers in Eastern Germany 1925–1934* (New Haven, 1984).

Bird, Keith W., *Erich Raeder: Admiral of the Third Reich* (Annapolis, MD, 2006).

Bird, Keith W., *Officers and Republic: The German Navy and Politics* (Ann Arbor, MI, 1982).

Bird, Keith W., *Weimar, the German Naval Officer Corps and the Rise of National Socialism* (Amsterdam, 1977).

Birn, Ruth Bettina, *Die Höheren SS- und Polizeiführer. Himmlers Vertreter im Reich und in den besetzten Gebieten* (Düsseldorf, 1986).

Blaazer, David, 'Finance and the End of Appeasement: The Bank of England, the National Government and the Czech Gold', *Journal of Contemporary History* 40 (2005), 25–40.

Black, Peter R., *Ernst Kaltenbrunner: Ideological Soldier of the Third Reich* (Princeton, NJ, 1984).

Black, Peter, 'Die Trawniki-Männer und die Aktion Reinhard', in Bogdan Musial (ed.), *'Aktion Reinhardt'. Der Völkermord an den Juden im Generalgouvernement 1941–1944* (Osnabrück, 2004), 309–52.

Blackbourn, David, *The Conquest of Nature: Water and the Making of Modern German Landscapes* (London, 2005).

Blanning, Tim, *The Triumph of Music: Composers, Musicians, and their Audiences, 1700 to the Present* (London, 2008).

Blaschke, Olaf, *Katholizismus und Antisemitismus im Deutschen Kaiserreich* (Göttingen, 1997).

Blaschke, Olaf and Kuhlemann, Frank-Michael (eds), *Religion im Kaiserreich. Milieus – Mentalitäten – Krisen* (Gütersloh, 1996).

Blodig, Vojtěch, 'Dějiny ghetta Terezín (1941–1945)', in Miloš Pojar (ed.), *Stín šoa nad Evropou* (Prague, 2001), 57–66.

Bloxham, Donald, *The Final Solution: A Genocide* (Oxford, 2009).

Bloxham, Donald, 'The Missing Camps of Aktion Reinhard', in Peter Gray and Kendrick Oliver (eds), *The Memory of Catastrophe* (Manchester, 2004), 118–31.

Boberach, Heinz (ed.), *Meldungen aus dem Reich, 1938–1945. Die geheimen Lageberichte des Sicherheitsdienstes der SS*, 18 vols (Herrsching, 1984–5).

Boelcke, Willi A., *Kriegspropaganda 1939–1945. Geheime Ministerkonferenzen im Reichspropagandaministerium* (Stuttgart, 1955).

Böhler, Joachim, *Auftakt zum Vernichtungskrieg. Die Wehrmacht in Polen 1939* (Frankfurt am Main, 2006).

Bohn, Robert, 'Die Errichtung des Reichskommissariats Norwegen', in idem (ed.), *Neutralität und totalitäre Aggression. Nordeuropa und die Grossmächte im Zweiten Weltkrieg* (Stuttgart, 1991), 129–47.

Bohn, Robert, *Reichskommissariat Norwegen. 'Nationalsozialistische Neuordnung' und Kriegswirtschaft* (Munich, 2000).

Bohn, Robert, ' "Ein solches Spiel kennt keine Regeln". Gestapo und Bevölkerung in Norwegen und Dänemark', in Paul and Mallmann (eds), *Die Gestapo im Zweiten Weltkrieg*, 463–81.

Bokovoy, Douglas, 'Verfolgung und Vernichtung', in idem and Stefan Meining (eds), *Versagte Heimat. Jüdisches Leben in Münchens Isarvorstadt* (Munich, 1994), 223–60.

Bornschein, Joachim, *Gestapochef Heinrich Müller. Technokrat des Terrors* (Leipzig, 2004).

Borodziej, Wodzimierz, *Terror und Politik. Die deutsche Polizei und die polnische Widerstandsbewegung im Generalgouvernement 1939–1944* (Mainz, 1999).

Botz, Gerhard, *Nationalsozialismus in Wien. Machtübernahme, Herrschaftssicherung, Radikalisierung* (rev. edn, Vienna, 2008).

Botz, Gerhard, *Wohnungspolitik und Judendeportation in Wien 1928–1945* (Vienna, 1975).

Bracher, Karl Dietrich, *The German Dictatorship: The Origins, Structure, and Consequences of National Socialism* (New York, 1970).

Bracher, Karl Dietrich, Sauer, Wolfgang and Schulz, Gerhard, *Die nationalsozialistische Machtergreifung. Studien zur Errichtung des totalitären Herrschaftssystems in Deutschland 1933/34* (Cologne and Opladen, 1960).

Brandes, Detlef, 'Kolaborace v Protektorátu Čechy a Morava', *Dějiny a současnost* 16 (1994), 25–9.

Brandes, Detlef, 'Nationalsozialistische Tschechenpolitik', in idem and Kural, Václav (eds), *Der Weg in die Katastrophe. Deutsch–tschechoslowakische Beziehungen 1938–1947* (Essen, 2004), 39–50.

Brandes, Detlef, *Die Tschechen unter deutschem Protektorat*, 2 vols (Munich, 1969 and 1975).

Brandes, Detlef, Ivaničková, Edita and Pešek, Jiří (eds), *Erzwungene Trennung. Vertreibungen und Aussiedlungen in und aus der Tschechoslowakei 1938–1947 im Vergleich mit Polen, Ungarn und Jugoslawien* (Essen, 1999).

Brechtken, Magnus, *'Madagascar für die Juden'. Antisemitische Idee und politische Praxis 1885–1945* (Munich, 1997).

Břečka, Jan, *Silver B neodpovídá. Historie čs. paraskupiny z Velké Británie v letech 2. světové války* (Brno, 2004).

Breitman, Richard, *The Architect of Genocide: Himmler and the Final Solution* (New York, 1991).

Breitman, Richard and Aronson, Shlomo, 'Eine unbekannte Himmler-Rede vom Januar 1943', *VfZ* 38 (1990), 337–48.

Breuer, Stefan, *Ordnungen der Ungleichheit. Die deutsche Rechte im Widerstreit ihrer Ideen, 1871–1945* (Darmstadt, 2001).

Breuer, Stefan, *Die Völkischen in Deutschland. Kaiserreich und Weimarer Republik* (Darmstadt, 2008).

Breymayer, Ursula and Ulrich, Bernd (eds), *Willensmenschen. Über deutsche Offiziere* (Frankfurt am Main, 1999).

Brissaud, André, *Canaris. Fürst des deutschen Geheimdienstes oder Meister des Doppelspiels?* (Frankfurt am Main, 1976).

Broszat, Martin, 'Hitler und die "Endlösung". Aus Anlass der Thesen von David Irving', *VfZ* 25 (1977), 739–75.

Broszat, Martin, *Nationalsozialistische Polenpolitik (1939–1945)* (Stuttgart, 1961).

Broszat, Martin and Mehringer, Hartmut (eds), *Bayern in der NZ-Zeit*, vol. 5: *Die Parteien KPD, SPD, BVP in Verfolgung und Widerstand* (Munich, 1983).

Browder, George C., 'Die Anfänge des SD. Dokumente aus der Organisationsgeschichte des Sicherheitsdienstes des Reichsführers SS', *VfZ* 27 (1979), 299–324.

Browder, George C., *Foundations of the Nazi Police State: The Formation of Sipo and SD* (Lexington, MA, 1990).

Browder, George C., *Hitler's Enforcers: The Gestapo and the SS Security Service in the Nazi Revolution* (New York, 1996).

Browder, George C., 'The Numerical Strength of the Sicherheitsdienst des RFSS', *Historical Social Research* 28 (1983), 30–41.

Browning, Christopher R., 'A Final Hitler Decision for the "Final Solution"? The Riegner Telegram Reconsidered', *Holocaust and Genocide Studies* (1996), 3–10.

Browning, Christopher R., *The Final Solution and the German Foreign Office: A Study of Referat DIII of Abteilung Deutschland 1940–43* (New York and London, 1978).

Browning, Christopher R., *Judenmord. NS-Politik, Zwangsarbeit und das Verhalten der Täter* (Frankfurt am Main, 2001).

Browning, Christopher R., *Ordinary Men: Police Battalion 101 and the Final Solution in Poland* (New York, 1992).

Browning, Christopher R., *The Origins of the Final Solution: The Evolution of Nazi Jewish Policy, September 1939–March 1942* (Lincoln, NB, 2004).

Browning, Christopher R., *The Path to Genocide: Essays on Launching the Final Solution* (Cambridge, 1992).

Bruendel, Steffen, *Volksgemeinschaft oder Volksstaat. Die 'Ideen von 1914' und die Neuordnung Deutschlands im Ersten Weltkrieg* (Berlin, 2003).

Brunner, Bernhard, *Der Frankreich-Komplex. Die nationalsozialistischen Verbrechen in Frankreich und die Justiz der Bundesrepublik Deutschland* (Göttingen, 2004).

Bryant, Chad, *Prague in Black: Nazi Rule and Czech Nationalism* (Cambridge, MA, 2007).

Buchheim, Hans, 'Die SS – Das Herrschaftsinstrument', in idem, Martin Broszat, Hans-Adolf Jacobsen and Helmut Krausnick, *Anatomie des SS-Staates* (3rd edn, Munich, 1994), vol. 1, 113–36.

Buchheim, Hans, Broszat Martin, Jacobsen, Hans-Adolf and Krausnick, Helmut, *Anatomie des SS-Staates* (3rd edn, Munich, 1994).

Büchler, Yehoshua 'The Deportation of Slovakian Jews to the Lublin District of Poland in 1942', *Holocaust and Genocide Studies* 6 (1991), 151–66.

Büchler, Yehoshua, 'A Preparatory Document for the Wannsee Conference', *Holocaust and Genocide Studies* 9 (1995), 121–9.

Burgdorff, Stephan (ed.), *Der Zweite Weltkrieg. Wendepunkte der deutschen Geschichte* (Munich, 2005).

Burian, Michal, Knížek, Aleš, Rajlich, Jiří and Stehlík, Eduard, *Assassination. Operation Anthropoid 1941–1942* (Prague, 2002).

Burleigh, Michael, *Death and Deliverance: Euthanasia in Germany, c.1900–1945* (Cambridge, 1994).

Burleigh, Michael and Wippermann, Wolfgang, *The Racial State: Germany 1933–1945* (Cambridge, 1991).

Burrin, Philippe, *Hitler and the Jews: The Genesis of the Holocaust* (London, 1994).

Büsch, Otto and Feldman, Gerald D. (eds), *Historische Prozesse der deutschen Inflation 1914–1924* (Berlin, 1978).

Busch, Sabine, *Hans Pfitzner und der Nationalsozialismus* (Stuttgart, 2001).

Büttner, Ursula, 'Der Aufstieg der NSDAP', in Forschungsstelle für Zeitgeschichte in Hamburg (ed.), *Hamburg im 'Dritten Reich'* (Göttingen, 2005).

Calic Edouard, *Reinhard Heydrich: The Chilling Story of the Man Who Masterminded the Nazi Death Camps* (New York, 1985).

Calic, Edouard, *Reinhard Heydrich. Schlüsselfigur des Dritten Reiches* (Düsseldorf, 1982).

Čapka, František, *Protektorát Čechy a Morava* (Brno, 1993).

Caplan, Jane, 'Political Detention and the Origin of the Concentration Camps in Nazi Germany, 1933–1935/6', in Neil Gregor (ed.), *Nazism, War and Genocide: New Perspectives on the History of the Third Reich* (Exeter, 2008), 22–41.

Caplan, Jane and Wachsmann, Nikolaus (eds), *Concentration Camps in Nazi Germany: The New Histories* (London, 2009).

Čelovský, Boris (ed.), *Germanisierung und Genozid. Hitlers Endlösung der tschechischen Frage. Deutsche Dokumente 1933–1945* (Brno and Dresden, 2005).

Červinka, František, *Česká kultura a okupace* (Prague, 2002).

Cesarani, David, *Becoming Eichmann: Rethinking the Life, Crimes and Trial of a Desk Murderer* (Cambridge, MA, 2006).

Chiari, Bernhard, *Alltag hinter der Front. Besatzung, Kollaboration und Widerstand in Weissrussland 1941–1944* (Düsseldorf, 1998).

Choumoff, Pierre Serge, *Nationalsozialistische Massentötungen durch Giftgas auf österreichischem Gebiet 1940–1945* (Vienna, 2000).

Clark, Christopher, 'Religion and Confessional Conflict', in Retallack (ed.), *Imperial Germany*, 83–105

Clavin, Patricia, *The Great Depression in Europe, 1929–1939* (Basingstoke, 2000).

Collingham, Lizzie, *The Taste of War: World War Two and the Battle for Food* (London, 2011).

Connelly, John, 'Nazis and Slavs: From Racial Theory to Racist Practice', *Central European History* 32 (1999), 1–33.

Conway, John S., *The Nazi Persecution of the Churches, 1933–45* (London, 1968).

Conze, Eckart, 'Adel unter dem Totenkopf. Die Idee eines Neuadels in den Gesellschaftsvorstellungen der SS', in idem and Monika Wienfort (eds), *Adel und Moderne. Deutschland im europäischen Vergleich im 19. und 20. Jahrhundert* (Cologne, 2004), 151–76.

Cornwall, Mark, ' "A Leap into Ice-Cold Water": The Manoeuvres of the Henlein Movement in Czechoslovakia, 1933–8', in idem and Evans (eds), *Czechoslovakia in a Nationalist and Fascist Europe*, 123–42.

Cornwall, Mark, ' "National Reparation?": The Czech Land Reform and the Sudeten Germans 1918–1938', *Slavonic and East European Review* 75 (1997), 259–80.

Cornwall, Mark, 'Stirring Resistance from Moscow: The German Communists of Czechoslovakia and Wireless Propaganda in the Sudetenland, 1941–1945', *German History* 24 (2006), 212–42.

Cornwall, Mark and Evans, R. J. W. (eds), *Czechoslovakia in a Nationalist and Fascist Europe 1918–1948* (Oxford, 2007).

Crampton, Richard J., *Eastern Europe in the Twentieth Century – and After* (London and New York, 1997).

Crampton, Richard J., 'Edvard Beneš', in Steven Casey and Jonathan Wright (eds), *Mental Maps in the Era of the Two World Wars* (Basingstoke, 2008), 135–56.

Čvaćara, Jaroslav, *Někomu život, někomu smrt. Československý odboj a nacistická okupační moc 1939–1941* (Prague, 2002).

Dahlhaus, Carl, *Nineteenth-Century Music* (Berkeley, CA, 1989).

Dallin, Alexander, *German Rule in Russia, 1941–1945: A Study of Occupation Policies* (rev. edn, Boulder, CO, 1981).

Dams, Carsten and Michael Stolle, *Die Gestapo. Herrschaft and Terror in Dritten Reich* (Munich, 2008).

Danker, Uwe, 'NS-Opfer und Täter. Versorgung mit zweierlei Mass. Lina Heydrich und Dr. Norbert L. mit Rentenangelegenheiten vor Gericht', *Demokratische Geschichte. Jahrbuch zur Arbeiterbewegung und Demokratie in Schleswig-Holstein* 10 (1996), 277–305.

Dean, Martin, *Collaboration in the Holocaust: Crimes of the Local Police in Belorussia and Ukraine, 1941–44* (New York, 2000).

Dederichs, Mario R., *Heydrich: The Face of Evil* (London, 2006).

Demps, Laurenz, *Der Invalidenfreidhof. Denkmal preussisch-deutscher Geschichte in Berlin* (Stuttgart, 1996).

Denkowski, Charles von, 'Zur Verschmelzung von SS und Polizei als Reichssicherheitshauptamt', *Kriminalistik* 57 (2003), 525–32.

Deschner, Günther, *Heydrich: The Pursuit of Total Power* (London, 1981).

Dieckmann, Christoph, 'Deutsche Besatzungspolitik und Massenverbrechen in Litauen 1941 bis 1944. Täter, Zuschauer, Opfer', unpublished PhD thesis, University of Freiburg, 2002.

Dieckmann, Christoph, 'The War and the Killing of the Lithuanian Jews', in Ulrich Herbert (ed.), *National Socialist Extermination Policies: Contemporary German Perspectives and Controversies* (New York and Oxford, 2000), 240–75.

Dieckmann, Christoph, Quinkert, Babette and Tönsmeyer, Tatjana (eds), *Kooperation und Verbrechen. Formen der 'Kollaboration' im östlichen Europa 1939–1945* (Göttingen, 2003).

Diehl, Paula (ed.), *Körper im Nationalsozialismus. Bilder und Praxen* (Munich, 2006).

Diehl, Paula, *Macht – Mythos – Utopie. Die Körperbilder der SS-Männer* (Berlin, 2005).

Dierker, Wolfgang, *Himmlers Glaubenskrieger. Der Sicherheitsdienst der SS und seine Religionspolitik 1933–1941* (Paderborn, 2002).

Diewald-Kerkmann, Gisela, *Politische Denunziation im NS-Regime oder die kleine Macht der 'Volksgenossen'* (Bonn, 1995).

Dillon, Christopher, '"We'll Meet Again in Dachau": The Early Dachau SS and the Narrative of Civil War', *Journal of Contemporary History* 45 (2010), 535–54.

Dimond, Mark, 'The Sokol and Czech Nationalism, 1918–48', in Cornwall and Evans, *Czechoslovakia in a Nationalist and Fascist Europe*, 185–206.

Distel, Barbara and Jakusch, Ruth (eds), *Konzentrationslager Dachau, 1933–1945* (Brussels, 1978).

Doerries, Reinhard (ed.), *Hitler's Last Chief of Foreign Intelligence: Allied Interrogations of Walter Schellenberg* (London, 2003).

Doležal, Jiří, *Česká kultura za protektorátu* (Prague, 1996).

Domröse, Ortwin, *Der NS-Staat in Bayern von der Machtergreifung bis zum Röhm-Putsch* (Munich, 1974).

Donson, Andrew, *Youth in the Fatherless Land: War Pedagogy, Nationalism and Authority in Germany, 1914–1918* (Cambridge, MA, 2010).

Dörner, Bernward, 'NS-Herrschaft und Denunziation. Anmerkungen zu Defiziten in der Denunziationsforschung', *Historical Social Research* 26 (2001), 55–69.

Döscher, Hans-Jürgen, *Reichskristallnacht. Die Novemberpogrome* (Munich, 2000).

Drdáčková, Eva, *Správní uspořádání protektorátu do Heydrichovy správní reformy (1939–1942)* (Plzeň, 2004).

Dreessen, Carl, *Die deutsche Flottenrüstung in der Zeit nach dem Vertrag von Versailles bis zum Beginn des Zweiten Weltkrieges und ihre Darstellung und Behandlung im Nürnberger Prozess von 1945/46* (Hamburg, 2000).

Drobisch, Klaus and Wieland, Günther, *System der NS-Konzentrationslager, 1933–1939* (Berlin, 1993).

Duhnke, Horst, *Die KPD von 1933 bis 1945* (Cologne, 1972).

Dülffer, Jost, *Weimar, Hitler und die Marine. Reichspolitik und Flottenbau 1920–1933* (Düsseldorf, 1973).

Dunger, Matthias, 'Städtebauliche Planung und Wohnungsbau im 19. Jahrhundert in Halle/S.', unpublished PhD thesis, University of Halle, 1991.

Dunker, Ulrich, *Der Reichsbund jüdischer Frontsoldaten 1919–1938* (Düsseldorf, 1977).

Ehmann, Annegret, 'From Colonial Racism to Nazi Population Policy: The Role of the So-Called Mischlinge', in Michael Berenbaum and Abraham J. Peck (eds), *The History of the Holocaust: The Known, the Unknown, the Disputed, and the Reexamined* (Bloomington, IN, 1998), 128–9.

Eiber, Ludwig, 'Unter Führung des NSDAP-Gauleiters. Die Hamburger Staatspolizei (1933–1937)', in Paul and Mallmann (eds), *Die Gestapo. Mythos und Realität*, 101–17.

Eisenberg, Christine, 'Massensport in der Weimarer Republik. Ein statistischer Überblick', *Archiv für Sozialgeschichte* 33 (1993), 137–77.

Elvert, Jürgen, 'Carl Schmitt. Ein Vordenker nationalsozialistischer Grossraumplanung?', *Historische Mitteilungen* 19 (2007), 260–76.

Epstein, Catherine, *Model Nazi: Arthur Greiser and the Occupation of Western Poland* (Oxford, 2010).

Essner, Cornelia, *Die 'Nürnberger Gesetze' oder die Verwaltung des Rassewahns, 1933–1945* (Paderborn, 2002).

Evans, Richard J., 'Coercion and Consent in Nazi Germany', *Proceedings of the British Academy* 151 (2007), 53–81.

Evans, Richard J., *The Coming of the Third Reich* (London, 2004).

Evans, Richard J., 'The Emergence of Nazi Ideology', in Jane Caplan (ed.), *Nazi Germany* (Oxford, 2008), 26–47.

Evans, Richard J., *The Third Reich in Power* (London, 2005).

Evans, Richard J., *The Third Reich at War 1939–1945* (London, 2008).

Fabréguet, Michel, *Mauthausen: Camp de concentration national-socialiste en Autrich rattachée* (Paris, 1999).

Falter, Jürgen, Lindenberger, Thomas and Schumann, Siegfried, *Wahlen und Abstimmungen in der Weimarer Republik. Materialien zum Wahlverhalten 1919–1933* (Munich, 1986).

Fauth, Tim, *Deutsche Kulturpolitik im Protektorat Böhmen und Mähren, 1939–1941* (Göttingen, 2004).

Fedorović, Tomáš, 'Zánik města Terezín a jeho přeměna v ghetto', *Terezínské listy* (2004), 15–43.

Feldman, Gerald D., *The Great Disorder: Politics, Economics and Society in the German Inflation 1914–1924* (Oxford 1993).

Fest, Joachim C., 'The Successor', in idem, *The Face of the Third Reich: Portraits of the Nazi Leadership* (New York, 1970), 98–114.

Feuchert, Sascha, Leibfried, Erwin and Riecke, Jörg (eds), *Die Chronik des Ghettos Lodz/Litzmannstadt* (Göttingen, 2006).

Fieberg, Gerhard (ed.), *Im Namen des deutschen Volkes. Justiz und Nationalsozialismus* (Cologne, 1989).

Fiedler, Jiří, *Atentát 1942* (Brno, 2002).

Fischer, Albert, *Hjalmar Schacht und Deutschlands 'Judenfrage'. Der 'Wirtschaftsdiktator' und die Vertreibung der Juden aus der deutschen Wirtschaft* (Cologne, 1995).

Flachowsky, Karin, 'Neue Quellen zur Abstammung Reinhard Heydrichs', *VfZ* 48 (2000), 319–27.

Fonzi, Paolo, 'Nazionalsocialismo e nuovo ordine europeo: la discussione sulla "Grossraumwirtschaft"', *Studi Storici* 45 (2004), 313–65.

Foot, Michael R. D., *SOE: An Outline History of the Special Operations Executive, 1940–1946* (London, 1984).

Forschbach, Edmund, *Edgar J. Jung. Ein Konservativer Revolutionär, 30. Juni 1934* (Pfullingen, 1984).

Förster, Roland G. (ed.), *'Unternehmen Barbarossa'. Zum historischen Ort der deutsch-sowjetischen Beziehungen von 1933 bis Herbst 1941* (Munich, 1993).

Fraenkel, Heinrich and Manvell, Roger, *Himmler. Kleinbürger und Massenmörder* (Frankfurt am Main, 1965).

Frajdl, Jiří, *Protektorátní kolaborantské a fašistické organizace, 1939–1945* (Prague, 2003).

Francev, Vladimír, 'Panzerjäger – Program. Nový úkol pro protektorátní průmysl', *Válečný rok 1944* (Prague 2002), 320–3.

Frankenstein, Norbert von, *'Seeteufel' Felix Graf Luckner. Wahrheit und Legende* (Hamburg, 1997).

Frei, Norbert, 'Zwischen Terror und Integration. Zur Funktion der politischen Polizei im Nationalsozialismus', in Christoph Dipper, Rainer Hudemann and Jens Petersen (eds), *Faschismus und Faschismen im Vergleich. Wolfgang Schieder zum 60. Geburtstag* (Cologne, 1998), 217–28.

Freitag, Werner and Minner, Katrin (eds), *Vergnügen und Inszenierung. Stationen städtischer Festkultur in Halle* (Halle an der Saale, 2004).

Freitag, Werner, Minner, Katrin and Ranft, Andreas (eds), *Geschichte der Stadt Halle*, vol. 2: *Halle im 19. und 20. Jahrhundert* (Halle an der Saale, 2006).

Freund, Florian and Perz, Bertrand, 'Mauthausen-Stammlager', in Benz and Distel (eds), *Der Ort des Terrors*, vol. 4: *Flossenbürg, Mauthausen, Ravensbrück*, 293–346.

Frevert, Ute, *Women in German History: From Bourgeois Emancipation to Sexual Liberation* (Oxford and Washington, DC, 1990).

Friedländer, Henry, *The Origins of Nazi Genocide: From Euthanasia to the Final Solution* (Chapel Hill, NC, 1995).

Friedländer, Saul, *Nazi Germany and the Jews*, vol. 1: *The Years of Persecution, 1933–1939* (New York, 1997).

Friedländer, Saul, *Nazi Germany and the Jews*, vol. 2: *The Years of Extermination, 1939–1945* (New York, 2007).

Friedman, Milton and Jacobson Schwartz, Anna, *The Great Contraction, 1929–1933* (Princeton, NJ, 2008).

Frisch, Walter, *German Modernism: Music and the Arts* (Berkeley, CA, 2005).

Frommer, Benjamin, *National Cleansing: Retribution against Nazi Collaborators in Postwar Czechoslovakia* (Cambridge, 2005).

Früh, Eckart, 'Terror und Selbstmord in Wien nach der Annexion Östereichs', in Felix Kreissler (ed.), *Fünfzig Jahre danach. Der Anschluss von innen und aussen gesehen* (Vienna and Zurich, 1989), 216–23.

Fulbrook, Mary (ed.), *Twentieth-Century Germany: Politics, Culture, and Society 1918–1990* (London, 2001).

Gailus, Manfred, *Protestantismus und Nationalsozialismus. Studien zur Durchdringung des protestantischen Sozialmilieus in Berlin* (Cologne, 2001).

Garbe, Detlef, *Zwischen Widerstand und Martyrium. Die Zeugen Jehovas im 'Dritten Reich'* (Munich, 1993).

Gebel, Ralf, *'Heim ins Reich'. Konrad Henlein und der Reichsgau Sudetenland (1938–1945)* (Munich, 1999).

Gebhart, Jan, 'Historiography on the Period 1938–1945', *Historica* 7/8 (2000–1), 145–63.

Gebhart, Jan, 'Migrace českého obyvatelstva v letech 1938–1939', *Český Časopis Historický* 3 (1998), 561–73.

Gedye, G. E. R., *Fallen Bastions: The Central European Tragedy* (London, 1939).

Geinitz, Christian, *Kriegsfurcht und Kampfbereitschaft. Das Augusterlebnis in Freiburg. Eine Studie zum Kriegsbeginn 1914* (Essen, 1998).

Gellately, Robert, 'Allwissend und allgegenwärtig? Entstehung, Funktion und Wandel des Gestapo-Mythos', in Paul and Mallmann (eds), *Die Gestapo. Mythos und Realität*, 47–70.

Gellately, Robert, *The Gestapo and German Society: Enforcing Racial Policy 1933–1945* (Oxford, 1990).

Gellately, Robert, *Hingeschaut und weggesehen: Hitler und sein Volk* (Munich, 2002).

Gellately, Robert, 'Social Outsiders and the Consolidation of Hitler's Dictatorship', in Neil Gregor (ed.), *Nazism, War and Genocide: Essays in Honour of Jeremy Noakes* (Exeter, 2005), 56–74.

Gellately, Robert and Stoltzfus, Nathan (eds), *Social Outsiders in Nazi Germany* (Princeton, NJ, 2001).

Geller, Jay H., 'The Role of the Military Administration in German-Occupied Belgium, 1940–1944', *Journal of Military History* 63 (1999), 99–125.

Gentile, Emilio, *The Sacralization of Politics in Fascist Italy* (Cambridge, MA, 1996).

Geppert, Dominik and Gerwarth, Robert (eds), *Wilhelmine Germany and Edwardian Britain: Essays on Cultural Affinity* (Oxford, 2008).

Gerhard, Gesine, 'Food and Genocide: Nazi Agrarian Politics in the Occupied Territories of the Soviet Union', *Contemporary European History* 18 (2009), 45–65.

Gerlach, Christian, *Kalkulierte Morde. Die deutsche Wirtschafts- und Vernichtungspolitik in Weissrussland 1941 bis 1944* (Hamburg, 1999).

Gerlach, Christian, 'Die Wannsee-Konferenz, das Schicksal der deutschen Juden und Hitlers politische Grundsatzentscheidung, alle Juden Europas zu ermorden', *WerkstattGeschichte* 6 (1997), 7–44.

Gerstner, Alexandra, *Neuer Adel: Aristokratische Elitekonzeptionen zwischen Jahrhundertwende und Nationalsozialismus* (Darmstadt, 2008).

Gerwarth, Robert, 'The Central European Counter-Revolution: Paramilitary Violence in Germany, Austria and Hungary after the Great War', *Past and Present* 200 (2008), 175–209.

Gerwarth, Robert and Malinowski, Stephan, 'Hannah Arendt's Ghosts: Reflections on the Disputable Path from Windhoek to Auschwitz', *Central European History* 42 (2009), 279–300.

Geyer, Martin H., *Verkehrte Welt. Revolution, Inflation und Moderne, München 1914–1924* (Göttingen, 1998).

Gilbert, Martin, *Kristallnacht: Prelude to Disaster* (London, 2006).

Glettler, Monika, Lipták, Lubomír and Míšková, Alena (eds), *Geteilt, besetzt, beherrscht. Die Tschechoslowakei 1938–1945. Reichsgau Sudetenland, Protektorat Böhmen und Mähren, Slowakei* (Essen, 2004).

Goldhagen, Daniel Jonah, *Hitler's Willing Executioners: Ordinary Germans and the Holocaust* (London, 1997).

Golla, Karl-Heinz, *Der Fall Griechenlands 1941* (Hamburg, 2007).

Goshen, Seev, 'Eichmann und die Nisko-Aktion im Oktober 1939. Eine Fallstudie zur NS-Judenpolitik in der letzten Etappe vor der Endlösung', *VfZ* 29 (1981), 74–96.

Gottwald, Alfred and Schulle, Diana, *Die Judendeportationen aus dem Deutschen Reich von 1941–1945. Eine kommentierte Chronologie* (Wiesbaden, 2005).

Graf, Christoph, *Politische Polizei zwischen Demokratie und Diktatur. Die Entwicklung der preussischen Politischen Polizei vom Staatsschutzorgan der Weimarer Republik zum Geheimen Staatspolizeiamt des Dritten Reiches* (Berlin, 1983).

Graml, Hermann, *Reichskristallnacht. Antisemitismus und Judenverfolgung im Dritten Reich* (Munich, 1998).

Gregor, Neil, 'Hitler' in Steven Casey and Jonathan Wright (eds.), *Mental Maps in the Era of Two World Wars* (Basingstoke, 2008), 177–202.

Grenville, John A. S., 'Die "Endlösung" und die "Judenmischlinge" im Dritten Reich', in Ursula Büttner, Werner Johe and Angelika Voss (eds), *Das Unrechtsregime. Internationale Forschung über den Nationalsozialismus* (Hamburg, 1986), vol. 2, 91–121.

Gruchmann, Lothar, '"Blutschutzgesetz" und Justiz. Zur Entstehung und Auswirkung des Nürnberger Gesetzes vom 15. September 1935', *VfZ* 31 (1983), 418–42.

Gruchmann, Lothar (ed.), *Johann Georg Elser. Autobiographie eines Attentäters* (Stuttgart, 1970).

Gruner, Wolf, 'The Factory Action and the Events at the Rosenstrasse in Berlin: Facts and Fictions about 27 February 1943 – Sixty Years Later', *Central European History* 36 (2003), 178–208.

Gruner, Wolf, 'Poverty and Persecution: The Reichsvereinigung, the Jewish Population, and anti-Jewish Policy in the Nazi State, 1939–1945', *Yad Vashem Studies* 27 (1999), 23–60.

Haar, Ingo and Fahlbusch, Michael (eds), *German Scholars and Ethnic Cleansing, 1920–1945* (Oxford, 2005).

Haasis, Hellmut, *Tod in Prag. Das Attentat auf Reinhard Heydrich* (Reinbek, 2002).

Hachmeister, Lutz, *Der Gegnerforscher. Die Karriere des SS-Führers Franz Alfred Six* (Munich, 1998).

Hartmann, Christian, *Wehrmacht im Ostkrieg. Front und militärisches Hinterland 1941–42* (Munich, 2009).

Hartmann, Christian and Slutsch, Sergej, 'Franz Halder und die Kriegsvorbereitungen im Frühjahr 1939. Eine Ansprache des Generalstabschefs des Heeres', *VfZ* 45 (1997), 467–95.

Harvey, Elisabeth, 'Culture and Society in Weimar Germany: The Impact of Modernism and Mass Culture', in Mary Fulbrook (ed.), *Twentieth-Century Germany: Politics, Culture, and Society 1918–1990* (London, 2001), 279–97.

Hauser, Andrea, *Halle wird Grossstadt. Stadtplanung, Grossstadtleben und Raumerfahrungen in Halle an der Saale 1870 bis 1914* (Halle an der Saale, 2006).

Havlíková, Jana (ed.), *Museli pracovat pro Říši. Nucené pracovní nasazení českého obyvatelstva v letech 2. světové války. Doprovodná publikace k výstavě* (Prague, 2004).

Hawkins, Mike, *Social Darwinism in European and American Thought, 1860–1945* (Cambridge, 1997).

Headland, Ronald, *Messages of Murder: A Study of the Reports of the Einsatzgruppen of the Security Police and the Security Service* (Rutherford, NJ, 1992).

Heiber, Helmut, 'Der Generalplan Ost', *VfZ* 6 (1958), 281–325.

Heiber, Helmut, 'Zur Justiz im Dritten Reich. Der Fall Eliáš', *VfZ* 3 (1955), 275–396.

Heinemann, Isabel, '"Another Type of Perpetrator": The SS Racial Experts and Forced Population Movements in the Occupied Regions', *Holocaust and Genocide Studies* 15 (2001), 387–411.

Heinemann, Isabel, '"Deutsches Blut". Die Rasseexperten der SS und die Volksdeutschen', in Jerzy Kochanowski and Maike Sach (eds), *Die 'Volksdeutschen' in Polen, Frankreich, Ungarn und der Tschechoslowakei. Mythos und Realität* (Osnabrück, 2006), 163–82.

Heinemann, Isabel, '"Ethnic Resettlement" and Inter-Agency Cooperation in the Occupied Eastern Territories', in Gerald D. Feldman and Wolfgang Seibel (eds), *Networks of Nazi Persecution: Bureaucracy, Business, and the Organization of the Holocaust* (Oxford and New York, 2004), 213–35.

Heinemann, Isabel, *'Rasse, Siedlung, deutsches Blut'. Das Rasse- und Siedlungshauptamt der SS und die rassenpolitische Neuordnung Europas* (Göttingen, 2003).

Heinemann, John L., *Hitler's First Foreign Minister: Constantin Freiherr von Neurath, Diplomat and Statesman* (Berkeley, CA, 1979).

Herbert, Ulrich, *Best. Biographische Studien über Radikalismus, Weltanschauung und Vernunft, 1903–1989* (Bonn, 1996).

Herbert, Ulrich, *Hitler's Foreign Workers: Enforced Foreign Labor in Germany under the Third Reich* (Cambridge and New York, 1997).

Herbert, Ulrich, 'Ideological Legitimization and Political Practice of the Leadership of the National Socialist Secret Police', in Hans Mommsen (ed.), *The Third Reich between Vision and Reality: New Perspectives on German History, 1918–1945* (Oxford, 2001), 99–108.

Herbert, Ulrich, 'Traditionen des Rassismus', in idem (ed.), *Arbeit, Volkstum, Weltanschauung. Über Fremde und Deutsche im 20. Jahrhundert* (Frankfurt am Main, 1995), 11–29.

Herbert, Ulrich, 'Von der "Reichskristallnacht" zum "Holocaust". Der 9. November und das Ende des "Radauantisemitismus"', in idem (ed.), *Arbeit, Volkstum, Weltanschauung*, 59–77.

Herbert, Ulrich, Orth, Karin and Dieckmann, Christoph (eds), *Die nationalsozialistischen Konzentrationslager: Entwicklung und Struktur*, 2 vols (Frankfurt, 2002).

Herbst, Ludolf, *Das nationalsozialistische Deutschland, 1933–1945. Die Entfesselung der Gewalt. Rassismus und Krieg* (Frankfurt am Main, 1996).

Herf, Jeffrey, *The Jewish Enemy: Nazi Propaganda during World War II and the Holocaust* (Cambridge, MA, 2006).

Hermann, Angela, 'Hitler und sein Stosstrupp in der "Reichskristallnacht"', *VfZ* 56 (2008), 603–20.

Hesse, Hans (ed.), *Persecution and Resistance of Jehovah's Witnesses during the Nazi Regime, 1933–1945* (Bremen, 2001).

Heumos, Peter, *Die Emigration aus der Tschechoslowakei nach Westeuropa und dem Nahen Osten* (Munich, 1989).

Hilberg, Raul, *The Destruction of the European Jews* (London, 1961).

Hildebrand, Klaus, *Das vergangene Reich. Deutsche Aussenpolitik von Bismarck bis Hitler, 1871–1945* (Stuttgart, 1995).

Hildesheimer, Esriel, *Jüdische Selbstverwaltung unter dem NS-Regime. Der Existenzkampf der Reichsvertretung und Reichsvereinigung der Juden in Deutschland* (Tübingen, 1994).

Hillmann, Jörg and Scheiblich, Reinhard, *Das rote Schloss am Meer. Die Marineschule Mürwik seit ihrer Gründung* (Hamburg, 2002).

Hilmes, Oliver, *Herrin des Hügels. Das Leben der Cosima Wagner* (Munich, 2007).

Hoch, Anton and Gruchmann, Lothar, *Georg Elser. Der Attentäter aus dem Volke. Der Anschlag auf Hitler im Münchner Bürgerbräu 1939* (Frankfurt am Main, 1980).

Hockerts, Hans Günter, *Die Sittlichkeitsprozesse gegen katholische Ordensangehörige und Priester 1936/1937. Eine Studie zur nationalsozialistischen Herrschaftstechnik und zum Kirchenkampf* (Mainz, 1971).

Hoensch, Jörg K. and Kováć, Dušan (eds), *Das Scheitern der Verständigung. Tschechen, Deutsche und Slowaken in der Ersten Republik* (Essen, 1994).

Hoerz, Peter F., *Jüdische Kultur im Burgenland. Historische Fragmente – volkskundliche Analysen* (Vienna, 2006).

Höhne, Heinz, *Canaris. Patriot im Zwielicht* (Munich, 1976).

Höhne, Heinz, *Mordsache Röhm. Hitlers Durchbruch zur Alleinherrschaft, 1933–1934* (Reinbek bei Hamburg, 1984).

Höhne, Heinz, *Der Orden unter dem Totenkopf. Die Geschichte der SS* (Munich, 1984).

Hořák, Martin and Jelínek, Tomáš, *Nacistická perzekuce obyvatel českých zemí* (Prague, 2006).

Hořejš, Miloš, 'Spolupráce Böhmisch-Mährische Landgesellschaft, Bodenamt für Böhmen und Mähren a Volksdeutsche Mittelstelle na germanizaci české půdy na Mělnicku a Mladoboleslavsku (1939–1945)', *Terezínské listy* 34 (2006), 89–124.

Huber, Axel, '"Du, Reinhard Heydrich, bist ein wahrhaft gutter SS-Mann gewesen". Totenkult und Heldenmythos nach dem Tod von SS-Gruppenführer Reinhard Heydrich', unpublished MA thesis, University of Konstanz, 2009.

Hübinger, Paul Egon, 'Thomas Mann und Reinhard Heydrich in den Akten des Reichsstatthalters von Epp', *VfZ* 28 (1980), 111–43.

Hüser, Karl, *Wewelsburg 1933 bis 1945 – Kult- und Terrorstätte der SS. Eine Dokumentation* (2nd edn, Paderborn, 1987).

Husson, Edouard, 'Comment écrire la biographie d'un acteur de l'appareil de terreur du IIIe Reich? L'exemple de Reinhard Heydrich (1904–1942)', *Revue d'Allemagne et des Pays de Langue Allemande* 33 (2001), 439–51.

Husson, Edouard, 'Die Entscheidung zur Vernichtung aller europäischen Juden. Versuch einer Neuinterpretation', in Klaus Hildebrand, Udo Wengst and Andreas Wirsching (eds), *Geschichtswissenschaft und Zeiterkenntnis. Von der Aufklärung bis zur Gegenwart. Festschrift für Horst Möller* (Munich, 2008), 277–89.

Husson, Edouard, *Heydrich et la solution finale* (Paris, 2008).

Hüttenberger Peter, 'Nationalsozialistische Polykratie', *Geschichte und Gesellschaft* 2 (1976), 417–42.

Ivanov, Miroslav, *Der Henker von Prag. Das Attentat auf Heydrich* (Berlin, 1993).

Jacobsen, Hans-Adolf, 'Kommissarbefehl und Massenexekution sowjetischer Kriegsgefangener', in Buchheim et al., *SS*, doc., 1, 449–544.

Jahn, Peter, and Rürup, Reinhard (eds), *Erobern und Vernichten. Der Krieg gegen die Sowjetunion 1941–1945* (Berlin, 1991).

Jančík, Drahomír, Kubů, Eduard and Kuklík, Jan (eds), *Arizace a restituce židovského majetku v českých zemích (1939–2000)* (Prague, 2003).

Jansen, Christian and Weckbecker, Arno, 'Eine Miliz im "Weltanschuungskrieg". Der "Volksdeutsche Selbstschutz" in Polen 1939/40', in Wolfgang Michalka (ed.), *Der Zweite Weltkrieg. Analysen, Grundzüge, Forschungsbilanz* (2nd edn, Munich, 1990), 482–500.

Jansen, Christian and Weckbecker, Arno, *Der 'Volksdeutsche Selbstschutz' in Polen 1939/40* (Munich, 1992).

Jansen, Hans, *Der Madagaskar-Plan. Die beabsichtigte Deportation der europäischen Juden nach Madagascar* (Munich, 1997).

Janssen, Karl-Heinz and Tobias, Fritz, *Der Sturz der Generäle. Hitler und die Blomberg–Fritsch-Krise 1938* (Munich, 1994).

Jastrzębski, Włodzimierz, *Der Bromberger Blutsonntag. Legende und Wirklichkeit* (Poznań, 1990).

Jaworski, Rudolf, *Vorposten oder Minderheit? Der Sudetendeutsche Volkstumskampf in den Beziehungen zwischen der Weimarer Republik und der ČSR* (Stuttgart, 1977).

Jefferies, Matthew, *Imperial Culture in Germany, 1871–1918* (Basingstoke and New York, 2003).

Jelavich, Barbara, *Modern Austria: Empire and Republic, 1815–1986* (Cambridge, 1987).

Jelínek, Zdeněk, 'K problematice atentátu na Reinharda Heydricha', *Historie a vojenství* 40 (1991), 65–101.

Jelínek, Zdeněk, *Operace Silver A* (Prague, 1992).

Jellonek, Burkhard, *Homosexuelle unter dem Hakenkreuz. Die Verfolgung von Homosexuellen im Dritten Reich* (Paderborn, 1990)

Jochmann, Werner, *Gesellschaftskrise und Judenfeindschaft in Deutschland 1870–1945* (Hamburg, 1988).

Johnson, Eric A., *Nazi Terror: The Gestapo, Jews, and Ordinary Germans* (New York, 1999).

Jung, Otmar, *Plebiszit und Diktatur. Die Volksabstimmungen der Nationalsozialisten. Die Fälle 'Austritt aus dem Völkerbund' (1933), 'Staatsoberhaupt' (1934) und 'Anschluss Österreichs' (1938)* (Tübingen, 1995).

Kahrs, Horst, 'Von der "Grossraumwirtschaft" zur "Neuen Ordnung". Zur strategischen Orientierung der deutschen Eliten 1932–1943', in Götz Aly (ed.), *Modelle für ein deutsches Europa. Ökonomie und Herrschaft im Grosswirtschaftsraum* (Berlin, 1992), 9–28.

Kaienburg, Hermann, *Das Konzentrationslager Neuengamme 1938–1945* (Berlin, 1997).

Kaienburg, Hermann, 'Sachsenhausen-Stammlager', in Benz and Distel (eds), *Ort des Terrors*, vol. 3: *Sachsenhausen, Buchenwald*, 17–72.

Kaiser, Wolf, 'Die Wannsee-Konferenz. SS-Führer und Ministerialbeamte im Einvernehmen über die Ermordung der europäischen Juden', in Heiner Lichtenstein and Otto R. Romberg (eds), *Täter – Opfer – Folgen. Der Holocaust in Geschichte und Gegenwart* (2nd edn, Bonn, 1997), 24–37.

Kárný, Miroslav, '"Heydrichiaden". Widerstand und Terror im "Protektorat Böhmen und Mähren"', in Loukia Droulia and Hagen Fleischer (eds), *Von Lidice bis Kalavryta. Widerstand und Besatzungsterror. Studien zur Repressalienpraxis im Zweiten Weltkrieg* (Berlin 1999), 51–63.

Kárný, Miroslav, 'Heydrichova cesta do Paříže (5.5.1942)', *Historie a vojenství* 41 (1992), 95–108.

Kárný, Miroslav, 'Konečné řešení'. Genocida českých židů v německé protektorátní politice (Prague, 1991).

Kárný, Miroslav, 'Die Logik von München. Das Protektorat Böhmen und Mähren', in Dietrich Eichholtz and Kurt Pätzold (eds), *Der Weg in den Krieg* (Berlin, 1989), 279–308.

Kárný, Miroslav, 'Die materiellen Grundlagen der Sozialdemagogie in der Protektoratspolitik Heydrichs', *Historica* 19 (1989), 123–59.

Kárný, Miroslav, 'Nisko in der Geschichte der Endlösung', *Judaica Bohemiae* 23 (1987), 69–84.

Kárný, Miroslav, 'Der "Reichsausgleich" in der deutschen Protektoratspolitik', in Ulrich Herbert (ed.), *Europa und der 'Reichseinsatz'. Ausländische Zivilarbeiter, Kriegsgefangene und KZ-Häftlinge in Deutschland 1938–1945* (Essen, 1991), 26–50.

Kárný, Miroslav, 'Zur Statistik der jüdischen Bevölkerung im sogenannten Protektorat', *Judaica Bohemiae* 23 (1987), 9–19.

Kasten, Bernd, *'Gute Franzosen'. Die französische Polizei und die deutsche Besatzungsmacht im besetzten Frankreich 1940–1944* (Sigmaringen, 1993).

Kay, Alex J., *Exploitation, Resettlement, Mass Murder: Political and Economic Planning for German Occupation Policy in the Soviet Union, 1940–1941* (New York and Oxford, 2006).

Kay, Alex J., 'Germany's Staatssekretäre, Mass Starvation and the Meeting of 2 May 1941', *Journal of Contemporary History* 41 (2006), 685–700.

Kempner, Robert, *Eichmann und Komplizen* (Zurich, Stuttgart, Vienna, 1961).

Kenmann, Alfons, 'Störfaktor and der "Heimatfront". Jugendliche Nonkonformität und die Gestapo', in Paul and Mallmann (eds), *Gestapo im Zweiten Weltkrieg*, 179–200.

Kershaw, Ian, *Hitler 1889–1936: Hubris* (London, 1998).

Kershaw, Ian, *Hitler 1936–1945: Nemesis* (London, 2000).

Kershaw, Ian, 'Improvised Genocide? The Emergence of the "Final Solution" in the Warthegau', *Transactions of the Royal Historical Society*, 6th series (1992), 51–98.

Kershaw, Ian, '"Working towards the Führer": Reflections on the Nature of the Hitler Dictatorship', *Contemporary European History* 2 (1993), 103–18.

Kerstingjohänner, Helmut, *Die deutsche Inflation 1919–1923. Politik und Ökonomie* (Frankfurt am Main, 2004).

Kessemeier, Gesa, *Sportlich, sachlich, männlich. Das Bild der 'Neuen Frau' in den Zwanziger Jahren* (Dortmund, 2000).

Kettenacker, Lothar, *Nationalsozialistische Volkstumspolitik im Elsass* (Stuttgart, 1973).

Kindleberger, Charles P., *Die Weltwirtschaftskrise, 1929–1939* (Munich, 1973).

Klarsfeld, Serge, *Vichy – Auschwitz. Die Zusammenarbeit der deutschen und französischen Behörden bei der 'Endlösung der Judenfrage' in Frankreich* (Nördlingen, 1989).

Klarsfeld, Serge and Steinberg, Maxime, *Die Endlösung der Judenfrage in Belgien* (New York, 1980).

Klein, Fritz, 'Between Compiègne and Versailles: The Germans on the Way from a Misunderstood Defeat to an Unwanted Peace', in Manfred F. Boemeke, Gerald D. Feldman and Elisabeth Glaser (eds), *The Treaty of Versailles: A Reassessment after 75 Years* (New York, 1998), 203–20.

Klein, John W., 'Hans Pfitzner and the Two Heydrichs', *Music Review* 26 (1965), 308–17.

Klenner, Jochen, *Verhältnis von Partei und Staat 1933–1945, dargestellt am Beispiel Bayerns* (Munich, 1974).

Koehl, Robert Lewis, *The Black Corps: The Structure and Power Struggles of the Nazi SS* (Madison, WI, 1983).

Koehl, Robert Lewis, 'The Character of the Nazi SS', *Journal of Modern History* 34 (1962), 275–83.

Koehl, Robert Lewis, *German Resettlement and Population Policy, 1939–1945: A History of the Reich Commission for the Strengthening of Germandom* (Cambridge, MA, 1957).

Kogon, Eugen, *Der SS-Staat. Das System der deutschen Konzentrationslager* (Munich, 1946).

Kogon, Eugen, Langbein, Hermann and Rückerl, Adalbert, *Nationalsozialistische Massentötungen durch Giftgas* (Frankfurt, 1983).

Kohlhaas, Elisabeth, 'Die Mitarbeiter der regionalen Staatspolizeistellen. Quantitative und qualitative Befunde zur Personalausstattung der Gestapo', in Paul and Mallmann (eds), *Die Gestapo. Mythos und Realität*, 219–35.

Kokoška, Jaroslav and Kokoška, Stanislav, *Spor o agenta A-54* (Prague, 1994).

Konrád, Ota, 'Die deutschen Hochschullehrer in Prag vor und nach 1938/39. Versuch einer Bestandsaufnahme', in Jerzy Kochanowski and Maike Sach (eds), *Die 'Volksdeutschen' in Polen, Frankreich, Ungarn und der Tschechoslowakei. Mythos und Realität* (Osnabrück, 2006), 147–62.

Koonz, Claudia, *The Nazi Conscience* (Cambridge, MA, 2003).

Kracik, Jörg, *Die Politik des deutschen Aktivismus in der Tschechoslowakei 1920–1938* (Frankfurt am Main, 1999).

Krause, Andreas, *Scapa Flow. Die Selbstversenkung der wilhelminischen Flotte* (Berlin, 1999).

Krausnick, Helmut, 'Die Einsatzgruppen vom Anschluss Österreichs bis zum Feldzug gegen die Sowjetunion. Entwicklung und Verhältnis zur Wehrmacht', in idem and Hans-Heinrich Wilhelm, *Die Truppe des Weltanschauungskrieges. Die Einsatzgruppen der Sicherheitspolizei und des SD, 1938–1942* (Stuttgart, 1981), 13–278.

Krausnick, Helmut, 'Hitler und die Morde in Polen. Ein Beitrag zum Konflikt zwischen Heer und SS um die Verwaltung der besetzten Gebiete', *VfZ* 11 (1963), 196–209.

Krausnick, Helmut and Willhelm, Hans-Heinrich, *Die Truppe des Weltanschauungskrieges. Die Einsatzgruppen der Sicherheitspolizei und des SD, 1938–1942* (Stuttgart, 1981), 13–278.

Krejčí, Jaroslav, 'The Bohemian-Moravian War Economy', in Michael Charles Kaser and Edward Albert Radice (eds), *The Economic History of Eastern Europe, 1919–1975* (Oxford, 1986).

Krejčová, Helena, Svobodová, Jana and Hyndráková, Anna (eds), *Židé v Protektorátu. Hlášení Židovské náboženské obce v roce 1942. Dokumenty* (Prague, 1997).

Kroener, Bernhard R., Müller, Rolf-Dieter and Umbreit, Hans, *Das Deutsche Reich und der Zweite Weltkrieg*, vol. 5/1: *Kriegsverwaltung, Wirtschaft, und personelle Ressourcen* (Stuttgart, 1988).

Kubů, Eduard, '"Die Bedeutung des deutschen Blutes im Tschechentum". Der "wissenschaftspädagogische" Beitrag des Soziologen Karl Valentin Müller zur Lösung des Problems der Germanisierung Mitteleuropas', *Bohemia. Zeitschrift für Geschichte und Kultur der böhmischen Länder* 45 (2004), 93–114.

Kubů, Eduard, 'Die Kreditanstalt der Deutschen 1911–1945. Ein Beitrag zum Wirtschaftsnationalismus der Deutschen in den böhmischen Ländern und ihrem Verhältnis Deutschland', *Zeitschrift für Unternehmensgeschichte* 45 (2000), 3–29.

Kubů, Eduard and Jančík, Drahomír, *'Arizace' a arizátoři. Drobný a střední židovský majetek v úvěrech Kreditanstalt der Deutschen (1939–45)* (Prague, 2005).

Kühl, Stefan, *Die Internationale der Rassisten. Aufstieg und Niedergang der internationalen Bewegung für Eugenetik und Rassenhygiene im 20. Jahrhundert* (Frankfurt am Main and New York, 1997).

Kuklík, Jan, 'Oduznání mnichovské dohody za druhé světové války', *Historie a vojenství* 46 (1997), 49–68.

Kulischer, Eugene M., *Europe on the Move: War and Population Changes, 1917–1947* (New York, 1948).

Kulka, Otto Dov, 'Die Nürnberger Rassegesetze und die deutsche Bevölkerung im Lichte geheimer NS Lage- und Stimmungsberichte', *VfZ* 32 (1984), 582–624.

Kulka, Otto Dov and Jäckel, Eberhard (eds), *Die Juden in den geheimen NS-Stimmungsberichten 1933–1945* (Düsseldorf, 2004).

Kundrus, Birthe, 'Kontinuitäten, Parallelen, Rezeptionen. Überlegungen zur Kolonialisierung des Nationalsozialismus', *WerkstattGeschichte* 43 (2006), 45–62.

Kural, Václav, *Vlastenci proti okupaci. Ústřední vedení odboje domácího 1940–1943* (Prague, 1997).

Kural, Václav, 'Von Masaryks "Neuem Europoa" zu den Grossraumplänen Hitler-Deutschlands', in Richard Plaschka (ed.), *Mitteleuropa-Konzeptionen in der ersten Hälfte des 20. Jahrhunderts* (Vienna, 1995), 351–7.

Kwiet, Konrad, 'Die Kennzeichnung mit dem Judenstern im Herbst 1941', in Wolfgang Benz (ed.), *Die Juden in Deutschland 1933–1945. Leben unter nationalsozialistischer Herrschaft* (Munich, 1988), 614–31.

Kwiet, Konrad, 'Rehearsing for Murder: The Beginning of the Final Solution in Lithuania in June 1941', *Holocaust and Genocide Studies* 12 (1998), 3–26.

Kwiet, Konrad, *Reichskommissariat Niederlande. Versuch und Scheitern nationalsozialistischer Neuordnung* (Stuttgart, 1968).

Lang, Jochen von, *Der Adjutant Karl Wolff. Der Mann zwischen Hitler und Himmler* (Munich, 1985).

Laqueur, Walter, *The Changing Face of Antisemitism: From Ancient Times to the Present Day* (Oxford, 2006).

Lehmann, Joachim, 'Herbert Backe – Technokrat und Agrarideologe', in Ronald Smelser (ed.), *Die braune Elite* (Darmstadt, 1993), vol. 2, 1–12.

Lehmann, Joachim, 'Verantwortung für Überleben, Hunger und Tod. Zur Stellung von Staatssekretär Herbert Backe im Entscheidungsgefüge von Ernährungs- und Landwirtschaft, Agrar- und Agressionspolitik in Deutschland während des Zweiten Weltkrieges sowie deren Voraussetzungen', in Ernst Münch (ed.), *Festschrift für Gerhard Heitz zum 75. Geburtstag* (Rostock, 2000), 509–26.

Lemberg, Hans, 'Prag im Zerrspiegel. Die Propagierung des "deutschen Prag" in der Protektoratszeit', in *Magister noster. Sborník statí věnovaných in memoriam Prof. Dr. Janu Havránkovi* (Prague, 2005), 383–94.

Lemmermann, Heinz, *Kriegserziehung im Kaiserreich. Studien zur politischen Funktion von Schule und Schulmusik 1890–1918*, 2 vols (Lilienthal bei Bremen, 1984), vol. 2, 671.

Lethen, Helmut, *Cool Conduct: The Culture of Distance in Weimar Germany* (Berkeley, CA, 2002).

Lewis, Wallace L., *The Survival of the German Navy 1917–1920: Officers, Sailors and Politics* (Ann Arbor, MI, 1983).

Lewy, Guenter, *The Nazi Persecution of the Gypsies* (Oxford, 2001).

Lexa, John G., 'Anti-Jewish Laws and Regulations in the Protectorate of Bohemia and Moravia', in Avigdor Dagan (ed.), *The Jews of Czechoslovakia*, 4 vols (Philadelphia, 1968–84), vol. 3, 75–103.

Lilienthal, Georg, *Der 'Lebensborn e. v.'. Ein Instrument nationalsozialistischer Rassenpolitik* (Frankfurt, 1993).

Lilla, Joachim, *Der Preussische Staatsrat 1921–1933. Ein biographisches Handbuch* (Düsseldorf, 2005).

Lilla, Joachim, *Statisten in Uniform. Die Mitglieder des Reichstags 1933–1945. Ein biographisches Handbuch* (Düsseldorf, 2004).

Liulevicius, Vejas Gabriel, *The German Myth of the East: 1800 to the Present* (Oxford, 2009).

Liulevicius, Vejas Gabriel, 'Der Osten als apokalyptischer Raum. Deutsche Fronterfahrungen im und nach dem Ersten Weltkrieg', in Gregor Thum (ed.), *Traumland Osten. Deutsche Bilder vom östlichen Europa im 20. Jahrhundert* (Göttingen, 2006), 47–65.

Longerich, Peter, *Die braunen Bataillone. Geschichte der SA* (Munich, 1989).

Longerich, Peter, *'Davon haben wir nichts gewusst!' Die Deutschen und die Judenverfolgung 1933–1945* (Munich, 2006).

Longerich, Peter (ed.), *Die Ermordung der europäischen Juden. Eine umfassende Dokumentation des Holocaust 1941–1945* (Munich, 1989).

Longerich, Peter, *Heinrich Himmler. Biographie* (Munich, 2008).

Longerich, Peter, *Joseph Goebbels. Biographie*, (Munich, 2010).

Longerich, Peter, *Politik der Vernichtung. Eine Gesamtdarstellung der nationalsozialistischen Judenverfolgung* (Munich and Zurich, 1998).

Loock, Hans-Dietrich, *Quisling, Rosenberg und Terboven. Zur Vorgeschichte und Geschichte der nationalsozialistischen Revolution in Norwegen* (Stuttgart, 1970).

Löw, Andrea, *Juden im Getto Litzmannstadt. Lebensbedingungen, Selbstwahrnehmung, Verhalten* (Göttingen, 2006).

Lower, Wendy, *Nazi Empire-Building and the Holocaust in Ukraine* (Chapel Hill, NC, 2005).

Lower, Wendy, 'A New Ordering of Space and Race. Nazi Colonial Dreams in Zhytomyr, Ukraine 1941–1944', *German Studies Review* 25 (2002), 227–54.

Lozowick, Yaacov, *Hitlers Bürokraten. Eichmann, seine willigen Vollstrecker und die Banalität des Bösen* (Zurich, 2000).

Luh, Andreas, *Der deutsche Turnverband in der ersten Tschechoslowakischen Republik. Vom völkischen Vereinsbetrieb zur volkspolitischen Bewegung* (Munich, 1988).

Lukeš, Igor and Goldstein, Eric (eds), *The Munich Crisis, 1938: Prelude to World War II* (London, 1999).

Luža, Radomír, *V Hitlerově objetí. kapitoly z českého odboje* (Prague, 2006).

MacDonald, Callum, *The Killing of SS Obergruppenführer Reinhard Heydrich: 27 May 1942* (London, 1992).

MacDonald, Callum, *Heydrich: Anatomie eines Attentats* (Munich, 1990).

McElligott, Anthony, *Contested City: Municipal Politics and the Rise of Nazism in Altona, 1917–1937* (Ann Arbor, MI, 1998).

Madajczyk, Czeslaw, 'Besteht ein Synchronismus zwischen dem "Generalplan Ost" und der Endlösung der Judenfrage?' in Wolfgang Michalka (ed.), *Der Zweite Weltkrieg. Analysen, Grundzüge, Forschungsbilanz* (2nd edn, Munich, 1990), 844–57.

Madajczyk, Czeslaw, *Die Okkupationspolitik Nazideutschlands in Polen 1939–1945* (Cologne, 1988).

Madajczyk, Czeslaw (ed.), *Vom Generalplan Ost zum Generalsiedlungsplan* (Munich, 1994).

Mai, Uwe, *Rasse und Raum. Agrarpolitik, Sozial und Raumplanung im NS-Staat* (Paderborn, 2002).

Malinowski, Stephan, *Vom König zum Führer. Deutscher Adel und Nationalsozialismus* (Frankfurt am Main, 2003).

Mallmann, Klaus-Michael, Böhler, Jochen and Matthäus, Jürgen, *Einsatzgruppen in Polen. Darstellung und Dokumentation* (Darmstadt, 2008).

Mallmann, Klaus-Michael and Paul, Gerhard (eds), *Karrieren der Gewalt. Nationalsozialistische Täterbiographien* (Darmstadt, 2004).

Mallmann, Klaus-Michael and Paul, Gerhard, *Herrschaft und Alltag. Ein Industrierevier im Dritten Reich* (Bonn, 1991).

Mang, Thomas, *Gestapo – Leitstelle Wien – Mein Name ist Huber* (Münster, 2004).

Mann, Reinhard, *Protest und Kontrolle im Dritten Reich. Nationalsozialistische Herrschaft im Alltag einer rheinischen Grossstadt* (Frankfurt am Main, 1987).

Manoschek, Walter, *'Serbien ist judenfrei'. Militärische Besatzungspolitik und Judenvernichtung in Serbien 1941/42* (Munich, 1993).

Maršálek, Hans, *Die Geschichte des Konzentrationslagers Mauthausen* (Vienna, 1980).

Maršálek, Pavel, *Protektorát Čechy a Morava. Státoprávní a politické aspekty nacistického okupačního režimu v českých zemích 1939–1945* (Prague, 2002).

Marssolek, Inge and Ott, René, *Bremen im 'Dritten Reich'. Anpassung – Widerstand – Verfolgung* (Bremen, 1986).

Mason, Timothy W., *Sozialpolitik im Dritten Reich. Arbeiterklasse und Volksgemeinschaft* (Opladen, 1977).

Mastny, Vojtech, *The Czechs under Nazi Rule: The Failure of National Resistance, 1939–42* (New York, 1971).

Matthäus, Jürgen, '"Operation Barbarossa" and the Onset of the Holocaust', in Browning, *The Origins of the Final Solution*, 253–5.

Matušů, Marie, *Muži pro speciální operace* (Prague, 2004).

Mazower, Mark, *Hitler's Empire: Nazi Rule in Occupied Europe* (London, 2008).

Mazower, Mark, *Inside Hitler's Greece: The Experience of Occupation 1941–1944* (New Haven, 1993).

Meershoek, Guus, 'Machtentfaltung und Scheitern. Sicherheitspolizei und SD in den Niederlanden', in Paul and Mallmann (eds), *Gestapo im Zweiten Weltkrieg*, 383–402.

Meershoeck, Guus, et al. (eds), *Repression und Kriegsverbrechen. Die Bekämpfung von Widerstands- und Partisanenbewegungen gegen die deutsche Besatzung in West- und Südosteuropa* (Berlin and Göttingen, 1997).

Mehringer, Hartmut, 'Die KPD in Bayern 1919–1945. Vorgeschichte, Verfolgung und Widerstand', in Broszat and idem (eds), *Bayern in der NS-Zeit*, vol. 5: *Die Parteien KPD, SPD, BVP in Verfolgung und Widerstand*, 1–286.

Meier, Kurt, *Kreuz und Hakenkreuz. Die evangelische Kirche im Dritten Reich* (Munich, 1992).

Melzer, Emanuel, 'Relations between Poland and Germany and their Impact on the Jewish Problem in Poland (1935–1938)', *Yad Vashem Studies* 12 (1977), 193–229.

Meyer, Ahlrich, *Die deutsche Besatzung in Frankreich 1940–1944. Widerstandsbekämpfung und Judenverfolgung* (Darmstadt, 2000).

Meyer, Beate, *'Jüdische Mischlinge'. Rassenpolitik und Verfolgungserfahrung 1933–1945* (Hamburg, 1999).

Michman, Dan, 'Why Did Heydrich Write the "Schnellbrief"? A Remark on the Reason and on its Significance', *Yad Vashem Studies* 32 (2004), 433–7.

Mikolajczyk, Steffen, 'Eine aufstrebende Industriestadt huldigt der Monarchie. Der Kaiserbesuch 1903', in Werner Freitag and Katrin Minner (eds), *Vergnügen und Inszenierung. Stationen städtischer Festkultur in Halle* (Halle an der Saale, 2004), 206–13.

Milotová, Jaroslava, '"Cizorodí" dělníci a jejich pracovní nasazení v nacistickém Německu v letech 1939–1945', in Havlíková (ed.), *Museli pracovat pro Říši*, 25–40.

Milotová, Jaroslava, 'Personální aspekty tzv. Heydrichovi správní reformy', *Paginae historiae* 1 (1993), 196–218.

Milotová, Jaroslava, 'Výsledky Heydrichovi správní reformy z pohledu okupačního aparátu', *Paginae historiae* 2 (1994), 161–74.

Milton, Sybil H., 'The Expulsion of Polish Jews from Germany, October 1938 to July 1939: A Documentation', *Leo Baeck Institute Yearbook* 29 (1984), 169–74.

Milton, Sybil H., '"Gypsies" as Social Outsiders in Nazi Germany', in Gellately and Stoltzfus (eds), *Social Outsiders in Nazi Germany*, 212–32.

Míšková, Alena, 'Die Deutsche Universität Prag im Vergleich mit anderen deutschen Universitäten der Kriegszeit', in Hans Lemberg (ed.), *Universitäten in nationaler Konkurrenz. Zur Geschichte der Prager Universitäten im 19. und 20. Jahrhundert* (Munich, 2003), 177–94.

Míšková Alena, 'Rassenforschung und Oststudien an der Deutschen (Karls-) Universität in Prag', in Brandes et al. (eds), *Erzwungene Trennung*, 37–50.

Mommsen, Hans, *Auschwitz. 17. Juli 1942* (Munich, 2002).

Mommsen, Hans, 'Der nationalsozialistische Polizeistaat und die Judenverfolgung vor 1938', *VfZ* 10 (1962), 68–87.

Mommsen, Hans, 'The Realization of the Unthinkable: The "Final Solution of the Jewish Question" in the Third Reich', in Gerhard Hirschfeld (ed.), *The Policies of Genocide: Jews and Soviet Prisoners of War in Nazi Germany* (London, 1986), 97–144.

Moorhouse, Roger, *Berlin at War: Life and Death in Hitler's Capital, 1939–45* (London, 2010).

Moorhouse, Roger, *Killing Hitler: The Third Reich and the Plots against the Führer* (London, 2006).

Morsch, Günter (ed.), *Mord und Massenmord im Konzentrationslager Sachsenhausen 1936–1945* (Berlin, 2005).

Moser, Jonny, 'Nisko: The First Experiment in Deportation', *Simon Wiesenthal Center Annual* 2 (1985), 1–30.

Moser, Jonny, 'Österreich', in Wolfgang Benz (ed.), *Dimension des Völlkermords, Die Zahl der jüdischen Opfer des Nationalsozialismus* (Munich, 1991), 67–93

Moser, Jonny, 'Die Zentralstelle für jüdische Auswanderung in Wien', in Kurt Schmid and Robert Streibel (eds), *Der Pogrom 1938. Judenverfolgung in Österreich und Deutschland* (Vienna, 1990).

Moulis, Miloslav and Tomášek, Dušan, *K. H. Frank. Vzestup a pád karloovarského knihkupce* (Prague, 2003).

Mucha, Josef and Petrželka, Karel, *O některých současných problémech národnostně smíšených manželství* (Prague, 1946).

Mühlen, Patrick von zur, *Rassenideologien. Geschichte und Hintergründe* (Berlin and Bonn-Bad Godesberg, 1977).

Müller, Klaus-Jürgen, *Das Heer und Hitler. Armee und nationalsozialistisches Regime, 1933–1940* (Stuttgart, 1969).

Müller, Michael, *Canaris. Hitlers Abwehrchef. Biographie* (Berlin, 2006).

Müller, Rolf-Dieter, *Hitlers Ostkrieg und die deutsche Siedlungspolitik. Die Zusammenarbeit von Wehrmacht, Wirtschaft und SS* (Frankfurt, 1991).

Müller, Sven Oliver and Torp, Cornelius (eds), *Imperial Germany Revisited: Continuing Debates and New Perspectives* (Oxford and New York, 2010).

Musial, Bogdan, *Deutsche Zivilverwaltung und Judenverwaltung im Generalgouvernement. Eine Fallstudie zum Distrikt Lublin 1939–1944* (Wiesbaden, 1999).

Musial, Bogdan, 'Konterrevolutionäre Elemente sind zu erschiessen'. *Die Brutalisierung des deutsch–sowjetischen Krieges im Sommer 1941* (Berlin and Moscow, 2000).

Musial, Bogdan, 'The Origins of "Operation Reinhard": The Decision-Making Process for the Mass Murder of the Jews in the Generalgouvernement', *Yad Vashem Studies* 28 (2000), 113–53.

Musilová, Dana, 'Problémy sociálně ekonomického vývoje v letech 1939–1945 v protektorátu Čechy a Morava', *Historický obzor* 3 (1992), 149–52.

Naumann, Uwe, *Faschismus als Groteske. Heinrich Manns Roman 'Lidice'* (Worms, 1980).

Nečas, Ctibor, *Holocaust českých Romů* (Prague, 1999).

Nelles, Dieter, 'Organisation des Terrors im Nationalsozialismus', *Sozialwissenschaftliche Literatur-Rundschau* 25 (2002), 5–28.

Němeček, Jan, 'Německá okupační politika v protektorátu a český protiněmecký odpor', in *Historické, právní a mezinárodní souvislosti Dekretů prezidenta republiky* (Prague, 2003).

Němeček, Jan, 'Rok 1942 v československém zahraničním odboji', in *Rok 1942 v českém odboji. Sborník příspěvků z vědecké konference* (Prague, 1999), 19–24.

Nesládková, Ludmila (ed.), *The Case Nisko in the History of the Final Solution of the Jewish Problem* (Ostrava, 1995).

Nessou, Anestis, *Griechenland 1941–1944* (Osnabrück, 2009).

Neuberger, Helmut, *Freimaurerei und Nationalsozialismus. Die Verfolgung der deutschen Freimaurerei durch völkische Bewegung und Nationalsozialismus 1918–1945*, 2 vols (Hamburg, 1980).

Neufeld, Hans-Joachim, Huck, Jürgen and Tessin, Georg, *Zur Geschichte der Ordnungspolizei, 1936–1945* (Koblenz, 1957).

Nicholas, Lynn H., *The Rape of Europa: The Fate of Europe's Treasures in the Third Reich and the Second World War* (New York, 1994).

Nicosia, Francis R., 'The End of Emancipation and the Illusion of Preferential Treatment: German Zionism, 1933–1938', *Leo Baeck Institute Year Book* 36 (1991), 243–65.

Nicosia, Francis R., 'Ein nützlicher Feind: Zionismus im nationalsozialistischen Deutschland 1933–1939', *VfZ* 37 (1989), 367–400.

Noakes, Jeremy, 'The Development of Nazi Policy towards the German-Jewish "Mischlinge" 1933–1945', *Leo Baeck Institute Yearbook* 34 (1989), 291–354.

Obst, Dieter, '*Reichskristallnacht*'. *Ursachen und Verlauf des antisemitischen Pogroms vom November 1938* (Frankfurt, 1991).

Ogorreck, Ralf, *Die Einsatzgruppen und die 'Genesis der Endlösung'* (Berlin, 1996).

Olshausen, Klaus, *Zwischenspiel auf dem Balkan. Die deutsche Politik gegenüber Jugoslawien und Griechenland von März bis Juli 1941* (Stuttgart, 1973).

Ophir, Baruch Z. and Wiesemann, Falk, *Die jüdischen Gemeinden in Bayern, 1918–1945* (Munich, 1979).

Orth, Karin, 'Rudolf Höss und die "Endlösung" der Judenfrage. Drei Argumente gegen deren Datierung auf den Sommer 1941', *WerkstattGeschichte* 18 (1997), 45–57.

Orth, Karin, *Das System der nationalsozialistischen Konzentrationslager. Eine politische Organisationsgeschichte* (Hamburg, 1999).

Osterloh, Jörg, *Nationalsozialistische Judenverfolgung im Reichsgau Böhmen und Sudetenland, 1938–1945* (Munich, 2006).

Ottmer, Hans-Martin, *'Weserübung'. Der deutsche Angriff auf Dänemark und Norwegen im April 1940* (Munich, 1994).

Overy, Richard, 'Business in the "Grossraumwirtschaft". Eastern Europe, 1938–1945', in Harold James (ed.), *Enterprise in the Period of Fascism in Europe* (Burlington, VT, 2002), 151–77.

Overy, Richard, *Interrogations: The Nazi Elite in Allied Hands, 1945* (New York, 2001).

Pasák, Tomáš, *Emil Hácha (1938–1945)* (Prague, 1997).

Patzold, Kurt and Schwartz, Erika (eds), *Tagesordnung. Judenmord. Die Wannsee Konferenz am 20. Januar 1942. Eine Dokumentation zur Organisation der 'Endlösung'* (Berlin, 1992).

Paul, Gerhard and Mallmann, Klaus-Michael (eds), *Die Gestapo im Zweiten Weltkrieg. 'Heimatfront' und besetztes Europa* (Darmstadt, 2000).

Paul, Gerhard and Mallmann, Klaus-Michael (eds), *Die Gestapo. Mythos und Realität* (Darmstadt, 1995).

Paul, Gerhard, '"Kämpfende Verwaltung". Das Amt IV des Reichssicherheitshauptamtes als Führungsinstanz der Gestapo', in idem and Mallmann (eds), *Gestapo im Zweiten Weltkrieg*, 42–81.

Pavlowitch, Stevan, *Hitler's New Disorder: The Second World War in Yugoslavia* (London, 2008).

Penton, James, *Jehovah's Witnesses and the Third Reich: Sectarian Politics under Persecution* (Toronto, 2004).

Pernes, Jiří, *Až na dno zrady. Emanuel Moravec* (Prague, 1997).

Petrick, Fritz, *Die Okkupationspolitik des deutschen Faschismus in Dänemark und Norwegen, 1940–45* (Berlin, 1992).

Peukert, Detlev J. K., *Inside Nazi Germany: Conformity, Opposition, and Racism in Everyday Life* (New Haven and London, 1987).

Pierenkemper, Toni and Tilly, Richard, *The German Economy during the Nineteenth Century* (New York, 2004).

Pinwinkler, Alexander, '"Assimilation" und "Dissimilation" in der Bevölkerungsgeschichte ca. 1918–1960', in Rainer Mackensen (ed.), *Bevölkerungsforschung und Politik in Deutschland im 20. Jahrhundert* (Wiesbaden, 2006), 23–48.

Piper, Ernst, *Alfred Rosenberg. Hitlers Chefideologe* (Munich, 2005).

Pohl, Dieter, 'Die grossen Zwangsarbeiterlager der SS- und Polizeiführer für Juden im Generalgouvernement 1942–1945', in Herbert et al. (eds), *Die nationalsozialistischen Konzentrationslager*, vol. 1, 415–38.

Pohl, Dieter, *Die Herrschaft der Wehrmacht. Deutsche Militärbesetzung und einheimische Bevölkerung in der Sowjetunion 1941–1944* (Munich, 2008).

Pohl, Dieter, *Nationalsozialistische Judenverfolgung in Ostgalizien 1941–1944. Organisation und Durchführung eines staatlichen Massenverbrechens* (Munich, 1996).

Pohl, Dieter, 'Schauplatz Ukraine. Der Massenmord an den Juden im Militärverwaltungsgebiet und im Reichskommissariat 1941–1943', in Norbert Frei, Sybille Steinbacher and Bernd C. Wagner (eds), *Ausbeutung, Vernichtung, Öffentlichkeit. Neue Studien zur nationalsozialistischen Lagerpolitik* (Munich, 2000), 135–73.

Pohl, Dieter, *Von der Judenpolitik' zum Judenmord. Der Distrikt Lublin des Generalgouvernements 1939–1944* (Frankfurt am Main, 1993).

Pollmeier, Heiko, 'Inhaftierung und Lagererfahrung deutscher Juden im November 1938', *Jahrbuch für Antisemitismusforschung* 8 (1999), 107–30.

Popplow, Ulrich, 'Reinhard Heydrich oder die Aufnordung durch den Sport', *Olympisches Feuer. Zeitschrift der deutschen Olympischen Gesellschaft* 8 (1963), 14–20.

Potthast, Jan Björn, *Das jüdische Zentralmuseum der SS in Prag. Gegnerforschung und Völkermord im Nationalsozialismus* (Frankfurt am Main, 2002).

Přibye, Lukáš, 'Das Schicksal des dritten Transports aus dem Protektorat nach Nisko', *Theresienstädter Studien und Dokumente* 7 (2000), 297–342.

Prien, Jochen, *Geschichte des Jagdgeschwaders 77*, vol. 1, *1934–1941* (Eutin, 1992).

Procházka, Theodor, *The Second Republic: The Disintegration of Post-Munich Czechoslovakia, October 1938–March 1939* (Boulder, CO, 1981).

Průcha, Václav, *Hospodářské a sociální dějiny Československa 1918–1992, 1. díl období 1918–1945* (Brno, 2004).

Pulzer, Peter G., *Die Entstehung des politischen Antisemitismus in Deutschland und Österreich 1867–1914* (2nd edn, Göttingen, 2004).

Puntenius, Michael, 'Das Gesicht des Terrors. Reinhard Heydrich (1904–1942)', in idem, *Gelehrte, Weltanschauer, auch Poeten. Literarische Porträts berühmter Hallenser* (Halle, 2006), 199–201.

Puschner, Uwe, *Die völkische Bewegung im wilhelminischen Kaiserreich. Sprache, Rasse, Religion* (Darmstadt, 2001).

Querg, Thorsten J., *Spionage und Terror. Das Amt VI des Reichssicherheitshauptamtes 1939–1945*. Phil. Diss., Freie Universität Berlin, Berlin 1997.

Querg, Thorsten, 'Wilhelm Höttl. Vom Informanten zum Sturmbannführer im Sicherheitsdienst der SS', in Barbara Danckwortt, Thorsten Querg and Claudia Schöningh (eds), *Historische Rassismusforschung. Ideologie – Täter – Opfer* (Hamburg and Berlin, 1995), 208–30.

Rabinovici, Doron, *Instanzen der Ohnmacht. Wien 1938–1945. Der Weg zum Judenrat* (Frankfurt, 2000).

Ramme, Alwin, *Der Sicherheitsdienst der SS. Zu seiner Funktion im faschistischen Machtapparat und im Besatzungsregime des sogenannten Generalgouvernements* (East Berlin, 1970).

Rapp, Petra Madeleine, *Die Devisenprozesse gegen katholische Ordensangehörige und Geistliche im Dritten Reich* (Bonn, 1981).

Rebentisch, Dieter and Teppe, Karl (eds), *Verwaltung contra Menschenführung im Staate Hitlers. Studien zum politisch-administrativen System* (Göttingen, 1986).

Rehding, Alexander, *Hugo Riemann and the Birth of Modern Musical Thought* (Cambridge, 2003).

Reichardt, Sven, *Faschistische Kampfbünde. Gewalt und Gemeinschaft im italienischen Squadrismus und in der deutschen SA* (Cologne, 2002).

Reichardt, Sven, 'Gewalt, Körper, Politik. Paradoxien in der Kulturgeschichte der Zwischenkriegszeit', in Wolfgang Hardtwig (ed.), *Politische Kulturgeschichte der Zwischenkriegszeit 1918–1939* (Göttingen, 2005), 205–39.

Reiche, Eric G., *The Development of the SA in Nürnberg, 1922–1934* (Cambridge, 1986).

Reichelt, Katrin, 'Kollaboration und Holocaust in Lettland, 1941–1945', in Wolf Kaiser (ed.), *Täter im Vernichtungskrieg. Der Überfall auf die Sowjetunion und der Völkermord and den Juden* (Munich, 2002).

Reitlinger, Gerald, *The SS: Alibi of a Nation 1922–1945* (New York, 1956).

Reittererová, Vlasta, 'Das Mozartjahr 1941 in Prag. Ein Beitrag zur Geschichte des Musiklebens im Protektorat Böhmen und Mähren', in *Přednášky z 47. běhu Letní školy slovanských studií* (Prague, 2004), 184–206.

Retallack, James (ed.), *Imperial Germany, 1871–1918* (Oxford, 2008).

Reulecke, Jürgen, *Geschichte der Urbanisierung in Deutschland* (Frankfurt am Main, 1985).

Richardi, Hans-Günter, *Schule der Gewalt. Die Anfänge des Konzentrationslagers Dachau 1933–1934. Ein dokumentarischer Bericht* (Munich, 1983).

Riess, Volker, *Die Anfänge der Vernichtung 'lebensunwerten Lebens' in den Reichsgauen Danzig-Westpreussen und Wartheland 1939/40* (Frankfurt am Main, 1995).

Robel, Gert, 'Sowjetunion', in Benz (ed.), *Dimension des Völkermordes*, 499–560.

Rohde, Horst, 'Hitler's First Blitzkrieg and its Consequences for North-Eastern Europe', in Militärgeschichtliches Forschungsamt (ed.), *Germany and the Second World War*, 10 vols (Oxford, 1990–), vol. 2: *Germany's Initial Conquests*, 101–26.

Röhr, Werner, 'Das Sudetendeutsche Freikorps – Diversionsinstrument der Hitler-Regierung bei der Zerschlagung der Tschechoslowakei', *Militärgeschichtliche Mitteilungen* 52 (1993), 35–66.

Roseman, Mark (ed.), *Generations in Conflict: Youth Revolt and Generation Formation in Germany, 1770–1968* (Cambridge, 2003).

Roseman, Mark, *The Villa, the Lake, the Meeting: Wannsee and the Final Solution* (London and New York, 2002).

Rosenkranz, Herbert, 'Entrechtung, Verfolgung und Selbsthilfe der Juden in Österreich', in Gerald Stourzh and Birgitta Zaar (eds), *Österreich, Deutschland und die Mächte. Internationale und Österreichische Aspekte des 'Anschlusses' vom März 1938* (Vienna, 1990), 367–417.

Ross, Corey, 'Entertainment, Technology and Tradition: The Rise of Recorded Music from the Empire to the Third Reich', in Karl Christian Führer and Corey Ross (eds), *Mass Media, Culture and Society in Twentieth-Century Germany* (Basingstoke, 2006), 25–43.

Ross, Corey, *Media and the Making of Modern Germany: Mass Communications, Society and Politics from the Empire to the Third Reich* (Oxford, 2008).

Rossino, Alexander B., *Hitler Strikes Poland: Blitzkrieg, Ideology and Atrocity* (Lawrence, KS, 2003).

Rossino, Alexander B., 'Nazi Anti-Jewish Policy during the Polish Campaign: The Case of the Einsatzgruppe von Woyrsch', *German Studies Review* 24 (2001), 35–53.

Rössler, Mechtild and Schleiermacher, Sabine (eds), *Der 'Generalplan Ost'. Hauptlinien der nationalsozialistischen Planungs- und Vernichtungspolitik* (Berlin, 1993).

Roth, Karl Heinz, 'Heydrichs Professor. Historiographie des "Volkstums" und der Massenvernichtungen. Der Fall Hans Joachim Beyer', in Peter Schöttler (ed.), *Geschichtsschreibung als Legitimationswissenschaft* (Frankfurt, 1997), 262–342.

Roth, Karl Heinz, 'Konrad Meyers erster "Generalplan Ost" (April/Mai 1940)', *Mitteilungen der Dokumentationsstelle zur NS-Sozialpolitik* 1 (1985), 45–52.

Rothkirchen, Livia, *The Jews of Bohemia and Moravia: Facing the Holocaust* (Lincoln, NB, 2006).

Runzheimer, Jürgen, 'Die Grenzzwischenfälle am Abend vor dem Angriff auf Polen', in Wolfgang Benz and Hermann Graml (eds), *Sommer 1939. Die Grossmächte und der Europäische Krieg* (Stuttgart, 1979), 107–47.

Runzheimer, Jürgen, 'Der Überfall auf den Sender Gleiwitz im Jahr 1939', *VfZ* 10 (1962), 408–26.

Rürup, Reinhard, 'Das Ende der Emanzipation. Die antijüdische Politik in Deutschland von der "Machtergreifung" bis zum Zweiten Weltkrieg', in Arnold Paucker, Sylvia Gilchrist and Barbara Suchy (eds), *Die Juden im nationalsozialistischen Deutschland* (Tübingen, 1986), 97–114.

Rürup, Reinhard, *Topographie des Terrors. Gestapo, SS und Reichssicherheitshauptamt auf den 'Prinz-Albrecht-Gelände'. Eine Dokumentation* (Berlin, 1987).

Rutherford, Phillip Terrell, *Prelude to the Final Solution: The Nazi Program for Deporting Ethnic Poles 1939–1941* (Lawrence, KS, 2007).

Safrian, Hans, *Die Eichmann-Männer* (Vienna, 1993).

Safrian, Hans, 'Expediting Expropriation and Expulsion: The Impact of the "Vienna Model" on Anti-Jewish Policies in Nazi Germany, 1938', *Holocaust and Genocide Studies* 14 (2000), 390–414.

Salewski, Michael, *Die Deutschen und die See. Studien zur deutschen Marinegeschichte des 19. und 20. Jahrhunderts*, 2 vols (Stuttgart, 1998 and 2002).

Sasse, Konrad, 'Aus Halles Musikleben von der Mitte des 19. Jahrhunderts bis 1945', in Rat der Stadt Halle (ed.), *Halle als Musikstadt* (Halle an der Saale, 1954), 40–52.

Sauer, Bernhard, *Schwarze Reichswehr und Fememorde. Eine Milieustudie zum Rechtsradikalismus in der Weimarer Republik* (Berlin, 2004).

Sauer, Wolfgang, *Die Mobilmachung der Gewalt* (Cologne, 1974).

Schäfer, Kirstin A., *Werner von Blomberg. Hitlers erster Feldmarschall* (Paderborn, 2006).

Schaser, Angelika, 'Gendered Germany', in Retallack (ed.), *Imperial Germany*, 128–50.

Scheffler, Wolfgang, 'Der Brandanschlag im Berliner Lustgarten im Mai 1942 und seine Folgen. Eine quellenkritische Betrachtung', *Berlin in Geschichte und Gegenwart. Jahrbuch des Landesarchivs Berlin* 3 (1984), 91–118.

Scheil, Stefan, *Die Entwicklung des politischen Antisemitismus in Deutschland zwischen 1881 und 1912* (Berlin, 1999).

Schelvis, Jules, *Vernichtungslager Sobibór. Dokumente – Texte – Materialien* (Berlin, 1998).

Schenk, Dieter, *Hitlers Mann in Danzig. Albert Forster und die NS-Verbrechen in Danzig-Westpreussen* (Bonn, 2000).

Schildberger, František, *Ležáky* (Hradec Králové, 1982).

Schleunes, Karl A. (ed.), *Legislating the Holocaust: The Bernhard Loesener Memoirs and Supporting Documents*, trans. Carol Scherer (Boulder, CO, 2001).

Schmidl, Erwin A., *Der 'Anschluss' Österreichs. Der deutsche Einmarsch im März 1938* (Vienna, 1994).

Schmidl, Erwin A., *März 38. Der deutsche Einmarsch in Österreich* (Vienna, 1987).

Schmidt, Ulf, 'Reassessing the Beginning of the "Euthanasia" Programme', *German History* 17 (1999), 543–50.

Schmidt-Hartmann, Eva, 'Tschechoslowakei', in Benz (ed.), *Dimension des Völkermords*, 353–80.

Schmiechen-Ackermann, Detlef, 'Der "Blockwart". Die unteren Parteifunktionen im national-sozialistischen Terror- und Überwachungsapparat', *VfZ* 48 (2000), 575–602.

Schmoller, Gustav von, 'Heydrich im Protektorat Böhmen und Mähren', *VfZ* 27 (1979), 626–45.

Schmuhl, Hans-Walter, 'Halle in der Weimarer Republik und im Nationalsozialismus', in Freitag et al. (eds), *Geschichte der Stadt Halle*, vol. 2, 237–302.

Schmuhl, Hans-Walter, *Rassenhygiene, Nationalsozialismus, Euthanasie. Von der Verhütung zur Vernichtung 'lebensunwerten Lebens' 1890–1945* (Göttingen, 1987).

Schreiber, Carsten, *Elite im Verborgenen. Ideologie und regionale Herrschaftspraxis des Sicherheitsdienstes der SS und seines Netzwerks am Beispiel Sachsen* (Munich, 2008).

Schuhladen-Krämer, Jürgen, 'Die Exekutoren des Terrors', in Michael Kissener and Joachim Scholtyseck (eds), *Die Führer der Provinz. NS-Biographien aus Baden und Württemberg* (Konstanz, 1997), 405–43.

Schulte, Jan Erik (ed.), *Die SS, Himmler und die Wewelsburg* (Paderborn, 2009).

Schulte, Jan Erik, *Zwangsarbeit und Vernichtung. Das Wirtschaftsimperium der SS. Oswald Pohl und das SS-Wirtschafts-Verwaltungshauptamt 1933–1945* (Paderborn, 2001).

Schulz, Andreas and Grebner, Gundula, *Generationswechsel und historischer Wandel* (Munich, 2003).

Schulze, Hagen, *Freikorps und Republik* (Boppard, 1968).

Schumann, Dirk, *Politische Gewalt in der Weimarer Republik. Kampf um die Strasse und Furcht vor dem Bürgerkrieg* (Essen, 2001).

Schwarz, Gudrun, *Eine Frau an seiner Seite. Ehefrauen in der SS-Sippengemeinschaft* (Hamburg, 1997).

Schwegel, Andreas, *Der Polizeibegriff im NS-Staat. Polizeirecht, juristische Publizistik und Judikative 1931–1944* (Tübingen, 2005).

Seeger, Andreas, *'Gestapo-Müller'. Die Karriere eines Schreibtischtäters* (Berlin, 1996).

Seidel, Doris, 'Die jüdische Gemeinde Münchens, 1933–1945', in Angelika Baumann and Andreas Heussler (eds), *München arisiert. Entrechtung und Enteignung der Juden in der NS-Zeit* (Munich, 2004).

Semerdjiev, Stefan, 'Reinhard Heydrich. Der deutsche Polizeichef als Jagdflieger', *Deutsche Militärzeitschrift* 41 (2004), 36–8.

Sereny, Gitta, *Das Ringen mit der Wahrheit. Albert Speer und das deutsche Trauma* (Munich, 1995).

Serrier, Thomas, *Entre Allemagne et Pologne. Nations et identités frontalières, 1848–1914* (Paris, 2002).

Severová, Dana, 'Sociální politika nacistů v takzvaném Protektorátu v letech 1939–1945', *Dějiny socialistického Československa* 7 (1985), 184–90.

Siemens, Daniel, *Horst Wessel. Tod und Verklärung eines Nationalsozialisten* (Munich, 2009).

Silberklang, David, 'Die Juden und die ersten Deportationen aus dem Distrikt Lublin', in Bogdan Musial (ed.), *'Aktion Reinhardt'. Der Völkermord an den Juden im Generalgouvernement 1941–1944* (Osnabrück, 2004), 141–64.

Simmert, Johannes and Herrmann, Hans-Walter, *Dokumentation zur Geschichte der jüdischen Bevölkerung in Rheinland-Pfalz und im Saarland von 1800*, vol 6: *Die nationalsozialistische Judenverfolgung in Rheinland-Pfalz 1933–1945. Das Schicksal der Juden im Saarland, 1920–1945* (Koblenz, 1974).

Skriebeleit, Jörg, 'Flossenbürg-Stammlager', in Benz and Distel (eds), *Ort des Terrors*, vol. 4: *Flossenbürg, Mauthausen, Ravensbrück*, 17–66.

Sládek, Oldrich, 'Standrecht und Standgericht. Die Gestapo in Böhmen und Mähren', in Mallmann and Paul (eds), *Gestapo im zweiten Weltkrieg*, 317–39.

Smelser, Ronald M., *The Sudeten Problem 1933–1938. Volkstumpolitik and the Formulation of Nazi Foreign Policy* (Folkestone, 1975).

Smilovitsky, Leonid, 'Righteous Gentiles, the Partisans and Jewish Survival in Belorussia, 1941–44', *Holocaust and Genocide Studies* 11 (1997), 301–29.

Smith, Bradley F., *Heinrich Himmler: A Nazi in the Making, 1900–1921* (Stanford, CA, 1974).

Snyder, Timothy, *Bloodlands: Europe Between Hitler and Stalin* (London, 2010).

Spiess, Alfred and Lichtenstein, Heiner, *Unternehmen Tannenberg. Der Anlass zum Zweiten Weltkrieg* (2nd rev. edn, Frankfurt am Main and Berlin, 1989).

Stahel, David, *Operation Barbarossa and Germany's Defeat in the East* (Cambridge, 2009).

Steigmann-Gall, Richard, *The Holy Reich: Nazi Conceptions of Christianity, 1919–1945* (Cambridge, 2003).

Steigmann-Gall, Richard, 'Religion and the Churches', in Jane Caplan (ed.), *Nazi Germany* (Oxford, 2008), 146–67.

Stein, Harry, 'Buchenwald-Stammlager', in Benz and Distel (eds), *Ort des Terrors*, vol. 3: *Sachsenhausen, Buchenwald*, 301–56.

Stein, Harry, 'Das Sonderlager im Konzentrationslager Buchenwald nach den Pogromen 1938', in Monica Kingreen (ed.), *'Nach der Kristallnacht'. Jüdisches Leben und antijüdische Politik in Frankfurt am Main 1938–1945* (Frankfurt am Main, 1999), 19–54.

Steinbacher, Sybille, *'Musterstadt' Auschwitz. Germanisierungspolitik und Judenmord in Ostoberschlesien* (Munich, 2000).

Steinkamp, Peter, 'Lidice 1942', in Gerd R. Ueberschär (ed.), *Orte des Grauens. Verbrechen im Zweiten Weltkrieg* (Darmstadt, 2003), 126–35.

Steinweis, Alan E., 'German Cultural Imperialism in Czechoslovakia and Poland, 1938–1945', *International History Review* 13 (1991), 466–80.

Steinweis, Alan E., *Kristallnacht 1938* (Cambridge, MA, 2009).

Steur, Claudia, 'Eichmanns Emissäre. Die "Judenberater" in Hitlers Europa', in Paul and Mallmann (eds), *Die Gestapo im Zweiten Weltkrieg*, 403–36.

Steur, Claudia, *Theodor Dannecker. Ein Funktionär der 'Endlösung'* (Essen, 1997).

Stevenson, Scott, *The Final Battle: Soldiers of the Western Front and the German Revolution of 1918* (Cambridge, 2009).

Stibbe, Matthew, *Women in the Third Reich* (London, 2003).

Stokes, Lawrence D., 'The Sicherheitsdienst (SD) of the Reichsführer SS and German Public Opinion, September 1939–June 1941', unpublished PhD thesis, Johns Hopkins University, 1972.

Stoldt, Hans-Ulrich, 'Operation Anthropoid', in Stephan Burgdorff (ed.), *Der Zweite Weltkrieg. Wendepunkte der deutschen Geschichte* (Munich, 2005), 171–5.

Stolle, Michael, *Die Geheime Staatspolizei in Baden. Personal, Organisation, Wirkung und Nachwirken einer regionalen Verfolgungsbehörde im Dritten Reich* (Konstanz, 2001).

Stoltzfus, Nathan, 'The Limits of Policy: Social Protection of Intermarried German Jews in Nazi Germany', in Gellately and Stoltzfus (eds), *Social Outsiders in Nazi Germany*, 117–44.

Strauss, Herbert A., 'Jewish Emigration from Germany: Nazi Policies and Jewish Responses', *Leo Baeck Institute Yearbook* 25 (1980), 313–61; and 26 (1981), 343–409.

Strebel, Bernhard, *Das KZ Ravensbrück. Geschichte eines Lagerkomplexes* (Paderborn, 2003).

Streit, Christian, *Keine Kameraden. Die Wehrmacht und die sowjetischen Kriegsgefangenen 1941–1945* (Stuttgart, 1978).

Šustek, Vojtěch, 'Josef Pfitzner a germanizace města Prahy', in *Osm set let pražské samosprávy. Sborník příspěvků z 18. vědecké konference Archivu hlavního města Prahy* (Prague, 2002), 167–81.

Sydnor, Charles, 'Executive Instinct. Reinhard Heydrich and the Planning for the Final Solution', in Michael Berenbaum and Abraham Peck (eds), *The Holocaust and History: The Known, the Unknown, the Disputed and the Re-examined* (Bloomington, IN, 1998), 159–86.

Sydnor, Charles, 'Reinhard Heydrich. Der "ideale Nationalsozialist"', in Ronald Smelser and Enrico Syring (eds), *Die SS. Elite unter dem Totenkopf. 30 Lebensläufe* (Paderborn, 2000), 208–19.

Tampke, Jürgen, *Czech–German Relations and the Politics of Central Europe. From Bohemia to the EU* (London, 2003).

Teichová, Alice, 'Instruments of Economic Control and Exploitation: The German Occupation of Bohemia and Moravia', in Richard Overy, Gerhard Otto and Johannes ten Cate (eds), *Die 'Neuordnung' Europas. NS-Wirtschaftspolitik in den besetzten Gebieten* (Berlin, 1997), 83–108.

Teichová, Alice, 'The Protectorate of Bohemia and Moravia (1939–1945): The Economic Dimension', in Mikulas Teich (ed.), *Bohemia in History* (Cambridge, 1998), 267–305.

Ther, Philipp, 'Deutsche Geschichte als imperiale Geschichte. Polen, slawophone Minderheiten und das Kaiserreich als kontinentales Empire', in Sebastian Conrad and Jürgen Osterhammel (eds), *Das Kaiserreich transnational. Deutschland in der Welt, 1871–1914* (Göttingen, 2004), 129–48.

Tönsmeyer, Tatjana, *Das Dritte Reich und die Slowakei 1939–1945. Politischer Alltag zwischen Kooperation und Eigensinn* (Paderborn, 2003).

Tooze, Adam, *Wages of Destruction: The Making and Breaking of the Nazi Economy* (London, 2006).

Toury, Jacob, 'Ein Auftakt zur "Endlösung". Judenaustreibungen über nichtslawische Reichsgrenzen 1933–1939', in Ursula Büttner, Werner Johe and Angelika Voss (eds), *Das Unrechtsregime. Internationale Forschung über den Nationalsozialismus* (Hamburg, 1986), vol. 2, 164–9.

Toury, Jacob, 'Die Entstehungsgeschichte des Austreibungsbefehls gegen die Juden der Saarpfalz und Badens', *Jahrbuch des Instituts für Deutsche Geschichte* 15 (1986), 431–64.

Tregenza, Michael, 'Belzec Death Camps', *Wiener Library Bulletin* 30 (1977), 8–25.

Tuchel, Johannes, *Am Grossen Wannsee 56–58. Von der Villa Minoux zum Haus der Wannsee-Konferenz* (Berlin, 1992).

Tuchel, Johannes, 'Gestapa und Reichssicherheitshauptamt. Die Berliner Zentralinstitutionen der Gestapo', in Paul and Mallmann (eds), *Die Gestapo. Mythos und Realität*, 84–100.

Tuchel, Johannes, *Konzentrationslager. Organisationsgeschichte und Funktion der 'Inspektion der Konzentrationslager' 1934–1938* (Boppard, 1991).

Tuchel, Johannes, 'Reinhard Heydrich und die "Stiftung Nordhav". Die Aktivitäten der SS-Führung auf Fehmarn', *Zeitschrift der Gesellschaft für Schleswig-Holsteinische Geschichte* 117 (1992), 199–225.

Tuchel, Johannes and Schattenfroh, Reinold, *Zentrale des Terrors. Prinz-Albrecht-Str. 8. Das Hauptquartier der Gestapo* (Berlin, 1987).

Tullner, Mathias, *Halle 1806 bis 2006. Industriezentrum, Regierungssitz, Bezirksstadt. Eine Einführung in die Stadtgeschichte* (Halle an der Saale, 2007).

Turner, Henry Ashby, *Hitler's Thirty Days to Power: January 1933* (London, 1997).

Twigge, Stephen, Hampshire, Edward and Macklin, Graham, *British Intelligence: Secrets, Spies and Sources* (Kew, 2008).

Ullrich, Volker, *Die nervöse Grossmacht. Aufstieg und Untergang des Kaiserreiches, 1871–1918* (3rd edn, Munich, 2007).

Ullrich, Volker, *Vom Augusterlebnis zur Novemberrevolution. Beiträge zur Sozialgeschichte Hamburgs und Nordeutschlands im Ersten Weltkrieg* (Bremen, 1999).

Umbreit, Hans, *Deutsche Militärverwaltungen 1938/39. Die militärische Besetzung der Tschechoslowakei und Polens* (Stuttgart, 1977).

Vaněk, Ladislav, *Atentát na Heydricha* (Prague, 1962).

Verhey, Jeffrey, *The Spirit of 1914: Militarism, Myth and Mobilization in Germany* (Cambridge, 2000).

Voigt, Rüdiger (ed.), *Grossraum-Denken. Carls Schmitts Kategorie der Grossraumordnung* (Stuttgart, 2008).

Wachsmann, Nikolaus, 'The Dynamics of Destruction: The Development of the Concentration Camps, 1933–1945', in Jane Caplan and idem (eds), *Concentration Camps in Nazi Germany: The New Histories* (London, 2009), 17–43.

Wachsmann, Nikolaus, *Hitler's Prisons: Legal Terror in Nazi Germany* (New Haven and London, 2004).

Wagner, Patrick, *Hitlers Kriminalisten. Die deutsche Kriminalpolizei und der Nationalsozialismus* (Munich, 2002).

Wagner, Patrick, *Volksgemeinschaft ohne Verbrecher. Konzeptionen und Praxis der Kriminalpolizei in der Zeit der Weimarer Republik und des Nationalsozialismus* (Hamburg, 1996).

Waite, Robert, *Vanguard of Nazism: The Free Corps Movement in Postwar Germany, 1918–23* (Cambridge, MA, 1952).

Waldman, Eric, *The Spartacist Uprising of 1919 and the Crisis of the German Socialist Movement: A Study of the Relation of Political Theory and Party Practice* (Milwaukee, WI, 1958).

Wannenmacher, Walter, 'Reinhard Heydrich', *Böhmen und Mähren* (1942).

Warmbrunn, Werner, *The German Occupation of Belgium, 1940–1944* (New York, 1993).

Watt, Donald Cameron, *How War Came: The Immediate Origins of the Second World War, 1938–1939* (London, 1989).

Weale, Adrian, *The SS: A New History* (London, 2010).

Weber, Reinhard, *Das Schicksal der jüdischen Rechtsanwälte in Bayern nach 1933* (Munich, 2006).

Weber, Wolfram, *Die innere Sicherheit im besetzten Belgien und Nordfrankreich 1940–1944. Ein Beitrag zur Geschichte der Besatzungsverwaltungen* (Düsseldorf, 1978).

Wegner, Bernd, *Hitlers politische Soldaten. Die Waffen-SS 1933–1945. Leitbild, Struktur und Funktion einer nationalsozialistischen Elite* (Paderborn, 1997).

Wehler, Hans-Ulrich, *Deutsche Gesellschaftsgeschichte*, vol. 3: *Von der deutschen Doppelrevolution bis zum Beginn des Ersten Weltkrieges, 1849–1914* (2nd edn, Munich, 2007).

Weigelt, Wolfgang, 'Nauen/Stolpshof', in Benz and Distel (eds), *Der Ort des Terrors*, vol. 3: *Sachsenhausen, Buchenwald*, 231–2.

Weikart, Richard, *From Darwin to Hitler: Evolutionary Ethics, Eugenics, and Racism in Germany* (Basingstoke, 2004).

Weinberg, Gerhard L., *Hitler's Foreign Policy 1933–1939: The Road to World War II* (New York, 2005).

Weingart, Peter, Kroll, Jürgen and Bayertz, Kurt, *Rasse, Blut und Gene. Geschichte der Eugenik und Rassenhygiene in Deutschland* (Frankfurt am Main, 1988).

Weiss, Aharon, 'The Holocaust and the Ukrainian Victims', in Michael Berenbaum (ed.), *A Mosaic of Victims: Non-Jews Persecuted and Murdered by the Nazis* (New York, 1990), 109–15.

Weisz, Franz, 'Personell vor allem ein "ständestaatlicher" Polizeikörper. Die Gestapo in Österreich', in Paul and Mallmann (eds), *Gestapo im Zweiten Weltkrieg*, 439–62.

Weitbrecht, Dorothee, 'Ermächtigung zur Vernichtung. Die Einsatzgruppen in Polen im Herbst 1939', in Klaus-Michael Mallmann and Bogdan Musial (eds), *Genesis des Genozids. Polen 1939–1941* (Darmstadt, 2004), 57–70.

Weitbrecht, Dorothee, *Der Exekutionsauftrag der Einsatzgruppen in Polen* (Filderstadt, 2001).

Weitz, Eric D., *A Century of Genocide: Utopias of Race and Nation* (Princeton, NJ, 2003).

Welch, David, *Germany, Propaganda and Total War, 1914–1918* (New Brunswick, NJ, 2000).

Welzer, Harald, *Täter. Wie aus ganz normalen Nenschen Massenmördern werden* (Frankfurt, 2005).

Westermann, Edward B., *Hitler's Police Battalions: Enforcing Racial War in the East* (Lawrence, KS, 2005).

Wetzel, Juliane, 'Frankreich und Belgien', in Benz (ed.), *Dimension des Völkermordes*, 105–35.

Weyrauch, Walter Otto, *Gestapo V-Leute. Tatsachen und Theorie des Geheimdienstes. Untersuchungen zur Geheimen Staatspolizei während der nationalsozialistischen Herrschaft* (Frankfurt am Main, 1989).

Whiting, Charles, *Heydrich: Henchman of Death* (Barnsley, 1999).

Wiedemann, Andreas, *Die Reinhard-Heydrich-Stiftung in Prag 1942–1945* (Dresden, 2000).

Wighton, Charles, *Heydrich: Hitler's Most Evil Henchman* (London, 1962).

Wildt, Michael, 'Before the "Final Solution": The Judenpolitik of the SD, 1935–1938', *Leo Baeck Institute Year Book* (1998), 241–69.

Wildt, Michael, *Generation des Unbedingten. Das Führungskorps des Reichssicherheitshauptamtes* (Hamburg, 2002).

Wildt, Michael, 'Der Hamburger Gestapochef Bruno Streckenbach. Eine nationalsozialistische Karriere', in Frank Bajohr and Joachim Szodrzynski (eds), *Hamburg in der NS-Zeit. Ergebnisse neuerer Forschungen* (Hamburg, 1995), 93–123.

Wildt, Michael (ed.), *Die Judenpolitik des SD 1935 bis 1938. Eine Dokumentation* (Munich, 1995).

Wildt, Michael (ed.), *Nachrichtendienst, politische Elite und Mordeinheit. Der Sicherheitsdienst des Reichsführes SS* (Hamburg, 2003).

Wildt, Michael, 'Radikalisierung und Selbstradikalisierung 1939. Die Geburt des Reichssicherheitshauptamtes aus dem Geist des völkischen Massenmordes', in Paul and Mallmann (eds), *Die Gestapo im Zweiten Weltkrieg*, 11–41.

Wildt, Michael, 'Das Reichssicherheitshauptamt. Radikalisierung und Selbstradikalisierung einer Institution', *Mittelweg* 36 (1998), 33–40.

Wildt, Michael, 'The Spirit of the Reich Security Main Office (RSHA)', *Totalitarian Movements and Political Religions* 6 (2005), 333–49.

Wilhelm, Friedrich, *Die Polizei im NS-Staat. Die Geschichte ihrer Organisation im Überblick* (2nd edn, Paderborn, 1999).

Wilhelm, Hans-Heinrich, *Die Einsatzgruppe A der Sicherheitspolizei und des SD 1941/42* (Frankfurt am Main, 1996).

Williams, Max, *Reinhard Heydrich: The Biography*, 2 vols (Church Stretton, 2001 and 2003).

Winkler, Heinrich August, 'Die Revolution von 1918/19 und das Problem der Kontinuität in der deutschen Geschichte', *Historische Zeitschrift* 250 (1990), 303–19.

Winkler, Heinrich August, *Von der Revolution zur Stabilisierung. Arbeiter und Arbeiterbewegung in der Weimarer Republik 1918 bis 1924* (Berlin and Bonn, 1984).

Witte, Peter, 'Two Decisions Concerning the "Final Solution of the Jewish Question": Deportations to Lodz and the Mass Murder in Chelmno', *Holocaust and Genocide Studies* 9 (1995), 318–45.

Witte, Peter and Tyas, Stephen, 'A New Document on the Deportation and Murder of Jews during "Einsatz Reinhard" 1942', *Holocaust and Genocide Studies* 15 (2001), 468–86.

Wysocki, Gerd, 'Lizenz zum Töten. Die "Sonderbehandlungs"-Praxis der Stapo-Stelle Braunschweig', in Paul and Mallmann (eds), *Gestapo im Zweiten Weltkrieg*, 237–54.

Wysocki, Gerhard, *Die Geheime Staatspolizei im Land Braunschweig. Polizeirecht und Polizeipraxis im Nationalsozialismus* (Frankfurt am Main and New York, 1997).

Yahill, Leni, 'Madagascar, Phantom of a Solution for the Jewish Question', in Bela Vago and George L. Mosse (eds), *Jews and Non-Jews in Eastern Europe, 1918–1945* (New York, 1974), 315–34.

Zahra, Tara, *Kidnapped Souls: National Indifference and the Battle for Children in the Bohemian Lands, 1900–1948* (Ithaca, NY, and London, 2008).

Záměćník, Stanislav, 'Dachau-Stammlager' in Benz and Distel (eds), *Ort des Terrors*, vol. 2: *Frühe Lager, Dachau, Emslandlager*, 233–74.

Zbikowski, Andrzej, 'Local Anti-Jewish Pogroms in the Occupied Territories of Eastern Poland, June–July 1941', in Lucjan Dobroszycki and Jeffrey S. Gurock (eds), *The Holocaust in the Soviet Union: Studies and Sources on the Destruction of the Jews in the Nazi-Occupied Territories of the USSR, 1941–1945* (Armonk, NY, 1993), 173–9.

Zeman, Zbyněk, *The Life of Edvard Beneš, 1884–1948: Czechoslovakia in Peace and War* (Oxford, 1997).

Zimmermann, Michael, *Rassenutopie und Genozid. Die nationalsozialistische 'Lösung der Zigeunerfrage'* (Hamburg, 1996).

Zimmermann, Moshe, 'Utopie und Praxis der Vernichtungspolitik in der NS-Diktatur. Überlegungen in vergleichender Absicht', in *WerkstattGeschichte* 13 (1996), 60–71.

Zimmermann, Volker, *Die Sudetendeutschen im NS-Staat. Politik und Stimmung der Bevölkerung im Reichsgau Sudetenland (1938–1945)* (Essen, 1999).

Zipfel, Friedrich, *Kirchenkampf in Deutschland 1933–1945. Religionsverfolgung und Selbstbehauptung der Kirchen in der nationalsozialistischen Zeit* (Berlin, 1965).

Zumbini, Massimo Ferrari, *Die Wurzeln des Bösen. Gründerjahre des Antisemitismus. Von der Bismarckzeit zu Hitler* (Frankfurt am Main, 2003).

Index